# CBSE Class 11
# CHEMiSTRY
## Chapter-wise Question Bank

## NCERT + Exemplar + Practice Questions

## with Solutions

**Corporate Office**

# DISHA PUBLICATION

45, 2nd Floor, Maharishi Dayanand Marg,
Corner Market, Malviya Nagar, New Delhi - 110017
Tel : 49842349 / 49842350

Typeset by Disha DTP Team

**www.dishapublication.com**
Books &
ebooks for
School &
Competitive
Exams

**www.mylearninggraph.com**
Etests
for
Competitive
Exams

Write to us at **feedback_disha@aiets.co.in**

# Contents

# 1 Some Basic Concepts of Chemistry

**1.1** Calculate the molecular mass of the following:
(i) $H_2O$ (ii) $CO_2$ (iii) $CH_4$

**Ans.** (i) Molecular mass of $H_2O = 2$ (1.008 amu) + 16.00 amu
= 18.016 amu.

(ii) Molecular mass of $CO_2 = 12.01$ amu $+ 2 \times 16.00$ amu
= 44.01 amu.

(iii) Molecular mass of $CH_4 = 12.01$ amu + 4 (1.008 amu)
= 16.042 amu.

**1.2** Calculate the mass per cent of different elements present in sodium sulphate ($Na_2SO_4$).

**Ans.** Mass % of an element

$$= \frac{\text{Mass of that element in the compound}}{\text{Molar mass of the compound}} \times 100$$

Now, molar mass of
$Na_2SO_4 = 2 (23.0) + 32.0 + 4 \times 16.0 = 142$ g mol$^{-1}$

Mass percent of sodium,

$$Na = \frac{46}{142} \times 100 = 32.39\%$$

Mass percent of sulphur,

$$S = \frac{32}{142} \times 100 = 22.54\%$$

Mass percent of oxygen,

$$O = \frac{64}{142} \times 100 = 45.07\%$$

**1.3** Determine the empirical formula of an oxide of iron which has 69.9% iron and 30.1% dioxygen by mass.

**Ans.**

| Element | Symbol | %by mass | Atomic mass | Moles of the element | Simplest molar ratio | Simplest whole number molar ratio |
|---|---|---|---|---|---|---|
| Iron | Fe | 69.9 | 55.85 | $\frac{69.9}{55.85} = 1.25$ | $\frac{1.25}{1.25} = 1$ | 2 |
| Oxygen | O | 30.1 | 16.0 | $\frac{30.1}{16.0} = 1.88$ | $\frac{1.88}{1.25} = 1.5$ | 3 |

$\therefore$ Empirical formula = $Fe_2O_3$.

**1.4** Calculate the amount of carbon dioxide that could be produced when
(i) 1 mole of carbon is burnt in air.
(ii) 1 mole of carbon is burnt in 16 g of dioxygen.
(iii) 2 moles of carbon are burnt in 16 g of dioxygen.

**Ans.** The balanced equation for the combustion of carbon in dioxygen/air is

$$C(s) \ + \ O_2(g) \longrightarrow CO_2(g)$$

| 1 mole | 1 mole | 1 mole |
|---|---|---|
| (12 g) | (32 g) | (44 g) |

(i) In air, combustion is complete. Therefore, $CO_2$ produced from the combustion of 1 mole of carbon = 44g.

(ii) Since only 16 g of dioxygen is available, hence it can combine only with 0.5 mole of carbon, i.e., dioxygen is the limiting reactant. Hence, $CO_2$ produced = 22 g.

(iii) In this case dioxygen again is the limiting reactant. 16 g of dioxygen can combine only with 0.5 mole of carbon. $CO_2$ produced again is equal to 22 g.

**1.5** Calculate the mass of sodium acetate ($CH_3COONa$) required to make 500 mL of 0.375 molar aqueous solution. Molar mass of sodium acetate is 82.0245 g mol$^{-1}$.

**Ans.** 0.375 M aqueous solution means that sodium acetate is present in 1000 mL of solution.

$\therefore$ Moles of sodium acetate present in solution = 0.375/2

Molar mass of sodium acetate = 82.0245 g mol$^{-1}$

Mass of sodium acetate required
= 0.375/2 mole $\times$ 82.0245 g mol$^{-1}$ = 15.380 g.

**1.6** Calculate the concentration of nitric acid in moles per litre in a sample which has a density, 1.41 g mL$^{-1}$ and the mass per cent of nitric acid in it being 69%.

**Ans.** Mass percent of 69% means that 100 g of nitric acid solution contain 69 g of nitric acid by mass.

Molar mass of nitric acid ($HNO_3$)
= 1 + 14 + 48 = 63 g mol$^{-1}$

Moles in 69g of $HNO_3$ = 69/63 = 1.095 mole

Volume of 100 g nitric acid solution

$=100/1.41 = 70.92$ mL $= 0.07092$ L

Conc. of $HNO_3$ in moles per litre

$= 1.095 / 0.0792$ L $= 13.83$ M

**1.7 How much copper can be obtained from 100 g of copper sulphate ($CuSO_4$) ?**

**Ans.** One mole of $CuSO_4$ contains 1 mole (1 g atom) of Cu

Molar mass of $CuSO_4 = 63.5 + 32 + 4 \times 16 = 159.5$ g mol$^{-1}$.

Thus, amount of Cu that can be obtained from 159.5 g of $CuSO_4 = 63.5$ g

Cu that can be obtained from 100 g of $CuSO_4$

$= \dfrac{63.5}{159.5} \times 100$ g $= 39.81$ g

**1.8 Determine the molecular formula of an oxide of iron in which the mass per cent of iron and oxygen are 69.9 and 30.1 respectively.**

**Ans.** Calculation of Empirical Formula. Refer Q. 1.3

Empirical formula mass of $Fe_2O_3$

$$= 2 \times 55.85 + 3 \times 16.00 = 159.7 \text{ g mol}^{-1}$$

$$n = \frac{\text{Molar mass}}{\text{Empirical formula mass}} = \frac{159.8}{159.7} = 1$$

Hence, molecular formula are empirical formula, viz., $Fe_2O_3$.

**1.9 Calculate the atomic mass (average) of chlorine using the following data :**

| | % Natural Abundance | Molar Mass |
|---|---|---|
| $^{35}$Cl | 75.77 | 34.9689 |
| $^{37}$Cl | 24.23 | 36.9659 |

**Ans.** Fractional abundance of $^{35}$Cl $= 0.7577$

Molar mass $= 34.9689$

Fractional abundance of $^{37}$Cl $= 0.2423$

Molar mass $= 36.9659$

Average atomic mass

$= (0.7577) (34.9689 \text{ amu}) + (0.2423) (36.9659 \text{ amu})$

$= 26.4959 + 8.9568 = 35.4527$

**1.10 In three moles of ethane ($C_2H_6$), calculate the following :**

**(i) Number of moles of carbon atoms.**

**(ii) Number of moles of hydrogen atoms.**

**(iii) Number of molecules of ethane.**

**Ans.** (i) 1 mole of $C_2H_6$ contains 2 moles of carbon atoms. Hence 3 moles of $C_2H_6$ will contain C–atoms $= 6$ moles.

(ii) 1 mole of $C_2H_6$ contains 6 moles of hydrogen atoms. Hence 3 moles of $C_2H_6$ will contain H–atoms $= 18$ moles.

(iii) 1 mole of $C_2H_6$ contains $6.02 \times 10^{23}$ molecules. Hence 3 moles of $C_2H_6$ will contain ethane molecules $= 3 \times 6.02 \times 10^{23} = 18.06 \times 10^{23}$ molecules.

**1.11 What is the concentration of sugar ($C_{12}H_{22}O_{11}$) in mol L$^{-1}$ if its 20 g are dissolved in enough water to make a final volume up to 2L?**

**Ans.** Molar mass of sugar ($C_{12}H_{22}O_{11}$)

$= 12 \times 12 + 22 \times 1 + 11 \times 16 = 342$ g mol$^{-1}$

No. of moles in 20 g of sugar

$= \dfrac{20 \text{g}}{342 \text{g mol}^{-1}} = 0.0585$ mole

Molar concentration

$= \dfrac{\text{Moles of solute}}{\text{Volume of solution}} = \dfrac{0.0585}{2} = 0.0293$ M

**1.12 If the density of methanol is 0.793 kg L$^{-1}$, what is its volume needed for making 2.5 L of its 0.25 M solution?**

**Ans.** Molar mass of methanol ($CH_3OH$) = 32 g mol$^{-1}$

$= 0.032$ kg mol$^{-1}$

As Molarity

$$= \frac{\text{mass of solute}}{\text{molar mass of solute} \times \text{volume of solution}}$$

We can write molarity $= \dfrac{\text{density of solution}}{\text{molar mass of solute}}$

Thus the molarity of the given solution will be

$$\frac{0.793 \text{kg L}^{-1}}{0.032 \text{ kg mol}^{-1}} = 24.78 \text{ mol L}^{-1}$$

Applying $\underset{\substack{\text{(Given} \\ \text{solution)}}}{M_1 \times V_1} = \underset{\substack{\text{(Solution to} \\ \text{be prepared)}}}{M_2 \times V_2}$

$$24.78 \times V_1 = 0.25 \times 2.5 \text{ L}$$

or $\qquad V_1 = 0.02522$ L $= 25.22$ mL

**1.13 Pressure is determined as force per unit area of the surface. The SI unit of pressure, pascal is as shown below:**

$$1Pa = 1N \text{ m}^{-2}$$

**If mass of air at sea level is 1034 g cm$^{-2}$, calculate the pressure in pascal.**

**Ans.** Pressure is the force (i.e., weight) acting per unit area

But weight $=$ mg

Pressure $=$ Weight per unit area

$$= 1034 \text{ g} \times 9.8 \text{ ms}^{-2}/\text{cm}^2$$

$$= \frac{1034 \text{g} \times 9.8 \text{ms}^{-2}}{\text{cm}^2} \times \frac{1\text{kg} \times 100\text{cm} \times 100\text{cm}}{1000\text{g}}$$

$$\times \frac{1\text{N}}{1\text{m} \times 1\text{m}} \times \frac{1\text{Pa}}{\text{kg m s}^{-2}} = 1.01332 \times 10^5 \text{ Nm}^{-2}$$

$$= 1.01332 \times 10^5 \text{ Pa}$$

**1.14 What is the SI unit of mass? How is it defined?**

**Ans.** S.I. unit of mass is kilogram (kg). It is equal to the mass of the international prototype of the kilogram. It is defined as the mass of platinum–iridium cylinder that is stored in air–tight jar at International Bureau of Weights and Measures in France.

**1.15 Match the following prefixes with their multiples:**

| Prefixes | Multiples |
|---|---|
| (i) micro | $10^6$ |
| (ii) deca | $10^9$ |
| (iii) mega | $10^{-6}$ |
| (iv) giga | $10^{-15}$ |
| (v) femto | $10$ |

**Ans.** micro = $10^{-6}$, deca = 10, mega = $10^6$, giga = $10^9$, femto = $10^{-15}$.

**1.16 What do you mean by significant figures?**

**Ans.** The total number of digits in a number including the last digit whose value is uncertain is called the number of significant figures.

**1.17 A sample of drinking water was found to be severely contaminated with chloroform, $CHCl_3$, supposed to be carcinogenic in nature. The level of contamination was 15 ppm (by mass).**
**(i) Express this in percent by mass.**
**(ii) Determine the molality of chloroform in the water sample.**

**Ans. (i)** 15 ppm means 15 parts in million ($10^6$) parts.

$$\% \text{ by mass } \frac{15}{10^6} \times 100 = 15 \times 10^{-4} = 1.5 \times 10^{-3} \%$$

**(ii)** Molar mass of chloroform
$(CHCl_3) = 12 + 1 + 3 \times 35.5 = 119.5 \text{ g mol}^{-1}$
100 g of the sample contain chloroform
$= 1.5 \times 10^{-3}$ g
$\therefore$ 1000 g (1 kg) of the sample will contain chloroform $= 1.5 \times 10^{-2}$ g

$$\text{Now molality } = \frac{1.5 \times 10^{-2}}{119.5} = 1.255 \times 10^{-4} \text{ m}$$

$\therefore$ Molality = $1.255 \times 10^{-4}$m.

**1.18 Express the following in the scientific notation:**
**(i) 0.0048**      **(ii) 234,000**
**(iii) 8008**      **(iv) 500.0**
**(v) 6.0012**

**Ans. (i)** $4.8 \times 10^{-3}$      (ii) $2.34 \times 10^5$
(iii) $8.008 \times 10^3$      (iv) $5.000 \times 10^2$
(v) $6.0012 \times 10^0$

**1.19 How many significant figures are present in the following?**
**(i) 0.0025**      **(ii) 208**
**(iii) 5005**      **(iv) 126,000**
**(v) 500.0**      **(vi) 2.0034**

**Ans. (i)** 2      (ii) 3
(iii) 4      (iv) 3
(v) 4      (vi) 5

**1.20 Round up the following upto three significant figures:**
**(i) 34.216**      **(ii) 10.4107**
**(iii) 0.04597**      **(iv) 2808**

**Ans. (i)** 34.2      (ii) 10.4
(iii) 0.0460      (iv) 2.80

**1.21 The following data are obtained when dinitrogen and dioxygen react together to form different compounds :**

| | Mass of dinitrogen | Mass of dioxygen |
|---|---|---|
| (i) | 14 g | 16 g |
| (ii) | 14 g | 32 g |
| (iii) | 28 g | 32 g |
| (iv) | 28 g | 80 g |

**(a) Which law of chemical combination is obeyed by the above experimental data? Give its statement.**

**(b) Fill in the blanks in the following conversions:**
**(i) 1 km = ........... mm = ........... pm**
**(ii) 1 mg = ........... kg = ........... ng**
**(iii) 1 mL = ........... L = ........... dm$^3$**

**Ans. (a)** Fixing the mass of dinitrogen as 28g, masses of dioxygen combined will be 32, 64, 32 and 80 g in the given four oxides. These are in the ratio 1: 2:1: 2.5 or 2 : 4 : 2 : 5 which is a simple whole number ratio. Hence, the given data obey the law of multiple proportions.

**Definition** – When two elements combine to form two or more chemical compounds, then the masses of one of the elements which combine with a fixed mass of the other, bear a simple ratio to one another.

**(b) (i)** $1 \text{ km} = 1 \text{ km} \times \dfrac{1000 \text{ m}}{1 \text{ km}} \times \dfrac{10 \text{ mm}}{1 \text{ cm}}$

$\qquad = \dfrac{100 \text{ cm}}{1 \text{ m}} \times 10^6 \text{ mm}$

$1 \text{ km} = 1 \text{ km} \times \dfrac{1000 \text{ m}}{1 \text{ km}} \times \dfrac{1 \text{ pm}}{10^{-12} \text{m}}$

$\qquad = 10^{15} \text{ pm}$

**(ii)** $1 \text{ mg} = 1 \text{ mg} \times \dfrac{1 \text{ g}}{1000 \text{ mg}} \times \dfrac{1 \text{ kg}}{1000 \text{ g}}$

$\qquad = 10^{-6} \text{ kg}$

$1 \text{ mg} = 1 \text{ mg} \times \dfrac{1 \text{ g}}{1000 \text{ mg}} \times \dfrac{1 \text{ ng}}{10^{-9} \text{ g}} = 10^6 \text{ ng}$

**(iii)** $1 \text{ mL} = 1 \text{ mL} \times \dfrac{1 \text{L}}{1000 \text{ mL}} = 10^{-3} \text{ L}$

$1 \text{ mL} = 1 \text{ cm}^3 = \dfrac{1 \text{cm}^3 \times 1 \text{dm} \times 1 \text{dm} \times 1 \text{dm}}{10 \text{cm} \times 10 \text{ cm} \times 10 \text{cm}}$

$\qquad = 10^{-3} \text{ dm}^3$

**1.22 If the speed of light is $3.0 \times 10^8$ m s$^{-1}$, calculate the distance covered by light in 2.00 ns.**

**Ans.** Distance covered = Speed × Time
$= 3.0 \times 10^8 \text{ ms}^{-1} \times 2.00 \text{ ns}$
$= 3.0 \times 10^8 \text{ ms}^{-1} \times 2.00 \text{ns} \times \dfrac{10^{-9} \text{ s}}{1 \text{ns}} = 6.00 \times 10^{-1}$
$\qquad\qquad\qquad\qquad\qquad m = 0.600 \text{ m}$

**1.23** In a reaction

$$A + B_2 \longrightarrow AB_2$$

Identify the limiting reagent, if any, in the following reaction mixtures.

(i)   300 atoms of A + 200 molecules of B

(ii)  2 mol A + 3 mol B

(iii) 100 atoms of A + 100 molecules of B

(iv)  5 mol A + 2.5 mol B

(v)   2.5 mol A + 5 mol B

**Ans.** (i)   According to the given reaction, 1 atom of A reacts with 1 molecule of B. Therefore 200 molecules of B will react with 200 atoms of A and 100 atoms of A will be left unreacted. Hence, B is the limiting reagent while A is the excess reagent.

(ii)  According to the given reaction, 1 mol of A reacts with 1 mol of B. Therefore 2 mol of A will react with 2 mol of B. Hence, A is the limiting reactant.

(iii) No limiting reagent

(iv)  2.5 mol of B will react with 2.5 mol of A. Hence B is the limiting reagent.

(v)   2.5 mol of A will react with 2.5 mol of B . Hence A is the limiting reagent.

**1.24** Dinitrogen and dihydrogen react with each other to produce ammonia according to the following chemical equation:

$$N_2(g) + H_2(g) \longrightarrow 2NH_3(g)$$

(i)   Calculate the mass of ammonia produced if $2.00 \times 10^3$ g dinitrogen reacts with $1.00 \times 10^3$ g of dihydrogen.

(ii)  Will any of the two reactants remain unreacted?

(iii) If yes, which one and what would be its mass?

**Ans.** (i)   Balanced equation for preparation of ammonia is

$$N_2(g) + 3H_2(g) \longrightarrow 2NH_3(g)$$

1 mol of $N_2$, i.e., 28 g react with 3 mol of $H_2$, i.e., 6g of $H_2$. 2000 g of $N_2$ will react with

$$H_2 = \frac{6}{28} \times 2000 \ g = 428.6 \ g \ \text{but the amount of } H_2$$

actually present is 1000g, thus $H_2$ is in excess and remain unreacted. Thus, $N_2$ is the limiting reagent while $H_2$ is the excess reagent.

1 mol of $N_2$, i.e., 28 g of $N_2$ produce

$NH_3 = 2$ mol $= 34$ g 2000g of $N_2$ will produce $NH_3$

$$= \frac{34}{28} \times 2000g = 2428.57g$$

(ii)  $H_2$ will remain unreacted.

(iii) Mass left unreacted $= 1000g - 428.6$ g

$$= 571.4 \ g$$

**1.25** How are 0.50 mol $Na_2CO_3$ and 0.50 M $Na_2CO_3$ different?

**Ans.** Molar mass of $Na_2CO_3 = 2 \times 23 + 12 + 3 \times 16 = 106$ g mol$^{-1}$

0.50 mol $Na_2CO_3$ means $= 0.50 \times 106$ g $= 53$ g

0.50 M $Na_2CO_3$ means 0.50 mol i.e, 53 g $Na_2CO_3$ are present in 1 litre of the solution .

**1.26** If ten volumes of dihydrogen gas reacts with five volumes of dioxygen gas, how many volumes of water vapour would be produced?

**Ans.** $H_2$ and $O_2$ react according to the equation

$$2H_2(g) + O_2(g) \longrightarrow 2H_2O(g)$$

Therefore, 2 volumes of $H_2$ react with 1 volume of $O_2$ to produce 2 volumes of water. Hence, 10 volumes of $H_2$ will react completely with 5 volumes of $O_2$ to produce 10 volumes of water vapour.

**1.27** Convert the following into basic units:

(i)   28.7 pm        (ii)  15.15 pm

(iii) 25365 mg

**Ans.** (i)   $28.7 \ pm = 28.7 \ pm \times \dfrac{10^{-12} m}{1 pm}$

$$= 2.87 \times 10^{-11} \ m$$

(ii)  $15.15 \ pm = 15.15 \ pm. \times \dfrac{10^{-12} m}{1 pm}$

$$= 1.515 \times 10^{-5} \ m$$

(iii) $25365 \ mg = 25365 \ mg \times \dfrac{1g}{1000 mg} \times \dfrac{1 kg}{1000 g}$

$$= 2.5365 \times 10^{-2} kg$$

**1.28** Which one of the following will have largest number of atoms?

(i)   1 g of Au (s)        (ii)  1 g of Na (s)

(iii) 1 g of Li (s)        (iv)  1 g of $Cl_2$(g)

**Ans.** (i)   $1 \ g \ Au = \dfrac{1}{197} mol = \dfrac{1}{197} \times 6.022 \times 10^{23}$ atoms

$$= 0.030 \times 10^{23} \ \text{atoms} = 3.0 \times 10^{21} \ \text{atoms}$$

(ii)  $1 g \ Na = \dfrac{1}{23} mol = \dfrac{1}{23} \times 6.022 \times 10^{23}$ atoms

$$= 0.261 \times 10^{23} \ \text{atoms} = 2.61 \times 10^{22} \ \text{atoms}$$

(iii) $1 \ g \ Li = \dfrac{1}{7} mol = \dfrac{1}{7} \times 6.022 \times 10^{23}$ atoms

$$= 0.86 \times 10^{23} \ \text{atoms} = 8.6 \times 10^{22} \ \text{atoms}$$

(iv)  1 g $Cl_2$

$$= \frac{1}{71} mol = \frac{1}{71} \times 6.022 \times 10^{23} \ \text{molecules}$$

$$= \frac{2}{71} \times 6.022 \times 10^{23} \ \text{atoms}$$

$$= 1.69 \times 10^{22} \text{atoms}$$

Thus 1 g of Li has the largest number of atoms.

**1.29 Calculate the molarity of a solution of ethanol in water in which the mole fraction of ethanol is 0.040.**

**Ans.** Given mole fraction of ethanol = 0.040

$$\text{i.e., } X_{C_2H_5OH} = \frac{n_{(C_2H_5OH)}}{n_{(C_2H_5OH)} + n_{(H_2O)}}$$

$$= 0.040 \qquad \dots \text{(i)}$$

Now we have to find number of moles of ethanol in 1 L of the solution which is nearly = 1 L of water (because solution is dilute)

$$\text{No. of moles in 1L water} = \frac{1000g}{18\,g\,mol^{-1}}$$

$$= 55.55 \text{ moles}$$

Substituting $n(H_2O) = 55.55$ in eqn (i), we get

$$\frac{n_{(C_2H_5OH)}}{n_{(C_2H_5OH)} + 55.55} = 0.040$$

$$0.040\, n_{(C_2H_5OH)} + 55.55 \times 0.040 = n_{(C_2H_5OH)}$$

or $\quad 0.96\, n_{(C_2H_5OH)} = 55.55 \times 0.040$

or $\quad n_{(C_2H_5OH)} = 2.31$ mol

Hence, molarity of the solution = 2.31M

**1.30 What will be the mass of one $^{12}C$ atom in g?**

**Ans.** 1 mol of $^{12}C$ atoms = $6.022 \times 10^{23}$ atoms = 12g

thus, $6.022 \times 10^{23}$ atoms of $^{12}C$ have mass = 12g

$\therefore$ 1 atom of $^{12}C$ will have mass

$$= \frac{12}{6.022 \times 10^{23}}\, g = 1.9927 \times 10^{-23}\, g$$

**1.31 How many significant figures should be present in the answer of the following calculations?**

(i) $\quad \dfrac{0.02856 \times 298.15 \times 0.112}{0.5785}$

(ii) $\quad 5 \times 5.364$

(iii) $\quad 0.0125 + 0.7864 + 0.0215$

**Ans.** (i) The least precise term has 3 significant figures (in 0.112). Hence, the answer should have 3 significant figures.

(ii) Leaving the exact number (5), the second term has 4 significant figures. Hence, the answer should be 4 significant figures.

(iii) In the given addition the least number of decimal places in the term is 4. Hence the answer should have the 4 significant figures.

**1.32 Use the data given in the following table to calculate the molar mass of naturally occuring *argon* isotopes:**

| Isotope | Isotopic molar mass | Abundance |
|---|---|---|
| $^{36}$Ar | 35.96755 g mol$^{-1}$ | 0.337% |
| $^{38}$Ar | 37.96272 g mol$^{-1}$ | 0.063% |
| $^{40}$Ar | 39.9624 g mol$^{-1}$ | 99.600% |

**Ans.** Molar mass of Ar

$= 35.96755 \times 0.00337 + 37.96272 \times 0.00063 + 39.96924 \times 0.99600$

$= 39.948$ g mol$^{-1}$

**1.33 Calculate the number of atoms in each of the following**

(i) 52 moles of Ar  (ii) 52 u of He

(iii) 52 g of He.

**Ans.** (i) 1 mol of Ar = $6.022 \times 10^{23}$ atoms

52 mol of Ar = $52 \times 6.022 \times 10^{23}$ atom

$= 3.131 \times 10^{25}$ atoms

(ii) 4 u of He = 1 atom of He

$52$ u of He $= \dfrac{1}{4} \times 52$ atoms = 13 atoms

(iii) 1 mole of He = 4g of He = $6.022 \times 10^{23}$ atoms

$52$ g of He $= \dfrac{6.022 \times 10^{23}}{4} \times 52$ atoms

$= 7.8286 \times 10^{24}$ atoms

**1.34 A welding fuel gas contains carbon and hydrogen only. Burning a small sample of it in oxygen gives 3.38 g carbon dioxide, 0.690 g of water and no other products. A volume of 10.0 L (measured at STP) of this welding gas is found to weigh 11.6 g. Calculate (i) empirical formula, (ii) molar mass of the gas, and (iii) molecular formula.**

**Ans.** Amount of carbon in 3.38 g of

$$CO_2 = \frac{12}{44} \times 3.38\, g = 0.9218\, g$$

Amount of hydrogen in 0.690 g of

$$H_2O = \frac{2}{18} \times 0.690\, g = 0.0767\, g$$

As compound contains only C and H, therefore, total mass of the compound $= 0.9218 + 0.0767$

$= 0.9985$ g

% of C in the compound $= \dfrac{0.9218}{0.9985} \times 100 = 92.32$

% of H in the compound $= \dfrac{0.0767}{0.9985} \times 100 = 7.68$

| Element | % by mass | Atomic mass | Moles of the element | Simplest molar ratio | Simplest whole number molar ratio |
|---|---|---|---|---|---|
| C | 92.32 | 12 | $\dfrac{92.32}{12} = 7.69$ | 1 | 1 |
| H | 7.68 | 1 | $\dfrac{7.68}{1} = 7.68$ | 1 | 1 |

$\therefore$ Empirical Formula = CH

$\therefore$ 10.0 L of the gas at STP weigh = 11.6 g

22.4 L of the gas at STP will weigh

$$= \frac{11.6}{10.0} \times 22.4 = 25.984g \text{ or } 26 \text{ approx}$$

Molar mass = 26 g mol$^{-1}$

Empirical formula mass of CH = 12 + 1 = 13

$\therefore \quad n = \dfrac{\text{Molecular mass}}{\text{E.F.mass}} = \dfrac{26}{13} = 2$

$\therefore$ Molecular formula = $2 \times CH = C_2H_2$

**1.35 Calcium carbonate reacts with aqueous HCl to give $CaCl_2$ and $CO_2$ according to the reaction.**
$$CaCO_3\,(s) + 2HCl\,(aq) \rightarrow CaCl_2\,(aq) + CO_2(g) + H_2O(l)$$
**What mass of $CaCO_3$ is required to react completely with 25 mL of 0.75 M HCl?**

**Ans.** **Step 1 :** Calculate mass of HCl in 25mL of 0.75M HCl

1000 mL of 0.75 M HCl contain HCl = 0.75 mol
$$= 0.75 \times 36.5\ g\ = 27.375g$$

25 mL of 0.75 M HCl will contain HCl
$$= \frac{27.375}{1000} \times 25\ g = 0.6844\ g.$$

**Step 2 :** Calculate mass of $CaCO_3$ reacting completely with 0.6844 g of HCl
$$CaCO_3\,(s) + 2HCl\,(aq) \rightarrow CaCl_2\,(aq) + CO_2\,(g) + H_2O\,(l)$$
2 mol of HCl, i.e., $2 \times 36.5g$

$= 73g$ of HCl react completely with $CaCO_3$ = 1 mol
$$= 100\ g$$

$\therefore$ 0.6844 g of HCl will react completely with
$$CaCO_3\ =\ \frac{100 \times 0.6844}{73}g = 0.938\ g$$

**1.36 Chlorine is prepared in the laboratory by treating manganese dioxide ($MnO_2$) with aqueous hydrochloric acid according to the reaction**
$$4\,HCl\,(aq) +\ MnO_2(s) \rightarrow 2H_2O\,(\ell) + MnCl_2(aq) + Cl_2\,(g)$$
**How many grams of HCl react with 5.0 g of manganese dioxide?**

**Ans.** 1 mol of $MnO_2$, i.e., $55 + 32 = 87$ g of $MnO_2$ react with 4 moles of HCl, i.e., $4 \times 36.5$ g = 146 g of HCl.

Hence 5.0 g of $MnO_2$ will react with HCl
$$= \frac{146}{87} \times 5.0g = 8.40g$$

---

## SECTION B — PRACTICE QUESTIONS 

### MULTIPLE CHOICE QUESTIONS

1. Which one of the following pairs of compounds illustrate the law of multiple proportions ?
   (a) $H_2O$ and $Na_2O$  (b) $MgO$ and $Na_2O$
   (c) $Na_2O$ and $BaO$  (d) $SnCl_2$ and $SnCl_4$

2. If the true value for an experimental result is 6.23 and the results reported by three students $X$, $Y$ and $Z$ are :
   $X$ : 6.18 and 6.28
   $Y$ : 6.20 and 6.023
   $Z$ : 6.22 and 6.24
   Which of the following option is correct :
   (a) $X$ precise, $Y$ accurate, $Z$ precise and accurate.
   (b) $X$ precise and accurate, $Y$ not precise, $Z$ precise
   (c) Both $X$ & $Z$ precise & accurate, $Y$ not precise.
   (d) Both $X$ & $Y$ neither precise nor accurate, $Z$ both precise and accurate.

3. Irrespective of the source, pure sample, of water always yields 88.89% mass of oxygen and 11.11% mass of hydrogen. This is explained by the law of
   (a) conservation of mass  (b) multiple proportions
   (c) constant composition  (d) constant volume

4. The number of significant figures for the three numbers 161 cm, 0.161 cm, 0.0161 cm are
   (a) 3,4 and 5 respectively
   (b) 3,4 and 4 respectively
   (c) 3,3 and 4 respectively
   (d) 3,3 and 3 respectively

5. Consider the following statements.
   (i) Atoms of H, O, N and C have identical properties but different mass.
   (ii) Matter is divisible into atoms which are further indivisible.
   (iii) The ratio of N: H in $NH_3$ is 1 : 3 and N : O in nitric oxide is 2 : 1.
   (iv) Dalton's atomic theory support law of conservation of mass.
   Which of the following pairs of statements is true according to Dalton's atomic theory ?
   (a) (i) and (ii)  (b) (ii) and (iii)
   (c) (ii) and (iv)  (d) (i) and (iv)

6. Two samples of lead oxide were separately reduced to metallic lead by heating in a current of hydrogen. The weight of lead from one oxide was half the weight of lead obtained from the other oxide. The data illustrates
   (a) law of reciprocal proportions
   (b) law of constant proportions
   (c) law of multiple proportions
   (d) law of equivalent proportions

7. Equal volumes of two gases A and B are kept in a container at the same temperature and pressure. Avogadro's law is invalid if
   (a) the gases are reactive
   (b) the gases are non-reactive
   (c) gas A has more number of molecules than gas B.
   (d) None of these

**8.** Which has maximum number of molecules?
   (a)  $7 g N_2$        (b)  $2 g H_2$
   (c)  $16 g NO_2$      (d)  $16 g O_2$

**9.** One mole of $CO_2$ contains :
   (a)  3 g atoms of $CO_2$
   (b)  $18.1 \times 10^{23}$ molecules of $CO_2$
   (c)  $6.02 \times 10^{23}$ atoms of O
   (d)  $6.02 \times 10^{23}$ atoms of C

**10.** The weight of one molecule of a compound $C_{60}H_{122}$ is
   (a)  $1.2 \times 10^{-20}$ gram
   (b)  $1.4 \times 10^{-21}$ gram
   (c)  $5.025 \times 10^{23}$ gram
   (d)  $6.023 \times 10^{23}$ gram

**11.** What is the average atomic mass of bromine from the following data : (abundance is in %)

| Isotope | Mass | Abundance |
|---|---|---|
| $^{79}Br$ | 78.9183361 | 50.69 |
| $^{81}Br$ | 80.916289 | 49.31 |

   (a)  79.9        (b)  76.6
   (c)  75.9        (d)  69.9

**12.** The number of moles of oxygen in one litre of air containing 21% oxygen by volume, under standard conditions are
   (a)  0.0093 mole      (b)  0.21 mole
   (c)  2.10 mole       (d)  0.186 mole

**13.** The mass of 1 mole of electrons is
   (a)  $9.1 \times 10^{-28} g$
   (b)  1.008 mg
   (c)  0.55 mg
   (d)  $9.1 \times 10^{-27} g$

**14.** How many moles of magnesium phosphate, $Mg_3(PO_4)_2$ will contain 0.25 mole of oxygen atoms?
   (a)  $1.25 \times 10^{-2}$
   (b)  $2.5 \times 10^{-2}$
   (c)  0.02
   (d)  $3.125 \times 10^{-2}$

## ASSERTION & REASON QUESTIONS

**DIRECTIONS (Qs. 1-6) :** *Each of these questions contains an assertion followed by reason. Read them carefully and answer the question on the basis of following options. You have to select the one that best describes the two statements.*
   (a)  If both Assertion and Reason are correct and the Reason is a correct explanation of the Assertion.
   (b)  If both Assertion and Reason are correct but Reason is not a correct explanation of the Assertion.
   (c)  If the Assertion is correct but Reason is incorrect.
   (d)  If the Assertion is incorrect but the Reason is correct.

**1.** **Assertion :** If significant figures number is higher, then smaller is the uncertainty and higher is the precision.
   **Reason :** The uncertainty in the experiment or the calculated values is indicated by mentioning the number of significant figures.

**2.** **Assertion :** Gases completely occupy the container in which they are placed.
   **Reason :** Gases have definite shape and definite volume and intermolecular forces are large.

**3.** **Assertion :** Both 106g of sodium carbonate and 12g of carbon have same number of carbon atoms.
   **Reason :** Both contain 1g atom of carbon which contain $6.022 \times 10^{23}$ carbon atoms.

**4.** **Assertion :** 1L of $N_2$ and 1L of $H_2$ contain same of moles.
   **Reason :** Under similar conditions, both the gases have same number of moles.

**5.** **Assertion :** NaCl is used to calculate the formula mass instead of molecular mass.
   **Reason :** NaCl (sodium chloride) does not exists a single entity in solid state.

**6.** **Assertion :** Number of gram molecules of $Na_2CO_3$ in 5.3 g of $Na_2CO_3$ is 0.05.
   **Reason:** 1g molecule represents 1g of compound.

## CASE/PASSAGE BASED QUESTIONS

**DIRECTIONS (Qs. 1-5) :** *Read the following case/passage and answer the questions.*

To describe the structure of matter which could explain the experimental facts known at that time about elements, compounds and mixtures and also the laws of chemical combination. John Dalton in 1808 put forward a theory known as Dalton's atomic theory. According to this all matter is made up of tiny, indivisible particles called atoms. All atoms of a specific element are identical in mass size and other properties. However atoms of different element exhibit, different properties and vary in mass and size. Atoms can neither be created nor destroyed.

**1.** Which of the following law could not be explained by Dalton's atomic theory?
   (a)  Law of conservation of mass
   (b)  Law of constant proportion
   (c)  Law of multiple proportion
   (d)  Law of gaseous volume

**2.** Irrespective of a source, a given compound always contains same elements combined together in the same proportion by mass. This is known as
   (a)  Law of multiple proportion.
   (b)  Law of constant or  definite proportions
   (c)  Law of reciprocal proportions
   (d)  None of these

3. Which of the following statement is incorrect?
   (a) Law of conservation of mass, law of constant proportion, law of multiple proportions, law of reciprocal proportions are the laws with the mass relationships.
   (b) Mass and energy are interconvertible.
   (c) Law of multiple proportion was given by J. L. Proust.
   (d) Law of conservation of mass was given by A. Lavoisier.

4. In compound A, 1.00g of nitrogen unites with 0.57g of oxygen. In compound B, 2.00g of nitrogen combines with 2.24g of oxygen. In compound C, 3.00g of nitrogen combines with 5.11g of oxygen. These results obey the following law
   (a) law of constant proportion
   (b) law of multiple proportion
   (c) law of reciprocal proportion
   (d) Dalton's law of partial pressure

5. The molecular weight of $O_2$ and $SO_2$ are 32 and 64 respectively. At 15°C and 150 mm Hg pressure, one litre of $O_2$ contains 'N' molecules. The number of molecules in two litres of $SO_2$ under the same conditions of temperature and pressure will be :
   (a) N/2              (b) 1 N
   (c) 2 N              (d) 4 N

## VERY SHORT ANSWER QUESTIONS

1. How many significant figures are present in $6.023 \times 10^{23}$?
2. Is the law of constant composition true for all types of compounds? Explain why or why not.
3. In what smallest whole-number ratio must N and O atoms combine to make dinitrogen to tetroxide $N_2O_4$ ? What is the mole ratio of the elements in this compound ?
4. Write 0.0005729 in scientific notation.
5. Nitrogen and Oxygen form $N_2O$, NO, $NO_2$, $N_2O_4$, $N_2O_5$. Which Law of chemical combination is followed?
6. Q is an impure substance, is it an element, compound or a mixture?
7. Express the following results to the proper number of significant figures.

$$\frac{\left(1.38 \times 10^{-4}\right)(0.8)}{3.9}$$

8. Why air is not always regarded as homogeneous mixture?
9. What is the law called which deals with the ratios of volumes of the gaseous reactants and products?
10. What is the difference between 2H and $H_2$?
11. What are basic properties used to identify a substance?
12. Dinitrogen combines with dihydrogen to form ammonia according to the following reaction.

$$N_2(g) + 3H_2(g) \rightleftharpoons 2NH_3(g)$$

What is the ratio of their volumes under similar conditions of temperature and pressure?

13. Balance the equation
$$P_4(s) + O_2(g) \longrightarrow P_4O_{10}(s)$$
14. What is the S.I. unit of energy?
15. Calculate the total number of electrons present in 1.4 g of nitrogen gas?
16. A colourless liquid used in rocket engines, whose empirical formula is $NO_2$, has a molar mass of 92. What is its molecular formula?
17. Why are the atomic masses of most of the elements fractional?
18. How many grams of silver are in 0.263 mol of Ag ?
19. Calculate the mass of $6.022 \times 10^{22}$ atoms of He.
20. Which element is used as a standard for comparing atomic and molecular masses?
21. Boron occurs in nature in the form of two isotopes $^{11}_{5}B$ and $^{10}_{5}B$ in ratio of 81% and 19% respectively. Calculate its average atomic mass.
22. Alkaline solution of $KMnO_4$ reacts as follows:
$$2KMnO_4 + 2KOH \longrightarrow 2K_2MnO_4 + H_2O + [O]$$
Calculate the equivalent weight of $KMnO_4$ in basic medium.
23. Calculate the mass of ferric oxide that will be obtained by complete oxidation of 2 g of Fe.
[Atomic weights of Fe = 56 u,  O = 16 u]
24. Balance the equation
$$C_3H_8(g) + O_2(g) \longrightarrow CO_2(g) + H_2O(1)$$

## SHORT ANSWER QUESTIONS

1. What is derived unit? Derive the unit for density in SI unit?
2. The population of India based on 1981 census figure was 684 million. Express the results in scientific notation and calculate the number of significant figures.
3. (a) When 4.2 g of $NaHCO_3$ ( sodium hydrogen carbonate) is added to a solution of $CH_3COOH$ (acetic acid) weighing 10.0 g, it is observed that 2.2 g $CO_2$ is released into atmosphere. The residue is found to weigh 12.0 g. Show that three observations are in agreement with the law of conservation of mass.
   (b) If 6.3 g of $NaHCO_3$ are added to 15.0 g $CH_3COOH$ solution, the residue is found to weigh 18.0 g. What is the mass of $CO_2$ released in the reaction?
4. (a) Classify the following as pure substances or mixtures
   (b) Separate the pure substance into elements and compounds and divide the mixtures into homogeneous and heterogeneous categories:
   (i) graphite (ii) milk (iii) air (iv) diamond (v) petrol (vi) tap water (vii) distilled water (viii) oxygen (ix) 22 carat gold (x) steel (xi) iron (xii) iodized table salt (xiii) wood (xiv) cloud.

5. Give at least four points of difference between a compound and a mixture.

6. Explain how compounds differ from elements?

7. Explain how mixture differs from pure substance?

8. How many significant figures are there in $1.00 \times 10^6$?

9. What are various types of mixtures? Give at least one example in each case?

10. How many molecules of water of hydration are present in 39.2 mg of Mohr's salt ?    $[FeSO_4 . (NH_4)_2SO_4. 6H_2O]$

11. How many moles of hydrogen, phosphorous and oxygen are present in 0.213 moles of $H_3PO_4$ (Phosphoric acid)?

12. The cost of table salt (NaCl) and table sugar ($C_{12}H_{22}O_{11}$) are ₹ 2 per kg and ₹ 6 per kg respectively calculate their cost per mole.

13. The vapour density of a mixture of $NO_2$ and $N_2O_4$ is 38.3 at 27°C. Calculate the number of moles of $NO_2$ in 100 g of the mixture.

14. One mole of sugar contains .......................oxygen atoms.

15. Calculate the number of electrons present in 21g of nitride ions.

## LONG ANSWER QUESTIONS

1. (i) 0.9031g of mixture of NaCl and KCl on treatment with conc. $H_2SO_4$ yields 1.0784g of a mixture of $Na_2SO_4$ and $K_2SO_4$. Calculate the % composition of the mixture.

(ii) Calculate the percentage of the naturally occurring isotopes $^{35}Cl$ and $^{37}Cl$ that accounts for the mass of chlorine taken as 35.45.

2. (i) Concentrated aqueous sulphuric acid is 98% $H_2SO_4$ by mass and has a density of 1.84 g mL$^{-1}$. What volume of the concentrated acid is required to make 5.0L of 0.50 M $H_2SO_4$ solution? ( Mol. weight of sulphuric acid = 98)

(ii) You are given a solution of 14.8M $NH_3$. How many milliliters of this solution do you require to give 100 ml of 1M$NH_3$? How much of water will you add?

3. (i) Calculate the volume at STP occupied by (a) 14 g of nitrogen, (b) 1.5 moles of carbon dioxide and (c) $10^{21}$ molecules of oxygen.

(ii) Ammonia contains 82.35% of nitrogen and 17.65% of hydrogen. Water contains 88.90% of oxygen and 11.10% of hydrogen. Nitrogen trioxide contains 63.15% of oxygen and 36.85% of nitrogen. Show that these data illustrate the law of reciprocal proportions.

4. What are the limitations of a chemical equation? How could these limitations be removed?

5. A compound on analysis gave the following percentage composition:
Na = 14.31%, S = 9.97%, H = 6.22% O = 69.50%
Calculate the molecular formula of the compound on the assumption that all the hydrogen in the compound is present in combination with oxygen as water of crystallization. Molecular mass of the compound is 322.

**SOLUTIONS**

### *Multiple Choice Questions*

1. **(d)**    $SnCl_2$        $SnCl_4$
$119 : 2 \times 35.5$    $119 : 4 \times 35.5$
Chlorine ratio in both compounds is
    $= 2 \times 35.5 : 4 \times 35.5 = 1 : 2$

2. **(d)** Both $Y$ and $X$ are neither precise nor accurate as the two values in each of them are not close. With respect to $X$ & $Y$, the values of $Z$ are close & agree with the true value. Hence, both precise & accurate.

3. **(c)** The H : O ratio in water is fixed, irrespective of its source. Hence, it explains law of constant composition.

4. **(d)** We know that all non-zero digits are significant and the zeros at the beginning of a number are not significant. Therefore number 161 cm, 0.161 cm and 0.0161cm have 3, 3 and 3 significant figures respectively.

5. **(c)** For statement (i) : H, O, C, N = All have different chemical properties.
For statement (ii) : It is true as per Dalton's postulate.

For statement (iii) : N : O = 1 : 1 (NO)
For statement (iv) : Dalton's postulates says, atoms can neither be created nor destroyed.

6. **(c)**

7. **(d)** Avogadro's law is independent of the reactive or unreactive nature of the gases.
According to Avogadro's law equal volumes of gases at the same temperature and pressure should contain equal number of molecules.

8. **(b)** 2g of $H_2$ means one mole of $H_2$, hence contains $6.023 \times 10^{23}$ molecules. Others have less than one mole, so have less no. of molecules.

9. **(d)** 1 molecule of $CO_2$ has one atom of C and two atoms of oxygen.
$\therefore$   1 mole of $CO_2$ has
$= 6.02 \times 10^{23}$ atoms of C
$= 2 \times 6.02 \times 10^{23}$ atoms of O

**10.** **(b)** Molecular weight of $C_{60}H_{122}$ = $(12 \times 60) + 122$ = 842.

Therefore weight of one molecule

$$= \frac{\text{Molecular weight of } C_{60}H_{122}}{\text{Avagadro's number}}$$

$$= \frac{842}{6.023 \times 10^{23}} = 1.4 \times 10^{-21} g$$

**11.** **(a)** $(78.9183361) \times (0.5069) + (80.916289) \times (0.4931)$ = 79.9

**12.** **(a)** 21% of 1 litre is 0.21 litre.

22.4 litres = 1 mole at STP

$$\therefore \quad 0.21 \text{ litre} = \frac{0.21}{22.4} = 0.0093 \text{ mol}$$

**13.** **(c)** Mass of 1 electron = $9.11 \times 10^{-28}$ g

$\therefore$ Mass of 1 mole $(6.02 \times 10^{23})$ electrons

= $9.11 \times 10^{-28} \times 6.02 \times 10^{23}$g

= $55 \times 10^{-5}$ g = $55 \times 10^{-5} \times 10^{3}$ mg = 0.55 mg.

**14.** **(d)** 1 Mole of $Mg_3(PO_4)_2$ contains 8 mole of oxygen atoms

$\therefore$ 8 mole of oxygen atoms $\equiv$ 1 mole of $Mg_3(PO_4)_2$

0.25 mole of oxygen atom $\equiv \dfrac{1}{8} \times 0.25$ mole of $Mg_3(PO_4)_2$

= $3.125 \times 10^{-2}$ mole of $Mg_3(PO_4)_2$

### Assertion & Reason Questions

**1.** **(a)** Precision refers to the proximity of various measurements for the same quantity. However, accuracy is the agreement of a particular value to the true value of the result. Significant figures are meaningful digits which are known with certainly.

**2.** **(c)** Gas molecules have negligible intermolecular interaction. Therefore, molecules are completely free to move and occupy the volume of the container.

**3.** **(a)** 106 g of $NaHCO_3$ contains 12g of carbon. Thus both $NaHCO_3$ and carbon contain $6.022 \times 10^{23}$ atoms.

**4.** **(a)** At similar condition of temperature and pressure volume ratio of gases = Mole ratio = Number of molecular ratio.

**5.** **(a)** NaCl is an ionic compound therefore does not exist as a single entity in solid state. Formula mass of NaCl = At. mass of $Na^+$ + At. mass of $Cl^-$
= 23u + 35.5u = 58.5u.

**6.** **(c)** 1g molecule of $Na_2CO_3$ = 1 mol = 106g
Since       106 g $Na_2CO_3$ = 1g molecule

$$\therefore \quad 5.3 \text{ g } Na_2CO_3 = \frac{1 \times 5.3}{106} = 0.05$$

### Case/Passage Based Questions

**1.** **(d)**         **2.** **(b)**

**3.** **(c)** Law of multiple proportions was given by Dalton.

**4.** **(b)** Law of multiple proportion. As the ratio of oxygen which combine with fix weights of 1 g of nitrogen bears a simple whole number ratio
0.57 : 1.12 : 1.703 = 1 : 2 : 3

**5.** **(c)** According to Avogadro's law "equal volumes of all gases contain equal number of molecules under similar conditions of temperature and pressure". Thus if 1 L of one gas contains N molecules, 2 L of any other gas under the same conditions of temperature and pressure will contain 2N molecules.

### Very Short Answer Questions

**1.** Four

**2.** No, law of constant composition is not true for all types of compounds. It is true only for the compounds obtained from one isotope. For example, carbon exists in two common isotopes, $^{12}C$ and $^{14}C$. When it forms $CO_2$ from $^{12}C$, the ratio of masses is 12 : 32 = 3 : 8 but from $^{14}C$, the ratio will be 14 : 32 = 7 : 16 which is not same as in the first case.

**3.** 1 : 2

**4.** 0.0005729 could be written in scientific notations as $5.729 \times 10^{-4}$.

**5.** The Law of multiple proportions.

**6.** Q is a mixture.

**7.** $\dfrac{\left(1.38 \times 10^{-4}\right)(0.8)}{3.9} = 28.3 \times 10^{-6}$

**8.** This is due to the presence of dust particles.

**9.** Gay Lussac's law of combining volumes.

**10.** 2H represents two atoms of hydrogen and $H_2$ represents one molecule of hydrogen.

**11.** These are colour, density, solubility, melting point, boiling point, etc.

**12.** The ratio of their volumes is 1 : 3 : 2.

**13.** $P_4(s) + 5\ O_2(g) \longrightarrow P_4O_{10}(s)$

**14.** Joule

**15.** Number of moles of nitrogen gas = $\dfrac{1.4}{28}$ = 0.05 mole

Number of molecules of $N_2$ gas
= $0.05 \times 6.022 \times 10^{23}$ = $3.01 \times 10^{22}$ molecules
= $3.01 \times 10^{22} \times 14$ electrons = $4.214 \times 10^{23}$ electrons.

**16.** The formula mass is 46.

The number of times the empirical formula $NO_2$, occurs in the compound is = 92/46 =2.

The molecular formula is $N_2O_4$

**17.** This is because atomic masses are the relative masses of atoms as compared with an atom of C-12 isotope taken as 12.

**18.** No. of grams of Ag = (0.263 mol of Ag)

$$\frac{107.9 \text{g of Ag}}{1 \text{ mol of Ag}} = 28.4 \text{ g of Ag}$$

**19.** $6.022 \times 10^{23}$ atom of He weights 4 g

∴ $6.022 \times 10^{22}$ atoms of He will weighs

$$= \frac{4 \times 6.022 \times 10^{22}}{6.022 \times 10^{23}} = 0.4 \text{ g}$$

**20.** Carbon, $C^{12}$ isotope is used as a standard for comparing the atomic as well as molecular masses.

**21.** Average atomic weight $= \dfrac{11 \times 81 + 10 \times 19}{100} = 10.81$

**22.** Equivalent weight

$$= \frac{\text{Molecular Weight}}{\text{Number of Electrons gained}}$$

$$= \frac{158}{1} = 158 \text{ g} \quad \boxed{Mn^{7+} + e^- \rightarrow Mn^{6+}}$$

**23.** $4Fe + 3O_2 \rightarrow 2Fe_2O_3$

$4 \times 56$g of Fe gives $2 \times 160$ g of $Fe_2O_3$

2 g of Fe gives $\dfrac{2 \times 160}{4 \times 56} \times 2 = 2.857$ g of $Fe_2O_3$.

**24.** $C_3H_8(g) + 5O_2(g) \longrightarrow 3CO_2(g) + 4H_2O(l)$

### *Short Answer Questions*

**1.** The units for physical quantities such as area, volume, density etc which are derived from the SI units of basic physical quantities are called derived units.

Density = Mass / Volume

The SI unit of mass is kg and volume is m³, hence unit of density is kg m⁻³.

**2.** 1 million = $10^6$ hence 684 million = $684 \times 10^6$

The value in terms of scientific notation may be expressed as $6.84 \times 10^8$. It has three significant figures.

**3.** (a) $NaHCO_3$ + $CH_3COOH \longrightarrow$

    4.2 g       10.0 g

         $CH_3COONa + H_2O + CO_2 \uparrow$

         12.0 g        2.2 g

∴ Total mass of the reactants = Total mass of the products

Hence, the law of conservation of mass is followed.

(b) $NaHCO_3$ + $CH_3COOH \longrightarrow$

    6.3 g       15.0 g

         $\underbrace{CH_3COONa + H_2O + CO_2}_{18.0 \text{ g}}$

According to the Law of conservation of mass, The mass of reactants = The mass of the products

$6.3 + 15.0 \rightarrow$      $18.0 + x$

$21.3$        $\rightarrow$      $18.0 + x$

∴   x (The mass of $CO_2$ formed)

$= 21.3 - 18 = 3.3$ g.

**4.** (a) **Pure substances :** Graphite, diamond, distilled water, oxygen, iron.

**Mixtures :** Milk, air, petrol, tap water, 22 carat gold, steel, iodized table salt, wood, cloud.

(b) **Elements :** Graphite, diamond, iron,

**Compunds :** Distilled water, oxygen,

**Homogeneous mixtures :** Milk, air, wood, petrol, tap water, 22 carat gold. steel

**Heterogeneous mixtures :** Iodized table salt, cloud.

**5.**

| | Compound | | Mixture |
|---|---|---|---|
| 1 | Elements combine in definite ratio by mass. | 1 | Constituents may combine in any ratio. |
| 2 | They are homogeneous in nature. | 2 | They may or may not be homogeneous. |
| 3 | Components cannot be separated easily. | 3 | Components could be separated easily. |
| 4 | Properties are different from those of constituent elements. | 4 | Properties resemble with the constituents. |

**6.** **Definition:** A compound contains atoms of different elements chemically combined together in a fixed ratio. An element is a pure chemical substance made of same type of atom.

**Composition:** Compounds contain different elements in a fixed ratio arranged in a defined manner through chemical bonds. They contain only one type of molecule. Elements that compose the compound are chemically combined. Elements contain only one type of atom..

**Ability to break down:** A compound can be separated into simpler substances by chemical methods/reactions. Elements cannot be broken down into simpler substances by chemical reactions.

**7.**

| | Pure Substance | | Mixture |
|---|---|---|---|
| 1 | Pure substances are composed of only one type of atom or molecule. | 1 | Mixture contain two or more substances. |
| 2 | As it consists of only one type of substance the composition remains same throughout. | 2 | It is formed of more than one type of substance. Hence composition is different thoughtout. |
| 3 | Cannot be separated by physical methods. | 3 | Can be separated into constituting substance by physical methods. |

**8.** There are 3 significant figure in $1.00 \times 10^6$.

**9.** Mixtures can be broadly classified into 2 main categories. These are
   1. Homogeneous Mixtures
   2. Heterogeneous Mixtures

The mixtures in which the components have a uniform distribution throughout the mixture are known as homogeneous mixtures. For example, salt and water is homogeneous mixture

The mixtures in which the components do not have a uniform distribution throughout the mixture which means in which the components are unevenly distributed are said to be heterogeneous mixtures. For example, sand and water is an example of the heterogeneous mixture.

**10.** Molecular mass of Mohr's salt = 392 gm

392 gm of $FeSO_4.(NH_4)_2SO_4.6H_2O$ has $6 \times 6.023 \times 10^{23}$ molecules of water of crystallization hence, $39.2 \times 10^{-3}$ gm of Mohr's salt contains

$$= \frac{6 \times 6.023 \times 10^{23} \times 39.2 \times 10^{-3}}{392}$$

$= 3.61 \times 10^{20}$ molecules of water of crystallization.

**11.** In 1 mole of $H_3PO_4$ there are 1 mole of phosphorus, 3 moles of hydrogen and four moles of oxygen atoms. Thus 0.213 moles of $H_3PO_4$ consists of $3 \times 0.213 = 0.639$ moles of hydrogen.

Thus 0.213 moles of $H_3PO_4$ consists of $1 \times 0.213 = 0.213$ moles of phosphorus. Thus 0.213 moles of $H_3PO_4$ consists of $4 \times 0.213 = 0.852$ moles of oxygen.

**12.** (a)  Cost of table salt (NaCl) per mole

Gram molecular mass of NaCl

= 23 + 35.5 = 58.5 g

Now, 1000 g of NaCl cost = ₹ 2

∴    58.5 g of NaCl will cost

$$= \frac{2}{(1000g)} \times (58.5g)$$

= 0.117 Rupee = $0.117 \times 100$ = 12 paise (approx.)

(b)  Cost of table sugar ($C_{12}H_{22}O_{11}$) per mole

Gram molecular mass of ($C_{12}H_{22}O_{11}$)

= $12 \times 12 + 22 \times 1 = 16 \times 11 = 144 + 22 + 176 = 342$ g

Now,  1000 g of sugar cost = ₹ 6

∴ 342 g of sugar will cost $= \dfrac{6}{(1000g)} \times (342g)$

= 2.052 = 2.0 ₹ (approx.)

**13.** Vapour density of the mixture of $NO_2$ and $N_2O_4$ = 38.3

Molecular mass of the mixture

= 2 × Vapour density

= $2 \times 38.3$ = 76.6 u = 76.6 g

Mass of the mixture = 100g

No. of moles of the mixture $= \dfrac{100}{76.6}$

Let the mass of $NO_2$ in the mixture = x g

∴    Mass of $N_2O_4$ in the mixture = (100 – x) g

Molar mass of $NO_2$ = 14 + 32 = 46 u = 46 g

Molar mass of $N_2O_4$ = 28 + 64 = 92 u = 92 g

No. of moles of $NO_2 = \dfrac{x}{46}$

No. of moles of $N_2O_4 = \dfrac{(100-x)}{92}$

Total no. of moles in the mixture

$$= \frac{x}{46} + \frac{(100-x)}{92}$$

Equating (i) and (ii), $\dfrac{x}{46} + \dfrac{(100-x)}{92} = \dfrac{100}{76.6}$

$92x + 46(100 - x) = \dfrac{100}{76.6} \times 46 \times 92 = 5524.8$

$92x - 46x = 5524.8 - 4600 = 924.8$.

**14.** One mole of sugar $C_{12}H_{22}O_{11}$ contains $11 \times 6.023 \times 10^{23}$ oxygen atoms

= $66.253 \times 10^{23} = 6.6253 \times 10^{24}$ atoms of oxygen

**15.** 14 g of Nitride ion, $N^{3-}$ contains (7 + 3)

= 10 moles of electrons

21 g of $N^{3-} = \dfrac{21}{14} \times 10 \times 6.022 \times 10^{23}$ electrons

= $9.033 \times 10^{24}$ electrons.

### *Long Answer Questions*

**1.** (i)  $2NaCl + H_2SO_4 \longrightarrow Na_2SO_4 + 2HCl$

   117g            142g        ...(i)

$2KCl + H_2SO_4 \longrightarrow K_2SO_4 + 2HCl$

   149g           174g        ...(ii)

Mass of the mixture =  0.9031g

Let the mass of NaCl = xg

The mass of KCl = (0.9031– x)g

Mass of $Na_2SO_4 + K_2SO_4$ = 1.0784g

From equation (i),

117g NaCl gives  = 142g $Na_2SO_4$

x g of NaCl will give = 142x/117g $Na_2SO_4$

From equation (ii) 149g KCl gives 174g $K_2SO_4$

(0.9031– x)g KCl will give = 174(0.9031 – x)/149 g $K_2SO_4$

Since mass of $Na_2SO_4$ and $K_2SO_4$ = 1.0784g

Thus 142x/117+ 174(0.9031 – x)/149 = 1.0784

On solving,  x = 0.518g

∴    Mass of NaCl = 0.518g  and mass of KCl =  0.9031– 0.518 = 0.3851g

% NaCl = 0.518 × 100/0.9031 = 57.36%

and % of KCl = $\dfrac{0.3851}{0.9031} \times 100 = 42.64\%$

(ii) Suppose $^{35}Cl$ present is = x%. Then $^{37}Cl$ present is = (100 – x)%

$$= \dfrac{x \times 35 + (100 - x) \times 37}{100} = 35.45$$

Average atomic mass $= \dfrac{x \times 35 + (100 - x) \times 37}{100}$

$$= 35.45$$

or   35x + 3700 – 37x = 3545
or   2x = 155   or   x = 77.5%.
Hence $^{35}Cl$ = 77.5 % and $^{37}Cl$ = 22.5%

**2.** (i) First let us calculate the molarity using the density of solution

$$M = \dfrac{\%\ age\ of\ solute \times 10 \times density\ of\ solution}{Mol.\ Weight\ of\ solute}$$

$$= \dfrac{98\%}{98} \times 10 \times 1.84\,g/mL = 18.4M$$

Using $M_1 V_1 = M_2 V_2$ where $M_1$ = 18.4M ;
$V_1$ = ?; $M_2$ = 0.50M ; $V_2$ = 5.0L
By substituting the values
18.4 × $V_1$ = 0.50 × 5

$$V_1 = \dfrac{0.50 \times 5}{18.4} = 0.136L$$

(ii) Using $M_1 V_1 = M_2 V_2$
where $M_1$ = 14.8 M, $V_1$ = ?,
$M_2$ = 1M, $V_2$ = 100 ml
∴   14.8M × $V_1$ = 1M × 100 ml

or   $V_1 = \dfrac{1 \times 100}{14.8}$ ml = 6.76 ml

∴   Volume of water added
$$= 100ml - 6.76ml$$
$$= 93.24ml$$

**3.** (i) (a) Molecular mass of nitrogen = 28 u
1 mole of nitrogen 22.4 litres at STP
i.e., 28 g of nitrogen occupy = 22.4 litres at STP

∴   14 g of nitrogen occupy $= \dfrac{22.4}{28} \times 14$

$$= 11.2\ litres\ at\ STP$$

(b) 1 mole of carbon dioxide = 22.4 litres at STP
∴   1.5 moles of carbon dioxide will occupy

$$= \dfrac{22.4}{1} \times 1.5 = 33.6\ litres\ at\ STP$$

(c) 1 mole of $O_2$ molecules = 6.022 × $10^{23}$ molecules = 22.4 litres at STP
i.e., 6.022 × $10^{23}$ molecules of oxygen occupy 22.4 litres at STP
$10^{21}$ molecules of oxygen will occupy

$$= \dfrac{22.4}{6.022 \times 10^{23}} \times 10^{21}\ litres\ at\ STP$$

$$= 3.72 \times 10^{-2}\ litres\ at\ STP$$
$$= 3.72 \times 10^{-2} \times 10^3\ cm^3\ at\ STP$$
$$= 37.2\ cm^3\ at\ STP$$

(ii) In $NH_3$, 17.65 g of H combine with N = 82.35 g

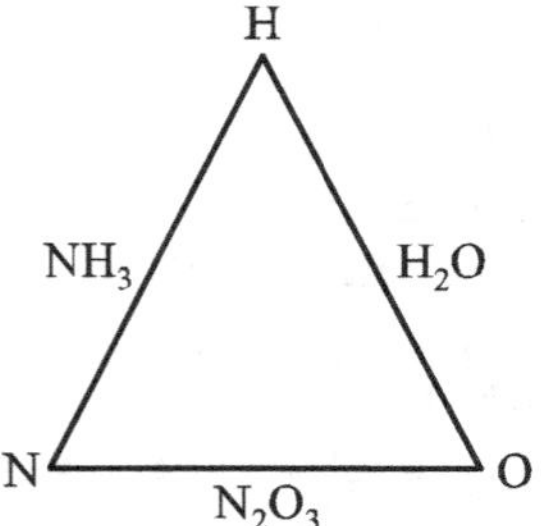


∴   1 g of H combine with

$$N = \dfrac{82.35}{17.65}\,g = 4.67\ g$$

In $H_2O$, 11.10 g of H combine with O = 88.90 g
∴   1 g of H combine with

$$O = \dfrac{88.90}{11.10}\,g = 8.01\ g$$

Ratio of the masses of N and O which combine with fixed mass (=1g) of H = 4.67 : 8.01 = 1 : 1.72
In $N_2O_3$, ratio of masses of N and O which combine with each other = 36.85 : 63.15 = 1:1.72. Thus, the two ratios are the same. Hence, it illustrates the law of reciprocal proportions.

**4.** Limitations of chemical equation and their removal is as follows:

(i) Physical states of the reactants and products are not given for example,
$$Zn + 2HCl \rightarrow ZnCl_2 + H_2$$
The suffixes like (s), (l), (g), (aq) are added to remove the drawbacks for example,
$$Zn(s) + 2HCl(aq) \rightarrow ZnCl_2(aq) + H_2(g)$$

(ii) Reaction conditions are not mentioned, which may be done by writing the conditions on the arrow between the reactants and the products for example,

$$H_2(g) + Cl_2(g) \xrightarrow{\text{Sunlight}} 2HCl(g)$$

(iii) Heat evolved or absorbed is not indicated, which may be done in terms of enthalpy change ($\Delta H$).

$$C(s) + O_2(g) \xrightarrow{\text{Combustion}} CO_2(g);$$
$$\Delta H = 393.5 \text{kJ}$$

$$N_2(g) + O_2(g) \xrightarrow{\text{Combustion}} 2NO(g);$$
$$\Delta H = 180 \text{ kJ}.$$

(iv) Concentrations of the reactants and the products are not mentioned. This drawback is removed by writing the prefix dil.(dilute) or conc. (concentrated) to a reactant. For example,

$$Zn(s) + \text{Dil. HCl} \longrightarrow ZnCl_2 + H_2(g)$$

(v) Rate of the reaction is not usually given and the same could be indicated (slow/fast) on the arrow.

(vi) Precipitation or the evolution of gas is normally not given, which may be indicated by the downward arrow ($\downarrow$) and the upward arrow ($\uparrow$) respectively.

For example,

$$AgNO_3(aq) + ZnCl(aq) \longrightarrow NaNO_3(aq) + AgCl(s)\downarrow$$

$$Zn(s) + 2HCl(aq) \longrightarrow ZnCl_2(aq) + H_2(g)\uparrow$$

| Element | Percentage | % age/Atomic mass | Simplest atomic ratio | Simplest whole number ratio |
|---|---|---|---|---|
| Na | 14.31 | $\dfrac{14.31}{23} = 0.622$ | 2 | 2 |
| S | 9.97 | $\dfrac{9.97}{32} = 0.311$ | 1 | 1 |
| H | 6.22 | $\dfrac{6.22}{1} = 6.22$ | 20 | 20 |
| O | 69.50 | $\dfrac{69.50}{16} = 4.34$ | 14 | 14 |

Empirical formula = $Na_2S\,H_{20}O_{14}$
Empirical formula mass
= $(2 \times 23) + 32 + 20 + 224 = 322$
Molecular mass = 322

$$n = \frac{322}{322} = 1$$

Molcular formula = n × Empirical formula
= $1 \times Na_2SH_{20}O_{14}$.
Since whole of the hydrogen is present as water molecules. Therefore, molecular formula
= $Na_2\,SO_4.10H_2O$.

SECTION C    NCERT EXEMPLAR QUESTIONS 

## MULTIPLE CHOICE QUESTIONS

1. A measured temperature on Fahrenheit scale is 200°F. What will this reading be on celsius scale?
   (a) 40 °C     (b) 94 °C
   (c) 93.3 °C     (d) 30 °C

2. What will be the molarity of a solution, which contains 5.85 g of NaCl(s) per 500 mL?
   (a) 4 mol L$^{-1}$     (b) 20 mol L$^{-1}$
   (c) 0.2 mol L$^{-1}$     (d) 2 mol L$^{-1}$

3. If 500 mL of a 5 M solution is diluted to 1500 mL, what will be the molarity of the solution obtained?
   (a) 1.5 M     (b) 1.66 M
   (c) 0.017 M     (d) 1.59 M

4. The number of atoms present in one mole of an element is equal to Avogadro number. Which of the following element contains the greatest number of atoms?
   (a) 4 g He     (b) 46 g Na
   (c) 0.40 g Ca     (d) 12 g He

5. If the concentration of glucose ($C_6H_{12}O_6$) in blood is 0.9 g L$^{-1}$, what will be the molarity of glucose in blood?
   (a) 5 M     (b) 50 M
   (c) 0.005 M     (d) 0.5 M

6. The empirical formula and molecular mass of a compound are $CH_2O$ and 180 g respectively. What will be the molecular formula of the compound?
   (a) $C_9H_{18}O_9$     (b) $CH_2O$
   (c) $C_6H_{12}O_6$     (d) $C_2H_4O_2$

7. One mole of any substance contains $6.022 \times 10^{23}$ atoms/molecules. Number of molecules of $H_2SO_4$ present in 100 mL of 0.02 M $H_2SO_4$ solution is........
   (a) $12.044 \times 10^{20}$ molecules
   (b) $6.022 \times 10^{23}$ molecules
   (c) $1 \times 10^{23}$ molecules
   (d) $12.044 \times 10^{23}$ molecules

8. Which of the following statements is correct about the reaction given below?
   $$4Fe(s) + 3O_2(g) \longrightarrow 2Fe_2O_3(g)$$
   (a) Total mass of iron and oxygen in reactants = total mass of iron and oxygen in product therefore it follows law of conservation of mass.

(b) Total mass of reactants = total mass of product, therefore, law of multiple proportions is followed.

(c) Amount of $Fe_2O_3$ can be increased by taking any one of the reactants (iron or oxygen) in excess.

(d) Amount of $Fe_2O_3$ produced will decrease if the amount of any one of the reactants (iron or oxygen) is taken in excess.

## ASSERTION & REASON QUESTIONS

**DIRECTIONS (Qs. 1-3) :** *Each of these questions contains an assertion followed by reason. Read them carefully and answer the question on the basis of following options. You have to select the one that best describes the two statements.*

(a) If both Assertion and Reason are correct and the Reason is a correct explanation of the Assertion.

(b) If both Assertion and Reason are correct but Reason is not a correct explanation of the Assertion.

(c) If the Assertion is correct but Reason is incorrect.

(d) If the Assertion is incorrect but the Reason is correct.

1. **Assertion :** One atomic mass unit is defined as one twelfth of the mass of one carbon-12 atom.
   **Reason :** Carbon-12 isotope is the most abundant isotope of carbon and has been chosen as standard.

2. **Assertion :** Significant figures for 0.200 is 3 whereas for 200 it is 1.
   **Reason :** Zero at the end or right of a number are significant provided they are not on the right side of the decimal point.

3. **Assertion :** Combustion of 16 g of methane gives 18 g of water.
   **Reason :** In the combustion of methane, water is one of the products.

## SHORT ANSWER QUESTIONS

1. 45.4L of dinitrogen reacted with 22.7 L of dioxygen and 45.4 L of nitrous oxide was formed. The reaction is given below:
$$2N_2(g) + O_2(g) \longrightarrow 2N_2O(g)$$
Which law is being obeyed in this experiment? Write the statement of the law.

2. The reactant which is entirely consumed in reaction is known as limiting reagent. In the reaction $2A + 4B \rightarrow 3C + 4D$, when 5 moles of A react with 6 moles of B, then
   (i) which is the limiting reagent?
   (ii) calculate the amount of C formed?

## LONG ANSWER QUESTIONS

1. Define the law of multiple proportions. Explain it with two examples. How does this law point to the existence of atoms?

2. A box contains some identical; red coloured balls, labelled as A, each weighing 2 grams. Another box contains identical blue coloured balls, labelled as B, each weighing 5 grams. Consider the combinations AB, $AB_2$, $A_2B$ and $A_2B_3$ and show that the law of multiple proportions is applicable.

## SOLUTIONS

### *Multiple Choice Questions*

1. **(c)** The relation between the temperatures on two scales is given by the following relationship :
$$°F = \frac{9}{5}T\,°C + 32$$
$$\therefore \quad T\,°C = (°F - 32) \times \frac{5}{9} = \frac{200-32}{9} \times 5$$
$$\Rightarrow \quad T°C = \frac{168 \times 5}{9} = 93.3\,°C$$

2. **(c)** $\text{Molarity} = \dfrac{\text{weight} \times 1000}{\text{molecular weight} \times \text{volume (mL)}}$
$$= \frac{5.85 \times 1000}{58.5 \times 500} = 0.2\,\text{mol L}^{-1}$$

3. **(b)** For dilution, a general formula is
$$\begin{array}{cc} M_1 V_1 & = & M_2 V_2 \\ \text{(Before dilution)} & & \text{(After dilution)} \end{array}$$
$$500 \times 5M = 1500 \times M_2$$
$$M_2 = \frac{5}{3} = 1.66\,\text{M}$$

4. **(d)** number of atoms = No. of moles $\times N_A$
$$\text{Moles of 4 g He} = \frac{4}{4} = 1\,\text{mol} \Rightarrow N_A\,\text{atoms}$$
$$46\,\text{g Na} = \frac{46}{23} = 2\,\text{mol}$$
$$\Rightarrow \quad 2\,N_A\,\text{atoms}$$
$$0.40\,\text{g Ca} = \frac{0.40}{40} = 0.1\,\text{mol} \Rightarrow 0.1\,N_A\,\text{atoms}$$
$$12\,\text{g He} = \frac{12}{4} = 3\,\text{mol} \Rightarrow 3\,N_A\,\text{atoms}$$
*i.e.*12 g He contains greatest number of atoms.

5. **(c)** In the given question, 0.9 g $L^{-1}$ means that 1000 mL (or 1L) solution contains 0.9 g of glucose.
   Molecular mass of glucose $(C_6H_{12}O_6)$
   = 180 u
   $\therefore$ Number of moles of glucose
   $$= \frac{0.9}{180} = 0.005\,\text{moles}$$
   $$= 5 \times 10^{-3}\,\text{mol glucose}$$
   Hence, 1000 mL or 1L solution contains 0.005 mole glucose or the molarity of glucose is 0.005 M.

**6.** **(c)** Given: Empirical formula mass of $CH_2O = 30$

Molecular mass $= 180$

$$n = \frac{\text{Molecular mass}}{\text{Empirical formula mass}} = \frac{180}{30} = 6$$

$\therefore$ Molecular formula $= n \times$ empirical formula

$= 6 \times CH_2O = C_6H_{12}O_6$

**7.** **(a)** Number of millimoles of $H_2SO_4$.

$=$ molarity $\times$ volume in mL

$= 0.02 \times 100 = 2$ millimoles

$= 2 \times 10^{-3}$ mol

Number of molecules

$=$ Number of moles $\times N_A$.

$= 2 \times 10^{-3} \times 6.022 \times 10^{23}$

$= 12.044 \times 10^{20}$ molecules

**8.** **(a)** According to the law of conservation of mass,

Total mass of reactants = Total mass of products

### Assertion & Reason Questions

**1.** **(a)** One atomic mass unit is defined as a mass exactly equal to one-twelfth of the mass of one carbon-12 atom. Carbon-12 has been choosen as standard as it is most abundant isotope of carbon.

**2.** **(c)** Zero at the end or right of a number are significant provided they are on the right side of the decimal point.

**3.** **(d)** $CH_4 + O_2 \longrightarrow CO_2 + 2H_2O$

1 mol of $CH_4$ given 2 mol of $H_2O$.

16 g of $CH_4 = 2 \times 18 = 36$ g of $H_2O$.

### Short Answer Questions

**1.** According to Gay Lussac's law of gaseous volumes, gases combine or are produced in a chemical reaction in a simple ratio by volume, provided that all gases are at the same temperature and pressure.

**2.** $2A + 4B \rightarrow 3C + 4D$

According to the above equation, 2 moles of 'A' require 4 moles of 'B' for the reaction.

Hence, for 5 moles of 'A', the moles of 'B' required = 5 mole of

$$A \times \frac{4 \text{ mole of B}}{2 \text{ mole of A}} = 10 \text{ mole of B}$$

But we have only 6 moles of 'B', hence, 'B' is the limiting reagent. So amount of 'C' formed is determined by amount of 'B'.

Since 4 moles of 'B' give 3 moles of 'C'. Hence 6 moles of 'B' will give

$$6 \text{ mole of B} \times \frac{3 \text{ mole of C}}{4 \text{ mole of B}} = 4.5 \text{ mole of C}$$

### Long Answer Questions

**1.** When two elements combine to form two or more chemical compounds, then the masses of one of the elements which combine with a fixed mass of the other bear a simple ratio to one another. This law is called law of multiple proportions.

For example, carbon combines with oxygen to form two compounds which are carbon dioxide and carbon monoxide.

The masses of oxygen which combine with a fixed mass of carbon in carbon dioxide and carbon monoxide are 32 and 16. Therefore oxygen bear; 32 : 16 ratio of 2 : 1.

Example 2: Sulphur combines with oxygen to form sulphur trioxide and sulphur dioxide. The masses of oxygen which combine with a fixed mass of sulphur in $SO_3$ and $SO_2$ are 48 and 32. Therefore oxygen bear a ratio of 48 : 32 or 3 : 2.

**2.**

|  | $AB$ | $AB_2$ | $A_2B$ | $A_2B_3$ |
|---|---|---|---|---|
| **Mass of A (in g)** | 2 | 2 | 4 | 4 |
| **Mass of B (in g)** | 5 | 10 | 5 | 15 |

If we fix the mass of A then mass of B combining with A will be

| 10g | 20g | 5g | 15g |
|---|---|---|---|
| 2 | 4 | 1 | 3 |

simple whole number ratio is obtained hence, law of multiple proportion is applicable.

# 2 — Structure of Atom

**2.1** **(i)** Calculate the number of electrons which will together weigh one gram.

**(ii)** Calculate the mass and charge of one mole of electrons.

**Ans. (i)** Mass of one electron $= 9.11 \times 10^{-31}$ kg,

i.e. $9.11 \times 10^{-31}$ kg = 1 electron

$$\therefore \ 10^{-3}\ \text{kg} = \frac{1}{9.11 \times 10^{-31}} \times 10^{-3} \text{electrons}$$

i.e. $10^{-3}$ kg $= 1.098 \times 10^{27}$ electrons.

**(ii)** Mass of one electron $= 9.11 \times 10^{-31}$ kg

$\therefore$ Mass of one mole of electrons

$= (9.11 \times 10^{-31}) \times 6.022 \times 10^{23}$

$= 5.486 \times 10^{-7}$ kg

Charge on one electron $= 1.602 \times 10^{-19}$ coulomb

$\therefore$ Charge on one mole of electrons

$= (1.602 \times 10^{-19}) \times (6.022 \times 10^{23})$

$= 9.65 \times 10^{4}$ coulombs.

**2.2** **(i)** Calculate the total number of electrons present in one mole of methane.

**(ii)** Find (a) the total number and (b) the total mass of neutrons in 7 mg of $^{14}$C.
(Assume that the mass of a neutron $= 1.675 \times 10^{-27}$ kg).

**(iii)** Find (a) the total number and (b) the total mass of protons in 34 mg of $NH_3$ at STP. Will the answer change if temperature and pressure are changed?

**Ans. (i)** 1 molecule of $CH_4$ contains electrons

$= 6 + 4 = 10$

$\therefore$ 1 mole, i.e., $6.022 \times 10^{23}$ molecules will contain electrons $= 6.022 \times 10^{24}$

**(ii) (a)** 1 g atom of $^{14}$C

$= 14$ g $= 6.022 \times 10^{23}$ atoms

$= (6.022 \times 10^{23}) \times 8$ neutrons

(as each $^{14}$C atom has $14 - 6 = 8$ neutrons)

Thus, 14 g or 14000 mg have

$8 \times 6.022 \times 10^{23}$ neutrons

$\therefore$ 7 mg will have neutrons

$$= \frac{8 \times 6.022 \times 10^{23}}{14000} \times 7$$

$= 2.4088 \times 10^{21}$

**(b)** $\because$ Mass of 1 neutron

$= 1.675 \times 10^{-27}$ kg

$\therefore$ Mass of $2.4088 \times 10^{21}$ neutrons

$= (2.4088 \times 10^{21}) \times (1.675 \times 10^{-27} \text{kg})$

$= 4.0347 \times 10^{-6}$ kg

**(iii) (a)** 1 mol of $NH_3$ = 17g of $NH_3$

$= 6.022 \times 10^{23}$ molecules of $NH_3$

$= (6.022 \times 10^{23}) \times (7 + 3)$ protons

$= 6.022 \times 10^{24}$ protons.

$\therefore$ 34 mg i.e., 0.034g of $NH_3$

$$= \frac{6.022 \times 10^{24}}{17} \times 0.034 \text{ protons}$$

$= 1.2044 \times 10^{22}$ protons.

**(b)** $\because$ Mass of one proton

$= 1.6726 \times 10^{-27}$ kg

$\therefore$ Mass of $1.2044 \times 10^{22}$ protons

$= (1.6726 \times 10^{-27}) \times (1.2044 \times 10^{22})$ kg

$= 2.0145 \times 10^{-5}$ kg.

**2.3** How many neutrons and protons are there in the following nuclei?

$$^{13}_{6}\text{C}, \quad ^{16}_{8}\text{O}, \quad ^{24}_{12}\text{Mg}, \quad ^{56}_{26}\text{Fe}, \quad ^{88}_{38}\text{Sr}$$

**Ans.**

| Nucleus | Z | A | protons (Z) | Neutrons (A–Z) |
|---|---|---|---|---|
| $^{13}_{6}\text{C}$ | 6 | 13 | 6 | $13 - 6 = 7$ |
| $^{16}_{8}\text{O}$ | 8 | 16 | 8 | $16 - 8 = 8$ |
| $^{24}_{12}\text{Mg}$ | 12 | 24 | 12 | $24 - 2 = 12$ |
| $^{56}_{26}\text{Fe}$ | 26 | 56 | 26 | $56 - 26 = 30$ |
| $^{88}_{38}\text{Sr}$ | 38 | 88 | 38 | $88 - 38 = 50$ |

**2.4** Write the complete symbol for the atom with the given atomic number (Z) and atomic mass (A).

**(i)** Z = 17, A = 35    **(ii)** Z = 92, A = 233

**(iii)** Z = 4, A = 9

**Ans. (i)** $^{35}_{17}\text{Cl}$    **(ii)** $^{233}_{92}\text{U}$    **(iii)** $^{9}_{4}\text{Be}$

**2.5** **Yellow light emitted from a sodium lamp has a wavelength ($\lambda$) of 580 nm. Calculate the frequency ($v$) and wave number ($\bar{v}$) of the yellow light.**

**Ans.** $\lambda = 580$ nm $= 580 \times 10^{-9}$ m

$$\text{Frequency, } v = \frac{c}{\lambda} = \frac{3.0 \times 10^8 \, ms^{-1}}{580 \times 10^{-9} \, m} = 5.17 \times 10^{14} s^{-1}$$

$$\text{Wave number, } \bar{v} = \frac{1}{\lambda} = \frac{1}{580 \times 10^{-9} \, m} = 1.72 \times 10^6 \, m^{-1}$$

**2.6** **Find energy of each of the photons which**
**(i)   correspond to light of frequency $3 \times 10^{15}$ Hz**
**(ii)  have wavelength of 0.50 Å.**

**Ans.** (i)  $v = 3 \times 10^{15}$ Hz
   $E = hv = (6.626 \times 10^{-34} Js) (3 \times 10^{15} s^{-1})$
   $= 1.988 \times 10^{-18} J$

(ii)  $\lambda = 0.50 \times 10^{-10}$ m,

$$E = hv = h\frac{c}{\lambda} = \frac{(6.626 \times 10^{-34} Js)(3 \times 10^8 \, ms^{-1})}{0.50 \times 10^{-10} \, m}$$

$$= 3.98 \times 10^{-15} J.$$

**2.7** **Calculate the wavelength, frequency and wave number of a light wave whose period is $2.0 \times 10^{-10}$s.**

**Ans.** $\text{Frequency } (v) = \dfrac{1}{\text{Period}} = \dfrac{1}{2.0 \times 10^{-10} \, s} = 5 \times 10^9 s^{-1}$

Wavelength,

$$\lambda = \frac{c}{v} = \frac{3.0 \times 10^8 \, ms^{-1}}{5 \times 10^9 \, s^{-1}} = 6.0 \times 10^{-2} \, m$$

$$\text{Wave number, } v = \frac{1}{\lambda} = \frac{1}{6 \times 10^{-2}} = 16.66 \, m^{-1}$$

**2.8** **What is the number of photons of light with a wavelength of 4000 pm that provide 1J of energy?**

**Ans.** $\lambda = 4000$ pm $= 4000 \times 10^{-12}$ m $= 4 \times 10^{-9}$ m

$$E = N \, hv = N h\frac{c}{\lambda}$$

$$\therefore N = \frac{E \times \lambda}{h \times c} = \frac{(J) \times (4 \times 10^{-9} \, m)}{(6.626 \times 10^{-34} Js)(3.0 \times 10^8 \, ms^{-1})}$$

$$= 2.012 \times 10^{16} \text{ photons}$$

**2.9** **A photon of wavelength $4 \times 10^{-7}$ m strikes on metal surface, the work function of the metal being 2.13 eV. Calculate**
**(i)   the energy of the photon (eV)**
**(ii)  the kinetic energy of the emission and**
**(iii) the velocity of the photoelectron**
$$(1 \text{ eV} = 1.6020 \times 10^{-19} \text{ J}).$$

**Ans.** (i)   $\text{Energy of the photon (E)} = hv = \dfrac{hc}{\lambda}$

$$= \frac{(6.626 \times 10^{-34} \, Js) \times (3 \times 10^8 \, ms^{-1})}{4 \times 10^{-7} \, m}$$

$$= 4.97 \times 10^{-19} \, J$$

$$= \frac{4.97 \times 10^{-19}}{1.602 \times 10^{-19}} \, eV = 3.10 \, eV$$

(ii)  $\text{Kinetic energy of emission } \left(\dfrac{1}{2} mv^2\right)$

$$= hv - hv_0 = 3.10 - 2.13 = 0.97 \text{ eV}$$

(iii)  $\dfrac{1}{2} mv^2 = 0.97 \, eV = 0.97 \times 1.602 \times 10^{-19} \, J$

i.e. $\dfrac{1}{2} \times (9.11 \times 10^{-31} \, kg) \times v^2 = 0.97 \times 1.602 \times 10^{-19} \, J$

or $v^2 = 0.341 \times 10^{12} = 34.1 \times 10^{10}$
or $v = 5.84 \times 10^5 \, m \, s^{-1}$

**2.10** **Electromagnetic radiation of wavelength 242 nm is just sufficient to ionise the sodium atom. Calculate the ionisation energy of sodium in kJ mol$^{-1}$.**

**Ans.** $E = Nhv = Nh\dfrac{c}{\lambda}$

$$= \frac{(6.02 \times 10^{23} \, mol^{-1}) \times (6.626 \times 10^{-34} \, Js) \times (3 \times 10^8 \, ms^{-1})}{242 \times 10^{-9} \, m}$$

$$= 4.945 \times 10^5 \, J \, mol^{-1} = 494.5 \text{ kJ mol}^{-1}$$

**2.11** **A 25 watt bulb emits monochromatic yellow light of wavelength of 0.57μm. Calculate the rate of emission of quanta per second.**

**Ans.** Energy emitted by the bulb = 25 watt = 25 Js$^{-1}$

$$(\because 1 \text{ watt} = 1 Js^{-1})$$

Energy of one photon $(E) = hv = h\dfrac{c}{\lambda}$

Here $\lambda = 0.57$ μm $= 0.57 \times 10^{-6}$ m
$(\because 1$ μm $= 10^{-6}$ m $)$
Putting $c = 3 \times 10^{-8}$ ms$^{-1}$
$h = 6.62 \times 10^{-34}$ Js, we get

$$E = \frac{(6.62 \times 10^{-34} \, Js)(3 \times 10^8 \, ms^{-1})}{0.57 \times 10^{-6} \, m} = 3.48 \times 10^{-19} \, J$$

$\because$   No. of photons emitted per sec

$$= \frac{25 \, Js^{-1}}{3.48 \times 10^{-19} \, J} = 7.18 \times 10^{19}$$

**2.12 Electrons are emitted with zero velocity from a metal surface when it is exposed to radiation of wavelength 6800 Å. Calculate threshold frequency ($v_0$) and work function ($W_0$) of the metal.**

**Ans.** Threshold wavelength ($\lambda_0$) = 6800 Å = $6800 \times 10^{-10}$ m

As $c = v\lambda$,

$$\therefore \quad v_0 = \frac{c}{\lambda_0} = \frac{3.0 \times 10^8 \, ms^{-1}}{6800 \times 10^{-10} \, m}$$

$= 4.41 \times 10^{14} \, s^{-1}$

Work function ($W_0$) = $hv_0$

$= (6.626 \times 10^{-34} \, Js)(4.41 \times 10^{14} s^{-1}) = 2.92 \times 10^{-19} J$

**2.13 What is the wavelength of light emitted when the electron in a hydrogen atom undergoes transition from an energy level with n = 4 to an energy level with n = 2?**

**Ans.** $\bar{v} = R\left(\dfrac{1}{n_1^2} - \dfrac{1}{n_2^2}\right) = 109677\left(\dfrac{1}{2^2} - \dfrac{1}{4^2}\right) cm^{-1}$

$$= 20564.4 \, cm^{-1}$$

$$v = \frac{1}{\lambda} = \frac{1}{20564.4 cm^{-1}} = 486 \times 10^{-7} \, cm$$

$= 486 \times 10^{-9} \, m = 486 \, nm$

**2.14 How much energy is required to ionise a H atom if the electron occupies $n = 5$ orbit? Compare your answer with the ionization enthalpy of H atom (energy required to remove the electron from $n = 1$ orbit).**

**Ans.** $E_n = -\dfrac{21.8 \times 10^{-19}}{n^2} J \, atoms^{-1}$

For ionization from 5th orbit, $n_1 = 5$, $n_2 = \infty$

$\therefore \quad \Delta E = E_2 - E_1 = -21.8 \times 10^{-19}$

$$\Delta E_5 = 21.8 \times 10^{-19}\left(\frac{1}{n_1^2} - \frac{1}{n_2^2}\right)$$

$$= 21.8 \times 10^{-19}\left(\frac{1}{5^2} - \frac{1}{\infty}\right) = 8.72 \times 10^{-20} \, J$$

For ionization from 1st orbit, $n_1 = 1$, $n_2 = \infty$

$$\Delta E_1 = 21.8 \times 10^{-19}\left(\frac{1}{1^2} - \frac{1}{\infty}\right) = 21.8 \times 10^{-19} \, J$$

So, $\dfrac{\Delta E_5}{\Delta E_1} = \dfrac{8.72 \times 10^{-20} J}{21.8 \times 10^{-19} J} = 0.04$

**2.15 What is the maximum number of emission lines when the excited electron of a H atom in $n = 6$ drops to the ground state?**

**Ans.** No. of lines produced when electron from *n*th shell drops to ground state

$$= \frac{n(n-1)}{2} = \frac{6(6-1)}{2} = 15$$

These are produced due to following transitions:

$6 \longrightarrow 5 \quad 5 \longrightarrow 4 \quad 4 \longrightarrow 3 \quad 3 \longrightarrow 2 \quad 2 \longrightarrow 1$

$6 \longrightarrow 4 \quad 5 \longrightarrow 3 \quad 4 \longrightarrow 2 \quad 3 \longrightarrow 1$

$6 \longrightarrow 3 \quad 5 \longrightarrow 2 \quad 4 \longrightarrow 1$

$6 \longrightarrow 2 \quad 5 \longrightarrow 1$

$6 \longrightarrow 1$

(5 lines)    (4 lines)    (3 lines)    (2 lines)    (1 line)

**2.16 (i) The energy associated with the first orbit in the hydrogen atom is $-2.18 \times 10^{-18}$ J atom$^{-1}$. What is the energy associated with the fifth orbit?**

**(ii) Calculate the radius of Bohr's fifth orbit for hydrogen atom.**

**Ans. (i)** $E_n = -\dfrac{2.18 \times 10^{-18}}{n^2} \, J$

$$\therefore E_5 = -\frac{2.18 \times 10^{-18}}{5^2} = -8.72 \times 10^{-20} \, J$$

(ii) For H–atom, $r_n = 0.529 \times n^2$ Å

$\therefore r_5 = 0.529 \times 5^2$

$= 13.225$ Å $= 1.3225$ nm.

**2.17 Calculate the wave number for the longest wavelength transition in the Balmer series of atomic hydrogen.**

**Ans.** For Balmer series, $n_1 = 2$.

Hence, $\bar{v} = R\left(\dfrac{1}{2^2} - \dfrac{1}{n_2^2}\right)$

$\bar{v} = \dfrac{1}{\lambda}$, For $\lambda$ to be longest (maximum) $\bar{v}$ should be minimum. This can be so when $n_2$ is minimum, i.e., $n_2 = 3$. Hence,

$$\bar{v} = (1.097 \times 10^7 \, m^{-1})\left(\frac{1}{2^2} - \frac{1}{3^2}\right)$$

$$= 1.097 \times 10^7 \times \frac{5}{36} \, m^{-1} = 1.523 \times 10^6 \, m^{-1}$$

**2.18 What is the energy in joules, required to shift the electron of the hydrogen atom from the first Bohr orbit to the fifth Bohr orbit and what is the wavelength of the light emitted when the electron returns to the ground state? The ground state electron energy is $-2.18 \times 10^{-11}$ ergs.**

**Ans.** As ground state electronic energy is $-2.18 \times 10^{-11}$ ergs, this means that

$$E_n = \frac{-2.18 \times 10^{-11}}{n^2} \, ergs$$

$$\Delta E = E_5 - E_1 = 2.18 \times 10^{-11}\left(\frac{1}{1^2} - \frac{1}{5^2}\right)$$

$$= 2.18 \times 10^{-11} \left(\frac{24}{25}\right) = 2.09 \times 10^{-11} \text{ ergs.}$$

$= 2.09 \times 10^{-18}$ J (1 erg $= 10^{-7}$J)

When electron returns to ground state (i.e., to n = 1), energy emitted $= 2.09 \times 10^{-18}$ J

As $E = h\nu = h\dfrac{c}{\lambda}$ or

$$\lambda = \frac{hc}{E} = \frac{(6.626 \times 10^{-34} \text{ Js})(3 \times 10^{10} \text{ cm s}^{-1})}{2.09 \times 10^{-18} \text{ J}}$$

$$= 9.51 \times 10^{-6} \text{cm} = 951 \times 10^{-8} \text{ cm} = 951 \text{ Å}$$

**2.19** **The electron energy in hydrogen atom is given by $E_n = (-2.18 \times 10^{-18})/n^2$J. Calculate the energy required to remove an electron completely from the n = 2 orbit. What is the longest wavelength of light in cm that can be used to cause this transition?**

**Ans.** $\Delta E = E_\infty - E_2 = 0 - \left(-\dfrac{2.18 \times 10^{-18} \text{ J atom}^{-1}}{2^2}\right)$

$$= 5.45 \times 10^{-19} \text{ J atoms}^{-1}$$

$\Delta E = h\nu = h\dfrac{c}{\lambda}$ or $\lambda = \dfrac{hc}{\Delta E}$

$$= \frac{(6.626 \times 10^{-34} \text{ Js}) \times (3 \times 10^8 \text{ ms}^{-1})}{5.45 \times 10^{-19} \text{ J}}$$

$$= 3.647 \times 10^{-7} \text{ m} = 3.647 \times 10^{-5} \text{cm.}$$

**2.20** **Calculate the wavelength of an electron moving with a velocity of $2.05 \times 10^7$ ms$^{-1}$.**

**Ans.** By de Broglie equation

$$\lambda = \frac{h}{mv} = \frac{6.626 \times 10^{-34} \text{ Js}}{(9.11 \times 10^{-31} \text{ kg})(2.05 \times 10^7 \text{ ms}^{-1})}$$

$$= 3.55 \times 10^{-11} \text{m} \qquad (1 \text{ J} = 1 \text{ kg m}^2 \text{ s}^{-2})$$

**2.21** **The mass of an electron is $9.1 \times 10^{-31}$ kg. If its K.E. is $3.0 \times 10^{-25}$ J, calculate its wavelength.**

**Ans.** $\text{K.E.} = \dfrac{1}{2}mv^2$

$$\therefore v = \sqrt{\frac{2 \text{K.E}}{m}} = \sqrt{\frac{2 \times 3.0 \times 10^{-25} \text{ J}}{9.1 \times 10^{-31} \text{kg}}} = 812 \text{ ms}^{-1}$$

$$(1 \text{ J} = 1 \text{ kg m}^2 \text{ s}^{-2})$$

By de Broglie equation,

$$\lambda = \frac{h}{mv} = \frac{6.626 \times 10^{-34} \text{ Js}}{(9.1 \times 10^{-31} \text{kg})(812 \text{ ms}^{-1})}$$

$$= 8.967 \times 10^{-7} \text{ m} = 8967 \text{ Å}$$

**2.22** **Which of the following are isoelectronic species i.e., those having the same number of electrons ?**
**Na$^+$, K$^+$, Mg$^{2+}$, Ca$^{2+}$, S$^{2-}$, Ar.**

**Ans.** No. of electrons :

Na$^+$ = 11 –1 = 10, K$^+$ = 19 –1 = 18,

Mg$^{2+}$ = 12–2 = 10, Ca$^{2+}$ = 20 –2 = 18,

S$^{--}$ = 16 + 2 = 18, Ar = 18.

Hence, isoelectronic species are (i) Na$^+$ and Mg$^{2+}$; (ii) K$^+$, Ca$^{2+}$, S$^{2-}$ and Ar.

**2.23** **(i)** **Write the electronic configurations of the following ions:**

    **(a)** **H$^-$**      **(b)** **Na$^+$**

    **(c)** **O$^{2-}$**      **(d)** **F$^-$**

   **(ii)** **What are the atomic numbers of elements whose outermost electrons are represented by**

    **(a)** **$3s^1$**      **(b)** **$2p^3$**

    **(c)** **$3p^5$?**

  **(iii)** **Which atoms are indicated by the following configurations ?**

    **(a)** **|He| $2s^1$**      **(b)** **|Ne| $3s^2 3p^3$**

    **(c)** **|Ar| $4s^2 3d^1$**

**Ans.** **(i)** (a) $_1$H = $1s^1$ $\therefore$ H$^-$ = $1s^2$

    (b) $_{11}$Na = $1s^2\, 2s^2 2p^6\, 3s^1$

       $\therefore$ Na$^+$ = $1s^2\, 2s^2\, 2p^6$

    (c) $_8$O = $1s^2\, 2s^2\, 2p^4$ $\therefore$ O$^{2-}$ = $1s^2\, 2s^2\, 2p^6$

    (d) $_9$F = $1s^2\, 2s^2\, 2p^5$ $\therefore$ F$^-$ = $1s^2\, 2s^2\, 2p^6$

  **(ii)** (a) $1s^2\, 2s^2\, 2p^6\, 3s^1$ (Z = 11)

    (b) $1s^2\, 2s^2\, 2p^3$ (Z = 7)

    (c) $1s^2\, 2s^2\, 2p^6\, 3s^2\, 3p^5$ (Z = 17)

  **(iii)** (a) [He] $2s^1 \rightarrow$ Lithium, Li

    (b) [Ne] $3s^2\, 3p^3 \rightarrow$ Phosphorus, P

    (c) [Ar] $4s^2\, 3d^1 \rightarrow$ Scandium, Sc

**2.24** **What is the lowest value of $n$ that allows $g$ orbitals to exist?**

**Ans.** For $g$–subshell, $\ell = 4$, As for a given value of $n$, $\ell$ can have values ranging from $\ell = 0$ to $n - 1$, to have $\ell = 4$, minimum value of $n = 5$

**2.25** **An electron is in one of the $3d$ orbitals. Give the possible values of $n$, $\ell$ and $m_\ell$ for this electron.**

**Ans.** For $3d$ orbital, $n = 3$, $\ell = 2$, $m = -2\, -1, 0, +1, +2$.

**2.26** **An atom of an element contains 29 electrons and 35 neutrons. Deduce (i) the number of protons and (ii) the electronic configuration of the element.**

**Ans.** For neutral atom, number of protons = number of electrons = 29

Thus, atomic number of the element = 29

Electronic configuration of element with Z = 29 will be

$1s^2\, 2s^2\, 2p^6\, 3s^2\, 3p^6\, 3d^{10}\, 4s^1$ or [Ar]$^{18}\, 3d^{10}\, 4s^1$, i.e., $_{29}$Cu.

**2.27** **Give the number of electrons in the species H$_2^+$, H$_2$ and O$_2^+$.**

**Ans.** H$_2$ = $_1$H + $_1$H = 2 electrons.

$\therefore$ H$_2^+$ has = 2 – 1 = 1 electron.

O$_2$ = $_8$O + $_8$O = 16 electrons.

$\therefore$ O$_2^+$ has = 16 – 1 = 15 electrons.

**2.28 (i) An atomic orbital has $n = 3$. What are the possible values of $l$ and $m_l$?**

**(ii) List the quantum numbers ($m_l$ and $l$) of electrons for 3d– orbital.**

**(iii) Which of the following orbitals are possible ? 1p, 2s, 2p and 3f.**

**Ans. (i)** When $n = 3$, $l = 0$, 1, 2

When $l = 0$, $m = 0$.

When $l = 1$, $m = -1$, 0, + 1.

When $l = 2$, $m = -2$, –1, 0, + 1, + 2.

**(ii)** For 3d–orbital, $n = 3$, $l = 2$

For $l = 2$, $m = -2$, –1, 0, + 1, + 2.

**(iii)** For any value of $n$ $l$ varies from 0 to $(n-1)$. Therefore 1p is not possible because when $n = 1$, $l = 0$ whereas for $p$ orbital $l$ should have minimum value of 1.

2s is possible because when $n = 2$, $l = 0$ (for $s$, $l = 0$)

2p is possible because when $n = 2$, $l = 0$, 1 (for $p$, $l = 1$)

3f is not possible because when $n = 3$, $l = 0$, 1, 2 (for $f$, $l = 3$)

**2.29 Using s, p, d notations, describe the orbital with the following quantum numbers:**

**(a) $n = 1, l = 0$   (b) $n = 3, l = 1$**

**(c) $n = 4, l = 2$   (d) $n = 4, l = 3$.**

**Ans.** (a) 1s (b) 3p (c) 4d (d) 4f.

**2.30 Explain, giving reasons, which of the following sets of quantum numbers are not possible.**

**(a) $n = 0, l = 0, m_l = 0, m_s = + 1/2$**

**(b) $n = 1, l = 0, m_l = 0, m_s = - 1/2$**

**(c) $n = 1, l = 1, m_l = 0, m_s = +1/2$**

**(d) $n = 2, l = 1, m_l = 0, m_s = -1/2$**

**(e) $n = 3, l = 3, m_l = -3, m_s = +1/2$**

**(f) $n = 3, l = 1, m_l = 0, m_s = +1/2$**

**Ans.** (a) Not possible because n can never be equal to zero. (b) Possible (c) Not possible (d) Possible (e) Not possible because when $n = 3$, $l \neq 3$ as value of $l$ varies from 0 to $n - 1$. (f) Possible.

**2.31 How many electrons in an atom may have the following quantum numbers ?**

**(a) $n = 4, m_s = - 1/2$   (b) $n = 3, l = 0$**

**Ans. (a)** Total electrons in $n = 4$ are $2n^2$, i,e., $2 \times 4^2 = 32$ Half of them, i.e., 16 electrons have $m_s = -\dfrac{1}{2}$.

**(b)** $n = 3$, $l = 0$ means 3s orbital which can have maximum 2 electrons.

**2.32 Show that the circumference of the Bohr orbit for the hydrogen atom is an integral multiple of the De Broglie wavelength associated with the electron revolving around the orbit.**

**Ans.** According to Bohr postulate of angular momentum,

$$mvr = n\frac{h}{2\pi} \qquad \text{or} \qquad 2\pi r = n\frac{h}{mv} \qquad \text{...(i)}$$

According to de Broglie equation, $\lambda = \dfrac{h}{mv}$ ...(ii)

Substituting this value in eqn. ($i$), we get $2\pi r = n\lambda$

Thus, the circumference ($2\pi r$) of the Bohr orbit for hydrogen atom is an integral multiple of de Broglie wavelength.

**2.33 What transition in the hydrogen spectrum would have the same wavelength as the Balmer transition, $n = 4$ to $n = 2$ of He$^+$ spectrum?**

**Ans.** For H–like particles in general

$$\bar{v} = \frac{2\pi^2 mZ^2 e^4}{ch^3}\left(\frac{1}{n_1^2} - \frac{1}{n_2^2}\right) = RZ^2\left(\frac{1}{n_1^2} - \frac{1}{n_2^2}\right)$$

$\therefore$ For He$^+$ spectrum, for Balmer transition, $n = 4$ to $n = 2$.

$$\bar{v} = \frac{1}{\lambda} = RZ^2\left(\frac{1}{2^2} - \frac{1}{4^2}\right) = R \times 4 \times \frac{3}{16} = \frac{3R}{4}$$

For hydrogen spectrum

$$\bar{v} = \frac{1}{\lambda} = R\left(\frac{1}{n_1^2} - \frac{1}{n_2^2}\right) = \frac{3}{4}R \text{ or } \frac{1}{n_1^2} - \frac{1}{n_2^2} = \frac{3}{4}$$

which can be so for $n_1 = 1$ and $n_2 = 2$, i.e., the transition is from $n = 2$ to $n = 1$

**2.34 Calculate the energy required for the process**

$$He^+ (g) \longrightarrow He^{2+} (g) + e^-$$

**The ionization energy for the H atom in the ground state is $2.18 \times 10^{-18}$ J atom$^{-1}$.**

**Ans.** For H–like particles, $E_n = \dfrac{2\pi^2 mZ^2 e^4}{n^2 h^2}$

For H–atom, I.E. $= E - E_1 = 0 - \left(-\dfrac{2\pi^2 me^4}{1^2 \times h^2}\right)$

$$= \frac{2\pi^2 me^4}{h^2} = 2.18 \times 10^{-18} J \text{ atoms}^{-1} \text{(Given)}$$

For the given process,

Energy required $= E_n - E_1 = 0 - \left(-\dfrac{2\pi^2 m \times 2^2 \times e^4}{1^2 \times h^2}\right)$

$$= 4 \times \frac{2\pi^2 me^4}{h^2}$$

$$= 4 \times 2.18 \times 10^{-18} = 8.72 \times 10^{-18} J$$

**2.35 If the diameter of a carbon atom is 0.15 nm, calculate the number of carbon atoms which can be placed side by side in a straight line across the length of scale of length 20 cm long.**

**Ans.** Diameter of carbon atom = 0.15nm

$= 0.15 \times 10^{-9}$ m $= 1.5 \times 10^{-10}$m

Length along which atoms are to be placed

$= 20$cm $= 20 \times 10^{-2}$m $= 2 \times 10^{-1}$ m

$\therefore$ No. of C-atoms which can be placed along the length

$$= \frac{2 \times 10^{-1}}{1.5 \times 10^{-10}} = 1.33 \times 10^9$$

**2.36** $2 \times 10^8$ **atoms of carbon are arranged side by side. Calculate the radius of carbon atom if the length of this arrangement is 2.4 cm.**

**Ans.** Total length = 2.4 cm.

Total number of atoms along the length = $2 \times 10^8$ atoms

$$\therefore \quad \text{Diameter of each atom} = \frac{2.4 \text{ cm}}{2 \times 10^8} = 1.2 \times 10^{-8}$$

$$\therefore \quad \text{Radius of the atom} = \frac{1.2 \times 10^{-8} \text{cm}}{2}$$

$$= 0.6 \times 10^{-8} \text{ cm} = 0.6 \times 10^{-9} \text{ m} = 0.6 \text{ nm}.$$

**2.37** **The diameter of zinc atom is 2.6 Å. Calculate (a) radius of zinc atom in pm and (b) number of atoms present in a length of 1.6 cm if the zinc atoms are arranged side by side lengthwise.**

**Ans.** (a) $\quad \text{Radius} = \dfrac{2.6\text{Å}}{2} = 1.3\text{Å}$

$$= 1.3 \times 10^{-10}\text{m} = 130 \times 10^{-12} \text{ m} = 130 \text{ pm}.$$

(b) Diameter of one atom = $2.6\text{Å} = 2.6 \times 10^{-10}$ m.

$\therefore$ No. of atoms present along the length

$$= \frac{1.6 \times 10^{-2}}{2.6 \times 10^{-10}} = 6.154 \times 10^7$$

**2.38** **A certain particle carries** $2.5 \times 10^{-16}$**C of static electric charge. Calculate the number of electrons present in it.**

**Ans.** Charge carried by one electron = $1.6022 \times 10^{-19}$C.

Electrons present in particle carrying $2.5 \times 10^{-16}$ C of charge

$$= \frac{2.5 \times 10^{-16}}{1.6022 \times 10^{-19}} = 1560$$

**2.39** **In Milikan's experiment, static electric charge on the oil drops has been obtained by shining X–rays. If the static electric charge on the oil drop is** $-1.282 \times 10^{-18}$ **C, calculate the number of electrons present on it.**

**Ans.** As in Q. 38 above , electrons present

$$= \frac{-1.282 \times 10^{-18}\text{C}}{-1.6022 \times 10^{-19}\text{C}} = 8$$

**2.40** **In Rutherford's experiment, generally the thin foil of heavy atoms like gold, platinum, etc., have been used to be bombarded by the α–particles. If the thin foil of light atoms like aluminium, etc., is used, what difference would be observed from the above results?**

**Ans.** Heavy atoms have a heavy nucleus carrying a large amount of positive charge. Hence some α-particles are easily deflected back on hitting the nucleus. Also a number of α–particles are deflected through small angles because of large positive charge on the nucleus. If light atoms are used, their nuclei will be light and moreover, they will have small positive charge on the nucleus. Hence, the number of particles deflected back and those deflected through some angle will be negligible or lesser.

**2.41** **Symbols** $^{79}_{35}$**Br and** $^{79}$**Br can be written whereas symbols** $^{35}_{79}$**Br and** $^{35}$**Br are not acceptable. Answer briefly.**

**Ans.** Atomic number of Bromine is fixed i.e, 35. However, different Bromine atoms may have different mass numbers (isotopes). Hence, it is essential to indicate mass number.

**2.42** **An element with mass number 81 contains 31.7% more neutrons as compared to protons. Assign the atomic symbol.**

**Ans.** Mass number = 81, i.e., p + n= 81

If protons = $x$, then neutrons

$$= x + \frac{31.7}{100}x = 1.317x$$

$$\therefore \quad x + 1.317\,x = 81$$

or $\quad 2.317x = 81$

or $\quad x = \dfrac{81}{2.317} = 35$

Thus, Protons = 35, i.e., atomic no. = 35

Hence, the symbol is $^{81}_{35}$Br

**2.43** **An ion with mass number 37 possesses one unit of negative charge. If the ion contains 11.1% more neutrons than the electrons, find the symbol of the ion.**

**Ans.** Suppose number of electrons in the ion = x

Then number of neutrons

$$= x + \frac{11.1}{100}x = 1.111x$$

No. of electrons in the neutral atom = x –1

$\therefore$ No. of protons = x –1

Mass number = No. of neutrons + No. of protons

$\therefore \quad 37 = 1.111x + x - 1 \quad$ or

2.111x = 38 $\quad$ or $\quad$ x = 18

Hence, the symbol of the ion will be $^{37}_{17}\text{Cl}^{-1}$

**2.44** **An ion with mass number 56 contains 3 units of positive charge and 30.4% more neutrons than electrons. Assign the symbol to this ion.**

**Ans.** Suppose number of electrons in the ion, $M^{3+}$ = x

$$\therefore \quad \text{No. of neutrons} = x + \frac{30.4}{100}x = 1.304x$$

No. of electrons in the neutral atom = x + 3

$\therefore$ No. of protons = x + 3

Mass no. = No. of protons + No. of neutrons

56 = x + 3 + 1.304 x $\quad$ or 2.304 x = 53 $\quad$ or x = 23

$\therefore$ No. of protons = Atomic no. = x + 3 = 23 + 3 = 26

Hence, the symbol of the ion will be $^{56}_{26}\text{Fe}^{3+}$ .

**2.45** **Arrange the following type of radiations in increasing order of frequency:**

(a) **radiation from microwave oven**

(b) **amber light from traffic signal**

(c) **radiation from FM radio**

(d) **cosmic rays from outer space and**

(e) **X–rays.**

**Ans.** Cosmic rays > X–rays > amber light > microwave > FM

**2.46** **Nitrogen laser produces a radiation at a wavelength of 337.1 nm. If the number of photons emitted is** $5.6 \times 10^{24}$**, calculate the power of this laser.**

**Ans.** $E = Nh\nu = Nh\dfrac{c}{\lambda}$

$$= \frac{(5.6 \times 10^{24})(6.626 \times 10^{-34}\text{ Js})(3.0 \times 10^8 \text{ ms}^{-1})}{(337.1 \times 10^{-9}\text{ m})}$$

$$= 3.3 \times 10^6 \text{J}$$

**2.47** Neon gas is generally used in the sign boards. If it emits strongly at 616 nm, calculate
(a) the frequency of emission
(b) distance traveled by this radiation in 30 s
(c) energy of quantum and
(d) number of quanta present if it produces 2 J of energy.

**Ans.** $\lambda = 616$ nm $= 616 \times 10^{-9}$ m
(a) Frequency,

$$\nu = \frac{c}{\lambda} = \frac{3.0 \times 10^8\, ms^{-1}}{616 \times 10^{-9}\, m} = 4.87 \times 10^{14}\, s^{-1}$$

(b) Velocity of the radiation $= 3.0 \times 10^8\, ms^{-1}$
$\therefore$ Distance travelled in 30 s
$= 30\, s \times 3 \times 10^8\, ms^{-1} = 9.0 \times 10^9 m$

(c) $E = h\nu = h\dfrac{c}{\lambda}$

$$= \frac{(6.626 \times 10^{-34}\, Js) \times 3.0 \times 10^8\, ms^{-1}}{616 \times 10^{-9}\, m} = 32.27 \times 10^{-20} J.$$

(d) No. of quanta in 2 J of energy

$$= \frac{2}{32.27 \times 10^{-20}} = 6.2 \times 10^{18}$$

**2.48** In astronomical observations, signals observed from the distant stars are generally weak. If the photon detector receives a total of $3.15 \times 10^{-18}$ J from the radiations of 600 nm, calculate the number of photons received by the detector.

**Ans.** Energy of one photon $= h\nu = h\dfrac{c}{\lambda}$

$$= \frac{(6.626 \times 10^{-34}\, Js)(3 \times 10^8\, ms^{-1})}{(600 \times 10^{-9}\, m)} = 3.313 \times 10^{-19}\, J$$

Total energy received $= 3.15 \times 10^{-18} J$

$\therefore$ No. of photons received $= \dfrac{3.15 \times 10^{-18}}{3.313 \times 10^{-19}} = 9.51 = 10$

**2.49** Lifetimes of the molecules in the excited states are often measured by using pulsed radiation source of duration nearly in the nano second range. If the radiation source has the duration of 2ns and the number of photons emitted during the pulse source is $2.5 \times 10^{15}$, calculate the energy of the source.

**Ans.** Frequency $= \dfrac{1}{2 \times 10^{-9}\, s} = 0.5 \times 10^9\, s^{-1}$

Energy $= N\, h\nu$
$= (2.5 \times 10^{15})\, (6.626 \times 10^{-34} Js)\, (0.5 \times 10^9\, s^{-1})$
$= 8.28 \times 10^{-10} J$

**2.50** The longest wavelength doublet absorption transition is observed at 589 and 589.6 nm. Calculate the frequency of each transition and energy difference between two excited states.

**Ans.** $\lambda_1 = 589 nm = 589 \times 10^{-9}$ m.

$$\therefore \nu_1 = \frac{c}{\lambda_1} = \frac{3.0 \times 10^8\, ms^{-1}}{589 \times 10^{-9}\, m} = 5.093 \times 10^{14} s^{-1}$$

$\lambda_2 = 589.6$ nm $= 589.6 \times 10^{-9} m$

$$\therefore \nu_2 = \frac{c}{\lambda_2} = \frac{3.0 \times 10^8\, ms^{-1}}{589.6 \times 10^{-9}\, m} = 5.088 \times 10^{14}\, s^{-1}$$

$\Delta E = E_2 - E_1 = h\, (\nu_1 - \nu_2)$
$= (6.626 \times 10^{-34} Js)\, (5.093 - 5.088\,) \times 10^{14}\, s^{-1}$
$= 3.31 \times 10^{-22}\, J$

**2.51** The work function for caesium atom is 1.9 eV. Calculate (a) the threshold wavelength and (b) the threshold frequency of the radiation. If the caesium element is irradiated with a wavelength 500 nm, calculate the kinetic energy and the velocity of the ejected photoelectron.

**Ans.** Work function $(W_0) = h\nu_0$

$$\therefore \nu_0 = \frac{W_0}{h} = \frac{1.9 \times 1.602 \times 10^{-19}\, J}{6.626 \times 10^{-34}\, Js}$$
$$(1eV = 1.602 \times 10^{-19}) = 4.59 \times 10^{14}\, s^{-1}$$

(a) $\lambda_0 = \dfrac{c}{\nu_0} = \dfrac{3.0 \times 10^8\, ms^{-1}}{4.59 \times 10^{14}\, s^{-1}} = 6.54 \times 10^{-7} m$
$= 654 \times 10^{-9}$ m $= 654$ nm

(b) K.E. of ejected electron $= h\, (\nu - \nu_0)$

$$= hc\left(\frac{1}{\lambda} - \frac{1}{\lambda_0}\right) = (6.626 \times 10^{-34}\, Js)(3.0 \times 10^8\, ms^{-1})$$

$$\times \left(\frac{1}{500 \times 10^{-9}\, m} - \frac{1}{654 \times 10^{-9}\, m}\right)$$

$$= \frac{6.626 \times 3.0 \times 10^{-26}}{10^{-9}}\left(\frac{154}{500 \times 654}\right) J$$

$$= 9.36 \times 10^{-20}\, J$$

$$K.E. = \frac{1}{2} mv^2 = 9.36 \times 10^{-20}\, J \text{ or kg m}^2\, s^{-2}$$

$$\therefore \frac{1}{2} \times (9.11 \times 10^{-31}\, kg)v^2 = 9.36 \times 10^{-20} kg\, m^2 s^{-2}$$

or $v^2 = 2.055 \times 10^{11}\, m^2\, s^{-2}$
$= 20.55 \times 10^{10}\, m^2 s^{-2}$
or $v = 4.53 \times 10^5\, ms^{-1}$.

**2.52** Following results are observed when sodium metal is irradiated with different wave lengths. Calculate (a) threshold wavelength and (b) Planck's constant.

| $\lambda$ (nm) | 500 | 450 | 400 |
|---|---|---|---|
| $v \times 10^{-5}$ (cms$^{-1}$) | 2.55 | 4.35 | 5.35 |

**Ans.** Suppose threshold wavelength
$= \lambda_0$ nm $= \lambda_0 \times 10^{-9}$ m

Then $h(\nu - \nu_0) = \dfrac{1}{2} mv^2$ or $hc\left(\dfrac{1}{\lambda} - \dfrac{1}{\lambda_0}\right) = \dfrac{1}{2} mv^2$

Substituting the given results of the three experiments, we get

$$\frac{hc}{10^{-9}}\left(\frac{1}{500}-\frac{1}{\lambda_0}\right)=\frac{1}{2}m(2.55\times10^{-7})^2 \qquad ...(i)$$

$$\frac{hc}{10^{-9}}\left(\frac{1}{450}-\frac{1}{\lambda_0}\right)=\frac{1}{2}m(4.35\times10^{-7})^2 \qquad ...(ii)$$

$$\frac{hc}{10^{-9}}\left(\frac{1}{400}-\frac{1}{\lambda_0}\right)=\frac{1}{2}m(5.35\times10^{-7})^2 \qquad ...(iii)$$

Dividing eqn. (ii) eqn. (i), we get

$$\frac{\lambda_0-450}{450\lambda_0}\times\frac{500\lambda_0}{\lambda_0-500}=\left(\frac{4.35}{2.55}\right)^2$$

or $\quad \dfrac{\lambda_0-450}{\lambda_0-500}=\dfrac{450}{500}\left(\dfrac{4.35}{2.55}\right)^2=2.619$

or $\quad \lambda_0-450=2.619\lambda_0-1309.5$
or $\quad 1.619\,\lambda_0=859.5$
$\therefore \qquad\qquad \lambda_0=531$ nm

Substituting this value in eqn. (iii), we get

$$\frac{h\times(3\times10^8)}{10^{-9}}\left(\frac{1}{400}-\frac{1}{531}\right)$$

$$=\frac{1}{2}(9.11\times10^{-31})(5.35\times10^{-7})^2$$

or $\quad h=6.66\times10^{-34}$ J s

**2.53** **The ejection of the photoelectron from the silver metal in the photoelectric effect experiment can be stopped by applying the voltage of 0.35 V when the radiation 256.7 nm is used. Calculate the work function for silver metal.**

**Ans.** Energy of the incident radiation = Work function + Kinetic energy of photoelectron

Energy of incident radiation (E)

$$=h\nu=h\frac{c}{\lambda}=\frac{(6.626\times10^{-34}\,Js)(3.0\times10^8\,ms^{-1})}{(256.7\times10^{-9}\,m)}$$

$$=7.74\times10^{-19}\text{ J}$$
$$=4.83\text{ e V }(1e\text{ V}=1.602\times10^{-19}\text{ J})$$

The potential applied gives the kinetic energy to the electron.

Hence, kinetic energy of the electron = 0.35 eV
$\therefore$ Work function = 4.83 e V – 0.35 e V = 4.48 eV

**2.54** **If the photon of the wavelength 150 pm strikes an atom and one of its inner bound electrons is ejected out with a velocity of 1.5 × 10⁷ m s⁻¹, calculate the energy with which it is bound to the nucleus.**

**Ans.** Energy of the incident photon

$$=\frac{hc}{\lambda}=\frac{(6.626\times10^{-34}\,Js)(3.0\times10^8\,ms^{-1})}{(150\times10^{-12}\,m)}$$

$$=13.25\times10^{-16}\text{ J}$$

Energy of the electron ejected $=\dfrac{1}{2}mv^2$

$$=\frac{1}{2}(9.11\times10^{-31}\,kg)(1.5\times10^7\,ms^{-1})^2$$
$$=1.025\times10^{-16}\text{ J}$$

Energy with which the electron was bound to the nucleus
$$=13.25\times10^{-16}\text{ J}-1.025\times10^{-16}\text{ J}=12.225\times10^{-16}\text{J}$$

$$=\frac{12.225\times10^{-16}}{1.602\times10^{-19}}\text{eV}=7.63\times10^3\text{ eV}.$$

**2.55** **Emission transitions in the Paschen series end at orbit n = 3 and start from orbit n and can be represented as $\nu = 3.29 \times 10^{15}$ (Hz) [1/3² – 1/n²]. Calculate the value of n if the transition is observed at 1285 nm. Find the region of the spectrum.**

**Ans.** $\nu=\dfrac{c}{\lambda}=\dfrac{3.0\times10^8\,ms^{-1}}{1285\times10^{-9}\,m}=2.33\times10^{14}\,s^{-1}$ ....(i)

According to question, $\nu=3.29\times10^{15}\left(\dfrac{1}{3^2}-\dfrac{1}{n^2}\right)$ ....(ii)

By comparing equation (i) and (ii), we get,

or $\quad \dfrac{1}{n^2}=\dfrac{1}{9}-\dfrac{3.0\times10^8}{1285\times10^{-9}}\times\dfrac{1}{3.29\times10^{15}}$

$$=0.111-0.071=0.04=\frac{1}{25}$$
or $\quad n^2=25 \quad$ or $\quad n=5$

**2.56** **Calculate the wavelength for the emission transition if it starts from the orbit having radius 1.3225 nm and ends at 211.6 pm. Name the series to which this transition belongs and the region of the spectrum.**

**Ans.** Radius of $n$th orbit of H–like particles

$$=\frac{0.529\,n^2}{Z}\,Å=\frac{52.9\,n^2}{Z}\,pm$$

$$r_1=1.3225\text{ nm}=1322.5\text{ pm}=52.9\,n_1^2$$

$$r_2=211.6\text{ pm}=\frac{52.9\,n_2^2}{Z}$$

$\therefore \dfrac{r_1}{r_2}=\dfrac{1322.5}{211.6}=\dfrac{n_1^2}{n_2^2}=6.25 \quad$ or $\quad \dfrac{n_1}{n_2}=2.5$

$\therefore$ If $n_2=2,\ n_1=5$. Thus, the transition is from 5th orbit. It belongs to **Balmer series**.

$$\bar{\nu}=1.097\times10^7\,m^{-1}\left(\frac{1}{2^2}-\frac{1}{5^2}\right)$$

$$=1.097\times\frac{21}{100}\times10^7\,m^{-1}$$

or $\quad \lambda=\dfrac{1}{\bar{\nu}}=\dfrac{100}{1.097\times21\times10^7}\,m$

$$=434\times10^{-9}\text{ m}=434\,nm$$

Thus, it lies in the visible region

**2.57** Dual behaviour of matter proposed by de Broglie led to the discovery of electron microscope often used for the highly magnified images of biological molecules and other type of material. If the velocity of the electron in this microscope is $1.6 \times 10^6\,\text{ms}^{-1}$, calculate de Broglie wavelength associated with this electron.

**Ans.** $\lambda = \dfrac{h}{mv} = \dfrac{6.626 \times 10^{-34}\,\text{kg m}^2\,\text{s}^{-1}}{(9.11 \times 10^{-31}\,\text{kg})(1.6 \times 10^6\,\text{ms}^{-1})}$

$= 4.55 \times 10^{-10}\,\text{m} = 455\,\text{pm}$

**2.58** Similar to electron diffraction, neutron diffraction microscope is also used for the determination of the structure of molecules. If the wavelength used here is 800 pm, calculate the characteristic velocity associated with the neutron.

**Ans.** Mass of neutron $= 1.675 \times 10^{-27}\,\text{kg}$

$\lambda = \dfrac{h}{mv}$ or $v = \dfrac{h}{m \times \lambda}$

$= \dfrac{6.626 \times 10^{-34}\,\text{kg m}^2\text{s}^{-1}}{1.675 \times 10^{-27}\,\text{kg} \times (800 \times 10^{-12}\,\text{m})}$

$= 4.94 \times 10^2\,\text{ms}^{-1}$

**2.59** If the velocity of the electron in Bohr's first orbit is $2.19 \times 10^6\,\text{ms}^{-1}$, calculate the de Broglie wavelength associated with it.

**Ans.** $\lambda = \dfrac{h}{mv} = \dfrac{6.626 \times 10^{-34}\,\text{kg m}^2\text{s}^{-1}}{(9.11 \times 10^{-31}\,\text{kg})(2.19 \times 10^6\,\text{ms}^{-1})}$

$= 3.32 \times 10^{-10}\,\text{m} = 332 \times 10^{-12}\,\text{m} = 332\,\text{pm}$

**2.60** The velocity associated with a proton moving in a potential difference of 1000 V is $4.37 \times 10^5\,\text{ms}^{-1}$. If the hockey ball of mass 0.1 kg is moving with this velocity, calculate the wavelength associated with this velocity?

**Ans.** $\lambda = \dfrac{h}{mv} = \dfrac{6.626 \times 10^{-34}\,\text{kg m}^2\text{s}^{-1}}{(0.1\,\text{kg})(4.37 \times 10^5\,\text{ms}^{-1})}$

$= 1.516 \times 10^{-38}\,\text{m}$

**2.61** If the position of the electron is measured within an accuracy of $\pm\,0.002$ nm, calculate the uncertainty in the momentum of the electron. Suppose the momentum of the electron is $h/4\pi$ m $\times\,0.05$ nm, is there any problem in defining this value.

**Ans.** $\Delta x = 0.002\,\text{nm} = 2 \times 10^{-3}\,\text{nm} = 2 \times 10^{-12}\,\text{m}$

$\Delta x \times \Delta p = \dfrac{h}{4\pi}$

$\therefore \Delta p = \dfrac{h}{4\pi \Delta x} = \dfrac{6.626 \times 10^{-34}\,\text{kg m}^2\text{s}^{-1}}{4 \times 3.14 \times (2 \times 10^{-12}\,\text{m})}$

$= 2.638 \times 10^{-23}\,\text{kg ms}^{-1}$

Actual momentum

$= \dfrac{h}{4\pi \times 0.05\,\text{nm}} = \dfrac{h}{4\pi \times 5 \times 10^{-11}\,\text{m}}$

$= \dfrac{6.626 \times 10^{-34}\,\text{kg m}^2\text{s}^{-1}}{4 \times 3.14 \times 5 \times 10^{-11}\,\text{m}}$

$= 1.055 \times 10^{-24}\,\text{kg ms}^{-1}$

This value cannot be defined as the actual magnitude of the momentum is smaller than the uncertainty in momentum, which is impossible.

**2.62** The quantum numbers of six electrons are given below. Arrange them in order of increasing energies. If any of these combination (s) has/have the same energy

(i) $n = 4$, $l = 2$, $m_\ell = -2$, $m_s = -1/2$
(ii) $n = 3$, $l = 2$, $m_\ell = -1$, $m_s = +1/2$
(iii) $n = 4$, $l = 1$, $m_\ell = 0$, $m_s = +1/2$
(iv) $n = 3$, $l = 2$, $m_\ell = -2$, $m_s = -1/2$
(v) $n = 3$, $l = 1$, $m_\ell = -1$, $m_s = +1/2$
(vi) $n = 4$, $l = 1$, $m_\ell = 0$, $m_s = +1/2$

**Ans.** The orbitals occupied by the electrons are (i) 4$d$ (ii) 3$d$ (iii) 4$p$ (iv) 3$d$ (v) 3$p$ (vi) 4$p$. Their energies will be in the order: (v) < (ii) = (iv) < (iii) = (vi) < (i)

**2.63** The bromine atom possesses 35 electrons. It contains 6 electrons in 2$p$ orbital, 6 electrons in 3$p$ orbital and 5 electrons in 4$p$ orbital. Which of these electron experiences the lowest effective nuclear charge?

**Ans.** 4$p$ electrons being farthest from the nucleus experience the lowest effective nuclear charge.

**2.64** Among the following pairs of orbitals which orbital will experience the larger effective nuclear charge?

(i) 2$s$ and 3$s$        (ii) 4$d$ and 4$f$
(iii) 3$d$ and 3$p$

**Ans.** (i) 2$s$ is closer to the nucleus than 3$s$. Hence 2$s$ will experience larger effective nuclear charge.

(ii) 4$d$

(iii) 3$p$ (for same reason)

**2.65** The unpaired electrons in Al and Si are present in 3p orbital. Which electrons will experience more effective nuclear charge from the nucleus?

**Ans.** Silicon has greater nuclear charge (+4) than aluminium (+3). Hence, the unpaired 3p electron of silicon will experience more effective nuclear charge.

**2.66** Indicate the number of unpaired electrons in:

(a) P                  (b) Si
(c) Cr              (d) Fe and
(e) Kr

**Ans.** (a) $_{15}\text{P} = 1s^2\,2s^2\,2p^6\,3s^2\,3p_x^1 3p_y^1 3p_z^1$.

No. of unpaired electrons $= 3$

(b) $_{14}\text{Si} = 1s^2\,2s^2\,2p^6\,3s^2\,3p_x^1 3p_y^1$.

No. of unpaired electrons $= 2$

(c) $_{24}\text{Cr} = 1s^2\,2s^2\,2p^6\,3s^2\,3p^6\,3d^5 4s^1$.
No. of unpaired electrons $= 6$

(d) $_{26}\text{Fe} = 1s^2\,2s^2\,2p^6\,3s^2\,3p^6\,3d^6\,4s^2$ number of unpaired electrons $= 4$ in (3$d$).

(e) $_{36}\text{Kr} = $ Noble gas. All orbitals are filled. Unpaired electrons $= 0$

**2.67** (a) How many sub–shells are associated with $n = 4$?

(b) How many electrons will be present in the sub-shells having $m_s$ value of $-1/2$ for $n = 4$ ?

**Ans.** (a) $n = 4$, $l = 0, 1, 2, 3$ (4 subshells , viz., $s, p, d$ and $f$)

(b) No. of electrons in 4th shell.
$= n^2 = 4^2 = 16$
Each orbital has one electron with $m_s = -1/2$
Hence there will be 16 electrons with $m_s = -1/2$.

## SECTION B — PRACTICE QUESTIONS

### Multiple Choice Questions

1. Which of the following pairs have identical values of e/m?
   (a) A proton and a neutron
   (b) A proton and deuteron
   (c) Deuteron and an $\alpha$-particle
   (d) An electron and $\gamma$-rays

2. The increasing order for the values of e/m (charge/mass) is
   (a) e, p, n, $\alpha$
   (b) n, p, e, $\alpha$
   (c) n, p, $\alpha$, e
   (d) n, $\alpha$, p, e

3. What is the ratio of mass of an electron to the mass of a proton?
   (a) 1 : 2
   (b) 1 : 1
   (c) 1 : 1837
   (d) 1 : 3

4. Millikan performed an experiment method to determine which of the following?
   (a) Mass of the electron
   (b) Charge of the electron
   (c) e/m ratio of electron
   (d) Both (a) and (b)

5. What is the optimum conditions required to study the conduction of electricity through gases.
   (a) High pressure and low voltage
   (b) High pressure and high voltage
   (c) Low pressure and high voltage
   (d) Low pressure and low voltage

6. When atoms are bombarded with alpha particles, only a few in million suffer deflection, others pass out undeflected.
   This is because
   (a) the force of repulsion on the moving alpha particle is small
   (b) the force of attraction between alpha particle and oppositely charged electrons is very small
   (c) there is only one nucleus and large number of electrons
   (d) the nucleus occupies much smaller volume compared to the volume of the atom

7. Which of the following does not contain number of neutrons equal to that of $_{18}^{40}\text{Ar}$ ?
   (a) $_{19}^{41}\text{K}$
   (b) $_{21}^{43}\text{Sc}$
   (c) $_{21}^{40}\text{Sc}$
   (d) $_{20}^{42}\text{Ca}$

8. Which of the following pairs will have same chemical properties ?
   (a) $_{6}^{14}\text{C}$ and $_{7}^{15}\text{N}$
   (b) $O^{2-}$ and $F^-$
   (c) $_{18}^{40}\text{Ar}$ and $_{19}^{40}\text{K}$
   (d) $_{17}^{35}\text{Cl}$ and $_{17}^{37}\text{Cl}$

9. From the data given below A, B, C and D respectively are,
   (A) 10 $e^-$, atomic no. 11
   (B) 10 $e^-$, atomic no. 6
   (C) 10 $e^-$, atomic no. 10
   (D) 10 $e^-$, atomic no. 9
   (a) $Na^+$, $C^{4-}$, Ne, $F^-$
   (b) $C^{4-}$, Ne, $Na^-$, $F^-$
   (c) $F^-$, $Na^+$, Ne, $C^{4-}$
   (d) $F^-$, $Na^+$, $C^{4-}$, Ne

10. Which one of the following is not the characteristic of Planck's quantum theory of radiation ?
    (a) The energy is not absorbed or emitted in whole number or multiple of quantum
    (b) Radiation is associated with energy
    (c) Radiation energy is not emitted or absorbed continuously but in the form of small packets called quanta
    (d) This magnitude of energy associated with a quantum is proportional to the frequency.

11. The value of Planck's constant is $6.63 \times 10^{-34}$ Js. The velocity of light is $3.0 \times 10^8$ m s$^{-1}$. Which value is closest to the wavelength in nanometers of a quantum of light with frequency of $8 \times 10^{15}$ s$^{-1}$ ?
    (a) $3 \times 10^7$
    (b) $2 \times 10^{-25}$
    (c) $5 \times 10^{-18}$
    (d) $4 \times 10^1$

12. Which of the following statements are not correct about electromagnetic radiation ?
    (i) Electromagnetic waves require medium to travel.
    (ii) Different electromagnetic radiations travel at same speed in vaccum.
    (iii) The oscillating electric and magnetic fields produced by oscillating charged particles are perpendicular to each other, but not to the direction of propagation.
    (iv) The oscillating electric field and magnetic field are perpendicular to each other, and also to the direction of propagation.
    (a) (i), (ii) and (iii)
    (b) (ii) and (iii)
    (c) (i) and (iii)
    (d) (i) and (iv)

13. A 600 W mercury lamp emits monochromatic radiation of wavelength 331.3 nm. How many photons are emitted from the lamp per second? ($h = 6.626 \times 10^{-34}$ Js; velocity of light = $3 \times 10^8$ ms$^{-1}$)
    (a) $1 \times 10^{19}$
    (b) $1 \times 10^{20}$
    (c) $1 \times 10^{21}$
    (d) $1 \times 10^{23}$

14. An electron from one Bohr stationary orbit can go to next higher orbit
    (a) by emission of electromagnetic radiation
    (b) by absorption of any electromagnetic radiation
    (c) by absorption of electromagnetic radiation of particular frequency
    (d) without emission or absorption of electromagnetic radiation

15. The energy of an electron in second Bohr orbit of hydrogen atom is :
    (a) $-5.44 \times 10^{-19}$ eV
    (b) $-5.44 \times 10^{-19}$ cal
    (c) $-5.44 \times 10^{-19}$ kJ
    (d) $-5.44 \times 10^{-19}$ J
16. The wavelength of the radiation emitted, when in a hydrogen atom electron falls from infinity to stationary state 1, would be (Rydberg constant $= 1.097 \times 10^7$ m$^{-1}$)
    (a) 406 nm
    (b) 192 nm
    (c) 91 nm
    (d) $9.1 \times 10^{-8}$ nm
17. What does negative sign in the electronic energy for hydrogen atom convey.
    (a) Energy of electron when $n = \infty$
    (b) The energy of electron in the atom is lower than the energy of a free electron in motion
    (c) The energy of electron in the atom is lower than the energy of a free electron of rest
    (d) The energy of electron decreases as it moves away from nucleus

## ASSERTION & REASON QUESTIONS

**DIRECTIONS (Qs. 1-9) :** *Each of these questions contains an assertion followed by reason. Read them carefully and answer the question on the basis of following options. You have to select the one that best describes the two statements.*

(a) If both Assertion and Reason are correct and the Reason is a correct explanation of the Assertion.

(b) If both Assertion and Reason are correct but Reason is not a correct explanation of the Assertion.

(c) If the Assertion is correct but Reason is incorrect.

(d) If the Assertion is incorrect but the Reason is correct.

1. **Assertion:** Characteristics of cathode rays (electron) do not depend upon the material of electrode and the nature of gas present in cathode ray tube.
   **Reason:** Electrons are basic constituents of all the atoms $q = \pm ne$.
2. **Assertion:** Millikan was able to measure the mass of oil droplets.
   **Reason:** He concluded that the magnitude of electrical charge, $q$, on the droplet is always an integral multiple of electrical charge, $e$, that is, $q = \pm ne$, where, $n = 1, 2, 3....$
3. **Assertion:** Nature of cathode rays in magnetic field or electric field is similar to negatively charged particles.
   **Reason:** Cathode rays consist of negatively charged particles.
4. **Assertion:** Isobars are different element atoms.
   **Reason:** Isobars have different chemical properties.
5. **Assertion :** Black body is an ideal body that emits and absorbs radiations of all frequencies.
   **Reason :** The frequency of radiation emitted by a body goes from a lower frequency to higher frequency with an increase in temperature.
6. **Assertion :** The radius of the first orbit of hydrogen atom is 0.529Å.
   **Reason :** Radius of each circular orbit $(r_n) = 0.529$Å $(n^2/Z)$, where $n = 1, 2, 3$ and $Z =$ atomic number.
7. **Assertion:** White light is the combination of seven colours of visible light.
   **Reason:** Blue colour has higher frequency and red colour has lowest frequency.
8. **Assertion:** Thomson suggested that atom is spherical in shape and completely neutral.
   **Reason:** This is because positive and negative charges are present in equal number.
9. **Assertion:** The kinetic energy of the photoelectrons is directly proportional to the intensity of incident light.
   **Reason:** The rate of emission of photoelectrons is inversely proportional to the intensity of incident light.

## MATCH THE COLUMN

1. Match the columns.

| Column-I | Column-II |
|---|---|
| (A) $^1_1$H, $^2_1$H and $^3_1$H | (p) Isobars |
| (B) $^{14}_6$C and $^{14}_7$N | (q) Isotopes |
| (C) Na$^+$ and Mg$^{2+}$ | (r) Isoelectronic species |

   (a) A – (p), B – (q), C – (r)
   (b) A – (q), B – (p), C – (r)
   (c) A – (r), B – (q), C – (p)
   (d) A – (p), B – (r), C – (q)

## VERY SHORT ANSWER QUESTIONS

1. Name a species which has no neutron.
2. What type of spectrum is obtained when light emitted from discharge tube containing hydrogen gas is analysed with a spectroscope?
3. Which experiment led to the discovery of neutrons?
4. The atomic number of Uranium is 92. How many electrons are there in the neutral atom? How many electrons and protons are there in the U$^{+2}$ ion?
5. Name the element whose isotope has mass number 14 and 8 neutrons.
6. An element of atomic weight $Z$ consists of two isotopes of mass number $Z - 1$ and $Z + 2$. Calculate the % of higher isotope.
7. What did Rutherford's alpha scattering experiment prove?
8. What is the ratio of mass of electron to the mass of proton?
9. How does the intensity of spectral line vary with wave length?
10. What is Stark effect?
11. What is Zeeman effect?
12. Explain why are Bohr's orbitals also called energy levels?
13. Which has the greater energy–a photon of violet light or a photon of green light?

14. Name the experiment evidence to support the wave nature of light.

15. How is photon different from proton?

16. When moving with the same velocity which one of the following particles has the largest de Broglie wavelength and why? (a) Electron (b) Proton (c) $\alpha$-particle

17. One photon of ultraviolet light can eject a photo electron from the surface of a certain metal. When the same metal is irradiated with 2 photons of red light having total energy equal to that of ultraviolet light; will photoelectron be ejected?

18. If the electron absorbs 12.1 eV of energy, it will jump to which orbit? (Given energy of electron is –13.6eV)

19. If the wavelength of green light is about 5000 Å, what is its frequency? ( $c = 3 \times 10^8$ m/s)

20. Calculate the kinetic energy of the ejected electron when ultra-violet radiation of frequenc $1.6 \times 10^{15}$ $s^{-1}$ strikes the surface of potassium metal. Threshold frequency of potassium is $5 \times 10^{14}$ $s^{-1}$. ($h = 6.63 \times 10^{-34}$ Js)

## SHORT ANSWER QUESTIONS

1. Explain how can you say electrons and protons are fundamental particles of all the atoms.

2. What is the origin of anode rays in the discharge tube? Name the particles which form anode rays.

3. Describe the drawback of Rutherford's model of atom.

4. What is the evidence that cathode rays are a part of all matter?

5. Why does the charge to mass ratio of positive rays depends on the gas taken in the discharge tube whereas charge to mass ratio of cathode rays is same for all gases?

6. Calculate the wavelength of de–Broglie waves associated with a proton of kinetic energy 500eV.
(given : $m_p = 1.67 \times 10^{-27}$kg,
$h = 6.626 \times 10^{-34}$Js and $1eV = 1.6 \times 10^{-19}$J)

7. Calculate and compare the energies of two radiations one with a wavelength of 800 nm and other with wavelength of 400 nm.

8. Calculate the wavelength of an electron that has been accelerated in a particle accelerator through a potential difference of 100 million volts. ($1$ eV $= 1.6 \times 10^{-19}$ J, $m_e = 9.1 \times 10^{-31}$ kg, $h = 6.6 \times 10^{-34}$ Js, $c = 3.0 \times 10^8$ ms$^{-1}$)

9. In photoelectric effect experiment irradiation of a metal with light of frequency $5 \times 10^{20}$ $s^{-1}$ yields electrons with maximum K.E. $= 6.63 \times 10^{-14}$ J. Calculate $v_0$ (threshold frequency) for the metal.

10. With what velocity must an electron travel so that its momentum is equal to that of a photon of wavelength = 5200 Å?

11. What is the wavelength for the electron accelerated by $1.0 \times 10^4$ volts ?

12. The first member ($H_\alpha$ line) of the Balmer series of hydrogen has a wavelength of 6563 Å. Calculate the wavelength of the second member ($H_\beta$ line).

13. Iodine molecule dissociates into atoms after absorbing light of 4500 Å. If one quantum of radiation is absorbed by each molecule, calculate the kinetic energy of iodine atoms. (Bond energy of $I_2 = 240$ kJ mol$^{-1}$)

14. Energy in a Bohr orbit is given to be equal to $-\dfrac{B}{n^2}$, where $B = 2.179 \times 10^{-18}$ J. Calculate the wavelength of the emitted radiation when electron jumps from the third orbit to the second.

15. A sheet of silver is illuminated by mono-chromatic ultraviolet radiations of wavelength = 1810 Å. What is the maximum energy of the emitted electron ? Threshold wavelength of silver is 2640 Å.

16. An electron beam can undergo diffraction by crystals. Through what potential should a beam of electrons be accelerated so that its wavelength becomes equal to 1.54 Å.

17. Two particles A and B are in motion. If the wavelength associated with particle A is $5 \times 10^{-8}$m, calculate the wavelength associated with particle B if its momentum is half of A.

18. A photon of wavelength $4 \times 10^{-7}$ m strikes on metal surface, the work function of the metal being 2.13 eV. Calculate
   (a) the energy of the photon in eV.
   (b) the kinetic energy of the emitted electron in joules.
   (c) the velocity of the photoelectron.
      ($1$ eV $= 1.6020 \times 10^{-19}$ J)

19. One of the lines in the Balmer series of the hydrogen atom emission spectrum is at 397 nm. It results from a transition from an upper energy level to $n = 2$. What is the principal quantum number of the upper level?

20. Ionization energy of a H-atom is 13.6 eV/atom. It requires a photon of energy 1.5 times the minimum which is required to remove the electron. Calculate the wavelength of the emitted electron.

21. What is the frequency and wavelength of a photon emitted during a transition from the $n = 5$ state to the $n = 2$ state in the hydrogen atom.

22. Calculate (i) wave number (ii) frequency of yellow radiation having wavelength of 5800 Å.

23. What are the main points of Planck's quantum theory?

24. Which of the following relate to light as wave, particle, or both?
   (A) diffraction           (B) photoelectric effect
   (C) $E = mc^2$            (D) $E = hv$

25. An electron in a hydrogen atom in its ground state absorbs 1.5 times as much energy as the minimum required for it to escape from the atom. What is the wavelength of the emitted electron?

**26.** An electron and a proton are possessing the same amount of kinetic energy. Which of the two have greater wavelength?

**27.** When light of frequency v is thrown on a metal surface with threshold frequency $v_0$, photo-electrons are emitted with maximum kinetic energy $= 1.3 \times 10^{-18}$J. If the ratio, $v : v_0 = 3 : 1$, calculate the threshold frequency $v_0$.

**28.** Define (i) Photo–electric effect (ii) Black body radiations.

## LONG ANSWER QUESTIONS

**1.** (i) Calculate the wavelength of photon which will be emitted when the electron of hydrogen atom jumps from the fourth shell to the first shell. The ionization energy of hydrogen atom is $1.312 \times 10^3$ kJ mol$^{-1}$.

(ii) Which orbital in each of the following pairs is lower in energy in a multi-electron system?

   (a) 2s, 2p         (b) 3p, 3d

   (c) 3s, 4s         (d) 4d, 5f

**2.** Complete the following statements:

(a) Two electrons in the same ————— must have opposite spins.

(b) The presence of unpaired electrons in an atom gives rise to ————— .

(c) When 'l' = 3, $m_l$ may have value from ————— to ————— .

(d) The neutral fourth–period atom having a total of six 'd' electrons is ————— .

(e) Orbitals with the same energy are said to be ————— .

(f) The electronic configuration of Sn is [Kr] ————— .

(g) The 2p orbitals of an atom have identical shapes but differ in their ————— .

(h) A nodal surface is one at which the probability of finding an electron is ————— .

(i) Electronic configuration of Li is not $1s^3$, it is in accordance with ————— .

(j) Balmer series in hydrogen spectrum is observed in the ————— region.

**3.** (i) Find the number of photons emitted per second by a 25 watt source of monochromatic light of wavelength 6000 Å ?

(ii) A certain photochemical reaction is found to require $7.61 \times 10^{-17}$J energy per molecule. Calculate the number of photons per molecule for light of wavelength 300nm that is just sufficient to initiate the reaction.

**4.** (i) What are the two longest wavelength lines (in nanometers) in the Lyman series of hydrogen spectrum ?

(ii) In a hydrogen atom, the energy of an electron in first Bohr's orbit is $13.12 \times 10^5$ J mol$^{-1}$. What is the energy required for its excitation to Bohr's second orbit ?

**5.** What were the weaknesses or limitations of Bohr's model of atoms ? Briefly describe the quantum mechanical model of atom ?

**6.** (i) Write outer electronic configuration of Cr atom. Why are half filled orbitals more stable ?

(ii) State Heisenberg's uncertainty principle. An electron has a velocity of 50 ms$^{-1}$ accurate upto 99.99%. Calculate the uncertainty in locating its position. (Mass of electron $= 9.1 \times 10^{-31}$ kg, $h = 6.6 \times 10^{-34}$ Js)

## SOLUTIONS

### *Multiple Choice Questions*

**1.** (c) Deuteron and an $\alpha$-particle have identical values of $e/m$.

**2.** (d) $\dfrac{e}{m}$ for  (i) neutron $= \dfrac{0}{1} = 0$

          (ii) $\alpha$-particle $= \dfrac{2}{4} = 0.5$

          (iii) proton $= \dfrac{1}{1} = 1$

          (iv) electron $= \dfrac{1}{1/1837} = 1837$

**3.** (c)

**4.** (b) Millikan determined the value of charge on the electron by using oil drop experiment.

**5.** (c) The electrical discharge through the gases could be observed only at low pressure and high voltage.

**6.** (d) The nucleus occupies much smaller volume compared to the volume of the atom.

**7.** (c) $_{18}Ar^{40}$ contains 22 neutrons and $_{21}Sc^{40}$ contains 19 neutrons. The number of neutrons $= (A - Z)$

**8.** (d) $_{17}Cl^{35}$ and $_{17}Cl^{37}$ are isotopes, so they will have same chemical properties.

**9.** (a) Isoelectronic species

**10.** (a) Energy is always absorbed or emitted in whole number or multiples of quantum.

**11.** (d) $E = h v = \dfrac{hc}{\lambda}$ or $\lambda = \dfrac{c}{v}$

$$\Rightarrow \lambda = \dfrac{3 \times 10^8}{8 \times 10^{15}} = 3.75 \times 10^{-8} \, m$$

In nanometer $\lambda = 3.75 \times 10$ nm which is closest to $4 \times 10^1$ nm

**12.** (c) The oscillating fields are perpendicular to the direction of propagation.

**13.** **(c)** Energy of a photon, $E = \dfrac{hc}{\lambda}$

$$= \frac{6.6 \times 10^{-34}\,(\text{Js}) \times 3 \times 10^8\,(\text{ms}^{-1})}{331.3 \times 10^{-9}\,(\text{m})} = 6 \times 10^{-19}\,\text{J}$$

No. of photons emitted per second

$$= \frac{600\,(\text{J})}{6 \times 10^{-19}\,(\text{J})} = 10^{21} \quad [1 \text{ watt} - \text{second} = \text{joule}]$$

**14.** **(c)** Since the energy difference between two consecutive Bohr orbits is quantized and the energy of higher orbit is more than that of lower orbit, so an electron from one Bohr stationary orbit can go to next higher orbit by absorption of electromagnetic radiation of particular wavelength or frequency.

**15.** **(d)** For H atom, $E_n = -\dfrac{13.6 Z^2}{n^2}\,\text{eV}$

For second orbit, $n = 2$

$Z =$ At. no. $= 1$ (for hydrogen)

$$\therefore\ E_2 = -\frac{13.6 \times (1)^2}{(2)^2} = \frac{-13.6}{4}\,\text{eV}$$

$$= \frac{-13.6 \times 1.6 \times 10^{-19}}{4}\,\text{J} = -5.44 \times 10^{-19}\,\text{J}$$

**16.** **(c)** $\dfrac{1}{\lambda} = R\left(\dfrac{1}{n_1^2} - \dfrac{1}{n_2^2}\right)$

$$\frac{1}{\lambda} = 1.097 \times 10^7 \left(\frac{1}{1} - \frac{1}{\infty}\right) = 1.097 \times 10^7\,\text{m}^{-1}$$

$$\lambda = 91.15 \times 10^{-9}\,\text{m} \approx 91\,\text{nm}$$

**17.** **(c)** Energy of free $e^-$ at rest ($n = \infty$) is zero.

### Assertion & Reason Questions

**1.** **(a)** Cathode rays are made up of electrons which are basic constituents of all atoms, so characteristics of cathode rays do not depend upon the material of electrode and the nature of gas present in the cathode ray tube.

**2.** **(a)** In various experiment, with different oil drops, the charge on the drops was found to be in the multiple of $1.602 \times 10^{-19}$C, thus, the lowest value of the charge on any oil drop was found to be $1.602 \times 10^{-19}$C.

**3.** **(a)** Cathode rays consist of negatively charged particles having e/m equal to that of an electron. Thus, the cathode rays are stream of electrons.

**4.** **(b)** Isobars are different elements which have same atomic mass, but different atomic number. They have different chemical properties.

**5.** **(b)** Energy increases with increase in temperature and so the frequency.

**6.** **(a)** Both assertion and reason are true and reason is the correct explanation of assertion.

Radius, $r_n = \dfrac{n^2 h^2}{4\pi e^2 mZ} = \dfrac{n^2}{Z} \times 0.529\text{Å}.$

For first orbit of H-atom

$$n = 1$$

$$r_1 = \frac{(1)^2}{1} \times 0.529\,\text{Å} = 0.529\,\text{Å}$$

**7.** **(b)** When white light is passed through a prism, it splits into seven colours violet (V), indigo (I), blue (B), green (G), yellow (Y), orange (O) and red (R), violet colour light has lowest wavelength and highest frequency and red colour light has highest wavelength and have lowest frequency.

**8.** **(a)**

**9.** **(c)** Rate of emission of photoelectrons is directly proportional to the intensity of incident light.

### Match the Column

**1.** **(b)** Isotopes have same atomic number. Isobars have same mass number, whereas isoelectronic species have same number of electrons although the (A) has same number of electrons but the protons they carry are same while in case of isolelectronic species number of protons they carry are different.

### Very Short Answer Questions

**1.** Hydrogen

**2.** Emission line spectrum.

**3.** Neutrons were discovered by Chadwick in 1932. Neutrons are produced when Chadwick bombarded a thin foil of beryllium with fast moving $\alpha$-particles. These neutral particles were found to have mass $1.675 \times 10^{-27}$ kg.

$$_{4}^{9}\text{Be} + _{2}^{4}\text{He} \rightarrow _{6}^{12}\text{C} + _{0}^{1}\text{n}$$

**4.** For a neutral atom, $U$,

Atomic number = number of protons – number of electrons

$\therefore$ Number of electrons = 92

$\therefore$ $U^{+2}$ has 90 electrons whereas the number of protons = 92

**5.** Atomic number = Mass number – Number of neutrons

Atomic no. $= 14 - 8 = 6$, so the element is carbon

**6.** Let the % of higher isotope $(Z + 2)$ is $x$, other isotope $(Z - 1)$ will be $(100 - x)$

Average atomic weight $(Z) = \dfrac{x(Z+2) + (100 - x)(Z-1)}{100}$

$= 100Z = Zx + 2x + 100Z - 100 - Zx + x$

$3x = 100 \quad \Rightarrow \quad x = 33.33\%$

7. Atoms contain massive, positively charged centers called nuclei and most of the space inside the atom is empty.

8. $\dfrac{9.1 \times 10^{-28}\,\text{g for electron}}{1.67 \times 10^{-24}\,\text{g for proton}} = 5.45 \times 10^{-4} = 1/1837$

9. With the decrease in the wavelength of light the intensity decreases.

10. The phenomenon of splitting up of a spectral line into closely spaced lines under the influence of an electric field is called Stark effect.

11. It is the phenomenon of splitting up of a spectral line into closely spaced lines under the influence of a magnetic field.

12. This is because each of them is associated with a definite amount of energy.

13. A photon of violet light has shorter wavelength and thus a higher energy.

$$\left[ E = h\nu = h\dfrac{c}{\lambda} \right]$$

14. The phenomenon of interference and diffraction support the wave nature of light.

15. A photon is the quantum of light and its energy is equal to $h\nu$, while a proton is a positively charged particle present in nucleus of an atom.

16. Electron will have largest wavelength because it has least mass.

17. No, because threshold frequency of electron will not be crossed by red photons, and one electron interacts with only one photon.

18. Energy of electron after absorption is
$$= -13.6\ \text{eV} + 12.1\ \text{eV} = -1.5\ \text{eV}$$
For hydrogen $E_n = -13.6 / n^2$
Thus, $-1.5 = -13.6 / n^2$
or $n^2 = 9$ or $n = 3$ i.e. i.e. it would jump to 3rd orbit.

19. $\nu = c/\lambda = 3.0 \times 10^8\,\text{m/s} /(5000 \times 10^{-10}\,\text{m}) = 6.0 \times 10^{14}\ \text{sec}^{-1}$.

20. Given that, $\nu = 1.6 \times 10^{15}\,\text{s}^{-1}$;
$\nu_0 = 5 \times 10^{14}\,\text{s}^{-1}$ ; $h = 6.63 \times 10^{-34}\,\text{Js}$
$\text{K.E.} = h(\nu - \nu_0)$
$= 6.63 \times 10^{-34}(16 \times 10^{14} - 5 \times 10^{14})$
$\quad = 6.63 \times 10^{-34} \times 11 \times 10^{14} = 7.29 \times 10^{-19}\,\text{J}$

### *Short Answer Questions*

1. The charge over mass ratio of negatively charged particles remains the same irrespective of nature of gas used in discharge tube and material of electrodes which shows that electrons are fundamental particle of all the atoms. Atom, as a whole is neutral and electrons are present in all the atoms, therefore, there must be equal number of positively charged particles in all the atoms.

2. They are obtained by ionisation of gas with the help of cathode rays. They consist of positively charged particle called protons.

3. Maxwell proved that when charged particle revolves under force of attraction, it continuously radiates energy. Electron is a charged particle and revolving under force of attraction, it should radiate energy and ultimately it should fall into the nucleus which actually does not happen. It means there is something wrong with Rutherford's model of atom.

4. Cathode rays are particles of matter with a definite mass-to-charge ratio. Cathode rays are independent of the gas in the discharge tube or the kind of material making up the electrodes. These are the evidences to prove that cathode rays are part of all matter.

5. Cathode rays, no matter what the source is , are composed of electrons– all of which have same charge to mass ratio. The ions formed after the loss of electrons might have the same magnitude of charge, but different masses. Hence they will have different charge to mass ratio.

6. Given that KE $= 500\ \text{eV} = 500 \times 1.6 \times 10^{-19}\,\text{J}$;
$m_p = 1.67 \times 10^{-27}\,\text{kg}$

$\text{KE} = \dfrac{1}{2}\,mv^2$

or $\quad 2\text{KE} = mv^2 \qquad\qquad \text{...(i)}$
Multiply eqn(i) with m we get
$\quad 2m\text{KE} = m^2v^2$
or $mv = \sqrt{2m\text{KE}}$
By de–Broglie equation $\lambda = h / mv$
$= h / \sqrt{2m\text{KE}}$

$= \dfrac{6.626 \times 10^{-34}}{\sqrt{2 \times 1.67 \times 10^{-27} \times 500 \times 1.6 \times 10^{-19}}}$

$= \dfrac{6.626 \times 10^{-34}}{\sqrt{26.72 \times 10^{-44}}} = \dfrac{6.626 \times 10^{-34}}{5.169 \times 10^{-22}} = 1.28 \times 10^{-12}\,\text{m}$

7. $E_1 = h\dfrac{c}{\lambda}$

$E_1 = \dfrac{6.626 \times 10^{-34} \times 3 \times 10^8}{800 \times 10^{-9}\,\text{m}} = 2.48 \times 10^{-19}\ \text{J}$ ;

$E_2 = \dfrac{6.626 \times 10^{-34} \times 3 \times 10^8}{400 \times 10^{-9}\,\text{m}} = 4.97 \times 10^{-19}\ \text{J}$

$\dfrac{E_1}{E_2} = \dfrac{1}{2}$ or $E_2 = 2E_1$

8. K.E. of the electron $= 100\ \text{MeV} = 100 \times 10^6\ \text{eV}$
$= 10^8\,\text{eV} = 10^8\ \text{eV} \times 1.6 \times 10^{-19}\ \text{J/eV} = 1.6 \times 10^{-11}\,\text{J}$

$\lambda = \dfrac{hc}{K.E.} = \dfrac{6.6 \times 10^{-34}\ \text{Js} \times 3 \times 10^8\ \text{ms}^{-1}}{1.6 \times 10^{-11}\ \text{J}}$

$\lambda = 1.24 \times 10^{-14}\ \text{m}$

**9.** $hv = hv_0 + K.E., \; h(v - v_0) = K.E.$

$$v - v_0 = \frac{K.E.}{h} = \frac{6.63 \times 10^{-14}\,\text{J}}{6.63 \times 10^{-34}\,\text{Js}} = 1 \times 10^{20}\,\text{s}^{-1}$$

$$5 \times 10^{20} - 1 \times 10^{20} = v_0 \Rightarrow v_0 = 4 \times 10^{20}\,\text{s}^{-1} \text{or Hz}$$

**10.** According to de Broglie equations, $\lambda = \dfrac{h}{mv}$

Momentum of electron, $mv = \dfrac{h}{\lambda}$

$$= \frac{\left(6.626 \times 10^{-34}\,\text{kg m}^2\text{s}^{-1}\right)}{\left(5200 \times 10^{-10}\,\text{m}\right)}$$

$$= 1.274 \times 10^{-27}\,\text{kg ms}^{-1} \qquad \qquad \text{...(i)}$$

The momentum of electron can also be calculated as
$mv = (9.1 \times 10^{-31}\,\text{kg}) \times v$       ...(ii)
Comparing (i) and (ii)
$(9.1 \times 10^{-31}\,\text{kg}) \times v = (1.274 \times 10^{-27}\,\text{kg ms}^{-1})$

$$v = \frac{\left(1.274 \times 10^{-27}\,\text{kg ms}^{-1}\right)}{\left(9.1 \times 10^{-31}\,\text{kg}\right)} = 1.4 \times 10^3\,\text{ms}^{-1}$$

**11.** Calculation of the velocity of electron
Energy (kinetic energy) of electron $= 1.0 \times 10^4$ volts
$\qquad\qquad = 1.0 \times 10^4 \times 1.6 \times 10^{-19}\,\text{J}$
$\qquad\qquad = 1.6 \times 10^{-15}\,\text{J} = 1.6 \times 10^{-15}\,\text{kg m}^2\text{s}^{-2}$
or    $1/2\,mv^2 = 1.6 \times 10^{-15}\,\text{kg m}^2\,\text{s}^{-2}$

or    $v = \left(\dfrac{2 \times 1.6 \times 10^{-15}\,\text{kg m}^2\text{s}^{-2}}{9.1 \times 10^{-31}\,\text{kg}}\right)^{1/2}$

$\qquad = 5.93 \times 10^7\,\text{ms}^{-1}$

Calculation of the wavelength of electron

According to de Broglie equation, $\lambda = \dfrac{h}{mv}$;

$$\lambda = \frac{\left(6.626 \times 10^{-34}\,\text{kg m}^2 s^{-1}\right)}{\left(9.1 \times 10^{-31}\,\text{kg}\right) \times \left(5.93 \times 10^7\,\text{ms}^{-1}\right)}$$

$= 1.22 \times 10^{-11}\,\text{m}$

**12.** Given that,    $\lambda_1 = 6563\,\text{Å}$
According to Bohr's theory, the wavelengths of the Balmer series are given by

$$\bar{v} = \frac{1}{\lambda} = R_H \left\{ \frac{1}{2^2} - \frac{1}{n_1^2} \right\}$$

For first member, $n_i = 3$

$$\therefore \quad \frac{1}{\lambda_1} = R_H \left\{ \frac{1}{2^2} - \frac{1}{3^2} \right\} = \frac{5R_H}{36}$$

And for second member, $n_i = 4$

$$\therefore \quad \frac{1}{\lambda_2} = R_H \left( \frac{1}{2^2} - \frac{1}{4^2} \right) = \frac{3R_H}{16}$$

Dividing the two equations,

$$\frac{\lambda_2}{\lambda_1} = \frac{5R_H}{36} \times \frac{16}{3R_H} = \frac{20}{27}$$

$$\therefore \quad \lambda_2 = \frac{20}{27}\lambda_1 = \frac{20}{27} \times 6563 = 4861.5\,\text{Å}$$

**13.** Given that,
$\lambda = 4500 \times 10^{-10}\,\text{m}$
$h = 6.626 \times 10^{-34}\,\text{Js}$       (constant)
$c = 3 \times 10^8\,\text{ms}^{-1}$       (constant)
Energy absorbed by each iodine molecule is given by,

$$\frac{hc}{\lambda} = \frac{6.626 \times 10^{-34} \times 3 \times 10^8}{4500 \times 10^{-10}} = 4.417 \times 10^{-19}\,\text{J}$$

Also given, Bond energy of $I_2 = 240 \times 10^8\,\text{J mol}^{-1}$

$$\therefore \quad \text{Bond energy of } I_2 \text{ molecule} = \frac{240 \times 10^3}{6.023 \times 10^{23}}$$

$\qquad = 3.984 \times 10^{-19}\,\text{J}$
$\therefore$   K. E. of iodine molecule
$\qquad = 4.417 \times 10^{-19} - 3.984 \times 10^{-19} = 0.433 \times 10^{-19}\,\text{J}$

and K.E. of iodine atom $= \dfrac{0.433 \times 10^{-19}}{2} = 0.2165 \times 10^{-19}\,\text{J}$

**14.** We are given that, $E_n = -\dfrac{B}{n^2}$

When an electron jumps from the third orbit ($n = 3$) to the second ($n = 2$), then energy of photon is given by,

$E = hv = E_3 - E_2$

$$= -\frac{B}{3^2} - \left\{ -\frac{B}{2^2} \right\} = B \left\{ \frac{1}{4} - \frac{1}{9} \right\} = \frac{5B}{36}$$

But $hv = h\dfrac{c}{\lambda}$

$$\therefore \quad \frac{hc}{\lambda} = \frac{5B}{36}$$

or    $\lambda = \dfrac{36\,hc}{5B}$

$$= \frac{36 \times 6.63 \times 10^{-34} \times 3 \times 10^8}{5 \times 2.179 \times 10^{-18}}\,\text{m}$$

$= 6572 \times 10^{-10}\,\text{m} = 6572\,\text{Å}$

**15.** According to Einstein's photoelectric equation, the maximum energy of the emitted electron is given by

$$E_m = h(v - v_0) = h\left(\frac{c}{\lambda_1} - \frac{c}{\lambda_2}\right)$$

$$= hc\left(\frac{1}{\lambda_1} - \frac{1}{\lambda_2}\right)$$

Here, $\lambda_1 = 1810\ \text{Å} = 1810 \times 10^{-10}\ m$

$\lambda_2 = 2640\ \text{Å} = 2640 \times 10^{-10}\ m$

$h = 6.63 \times 10^{-34}\ \text{Js}$

$c = 3 \times 10^8\ \text{ms}^{-1}$

Hence, maximum energy of the emitted electron,

$$E_m = 6.63 \times 10^{-34} \times 3 \times 10^8$$

$$\left[\frac{1}{18 \times 10^{-10}} - \frac{1}{2640 \times 10^{-10}}\right] J$$

$$= 19.89 \times 10^{-26}\left[\frac{2640 \times 10^{-10} - 1810 \times 10^{-10}}{1810 \times 2640 \times 10^{-20}}\right] J$$

$$= 3.4553 \times 10^{-19}\ \text{J} = 2.16\ \text{ev} \quad (\because 1\ \text{ev} = 1.6 \times 10^{-19}\ \text{J})$$

**16.** Here, $\dfrac{1}{2} mV^2 = eV$

or $\dfrac{1}{2} m \dfrac{h^2}{m^2 \lambda^2} = eV$ $\qquad \left[\because \lambda = \dfrac{h}{mV}\right]$

or $V = \dfrac{1}{2} \dfrac{h^2}{m\lambda^2 e}$

Given that,

$\lambda = 1.54\ \text{Å} = 1.54 \times 10^{-10}\ m$

$h = 6.626 \times 10^{-34}\ \text{Js}$

$m = 9.108 \times 10^{-31}\ \text{kg}$

$e = 1.602 \times 10^{-19}\ \text{C}$

$$\therefore V = \frac{1}{2} \times \frac{\left(6.626 \times 10^{-34}\right)^2}{9.108 \times 10^{-31} \times \left(1.54 \times 10^{-10}\right)^2 \times 1.602 \times 10^{-19}}$$

$$= 63.3\ \text{Volts}$$

**17.** According to de Broglie's equation,

$$\lambda = \frac{h}{mv} = \frac{h}{p}$$

For particle A

$$\lambda_A = \frac{h}{p_A}$$

For particle B,

$$\lambda_B = \frac{h}{p_B}$$

$$\therefore \quad \frac{\lambda_A}{\lambda_B} = \frac{h}{p_A} \cdot \frac{p_B}{h}$$

$$\frac{\lambda_A}{\lambda_B} = \frac{p_B}{p_A}$$

But $p_B = \dfrac{1}{2} p_A$

$$\frac{\lambda_A}{\lambda_B} = \frac{1}{2} \frac{p_A}{p_A}$$

$$\frac{\lambda_A}{\lambda_B} = \frac{1}{2}$$

$$\therefore \quad \lambda_B = 2\lambda_A = 2 \times 5 \times 10^{-8}$$

$$\lambda_B = 10^{-7}\ m$$

**18.** $\lambda = 4 \times 10^{-7}\ m$

(a) Energy of the incident photon

$$E = h\frac{c}{\lambda}$$

$$E = \frac{6.626 \times 10^{-34}\ \text{Js} \times 3.0 \times 10^8\ \text{ms}^{-1}}{4 \times 10^{-7}\ m}$$

$$= 4.9695 \times 10^{-19}\ \text{J}$$

$$E = \frac{4.9695 \times 10^{-19}}{1.6020 \times 10^{-19}}\ \text{eV} = 3.102\ \text{eV}.$$

(b) Kinetic energy KE
= Energy of photon − Work function
= 3.102 − 2.13 = 0.972 eV
= 0.972 × 1.6020 × 10⁻¹⁹ J = 1.557 × 10⁻¹⁹ J

(iii) Velocity of the photoelectron $= v = \sqrt{\dfrac{2KE}{m_e}}$

$$v = \sqrt{\frac{2 \times 1.557 \times 10^{-19}}{9.1 \times 10^{-31}}}$$

$$\Rightarrow v = 5.85 \times 10^5\ \text{m s}^{-1}$$

**19.** For Balmer series

$$\frac{1}{\lambda} = 1.0097 \times 10^7\left(\frac{1}{2^2} - \frac{1}{n_H^2}\right)$$

$$\frac{1}{3.97 \times 10^{-7}\ m} = 1.97 \times 10^7\left(\frac{1}{4} - \frac{1}{n_H^2}\right)$$

$$\therefore \quad \frac{1}{4} - \frac{1}{n_H^2} = \frac{1}{3.97 \times 10^{-7} \text{ m} \times 1.097 \times 10^7 \text{ m}^{-1}} = 0.23$$

$$\therefore \quad \frac{1}{n_H^2} = \frac{1}{4} - 0.23 = 0.02$$

$$n_H^2 = \frac{1}{0.02} = 50$$

$$\therefore \quad n_H = 7$$

**20.** I.E. = Work function = 13.6 eV

Energy of the photon = $1.5 \times IE$

$$= 1.5 \times 13.6 \text{ eV}$$

We know that

$$h\nu = W + \text{KE}$$

$$\therefore \quad \text{KE} = h\nu - W = (1.5 \times 13.6) - 13.6$$

$$\text{KE} = 0.5 \times 13.6 \text{ eV} = 6.8 \text{ eV}$$

$$\text{KE} = 6.8 \times 1.6 \times 10^{-19} \text{ J}$$

But $6.8 \times 1.6 \times 10^{-19} = \dfrac{mv^2}{2}$

$$\therefore \quad v = \left( \frac{2 \times 6.8 \times 1.6 \times 10^{-19}}{9.1 \times 10^{-31}} \right)^{1/2}$$

$$v = 1.55 \times 10^6 \text{ m s}^{-1}$$

From de Broglie equation, we can write

$$\lambda = \frac{h}{mv} = \frac{6.26 \times 10^{-34}}{9.1 \times 10^{-31} \times 1.55 \times 10^6}$$

$$\lambda = 4.71 \times 10^{-10} \text{ m}$$

$$\lambda = 471 \text{ pm}$$

**21.** Since $n_L = 2$ and $n_H = 5$. This transition gives rise to a spectral line in the Balmer series.

We have

$$\Delta E = 2.178 \times 10^{-18} \left[ \frac{1}{n_L^2} - \frac{1}{n_H^2} \right] J$$

$$= 2.178 \times 10^{-18} \left( \frac{1}{2^2} - \frac{1}{5^2} \right)$$

$$= 2.178 \times 10^{-18} \times \frac{21}{100}$$

$$\Delta E = 4.57 \times 10^{-19} \text{ J}$$

The frequency of a photon is given by

$$\nu = \frac{\Delta E}{h} = \frac{4.57 \times 10^{-19} \text{ J}}{6.626 \times 10^{-34} \text{ Js}} = 6.90 \times 10^{14} \text{ s}^{-1}$$

and the wavelength

$$\lambda = \frac{c}{\nu} = \frac{3.0 \times 10^8 \text{ ms}^{-1}}{6.90 \times 10^{14} \text{ s}^{-1}} = 4.35 \times 10^{-7} \text{ m}$$

$$= 435 \text{ nm}$$

**22.** (i) wave number $\bar{\nu} = 1/\lambda = 1 / 5800 \times 10^{-10}$ m

$$= 1.724 \times 10^6 \text{ m}^{-1}$$

(ii) $\nu$ (frequency) = $c / \lambda$ $= \dfrac{3 \times 10^8 \text{ ms}^{-1}}{5800 \times 10^{-10} \text{ m}}$

$$= 5.172 \times 10^{14} \text{ s}^{-1}$$

**23.** The main points of this theory are as follows:

   (i)    The radiant energy is emitted or absorbed not continuosly but discontinuosly in the form of small discrete packets of energy. Each such packet of energy is called a quantum. In case of light, the quantum of energy is called photon.

  (ii)    The energy of each quantum is directly proportional to the frequency of radiation i.e. E $\propto \nu$ or

        E = h $\nu$ where 'h' is Planck's constant and its value is $6.626 \times 10^{-34}$ Js.

**24.** (A) wave motion      (B) particle

     (C) particle          (D) both

**25.** Since 13.6 eV is needed to ionize H–atom, its 1.5 times (i.e., $13.6 \times 1.5$) 20.4 eV have been absorbed by electron in hydrogen atom. Of this energy, 6.8 eV is converted to kinetic energy. The velocity of the electron is as follows:

$$6.8 \text{ eV} = 6.8 (1.6 \times 10^{-19} \text{ C}) \ (1\text{V})$$

$$= 1.088 \times 10^{-18} \text{ J}$$

$$\text{KE} = \frac{1}{2} mv^2$$

or $v = \sqrt{2\text{KE}/m}$

$$= \sqrt{2(1.088 \times 10^{-18} \text{ J}) / 9.1 \times 10^{-31} \text{ kg}}$$

$$= 1.55 \times 10^6 \text{ m/s}$$

According to de Broglie equation

$$\lambda = \frac{h}{mv} = \frac{6.63 \times 10^{-34} \text{ Js}}{(9.1 \times 10^{-31} \text{ kg})(1.55 \times 10^6 \text{ m/s})}$$

$$= 4.7 \times 10^{-10} \text{ m}$$

**26.** The kinetic energy of a particle is given by,

$$\text{KE} = \frac{1}{2} mv^2 \qquad \qquad \text{...(i)}$$

Multiply and divide eqn(i) by 'm'

$$= \frac{1}{2} m^2v^2/m \ = p^2 / 2m \qquad \qquad \text{...(ii)}$$

We Know that $\lambda = h / p$    or $p = h / \lambda$

By substituting value of p in eq (ii) we get,

$$K.E. = \frac{h^2}{2m\lambda^2}$$

$$\text{KE for electron} = \frac{h^2}{2m_e\lambda_e^2}$$

$$\text{And KE for proton} = \frac{h^2}{2m_p\lambda_p^2}$$

Since KE for electron = KE for proton

$$\frac{h^2}{2m_e\lambda_e^2} = \frac{h^2}{2m_p\lambda_p^2}$$

or $\quad \dfrac{\lambda_e}{\lambda_p} = \dfrac{\sqrt{m_p}}{\sqrt{m_e}}$

As $m_p > m_e$ thus $\lambda_e > \lambda_p$

**27.** Given that, K.E. $= 1.3 \times 10^{-18}$ J ; $v = 3v_0$ ;
$h = 6.626 \times 10^{-34}$ Js
Kinetic energy of electron $= h(v - v_0)$
$1.3 \times 10^{-18} = 6.626 \times 10^{-34}(3v_0 - v_0)$

$$v_0 = \frac{1.3 \times 10^{-18}}{6.626 \times 10^{-34} \times 2} = 9.81 \times 10^{14} \text{ Hz.}$$

**28.** (i) The phenomenon of emission of electrons from the metal surface when a light of suitable frequency equal to or greater than the threshold frequency strikes on it is called photo-electric effect. The emitted electrons are called photo-electrons.

(ii) A black body is a substance which absorbs all the light radiation falling on it and when it is heated to a high temperature it emits all the radiations. The radiations emitted by a black body are called black body radiations.

### Long Answer Questions

**1.** (i) For H atom,
$E_n = -1.312 \times 10^3$ kJmol$^{-1}$
$\quad = -1.312 \times 10^6$ Jmol$^{-1}$

$$= -\frac{1.312 \times 10^6}{6.023 \times 10^{23}} \text{ J atom}^{-1}$$

$$= -2.18 \times 10^{-18} \text{ J atom}^{-1}$$

Here, $n_{final} = 1$ ; $n_{initial} = 4$

$$E_{initial} = -\frac{2.18 \times 10^{-18}}{(4)^2} = -0.136 \times 10^{-18} \text{ J atom}^{-1}$$

$$E_{final} = -\frac{2.18 \times 10^{-18}}{(1)^2} = -2.18 \times 10^{-18} \text{ J atom}^{-1}$$

$\Delta E = E_{final} - E_{initial}$
$= -2.18 \times 10^{-18} (-0.316 \times 10^{-18}) = -1.864 \times 10^{-18}$ J
Also, $\Delta E = hc/\lambda$

$$\lambda = h c/\Delta E = \frac{6.626 \times 10^{-34} \times 3 \times 10^8}{1.864 \times 10^{-18}} = 10.66 \times 10^{-8} \text{ m}$$

(ii) (a) $2s < 2p$ $\qquad$ (b) $3p < 3d$
$\quad$ (c) $3s < 4s$ $\qquad$ (d) $4d < 5f$

**2.** (a) orbital $\qquad$ (b) para-magnetism
(c) $-3$ to $+3$ $\qquad$ (d) Fe
(e) degenerate $\qquad$ (f) $5s^2\, 4d^{10}\, 5p^2$
(g) orientations in space
(h) zero
(i) pauli's exclusion principle
(j) visible.

**3.** (i) We are given that P(Power) $= 25$ W ; t $= 1$ sec;
$\lambda = 6000$Å $= 6000 \times 10^{-10}$ m $= 6 \times 10^{-7}$m
Energy of one photon is $E = hv = hc / \lambda$

$$= \frac{6.63 \times 10^{-34} \times 3 \times 10^8}{6 \times 10^{-7}} = 3.315 \times 10^{-19} \text{ J}$$

∴ Number of photons emitted per second

$$= \frac{\text{Total energy emitted per sec}}{\text{Energy of one photon}} = \frac{25 \times 1}{3.315 \times 10^{-19}}$$

$$= 7.54 \times 10^{19}$$

(ii) Given that, $E = 7.61 \times 10^{-17}$J;
$\quad \lambda = 300$ nm $= 300 \times 10^{-9}$ m;
$h = 6.626 \times 10^{-34}$ Js
$c = 3 \times 10^8$ ms$^{-1}$
According to Planck's equation
$E = nhv = nhc/\lambda \Rightarrow n = E \lambda /hc$

$$= \frac{7.61 \times 10^{-17} \times 300 \times 10^{-9}}{6.626 \times 10^{-34} \times 3 \times 10^8} = 115 \text{ photons}$$

**4.** (i) According to Rydberg-Balmer equation.

$$\frac{1}{\lambda} = R\left[\frac{1}{n_1^2} - \frac{1}{n_2^2}\right] = R\left[\frac{1}{1^2} - \frac{1}{n_2^2}\right]$$

The wavelength ($\lambda$) will be longest when $n_2$ is the smallest i.e., $n_2 = 2$ and 3 for two longest wavelength lines.
For $n_2 = 2$ :

$$\frac{1}{\lambda} = \left(1.097 \times 10^{-2} \text{ nm}^{-1}\right)\left[\frac{1}{1^2} - \frac{1}{2^2}\right]$$

$$= \left(1.097 \times 10^{-2} \text{ nm}^{-1}\right) \times \frac{3}{4}$$

$$= 8.228 \times 10^{-3} \text{ nm}^{-1} \text{ or } \lambda = 121.54 \text{ nm}$$

For $n_2 = 3$ :

$$\frac{1}{\lambda} = \left(1.097 \times 10^{-2} \text{ nm}^{-1}\right)\left[\frac{1}{1^2} - \frac{1}{3^2}\right]$$

$$= \left(1.097 \times 10^{-2} \text{ nm}^{-1}\right) \times (8/9)$$

$$= 9.75 \times 10^{-3} \text{ nm}^{-1}; \lambda = 102.56 \text{ nm}$$

(ii) The expression for the energy of hydrogen of electron is :

$$E_n = -\frac{2\pi^2 m e^4}{n^2 h^2}$$

When $n = 1$,

$$E_1 = -\frac{2\pi^2 m e^4}{(1)^2 h^2} = -13.12 \times 10^5 \text{ J mol}^{-1}$$

When $n = 2$,

$$E_2 = -\frac{2\pi^2 m e^4}{(2)^2 h^2} = -\frac{13.12 \times 10^5}{4} \text{ J mol}^{-1}$$

$$= -3.28 \times 10^5 \text{ J mol}^{-1}$$

The energy required for the excitation is :

$$\Delta E = E_2 - E_1 = \left(-3.28 \times 10^5\right) - \left(-13.12 \times 10^5\right)$$

$$= 9.84 \times 10^5 \text{ J mol}^{-1}.$$

5. Limitations of Bohr's model of an atom :
   (i) It could not explain spectrum of multi-electron atoms.
   (ii) It could not explain Zeeman and stark effect.
   (iii) It could not explain shape of molecules.
   (iv) It was not in accordance with Heisenberg's uncertainty principle.

   **Quantum Mechanical Model :** It was developed on the basis of Heisenberg's uncertainty principal and dual behaviour of matter.

Main features of this model are given below :
(i) The energy of electrons in an atoms is quantized *i.e.* can have certain values.
(ii) It existence of quantized electronic energy levels is a direct result by the wave litre properties of electrons.
(iii) Both the exact position of exact velocity of an electron in an atom cannot be determined simultaneously.
(iv) The orbitals are filled increasing order of energy. All the information about the electron than atom is stored in orbital wave function $\Psi$.
(v) From the value of $\Psi^2$ at different points within atom, it is possible to predict the region around the nucleus where electron most probably will found.

6. (i) $Cr(24) : 1s^2\, 2s^2\, 2p^6\, 3s^2\, 3p^6\, 4s^1\, 3d^5$
   Half filled orbitals are more stable because of symmetrical distribution of electrons and exchange energy is maximum.

   (ii) It is impossible to determine the exact position and momentum of first moving sub-atomic particle like electron simultaneously.

$$\Delta V = 50 \times [(100 - 99.99)\%]$$

$$= 50 \times \frac{0.01}{100} = 50 \times 10^{-4}$$

$$= 5 \times 10^{-3} \text{ ms}^{-1}$$

$$\Delta x . \Delta V = \frac{h}{4m\pi}$$

$$\Rightarrow \Delta x = \frac{6.6 \times 10^{-34} \text{ Js}}{4 \times 9.1 \times 10^{-31}\text{kg} \times 3.142 \times 5 \times 10^{-3} \text{ ms}^{-1}}$$

$$\Delta x = \frac{6.6}{571.844} = 1.154 \times 10^{-2} \text{m}.$$

## SECTION C — NCERT EXEMPLAR QUESTIONS 

### MULTIPLE CHOICE QUESTIONS

1. Which of the following statements about the electron is incorrect?
   (a) It is a negatively charged particle.
   (b) The mass of electron is equal to the mass of neutron.
   (c) It is a basic constituent of all the atoms.
   (d) It is a constituent of cathode rays.

2. Which of the following properties of atom could be explained correctly by Thomson model of atom?
   (a) Overall neutrality of atom
   (b) Spectra of hydrogen atom
   (c) Position of electrons, protons and neutrons in atom
   (d) Stability of atom

3. Number of angular nodes for $4d$ orbital is ........... .
   (a) 4    (b) 3    (c) 2    (d) 1

4. Total number of orbitals associated with third shell will be ............... .
   (a) 2    (b) 4    (c) 9    (d) 3

5. Orbital angular momentum depends on ...........
   (a) $l$            (b) $n$ and $l$
   (c) $n$ and $m$    (d) $m$ and $s$

6. Chlorine exists in two isotopic forms Cl-37 and Cl-35, but its atomic mass is 35.5. This indicates the ratio of Cl-37 and Cl-35 is approximately
   (a) 1 : 2        (b) 1 : 1
   (c) 1 : 3        (d) 3 : 1

**7.** If travelling at same speeds, which of the following matter waves have the shortest wavelength?

(a) Electron
(b) Alpha particle ($He^{2+}$)
(c) Neutron
(d) Proton

**8.** The probability density plots of $1s$ and $2s$ orbitals are given in figure.

 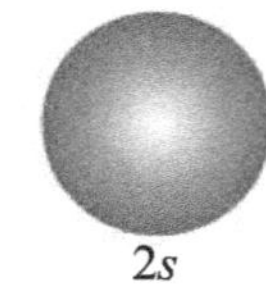

$1s$      $2s$

The density of dots in a region represents the probability density of finding electrons in the region. On the basis of above diagram which of the following statements is incorrect?

(a) $1s$ and $2s$ orbitals are spherical in shape.
(b) The probability of finding the electron is maximum near the nucleus.
(c) The probability of finding the electron at a given distance is equal in all directions.
(d) The probability density of electrons for $2s$ orbital decreases uniformly as distance from the nucleus increases.

## ASSERTION & REASON QUESTIONS

**DIRECTIONS (Qs. 1-2) :** *Each of these questions contains an assertion followed by reason. Read them carefully and answer the question on the basis of following options. You have to select the one that best describes the two statements.*

(a) If both Assertion and Reason are correct and the Reason is a correct explanation of the Assertion.
(b) If both Assertion and Reason are correct but Reason is not a correct explanation of the Assertion.
(c) If the Assertion is correct but Reason is incorrect.
(d) If the Assertion is incorrect but the Reason is correct.

**1.** **Assertion :** All isotopes of a given element show the same type of chemical behaviour.
**Reason :** The chemical properties of an atom are controlled by the number of electrons in the atom.

**2.** **Assertion :** It is impossible to determine the exact position and exact momentum of an electron simultaneously.
**Reason :** The path of an electron in an atom is clearly defined.

## SHORT ANSWER QUESTIONS

**1.** Table-tennis ball has a mass 10 g and a speed of 90 m/s. If speed can be measured within an accuracy of 4% what will be the uncertainty in speed and position?

**2.** Hydrogen atom has only one electron, so mutual repulsion between electrons is absent. However, in multielectron atoms mutual repulsion between the electrons is significant. How does this affect the energy of an electron in the orbitals of the same principal quantum number in multelectron atoms?

## LONG ANSWER QUESTIONS

**1.** Threshold frequency, $V_0$ is the minimum frequency which a photon must possess to eject an electron from a metal. It is different for different metals. When a photon of frequency $1.0 \times 10^{15}$ s$^{-1}$ was allowed to hit a metal surface, an electron having $1.988 \times 10^{-19}$ J of kinetic energy was emitted. Calculate the threshold frequency of this metal. Show that an electron will not be emitted if a photon with a wavelength equal to 600 nm hits the metal surface.

**2.** Calculate the energy and frequency of the radiation emitted when an electron jumps from $n = 3$ to $n = 2$ in a hydrogen atom.

## SOLUTIONS

### *Multiple Choice Questions*

**1.** **(b)** The mass of electron is very small as compared to the mass of the neutron.
Mass of electron = $9.1 \times 10^{-31}$ kg
Mass of neutron = $1.67 \times 10^{-27}$ kg

**2.** **(a)** J. J. Thomson, in 1898, proposed plum pudding model of atom. An important feature of this model is that the mass of the atom is assumed to be uniformly distributed over the atom. This model was able to explain the overall neutrality of the atom.

**3.** **(c)** Number of angular nodes = $l$
$l = 2$ for $d$-orbital
$\therefore$ Number of angular nodes = 2

**4.** **(c)** Total number of orbitals associated with $n^{th}$ shell = $n^2$
$\therefore$ Total number of orbitals associated with third shel
= $(3)^2 = 9$

**5.** **(a)** Orbital angular momentum,
$$mvr = \frac{h}{2\pi}\sqrt{l(l+1)}$$
Hence, it depends only on '$l$', $l$ can have values ranging from 0 to $(n - 1)$.

**6.** **(c)** The fractional atomic mass (35.5) of chlorine is due to the fact that in ordinary chlorine atom, Cl-37 and Cl-35 are present in the ratio of 1 : 3.

$\therefore$   Average atomic mass of Cl

$$= \frac{3 \times 35 + 1 \times 37}{4} = 35.5 \text{ amu}$$

**7.** **(b)** From de-Broglie equation, wavelength,

$$\lambda = \frac{h}{mv}$$

For same speed of different particles, $\lambda \propto \dfrac{1}{m}$

As $h$ is constant, greater the mass of matter waves, lesser is wavelength and vice-versa. Among these matter waves, alpha particle ($He^{2+}$) has higher mass, therefore, shortest wavelength.

**8.** **(d)** The probability density of electrons in $2s$ orbital first increases then decreases and after that it increases again as distance increases from nucleus.

### *Assertion & Reason Questions*

**1.** **(a)** All isotopes have same atomic number means same number of electrons and they bear similar chemical properties.

**2.** **(c)** The effect of Heisenberg Uncertainty Principal is significant only for motion of microscopic objects and is negligible for that of macroscopic objects.

### *Short Answer Questions*

**1.** Uncertainty in the speed of ball

$$= \frac{90 \times 4}{100} = \frac{360}{100} = 3.6 \text{ms}^{-1}$$

Uncertainty in position $= \dfrac{h}{4\pi m \Delta v}$

$$= \frac{6.626 \times 10^{-34} \text{ Js}}{4 \times 3.14 \times 10 \times 10^{-3} \text{ Kg g}^{-1} \times 3.6 \text{ms}^{-1}}$$
$$= 1.46 \times 10^{-33} \text{ m}$$

**2.** The energy of electron is determined by the value of n in hydrogen atom and by n + l in multielectron atom. So for a given principal quantum number electron of s, p, d and f orbitals have different energy.

### *Long Answer Questions*

**1.** **Hint:** $hv = hv_0 + \dfrac{1}{2} mv^2$

**2.** $\Delta E = -3.052 \times 10^{-19}$ J, $v = 4.606 \times 10^{16}$ Hz.

# 3. Periodic Classification of Properties



**3.1** **What is the basic theme of organisation in the periodic table?**

**Ans.** The basic theme of organisation of elements in the periodic table is to simplify and systematize the study of the properties of all the elements and millions of their compounds. On the basis of similarities in chemical properties, the various elements have now been divided into different groups. This has made the study simple because the properties of elements are now studied in form of groups rather than individually.

**3.2** **Which important property did Mendeleev use to classify the elements in his periodic table and did he stick to that?**

**Ans.** Mendeleev used atomic weight as the basis of classification of elements in the periodic table. He arranged known elements in order of increasing atomic weights grouping together elements with similar properties.

**3.3** **What is the basic difference in approach between the Mendeleev's Periodic Law and the Modern Periodic Law?**

**Ans.** Mendeleev Periodic Law states that the physical and chemical properties of the elements are periodic function of their atomic weights while Modern Periodic Law states that physical and chemical properties of the elements are a periodic function of their atomic numbers. Thus, the basic difference in approach between Mendeleev's Periodic Law and Modern Periodic Law is the change in the basis of classification of elements from atomic weight to atomic number.

**3.4** **On the basis of quantum numbers, justify that the sixth period of the periodic table should have 32 elements.**

**Ans.** In the modern periodic table, each period starts with the filling of a new principal energy level. Thus, the sixth period begins with the filling of principal quantum number, $n = 6$. When $n = 6$, $l = 0, 1, 2, 3$. But according to Aufbau's principle, the energy of $6d$ subshell is higher than that of $7s$–subshell but energies of $5d$– and $4f$ sub shells are lower than that of $6p$–subshell. Therefore, in 6th period, electrons can be filled in only $6s$, $4f$, $5d$ and $6p$–subshells whose energies increase in the order :

$6s < 4f < 5d < 6p$. Now $s$-subshell has one, $p$-subshell has three, $d$-subshell has five and $f$-subshell has seven orbitals. Hence, in all, there are $16 (1 + 3 + 5 + 7)$ orbitals that can be filled in this period. Since according to Pauli's exclusion principle each orbital, at the maximum, can accommodate two electrons, therefore, 16 orbitals, at the maximum, can have 32 electrons and hence sixth period has 32 elements.

**3.5** **In terms of period and group, where would you locate the element with Z = 114 ?**

**Ans.** The filling of the 6th period ends at $_{86}$Rn. Thereafter, the filling of 7th period starts. Like in 6th period, in 7th period also, the filling of four sub–shells, *i.e.,* $7s$, $7p$, $6d$ and $5f$ occurs. But according to Aufbau's principle, their energies increase in the order: $7s < 5f < 6d < 7p$. Therefore, after $_{86}$Rn, the next two elements with $Z = 87$ and $Z = 88$ are $s$-block elements, the next fourteen, i.e. $Z = 90$–103 are $f$-block elements, the next ten, *i.e.* $Z = 104$ –112 are $d$-block elements and the last six, i.e., $Z = 113$ –118 are $p$-block elements. Therefore, the element $Z = 114$ is the second $p$-block element (*i.e.* group 14) of the 7th period. Thus, the location of the element with $Z = 114$ in the periodic table is

Period = 7th   Block : $p$   Group : 14

**3.6** **Write the atomic number of the element present in the third period and seventeenth group of the periodic table.**

**Ans.** In the third period the filling up of only $3s$– and $3p$-orbitals occurs. Therefore, in this period there are only two $s$ -and six $p$-block elements. Since third period starts with $Z = 11$ and ends at $Z = 18$, therefore, elements with $Z = 11$ and $Z = 12$ are $s$-block elements. The next six elements with $Z = 13$ to 18 are $p$-block elements and belong to groups 13,14,15,16,17 and 18. Therefore, the element which will lie in seventeenth group will have $Z = 12 + 5 = 17$

**3.7** **Which element do you think would have been named by**
**(i)**    **Lawrence Berkeley Laboratory**
**(ii)**   **Seaborg's group ?**

**Ans.** (i)    Lawrencium ($Z = 103$) and Berkeliuin ($Z = 97$)
      (ii)   Seaborgium ($Z = 106$)

**3.8 Why do elements in the same group have similar physical and chemical properties ?**

**Ans.** Elements in the same group have similar electronic configuration and hence have similar physical and chemical properties.

**3.9 What does atomic radius and ionic radius really mean to you ?**

**Ans.** Atomic radius literally means size of the atom. It can be measured either by X–ray or by spectroscopic methods. In case of non–metals, atomic radius is called covalent radius. It is defined as one–half the distance between the nuclei of two covalently bonded atoms of the same element in a molecule. For example, the internuclear distance between two chlorine atoms in chlorine molecule is 198 pm. Therefore, the covalent radius of chlorine atom is 198/2 =99 pm (0.99 Å). In case of metals, atomic radius is called metallic radius. It is defined as one– half the distance between the two adjacent atoms in the crystal lattice. For example, the distance between two adjacent copper atoms in solid copper is 256 pm, therefore, the metallic radius of copper is 256/2 = 128 pm (1.28 Å). Ionic radius means size of the ion. An ion can be a cation or an anion. The size of a cation is always smaller than that of the parent atom because loss of one or more electrons increases the effective nuclear charge. As a result, force of attraction increases and hence the ionic size decreases. On the other hand, the size of the anion is larger than the parent atom because the addition of one or more electrons decreases the effective nuclear charge. As a result, the force of attraction decreases and hence the ionic size increases. For example, the ionic radius of $Na^+$ is 95 pm while the atomic radius of sodium is 186 pm. On the other hand, ionic radius of fluoride ion is 136 pm whereas the atomic radius of fluorine atom is only 72 pm.

**3.10 How do atomic radius vary in a period and in a group ? How do you explain the variation?**

**Ans.** The atomic radius increases down the group. This is because a new energy shell (i.e. principal quantum number increases by unity) is added at each succeeding element while the number of electrons in the valence shell remains to be the same. In other words, the electrons in the valence shell of each succeeding element lie farther and farther away from the nucleus. As a result, the force of attraction of the nucleus for the valence electrons decreases and hence the atomic size increases.In contrast, the atomic size decreases as we move from left to right in a period. This is because that within a period the outer electrons remain in the same shell but the nuclear charge increases by one unit at each succeeding element. Due to this increased nuclear charge, the attraction of the nucleus for the outer electrons increases and hence the atomic size decreases.

**3.11 What do you understand by isoelectronic species? Name the species that will be iso-electronic with each of the following atoms or ions.**

**(i) $F^-$** **(ii) Ar**
**(iii) $Mg^{2+}$** **(iv) $Rb^+$**

**Ans.** Ions of different elements which have the same number of electrons but different magnitude of the nuclear charge are called isoelectronic species.

(i) $F^-$ has 10 (9 + 1) electrons. Therefore, the species nitride ion, $N^{3-}$ (7 + 3); oxide ion; $O^{2-}$ (8 + 2), neon, Ne (10 + 0); sodium ion, $Na^+$ (11 – 1); magnesium ion, $Mg^{2+}$ (12 –2); aluminium ion, $Al^{3+}$ (13 – 3) etc. each one of which contains 10 electrons, are isoelectronic with it.

(ii) Ar has 18 electrons. Therefore, the species phosphide ion, $P^{3-}$ (15 + 3), sulphide ion; $S^{2-}$ (16 + 2); chloride ion, $Cl^-$ (17 + 1), potassium ion, $K^+$ (19 – 1), calcium ion, $Ca^{2+}$ (20 – 2), etc., each one of which contains 18 electrons, are isoelectronic with it.

(iii) $Mg^{2+}$ has 10 (12 – 2) electrons, therefore, the species $N^{3-}$, $O^{2-}$, $F^-$, Ne, $Na^+$, $Al^{3+}$, etc. each one of which contains 10 electrons, are isoelectronic with it.

(iv) $Rb^+$ has 36 (37 – 1) electrons. Therefore, the species bromide ion, $Br^-$ (35 + 1), krypton, Kr (36 + 0) and strontium $Sr^{2+}$ (38 – 2) each one of which has 36 electrons, are isoelectronic with it.

**3.12 Consider the following species:**
**$N^{3-}$, $O^{2-}$, $F^-$, $Na^+$, $Mg^{2+}$ and $Al^{3+}$.**
**(i) What is common in them ?**
**(ii) Arrange them in the order of increasing ionic radii?**

**Ans.** (i) Each one of these ions contains 10 electrons and hence all are isoelectronic ions.

(ii) The ionic radii of isoelectronic ions decrease with the increase in the magnitude of the nuclear charge. For example, consider the isoelectronic ions: $N^{3-}$, $O^{2-}$, $F^-$, $Na^+$, $Mg^{2+}$ and $Al^{3+}$. All these ions have 10 electrons but their nuclear charges increase in the order: $N^{3-}$ (+ 7), $O^{2-}$ (+ 8), $F^-$ (+ 9), $Na^+$ (+ 11), $Mg^{2+}$ (+ 12) and $Al^{3+}$ (+ 13). Therefore, their ionic radii decrease in the order: $N^{3-} > O^{2-} > F^- > Na^+ > Mg^{2+} > Al^{3+}$.

**3.13 Explain why cations are smaller and anions are larger in radii than their parent atoms.**

**Ans.** The ionic radius of a cation is always smaller than the parent atom because the loss of one or more electrons increases the effective nuclear charge. As a result, the force of attraction of nucleus for the electrons increases and hence the ionic radii decrease. In contrast, the ionic radius of an anion is always larger than its parent atom because the addition of one or more electrons decreases the effective nuclear charge. As a result, the force of attraction of the nucleus for the electrons decreases and hence the ionic radius increases.

**3.14 What is the significance of the terms –'isolated gaseous atom' and 'ground state' while defining the ionization enthalpy and electron gain enthalpy ?**

**Ans.** (i) Ionization enthalpy is the minimum amount of energy required to remove the most loosely bound electron from an isolated gaseous atom so as to convert it into a gaseous cation is called ionization enthalpy. The force with which an electron is attracted by the nucleus of an atom is appreciably affected by presence of other atoms within its molecule or in the neighborhood. Therefore, for the purpose of determination of ionization enthalpy, it is essential that these inter–atomic forces of attraction should be minimum. Since in the gaseous state, the atoms are widely separated, therefore, these inter–atomic forces are minimum. Further since it is not possible to isolate a single atom for the purpose of determination of its ionization enthalpy, therefore, the inter–atomic distances are further reduced by carrying out the measurement at a low pressure of the gaseous atom. It is because of these reasons, that the term isolated gaseous atom has been included in the definition of ionization enthalpy.

(ii) Electron gain enthalpy is the energy released when an isolated gaseous atom in the ground state accepts an extra electron to form the gaseous negative ion. The term isolated gaseous atom has already been explained above. The term ground state here means that the atom must be present in the most stable state, i.e., the ground state. The reason being that when the isolated gaseous atom is in the excited state, lesser amount of energy will be released when it gets converted into gaseous anion after accepting an electron. Therefore, for comparison purposes, the electron gain enthalpies of gaseous atoms must be determined in their respective most stable state, i.e., ground state.

**3.15 Energy of an electron in the ground state of the hydrogen atom is $-\,2.18 \times 10^{-18}$ J. Calculate the ionization enthalpy of atomic hydrogen in terms of J mol$^{-1}$.**

**Hint :** Apply the idea of mole concept to derive the answer.

**Ans.** The energy required to remove an electron in the ground state of hydrogen atom

$$= -\,(\text{its energy in the ground state})$$
$$= -\,(-\,2.18 \times 10^{-18}\ \text{J}) = 2.18 \times 10^{-18}\ \text{J}$$

Ionization energy per mole of hydrogen atoms

$$= \frac{2.8 \times 10^{-18} \times 6.02 \times 10^{23}}{1000} = 1312.36\ \text{kJ mol}^{-1}$$
$$= 1312.36 \times 10^{3}\ \text{J mol}^{-1}$$

**3.16 Among the second period elements the actual ionization enthalpies are in the order Li < B < Be < C < O < N < F < Ne.**

**Explain why**

**(i) Be has higher $\Delta_i$ H than B**

**(ii) O has lower $\Delta_i$ H than N and F ?**

**Ans.** (i) The ionization enthalpy, among other things, depends upon the type of electron to be removed from the same principal shell. In case of Be ($1s^2 2s^2$) the outermost electron is present in $2s$-orbital while in B ($1s^2 2s^2 2p^1$) it is present in $2p$-orbital. Since $2s$-electrons are more strongly attracted by the nucleus than $2p$-electrons, therefore, lesser amount of energy is required to knock out a $2p$-electron than a $2s$-electron. Consequently, $\Delta_i$H of Be is higher than that $\Delta_i$H of B.

(ii) The electronic configuration of N ($1s^2 2s^2 2p_x{}^1 2p_y{}^1 2p_z{}^1$) in which $2p$-orbitals are exactly half-filled is more stable than the electronic configuration of O ($1s^2 2s^2 2p_x{}^2, 2p_y{}^1, 2p_z{}^1$) in which the $2p$-orbitals are neither half-filled nor completely filled. Therefore, it is difficult to remove an electron from N than from O. As a result, $\Delta_i$H of N is higher than that of O. Further, the electronic configuration of F is $1s^2 2s^2 2p_x^2 2p_y^2 2p_z^1$. Because of higher nuclear charge (+9), the first ionization enthalpy of F is higher than that of O.

**3.17 How would you explain the fact that the first ionization enthalpy of sodium is lower than that of magnesium but its second ionization enthalpy is higher than that of magnesium?**

**Ans.** The electronic configurations of Na and Mg are:

Na : $1s^2 2s^2 2p^6 3s^1$    Mg: $1s^2 2s^2 2p^6 3s^2$

Thus, the first electron in both the cases has to be removed from the 3s–orbital but the nuclear charge of Na (+ 11) is lower than that of Mg (+ 12), therefore, the first ionization energy of sodium is lower than that of magnesium. After the loss of first electron, the electronic configuration of Na$^+$ is $1s^2 2s^2 2p^6$. Here, the electron is to be removed from inert (neon) gas configuration which is very stable and hence removal of second electron from sodium is very difficult. However, in case of magnesium, after the loss of first electron, the electronic configuration of Mg$^+$ is $1s^2 2s^2 2p^6 3s^1$. Here, the electron is to be removed from a $3s$ orbital which is much easier than to remove an electron from inert gas configuration. Therefore, the second ionization enthalpy of sodium is higher than that of magnesium.

**3.18 What are the various factors due to which the ionization enthalpy of the main group elements tends to decrease down the group ?**

**Ans.** Within the main group elements, the ionization enthalpy decreases regularly as we move down the group due to the following two factors.

(i) **Atomic size.** On moving down the group, the atomic size increases gradually due to the addition of one new principal energy shell at each succeeding element. As a result, the distance of the valence electrons from the nucleus increases. Consequently, the force of attraction of the nucleus for the valence electrons decreases and hence the ionization enthalpy decreases.

(ii) **Screening effect.** With the addition of new shells, the number of inner electron shells which shield the valence electrons increase. In other words, the shielding effect or the screening effect increases. As a result, the force of attraction of the nucleus for the valence electrons further decreases and hence the ionization enthalpy decreases.

**3.19** **The first ionization enthalpy values (in kJ mol$^{-1}$) of group 13 elements are :**

| B | Al | Ga | In | Tl |
|---|---|---|---|---|
| 801 | 577 | 579 | 558 | 589 |

**How would you explain this deviation from the general trend ?**

**Ans.** On moving down the group 13 from B to Al, the ionization enthalpy decreases as expected due to an increase in atomic size and screening effect which outweigh the effect of increased nuclear charge.

However $\Delta_i H$ of Ga is only slightly higher (2 kJ mol$^{-1}$) than that of Al while that of Tl is much higher than those of Al, Ga and In. These deviations can be explained as follows:

Al follows immediately after $s$–block elements while Ga and In follow after $d$–block elements and Tl after $d$– and $f$–block elements. These extra $d$–and $f$–electrons do not shield(or screen) the outer shell–electrons from the nucleus very effectively. As a result, the valence electrons remain more tightly held by the nucleus and hence larger amount of energy is needed for their removal. This explains why Ga has higher ionization enthalpy than Al. Further on moving down the group from Ga to In, the increased shielding effect (due to the presence of additional $4d$–electrons) outweighs the effect of increased nuclear charge ($49 - 31 = 18$ units) and hence the $\Delta_i H_1$ of In is lower than that of Ga. Thereafter, the effect of increased nuclear charge ($81 - 49 = 32$ units) outweighs the shielding effect due to the presence of additional $4f$ and $5d$ electrons and hence the $\Delta_i H_1$ of Tl is much higher than that of Al, Ga and In.

**3.20** **Which of the following pairs of elements would have a more negative electron gain enthalpy?**

**(i) O or F (ii) F or Cl**

**Ans.** (i) Both O and F lie in 2nd period. As we move from O to F, the atomic size decreases and the nuclear charge increases. Both these factors tend to increase the attraction of the nucleus for the incoming electron and hence electron gain enthalpy becomes more negative. Further, gain of one electron by F gives F$^-$ ion ($1s^2\ 2s^2\ 2p^6$) which has stable inert gas configuration while the gain of one electron by O gives O$^-$ ion ($1s^2\ 2s^2\ 2p^5$) which does not have stable inert gas configuration. Consequently, the energy released is much higher in going from F $\rightarrow$ F$^-$ than in going from O $\rightarrow$ O$^-$. In other words, electron gain enthalpy of F is much more negative ($-328$ kJ mol$^{-1}$) than that of oxygen ($-141$ kJ mol$^{-1}$).

(ii) In general, the electron gain enthalpy becomes less negative on moving down the group. But the electron gain enthalpy of chlorine ($-349$ kJ mol$^{-1}$) is more negative than that of fluorine ($-328$ kJ mol$^{-1}$). The reason for this deviation is the small size of F atom. Due to its small size, the electron–electron repulsions in the relatively compact $2p$–subshell are comparatively large and hence the incoming electron is not accepted with the same ease as is the case

with larger Cl atom. Consequently, electron gain enthalpy of Cl is more negative than that of F.

**3.21** **Would you expect the second electron gain enthalpy of O as positive, more negative or less negative than the first? Justify your answer.**

**Ans.** The second electron gain enthalpy of O is positive as explained below:

When an electron is added to O atom to form O$^-$ ion, energy is released. Thus, first electron gain enthalpy of O is negative.

$$O\,(g) + e^-(g) \rightarrow\ O^-\,(g);\ \Delta_{eg} H = -141\ \text{kJ mol}^{-1}$$

But when another electron is added to O$^-$ to form O$^{2-}$ ion, energy is absorbed to overcome the strong electrostatic repulsion between the negatively charged O$^-$ ion and the second electron being added. Thus, the second electron gain enthalpy of oxygen is positive.

$$O^-\,(g) + e^-\,(g) \longrightarrow\ O^{2-}\,(g);$$
$$\Delta_{eg} H = + 78\text{kJ mol}^{-1}$$

**3.22** **What is the basic difference between the terms electron gain enthalpy and electron-egativity ?**

**Ans.** Both electron gain enthalpy and electro-negativity refer to the tendency of the atom of an element to attract electrons. Whereas electron gain enthalpy refers to the tendency of an isolated gaseous atom to accept an additional electron to form a negative ion, electronegativity refers to the tendency of the atom of an element to attract the shared pair of electrons towards it in a covalent bond.

**3.23** **How would you react to the statement that the electronegativity of N on Pauling scale is 3.0 in all the nitrogen compounds?**

**Ans.** The electronegativity of any given atom is not constant. Therefore, the statement that the electro negativity of N on Pauling scale is 3.0 in all nitrogen compounds is wrong. Actually electronegativity varies with the state of hybridization and the oxidation state of the element. The electronegativity increases as the percentage of s–character of a hybrid orbital increases or the oxidation state of the element increases. For example, the electronegativity of N increases as we move from, sp$^3$ to sp$^2$ to sp hybrid orbital. Similarly, the electronegativity of N in NO$_2$ where oxidation state of N is +4 is higher than in NO where the oxidation state of N is +2.

**3.24** **Describe the theory associated with the radius of an atom as it (a) gains an electron (b) loses an electron.**

**Ans.** (a) When a neutral atom gains one electron to form an anion, its radius increases. The reason being that the number of electrons in the anion increases while its nuclear charge remains the same as the parent atom. Since the same nuclear charge now attracts greater number of electrons, therefore, force of attraction of the nucleus on the electrons of all the shells decreases (i.e., effective nuclear charge decreases) and hence the electron cloud expands. In other words, the distance between the centre of the nucleus and the last shell that contains electrons increases thereby increasing the ionic radius. Thus,

| Atom | Anion |
|---|---|
| 17 Electrons | 18 Electrons |
| + 17 Nuclear charge | + 17 |
| 99pm Ionic size | 181 pm |

(b) When a neutral atom loses one electron to form a cation, its atomic radius decreases. The reason being that the number of electrons in the cation decreases while its nuclear charge remains the same as the parent atom. Since the same nuclear charge now attracts lesser number of electrons, therefore, the force of attraction of the nucleus on the electrons of all the shells increases (i.e., effectivenuclear charges increases) and hence the size of cation decreases. Thus



| Atom | Cation |
|---|---|
| 11 Electrons | 10 |
| + 11 Nuclear charge | + 11 |
| 156 pm   Ionic size | 95 pm. |

**3.25 Would you expect the first ionization enthalpies for two isotopes of the same element to be the same or different ? Justify your answer.**

**Ans.** Two isotopes of the same element have same no. of electrons, same nuclear charge, same size and hence they are expected to have same ionization enthalpy.

**3.26 What are the major differences between metals and non-metals ?**

**Ans.** Elements which have a strong tendency to lose electrons to form cations are called metals while those which have a strong tendency to accept electrons to form anions are called non–metals. Thus, metals are strong reducing agents, they have low ionization enthalpies, have less negative electron gain enthalpies, low electronegativity, form basic oxides and ionic compounds.

Non–metals, on the other hand, are strong oxidizing agents, they have high ionization enthalpies, have high negative electron gain enthalpies, high electronegativity, form acidic oxides and covalent compounds.

**3.27 Use the periodic table to answer the following questions.**

**(a) Identify an element with five electrons in the outer subshell.**

**(b) Identify an element that would tend to lose two electrons.**

**(c) Identify an element that would tend to gain two electrons.**

**(d) Identify the group having metal, non-metal, liquid as well as gas at room temperature.**

**Ans.** (a) The general electronic configuration of the elements having five electrons in the outer subshell is $ns^2 np^5$.

This electronic configuration is characteristic of elements of group 17, i.e., halogens and their examples are F, Cl, Br, I, At, etc.

(b) The elements which have a tendency to lose two electrons must have two electrons in the valence shell. Therefore, their general configuration should be $ns^2$. This electronic configuration is characteristic of group 2 elements, i.e., alkaline earth metals and their examples are Mg, Ca, Sr, Ba, etc.

(c) The elements which have a tendency to accept two electrons must have six electrons in the valence shell. Therefore, their general electronic configuration is $ns^2 np^4$. This electronic configuration is characteristic of group 16 elements and their examples are O and S.

(d) A metal which is liquid at room temperature is mercury. It is a transition metal and belongs to group 12. A non–metal which is a gas at room temperature is nitrogen (group 15), oxygen (group 16), fluorine, chlorine (group 17) and inert gases (group 18).

A non–metal which is a liquid at room temperature is bromine (group 17).

**3.28 The increasing order of reactivity among group 1 elements is Li < Na < K < Rb < Cs whereas that among group 17 elements is F > Cl > Br > I. Explain.**

**Ans.** The elements of group 1 have only one electron in their respective valence shells and thus have a strong tendency to lose this electron. The tendency to lose electrons, in turn, depends upon the ionization enthalpy. Since the ionization enthalpy decreases down the group, therefore, the reactivity of group 1 elements increases in the same order: Li < Na < K < Rb < Cs. In contrast, the elements of group 17, have seven electrons in their respective valence shells and thus have a strong tendency to accept one more electron. The tendency to accept electrons, in turn, depends upon their electrode potentials. Since the electrode potentials of group 17 elements decrease in the order: F (+ 2.87 V) > Cl (1.36 V), Br (1.08 V) and I (+ 0.53V), therefore, their reactivity also decrease in the same order : F > Cl > Br > I.

**3.29 Write the general outer electronic configuration of $s$–, $p$–, $d$– and $f$–block elements :**

**Ans.** (i) $s$–Block elements: $ns^{1-2}$ where n = 2 – 7
(ii) $p$–Block elements: $ns^2 np^{1-6}$ where n = 2 – 6
(iii) $d$–Block elements: $(n-1) d^{1-10} ns^{0-2}$ where n = 4 – 7
(iv) $f$–Block elements :
$(n-2)f^{1-14} (n-1) d^{0-1} ns^2$ where n = 6 – 7

**3.30 Assign the position of the element having outer electronic configuration,**
(i) $ns^2 np^4$ **for n = 3**
(ii) $(n-1) d^2 ns^2$ **for n = 4 and**
(iii) $(n-2)f^7 (n-1) d^1 ns^2$ **for n = 6 in the periodic table.**

**Ans.** (i) When n = 3 , it suggests that the element belongs to third period. Since the last electron enters the p–orbital, therefore, the given element is a p–block element. Further since the valence shell contains

6 (2 + 4) electrons, therefore, group number of the element = 10 + no. of electrons in the valence shell = 10 + 6 = 16. The complete electronic configuration of the element is $1s^2 2s^2 2p^6 3s^2 3p^4$ and the element is S (Sulphur)

(ii) n = 4 suggests that the element lies in the 4th period. Since the d–orbitals are incomplete, therefore, it is a d–block element. The group number of the element = no. of d–electrons + no. of s –electrons = 2 + 2 = 4. Thus, the elements lies in group 4 and 4th period. The complete electronic configuration of the element is $1s^2 2s^2 2p^6 3s^2 3p^6 3d^2 4s^2$ and the element in Ti (Titanium).

(iii) n = 6 means that the element lies in the sixth period. Since the last electron goes to the f–orbital, therefore, the element is a f–block element. All f– block elements lie in group 3. The complete electronic configuration of the element is $[Xe] 4f^7 5d^1 6s^2$. The atomic number of the element 54 + 7 + 1 + 2 = 64 and the element Gd (Gadolinium).

**3.31 The first ( $\Delta_i H_1$ ) and the second ( $\Delta_i. H_2$ ) ionization enthalpies (in kJ mol $^{-1}$) and the( $\Delta_{eg}H$) electron gain enthalpy (in kJ mol$^{-1}$) of a few elements are given below:**

| Elements | $\Delta_i H_1$ | $\Delta_i H_2$ | $\Delta_{eg} H$ |
|---|---|---|---|
| I | 520 | 7300 | – 60 |
| II | 419 | 3051 | – 48 |
| III | 1681 | 3374 | – 328 |
| IV | 1008 | 1846 | – 295 |
| V | 2372 | 5251 | + 48 |
| VI | 738 | 1451 | – 40 |

**Which of the above elements is likely to be:**
**(a) the least reactive element**
**(b) the most reactive metal**
**(c) the most reactive non–metal**
**(d) the least reactive non–metal**
**(e) the metal which can form a stable binary halide of the formula MX$_2$ (X = halogen)**
**(f) the metal which can form a predo-minantly stable covalent halide of the formula MX (X = halogen) ?**

**Ans.** (a) The element V has highest first ionization enthalpy ($\Delta_i H_1$) and positive electron gain enthalpy ($\Delta_g H$) and hence it is the least reactive element. Since inert gases have positive $\Delta_i H_1$, therefore, the element V must be an inert gas. The values of $\Delta_i H_1$, $\Delta_i H_2$ and $\Delta_{eg} H$ match that of He.

(b) The element II which has the least first ionization enthalpy ($\Delta_i H_1$) and a low negative electron gain enthalpy ($\Delta_{eg} H$) is the most reactive metal. The values of $\Delta_i H_1$, $\Delta_i H_2$ and $\Delta_{eg}H$ match that of K (potassium).

(c) The element III which has high first ionization enthalpy ($\Delta_1 H_1$) and a very high negative electron gain enthalpy ($\Delta_{eg} H$) is the most reactive non–metal. The values of $\Delta_i H_1$, $\Delta_i H_2$ and $\Delta_{eg}H$ match that of F (fluorine).

(d) The element IV has a high negative electron gain enthalpy ($\Delta_{eg} H$) but not so high first ionization enthalpy ($\Delta_i H_i$). Therefore, it is the least reactive non–metal. The values of $\Delta_i H_1$, $\Delta_i H_2$ and $\Delta_{eg}H$ match that of I (Iodine).

(e) The element VI has low first ionization enthalpy ($\Delta_i H_1$) but higher than that of alkali metals. Therefore, it appears that the element is an alkaline earth metal and hence will form binary halide of the formula MX$_2$ (where X = halogen). The values of $\Delta_i H_1$, $\Delta_i H_2$ and $\Delta_{eg}H$ match that of Mg (magnesium).

(f) The element I has low first ($\Delta_i H_1$) but a very high second ionization enthalpy ($\Delta_i H_2$), therefore, it must be an alkali metal. Since the metal forms a predominantly stable covalent halide of the formula MX (X = halogen), therefore, the alkali metal must be least reactive. The values of $\Delta_i H_1$ $\Delta_i H_2$ and $\Delta_{eg}H$ match that of Li (lithium).

**3.32 Predict the formulas of the stable binary compounds that would be formed by the combination of the following pairs of elements.**
**(a) Lithium and oxygen**
**(b) Magnesium and nitrogen**
**(c) Aluminium and iodine**
**(d) Silicon and oxygen**
**(e) Phosphorus and fluorine**
**(f) Element 71 and fluorine**

**Ans.** (a) Lithium is an alkali metal (Group 1). It has only one electron in the valence shell, therefore, its valency is 1. Oxygen is a group 16 element with a valence of 2. Therefore, formula of the compound formed would be $Li_2O$ (Lithium oxide).

(b) Magnesium is an alkaline earth metal (Group 2) and hence has a valence of 2. Nitrogen is a group 15 element with a valence of 8 – 5 = 3. Thus, the formula of the compound formed would be $Mg_3N_2$ (Magnesium nitride).

(c) Aluminium is group 13 element with a valence of 3 while iodine is a halogen (group 17) with a valence of 1. Therefore, the formula of the compound formed would be $AlI_3$ (Aluminium iodide).

(d) Silicon is a group 14 element with a valence of 4 while oxygen is a group 16 element with a valence of 2. Hence the formula of the compound formed is $SiO_2$ (Silicon dioxide).

(e) Phosphorus is a group 15 element with a valence of 3 or 5 while fluorine is a group 17 element with a valence of 1. Hence the formula of the compound formed would be $PF_3$ or $PF_5$.

(f) Element with atomic number 71 is a lanthanoid called lutetium (Lu). Its common valence is 3. Fluorine is a group 17 (halogen) element with a valence of 1. Therefore, the formula of the compound formed would be $LuF_3$ (Lutetium fluoride).

**3.33 In the modern periodic table, the period indicates the value of :**

   (a) atomic number

   (b) atomic mass

   (c) principal quantum number

   (d) azimuthal quantum number

**Ans.** In the modern periodic table, each period begins with the filling of a new shell. Therefore, the period indicates the value of principal quantum number. Thus, option (c) is correct.

**3.34 Which of the following statements related to the modern periodic table is incorrect?**

   (a) The *p*–block has 6 columns, because a maximum of 6 electrons can occupy all the orbitals in a *p*–shell.

   (b) The *d*–block has 8 columns, because a maximum of 8 electrons can occupy all the orbitals in a *d*–subshell.

   (c) Each block contains a number of columns equal to the number of electrons that can occupy that subshell.

   (d) The block indicates value of azimuthal quantum number (*l*) for the last subshell that received electrons in building up the electronic configuration.

**Ans.** Statement (b) is incorrect while other statements are correct. The correct statement is: the *d*-block has 10 columns, because a maximum of 10 electrons can occupy all the orbitals in a *d*-subshell.

**3.35 Anything that influences the valence electrons will affect the chemistry of the element. Which one of the following factors does not affect the valence shell**

   (a) Valence principal quantum number (n)

   (b) Nuclear charge (Z)

   (c) Nuclear mass

   (d) Number of core electrons.

**Ans.** Nuclear mass does not affect the valence shell because nucleus consists of protons and neutrons. Where protons i.e. nuclear charge affects the valence shell but neutrons do not. Thus, option (c) is wrong.

**3.36 The size of isoelectronic species – $F^-$, Ne and $Na^+$ is affected by**

   (a) nuclear charge (Z)

   (b) valence principal quantum number (n)

   (c) electron–electron interaction in the outer orbitals

   (d) none of the factors because their size is the same.

**Ans.** The size of the isoelectronic ions depends upon the nuclear charge (Z). As the nuclear charge increases the size decreases. For example, $F^-$ (+ 9) > Ne (+ 10) > $Na^+$ (+ 11). Therefore, statement (a) is correct while all other statements are wrong.

**3.37 Which one of the following statements is incorrect in relation to ionization enthalpy?**

   (a) Ionization enthalpy increases for each successive electron.

   (b) The greatest increase in ionization enthalpy is experienced on removal of electron from core noble gas configuration.

   (c) End of valence electrons is marked by a big jump in ionization enthalpy.

   (d) Removal of electron from orbitals bearing lower *n* value is easier than from orbital having higher *n* value.

**Ans.** Statement (d) is incorrect. The correct statement is: Removal of electron from orbitals bearing lower n value is difficult than from orbital having higher n value. All other statements are correct.

**3.38 Considering the elements B, Al, Mg and K, the correct order of their metallic character is :**

   (a) B > Al > Mg > K

   (b) Al > Mg > B > K

   (c) Mg > Al > K > B

   (d) K > Mg > Al > B

**Ans.** In a period, metallic character increases as we move from right to left. Therefore, metallic character of K, Mg and Al decreases in the order: K > Mg > Al. However, within a group, the metallic character, increases from top to bottom. Thus, Al is more metallic than B. Therefore, the correct sequence of decreasing metallic character is: K > Mg > Al > B, i.e., option (d) is correct.

**3.39 Considering the elements B, C, N, F and Si, the correct order of their non–metallic character is**

   (a) B > C > Si > N > F

   (b) Si > C > B > N > F

   (c) F > N > C > B > Si

   (d) F > N > C > Si > B

**Ans.** In a period, the non–metallic character decreases from right to left . Thus, among B, C, N and F, non–metallic character decreases in the order: F > N > C > B. However, within a group, non–metallic character decreases from top to bottom. Thus, C is more non–metallic than Si. Therefore, the correct sequence of decreasing non–metallic character is : F > N > C > B > Si, i.e., option (c) is correct.

**3.40 Considering the elements F, Cl, O and N the correct order of their chemical reactivity in terms of oxidizing property is:**

   (a) F > Cl > O > N    (b) F > O > Cl > N

   (c) Cl > F > O > N    (d) O > F > N > Cl

**Ans.** Within a period, the oxidizing character increases from left to right. Therefore, among F, O and N, oxidizing power decreases in the order: F > O > N. However, within a group, oxidizing power decreases from top to bottom. Thus, F is a stronger oxidizing agent than Cl. Further because O is more electronegative than Cl, therefore, O is a stronger oxidizing agent than Cl. Thus, over all decreasing order of oxidizing power is : F > O > Cl > N i.e., option (b) is correct.

| SECTION B | PRACTICE QUESTIONS |

## MULTIPLE CHOICE QUESTIONS

1. Lothar Meyer plotted the physical properties such as atomic volume, melting point and ...X... against atomic weight. Here, X refers to
   (a) mass  (b) boiling point
   (c) surface tension  (d) None of these

2. If atomic number of X is 42, then atomic number of $e$ is

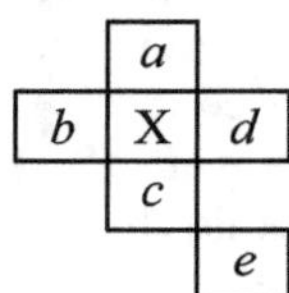

   (a) 106  (b) 74
   (c) 75  (d) 107

3. Select the correct chronological order for the discoveries of the following scientists.
   Dobereiner, Newlands, Chancourtois, Mendeleev
   (a) Chancourtois, Dobereiner, Newlands, Mendeleev
   (b) Dobereiner, Chancourtois, Newlands, Mendeleev
   (c) Dobereiner, Newlands, Chancourtois, Mendeleev
   (d) Chancourtois, Newlands, Dobereiner, Mendeleev

4. Which of the following is correct about Eka-Aluminium and Eka-Silicon ?
   (a) Oxides of Eka-Aluminium is $Ga_2O_3$ and Eka-Silicon is $GeO_2$
   (b) Oxides of Eka-Aluminium is $Al_2O_3$ and Eka-Silicon is $Si_2O_3$
   (c) Melting point of Eka-Aluminium is lower than the melting point of Eka-Silicon
   (d) Both (a) and (c)

5. Which of the following statement(s) about the modern periodic table is/are incorrect ?
   (i) The elements in the modern periodic table are arranged on the basis of their decreasing atomic number
   (ii) The elements in the modern periodic table are arranged on the basis of their increasing atomic masses
   (iii) Isotopes are placed in adjoining group(s) in the periodic table
   (iv) The elements in the modern periodic table are arranged on the basis of their increasing atomic number
   (a) (i) only  (b) (i), (ii) and (iii)
   (c) (i), (ii) and (iv)  (d) (iv) only

6. The symbol and IUPAC name for the element with atomic number 120, respectively are
   (a) Ubn and unbinilium  (b) Ubn and unbiunium
   (c) Ubn and unnibium  (d) Ubn and unnilium

7. The elements with atomic numbers 9, 17, 35, 53 and 85 belong to
   (a) alkali metals  (b) alkaline earth metals
   (c) halogens  (d) noble gases

8. The element with positive electron gain enthalpy is
   (a) hydrogen  (b) sodium
   (c) oxygen  (d) neon

9. Which of the following property of element is directly related to electronegativity?
   (a) Atomic radius
   (b) Ionization enthalpy
   (c) Non-metallic character
   (d) None of these

10. Which ionisation potential (IP) in the following equations involves the greatest amount of energy ?
    (a) $Na \rightarrow Na^+ + e^-$  (b) $K^+ \rightarrow K^{2+} + e^-$
    (c) $C^{2-} \rightarrow C^{3+} + e^-$  (d) $Ca^+ \rightarrow Ca^{2+} + e^-$

11. The correct order of decreasing electronegativity values among the elements I-beryllium, II-oxygen, III-nitrogen and IV-magnesium is
    (a) II > III > I > IV  (b) III > IV > II > I
    (c) I > II > III > IV  (d) I > II > IV > III

12. Which is the correct order of electronegativity ?
    (a) F > N < O > C  (b) F > N > O > C
    (c) F > N > O < C  (d) F < N < O = C

## ASSERTION & REASON QUESTIONS

**DIRECTIONS (Qs. 1-6) :** *Each of these questions contains an assertion followed by reason. Read them carefully and answer the question on the basis of following options. You have to select the one that best describes the two statements.*
(a) If both Assertion and Reason are correct and the Reason is a correct explanation of the Assertion.
(b) If both Assertion and Reason are correct but Reason is not a correct explanation of the Assertion.
(c) If the Assertion is correct but Reason is incorrect.
(d) If the Assertion is incorrect but the Reason is correct.

1. **Assertion :** Second period consists of 8 elements.
   **Reason :** Number of elements in each period is four times the number of atomic orbitals available in the energy level that is being filled.

2. **Assertion :** Helium is placed in group 18 along with *p*-block elements.
   **Reason :** It shows properties similar to *p*-block elements.

3. **Assertion :** In Mendeleev's periodic table, elements are classified according to their atomic masses.
   **Reason :** Atomic number is equal to the number of protons.

**4.** **Assertion :** Atomic size increases along a period.

**Reason :** Effective nuclear charge increases as the atomic number increases resulting in the increased attraction of electrons to the nucleus.

**5.** **Assertion :** First ionisation enthalpy is higher the second ionisation enthalpy.

**Reason :** Ionisation enthalpy is the tendency of an element to gain electrons.

**6.** **Assertion :** KCl is an ionic compound.

**Reason :** Electronegativity difference between K and Cl is greater than 1.7.

## CASE/PASSAGE BASED QUESTIONS

**DIRECTIONS (Qs. 1-5) :** *Read the following case/passage and answer the questions.*

Periodic trends are observed in atomic sizes, ionization enthalpies, electron gain enthalpies electronagativity and valence. The atomic radii decrease, while going from left to right in a period and increase with atomic number in a group. Ionization enthalpies generally increase across a period and decrease down a group. Electronegativity also show similar trend. Electron gain enthalpies in general become more negative across a period and less negative down a group.

**1.** Which of the following represents the correct order of increasing electron gain enthalpy with negative sign for the elements O, S, F and Cl ?

(a) $Cl < F < O < S$     (b) $O < S < F < Cl$

(c) $F < S < O < Cl$     (d) $S < O < Cl < F$

**2.** Which of the following statement(s) is/are incorrect?

(i) Ionization enthalpy is expressed in units of $kJmol^{-1}$.

(ii) Ionization enthalpy is always positive.

(iii) Second ionization enthalpy will be higher than the third ionization enthalpy.

(a) Only (ii)     (b) Only (iii)

(c) (ii) and (iii)     (d) None of these

**3.** As we move across the second period from C to F ionisation enthalpy increases but the trend from C to F for ionisation enthalpy is $C < O < N < F$. This is because

(a) atomic radii of O > atomic radii of N

(b) electronic configuration of N is more stable than electronic configuration of O

(c) atomic radii of N > atomic radii of O

(d) None of these

**4.** Arrange S, P, As in order of increasing ionisation energy

(a) $S < P < As$     (b) $P < S < As$

(c) $As < S < P$     (d) $As < P < S$

**5.** Which of the following will have the least negative electron gain enthalpy?

(a) P     (b) S

(c) Cl     (d) F

## VERY SHORT ANSWER QUESTIONS

**1.** Which *p*- block elements exist as liquid at room temperature?

**2.** Arrange the anions in order of increasing radius; $Cl^-$, $Br^-$, $N^{3-}$, $O^{2-}$. Give reason for your answer.

**3.** Arrange the oxides in order of increasing basic character; BeO, MgO, CaO, BaO. Give reason for your answer.

**4.** Arrange the oxides in order of increasing acidic character; $Li_2O$, BeO, $B_2O_3$, $CO_2$. Give reason for your answer.

**5.** Why were the names eka-aluminium and eka-silicon given to gallium and germanium by Mendeleev?

**6.** What are representative element ?

**7.** What are inner transition metals ?

**8.** Why *d*-block elements are called transition elements ?

**9.** What is the difference between Mendeleev's and the modern periodic law ?

**10.** State Dobereiner's law of triads, giving examples.

**11.** What is meant by Newland's law of octaves ?

**12.** What is meant by periodicity of properties ?

**13.** With which quantum number does every period in periodic table begin ?

**14** To which series do man-made elements belong?

**15.** Name a lanthanoid which is man-made?

**16.** Why Group –2 elements have positive electron gain enthalpy?

**17.** Ga atom loose electron(s) to form $Ga^+$ , $Ga^{2+}$, $Ga^{3+}$ ions. Which step will have highest ionization energy?

**18.** Compare the size of $Al^{3+}$ , $Mg^{2+}$ and $Ca^{2+}$.

**19.** Arrange the following elements in the increasing order of metallic character. B, Al, Mg, K

**20.** Arrange the following elements in the increasing order of non-metallic character. C, Si, N, F

**21.** Which of the following ion has the smallest radius ? $Li^+$, $Na^+$, $K^+$, $Be^{2+}$, $Mg^{2+}$

**22.** Name the elements with the lowest and the highest ionisation energy.

**23.** Define van der Waal's radius of an atom.

**24.** Predict the position of the element in the Periodic Table satisfying the electronic configuration $(n-1)\,d^1\,ns^2$ for $n = 4$.

**25.** Why do noble gases have bigger atomic size than halogens ?

**26.** Among (the non-radioactive) halogens the element that has the lowest electron affinity is ..................

## SHORT ANSWER QUESTIONS

**1.** Give four defects of Mendeleev's periodic table.

**2.** Why are group 1 elements called alkali metals and group 17 are called halogens?

**3.** Use the Periodic Table to determine the number of electrons in each of the *s, p* and *d* orbitals outside the precious noble gas core of the following elements.

(i) Silicon     (ii) Chlorine

(iii) Manganese     (iv) Cobalt

**4.** The elements $Z = 117$ and $Z = 120$ have not yet been discovered. In which family/group would you place these elements and also give the electronic configuration in each case.

**5.** What are the defects in Modern Periodic Table?

**6.** Explain why the first ionization potential for copper is higher than that of potassium, whereas the second ionization potentials for both metals are in the reverse order.

**7.** Arrange the following set of atoms in order of increasing ionization energy: Zn, Ga, K. Also discuss the reason.

**8.** The first ($IE_1$) and second ($IE_2$) ionisation energies (kJ/mol) of a new element designated by Roman numerals are shown below :

|         | I    | II   | III  | IV   |
|---------|------|------|------|------|
| $IE_1$  | 2372 | 520  | 900  | 1680 |
| $IE_2$  | 5251 | 7300 | 1760 | 3380 |

Which of these elements is likely to be (a) a reactive metal, (b) a reactive non-metal, (c) a noble gas, (d) a metal that forms a binary halide of the formula, $AX_2$?

**9.** Give the order in which the melting points of halides of sodium decrease and why ?

**10.** Arrange the following in increasing order :
(i) $BeCO_3, BaCO_3, CaCO_3, MgCO_3$ (Thermal stability)
(ii) $BeCl_2, BaCl_2, SrCl_2, CaCl_2$ (Ionic character).

**11.** (i) Name the most metallic element in second period and most non-metallic element.
(ii) The element with (a) largest atomic radius, (b) smallest atomic radius in third period.
(iii) The element having general electronic configuration $ns^2np^4$ in fourth period.

**12.** Show by a chemical reaction with water that $Na_2O$ is a basic oxide and $Cl_2O_7$ is an acidic oxide.

**13.** What is screening or shielding effect ? How does it influence the ionization enthalpy ?

**14.** The ions $Na^+$ and $Mg^{2+}$ occur in chemical compounds, but the ions $Na^{2+}$ and $Mg^{3+}$ do not. Explain.

**15.** Give reason : ionic compounds of the halogen contain singly charged $X^-$ ion and not doubly charged $X^{2-}$ ion.

**16.** How much energy in kJ will be required to convert all the magnesium atoms into magnesium ions present in 12 mg of the metal vapours ? $IE_1$, $IE_2$ for Mg being 7.646 and 15.035 eV respectively.

**17.** Calculate the electron affinity of iodine in electron volts if $4.9 \times 10^{-3}$ J of energy is released when one million atoms of iodine are converted into iodide ions according to the equation :

$$I\,(g) + e^- \rightarrow I^-\,(g)$$

**18.** Arrange the given compounds in order of increasing acidic strength; $CH_4$, $NH_3$, $H_2O$, HF. Give reason for your answer.

**19.** Define (i) metallic radius (ii) covalent radius.

**20.** Why are electron gain enthalpies of Be and Mg positive ?

## LONG ANSWER QUESTIONS

**1.** Name the four blocks of elements in the periodic table and list the difference in their electronic configurations. Give examples of each type of elements. Write at least four characteristics of each block.

**2.** Discuss the trends in atomic sizes of elements in periodic table.

**3.** (i) Explain the terms (a) screening effect, (b) penetration effect, (c) metallic character.
(ii) Why are electron affinities of noble gases zero ? Arrange halogens in increasing order of electron affinity.

**4.** The second ionization enthalpy ($IE_2$) of the elements of the second period are given below :

| Element : | $IE_2$ (kJ/mol) : |
|-----------|-------------------|
| Li        | 7294              |
| Be        | 1756              |
| B         | 2430              |
| C         | 2354              |
| N         | 2856              |
| O         | 3396              |
| F         | 3377              |
| Ne        | 3966              |

(i) Explain
(a) Why is $IE_2$ of Li so much higher than for all other elements of this period ?
(b) What is the general trend from Be to Ne of increasing $IE_2$?
(c) Why $IE_2$ of F is just about the same or very slightly less than that of oxygen ?
(ii) Would you predict the $IE_2$ of Na in kJ/mol is
(a) greater than 7294
(b) between 3966 and 7294 or
(c) less than 3966 ? Explain.

**5.** What are the IUPAC rules for writing the names and symbols of the elements having atomic numbers more than 100 ?

## SOLUTIONS

### Multiple Choice Questions

1. **(b)** Lothar Meyer plotted the physical properties such as atomic volume, melting point and boiling point against atomic weight and obtained a periodically repeated pattern.
2. **(d)**
3. **(b)** Correct order is Dobereiner, Chan-courtois, Newlands, Mendeleev.
4. **(d)** Oxides of Eka-Aluminium = $Ga_2O_3$
   Oxides of Eka-Silicon = $SiO_2$
   Melting point of Eka-Aluminium = Low (302 K)
   Melting point of Eka-Silicon = High (1231 K)
5. **(b)**
6. **(a)** Atomic number (Z) = 120
   IUPAC name = Unbinilium
   Symbol = Ubn
7. **(c)** The elements have 7 electrons in the valence shell.
8. **(d)** Noble gases have positive values of electron gain enthalpy because the anion is higher in energy than the isolated atom and electron.
9. **(c)** The increase in the electronegativities across a period is accompanied by an increase in non-metallic properties (or decrease in metallic properties) of elements.
10. **(c)** highest positive charge on $C^{2+}$.
11. **(a)** Electronegativity values of given elements are as follows:
    Be – 1.5 (I)      Mg – 1.2 (IV)
    O – 3.5 (II)      N – 3.0 (III)
    *i.e.* II > III > I > IV
12. **(a)** Electronegativity increases along a period.

### Assertion & Reason Questions

1. **(c)** Number of elements in each period is twice the number of atomic orbitals available in the energy level that is being filled.
2. **(c)** He $(1s^2)$ should be placed along with *s*-block elements because of its electronic configuration but it has a completely filled valence shell and as a result it exhibits properties of noble gases, thus it is placed along with noble gases $(ns^2, np^6)$.
3. **(b)** Mendeleev arranged the elements in the increasing order of their atomic mass in the form of a table. Properties of the elements are periodic functions of their atomic masses.
4. **(d)** Atomic size generally decreases along a period.
5. **(d)** First ionisation enthalpy is lower than the second ionisation enthalpy, because on removal of one electron, atom changes into cation. Cation has higher effective nuclear charge than parent atom; therefore, second ionisation is higher than the first. Ionisation enthalpy is the energy required when an electron is removed form an isolated and gaseous atom.
6. **(a)** K is highly electropositive atom and Cl is highly electro negative atom, therefore, electronegativity difference is greater than 1.7, hence, KCl is an ionic compound.

### Case/Passage Based Questions

1. **(b)** O < S < F < Cl
   Electron gain enthalpy –141, –200, – 333, – 349 kJ $mol^{-1}$
2. **(b)** Second ionization enthalpy will be higher than the first ionization enthalpy but lower than the third ionization enthalpy.
3. **(b)**
4. **(c)** I.E. decreases down the group.
5. **(a)** Adding an electron to the $3p^3$ stable orbital leads to greater repulsion than adding an electron to the $3p^4$ orbital. Hence, phosphorus has the least negative electron gain enthalpy.

### Very Short Answer Questions

1. Gallium and Bromine.
2. $O^{2-} < N^{3-} < Cl^- < Br^-$. Ionic radius increases down a group and decreases across a period
3. BeO < MgO < CaO < BaO. On moving down a group metallic character increases. Metallic oxides are basic in nature. Ba is most metallic.
4. $Li_2O < BeO < B_2O_3 < CO_2$ on moving across a period non-metallic character increases. Non-metallic oxides are acidic in nature. C is most non-metallic.
5. Mendeleev named these elements as eka-aluminium and eka-silicon because he believed that they would be similar to aluminium and silicon respectively in their properties.
6. The elements of group 1 (alkali metals) group 2 (alkaline earth metals) and group 13 to 17 constitute the representative elements. They are elements of *s*-block and *p*-block.
7. Lanthanoids (the fourteen elements after Lanthanum) and actinides (the fourteen elements after actinium) are called inner transition elements.
8. They represent change or transition from strongly metallic *s*-block to largely covalent *p*-block elements.
9. Mendeleev's Periodic Law was based on atomic masses while the modern periodic law was based on the atomic number.
10. It states that those triads in which the atomic weight of middle element was average of the atomic weight of first and third, such elements resemble in the physical and chemical properties, e.g.

    Li      Na      K
    7      $\dfrac{7+39}{2} = 23$      39
11. It states if elements are arranged in increasing order of their atomic weights, properties of every 8th element resemble with the first element.
12. The reccurrence of similar properties after a definite interval is called periodicity of properties.
13. Principal quantum number.
14. Actinoid series (*f*-block elements).
15. Promethium (Pm), atomic number 61 is man-made element.

16. Since they have fully filled $s$–subshell thus they have no tendency to accept electron.

17. $Ga^{2+} \longrightarrow Ga^{3+} + e^-$

18. $Al^{3+} < Mg^{2+} < Ca^{2+}$. All are isoelectronic.

19. Metallic character increases down the group and decreases along the period. The correct order is
$$B < Al < Mg < K$$

20. The correct order is
$$Si < C < N < F$$

21. $Be^{2+}$. Be is a second period element, thus smaller than higher period elements ($Na^+$, $K^+$, $Mg^{2+}$). The $Be^{2+}$ is isoelectronic with $Li^+$ but has a greater nuclear charge. Therefore, $Be^{2+}$ is smaller in size than $Li^+$.

22. Cs, He.

23. It is one half of the distance between the centres of nuclei of two nearest non-bonded atoms of the adjacent molecules of the element in the solid state.

24. $(n-1)\,d^1\,ns^2 = 3d^1\,4s^2$
$\therefore$ It lies in the 4th period and III B (or 3rd) group.

25. Noble gases have bigger atomic size than halogens because van der Waal's radii are bigger than covalent radii.

26. Iodine.

### *Short Answer Questions*

1. (a) Isotopes should be given separate place because they have different atomic mass.
   (b) The increasing order of atomic weight is not maintained.
   (c) Some elements in the same group differ in their properties.
   (d) The position of hydrogen is not justified.

2. Group 1 elements are called alkali metals because their hydroxides form soluble bases called alkalies and their ashes are alkaline in nature.
   Group 17 are called halogens because they are salt-producer.

3. (i) $Si(Z = 14)$ : $[Ne]\ 3s^2\ 3p^2$
   Number of electrons in $s$-orbital = 2
   Number of electrons in $p$-orbital = 2
   (ii) $Cl(Z = 17)$ : $[Ne]\ 3s^2\ 3p^5$
   Number of electrons in $s$-orbital = 2
   Number of electrons in $p$-orbital = 5
   (iii) Mn $(Z = 25)$ : $[As]\ 3d^5\ 4s^2$
   Number of electrons in $d$-orbital = 5
   Number of electrons in $s$-orbital = 2
   (iv) Co $(Z = 27)$ : $[Ar]\ 3d^7\ 4s^2$
   Number of electrons in $d$-orbital = 5
   Number of electrons in $s$-orbital = 2

4. The element with $Z = 117$ would belong to group 17 and halogen family. The electronic configuration would be $[Rn]\ 5f^{14}\ 6d^{10}\ 7s^2\ 7p^5$
   The element with $Z = 120$ belong to group 2 (alkaline earth metal) family with a electronic configuration would be $[Uuo]\ 8s^2$

5. The defects are:
   (i) Position of hydrogen is uncertain, since although it has been placed in Group–1 with alkali metals but it also shows properties similar to elements of Group–17.

(ii) Lanthanides and actinides have not been accommodated in main body of the periodic table.

6. Copper and potassium both belongs to 4th period. Copper is present in group II whereas potassium is present in group I. Thus first ionisation energy of copper will be higher as ionisation energy increases on moving left to right in a period. In case of second ionisation energy potassium acquire inert gas ($ns^2\,np^6$) configuration. Thus removal of second electron will be difficult from $3s^2\ 3p^6$ configuration of potassium in comparison to $3d^{10}$ configuration of copper.

7. K < Ga < Zn. K having the largest atomic radii out of given elements. Thus has least ionization energy. The electron removed from Zn is from a completely filled 4s orbital while in case of Ga it is from partially filled 4p orbital. The 4p electrons is at higher energy and is less tightly held by nucleus than 4s electron. Thus, it is more easily removed.

8. (a) II    (b) IV    (c) I    (d) III.

9. NaF > NaCl > NaBr > NaI. Greater the difference in electronegativity, more will be ionic character, higher will be melting point due to high lattice energy.

10. (i) $BeCO_3 < MgCO_3 < CaCO_3 < BaCO_3$
    (ii) $BeCl_2 < CaCl_2 < SrCl_2 < BaCl_2$.

11. (i) Most metallic element is Li and most non-metallic element is F.
    (ii) Na has largest atomic radius, Cl has smallest atomic radius.
    (iii) Se(34) : $1s^2\ 2s^2\ 2p^6\ 3s^2\ 3p^6 4s^2 3d^{10} 4p^4$ is element in fourth period with general electronic configuration $ns^2\,np^4$.

12. $Na_2O$ reacts with water to form sodium hydroxide which turns red litmus blue.

$$\underset{\text{Sod. oxide}}{Na_2O} + H_2O \longrightarrow \underset{\text{Sod. hydroxide}}{2NaOH}$$

Therefore, $Na_2O$ is a basic oxides.
In contrast, $Cl_2O_7$ reacts with water to form perchloric acid which turns blue litmus red.

$$Cl_2O_7 + H_2O \longrightarrow \underset{\text{perchloric acid}}{2HClO_4}$$

Therefore, $Cl_2O_7$ is an acidic oxide.

13. In a multielectron atom, the electrons present in the inner shells shield the electrons in the valence shell from the attraction of the nucleus or they act as a screen between the nucleus and these electrons. This is known as shielding effect or screening effect.
    As the screening effect increases, the effective nuclear charge decreases. Consequently, the force of attraction by the nucleus for the valence shell electrons decreases and hence the ionization enthalpy decreases.

14. $Na^{2+}$ and $Mg^{3+}$ do not occur in chemical compounds because $Na^+$ and $Mg^{2+}$, both have a stable noble gas configuration of neon. The removal of electron either from $Na^+$ (to form $Na^{2+}$) or $Mg^{2+}$ (to form $Mg^{3+}$) requires a very large amount of energy.

15. Halogens are short of one electron to complete nearest noble gas electronic configuration. And they can attain the noble gas configuration by picking up an electron and

from $X^-$. Once the shell is complete, then additional electron would have to begin a new shell which leads to unstable electronic configuration. That's why $X^{2-}$ does not exist.

**16.** $IE_1 + IE_2$ for $Mg = 7.646 + 15.035$  or $22.681$ eV

or   $22.681 \times 96.49 = 2188.489$ kJ mol$^{-1}$

1 mole of Mg (24g) = 2188.5 kJ

$$1.2 \times 10^{-3}\text{g of Mg} = \frac{2188.5}{24} \times 12 \times 10^{-3} \text{ kJ}$$

$= 1094.25$ J

**17.** $10^6$ atoms of I when change to I$^-$, energy released is $4.9 \times 10^{-13}$ J.

$$1 \text{mole of atoms} = \frac{4.9 \times 10^{-13}}{10^6} \times 6.023 \times 10^{23} \text{ J}$$

$= 29.5 \times 10^4 \times 10^{-3} = 295$ kJ mol$^{-1}$

$$= \frac{295}{96.49} = 3.057 \text{ eV}.$$

**18.** $CH_4 < NH_3 < H_2O < HF$. Electronegativity increases across a period. Thus electronegativity difference between hydrogen and other element increases. More will be the electronegativity difference more will be acidic character.

**19.** (i) *Metallic radius* is defined as the half the internuclear distance separating the metal ions in the metallic crystal.

(ii) *Covalent radius* is defined as the half the distance between the centre of the nuclei of the two bonded atoms in a covalent bond. the covalent radius $= \dfrac{a}{2}$.

**20.** They have fully filled *s*-orbitals and hence have no tendency to accept an additional electron. That's why energy is needed if an extra electron has to added. Therefore electron gain enthalpies of Be and Mg are positive.

### *Long Answer Questions*

**1.** Four blocks of periodic table are known as *s*-, *p*- *d*- and and *f*-block elements.

**General characteristics of *s*-Block elements :**

General electronic configuration ns$^{1-2}$.

(i) They are soft metals with low melting and boiling points.

(ii) They are highly reactive metals and forms univalent and bivalent ions by losing one or two valence electrons respectively.

(iii) They have low ionisation energies and thus are highly electropositive.

(iv) They act as strong reducing agents. Examples are : Na, Mg, etc.

**General characteristics of *p*-Block elements :**

General electronic configuration ns$^2$np$^{1-6}$

(i) p-Block elements include both metals and non-metals. The metallic character decreases and non-

metallic nature of elements increases as we move along a period from left to right.

(ii) Their ionisation energies are relatively higher as compared to s-block elements.

(iii) They form covalent compounds.

(iv) Majority of them show more than one oxidation state in their compounds. Examples are : O, F, etc.

**General characteristics of d-Block elements :**

General electronic configuration ns$^2$(n–1)d$^{1-10}$

(i) They are hard metals having high melting and boiling points.

(ii) They exhibit several oxidation states.

(iii) Their ionisation energies lie between s- and p-block elements.

(iv) They form both the ionic and covalent compounds. Examples are : Cr, Fe, etc.

**General characteristics of *f*-Block elements :**

General electronic configuration $(n-2)f^{1-14}$ $(n-1)d^{0-1} ns^2$

(i) They are heavy metals.

(ii) They show high melting and boiling points.

(iii) They show variable oxidation states.

(iv) They have the tendency to form complexes.

**2.** **Variation of atomic radii in a period : Atomic radii (covalent or vander Waal's) decreases with increase in the atomic number in a given period.** The decrease of atomic radii along a period is due to increase in magnitude of nuclear charge while the number of shells remain the same. Due to increased nuclear charge on moving left to right along a period the electrons of all the shells are pulled closer to the nucleus resulting into decrease in size of atomic radii.

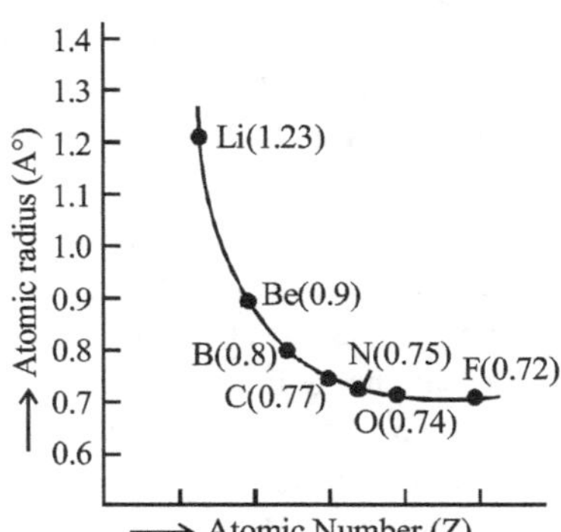


Variation of atomic radii in a period

**Variation of atomic radii in a group : The atomic radii of elements increases from top to bottom in a given group.** The increase in size on descending a group is due to addition of extra shell (i.e. the number of principal quantum number increases) which outweights the effect of increased nuclear charge. Consequently, the distance of the outermost electron from the nucleus gradually increases down a group i.e. size of atom increases on going down a group.

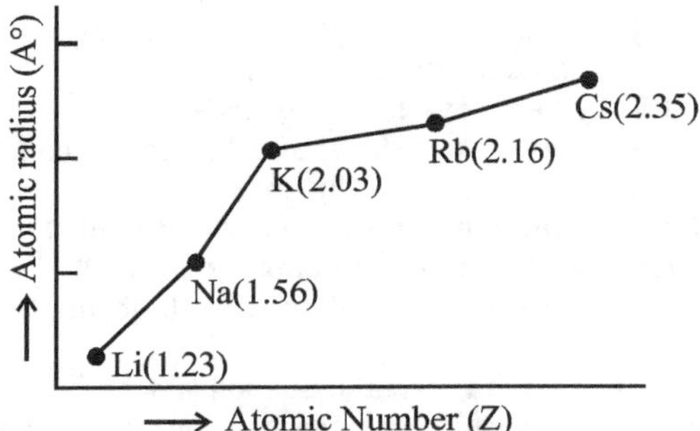



(Variation of atomic radius down a group)

3. (i) (a) **Screening effect.** The inner electrons between valence electron and nucleus shield the valence electron from nucleus; it is called shielding effect.

(b) **Penetration effect.** Due to shape of the orbital, $s$ electron penetrates nearer to the nucleus than $p$, $d$ or $f$-electrons and are more tightly held.

(c) **Metallic character.** Lower the ionisation energy, more will be tendency to lose electron, higher will be metallic character.

(ii) The electron affinity of noble gases is zero because they have stable electronic configurations. $Cl > F > Br > I$ is increasing order of electron affinity.

4. (i) (a) For lithium, the outer electron is $2s$ electron, but for $Li^+$ the outer electron is a $1s$ electron, closer to the nucleus and lower in energy than the $2s$ electron. Moreover, it is difficult to break the noble gas configuration in $Li^+$. Hence, $IE_2$, for Li is so much higher than for all other elements of their period.

(b) Once the first electron is removed, the effective nuclear charge increases, and the size of $M^+$ is less than a M-atom. So, the electrons in $M^+$ are more strongly held by the nucleus. Hence $IE_2$ increases from Be to Ne.

(c) After the removal of one electron, the $O^+$ has an electronic configuration of $1s^2\ 2s^2\ 2p^3$ whereas $F^+$ has an electronic configuration of $1s^2\ 2s^2\ 2p^3$. As $2p$ subshell is half-filled in $O^+$, so, $O^+$ is more stable than $F^+$. Hence, more energy is required to remove an electron from $O^+$ than from $F^+$.

(ii) The $IE_2$ of Na is between 3960 and 7294 kJ/mol (it is 4560 kJ/mol). The $Na^+$ has a noble gas core than Na which has one loosely held electron in $3s$-subshell. The energy needed to remove an electron from the noble-gas core of an atom is always much larger than that needed to remove a valence electron. The core electrons having lower principal quantum numbers are so close to the nucleus that they are strongly attracted to it.

5. These are :

(i) The names are derived from the atomic numbers using the roots for 0 and the numbers from 1 to 9. The suffix ium is added to the name.

(ii) In some cases, the names are shortened. For example, biium is shortened to bium.

(iii) The symbol of element is then obtained from the first letters of the roots of numbers which make up the atomic number of the given element. The symbol of the element consists of three letters.

Roots for the IUPAC names of the elements are :

| Digit | Root | Abbreviations |
|---|---|---|
| 0 | nil | $n$ |
| 1 | un | $u$ |
| 2 | bi | $b$ |
| 3 | tri | $t$ |
| 4 | quad | $q$ |
| 5 | pent | $p$ |
| 6 | hex | $h$ |
| 7 | sept | $s$ |
| 8 | oct | $o$ |
| 9 | enn | $e$ |

The IUPAC names of the elements having atomic numbers 101 to 120 are :

| Atomic No. (Z) | IUPAC Name | Symbols |
|---|---|---|
| 101 | Unnilunium | Unu |
| 102 | Unnilbium | Unb |
| 103 | Unniltrium | Unt |
| 104 | Unnilquadium | Unq |
| 105 | Unnilpentium | Unp |
| 106 | Unnilhexium | Unh |
| 107 | Unnilseptium | Uns |
| 108 | Unniloctium | Uno |
| 109 | Unnilennium | Une |
| 110 | Ununnilium | Uun |
| 111 | Unununium | Uun |
| 112 | Ununbium | Uuu |
| 113 | Ununtrium | Uub |
| 114 | Ununquadium | Uuq |
| 115 | Ununpentium | Uup |
| 116 | Ununhexium | Uuh |
| 117 | Ununseptium | Uus |
| 118 | Ununoctium | Uuo |
| 119 | Ununennium | Uue |
| 120 | Unbinilum | Ubn |

## SECTION C | NCERT EXEMPLAR QUESTIONS 

### MULTIPLE CHOICE QUESTIONS

1. The order of screening effect of electrons of $s$, $p$, $d$ and $f$ orbitals of a given shell of an atom on its outer shell electrons is
   (a) $s > p > d > f$    (b) $f > d > p > s$
   (c) $p < d < s > f$    (d) $f > p > s > d$

2. Among halogens, the correct order of amount of energy released in electron gain (electron gain enthalpy) is
   (a) $F > Cl > Br > I$    (b) $F < Cl < Br < I$
   (c) $F < Cl > Br > I$    (d) $F < Cl < Br < I$

3. The elements in which electrons are progressively filled in $4f$-orbital are called
   (a) actinoids
   (b) transition elements
   (c) lanthanoids
   (d) halogens

4. Which of the following is the correct order of size of the given species
   (a) $I > I^- > I^+$    (b) $I^+ > I^- > I$
   (c) $I > I^+ > I^-$    (d) $I^- > I > I^+$

5. The first ionisation enthalpies of Na, Mg, Al and Si are in the order
   (a) $Na < Mg > Al < Si$
   (b) $Na > Mg > Al > Si$
   (c) $Na < Mg < Al < Si$
   (d) $Na > Mg > Al < Si$

6. The formation of oxide ion $O^{2-}(g)$, from oxygen atom requires first an exothermic and then an endothermic step as shown below
   $O(g) + e^- \rightarrow O^-(g); \Delta H^\circ = -141 \text{ kJ mol}^{-1}$
   $O^-(g) + e^- \rightarrow O^{2-}(g); \Delta H^\circ = +780 \text{ kJ mol}^{-1}$
   Thus, process of formation of $O^{2-}$ in gas phase is unfavourable even though $O^{2-}$ is isoelectronic with neon. It is due to the fact that
   (a) oxygen is more electronegative
   (b) addition of electron in oxygen results in larger size of the ion
   (c) electron repulsion outweighs the stability gained by achieving noble gas configuration
   (d) $O^-$ ion has comparatively smaller size than oxygen atom

### ASSERTION & REASON QUESTIONS

**DIRECTIONS (Qs. 1-2) :** *Each of these questions contains an assertion followed by reason. Read them carefully and answer the question on the basis of following options. You have to select the one that best describes the two statements.*
(a) If both Assertion and Reason are correct and the Reason is a correct explanation of the Assertion.
(b) If both Assertion and Reason are correct but Reason is not a correct explanation of the Assertion.
(c) If the Assertion is correct but Reason is incorrect.
(d) If the Assertion is incorrect but the Reason is correct.

1. **Assertion :** Generally, ionisation enthalpy increases from left to right in a period.
   **Reason :** When successive electrons are added to the orbitals in the same principal quantum level, the shielding effect of inner core of electrons does not increase very much to compensate for the increased attraction of the electron to the nucleus.

2. **Assertion :** Electron gain enthalpy becomes less negative as we go down a group.
   **Reason :** Size of the atom increases on going down the group and the added electron would be farther from the nucleus.

### SHORT ANSWER QUESTIONS

1. Identify the group and valency of the element having atomic number 119. Also predict the outermost electronic configuration and write the general formula of its oxide.

2. Nitrogen has positive electron gain enthalpy whereas oxygen has negative. However, oxygen has lower ionisation enthalpy than nitrogen. Explain.

3. Explain the following :
   (a) Electronegativity of elements increase on moving from left to right in the periodic table.
   (b) Ionisation enthalpy decrease in a group from top to bottom.

4. Among the elements B, Al, C and Si :
   (a) Which has the highest first ionisation enthalpy ?
   (b) Which has most negative electron gain enthalpy ?
   (c) Which has the largest atomic radius ?
   (d) Which has the most metallic character ?

### LONG ANSWER QUESTIONS

1. Discuss the factors affecting electron gain enthalpy and the trend in its variaiton in the periodic table.

2. Define ionisation enthalpy. Discuss the factors affecting ionisation enthalpy of the elements and its trends in the periodic table.

## SOLUTIONS

### *Multiple Choice Questions*

1. **(a)** For a given shell, screening effect decreases in the order : $s > p > d > f$.

2. **(c)** As we move in a group from Cl to I, the electron gain enthalpy (*i.e.*, energy released in electron gain) become less and less negative due to corresponding increase in the atomic size.

   However, the electron gain enthalpy of F is less negative than that of Cl due to its small size. Thus, the negative electron gain enthalpy among halogens follows the order:

   $$F < Cl > Br > I$$

3. **(c)** The elements in which electrons are filled in 4*f*-orbital are called lanthanoids. Lanthanoids consist of elements from Z = 58 (cerium) to 71 (lutetium).

4. **(d)** Generally, cations are smaller in size while anions are bigger in size than the neutral atom.

5. **(a)** Electronic configuration for the given elements will be :

   $Na = [Ne]3s^1$, $Mg = [Ne]3s^2$, $Al = [Ne]3s^23p^1$,
   $Si = [Ne] 3s^23p^2$

   Ionisation enthalpy increases along a period but I.E of Mg is higher than Al because of completely filled $3s$ orbital in Mg.

6. **(c)** $O^{2-}$ has noble gas configuration and isoelectronic with neon but its formation is unfavourable due to strong electronic repulsion between the negatively charged $O^-$ ion and the electron being added.

   Thus, the electron repulsion will be more than the stability gained by achieving noble gas configuration.

### *Assertion & Reason Questions*

1. **(a)** Ionization enthalpy depends upon two factors:
   (a) the attraction of electrons towards the nucleus, and
   (b) the repulsion of electrons from each other.

2. **(b)** The electron gain enthalpy decreases from top to bottom in a group.

### *Short Answer Questions*

1. Group : 1, Valency : 1
   Outermost electronic configuration = $8s^1$
   Formula of Oxide = $M_2O$

2. The outermost electronic configuration of nitrogen $\left(2s^2\ 2p_x^1\ 2p_y^1\ 2p_z^1\right)$ is very stable because *p*-orbital is half filled. Addition of extra electron to any of the $2p$ orbital requires energy.

   Oxygen has 4 electrons in $2p$ orbitals and acquires stable configuration i.e., $2p^3$ configuration after removing one electron.

3. (a) Decrease in size of atom and increase in nuclear charge.
   (b) Increase in atomic size.

4. (a) Carbon has highest first ionisation enthalpy.
   (b) Carbon has most negative electron gain enthalpy.
   (c) Al has largest atomic radius.
   (d) Al has most metallic character.

### *Long Answer Questions*

1. The factors affecting electron gain enthalpy and the trend in its variation in the periodic table are:

   (1) **Atomic Size:** As we go down the group electron gain enthalpy decreases as the distance of the nucleus from the outermost shell increases which decreases its tendency to gan electron and electron gain enthalpy becomes less negative.

   (2) **Effective Nuclear Charge:** As we go from left to right in a period the effective nuclear charge increases and when we move down the group it decreases which results in the attraction of electrons from the outermost shell.

   (3) **Electronic Configuration:** The tenency to gain electrons depends upon the stability of an element. Elemens having completely or half-filled stable orbitals have a very low lendency to gain electron thus they have very low electron gan enthalpy.

   (4) **Trends:** Across a period the electron gain enthalpy becomes more negative. Down the group, the electron gain enthalpy becomes less negative.

2. Ionisation enthalpy is the energy required by an isolated and gaseous atom in its ground state to remove an electron.
   **Effective nuclear charge:** Due to the screening effect, the valence electrons are shielded by the inner core electrons. This effective nuclear charge is less than the actual charge present on the atom.
   **Penetrated orbitals:** It is difficult to remove an electron from the orbitals that are closer to the nucleus and are penetrated towards the nucleus. The order of penetration is given by: $s > p > d > f$.
   **Stability of orbitals:** Half-filled and filled orbitals have a high ionisation enthalpy as they don't want to lose their stability. Across a period the ionisation enthalpy increases along the period. Down the group, the ionisation enthalpy decreases.

# 4   Chemical Bonding

**4.1**   **Explain the formation of a chemical bond.**

**Ans.** The atoms of different elements combine with each other in order to complete their respective octets or duplet to attain nearest noble gas configuration.

**4.2**   **Write Lewis dot symbols for atoms of the following elements : Mg, Na, B, O, N, Br.**

**Ans.** $_{12}$Mg = 2, 8 2 $\therefore$ Lewis symbol = Mg :

$_{11}$Na = 2, 8, 1 $\therefore$ Lewis symbol = $\overset{\bullet}{N}a$

$_{2}$B = 2, 3 $\therefore$ Lewis symbol = $\cdot \overset{\bullet}{B} \cdot$

$_{8}$O = 2, 6 $\therefore$ Lewis symbol = $: \overset{\bullet\bullet}{O} :$

$_{7}$N = 2, 5 $\therefore$ Lewis symbol = $: \overset{\bullet}{\underset{\bullet}{N}} \cdot$

$_{35}$Br = 2,8,18,7 $\therefore$ Lewis symbol = $: \overset{\bullet\bullet}{\underset{\bullet\bullet}{Br}} \cdot$

**4.3**   **Write Lewis symbols for the following atoms and ions : S and $S^{2-}$ : Al and $Al^{3+}$ ; H and $H^-$.**

**Ans.** $_{10}$S = 2, 8, 6 $\therefore$ Lewis symbol = $: \overset{\bullet\bullet}{S} :$ ,

$S^{2-}$ ion $= \left[ : \overset{\bullet\bullet}{\underset{\bullet\bullet}{S}} : \right]^{2-}$

$_{13}$Al = 2,8,3

$\therefore$ Lewis symbol = $\cdot \overset{\bullet}{A}l \cdot$, $Al^{3+}$ ions =[ Al]$^{3+}$

$_{1}$H = 1 $\therefore$ Lewis symbol = H; $H^-$ ions = $\overset{\bullet}{H} \cdot$

**4.4**   **Draw the Lewis structures for the following molecules and ions : $H_2S$, $SiCl_4$, $BeF_2$, $CO_3^{2-}$, HCOOH**

**Ans.** (i)   $H_2S = \overset{\displaystyle :S:}{\underset{H \quad H}{\wedge}}$

(ii)   $SiCl_4 = :\overset{\bullet\bullet}{\underset{\bullet\bullet}{Cl}} \diagdown \overset{\displaystyle :\overset{\bullet\bullet}{Cl}:}{\underset{\displaystyle :\overset{\bullet\bullet}{Cl}:}{Si}} \diagup \overset{\bullet\bullet}{\underset{\bullet\bullet}{Cl}}:$

(iii)   $BeF_2 = :\overset{\bullet\bullet}{\underset{\bullet\bullet}{F}} - \overset{\bullet\bullet}{\underset{\bullet\bullet}{Be}} - \overset{\bullet\bullet}{\underset{\bullet\bullet}{F}}:$

(iv)   $CO_3^{2-} = \left[ \begin{array}{c} :\overset{\bullet\bullet}{O}: \\ \| \\ C \\ \diagup \diagdown \\ :\overset{\bullet\bullet}{\underset{\bullet\bullet}{O}}: \quad :\overset{\bullet\bullet}{\underset{\bullet\bullet}{O}}: \end{array} \right]^{2-}$

(v)   HCOOH = $H - \overset{\displaystyle :\overset{\bullet\bullet}{O}:}{\underset{}{\overset{\|}{C}}} - \overset{\bullet\bullet}{\underset{\bullet\bullet}{O}} - H$

**4.5**   **Define octet rule. Write its significance and limitations.**

**Ans.** **Octet Rule:** Elements combine with each other in order to complete their respective octets i.e. , 8 electrons in their outermost shell.

**Significance of octet rule:** It helps to explain why different atoms combine with each other to form ionic compounds or covalent compounds.

**Limitations of octet rule:** The octet rule fails to explain

(i)   the formation of molecules in which the central atom has less than eight electrons in the valence shell such as $BeCl_2$ , $BF_3$, etc.

(ii)   the formation of molecules in which the central atom has more than eight electrons in the valence shell such as $PF_5$, $SF_6$, etc.

(iii)   the formation of compounds of noble gases especially xenon and krypton such as $XeF_2$, $XeF_6$, etc.

(iv)   odd electron molecules like NO, $NO_2$.

**4.6**   **Write the favourable factors for the formation of ionic bond.**

**Ans.** (i)   Low ionization enthalpy of the metal atom.

(ii)   High electron gain enthalpy of the non–metal atom.

(iii)   High lattice enthalpy of the compound formed.

**4.7**   **Discuss the shape of the following molecules using the VSEPR model: $BeCl_2$, $BCl_3$, $SiCl_4$, $AsF_5$, $H_2S$, $PH_3$**

**Ans.** (i)   $BeCl_2$ = Cl: Be :Cl. The central atom has only two bond pairs and no lone pair. Hence linear.

(ii)   $BCl_3 = $ Cl: $\overset{\displaystyle Cl}{\underset{}{\overset{\bullet\bullet}{B}}}$ :Cl. The central atom has only 3 bond pairs and no lone pair. Hence, it has triangular planar shape.

(iii)   $SiCl_4 = $ Cl: $\overset{\displaystyle \overset{\bullet\bullet}{Cl}}{\underset{\displaystyle \overset{\bullet\bullet}{Cl}}{Si}}$ :Cl. Bond pairs = 4, lone pair = 0. Shape = Tetrahedral

(iv) $AsF_5 = $ F : As : F.  Bond pairs = 5, lone pair = 0.

Shape = Trigonal bipyamidal

(v) $H_2S = $ H : S : H. Bond pairs = 2, lone pairs = 2.

Shape = Bent/V– shaped

(vi) $PH_3 = $ H : P : H.  Bond pairs = 3, lone pair = 1.

Shape = Trigonal pyramidal

**4.8 Although geometries of $NH_3$ and $H_2O$ molecules are distorted tetrahedral, bond angle in water is less than that of ammonia. Discuss.**

**Ans.** In $NH_3$, there is only one lone pair on N–atom to repel the bond pairs whereas in $H_2O$, there are two lone pairs on O–atom to repel the bond pairs. Hence, the repulsions on bond pairs are greater in $H_2O$ than in $NH_3$ and hence the bond angle is less.

**4.9 How do you express the bond strength in terms of bond order?**

**Ans.** Greater the bond order, stronger is the bond.

**4.10 Define the bond length.**

**Ans.** The equilibrium distance between the centers of nuclei of the two bonded atoms is called its bond length.

**4.11 Explain the important aspects of resonance with reference to the $CO_3^{2-}$ ion.**

**Ans.** $CO_3^{-2}$ has resonance in its structure due to which the bond lengths between C–O are equal.

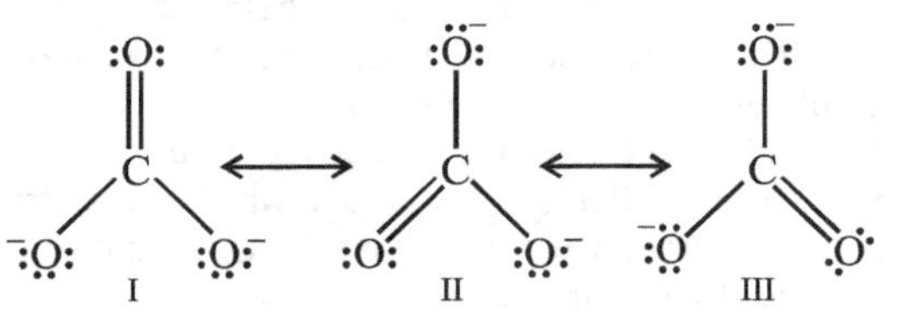

**4.12 $H_3PO_3$ can be represented by structures 1 and 2 shown below. Can these two structures be taken as the canonical forms of the resonance hybrid representing $H_3PO_3$ ? If not, give reasons for the same**

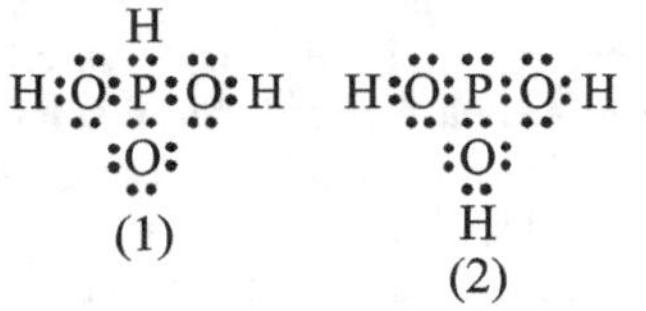

**Ans.** No, these cannot be taken as canonical forms because the positions of atoms have changed.

**4.13 Write the resonance structures for $SO_3$, $NO_2$ and $NO_3^-$.**

**Ans.** (i) $SO_3$:

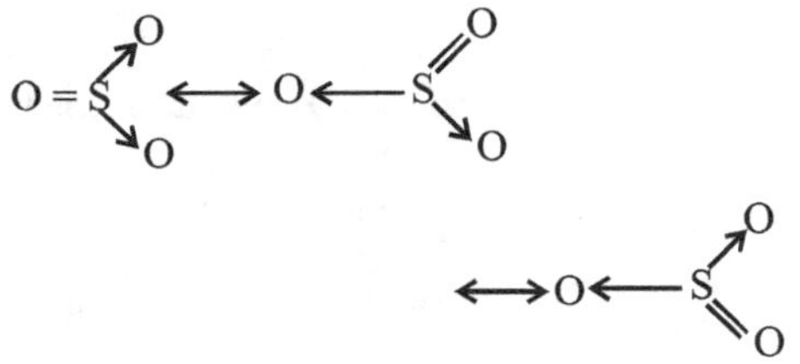

(ii) $NO_2$:

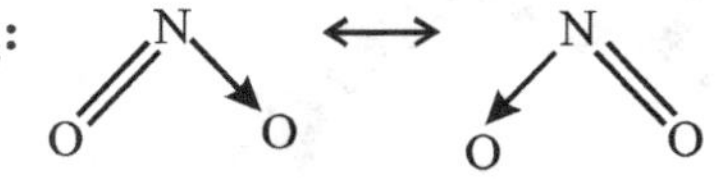

(iii) $NO_3^-$:

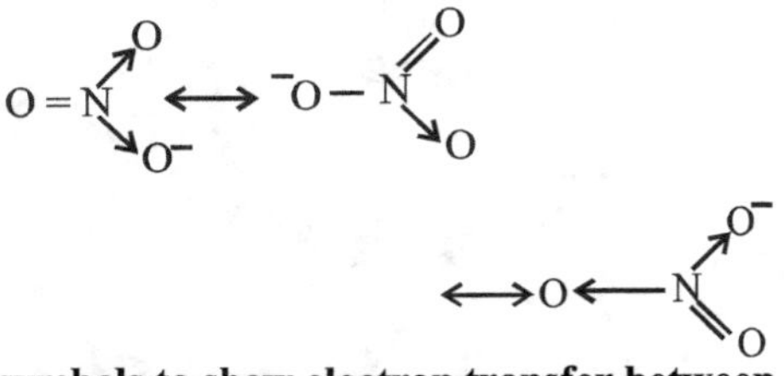

**4.14 Use Lewis symbols to show electron transfer between the following atoms to form cations and anions: (a) K and S (b) Ca and O (c) Al and N.**

**Ans.** (a) $K^+ \left[ :S: \right]^{2-}$ or $K_2S$

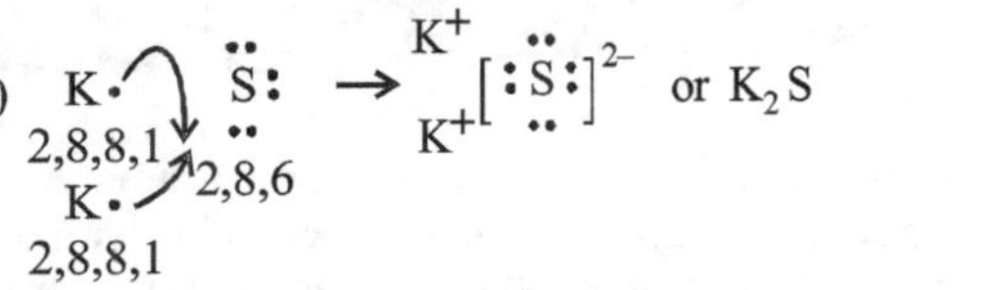

(b) $Ca^{2+} \left[ :O: \right]$ or $Ca^{2+}O^{2-}$ or $CaO$

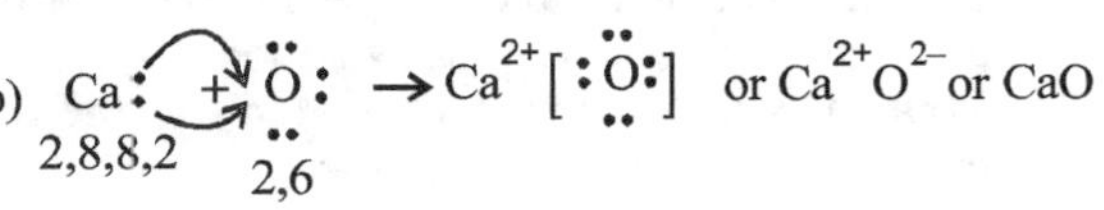

(c) $Al^{3+} \left[ :N: \right]$ or $Al^{3+}N^{3-}$ or $AlN$

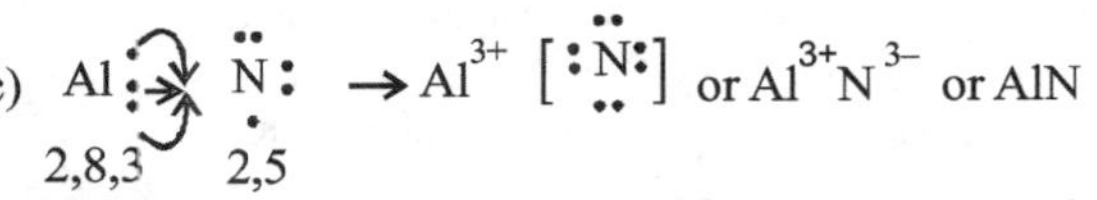

**4.15 Although both $CO_2$ and $H_2O$ are triatomic molecules, the shape of $H_2O$ molecule is bent while that of $CO_2$ is linear. Explain this on the basis of dipole moment.**

**Ans.** The dipole moment studies show that net dipole moment of $CO_2$ molecule is zero. This is possible only if $CO_2$ is a linear molecule (O = C = O) so that dipole moments of C–O are equal and opposite and hence cancel out. On the other hand, $H_2O$ molecule is found to have a net dipole moment (1.84 D) though it contains 2 O–H bonds. This shows that it is a bent molecule.

**4.16 Write the significance/applications of dipole moment.**

**Ans.** Applications of dipole moment are : (a) in determining polarity of bonds (b) in calculation of percentage ionic character (c) to distinguish between *cis* and *trans* isomers (d) to distinguish between *ortho*, *meta* and *para* isomers.

**4.17 Define electronegativity. How does it differ from electron gain enthalpy?**

**Ans.** Electronegativity of an element is the tendency of its atom to attract the shared pair of electrons towards itself in a covalent bond.

Electronegativity denotes the relative attraction of covalently bonded atoms for the bonding electron pairs while electron affinity is the energy released when an electron is added to a gaseous atom or ion to form a gaseous ion. Electronegativity is applicable to a compound whereas electron gain enthalpy is applicable to an isolated gaseous atom.

**4.18 Explain with the help of suitable example polar covalent bond.**

**Ans.** When two dissimilar atoms having different electronegativities combine together to form a covalent bond, the shared pair of electrons does not lie at equal distances from the nuclei of both the bonded atoms but shifts towards the atom having greater electronegativity. Since the more electronegative atom attracts the electrons more strongly, the distribution of electrons gets distorted. As a result, one end of the molecule, having more electronegative atom becomes slightly negatively charged while the other acquires slightly positive charge. Thus, positive and negative poles are developed and this type of bond is called polar covalent bond.

For example in HCl, chlorine being more electronegative than hydrogen will pull bonding electrons towards itself and develop a negative charge while hydrogen will have a partial positive charge.

$$\overset{\delta^+}{H} \rightarrowtail \overset{\delta^-}{Cl} \Rightarrow H-Cl$$

**4.19 Arrange the bonds in order of increasing ionic character in the molecules : LiF, K$_2$O, N$_2$, SO$_2$ and ClF$_3$**

**Ans.** $N_2 < SO_2 < ClF_3 < K_2O < LiF$

**4.20 The skeletal structure of CH$_3$COOH as shown below is correct, but some of the bonds are shown incorrectly. Write the correct Lewis structure for acetic acid.**

$$\begin{array}{c} H \quad\ \ :\!\overset{\displaystyle ..}{O}\!: \\ |\qquad | \\ H\!=\!C\!-\ \!C\!-\!\underset{..}{\overset{..}{O}}\!-\!H \\ | \\ H \end{array}$$

**Ans.**

$$\begin{array}{c} H \quad\ \ :\!\overset{\displaystyle ..}{O}\!: \\ |\qquad \| \\ H\!-\!C\!-\ \!C\!-\!\underset{..}{\overset{..}{O}}\!-\!H \\ | \\ H \end{array}$$

**4.21 Apart from tetrahedral geometry, another possible geometry for CH$_4$ is square planar with the four H atoms at the corners of the square and the C atom at its centre. Explain why CH$_4$ is not square planar?**

**Ans.** Electronic configuration of C–atom is $1s^2\,2s^2 2p_x^{\,1}\,2p_y^{\,1}$ Hence, it undergoes $sp^3$ hybridisation which gives a tetrahedral shape. For square planar, the hybridisation required is $dsp^2$ which is not possible for C–atom in CH$_4$.

**4.22 Explain why BeH$_2$ molecule has a zero dipole moment although the Be–H bonds are polar?**

**Ans.** This is because BeH$_2$ molecule is linear (H–Be–H) so that the two Be–H bond moments are equal and opposite and hence cancel out.

**4.23 Which out of NH$_3$ and NF$_3$ has higher dipole moment and why?**

**Ans.**

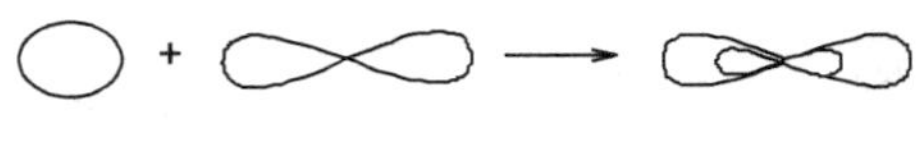


NH$_3$ has higher dipole moment than NF$_3$. This is explained on the basis of the following two reasons.

(1) The dipole formed between the lone pair and N atom has to be taken into consi-deration which is in the direction of the lone pair.

(2) F is more electronegative than N, therefore direction of bond is from N to F whereas N is more electronegative than H, the direction of the bond is from H to N .Thus (see diag.) resultant moment of N –H bonds add up to the bond moment of lone pair, whereas that of 3 N–F bonds partly cancels the resultant moment of lone pair. Hence, the net dipole moment of NF$_3$ is less than that of NH$_3$.

**4.24 What is meant by hybridisation of atomic orbitals? Describe the shapes of $sp$, $sp^2$ and $sp^3$ hybrid orbitals?**

**Ans.** Hybridization is defined as the mixing of the atomic orbitals belonging to the same atom but having slightly different energies so that a redistribution of energy takes place between them resulting in the formation of new orbitals of equal energies and identical shapes. The new orbitals thus formed are known as hybrid orbitals..

*sp*– **hybridization** :– when one s and one p orbital belonging to the same main shell of an atom mix together to form two new equivalent orbitals type of hybridisation is called *sp* hybridisation.

$$\bigcirc + \infty \longrightarrow \infty$$

$$\quad s \qquad\qquad p \qquad\qquad sp$$

*sp$^2$*–**hybridization** :– when one $s$ and two $p$ orbitals of the same shell of an atom mix to form three new equivalent orbitals, the type of hybridization is called $sp^2$ hybrid orbitals.

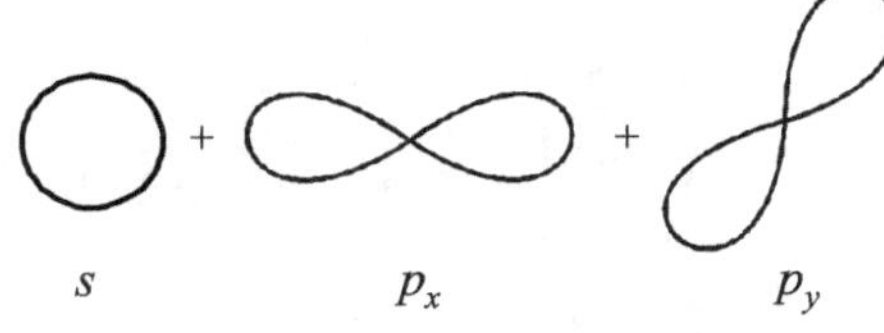

$$sp^2$$

$sp^3$**–hybridization :–** when one $s$ and three $p$ orbitals of the same shell of an atom mix to form four new equivalent orbitals, the type of hybridization is called $sp^3$ hybrid orbitals.

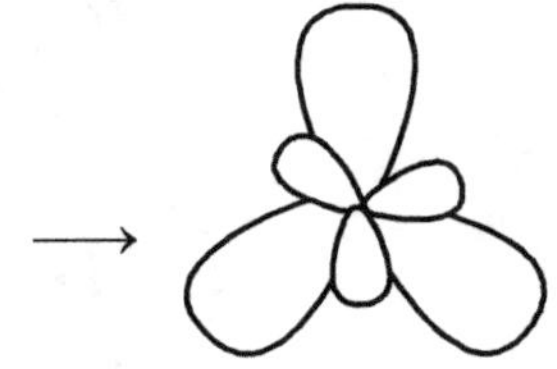

$$s \qquad p_x \qquad p_y \qquad p_z \qquad sp^3$$

**4.25  Describe the change in hybridisation (if any) of the Al atom in the following reaction :**
$$AlCl_3 + Cl^- \longrightarrow AlCl_4^-$$
**Ans.** E.C. of $_{13}Al = 1s^2\,2s^2\,2p^6\,3s^2\,3p^1$ (Ground state) or $1s^2\,2s^2\,2p^6\,3s^1\,3p_x^{\,1}\,3p_y^{\,1}$ (Excited state). Hence, it undergoes, $sp^2$ hybridization to give it planar triangular structure. To form $AlCl_4^{-1}$, the empty $3p_z$ orbital is also involved so that hybridization is $sp^3$ and the shape is tetrahedral.

**4.26  Is there any change in the hybridisation of B and N atoms as a result of the following reaction?**
$$BF_3 + NH_3 \longrightarrow F_3B.NH_3$$
**Ans.** In $BF_3$, B is $sp^2$ hybridized and in $NH_3$, N is $sp^3$ hybridized. After the reaction, hybridization of B changes to $sp^3$ but that of N remains unchanged.

**4.27  Draw diagrams showing the formation of a double bond and a triple bond between carbon atoms in $C_2H_4$ and $C_2H_2$ molecules.**
**Ans.** $C_2H_4$:

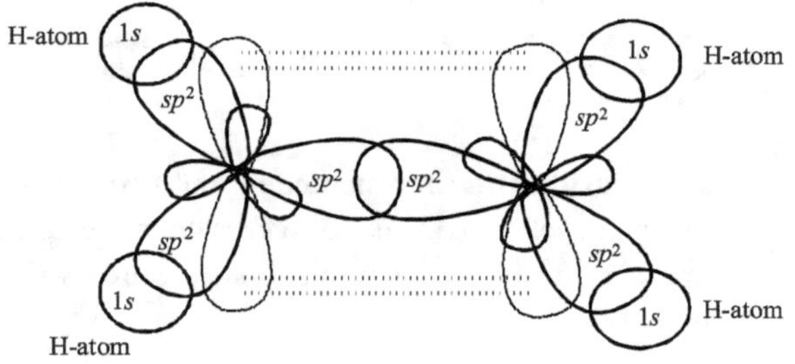


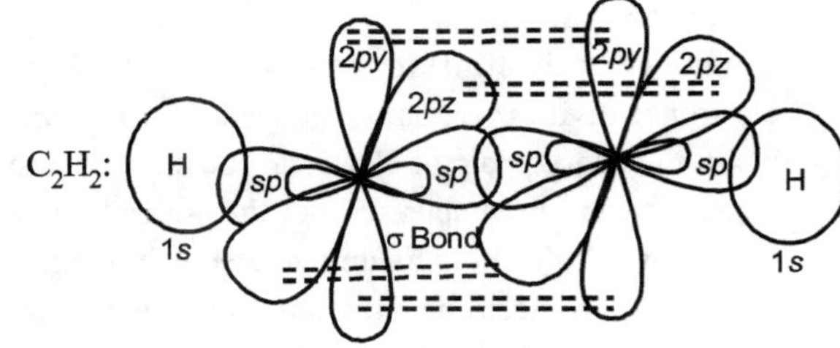


**4.28  What is the total number of sigma and pi bonds in the following molecules ?**
(a)  $C_2H_2$          (b)  $C_2H_4$

**Ans.** (a)  $H\overset{\sigma}{-}C\overset{\overset{\pi}{\overset{\sigma}{\equiv}}}{\underset{\pi}{}}C\overset{\sigma}{-}H$ $(3\sigma, 2\pi)$

(b)  $\overset{H}{\underset{H}{>}}C\overset{\pi}{\underset{\pi}{=}}C\overset{H}{\underset{H}{<}}$ $(5\sigma, 1\pi)$

**4.29  Considering $x$–axis as the internuclear axis which out of the following will not form a sigma bond and why ?**
(a)  $1s$ and $1s$          (b)  $1s$ and $2p_x$
(c)  $2p_y$ and $2p_y$       (d)  $1s$ and $2s$

**Ans.** Only (c) will not form a $\sigma$–bond because taking $y$–axis as the intermolecular axis, there will be lateral (sideway) overlap between the two $2p_y$ orbitals forming a $\pi$ bond.

**4.30  Which hybrid orbitals are used by carbon atoms in the following molecules ?**
(a)  $CH_3–CH_3$
(b)  $CH_3–CH = CH_2$
(c)  $CH_3–CH_2–OH$
(d)  $CH_3–CHO$
(e)  $CH_3COOH$.

**Ans.** (a)  $H-\overset{\overset{\textstyle H}{|}}{\underset{\underset{\textstyle H}{|}}{C}}-\overset{\overset{\textstyle H}{|}}{\underset{\underset{\textstyle H}{|}}{C}}-H$.

Both C—atoms use $sp^3$ hybrid orbitals.

(b)  $H-\overset{\overset{\textstyle H}{|}}{\underset{\underset{\textstyle H}{|}}{\overset{1}{C}}}-\overset{\overset{\textstyle H}{}}{\overset{2}{C}}=\overset{\overset{\textstyle H}{}}{\underset{\underset{\textstyle H}{}}{\overset{3}{C}}}$ , $C_1 = sp^3, C_2 = sp^2,$

$C_3, = sp^2$

(c)  $H-\overset{\overset{\textstyle H}{|}}{\underset{\underset{\textstyle H}{|}}{C}}-\overset{\overset{\textstyle H}{|}}{\underset{\underset{\textstyle H}{|}}{C}}-\overset{..}{\underset{..}{O}}{:}$

Both C–atoms use $sp^3$ hybrid orbitals.

(d) $H-\overset{\displaystyle 1}{\underset{\displaystyle H}{\overset{\displaystyle H}{C}}}-\overset{\displaystyle 2}{C}\overset{H}{\underset{O}{\diagup}}$ . $C_1 = sp^3$, $C_2 = sp^2$

(e) $H-\overset{\displaystyle 1}{\underset{\displaystyle H}{\overset{\displaystyle H}{C}}}-\overset{\displaystyle 2}{\underset{}{\overset{O}{C}}}-O-H$ . $C_1 = sp^3$, $C_2 = sp^2$

**4.31 What do you understand by bond pairs and lone pairs of electrons ? Illustrate by giving one example of each type?**

**Ans.** Covalent bonds are formed by mutual sharing of electrons between the two atoms. The shared pairs of electrons thus present between the bonded atoms are called bond pairs. All the electrons of an atom may not participate in the bonding. The electron pairs present on the atoms which do not take part in bonding are called lone pairs of electrons. For example, in

$CH_4$ $\left( H:\overset{\displaystyle \cdot\cdot}{\underset{\displaystyle \cdot\cdot}{C}}:H \right)$, there are only 4 bond pairs but in

$H_2O$ $\left( \overset{\displaystyle \cdot\cdot}{\underset{\displaystyle H\ \ H}{:O:}} \right)$, there are two bond pairs and two lone pairs.

**4.32 Distinguish between a sigma and a pi bond.**

**Ans.**

| Sigma bond | Pi bond |
|---|---|
| 1. It is formed by overlap of orbitals along internuclear axis. | 1. It is formed by sideways overlapping of orbitals. |
| 2. It is formed by overlapping of s-s orbital, s-p orbital and p-p orbital. | 2. It is formed by overlap of p-p and p-d orbitals. |
| 3. The electron cloud of a sigma bond is symmetrical about the internuclear axis and the overlapping is quite large, thus sigma bonds are strong. | 3. As the electron clouds overlap above and below the plane of internuclear axis, the overlapping is small, thus pi bonds are weak. |
| 4. Free rotation about a sigma bond is possible. | 4. Free rotation about a pi bond is not possible, since on rotating the overlapping vanishes and the bond breaks. |
| 5. Bond length is longer. | 5. Bond length is shorter. |
| 6. No preset conditions are required for the formation of bond. | 6. Pi bonds are always formed after sigma bonds have formed. |

**4.33 Explain the formation of $H_2$ molecule on the basis of valence bond theory.**

**Ans.**

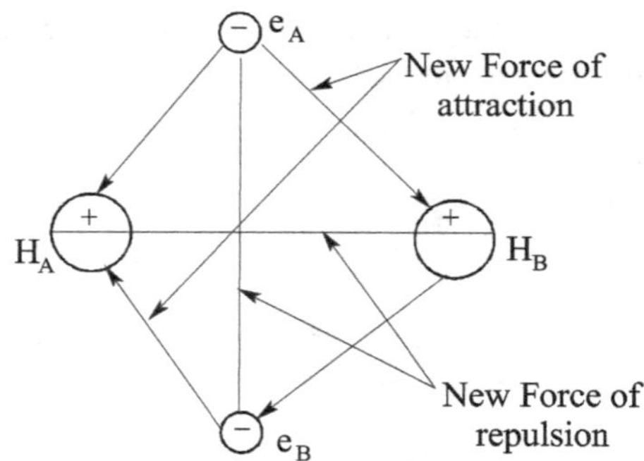


Consider two hydrogen atoms A and B with electron $e_A$ and $e_B$ respectively. $H_A$ represents the nucleus of hydrogen atom 'A' and $H_B$ for hydrogen atom 'B'. When the two hydrogen atoms approach each other, the following two forces come into existence:

(a) Attractive forces between (i) electron $e_A$ and nucleus $H_B$ (ii) electron $e_B$ and nucleus $H_A$.

(b) Repulsive forces between (i) electron $e_A$ and electron $e_B$ (ii) nucleus $H_A$ and nucleus $H_B$.

The attractive forces tend to bring the atom close to each other, whereas repulsive forces tend to push them apart. Since the magnitude of attractive forces is greater than the repulsive forces, as a result, the energy of the system decreases and a molecule of hydrogen is formed.

**4.34 Write the important conditions required for the linear combination of atomic orbitals to form molecular orbitals.**

**Ans.** The main points are

(i) When two atomic orbitals combine they loose their original identity and form new orbitals which are termed as molecular orbitals.

(ii) Only those atomic orbitals combine to form molecular orbitals which have comparable energies and proper orientation. For example 1s would only combine with 1s and not with $2s$. $2p_x$ would only combine with $2p_x$ of other atom and so on.

(iii) The number of molecular orbitals formed is equal to the number of atomic orbitals which combine with one another.

(iv) The two atomic orbitals combine to give bonding molecular orbital and anti–bonding molecular orbital. The bonding molecular orbital has lower energy than anti–bonding molecular orbital and hence greater stability than the other.

(v) The filling up of molecular orbitals takes place according to the same rules as those of atomic orbitals.

**4.35 Use molecular orbital theory to explain why the $Be_2$ molecule does not exist.**

**Ans.** E.C. of $_4Be = 1s^2\ 2s^2$

M.O. E.C. of $Be_2 = \sigma_{1s}^2\ \sigma^*{}_{1s}^2\ \sigma_{2s}^2\ \sigma^*{}_{2s}^2$

$\therefore$ Bond order $= \dfrac{1}{2}(4-4) = 0$ .

Hence, $Be_2$ does not exist.

**4.36** **Compare the relative stability of the following species and indicate their magnetic properties:**

$O_2$, $O_2^+$, $O_2^-$ **(superoxide)**, $O_2^{2-}$ **(peroxide)**

**Ans.** The electronic configuration of

$O_2 = KK\sigma\,(2s)^2\,\sigma^*(2s)^2\,\sigma\,(2p_z)^2\,\pi\,(2p_y)^2\,\pi\,(2p_x)^2\,\pi^*(2p_y)^1\,\pi^*(2p_x)^1$

The number of bonding electrons ($N_b$) = 8, number of anti–bonding electrons ($N_a$) = 4

$$\text{Bond order} = \frac{N_b - N_a}{2} = 1/2\,(8-4) = 2\,,$$

It is paramagnetic due to presence of 2 unpaired electrons in the $\pi^*(2p_y)$ and $\pi^*(2p_z)$.

The electronic configuration of

$O_2^+ = KK\,\sigma(2s)^2\,\sigma^*(2s)^2\,\sigma(2p_z)^2\,\pi(2p_y)^2\,\pi(2p_x)^2\,\pi^*(2p_y)^1$

The number of bonding electrons ($N_b$) = 8, number of anti–bonding electrons ($N_a$) = 3

$$\text{Bond order} = \frac{N_b - N_a}{2} = 1/2\,(8-3) = 2\frac{1}{2}\,,$$

It is paramagnetic due to presence of 1 unpaired electrons in the $\pi^*(2p_y)$.

The electronic configuration of $O_2^{-1}$ (super-oxide) = $KK$

$\sigma\,(2s)^2\,\sigma^*(2s)^2\,\sigma(2p_z)^2\,\pi(2p_y)^2\,\pi(2p_x)^2\,\pi^*(2p_y)^2\,\pi^*(2p_z)^1$

The number of bonding electrons ($N_b$) = 8, number of anti–bonding electrons ($N_a$) = 5

$$\text{Bond order} = \frac{N_b - N_a}{2} = 1/2\,(8-5) = 1\frac{1}{2}\,,$$

It is paramagnetic due to presence of 1 unpaired electrons in the $\pi^*(2p_y)$.

The electronic configuration of $O_2^{2-}$ ( peroxide) = $KK\,\sigma$

$(2s)^2\,\sigma^*(2s)^2\,\sigma(2p_x)^2\,\pi(2p_y)^2$
$\pi(2p_z)^2\,\pi^*(2p_y)^2\,\pi^*(2p_z)^2$

The number of bonding electrons ($N_b$) = 8, number of anti-bonding electrons ($N_a$) = 6

$$\text{Bond order} = \frac{N_b - N_a}{2} = 1/2\,(8-6) = 1,$$

It is dia–magnetic due to presence of no unpaired electrons. The relative stability would be $O_2^+ > O_2 > O_2^-$ $> O_2^{2-}$ since higher the bond order more is the stability.

**4.37** **Write the significance of a plus and a minus sign shown in representing the orbitals.**

**Ans.** As orbitals are represented by wave functions, a plus sign in an orbital represents a positive wave function and a minus sign represents a negative wave function.

**4.38** **Describe the hybridisation in case of $PCl_5$. Why are the axial bonds longer as compared to equatorial bonds ?**

**Ans.** In $PCl_5$ the hybridization is $sp^3d$, thus it has a trigonal bi–pyramidal structure. This is because one of the $3s$ electron of '$p$' gets promoted to $3d$ orbital giving the electronic configuration $1s^2 2s^2 2p^6 3s^1 3p_x^1 3p_y^1 3p_z^1 3d^1$, thus it involves $sp^3d$ hybridization.

The equatorial and the axial bond lengths in $PCl_5$ are different. The axial bond lengths are longer than the equatorial bond length. This is due to minimize bond–pair bond–pair repulsion for the large sized chlorine atoms.

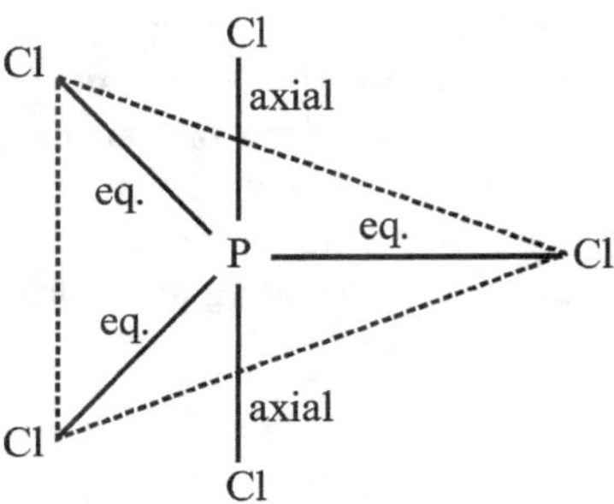


**4.39** **Define hydrogen bond. Is it weaker or stronger than the van der Waals forces ?**

**Ans.** **Hydrogen bond** – Whenever a molecule contains a hydrogen atom linked to a highly electron-egative atom (F,O,N), this atom attracts the shared pair of electrons more and so this end of the molecule becomes slightly negative while the other H–end becomes slightly positive. The negative end attracts the positive end as a result a weak bond is formed between them. This bond is called hydrogen bond.

...... $H^{\delta+} - X^{\delta-}$ ...... $H^{\delta+} - X^{\delta-}$ ...... $H^{\delta+} - X^{\delta-}$ ......

Hydrogen bond is stronger than the van der Waal's forces.

**4.40** **What is meant by the term bond order ? Calculate the bond order of: $N_2$, $O_2$, $O_2^+$ and $O_2^-$?**

**Ans.** Bond order is defined as half of the difference between the number of electrons present in the bonding and the anti–bonding orbitals i.e. B.O = 1/2 ( $N_b - N_a$).

The electronic configuration of

$O_2 = KK\,\sigma\,(2s)^2\,\sigma^*(2s)^2\,\sigma(2p_x)^2\,\pi(2p_y)^2\,\pi\,(2p_z)^2\,\pi^*(2p_y)^1$
$\pi^*(2p_z)^1$

The number of bonding electrons ($N_b$) = 8, number of anti–bonding electrons ($N_a$) = 4

$$\text{Bond order} = \frac{N_b - N_a}{2} = 1/2\,(8-4) = 2\,,$$

The electronic configuration of

$O_2^+ = KK\,\sigma(2s)^2\,\sigma^*(2s)^2\,\sigma(2p_x)^2\,\pi(2p_y)^2\,\pi(2p_z)^2\,\pi^*(2p_y)^1$

The number of bonding electrons ($N_b$) = 8, number of anti–bonding electrons ($N_a$) = 3

Bond order $= \dfrac{N_b - N_a}{2} = 1/2\,(8-3) = 2\dfrac{1}{2}$

The electronic configuration of $O_2^{-1}$ (superoxide) $= KK$ $\sigma(2s)^2\,\sigma*(2s)^2\;\sigma(2p_x)^2\pi(2p_y)^2\,\pi\,(2p_z)^2\,\pi*(2p_y)^2\,\pi*(2p_z)^1$
The number of bonding electrons $(N_b) = 8$, number of anti-bonding electrons $(N_a) = 5$

Bond order $= \dfrac{N_b - N_a}{2} = 1/2\,(8-5) = 1.5$

The electronic configuration of $N_2 = KK\;\sigma\,(2s)^2\,\sigma*(2s)^2$ $\sigma\,(2p_x)^2\,\pi(2p_y)^2\,\pi(2p_z)^2$
The number of bonding electrons $(N_b) = 8$, number of anti-bonding electrons $(N_{ab}) = 2$

Bond order $= \dfrac{N_b - N_a}{2} = 1/2\,(8-2) = 3$

The order of stability will be $N_2 > O_2^+ > O_2 > O_2^-$.

<table><tr><td>**SECTION B**</td><td># PRACTICE QUESTIONS</td></tr></table>

## Multiple Choice Questions

1. When a metal atom combines with non-metal atom, the non-metal atom will
   (a) lose electrons and decrease in size
   (b) lose electrons and increase in size
   (c) gain electrons and decrease in size
   (d) gain electrons and increase in size

2. The lowest energy structure is the one with the .......... formal charges on the atoms.
   (a) smallest      (b) highest
   (c) zero      (d) negative

3. Which of the following is the electron deficient molecule?
   (a) $C_2H_6$      (b) $B_2H_6$
   (c) $SiH_4$      (d) $PH_3$

4. Which of the following is/are not the condi-tion(s) for Lewis dot structure?
   (i) Each bond is formed as a result of sharing of an electron pair between the atoms.
   (ii) From the two combining atoms only one atom contribute electron(s) to the shared pair.
   (iii) The combining atoms attain the outer shell noble gas configurations as a result of the sharing of electrons.
   (a) (i) and (iii)      (b) (ii) and (iii)
   (c) (ii) only      (d) (iii) only

5. Which of the following molecule(s) obey the octet rule?
   (i) $[BF_4]^-$      (ii) $[AlCl_4]^-$
   (iii) $SO_2$,      (iv) $CCl_4$
   (a) (i), (ii), (iii), (iv)      (b) (ii), (iii), (iv)
   (c) (i), (iii), (iv)      (d) (i), (ii), (iv)

6. The correct sequence of increasing covalent character is represented by
   (a) $LiCl < NaCl < BeCl_2$
   (b) $BeCl_2 < LiCl < NaCl$
   (c) $NaCl < LiCl < BeCl_2$
   (d) $BeCl_2 < NaCl < LiCl$

7. Which of the following is correct representation of resonance?

   A. 

   B. 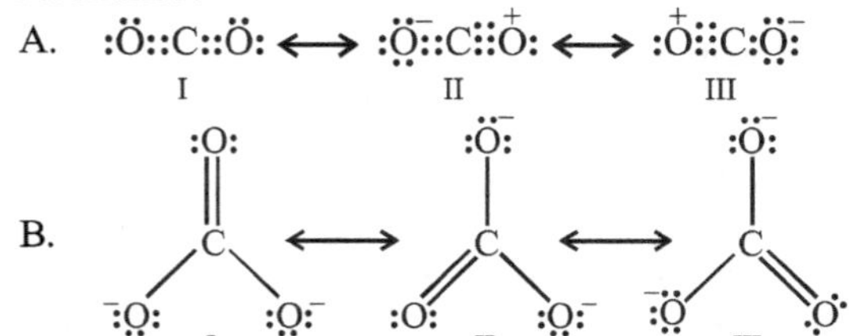

   Choose the correct option.
   (a) Only A      (b) Only B
   (c) Both A and B      (d) None of these

8. Which of the following statements is false ?
   (a) $H_2$ molecule has one sigma bond
   (b) HCl molecule has one sigma bond
   (c) Water molecule has two sigma bonds and two lone pairs
   (d) Acetylene molecule has three pi bonds and three sigma bonds

9. Which of the following is/are misconception(s) associated with resonance?
   (i) The molecule exist for a certain fraction of time in one cannonical form and for other fractions of time in other cannonical forms.
   (ii) The cannonical forms have no real exis-tence.
   (iii) There is no such equilibrium between the cannonical forms.
   (a) (i) only      (b) (ii) and (iii)
   (c) (i) and (iii)      (d) (iii) only

## Assertion & Reason Questions

**DIRECTIONS (Qs. 1-6) :** *Each of these questions contains an assertion followed by reason. Read them carefully and answer the question on the basis of following options. You have to select the one that best describes the two statements.*
(a) If both Assertion and Reason are correct and the Reason is a correct explanation of the Assertion.
(b) If both Assertion and Reason are correct but Reason is not a correct explanation of the Assertion.
(c) If the Assertion is correct but Reason is incorrect.
(d) If the Assertion is incorrect but the Reason is correct.

1. **Assertion :** The correct Lewis structure of $O_3$ may be drawn as

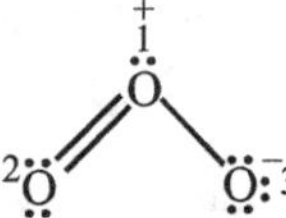

   **Reason :** The formal charges on atom 1, 2 and 3 are $+1$, 0 and $-1$ respectively.

2. **Assertion :** Sulphur compounds like $SF_6$ and $H_2SO_4$ have 12 valence electrons around S atom.

   **Reason :** All sulphur compounds do not follow octet rule.

3. **Assertion :** The lesser the lattice enthalpy, more stable is the ionic compound.

   **Reason :** The lattice enthalpy is greater for ions of highest charge and smaller radii.

4. **Assertion :** $CH_2Cl_2$ is non-polar and $CCl_4$ is polar molecule.

   **Reason :** Molecule with zero dipole moment is non-polar in nature.

5. **Assertion :** Lone pair-lone pair repulsive interactions are greater than lone pair-bond pair and bond pair-bond pair interactions.

   **Reason :** The space occupied by lone pair electrons is more as compared to bond pair electrons.

6. **Assertion :** $\pi$ bonds are weaker than $\sigma$ bonds.

   **Reason :** $\pi$ bonds are formed by the overlapping of *p-p* orbitals along their axes.

## CASE/PASSAGE BASED QUESTIONS

**DIRECTIONS (Qs. 1-5) :** *Read the following case/passage and answer the questions.*

Nyholm and Gillespie (1957) refined the VSEPR model by explaining the important difference between the lone pairs and bonding pairs of electrons. While the lone pairs are localised on the central atom, each bonded pair is shared between two atoms. As a result, the lone pair electrons in a molecule occupy more space as compared to the bonding pairs of electrons. This results in greater repulsion between lone pairs of electrons as compared to the lone pair - bond pair and bond pair - bond pair repulsions. These repulsion effects result in deviations from idealised shapes and alterations in bond angles in molecules.

The VSEPR Theory is able to predict geometry of a large number of molecules, especially the compounds of p-block elements accurately. It is also quite successful in determining the geometry quite-accurately even when the energy difference between possible structures is very small. The theoretical basis of the VSEPR theory regarding the effects of electron pair repulsions on molecular shapes is not clear and continues to be a subject of doubt and discussion.

1. Which of the following has square pyramid shape?
   - (a) $ClF_3$
   - (b) $SF_4$
   - (c) $XeF_4$
   - (d) $BrF_5$

2. Which of the following is the correct increasing order of lone pair of electrons on the central atom?
   - (a) $IF_7 < IF_5 < ClF_3 < XeF_2$
   - (b) $IF_7 < XeF_2 < ClF_2 < IF_5$
   - (c) $IF_7 < ClF_3 < XeF_2 < IF_5$
   - (d) $IF_7 < XeF_2 < IF_5 < ClF_3$

3. A $\sigma$-bonded molecule $MX_3$ is T-shaped. The number of non-bonding pairs of electron is
   - (a) 0
   - (b) 2
   - (c) 1
   - (d) can be predicted only if atomic number of M is known.

4. Which of the following structure is most stable ?

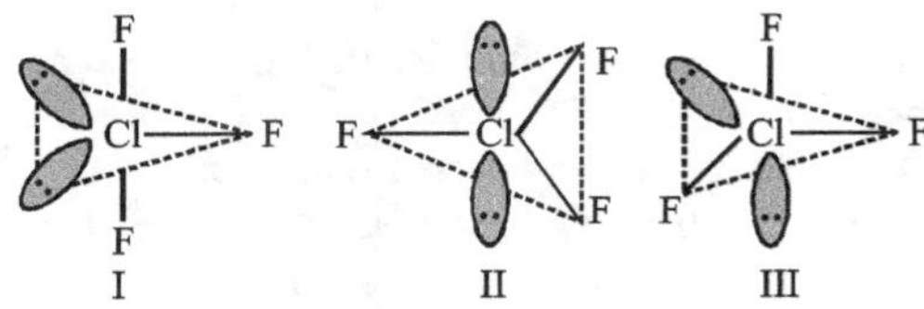

   Choose the correct option.
   - (a) Only I
   - (b) Only II
   - (c) Only III
   - (d) All three have same stability

5. Among the following molecules : $SO_2$, $SF_4$, $ClF_3$, $BrF_5$ and $XeF_4$, which of the following shapes does not describe any of the molecules mentioned?
   - (a) Bent
   - (b) Trigonal bipyramidal
   - (c) See-saw
   - (d) T-shape

## VERY SHORT ANSWER QUESTIONS

1. Define covalent bond according to orbital concept?
2. Why is solid NaCl non-conductor of electricity?
3. Why is NaCl harder than sodium metal?
4. Draw Lewis dot structure for $MgCl_2$ and $CH_4$.
5. Write Lewis formula for HCHO.
6. In writing Lewis dot structures of molecules, which atom is given central position?
7. How is bond order related to the stability of a molecule?
8. Write the type of hybridisation involve in $CH_4$, $C_2H_4$ and $C_2H_2$.
9. Which is more polar—$CO_2$ or $N_2O$? Give reason.
10. State the types of hybrid orbitals associated with (i) P in $PCl_5$ and (ii) S in $SF_6$.
11. Define covalent bonds according to quantum theory of valence bond theory (modern concept).
12. Out of NaCl and MgO, which has higher value of lattice energy?
13. Explain why reactions involving covalent compounds are generally slow?

14. Define dipole moment. Is it scalar or vector quantity?
15. Why are dipole moments of $CO_2$, $BF_3$, $CCl_4$, $PF_5$, $SF_6$ zero?
16. Can a $\pi$-bond be formed in the absence of a sigma bond?
17. What types of hybridisation are involved with the central atom of a molecule having following shapes:
    (i) planar, (ii) a regular tetrahedral, (iii) an equilateral triangle.
18. Which of the following structures contributes least towards resonance hybrid?

$$\overset{-}{N} = \overset{+}{N} = O \quad :N \equiv \overset{+}{N} - \ddot{O}:^- \quad :\overset{2-}{N} - \overset{+}{N} \equiv O^+:$$
$$\quad \text{I} \qquad\qquad \text{II} \qquad\qquad\qquad \text{III}$$

19. Which of the species have similar shape and why? $NO_2^-$, $NO_2^+$, $CO_2$, $O_3$.
20. Define lattice enthalpy and how is it related to the stability of the ionic compound.
21. How are bond order and bond length related to each other?
22. $ClF_3$ is T-shape molecule while $NF_3$ has a trigonal pyramidal shape. Explain.
23. State the hybridisation of the carbon labelled ($x$) and ($y$) in acetic acid.

$$H - \underset{\underset{H}{|}}{\overset{\overset{H}{|}}{C}}_{y} - \overset{\overset{O}{\|}}{C}_{x} - O - H$$

24. Which out of the two molecules OCS and $CS_2$ has a higher *dipole* moment and why?
25. What are the conditions of resonating structures?
26. Which is more stronger and why $\sigma$ or $\pi$ bond?
27. Which has got more s–character ethane or acetylene?

## SHORT ANSWER QUESTIONS

1. Three elements have the following Lewis symbols:

$$\dot{A} \quad \cdot \dot{B} \cdot \quad :\dot{\underset{..}{C}}:$$

    (a) Assign groups of the periodic table to these elements.
    (b) Which elements are expected to form ions and what is the expected charge over these ions?
    (c) Write the formulae and Lewis structures of the covalent compounds formed between
       (i) A and B       (ii) A and C
2. Write the electron-dot structures for

    (i) $CN^-$       (ii) $SO_3^{2-}$ and       (iii) $ClO_2^-$.
3. What do you understand by co-ordinate covalent bond? Give one example.
4. Covalent bonds are called directional bonds while ionic bonds are called non–directional. Why?
5. What are the conditions for writing the Lewis dot structures for molecules?

6. Use Lewis dot symbols to show electron transfer between the following atoms to form cations and anions:
    (a) Na and Cl   (b) Ca and O
7. Which elements are likely to form ionic bond and why?
8. Define a single covalent bond and double covalent bond.
9. "A non-polar molecule can have highly polar bonds". Justify the statement.
10. Chlorine is non-polar while HCl is a polar molecule. Explain.
11. Covalent bonds possess some ionic character also, explain why?
12. Out of the following four resonance structures for the $CO_2$ molecule, which are important for describing the bonding in the molecule and why?

$$\ddot{O} = C = \ddot{O} \qquad\qquad \overset{+}{O} \equiv C - \ddot{O}:^-$$
$$\qquad 1 \qquad\qquad\qquad\qquad 2$$
$$:\ddot{O}^- \equiv C - \overset{+}{O} \qquad\qquad :\ddot{O}^- - C^{2+} - \ddot{O}:^-$$
$$\qquad 3 \qquad\qquad\qquad\qquad 4$$

13. Give hybridization and shape of
    (a) $XeF_4$                    (b) $BrF_3$ .
14. Predict the dipole moment of a molecule of the type
    (i) $AX_4$ having a square planar geometry.
    (ii) $AX_5$ having a square pyramidal shape.
    (iii) $AX_6$ having an octahedral geometry.
15. Why are lone pair-lone pair repulsions stronger than lone pair-bond pair?
16. Explain the formation and difference between a sigma ($\sigma$) bond and a pi ($\pi$) bond.
17. Define Lattice energy. How is Lattice energy influenced by (i) Charge on the ions (ii) Size of the ions.
18. Calculate the percent ionic character of HCl. Given that the observed dipole moment is 1.03D and the bond length of HCl is 1.275 Å. Given $q = 4.8 \times 10^{-10}$ esu.

## LONG ANSWER QUESTIONS

1. Select the best Lewis structure(s) for the sulphate ion, $SO_4^{2-}$.
2. State the hybridization and draw the molecular structure of the following
    (a) $PF_5$ (b) $I_3^-$ (c) $NH_3$ (d) $XeO_3$ (e) $CH_4$
3. Determine the formal charges on the atoms in the two structures shown below for the molecule $POCl_3$. Which of these two structures is the better structure (i.e., which is preferred)?

$$\underset{\text{I}}{\overset{\displaystyle :\ddot{Cl}:}{:\ddot{Cl} - \underset{\underset{:\ddot{Cl}:}{|}}{P} = \ddot{O}:}} \qquad\qquad \underset{\text{II}}{\overset{\displaystyle :\ddot{Cl}:}{:\ddot{Cl} - \underset{\underset{:\ddot{Cl}:}{|}}{P} - \ddot{O}:}}$$

4. What are the characteristics of resonance?
5. Give difference between Bonding Molecular orbital and Anti–bonding molecular orbital.

## SOLUTIONS

### *Multiple Choice Questions*

1. **(d)** When a metal for example Na combines with a non metal e.g., $Cl_2$. Following reaction occurs
$$2Na + Cl_2 \longrightarrow 2NaCl$$
In this process Na loses one electron to form $Na^+$ and Cl accepts one electron to form $Cl^-$
$$Na \longrightarrow Na^+ + e^-$$
$$Cl + e^- \longrightarrow Cl^-$$
Therefore, in this process Cl gains electron and hence, its size increases.

2. **(a)** The lowest energy structure is the one with the smallest formal charges on the atoms.

3. **(b)** The compounds in which octet of central atom is incomplete are known as electron deficient compounds. Hence, $B_2H_6$ is an electron deficient compound.

4. **(c)** Each combining atom contributes at least one electron to the shared pair.

5. **(d)** 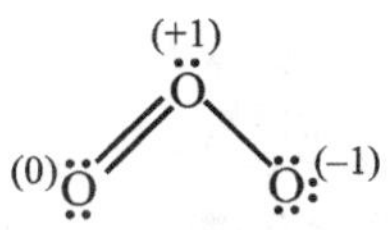

Total no. of valence electron around sulphur in $SO_2$ is 10, while in case of other molecules total no. of 8 electrons are present in each.

6. **(c)** As difference of electronegativity inc-reases % ionic character increases and covalent character decreases *i.e.*, electronegativity difference decreases, covalent character increases.
Further, greater the charge on the cation and smaller the size, more will be its polarising power. Hence, covalent character increases.

7. **(c)** Both representation of resonating structures in molecules of $CO_2$ and $CO_3^{2-}$ are correct.

8. **(d)** Structure of acetylene molecule
$$H \overset{1\sigma}{-} C \underset{2\pi}{\overset{1\sigma}{\equiv}} C \overset{1\sigma}{-} H$$
Thus, acetylene molecule has $3\sigma$ bonds and $2\pi$ bonds.

9. **(a)** The molecule does not exist for a certain fraction of time in one cannonical form and for other fractions of time in other cannonical forms. It exists as a resonance hybrid.

### *Assertion & Reason Questions*

1. **(a)** 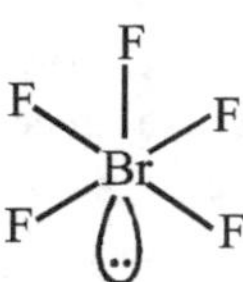

Formal charge = (total number of valence $e^-$ in the free atom) − (total number of non-bonding $e^-$) − $\dfrac{1}{2}$ (total number of bonding $e^-$)

Formal charge on O(1) $= 6 - 2 - \dfrac{1}{2}(6) = +1$

Formal charge on O(2) $= 6 - 4 - \dfrac{1}{2}(4) = 0$

Formal charge on O(3) $= 6 - 6 - \dfrac{1}{2} \times 2 = -1$

Hence, correct representation of $O_3$ is

2. **(c)** Sulphur forms many compounds in which the octet rule is obeyed. For example, $SCl_2$ has an octet of electrons around it.

3. **(d)** Assertion is false but reason is true.
The greater the lattice enthalpy, more stable is the ionic compound.

4. **(d)** Assertion is false but reason is true.
$CH_2Cl_2$ is polar while $CCl_4$ is non-polar because in $CCl_4$ net dipole moment cancels.

5. **(a)** While the lone pairs are localised on the central atom, each bonded pair is shared between two atoms. As a result, the lone pair electrons in a molecule occupy more space as compared to the bonding pairs of electrons. This results in greater repulsion between lone pairs of electrons as compared to the lone pair -bond pair and bond pair - bond pair repulsions.

6. **(c)** pi bonds are formed by the overlapping of *p-p* orbitals perpendicular to their axis *i.e.*, sidewise overlap.

### *Case/Passage Based Questions*

1. **(d)** $BrF_5$

2. **(a)** The number of lone pairs of electrons on central atom in various given species are

| Species | Number of lone pairs on central atom |
|---|---|
| $IF_7$ | 0 |
| $IF_5$ | 1 |
| $ClF_3$ | 2 |
| $XeF_2$ | 3 |

Thus the correct increasing order is
$$IF_7 < IF_5 < ClF_3 < XeF_2$$
$$\;0\quad\;\; 1\quad\;\;\; 2\quad\;\;\; 3$$

**3.** **(b)**

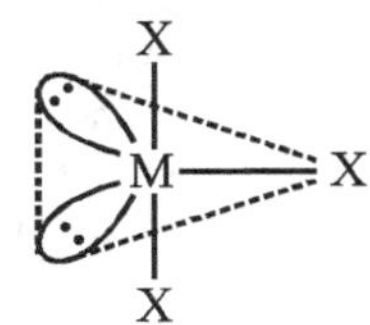

Number of lone pair = 2

**4.** **(a)** I is the most stable geometry because both the lone pairs are present at equatorial position. Due to which, repulsion is minimum in molecule as compared to the repulsion in other molecules where lone pair is in axial position.

**5.** **(b)** 

| | | |
|---|---|---|
| $SO_2$ | – | bent |
| $SF_4$ | – | see-saw |
| $ClF_3$ | – | T-shape |
| $BrF_5$ | – | square pyramidal |
| $XeF_4$ | – | square planar. |

### Very Short Answer Questions

**1.** Covalent bond can be formed by the overlap of the orbitals belonging to the two atoms having opposite spins of electrons.

**2.** In solid NaCl, $Na^+$ and $Cl^-$ are not free to move.

**3.** In NaCl, there is strong ionic bond between $Na^+$ and $Cl^-$ whereas in Na metal there is weak metallic bond.

**4.** $:\ddot{C}l^- : Mg^{2+} : \ddot{C}l^- :$ and $H : \overset{..}{\underset{..}{C}} : H$ (with H above and below)

**5.** $H \cdot \overset{\overset{\overset{O}{\cdot\cdot}}{\cdot\cdot}}{C} \cdot H$

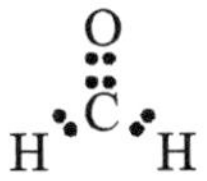

**6.** Generally least electronegative atom is given central position.

**7.** Higher the bond order greater is the stability.

**8.** $CH_4 = sp^3$
$C_2H_4 = sp^2$
$C_2H_2 = sp$

**9.** $N_2O$ is more polar than $CO_2$. This is because $CO_2$ is linear and symmetrical. Its net dipole moment is zero. $N_2O$ is linear but not symmetrical. It has a net dipole moment of $\sigma116D$.

**10.** (i) $sp^3d$ of P in $PCl_5$
(ii) $sp^3d^2$ of S in $SF_6$

**11.** It is formed by overlapping of half filled atomic orbitals.

**12.** MgO has higher value of lattice energy.

**13.** Covalent compounds have high bond dissociation energy that is why they react slowly.

**14.** Dipole moment is defined as product of charge and distance between atoms. $\boxed{\mu = e \times d.}$ It is a vector quantity.

**15.** They have symmetrical shape, individual bond moments get cancelled, therefore, net dipole moment is zero.

**16.** No.

**17.** (i) $sp^2$, (ii) $sp^3$, (iii) $sp^2$.

**18.** III, contributes least because like charges reside on adjacent atoms.

**19.** $NO_2^+$ and $CO_2$ are '$sp$' hybridised, therefore have linear shape.

**20.** The lattice enthalpy of an ionic solid is defined as the energy required to completely separate one mole of solid ionic compound into gaseous constituent ions.
The lattice enthalpy qualitatively measure the stability of an ionic compound.

**21.** Bond order and the bond length are inversely related.

$$\text{Bond order} \propto \frac{1}{\text{Bond length}}$$

**22.** In $ClF_3$, Cl, the central atom has five electron pair (three are bond pair and two are lone pair). It is a $AX_3L_2$ type molecule. $NF_3$ is $AX_3L$ type molecule and has a trigonal pyramidal shape.

**23.** The carbon atom x is $sp^2$ and carbon atom $y$ is $sp^3$ hybridised.

**24.** OCS will have a higher dipole moment than $CS_2$ although both are linear in shape. This is due to difference in electronegativity of O and S. In OCS, two dissimilar atoms are bonded to the central C atom.

$$O=C=O \qquad O=C=S$$
$$\mu_{net} = 0 \qquad \mu_{net} \neq 0$$
$$\text{or } \mu_1 = \mu_2 \qquad \text{or } \mu_1 > \mu_2$$

**25.** Different resonating structures of a substance have : (i) same positions of atoms (ii) same number of shared and unshared electrons (iii) almost equal energy.

**26.** $\sigma$ bond is more stronger than $\pi$ bonds. Because the electron cloud of a sigma bond is symmetrical about the internuclear axis and the overlapping is quite large.

**27.** Acetylene($C_2H_2$) having sp–hybridization has more s–character than ethane ($C_2H_6$) having $sp^3$ hybridization.

### Short Answer Questions

**1.** (a) A – group 1, B – group 14, C – group 17
(b) A, C are expected to form ions $A^+$ and $C^-$

(c) (i) $A : \overset{A}{\underset{A}{B}} : A$ (ii) $A^+ \left[ :\ddot{C}: \right]^- $ or $A^+Cl$

**2.** (a) $CN^-$ ion has $4 + 5 + 1 = 10$ electrons (4 from the C atom, 5 from the N atom, and 1 for the additional negative charge).

Therefore, the Lewis structure is

$$\left[:\overset{..}{C} + \cdot \overset{..}{N} : + \cdot\right]^- \longrightarrow \left[:C:::N:\right]^- \longrightarrow \left[:C\equiv N:\right]^-$$

(b) $SO_3^{-2}$ : Total number of electrons

$= 6 + 3 \times 6 + 2 = 26$. The Lewis structure is

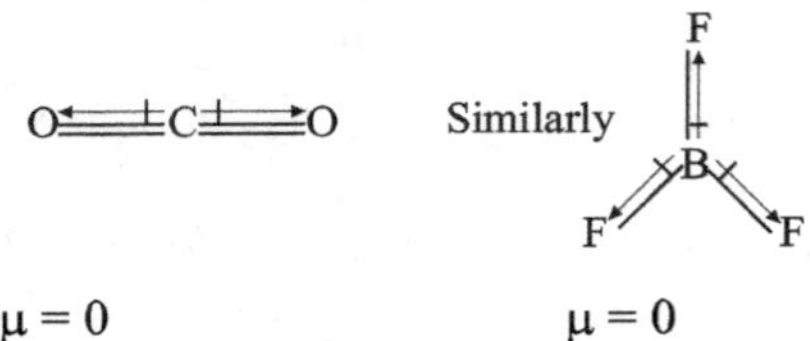

or

The $-2$ charge is present on the entire ion.

(c) $ClO_2^-$ : The total number of electrons

$= 7 + 2 \times 6 + 1 = 20$. The Cl is the central atom and O atoms are bonded to it. The Lewis structure is

$$[:\overset{..}{O}:\overset{..}{C}l:\overset{..}{O}:]^- \quad \text{or} \quad [:\overset{..}{O}-\overset{..}{C}l-\overset{..}{O}:]^-$$

**3.** Co-ordinate covalent or dative bond is formed by mutual sharing of electrons between the two atoms but the shared pair of electrons is donated only by one atom.

$$A + :B \rightarrow A:B$$

An example is the formation of the ammonium ion, in which all bonds are clearly identical

$$H^+ + :NH_3 \longrightarrow \left[\begin{matrix} H \\ \overset{..}{H:N:H} \\ H \end{matrix}\right]^+$$

**4.** In covalent bond, the shared pair of electrons are localized between the two atoms and also covalent bonds are formed by overlap of half filled atomic orbitals. Since orbitals are directional in nature covalent bonds are directional; while in ionic bond each ion is surrounded by a number of oppositely charged ions and there is no definite direction.

**5.** The following are conditions for writing Lewis dot structures for molecules :

(i) Each bond is formed as a result of sharing of an electron pair between the atoms.

(ii) Each combining atom contributes one electron to the shared pair.

(iii) The combining atoms attain the outer-shell noble gas configurations as a result of the sharing of electrons.

**6.** (a) $Na^\cdot + \cdot \overset{..}{\underset{..}{C}l}: \longrightarrow \left[Na^+\right]\left[Cl^-\right]$

(b) $Ca: + \overset{..}{O}: \longrightarrow \left[Ca^{2+}\right]\left[O^{2-}\right]$

**7.** The elements having low ionization enthalpy and high electron gain enthalpy give rise to the formation of ionic bond. Example NaCl. This is because elements with low ionization enthalpy would easily loose electron to form cation while elements, which are having high electron affinity, would pick up the electron easily and form anion. The positive cation would combine with negative anion with the release of energy called lattice enthalpy would result in the formation of ionic crystal.

**8.** A single covalent bond has only one shared pair of electron between the two atoms. For example $\fbox{H}\odot\fbox{H}$

If two atoms share two pairs of electrons, the covalent bond between them is called a double covalent bond. For example $\fbox{O}\ddot{:}\fbox{O}$

**9.** A non-polar molecule can have highly polar bonds because molecular dipole is a vector sum of various bond dipoles. For example, in $CO_2$ there are two strong $C = O$ dipoles but net dipole moment of the molecule is zero.

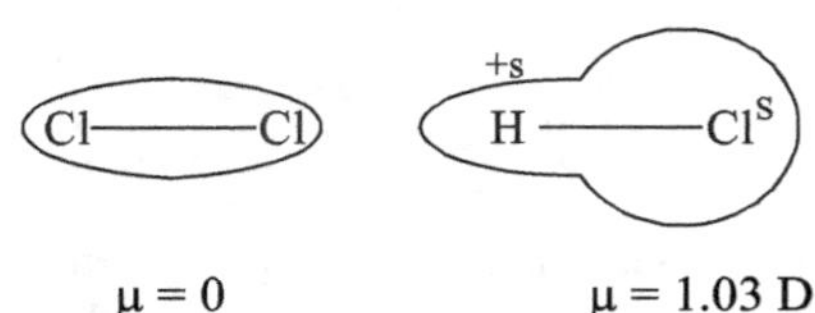

$$\mu = 0 \qquad\qquad \mu = 0$$

**10.** In chlorine molecule, two chlorine atoms with same electronegativity are held by a single covalent bond hence $Cl_2$ is non-polar. In HCl, the bond is polar due to different electro-negativities of H, Cl.

$$\fbox{Cl——Cl} \qquad \overset{+s}{H}———Cl^s$$

$$\mu = 0 \qquad\qquad \mu = 1.03\ D$$

**11.** Hundred percent covalent character is found in the covalent bonds between the atoms of the same element, however, in heteroatomic covalent bonds some percentage of ionic character is also present which goes on increasing with the increasing difference in the electronegativities of the bonded atoms.

**12.** The resonating structures 1, 2, 3 of the $CO_2$ molecule are important for describing the bonding in the molecule as both the C–O bond lengths are the same (115 pm) which lies between carbon-oxygen triple bond length (110 pm) and double bond length (121 pm).

**13.** (a) $XeF_4$–hybridization is $sp^3d^2$ and shape is octahedral or square planar.

(b) $BrF_3$–hybridization is $sp^3d$ and shape is T–shaped.

**14.** (i) Zero dipole moment.

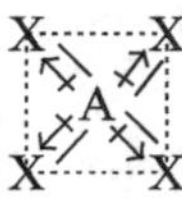

(ii) The molecule will have an appreciable dipole moment.

$$X \cdots \overset{\textstyle X}{\underset{\textstyle A}{\phantom{.}}} \cdots X$$

(iii) Zero dipole moment

**15.** The lone pairs are localized on the central atom, while each bonded pair is share between two atoms. Consequently, the lone pair electrons in a molecule occupy more space as compared to the bonding pair electrons. This causes greater repulsion between lone pairs of electrons as compared to the lone pair-bond pair and bond pair-bond pair repulsion.

**16.**

| | σ-bond | | π-bond |
|---|---|---|---|
| (a) | σ-bond is formed by the axial overlapping of half-filled atomic orbitals. | (a) | π-bond is formed by the lateral or sideways overlapping of atomic orbitals. |
| (b) | It is formed when two s-orbitals overlap or when one orbital with directional character (p-orbital) overlaps along its axis. | (b) | It is formed by the overlapping of two parallel p-orbitals which are available after σ-bonds have been formed. |
| (c) | A σ-bond has a cylindrical shape about the bond axis. | (c) | A π-bond has an electron distribution above and below the bond axis. |
| (d) | A σ-bond is a strong bond. | (d) | A π-bond is weaker than σ-bond. |
| (e) | It allows free rotation. | (e) | It restricts free rotation. |

**17.** Lattice energy is defined as the energy released when one mole of crystalline solid is formed by the combination of oppositely charged ions.

(i) As the magnitude of charge on an ion increases there will be greater force of interionic attraction and hence greater will be the value of Lattice energy.

(ii) Smaller the size of the ions user will be the internuclear distance and thus greater will be the Lattice energy.

**18.** $1 \text{ esu} = 3.335 \times 10^{-10} \text{C}$

$\therefore \quad 4.8 \times 10^{-10} \text{ esu}$

$$= 3.335 \times 10^{-10} \times 4.8 \times 10^{-10}$$

$$= 16 \times 10^{-20} = 1.6 \times 10^{-19}$$

Now, $\mu_{\text{ionic}} = q \times d$

$$= 1.6 \times 10^{-19} \times 1.275 \times 10^{-10}$$

$$= 2.04 \times 10^{-29} \text{ C.m}$$

Given $\mu_{\text{observed}} = 1.03D = 1.03 \times 3.35 \times 10^{-30} \text{ C.m}$
$$= 3.45 \times 10^{-30} \text{ C.m}$$

Now percent ionic

Character $= \dfrac{\mu_{\text{obs}}}{\mu_{\text{cal}}} \times 100$

$$= \frac{3.45 \times 10^{-30}}{2.04 \times 10^{-29}} \times 100 = 16.83\%$$

### *Long Answer Questions*

**1.** First, let's draw a Lewis structure that obeys the octet rule.

Now let's calculate formal charges.
For sulfur atom
formal charge $= 6 - 0 - 4 = +2$
For oxygen atom
formal charge $= 6 - 6 - 1 = -1$ Adding the formal charges to the Lewis structure gives the following structure

Now, we will try to reduce these formal charges. If we move an unshared pair of electrons from oxygen to the S–O bond makes the charge on the oxygen less negative and the charge on the sulfur less positive. Since there are two positive formal charges or sulfur, we need to do this twice to give sulfur a zero formal charge. This results in following structure

Notice, however, that in creating the double bonds, we had choices as to where locate them. There are four different arrangements for these double bonds, as shown below, are four resonance structures.

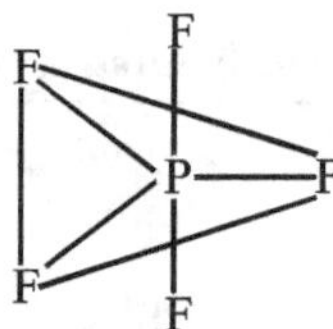

Thus, we consider the sulphate ion to be a resonance hybrid of these contributing structures.

2.  (a)  $PF_5^-$ hybridization $sp^3d$, molecular shape – Trigonal bipyramidal

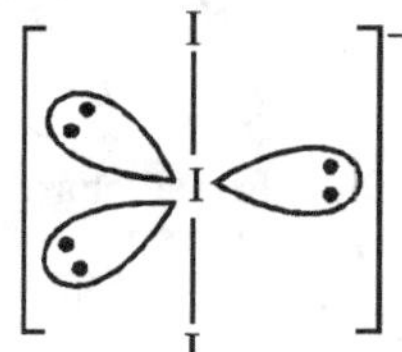

(b)  $I_3^{-1}$ – hybridization $sp^3d$, molecular shape – Linear

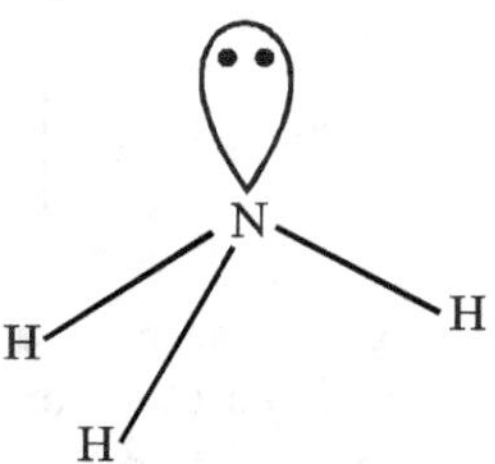

(c)  $NH_3$ – hybridization $sp^3$, molecular shape – Trigonal pyramidal

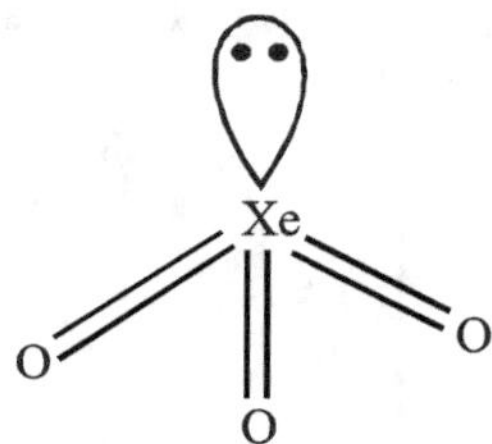

(d)  $XeO_3$ – hybridization $sp^3$, molecular shape – Pyramidal

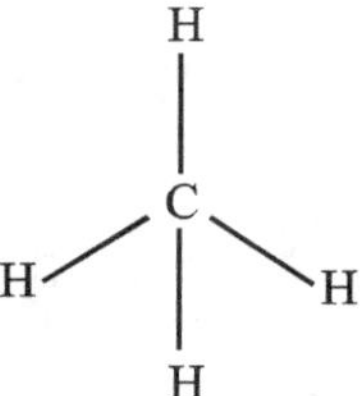

(e)  $CH_4$ – hybridization $sp^3$, molecular shape – Tetrahedral

3.  Formal change on atom in a Lewis structure is given as

$$= \begin{bmatrix} \text{total number of valence} \\ \text{electrons in the free atom} \end{bmatrix}$$

$$- \begin{bmatrix} \text{total number of non} \\ \text{bonding (lone pair)} \\ \text{electrons} \end{bmatrix} - \frac{1}{2}\begin{bmatrix} \text{total no. of} \\ \text{bonding (shared pair)} \\ \text{electrons} \end{bmatrix}$$

For calculating the formal charges; we just apply the formula given above. Then, to choose the better structure, we look for the one with the smallest formal charges on the atoms. We begin by calculating the formal charges. For the chlorines, which have valence electrons as isolated neutral atoms, we have

formal charge $= 7 - 6 - 1 = 0$

Each chlorine has a formal charge of zero in both structures. Now let's examine the other atoms.

**For structure I**
**Phosphorus:** formal charge $= 5 - 0 - 5 = 0$
Oxygen: formal charge $= 6 - 4 - 2 = 0$
**For structure II**
**Phosphorus:** formal charge $= 5 - 0 - 4 = +1$
Oxygen: formal charge $= 6 - 6 - 1 = -1$
Placing these formal charges on the respective Lewis structures gives

Finally, since structure I has the smallest formal charges, it is lower in energy and is the better Lewis structure for this molecule.

4.  Characteristics of resonance are following
(i)  The contributing structures do not have any real existence. Only the resonance hybrid has the real existence.
(ii)  As a result of resonance, the bond lengths of different bonds in a molecule becomes equal.
(iii)  The resonance hybrid has lower energy and hence greater stability than any of the contributing structures.
(iv)  Greater is the resonance energy, greater is the stability of the molecule.
(v)  Greater is the number of canonical forms especially with nearly same energy, greater is the stability of the molecule.

**5.** Difference between Bounding molecular orbital and Anti-bonding molecular orbital.

| Bonding molecular orbital | | Anti-bonding molecular orbital | |
|---|---|---|---|
| (a) | Molecular orbitals formed by the additive effect of the atomic orbitals is called bonding molecular orbitals. | (a) | Molecular orbitals formed by the subtractive effect of atomic is called anti-bonding molecular orbitals. |
| (b) | Probability of finding the electrons is more in the case of bonding molecular orbitals. | (b) | Probability of finding electrons is less in anti-bonding molecular orbitals. There is also a node between the anti-bonding molecular orbital between two nuclei where the electron density is zero. |
| (c) | These are formed by the combination of + and + and – with – part of the electron waves. | (c) | These are formed by the overlap of + with – part. |
| (d) | The electron density in the bonding molecular orbital in the inter-nuclear region is high. As a result, the nuclei are shielded from each other and hence the repulsion is very less. | (d) | The electron density in the anti-bonding molecular orbital in the internuclear region is very low and so the nuclei are directly exposed to each other. Therefore the nuclei are less shielded from each other. |
| (e) | The bonding molecular orbitals are represented by $\sigma$, $\pi$, $\delta$. | (e) | The corresponding anti-bonding molecular orbitals are represented by $\sigma^*$, $\pi^*$, $\delta^*$. |

## SECTION C — NCERT EXEMPLAR QUESTIONS

### MULTIPLE CHOICE QUESTIONS

**1.** Which of the following species has tetrahedral geometry?

(a) $BH_4^-$  (b) $NH_2^-$

(c) $CO_3^{2-}$  (d) $H_3O^+$

**2.** If the electronic configuration of an element is $1s^2\, 2s^2\, 2p^6\, 3s^2\, 3p^6\, 3d^2\, 4s^2$, the four electrons involved in chemical bond formation will be

(a) $3p^6$  (b) $3p^6,\, 4s^2$

(c) $3p^6,\, 3d^2$  (d) $3d^2,\, 4s^2$

**3.** Isostructural species are those which have the same shape and hybridisation. Among the given species identify the isostructural pairs.

(a) $[NF_3$ and $BF_3]$

(b) $[BF_4^-$ and $NH_4^+]$

(c) $[BCl_3$ and $BrCl_3]$

(d) $[NH_3$ and $NO_3^-]$

**4.** Hydrogen bonds are formed in many compounds *e.g.,* $H_2O$, HF, $NH_3$. The boiling point of such compounds depends to an extent on the strength of hydrogen bond and the number of hydrogen bonds. The correct decreasing order of the boiling points of above compounds is

(a) $HF > H_2O > NH_3$

(b) $H_2O > HF > NH_3$

(c) $NH_3 > HF > H_2O$

(d) $NH_3 > H_2O > HF$

**5.** In $NO_3^-$ ion, the number of bond pairs and lone pairs of electrons on nitrogen atom are

(a) 2, 2  (b) 3, 1

(c) 1, 3  (d) 4, 0

**6.** Which molecule/ion out of the following does not contain unpaired electrons?

(a) $N_2^+$  (b) $O_2$

(c) $O_2^{2-}$  (d) $B_2$

**7.** Which of the following options represents the correct bond order?

(a) $O_2^- > O_2 > O_2^+$

(b) $O_2^- < O_2 < O_2^+$

(c) $O_2^- > O_2 < O_2^+$

(d) $O_2^- < O_2 > O_2^+$

## ASSERTION & REASON QUESTIONS

**DIRECTIONS (Qs. 1-2) :** *Each of these questions contains an assertion followed by reason. Read them carefully and answer the question on the basis of following options. You have to select the one that best describes the two statements.*

(a) If both Assertion and Reason are correct and the Reason is a correct explanation of the Assertion.

(b) If both Assertion and Reason are correct but Reason is not a correct explanation of the Assertion.

(c) If the Assertion is correct but Reason is incorrect.

(d) If the Assertion is incorrect but the Reason is correct.

1. **Assertion :** Though the central atom of both $NH_3$ and $H_2O$ molecules are $sp^3$ hybridised. Yet $H - N - H$ bond angle is greater than that of $H - O - H$.
   **Reason :** This is because the nitrogen atom has one lone pair and oxygen atom has two lone pairs.

2. **Assertion :** Sodium chloride formed by the action of chlorine gas on sodium metal is a stable compound.
   **Reason :** This is because sodium and chloride ions acquire octet in sodium chloride formation.

## SHORT ANSWER QUESTIONS

1. Using molecular orbital theory, compare the bond energy and magnetic character of $O_2^+$ and $O_2^-$ species.

2. Structures of molecules of two compounds are given below :

<br>

(I)                 (II)

(a) Which of the two compounds will have intermolecular hydrogen bonding and which compound is expected to show intramolecular hydrogen bonding.

(b) The melting point of a compound depends on, among other things, the extent of hydrogen bonding. On this basis explain which of the above two compounds will show higher melting point.

(c) Solubility of compounds in water depends on power to form hydrogen bonds with water. Which of the above compounds will form hydrogen bonds with water easily and be more soluble in it.

## LONG ANSWER QUESTION

1. Briefly describe the valence bond theory of covalent bond formation by taking an example of hydrogen. How can you interpret energy changes taking place in the formation of dihydrogen?

---

## SOLUTIONS

### *Multiple Choice Questions*

1. **(a)** $BH_4^- \Rightarrow$ 4 bond pairs and 0 lone pair $\rightarrow sp^3$ hybridised.
   $\therefore$ Tetrahedral geometry.

2. **(d)** The given electronic configuration shows that the element belongs to $d$-block of the periodic table and known to be a transition element. In transition elements, electrons of $ns$ and $(n-1)d$ subshell take part in bond formation.

3. **(b)** $BF_4^-$ and $NH_4^+$ both the species are tetrahedral and $sp^3$ hybridised.

4. **(b)** Strength of H-bonding is in the order :
   $$HF > H_2O > NH_3$$
   Also, each $H_2O$ molecule is linked to four other $H_2O$ molecules through H-bonds while each HF molecule is linked only to two other HF molecules.

Hence, decreasing order of b.p. will be : $H_2O > HF > NH_3$

5. **(d)** In $NO_3^-$ ion,
   number of bond pairs (or shared pairs) = 4
   number of lone pairs = 0

$$O = \overset{+}{N} - O^-$$
$$|$$
$$O^-$$

6. **(c)** The electronic configuration of the given molecules are :

$$N_2^+ = \sigma 1s^2 \sigma^* 1s^2 \sigma 2s^2 \sigma^* 2s^2 \pi 2p_x^2$$

$$= \pi p_y^2 \sigma 2p_z^1$$

1 unpaired $e^-$

$$O_2 = \sigma 1s^2 \sigma^* 1s^2 \sigma 2s^2 \sigma^* 2s^2 \sigma 2p_z^2 \pi 2p_x^2$$

$$\approx \pi 2p_y^2$$

$\pi * 2p_x^1 \approx \pi * 2p_y^1$ ; 2 unpaired $e^-s$

$O_2^{2-} = \sigma 1s^2 \sigma * 1s^2 \sigma 2s^2 \sigma * 2s^2 \sigma 2p_z^2 \pi 2p_x^2$

$\approx \pi 2p_y^2$

$\pi * 2p_x^2 \approx \pi * 2p_y^2$ ; no unpaired $e^-s$

$B_2 = \sigma 1s^2 \sigma * 1s^2 \sigma 2s^2 \sigma * 2s^2 \pi 2p_x^1 \approx \pi 2p_y^1$;

2 unpaired $e^-s$

**Trick :** We know that $O_2$ molecule has 2 unpaired electrons. Thus, $O_2^{2-}$ will not have any unpaired electrons.

**7.** **(b)** E.C of $O_2$ :

$\sigma 1s^2 \, \sigma * 1s^2 \, \sigma 2s^2 \, \sigma * 2s^2 \, \sigma 2p_z^2 \pi 2p_x^2 \approx \pi 2p_y^2$

$\pi * 2p_x^1 \approx \pi * 2p_y^1$

$\text{B.O} = \frac{1}{2}(N_b - N_a) = \frac{1}{2}(10-6) = 2$

E.C of $O_2^+$ :

$\sigma 1s^2 \sigma * 1s^2 \sigma 2s^2 \sigma * 2s^2 \sigma 2p_z^2 \pi 2p_x^2 \approx \pi 2p_y^2$

$\pi * 2p_x^1 \approx \pi * 2p_y^0$

$\text{B.O} = \frac{1}{2}(10-5) = 2.5$

E.C of $O_2^-$ :

$\sigma 1s^2 \sigma * 1s^2 \sigma 2s^2 \sigma * 2s^2 \sigma 2p_z^2 \pi 2p_x^2 \approx \pi 2p_y^2$

$\pi * 2p_x^2 \approx \pi * 2p_y^1$

Bond order $= \frac{1}{2}(10-7) = 1.5$

Hence, the correct order of bond order will be :

$O_2^- < O_2 < O_2^+$ .

Assertion & Reason Questions

**1.** **(a)** Assertion and reason are correct and reason is the correct explanation of assertion.

lp – lp repulsion > lp – bp repulsion.

Due to this $H - \overset{..}{N} - H$ bond angle is greater than

$H - \overset{..}{\underset{..}{O}} - H$ bond angle.

**2.** **(a)**

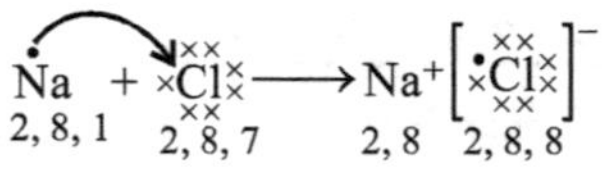

$$\overset{\bullet}{\underset{2,8,1}{Na}} + \underset{2,8,7}{\times\overset{\times\times}{\underset{\times\times}{Cl}}\times} \longrightarrow \underset{2,8}{Na^+} \underset{2,8,8}{\left[\times\overset{\times\times}{\underset{\times\times}{Cl}}\times\right]^-}$$

Short Answer Questions

**1.** **(i)** According to molecular orbital theory electronic configuration of $O_2^+$ and $O_2^-$ species are as follows :

$O_2^+ : (\sigma 1s)^2 (\overset{*}{\sigma} 1s^2)(\sigma 2s)^2 (\overset{*}{\sigma} 2s^2)(\sigma 2p_z)^2$

$$(\pi 2p_x^2 , \pi 2p_y^2)(\overset{*}{\pi} 2p_x^1)$$

$O_2^- : (\sigma 1s)^2 (\overset{*}{\sigma} 1s^2)(\sigma 2s)^2 (\overset{*}{\sigma} 2s^2)(\sigma 2p_z)^2$

$$(\pi 2p_x^2 , \pi 2p_y^2)(\overset{*}{\pi} 2p_x^2 , \overset{*}{\pi} 2p_y^1)$$

Bond order of $O_2^+ = \dfrac{10-5}{2} = \dfrac{5}{2} = 2.5$

Bond order of $O_2^- = \dfrac{10-7}{2} = \dfrac{3}{2} = 1.5$

Higher bond order of $O_2^+$ shows that it is more stable than $O_2^-$ . Both the species have unpaired electrons. So both are paramagnetic in nature.

**2.** **(a)** Compound (I) will form intramolecular hydrogen bond because $NO_2$ and OH group are close together in comparison to that in compound (II)

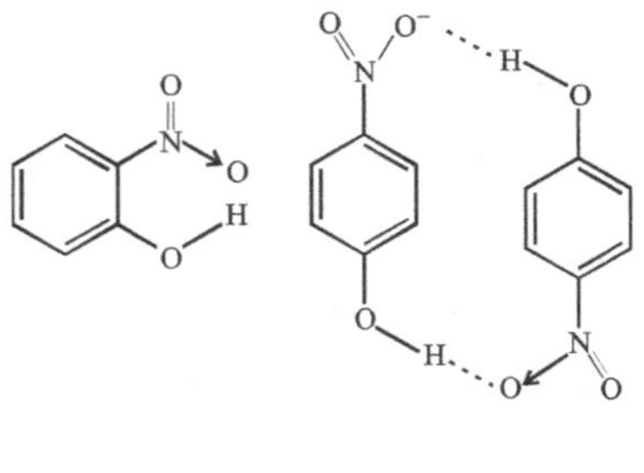

$\qquad$ (I) $\qquad\qquad\qquad$ (II)

**(b)** Compound (II) will have higher melting point because it forms intermolecular hydrogen bonds. Thus, more and more molecules are joined together through hydrogen bond formation.

(c) Due to intermolecular hydrogen bonding compound (I) will not be able to form hydrogen bonds with water thus will be less soluble in it while compound (II) can form hydrogen bond with water more easily and will be soluble in water.

### *Long Answer Question*

1. The valence bond theory was put forward by Heitler and London in 1927. It was later improved and developed by L. Pauling and J.C. Slater in 1931. The valence bond theory is based on the knowledge of atomic orbitals and electronic configurations of elements, overlap criteria of atomic orbitals and stability of molecule.

   The main points of valence bond theory are

   (i) Atoms do not lose their identity even after the formation of the molecule.

   (ii) The bond is formed due to the interaction of only the valence electrons as the two atoms come close to each other. The inner electrons do not participate in the bond formation.

   (iii) During the formation of bond, only the valence electrons from each bonded atom lose their identity. The other electrons remain unaffected.

   (iv) The stability of bond is accounted by the fact that the formation of bond is accompanied by release of energy. The molecule has minimum energy at a certain distance between the atoms known as internuclear distance. Larger the decrease in energy, stronger will be the bond formed.

# 5. States of Matter

**5.1** What will be the minimum pressure required to compress 500 dm³ of air at 1 bar to 200 dm³ at 30°C?

**Ans.** $P_1 = 1$ bar,  $V_1 = 500$ dm³
$P_2 = ?$,  $V_2 = 200$ dm³
As temperature remains constant at 30°C,
$P_1V_1 = P_2V_2$
1 bar × 500 dm³ = $P_2$ × 200 dm³

or  $P_2 = \dfrac{500}{200}$ bar = 2.5 bar

**5.2** A vessel of 120 mL capacity contains a certain amount of gas at 35°C and 1.2 bar pressure. The gas is transferred to another vessel of volume 180 mL at 35°C. What would be its pressure ?

**Ans.** $V_1 = 120$ mL,  $P_1 = 1.2$ bar,  $T_1 = 35°C$
$V_2 = 180$ mL,  $P_2 = ?$,  $T_2 = 35°C$
As température remains constant, $P_1V_1 = P_2V_2$
(1.2 bar) (120 mL) = $P_2$ (180 mL)
or  $P_2 = 0 \cdot 8$ bar

**5.3** Using the equation of state, PV = n RT, show that at a given temperature, density of a gas is proportional to gas pressure, P.

**Ans.** Using PV = nRT

$$PV = \frac{wRT}{M}, \text{ where } n = \text{No. of moles } = \frac{\text{weight}(w)}{\text{Mol.Mass}(M)}$$

$$\therefore \ P = \frac{wRT}{VM}$$

$$P = d\frac{RT}{M}, \text{ where density d = weight / Volume}$$

$$\text{or } d = \frac{MP}{RT}$$

Thus, for a given temperature (M and R are constant) , the density of gas is proportional to gas pressure i.e. $d \propto P$.

**5.4** At 0°C, the density of a certain oxide of a gas at 2 bar is same as that of dinitrogen at 5 bar. What is the molecular mass of the oxide ?

**Ans.** Using the expression,  $d = \dfrac{MP}{RT}$

$\therefore \ d_1 = d_2$

$$\Rightarrow \frac{M_1P_1}{RT} = \frac{M_2P_2}{RT}$$

$$\Rightarrow \frac{2 \times M_1}{RT} = \frac{5 \times 28}{RT}$$

$M_1 = 70$ u

**5.5** Pressure of 1 g of an ideal gas A at 27°C is found to be 2 bar. When 2 g of another ideal gas B is introduced in the same flask at same temperature, the pressure becomes 3 bar. Find the relationship between their molecular masses.

**Ans.** Suppose molecular masses of A and B are $M_A$ and $M_B$ respectively. Then their number of moles will be

$$n_A = \frac{1}{M_A}, n_B = \frac{2}{M_B} \qquad \left( \because n = \frac{\text{given mass}}{\text{molar mass}} \right)$$

$P_A = 2$ bar, $P_A + P_B = 3$ bar, i.e.,  $P_B = 1$ bar
Applying the relation PV = nRT
$P_AV = n_ART$,   $P_BV = n_BRT$

$$\therefore \ \frac{P_A}{P_B} = \frac{n_A}{n_B} = \frac{P_A}{P_B} = \frac{1/M_A}{2/M_B}$$

$$\text{or } \frac{M_B}{M_A} = 2 \times \frac{P_A}{P_B} = 2 \times \frac{2}{1} = 4 \text{ or } M_B = 4 M_A$$

**5.6** The drain cleaner, Drainex contains small bits of aluminium which react with caustic soda to produce dihydrogen. What volume of dihydrogen at 20°C and 1 bar will be released when 0.15 g of aluminium reacts?

**Ans.**
$$\underset{2 \times 27g}{2Al} + 2NaOH + 2H_2O \longrightarrow 2NaAlO_2 + \underset{3 \times 22.4 \text{ L}}{3H_2}$$

$H_2$ produced at STP from 0.15 g Al

$$= \frac{3 \times 22400 \times 0.15}{54} \text{ml} = 186.7 \text{ ml}$$

$$\underset{\text{(STP)}}{\frac{P_1V_1}{T_1}} = \underset{\text{(Required conditions)}}{\frac{P_2V_2}{T_2}}$$

We know 1 bar = 0.987 atm

$$\frac{1\,\text{atm} \times 186.7\,\text{ml}}{273\,\text{K}} = \frac{0.987\,\text{atm} \times V_2}{293\,\text{K}}$$

or $V_2$ = 203 ml

**5.7** **What will be the pressure exerted by a mixture of 3.2 g of methane and 4.4 g of carbon dioxide contained in a 9 dm$^3$ flask at 27°C ?**

**Ans.** $P = \dfrac{n}{V}\ RT = \dfrac{wRT}{MV}$

$$n_{CH_4} = \frac{3.2}{16}\,\text{mol} = 0.2\,\text{mol}$$

$$n_{CO_2} = \frac{4.4}{44}\,\text{mol} = 0.1\,\text{mol}$$

$$PV = \left(n_{CH_4} + n_{CO_2}\right)RT$$

$$\frac{0.3 \times 0.0821\,\text{dm}^3\text{atm}\,\text{K}^{-1}\text{mol}^{-1} \times 300\,\text{K}}{9\,\text{dm}^3}$$

$P_{total}$ = 0.82 atm

**5.8** **What will be the pressure of the gaseous mixture when 0.5 L of H$_2$ at 0.8 bar and 2.0 L of dioxygen at 0.7 bar are introduced in a 1 L vessel at 27°C ?**

**Ans.** Partial pressure of H$_2$ in 1L vessel
$P_1$ = 0.8 bar, $V_1$ = 0.5L,
$P_2$ = ? $V_2$ = 1.0 L
Temperature remaining constant,
$P_1 V_1 = P_2 V_2$ (Boyle's Law)
or, 0.8 bar × 0.5L = $P_2$ × 1.0 L
or $P_{H_2}$ = 0.40 bar

Partial pressure of O$_2$ in 1L vessel
$P'_1$ = 0.7 bar, $V'_1$ = 2.0 L, $P'_2$ = ? $V'_2$ = 1.0 L
Temperature remaining constant
$P'_1 V'_1 = P'_2 V'_2$
or, 0.7 bar × 2.0 L = $P'_2$ × 1.0 L
or, $P'_2$ = 1.4 bar or, $P_{O_2}$ = 1.4 bar

Total pressure = $P_{H_2}$ + $P_{O_2}$ = 0.4 bar + 1.4 bar = 1.8 bar

**5.9** **Density of a gas is found to be 5.46 g/dm$^3$ at 27°C at 2 bar pressure. What will be its density at STP ?**

**Ans.** $d = \dfrac{MP}{RT}$

For the same gas at different temperature and pressure

$$\frac{d_1}{d_2} = \frac{P_1}{T_1} \times \frac{T_2}{P_2}$$

Given that
$d_1$ = 5.46 g dm$^{-3}$,
$T_1$ = 27° C = 300 K, $P_1$ = 2 bar
At S.T.P.
$d_2$ = ?, $T_2$ = 0°C = 273K, $P_2$ = 1 bar

$$\frac{5.46\,\text{g dm}^{-3}}{d_2} = \frac{2\,\text{bar}}{300\,\text{K}} \times \frac{273\,\text{K}}{1\,\text{bar}}$$

or, $d_2$ = 3 g dm$^{-3}$

**5.10** **34.05 mL of phosphorus vapour weighs 0.0625 g at 546°C and 0.1 bar pressure. What is the molar mass of phosphorus ?**

**Ans.** Volume at 0°C and 1 bar pressure $= \dfrac{P_1 V_1}{T_1} = \dfrac{P_2 V_2}{T_2}$

or, $\dfrac{0.1\,\text{bar} \times 34.05\,\text{mL}}{(546+273)\,\text{K}} = \dfrac{1 \times V_2}{273\,\text{K}}$

$$V_2 = \frac{0.1 \times 34.05 \times 273}{(819\,\text{K})}$$

or, $V_2$ = 1.135 mL.

∴ Weight of 1.135 mL of vapour at 0°C and 1 bar pressure = 0.0625 g

∴ Weight of 22700 mL of vapour at 0°C and 1 bar pressure

$$= \frac{0.0625}{1.135} \times 22700 = 1250\,\text{g}$$

∴ Molar mass = 125 g mol$^{-1}$

**5.11** **A student forgot to add the reaction mixture to the round bottomed flask at 27°C but instead he/she placed the flask on the flame. After a lapse of time, he realized his mistake, and using a pyrometer he found the temperature of the flask was 477°C. What fraction of air would have been expelled out ?**

**Ans.** Let us assume that volume of vessel = V cm$^3$
or, volume of air in the flask at 27°C = V cm$^3$

Since, $\dfrac{V_1}{T_1} = \dfrac{V_2}{T_2}$ or $\dfrac{V}{300} = \dfrac{V_2}{750}$

or, $V_2$ = 2.5 V

∴ Volume expelled = 2.5 V – V = 1.5 V

∴ Fraction of air expelled $= \dfrac{1.5V}{2.5V} = \dfrac{3}{5}$

**5.12** **Calculate the temperature of 4.0 mole of a gas occupying 5 dm$^3$ at 3.32 bar. (R = 0.083 bar dm$^3$ K$^{-1}$ mol$^{-1}$).**

**Ans.** $PV = nRT$

or $T = \dfrac{PV}{nR} = \dfrac{3.32\,\text{bar} \times 5\,\text{dm}^3}{4.0\,\text{mol} \times 0.083\,\text{bar dm}^3\text{K}^{-1}\text{mol}^{-1}} = 50\,\text{K}$

**5.13** **Calculate the total number of electrons present in 1.4 g of dinitrogen gas**

**Ans.** Gram molecular mass of dinitrogen = 28 g
28 g of dinitrogen contains 6.023 × 10$^{23}$ molecules.
∴ 1.4 g of dinitrogen would contain

$$= \frac{6.023 \times 10^{23} \times 1.4}{28} = 3.011 \times 10^{22}\ \text{molecules}$$

Since 1 atom of nitrogen consists of 7 electrons then one nitrogen molecule would contain 14 electrons 3.011 × 10$^{22}$ molecules of nitrogen would contain = 14 × 3.011 × 10$^{22}$
= 4.215 × 10$^{23}$ electrons.

**5.14** How much time would it take to distribute one Avogadro number of wheat grains, if $10^{10}$ grains are distributed each second?

**Ans.** One Avogadro number of wheat grains $6.022 \times 10^{23}$ grains
Time required to distribute $10^{10}$ grains = 1 sec
Time required to distribute $6.022 \times 10^{23}$ grains

$$= \frac{6.023 \times 10^{23}}{10^{10}} \sec = 6.022 \times 10^{13} \sec$$

$$= \frac{6.022 \times 10^{13}}{60 \times 60 \times 24 \times 365} \text{years} = 19.09 \times 10^{5} \text{ years.}$$

**5.15** Calculate the total pressure in a mixture of 8 g of dioxygen and 4g of dihydrogen confined in a vessel of 1 dm$^3$ at 27°C. R = 0.083 bar dm$^3$ K$^{-1}$ mol$^{-1}$.

**Ans.** Molar mass of $O_2$ = 32g mol$^{-1}$
∴ 8g of $O_2$ = 8 / 32 g mol$^{-1}$ = 0.25 mol
Molar mass of $H_2$ = 2 g mol$^{-1}$
∴ 4g of $H_2$ = 4 / 2 g mol$^{-1}$ = 2 mol
∴ Total number of moles (n)
= 2 mol + 0.25 mol = 2.25 mol
V = 1 dm$^3$, T = 27° C
= 300 K , R = 0.083 bar dm$^3$ K$^{-1}$ mol$^{-1}$

$$PV = n\,RT \text{ or, } P = \frac{nRT}{V}$$

$$= \frac{2.25\text{mol} \times 0.083\text{bar dm}^3\text{K}^{-1}\text{mol}^{-1} \times 300\text{K}}{1\text{dm}^3}$$

= 56.025 bar

**5.16** Pay load is defined as the difference between the mass of displaced air and the mass of the balloon. Calculate the pay load when a balloon of radius 10 m, mass 100 kg is filled with helium at 1.66 bar at 27°C. (Density of air = 1.2 kg m$^{-3}$ and R = 0.083 bar dm$^3$ K$^{-1}$ mol$^{-1}$).

**Ans.** Volume of the balloon
= $4/3\pi\,r^3$ = 4/3 × 22/7 × (10m)$^3$ = 4190.5 m$^3$
Volume of He filled at 1.66 bar and 27°C
= 4190.5 m$^3$
Calculation of mass of He PV = nRT = (w/M) RT

$$\text{or, } w = \frac{MPV}{RT}$$

$$= \frac{4 \times 10^{-3}\text{kg mol}^{-1} \times 1.66\text{bar} \times 4190.5 \times 10^3\text{dm}^3}{0.083\text{bar dm}^3\text{K}^{-1}\text{mol}^{-1} \times 300\text{K}}$$

= 1117.5 kg
∴ Total mass of (balloon + He)
= 100 + 1117.5 = 1217.5 kg
Maximum mass of the air that can be displaced by the balloon to go up = Volume × Density
or, 4190.5 m$^3$ × 1.2 kg m$^{-3}$ = 5028.6 kg
payload = 5028.6 −1217.5 kg = 3811.1 kg

**5.17** Calculate the volume occupied by 8.8 g of CO$_2$ at 31.1°C and 1 bar pressure. R = 0.083 bar L K$^{-1}$ mol$^{-1}$.

**Ans.** $PV = nRT$ or, $V = \dfrac{nRT}{P} = \dfrac{wRT}{MP}$ $\left(\text{because n} = \dfrac{w}{M}\right)$

$$V = \frac{8.8\text{g}}{44\text{g mol}^{-1}} \times \frac{0.083\text{ bar L K}^{-1}\text{mol}^{-1} \times (273 + 31.1)\text{K}}{1\text{bar}}$$

= 5.05 L.

**5.18** 2.9 g of a gas at 95°C occupied the same volume as 0.184 g of dihydrogen at 17°C, at the same pressure. What is the molar mass of the gas ?

**Ans.** Let the molar mass of the gas be $M_x$
We know $P_1 = P_2$ and $V_1 = V_2$
or $P_1 V_1 = P_2 V_2$
or $n_1 RT_1 = n_2 RT_2$ or $n_1 T_1 = n_2 T_2$

$$\text{or } \frac{W_1}{M_1} T_1 = \frac{W_2}{M_2} T_2$$

$$\therefore \frac{2.9}{M_x} \times (95 + 273) = \frac{0.184}{2} \times (17 + 273)$$

$$\text{or } M_x = \frac{2.9 \times 368 \times 2}{0.184 \times 290} = 40\text{g mol}^{-1}$$

**5.19** A mixture of dihydrogen and dioxygen at one bar pressure contains 20% by weight of dihydrogen. Calculate the partial pressure of dihydrogen.

**Ans.** $\because$ Moles $= \dfrac{\text{given mass}}{\text{molar mass}}$

$n_{H_2}$ = 20 / 2 = 10 moles,
$n_{O_2}$ = 80 / 32 = 2.5 moles

$$P_{H_2} = \frac{n_{H_2}}{n_{H_2} + n_{O_2}} \times P_{Total} = \frac{10}{10 + 2.5} \times 1\text{bar.} = 0.8\text{ bar}$$

**5.20** What would be the SI unit for the quantity $pV^2T^2/n$?

**Ans.** $$\frac{\text{Nm}^{-2} \times (\text{m}^3)^2 \times \text{K}^2}{\text{mol}} = \text{Nm}^4\text{K}^2\text{mol}^{-1}$$

**5.21** In terms of Charle's law explain why −273°C is the lowest possible temperature?

**Ans.** At −273°C, volume of the gas becomes equal to zero, i.e., the gas ceases to exist.

**5.22** Critical temperature for carbon dioxide and methane are 31.1°C and − 81.9°C respectively. Which of these has stronger intermolecular forces and why?

**Ans.** Higher the critical temperature, more easily the gas can be liquefied, i.e., greater are the intermolecular forces of attraction. Hence, CO$_2$ has stronger intermolecular forces than CH$_4$.

**5.23** Explain the physical significance of the van der Waal's parameters?

**Ans.** '$a$' is a measure of the magnitude of the intermolecular forces of attraction while b is a measure of the effective size of the gas molecules.

## SECTION B — PRACTICE QUESTIONS

### MULTIPLE CHOICE QUESTIONS

1. 600 c.c. of a gas at a pressure of 750 mm of Hg is compressed to 500 c.c. Taking the temperature to remain constant, the increase in pressure, is
   (a) 150 mm of Hg
   (b) 250 mm of Hg
   (c) 350 mm of Hg
   (d) 450 mm of Hg

2. On a ship sailing in pacific ocean where temperature is 23.4°C, a balloon is filled with 2 L air. What will be the volume of the balloon when the ship reaches Indian ocean, where temperature is 26.1°C ?
   (a) 2.018 L
   (b) 2.8 L
   (c) 3.5 L
   (d) 1.5 L

3. The correct value of the gas constant '$R$' is close to :
   (a) 0.082 litre-atmosphere K
   (b) 0.082 litre-atmosphere $K^{-1}$ $mol^{-1}$
   (c) 0.082 litre – $atmosphere^{-1}$ K $mol^{-1}$
   (d) 0.082 litre $^{-1}$ atmosphere $^{-1}$ K mol

4. If three unreactive gases having partial pressures $P_A$, $P_B$ and $P_C$ and their moles are 1, 2 and 3 respectively then their total pressure will be
   (a) $P = P_A + P_B + P_C$
   (b) $P = \dfrac{P_A + P_B + P_C}{6}$
   (c) $P = \dfrac{\sqrt{P_A + P_B + P_C}}{3}$
   (d) None of these

5. Value of universal gas constant (R) depends upon
   (a) Number of moles of gas
   (b) Volume of gas
   (c) Temperature of gas
   (d) None of these

6. What is the ratio of pressure of the 2 g of hydrogen to that of 4 g of helium at temperature of 298 K, 20 mL volume? (consider the ideal behaviour)
   (a) 1 : 2
   (b) 2 : 1
   (c) 1 : 1
   (d) 2 : 2

7. The van der Waal's constant '$a$' for four gases P, Q, R and S are 4.17, 3.59, 6.71 and 3.8 atm $L^2$ $mol^{-2}$ respectively. Therefore, the ascending order of their liquefaction is
   (a) R < P < S < Q
   (b) Q < S < R < P
   (c) Q < S < P < R
   (d) R < P < Q < S

8. An ideal gas can't be liquefied because
   (a) its critical temperature is always above 0°C
   (b) Its molecules are relatively smaller in size
   (c) it solidifies before becoming a liquid
   (d) forces between its molecules are negligible

9. Select the one that when used would be considered as best condition for liquefaction of a gas.
   (a) Increasing the temperature.
   (b) Decreasing the pressure.
   (c) Increasing the pressure and decreasing the temperature.
   (d) Decreasing the pressure and increasing the temperature.

10. Which of the following phenomena is caused by surface tension ?
    (a) Particles at the bottom of river remain separated but they stick together when taken out.
    (b) A liquid rise in a thin capillary.
    (c) Small drops of mercury form spherical bead instead of spreading on the surface.
    (d) All of the above

11. The correct order of viscosity of the following liquids will be
    (a) Water < methyl alcohol < dimethyl ether < glycerol
    (b) methyl alcohol < glycerol < water < dimethyl ether
    (c) dimethyl ether < methyl alcohol < water < glycerol
    (d) glycerol < dimethyl ether < water < methyl alcohol

12. A liquid can exist only
    (a) between triple point and critical temperature
    (b) at any temperature above the melting point
    (c) between melting point and critical temperature
    (d) between boiling and melting temperature

### ASSERTION & REASON QUESTIONS

**DIRECTIONS (Qs. 1-6) :** *Each of these questions contains an assertion followed by reason. Read them carefully and answer the question on the basis of following options. You have to select the one that best describes the two statements.*
(a) If both Assertion and Reason are correct and the Reason is a correct explanation of the Assertion.
(b) If both Assertion and Reason are correct but Reason is not a correct explanation of the Assertion.
(c) If the Assertion is correct but Reason is incorrect.
(d) If the Assertion is incorrect but the Reason is correct.

1. **Assertion :** Plot of $p$ vs $1/V$ is a straight line.
   **Reason :** At constant temperature, pressure is directly proportional to volume.

2. **Assertion :** At low pressure and high temperature, some gases like $Cl_2$, $N_2$ and $CH_4$ behave as ideal gas.
   **Reason :** At low temperature and high pressure, real gases behave as ideal gas.

3. **Assertion :** Non-polar molecular substances have London forces.
   **Reason :** London forces are the weakest intermolecular forces that depend on the molecular mass of substances.

4. **Assertion:** High value of van der Waals' constant '$a$', favours the liquefaction of gas.
   **Reason:** The van der Waals constant '$a$' depends on the volume occupies by gas molecules.

**5.** **Assertion:** At constant temperature, visocisity of liquid remains same.
**Reason:** When temperature increases of a liquid, viscosity decreases as the kinetic energy inc.

**6.** **Assertion:** For an ideal gas, the graph of Z (compressibility factor) vs. p (pressure) will be a straight line.

**Reason:** $Z = \dfrac{pV}{nRT} = 1$ for an ideal gas as $pV = nRT$.

## CASE/PASSAGE BASED QUESTIONS

**DIRECTIONS (Qs. 1-5) :** *Read the following case/passage and answer the questions.*

Van der Waals equation is an equation relating the relationship between the pressure, volume, temperature, and amount of real gases. For a real gas containing '$n$' moles, the equation is written as;

$$\left(P + \frac{an^2}{V^2}\right)(V - nb) = nRT$$

where, $P$, $V$, $T$, $n$ are the pressure, volume, temperature and moles of the gas. '$a$' and '$b$' constants specific to each gas.
As constant temperature, a decrease in pressure increases the volume(V). Hence at low pressures, the volume will be larger.

So, the correction factor in pressure $\left(a\dfrac{n^2}{V^2}\right)$ becomes very small and negligible.
Again the volume of the gas will be larger compared to the volume of the molecules ($n$, $b$). Hence, the volume correction also will be small and negligible.
As the correction factor becomes negligible, pressure and volume of the real gases will be equal to that of ideal gases. Interestingly, all real gases behave like ideal gases at low pressures and high temperatures.

**1.** A gas described by van der Waal's equation
(i) behaves similar to an ideal gas in the limit of large molar volume
(ii) behaves similar to an ideal gas in the limit of large pressure
(iii) is characterised by van der Waal's coefficients that are dependent on the identity of the gas but are independent of the temperature
(iv) has the pressure that is lower than the pressure exerted by the same gas behaving ideally
(a) (i) and (ii)      (b) (i) and (iii)
(c) (i), (ii) and (iii)      (d) (ii) and (iv)

**2.** In van der Waal's equation of state of the gas law, the constant '$b$' is a measure of
(a) volume occupied by the molecules
(b) intermolecular attraction
(c) intermolecular repulsions
(d) intermolecular collisions per unit volume

**3.** Which of the following statements are correct ?
(i) Real gases show deviations from ideal gas law because molecules interact with each other.
(ii) Due to interaction of molecules the pressure exerted by the gas is given as :
$$p_{real} = p_{ideal} + \frac{an^2}{V^2}$$
(iii) Value of '$a$' is measure of magnitude of intermolecular attractive forces within the gas and depends on temperature and pressure of gas.
(iv) At high pressure, volume occupied by the molecules also becomes significant because instead of moving in volume V, these are now restricted to volume (V-nb)
(a) (i) and (iv)      (b) (i), (ii) and (iii)
(c) (i), (iii) and (iv)      (d) (i) and (iii)

**4.** In van der Waal's equation of state for a non ideal gas, the term that accounts for intermolecular forces is
(a) $(V - b)$      (b) $RT$
(c) $\left(P + \dfrac{a}{V^2}\right)$      (d) $(RT)^{-1}$

**5.** The compressibility factor for a real gas at high pressure is :
(a) $1 + \dfrac{RT}{Pb}$      (b) $1$
(c) $1 + \dfrac{Pb}{RT}$      (d) $1 - \dfrac{Pb}{RT}$

## VERY SHORT ANSWER QUESTIONS

**1.** State Charle's Law.
**2.** Is volume directly or inversely proportional to pressure at constant temperature ?
**3.** Given are the boiling point of different liquids $CS_2 = 46.3°$ C ; $H_2O = 100°C$ ; $CCl_4 = 77°C$. In which liquid the intermolecular forces of attraction are weakest?
**4.** Define Boyle's law.
**5.** Liquids are less compressible than gases. Explain.
**6.** The tyre of automobile is inflated to lesser pressure in summer than in winter. Why ?
**7.** The size of weather balloon becomes larger and larger as it ascends up into higher altitudes. Why?
**8.** State Graham's law of diffusion.
**9.** What do you mean by Boyle temperature ? Give
**10.** Give most common application of Dalton's law.
**11.** Name any three measurable properties of gases.
**12.** What is an isotherm ?
**13.** Liquid is transferred from a large beaker to a small beaker, what will be the effect on its vapour pressure ?
**14.** Why does a gas expand indefinitely ?
**15.** Explain, why the bubbles of a gas in a boiling liquid generally increase in volume as they approach the upper surface ?
**16.** What is the effect of temperature on the vapour pressure of a liquid ?

17. What is thermodynamic scale of temperature?
18. Why is it not possible to cool a gas at 0 K ?
19. What is the molar gas volume at STP for an ideal gas ?
20. What is the density of oxygen, $O_2$ in grams per litre at $25°C$ and $0.850$ atm ?
21. How is the mole fraction of a component gas related its partial pressure and the total pressure.
22. How does the vapour pressure depend on the amount of a liquid ?
23. What is the effect of pressure on (i) viscosity, (ii) surface tension, (iii) density of liquid ?
24. What is boiling point of water at (i) higher altitudes, (ii) in pressure cooker ?
25. Why is moist air lighter than dry air ?
26. What is an isobar ?
27. Define root mean square velocity.
28. What are critical constants of a gas ?
29. What is SI unit of (i) Viscosity (ii) Surface tension.
30. Define critical temperature of gas.
31. What are real gases ?
32. Why liquids diffuse slowly as compared to gases ?
33. An astronaut in an orbiting space-ships spilled a few drops of his drink, and the liquid floated around the cabin. In what geometric shape is each drop most likely to be found? Explain.

## SHORT ANSWER QUESTIONS

1. At STP a given quantity of gas occupies 5.00 litres. What is the temperature of this same quantity of gas at the same pressure when it occupies a volume of 10 litres?
2. What are the two practical implications of the Boyle's law?
3. A perfect gas at 340 K is heated at constant pressure until its volume has increased by 18 per cent. What is the final temperature of the gas?
4. A bacterial culture isolated from sewage produced 41.3 ml of methane, $CH_4$ at $31°C$ and 753 mm Hg. What is the volume of this methane at STP?
5. How many litres of chlorine gas, $Cl_2$, can be obtained at $40°C$ and 1.03 atm from 9.41 g of hydrogen chloride, according to the following equation?
$$2KMnO_4 \text{ (s)} + 16HCl \text{ (aq)} \rightarrow$$
$$8H_2O \text{ (}l\text{)} + 2KCl \text{ (aq)} + 2MnCl_2 \text{ (aq)} + 5Cl_2 \text{ (g)}$$
6. Explain why 15g of steam at $100°C$ melts more ice than 15g of liquid water at $100°C$?
7. Explain why liquids like ether and acetone are kept in cool places?
8. A cylinder contains nitrogen gas and a small amount of liquid water at a temperature of $25°C$ (the vapour pressure of water is 23.8 mm Hg). The total pressure is 600 mm Hg. A piston is pushed into the cylinder until the volume is halved. What is the final total pressure?

9. What names are given to the following ideal gas relationships ?
   (a) Volume and moles at constant T and $p$.
   (b) Pressure of non-reacting gases in mixture of constant T and V.
   (c) Volume and temperature in Kelvin at constant $p$ and $n$.
10. What is the volume of a sample of oxygen at a pressure of 2.50 atm, if its volume is 3.15 L at 1.00 atm ? The temperature remains constant.
11. A sample x of hydrogen gas is found to occupy 906 $cm^3$ of volume at 300 K. Calculate the temperature at which it will occupy 500 $cm^3$ of volume? (Assuming amount and pressure remains constant.)
12. A quantity of hydrogen is confined in a chamber of constant volume. When the chamber is immersed in a bath of melting ice, the pressure of the gas is 1000 torr. What is the temperature in Celsius, when the pressure in manometer indicates are absolute pressure of 400 torr ?
13. Calculate the value of R in S.I. units for one mole gas at STP.
14. Using the kinetic theory, account for the observed behaviour of gases described by Dalton's law.
15. Why in case of hydrogen and helium the compressibility factor is always greater than 1?
16. Why glycerin is more viscous than ethanol?
17. Viscosity of a liquid arises due to strong intermolecular forces existing between the molecules. Stronger the intermolecular forces, greater is the viscosity. Name the intermolecular forces existing in the following liquids and arrange them in the increasing order of their viscosities. Also give reason for the assigned order in one line.
    Water, hexane ($CH_3CH_2CH_2CH_2CH_2CH_3$), glycerine ($CH_2OHCH(OH)CH_2OH$)
18. What are the causes of deviations from ideal behaviour?
19. An open vessel at $27°C$ is heated until three-fifth of the air in it has been expelled. Assuming that the volume of the vessel remains constant, find the temperature to which the vessel has been heated.

## LONG ANSWER QUESTIONS

1. (i) A quantity of hydrogen is confined in a chamber of constant volume. When the chamber is immersed in a bath of melting ice, the pressure of the gas is 1000atm. (a) What is the Celsius temperature when the pressure manometer indicates an absolute pressure of 400 atm? (b) What pressure will be indicated when the chamber is brought to 100 °C?
   (ii) A steel tank containing air at 15 atm pressure at 15° C is provided with a safety valve that will yield at a pressure of 30 atm. To what minimum temperature must the air be heated to blow the safety valve?

2. Two flasks A and B have equal volume. Flask A contains $H_2$ and is maintained at 300 K while flask B contains an equal mass of $CH_4$ gas and is maintained at 600 K.
   (a) Which flask contains greater number of molecules? How many times more?
   (b) In which flask is the pressure greater? How many times greater?
3. (i) Derive the formula to calculate molar mass of gas from ideal gas equation
   (ii) Give difference between ideal and real gas.
4. (i) One mole of the $CO_2$ occupies 1.5 L at 25°C.

Calculate the pressure exerted by the gas using:
(a) an ideal gas equation
(b) van der Waal's equation if:
   a = 3.012 atm mol$^{-2}$ and
   b = 0.04 L mol$^{-1}$.
(ii) 1 L of $O_2$ and 1 L of $H_2$ are taken in a vessel of 2 L capacity at NTP. The gases are made to combine to form water.
Calculate:
(i) the moles and weight of water formed.
(ii) the amount of gas left in vessel.
(iii) the total pressure if the vessel is heated to 100°C.
(iv) moles of $O_2$ used for the formation of water.

## SOLUTIONS

### *Multiple Choice Questions*

1. **(a)** Given initial volume $(V_1)$ = 600 c.c.; Initial pressure $(P_1)$ = 750 mm of Hg and final volume $(V_2)$ = 500 c.c. according to Boyle's law,
$$P_1V_1 = P_2V_2$$
$$750 \times 600 = P_2 \times 500$$
or $P_2 = \dfrac{750 \times 600}{500} = 900$ mm of Hg

Therefore, increase of pressure = $(900 - 750) = 150$ mm of Hg.

2. **(a)** $V_1 = 2$ L, $T_2 = (26.1 + 273)$ K = 299.1 K, $V_2 = ?$
$T_1 = (23.4 + 273)$ K = 296.4 K

From Charle's law, $\dfrac{V_1}{T_1} = \dfrac{V_2}{T_2} \Rightarrow V_2 = \dfrac{V_1 T_2}{T_1}$

$\Rightarrow V_2 = \dfrac{2L \times 299.1K}{296.4K} = 2L \times 1.009$
$= 2.018$ L

3. **(b)** $R = 0.082$ litre atm K$^{-1}$ mol$^{-1}$.
4. **(a)** By Dalton's Law.
5. **(d)** Value of gas constant depends only upon units of measurement.
6. **(c)** Number of moles, temperature and volume are same.
7. **(c)** Easily liquefiable gases have greater intermolecular forces which is represented by high value of '$a$'. The greater the value of '$a$' more will be liquefiability.
So, the order is Q < S < P < R.
8. **(d)** In the ideal gas, the intermolecular forces of attraction are negligible and hence, it cannot be liquefied.
9. **(c)** It brings molecules of gases closer.
10. **(d)** All these phenomena are caused by surface tension.
11. **(c)** The correct order of viscosity of the given liquids is dimethyl ether < methyl alcohol < water < glycerol, due to increasing H-bonding.
12. **(d)** A substance exists as a liquid above its m. p. and below its b. p.

### *Assertion & Reason Questions*

1. **(c)** According to Boyle's law, at constant temperature for fixed amount of gas.
$P \propto 1/V$
$PV = $ constant
Therefore, plot of $p$ vs. $1/V$ at constant temperature is a straight line.
2. **(c)** $Cl_2$, $N_2$ and $CH_4$ behave as ideal gases at low pressure and high temperature because under these conditions molecular interactions are negligible and the volume occupied one gaseous molecule is negligible in comparison to the volume of gas.
3. **(b)** When two non-polar atoms or molecules attract to each other due to the formation of temporary dipoles is known as London forces. Interaction energy is inversely proportional to the sixth power of distance between two interacting particles ($1/r$, where '$r$' is the distance between two particles).
4. **(c)** Greater the value of van der Waals constant '$a$', greater is the intermolecular interaction. The critical temperature of a gas depends on the strength of the intermolecular forces, if critical temperature is higher than liquefaction of gases is higher.
5. **(a)** Viscosity is a measure of resistance to flow which arises due to the internal friction between layers of fluid flows. Strong intermolecular forces between molecules hold them together and resist movement of layers past one another.
When temperature of a liquid, increases viscosity decreases as the kinetic energy of molecules increases and internal friction between the liquid layers decreases.

6. **(a)** Compressibility (Z) $= \dfrac{PV}{nRT}$

For ideal gas, Z = 1 at all temperatures and pressures because PV = nRT. The graph of Z vs. P will be a straight line parallel to pressure axis. For gases which deviate from ideality, value of Z deviate from unity.

### *Case/Passage Based Questions*

1. **(b)**
   (i) At very large molar volume

   $$P + \frac{a}{V_m^2} \approx P \text{ and } V_m - b = V_m$$

   (iii) According to van der Waal's equation '$a$' and '$b$' are independent of temperature.

2. **(a)** In van der Waal's equation, '$b$' is for volume correction.

3. **(a)** For statement (ii), $P_{real} = P_{ideal} - \dfrac{an^2}{V^2}$

   For statement (iii), value of '$a$' is independent of temperature and pressure.

4. **(c)** $\left(P + \dfrac{a}{V^2}\right)(V - b) = RT$; Here $\left(P + \dfrac{a}{V^2}\right)$ represents the intermolecular forces.

5. **(c)** $\left(P + \dfrac{a}{V^2}\right)(V - b) = RT$ at high pressure $\dfrac{a}{V^2}$ can be neglected

   $PV - Pb = RT \quad$ and $\quad PV = RT + Pb$

   $$\frac{PV}{RT} = 1 + \frac{Pb}{RT}$$

   $$Z = 1 + \frac{Pb}{RT}; \quad Z > 1 \text{ at high pressure}$$

### *Very Short Answer Questions*

1. At constant pressure the volume of given mass of gas is directly proportional to absolute temperature.
2. Volume is inversely proportional to pressure according to Boyle's law.
3. $CS_2$
4. The volume of a given mass of gas is inversely proportional to pressure at constant temperature.
   $V \propto 1/P$ or $PV = $ constant.
5. Liquid molecules have stronger intermolecular forces of attraction as compared to gases, thus they are less compressible than gases.
6. Air expands more during summer than winter.
7. At higher altitudes, atmospheric pressure is less, therefore, air inside balloon exerts pressure and it becomes larger and larger.
8. It states that the rate of diffusion of gases is inversely proportional to square root of molecular masses at constant temperature and pressure.
9. Boyle temperature is a temperature at which most of real gases show ideal gas behaviour over wide range of pressure.
10. The air pressure decreases with increase in altitude. That is why jet aeroplane flying at high altitude need pressurization of the cabin so that partial pressure of oxygen is sufficient for breathing.
11. (i) Volume         (ii) Pressure
    (iii) Temperature

12. The graph plotted between P and V for a gas at constant temperature is called an isotherm.
13. There will be no effect on the vapour pressure of a liquid because vapour pressure is an intensive property.
14. Because the intermolecular forces of attraction among the molecules of a gas are negligible.
15. Because on approach of the upper surface, the pressure on them decreases and hence volume increases.
16. Vapour pressure is directly proportional to the temperature.
17. The temperature scale based on absolute zero ($0K = -273.15°C$) is known as the thermodynamic scale of temperature.
18. It is not possible to cool gas at 0K because all gases condenses to liquids or solids before this temperature is reached.
19. Molar gas volume (volume of one mole of gas) at $0°C$ and under 1 atm is 22.4 L or $22.4 \times 10^{-3}$ m³.
20. $d = \dfrac{PM}{RT}$

    $$d = \frac{0.850 \text{ atm} \times 32.0 \text{ g mol}^{-1}}{0.0821 \text{ L atm mol}^{-1} \times 298 \text{ K}} = 1.11 \text{ gL}^{-1}$$

21. Mole fraction equals the partial pressure divided by the total pressure.

    $$x_i = \frac{p_i}{P_{total}}$$

22. The vapour pressure is a kinetic phenomenon. It is independent of the amount of a liquid. It only depends on the temperature.
23. Increase in pressure increases viscosity, surface tension and density because force of attraction increases.
24. (i) $< 100°C$    (ii) $> 100°C$
25. Moist air has water vapour which has lower vapour density $(18/2 = 9)$ than dry air, which has vapour density equal to 14.4. That is why moist air is lighter than dry air.
26. The graph plotted between V and T at constant pressure is called an isobar.
27. It is the square root of the mean of the squares of different speeds of all the molecules of a gas.
28. Critical temperature, critical volume and critical pressure are called critical constants of a gas.
29. (i) Unit of viscosity is pas $Nm^{-2}$ S.
    (ii) Unit of surface tension $Nm^{-1}$.
30. The temperature above which a gas cannot be liquefied.
31. A gas which can deviate ideal gas behaviour at higher pressure and lower temperature is called a real gas.
32. In Liquids, the molecules are more compact in comparison to gases.
33. The drop would be spherical—the shape which gives the smallest surface area per unit volume, in response to surface tension.

### *Short Answer Questions*

1. Pressure is constant, so apply Charle's law.

   $$\frac{V_1}{T_1} = \frac{V_2}{T_2}$$

**1.** $V_1 = 5\,L\,;\ V_2\,;\ = 10\,L\,;\ T_1 = 273\ K\,;\ T_2 = ?$

$$T_2 = \frac{V_2 \times T_1}{V_1} = \frac{10 \times 273}{5} = 546\ K$$

**2.** The two practical implications of the Boyle's law are:
   (i) The density and pressure decreases with the increase in altitude. The decrease in pressure at high altitudes causes altitude sickness (headache, sluggish feeling) due to decrease in the oxygen intake in each breath.
   (ii) When a given mass of a gas is compressed, the same number of molecules occupy a smaller space. This means that the gas becomes denser. Air at the level is denser because it is compressed by the mass of air above it.

**3.** $V_1 = V;\ V_2 = \dfrac{18}{100}V + V = \dfrac{118}{100}V$

$T_1 = 340\ K \qquad T_2 = ?$

$$\frac{V_1}{T_1} = \frac{V_2}{T_2}\ \text{or}\ T_2 = \left(\frac{V_2}{V_1}\right)T_1$$

$$T_2 = \frac{\left(\dfrac{118V}{100}\right)}{V} \times 340K \quad T_2 = 401\ K.$$

**4.** $V_1 = 41.3\ ml \qquad V_2 = ?$
$P_1 = 753\ mm\ Hg \quad P_2 = 760\ mm\ Hg$
$T_1 = 31 + 273 = 304\ K \quad P_2 = 273\ K$

$$\therefore\quad V_2 = \frac{P_1}{P_2} \times \frac{T_2}{T_1} \times V_1 = \frac{753\ mm\ Hg \times 273K \times 41.3\ ml}{760\ mm\ Hg \times 304K}$$

$$V_2 = 36.7\ ml.$$

**5.** $n_{HCl} = \dfrac{9.41g}{36.5g\ mol^{-1}} = 0.26\ mol$

16 mol HCl liberates 5 mol $Cl_2$
$\therefore$ 0.26 mol HCl will liberate

$$5 \times \frac{0.26}{16} = 0.081\ mol\ Cl_2$$

$$PV = nRT$$

$$V_{Cl_2} = \frac{nRT}{P}$$

$$= \frac{0.081\ mol \times 0.0821\ L\ atm^{-1}K^{-1} \times 313K}{1.03\ atm}$$

$$V_{Cl_2} = 2.02L.$$

**6.** More heat is required for vapourisation than for melting. Melting needs only enough energy for the molecules to escape from their sites in the solid. For vapourisation, enough energy must be supplied to break most of the intermolecular attractions. That's why 15g of steam melts more ice than 15g of water at 100°C.

**7.** Liquid like ether and acetone are highly volatile due to weak intermolecular forces of attraction. The rate of evaporation of liquid decreases with decrease in temperature. Therefore, ether and acetone are kept in cool place to slow down their evaporation.

**8.** Given that,
$P_1 = 600 - 23.8 = 576.2\ mm\ of\ Hg$

$$V_2 = \frac{V_1}{2}$$

According to Boyle's law,
$$P_1V_1 = P_2V_2$$

$$\therefore\quad 576.2 \times V_1 = P_2 \times \frac{V_1}{2}$$

or $P_2 = 1152.4$
The final total pressure $= 1152.4 + 23.8 = 1176.2\ mm\ of\ Hg$

**9.** (a) Avogadro's Law
(b) Dalton's Law
(c) Charles's Law

**10.** $\left.\begin{array}{l} P_1 = 1.00\ atm \\ P_2 = 2.50\ atm \\ V_1 = 3.15\ L \\ V_2 = ? \end{array}\right\}$ Temperature and an amount of gas remains constant

From Boyle's law, we have
$$P_1 V_1 = P_2 V_2$$

or $\quad V_2 = \dfrac{1.00\ atm \times 3.15\ L}{2.50\ atm} = 1.26\ L.$

**11.** $T_1 = 300\ K \qquad T_2 = ?$
$V_1 = 906\ cm^3 \qquad V_2 = 500\ cm^3$

Using Charles law

$$\frac{V_1}{T_1} = \frac{V_2}{T_2}\quad \text{or}\quad T_2 = \left(\frac{V_2}{V_1}\right)T_1$$

$$T_2 = \left(\frac{500\ cm^3}{906\ cm^3}\right) \times 300\ K$$

$$\therefore\quad T_2 = 166\ K.$$

**12.** As melting ice implies 0°C.
$\therefore\quad T_1 = 273\ K \qquad P_1 = 1000\ torr$
$\qquad T_2 = ? \qquad\quad P_2 = 400\ torr$

$$\frac{P_1}{T_1} = \frac{P_2}{T_2}\ \text{(volume and amount of gas remains constant)}$$

$$\therefore\quad T_2 = \left(\frac{P_2}{P_1}\right)T_1 = \left(\frac{400\ torr}{1000\ torr}\right) \times 273\ K$$

$$= 109\ K = -164°C.$$

**13.** $R = \dfrac{PV}{nT};\ P = 1\ atm = 101.325 \times 10^3\ (Nm^{-2})$

$V = 22.4\ L = 22.4 \times 10^{-3}\ m^3$

$n = 1\ mol,\ T = 273\ K$

$$R = \frac{101.325 \times 10^3\ Nm^{-2} \times 22.4 \times 10^{-3}\ m^3}{1\ mol \times 273\ K}$$

$$R = 8.314\ J\ mol^{-1}\ K^{-1}$$

14. There are no attractive forces between the particles of an ideal gas. In the mixture of gases, each particle strikes the walls same number of times per second as if no other particles were present. Therefore, the pressure of a particular gas in a mixture is not changed by the presence of other gases.

15. $H_2$ and He being a very small molecules, the intermolecular forces of attraction in them are negligible i.e. '$a$' factor is very small so that $a/V^2$ is negligible. The van der waal's equation reduces to
    $P(V - b) = RT$ for 1 mole
    or $PV - bP = RT$ or $PV = RT + bP$ ...(i)
    Divide eqn. (i) by RT we get

    $$\frac{PV}{RT} = 1 + \frac{bP}{RT} \text{ We know PV /RT} = Z \text{, thus } Z = 1 + \frac{bP}{RT}$$

    i.e. $Z > 1$ and increases with increase in the value of P.

16. This is because of presence of three –OH groups in glycerol or glycerin as compared to only one –OH group in ethanol. Hence, the hydrogen bonding in glycerin is thrice as compared to alcohol molecule. Thus, there is a greater intermolecular force of attraction in glycerin than in ethanol; therefore, it is more viscous than alcohol.

17. In water and glycerine – Hydrogen bonding. Hexane – Dispersion forces / London forces. The order of viscosities of these liquids is hexane < water < glycerine. Hexane has weakest intermolecular forces and glycerine the strongest (three OH groups). Therefore, hexane has minimum viscosity and glycerine has maximum viscosity.

18. The causes of deviations from ideal behaviour are:
    (a) The molecules of a gas occupy a certain volume as can seen from the fact that gases can be liquified and solidified at low temperatures and high pressure.
    (b) The effect of applying high pressure is to bring the molecules closer to one another, thereby increasing the forces of attractions amongst them.

19. Given that,
    $T_1 = 27°C = 300K$
    $n_1 = 1$ mol

    $n_2 = 1 - \dfrac{3}{5} = 0.4$ mol

    The volume of the gas remains constant throughout the process therefore pressure also remains constant. Hence from

    $$n_1 RT_1 = n_2 RT_2$$

    or $T_2 = \dfrac{n_1}{n_2} \times T_1 = \dfrac{1}{0.4} \times 300 = 750$

    $T_2 = 477°C$

### Long Answer Questions

1. (i) (a) Data given $P_1 = 1000$ atm; $P_2 = 400$ atm ; $T_1 = 0°C + 273 = 273K$ ( since ice melts at $0°C$) ; $T_2 = ?$ at constant volume.

    $$\frac{P_1}{T_1} = \frac{P_2}{T_2} \quad \therefore T_2 = \frac{T_1 . P_2}{P_1} = \frac{273 \times 400}{1000}$$

    $$= 109 \text{ K} = 109 - 273 = -164° \text{ C}$$

(b) Here we have to calculate

$$P_2 = \frac{T_2 . P_1}{T_1} = \frac{(100 + 273) \times (1000 \text{ atm})}{(0 + 273)}$$

$$= 1.37 \times 10^3 \text{ atm}$$

(ii) Applying Charles law as volume is constant $\dfrac{P_1}{T_1} = \dfrac{P_2}{T_2}$

$P_1 = 15$ atm ; $P_2 = 30$ atm ; $T_1 = (15 + 273)K = 288K$ ; $T_2 = ?$

$$\frac{15 \text{ atm}}{288 \text{K}} = \frac{30 \text{ atm}}{T_2} \text{ or } T_2 = 576 \text{ K}$$

$$= (576 - 273) = 303°C$$

2. (a) Mass of gas in each flask = wg
    Number of molecules of $H_2$ in flask A

    $$n_{(H_2)A} = \frac{\text{Number of grams of } H_2 \times N_A}{\text{molar mass of } H_2}$$

    $$= \frac{wg \times 6.023 \times 10^{23} \text{ molecules / mol}}{2g \text{ mol}^{-1}}$$

    $$n_{(H_2)A} = \frac{1}{2} w \times 6.023 \times 10^{23} \text{ molecules}$$

    Number of molecules of $CH_4$ in flask B.

    $$n_{(CH_4)B} = \frac{wg \times 6,023 \times 10^{23} \text{ molecules / mol}}{16g / \text{mol}}$$

    $$= \frac{1}{16} w \times 6.023 \times 10^{23} \text{ molecules}$$

    $$\therefore \frac{\text{Number of molecules of } H_2}{\text{Number of molecules of } CH_4}$$

    $$= \frac{\dfrac{1}{2} w \times 6.023 \times 10^{23}}{\dfrac{1}{16} w \times 6.023 \times 10^{23}} = 8.$$

    Therefore, flask A contains eight times the number of molecules in flask B.

    (b) Partial pressure in flask A,

    $$P_{(H_2)A} = \frac{n_A RT_A}{V}$$

    and partial pressure in flask B,

    $$P_{(CH_4)B} = \frac{n_B RT_B}{V}$$

    $$\therefore \frac{P_{(H_2)A}}{P_{(CH_4)B}} = \frac{n_A}{n_B} \times \frac{T_A}{T_B} = 8 \times \frac{300}{600} = 4$$

    Therefore, the pressure in flask A is four times that in flask B.

**3.** **(i)** We know $PV = nRT$ or $PV = \dfrac{wRT}{M}$ where w is the mass of the gas and M is its molar mass.

$$\therefore M = \frac{wRT}{PV}$$

Knowing w, P (its pressure), V(volume), R(gas constant) and T(temperature) molar mass M can be calculated.

If density is known then $M = dRT / P$ where d = density $= w / M$.

**(ii)** Ideal gas are those which obeys gas laws (Boyle's law, Charle's law etc) or the gas equation $PV = nRT$ strictly for all the values of temperature and pressure. The molecules of ideal gas occupy negligible volume and exert negligible force of attraction on one another.

Real gases does not obey gas laws under all conditions of temperature and pressure. All gases in the universe are real. Real gases approach ideal behaviour only at high temperature and low pressure.

**4.** **(i)**

**(a)** According to ideal gas equation:

$$PV = nRT$$

$$P = \frac{nRT}{V} = \frac{1 \times 0.0821 \times 298}{1.5} = 16.29 \text{ atm.}$$

**(b)** According to van der Waal's gas equation:

$$\left(P + \frac{an^2}{V^2}\right)(V - nb) = nRT$$

$$P = \frac{nRT}{(V - nb)} - \left(\frac{an^2}{V^2}\right)$$

$$= \frac{1 \times 0.0821 \times 298}{(1.5 - 1 \times 0.04)} - \left(\frac{3.6 \times (1)^2}{(1.5)^2}\right) = 15.137 \text{ atm.}$$

**(ii)** $H_2 + \dfrac{1}{2}O_2 \longrightarrow H_2O$

Before reaction,

Volume of $H_2 = 1L$

Volume of $O_2 = 1L$

After reaction,

$1 \text{ L } H_2$ reacts with $\dfrac{1}{2}\text{L } O_2$ to yield $1 \text{ L } H_2O$

$\therefore$ Volume of $H_2$ left $= 1 - 1 = 0L$

Volume of $O_2$ left $= 1 - \dfrac{1}{2} = \dfrac{1}{2}L$

Valume of $H_2O$ formed $= 1L$

**(i)** According to ideal gas equation,

$$P V = nRT$$

or $n(H_2O) = \dfrac{PV}{RT} = \dfrac{1 \times 1}{0.0821 \times 273}$

$= 0.0446$ (at NTP)

Mass of $H_2O = n \times M = 0.0446 \times 18 = 0.8031$ g

**(ii)** At NTP,

$22.4$ L $O_2$ weights $= 32$ g

$\therefore$ $0.5$ L $O_2$ weights $= \dfrac{32 \times 0.5}{22.4} = 0.7143$g

**(iii)** Given that, T $= 100°$C $= 373$ K

$$V = 2L$$

$$n (H_2O) = 0.0446$$

$$n (O_2) = \frac{PV}{RT}$$

$n$ (total) $= 0.0446 + 0.0223 = \dfrac{1 \times 0.5}{0.0821 \times 273}$

$= 0.0223 = 0.0669$

$$P = \frac{nRT}{V} = \frac{0.0669 \times 0.0821 \times 373}{2}$$

$= 1.02$ atm

**(iv)** Volume of $O_2$ that reacts to yield $H_2O = 0.5L$

At NTP, $22.4$ L $= 1$ mol

$\therefore$ $0.5$ L $= \dfrac{0.5}{22.4} = 0.02$ mol $O_2$

reacts to yield $H_2O$

## SECTION C — NCERT EXEMPLAR QUESTIONS

### MULTIPLE CHOICE QUESTIONS

**1.** A person living in shimla observed that cooking food without using pressure cooker takes more time. The reason for this observation is that at high altitude

(a) pressure increases

(b) temperature decreases

(c) pressure decreases

(d) temperature increases

**2.** Which of the following property of water can be used to explain the spherical shape of rain droplets?

(a) Viscosity        (b) Surface tension

(c) Critical phenomena    (d) Pressure

**3.** Dipole-dipole forces act between the molecules possessing permanent dipole. Ends of dipoles possess 'partial charges'. The partial charge is

(a) more than unit electronic charge

(b) equal to unit electronic charge

(c) less than unit electronic charge

(d) double the unit electronic charge

4. As the temperature increases average kinetic energy of molecules increases. What would be the effect of increase of temperature on pressure provided the volume is constant?
   (a) Increases      (b) Decreases
   (c) Remains same      (d) Becomes half

5. Increase in kinetic energy can overcome intermolecular forces of attraction. How will the viscosity of liquid be affected by the increase in temperature?
   (a) Increase
   (b) No effect
   (c) Decrease
   (d) No regular pattern will be followed

6. How does the surface tension of a liquid vary with increase in temperature?
   (a) Remains same
   (b) Decreases
   (c) Increases
   (d) No regular pattern is followed

7. Gases possess characteristic critical temperature which depends upon the magnitude of intermolecular forces between the particles. Following are the critical temperatures of some gases.

| Gases | $H_2$ | He | $O_2$ | $N_2$ |
|---|---|---|---|---|
| Critical temperature in Kelvin | 33.2 | 5.3 | 154.3 | 126 |

From the above data, what would be the order of liquefaction of these gases? Start writing the order from the gas liquefying first
   (a) $H_2$, He, $O_2$, $N_2$      (b) He, $O_2$, $H_2$, $N_2$
   (c) $N_2$, $O_2$, He, $H_2$      (d) $O_2$, $N_2$, $H_2$, He

## ASSERTION & REASON QUESTIONS

**DIRECTIONS (Qs. 1-3) :** *Each of these questions contains an assertion followed by reason. Read them carefully and answer the question on the basis of following options. You have to select the one that best describes the two statements.*
(a) If both Assertion and Reason are correct and the Reason is a correct explanation of the Assertion.
(b) If both Assertion and Reason are correct but Reason is not a correct explanation of the Assertion.
(c) If the Assertion is correct but Reason is incorrect.
(d) If the Assertion is incorrect but the Reason is correct.

1. **Assertion :** Three states of matter are the result of balance between intermolecular forces and thermal energy of the molecules.
   **Reason :** Intermolecular forces tend to keep the molecules together but thermal energy of molecules tends to keep them apart.

2. **Assertion :** At constant temperature, pV vs V plot for real gases is not a straight line.
   **Reason :** At high pressure all gases have Z > 1 but at intermediate pressure most gases have Z < 1.

3. **Assertion :** Gases do not liquefy above their critical temperature, even on applying high pressure.
   **Reason :** Above critical temperature, the molecular speed is high and intermolecular attractions cannot hold the molecules together because they escape because of high speed.

## SHORT ANSWER QUESTIONS

1. At 15°C and 900 mm pressure, 0.4 gram of a certain gas occupied 3280 mL. If the pressure is changed to 1300 mm at constant temperature. What is the density of the gas?

2. Calculate the vapour density of a gas, 12.8g of which occupies 10L at a pressure of 750 mm at 27°C.

3. Which type of intermolecular forces exist among the following molecules?
   (i) $H_2S$ molecules
   (ii) $H_2O$ molecules
   (iii) $Cl_2$ and $CCl_4$ molecules
   (iv) $SiH_4$ molecules
   (v) Helium atoms
   (vi) He atoms and HCl molecules

4. Value of universal gas constant (R) is same for all gases. What is its physical significance?

5. Compressibility factor, Z, of a gas is given as $Z = \dfrac{pV}{nRT}$
   (i) What is the value of Z for an ideal gas ?
   (ii) For real gas what will be the effect on value of Z above Boyle's temperature ?

## LONG ANSWER QUESTIONS

1. The variation of vapour pressure of different liquids with temperature is shown in Fig. 5.6.
   (i) Calculate graphically boiling points of liquids A and B.
   (ii) If we take liquid C in a closed vessel and heat it continuously. At what temperature will it boil?
   (iii) At high altitude, atmospheric pressure is low (say 60 mm Hg). At what temperature liquid D boils?
   (iv) Pressure cooker is used for cooking food at hill station. Explain in terms of vapour pressure why is it so?

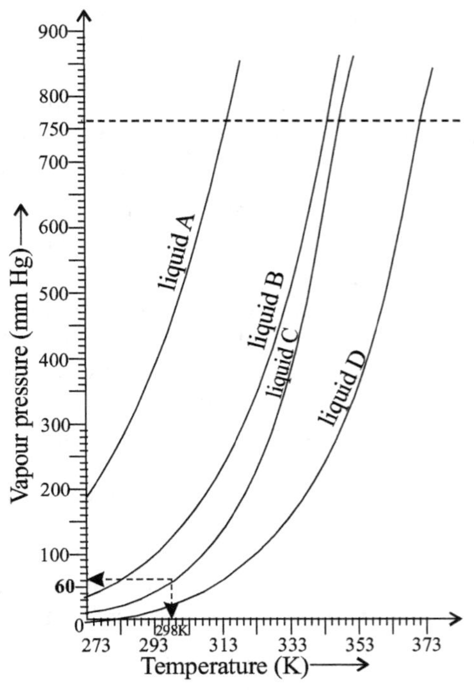



2. Isotherms of carbon dioxide at various temperatures are represented in fig. 5.5. Answer the following questions based on this figure.
   (i) In which state will $CO_2$ exist between the points 'a' and 'b' at temperature $T_1$?
   (ii) At what point will $CO_2$ start liquefying when temperature is $T_1$?
   (iii) At what point will $CO_2$ be completely liquefied when the temperature is $T_2$.
   (iv) Will condensation take place when the temperature is $T_3$.
   (v) What portion of the isotherm at $T_1$ represent liquid and gaseous $CO_2$ at equilibrium?

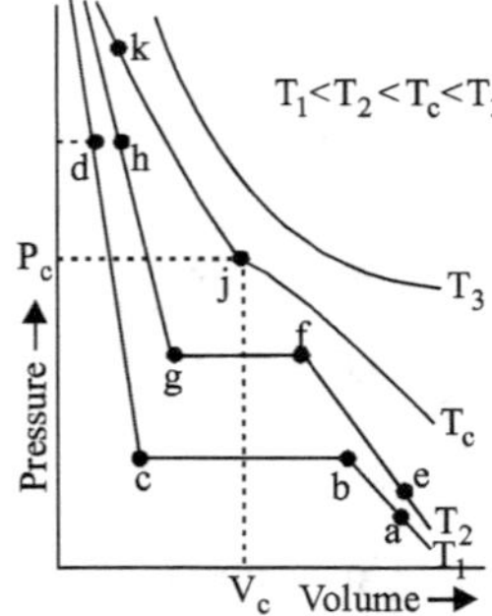



## SOLUTIONS

### Multiple Choice Questions

1. **(c)** At high altitude, pressure is low, hence, boiling point is low due to which things take more time to cook. However, in a pressure cooker, pressure is increased and hence, boiling point increases. Thus, in a pressure cooker food cook faster *i.e.* a less period of time.

2. **(b)** The property of surface tension explains the spherical shape of rain droplets. Surface tension tries to decrease the surface area of the liquid to the minimum. The rain droplets are spherical because for a given volume, a sphere has minimum surface area.

3. **(c)** Dipole-dipole forces act between the molecules possessing permanent dipole and ends of dipoles possess 'partial charges'. Partial charges present on ends of a dipole are always less than the unit electronic charge.

4. **(a)** From Gay-Lussac's law, at constant volume, as the temperature is increased, pressure increases.

5. **(c)** Kinetic energy of the molecules of liquid increases with increase of temperature, which can overcome the intermolecular forces. Hence, the liquid starts flowing. In other words, the viscosity of a liquid decreases with increase in temperature.

6. **(b)** The surface tension of liquids generally decreases with increase of temperature and becomes zero at the critical temperature. This is due to the fact that, with increase of temperature, the kinetic energy of the molecules increases and therefore, the intermolecular attraction decreases.

7. **(d)** Higher the critical temperature, more easily is the gas get liquified. Hence, order of liquefaction starting with the gas liquefying first will be : $O_2$, $N_2$, $H_2$, He.

### Assertion & Reason Questions

1. **(a)** Both assertion and reason are correct and reason is the correct explanation of assertion.

2. **(b)** At constant temperature pV vs. V plot for real gases is not a straight line as real gas molecules possess intermolecular force of attraction.

3. **(a)** Gases do not liquefy above their critical temperature because as the temperature increases kinetic energy of the molecules also increases and it become difficult to liquefy them.

### Short Answer Questions

1. $$\text{Density} = \frac{\text{Mass}}{\text{Volume}}$$

   $\therefore$ Density at 900 mm pressure

   $$= \frac{0.4}{3280} \, g/mL$$

   $$= 0.000122 \text{ g/mL}$$

   At constant temperature, Density $\times$ Pressure

   $$\therefore \quad \frac{d_1}{P_1} = \frac{d_2}{P_2} \qquad \text{or} \qquad d_2 = \frac{d_1 \times d_2}{P_1}$$

$d_1 = 0.000122$ g/mL      $d_2 = ?$

$P_1 = 900$ mm      $P_2 = 1300$ mm

$$\therefore \quad d_2 = \frac{0.000122 \times 1300}{900} = 0.0001762 \text{ g/mL}$$

Hence, density of gas at 1300 mm = 0.0001762 g/mL.

**2.** Vapour density (V.D.) $= \dfrac{W}{2} \times \dfrac{RT}{PV}$

Given,

$W = 12.8$g

$R = 0.082$ litre-atm degree$^{-1}$ mole$^{-1}$

$T = 273 + 27 = 300$ K

$P = \dfrac{750}{760}$ atm

$V = 10$L

Substituting these values, we get

$$\text{V.D.} = \frac{12.8 \times 0.082 \times 300}{\dfrac{750}{760} \times 10 \times 2} = 15.92.$$

**3.**   (i) Dipole-dipole interactions (because $H_2S$ is polar).

  (ii) Hydrogen bonding.

  (iii) London dispersion forces (because both are non-polar)

  (iv) London dispersion forces (because $SiH_4$ is non-polar).

  (v) London dispersion forces (because He atoms have symmetrical electron clouds).

  (vi) Dipole-induced dipole forces (because HCl is polar while He atom has symmetrical electron cloud).

**4.** Unit of R depends upon those units in which P, V and T are measured, $R = \dfrac{PV}{nT}$. If pressure is measured in Pascal, per mole volume is measured in m$^3$ and temperature is measured in Kelvin then. Units of 'R' are Pa m$^3$ K$^{-1}$ mol$^{-1}$ or J mol$^{-1}$K$^{-1}$. Joule is the unit of work done so 'R' is work done per mole per kelvin.

**5.**   (i) $Z = 1$ for ideal gas

  (ii) For a real gas $Z > 1$ above Boyle's temperature.

## Long Answer Questions

**1.**   (i) The boiling point of liquid A is: 315 K (approx) and the boiling point of B is: 345 K (approx.)

  (ii) In the closed vessel the liquid C will not boil because the pressure is kept on increasing in the vessel.

  (iii) According to the graph Temperature corresponding to 60 mm of hg = 313 K. So liquid D will boil at 313 K. So liquid D will boil at 313 K.

  (iv) Since the atmospheric pressure is low at high altitudes, water boils at low temperatures on hills. We already know that a liquid boils when its vapour pressure equals atmospheric pressure. Because a pressure cooker raises the boiling point of water and its heat content, food cooks faster.

**2.**   (i) $CO_2$ exists as in the gaseous state between the points 'a' and 'b' at temperature $T_1$ because from point 'a' to 'b' volume starts decreasing and the pressure increases and the gaseous molecules start to come closer but exist in the gaseous state only.

  (ii) At the temperaturte $T_1$, $CO_2$ starts liquefying at the point 'b'. Because at point 'b' the liquefication has just started or commences.

  (iii) At the temperature $T_2$, $CO_2$ will be completely liquefied at the point 'g'. Because in the curve at the temperature $T_2$ point 'f' to 'g' represents the phase where the gas is being converted to liquid and at point 'g' all the gas has been converted to liquid.

  (iv) As stated in the graph $T_3 > T_C > T_2 > T_1$. Temperature $T_3 > T_C$ i.e., the critical temperature so condensation will not take place when the temperature is $T_3$. Because critical temperature is the temperature of gas above which gas cannot be liquified howsoever high pressure is applied and $T_3$ is greater than $T_C$.

  (v) At the temperature $T_1$ curve the equilibrium of liquid and gaseous state of $CO_2$ is represented between the point's 'b' and 'c'. Because between the points 'b' and 'c', the pressure being the constant volume of a gas decreases till point 'c' so between these points $CO_2$ gas partially exists as in liquid and the gaseous state i.e., existing in equilibrium.

# 6

# Thermodynamics

**6.1** Choose the correct answer. A thermodynamic state function is a quantity
 (i) used to determine heat changes
 (ii) whose value is independent of path
 (iii) used to determine pressure volume work
 (iv) whose value depends on temperature only.

**Ans.** (ii) Whose value is independent of path.

**6.2** For the process to occur under adiabatic conditions, the correct condition is
 (i) $\Delta T = 0$  (ii) $\Delta p = 0$  (iii) $q = 0$  (iv) $w = 0$

**Ans.** (iii) $q = 0$

**6.3** The enthalpies of all elements in their standard states are :
 (i) unity
 (ii) zero
 (iii) $< 0$
 (iv) different for each element

**Ans.** (ii) zero

**6.4** $\Delta U^\circ$ of combustion of methane is $-X$ kJ mol$^{-1}$. The value of $\Delta H^\circ$ is
 (i) $= \Delta U^\circ$   (ii) $> \Delta U^\circ$   (iii) $< \Delta U^\circ$   (iv) $= 0$

**Ans.** The balanced equation for combustion of methane will be

$$CH_4(g) + 2O_2(g) \longrightarrow CO_2(g) + 2H_2O(\ell)$$

Thus, $\Delta n_g = (n_p - n_r)_g = 1 - 3 = -2$
$\Delta H^\circ = \Delta U^\circ + \Delta n_g RT = -X - 2RT$ Thus, $\Delta H^\circ < \Delta U^\circ$.
Hence, (iii) is the correct answer.

**6.5** The enthalpy of combustion of methane, graphite and dihydrogen at 298 K are, $-890 \cdot 3$ kJmol$^{-1}$, $-393.5$ kJ mol$^{-1}$ and $-285.8$ kJ mol$^{-1}$ respectively. Enthalpy of formation of $CH_4$ (g) will be
 (i) $-74.8$ kJmol$^{-1}$        (ii) $-52.27$ kJ mol$^{-1}$
 (iii) $+74.8$ kJ mol$^{-1}$      (iv) $+52.26$ kJ mol$^{-1}$

**Ans.** Given :
 (i) $CH_4(g) + 2O_2(g) \longrightarrow CO_2(g) + 2H_2O(\ell)$,
   $\Delta H = -890.3$ kJ mol$^{-1}$

 (ii) $C(s) + O_2(g) \longrightarrow CO_2(g)$, $\Delta H = -393.5$ kJ mol$^{-1}$

 (iii) $H_2(g) + \dfrac{1}{2} O_2(g) \longrightarrow H_2O(\ell)$, $\Delta H = -285.8$ kJ mol$^{-1}$

 Aim : $C(s) + 2H_2(g) \longrightarrow CH_4(g)$, $\Delta H = ?$
 Eqn. (ii) + 2 Eqn. (iii) − Eqn. (i) gives the required equation with
 $\Delta H = -393.5 + 2(-285.8) - (-890.3)$ kJ mol$^{-1}$
 $= -74.8$ kJmol$^{-1}$.
 Hence, (i) is the correct answer.

**6.6** A reaction, $A + B \longrightarrow C + D + q$ is found to have a positive entropy change. The reaction will be
 (i) possible at high temperature
 (ii) possible only at low temperature
 (iii) not possible at any temperature
 (iv) possible at any temperature

**Ans.** Here, $\Delta H = -$ve and $\Delta S = +$ve. $\Delta G = \Delta H - T\Delta S$. For the reaction to be spontaneous, $\Delta G$ should be $-$ve which will be so at any temperature, i.e., option (iv) is correct.

**6.7** In a process, 701 J of heat is absorbed by a system and 394 J of work is done by the system. What is the change in internal energy for the process ?

**Ans.** $q = +701$ J, $w = -394$ J, $\Delta E = ?$
 By first law of thermodynamics
 $\Delta E = q + w = +701$ J $+ (-394$ J$) = +307$ J
 i.e., internal energy of the system increases by 307 J.

**6.8** The reaction of cyanamide, $NH_2CN$ (s), with dioxygen was carried out in a bomb calorimeter, and $\Delta E$ was found to be $-742.7$ kJ mol$^{-1}$ at 298 K. Calculate enthalpy change for the reaction at 298 K.

$$NH_2CN(s) + \dfrac{3}{2} O_2(g) \longrightarrow N_2(g) + CO_2(g) + H_2O(\ell).$$

**Ans.** $\Delta n_g = (n_p - n_r)_g = 2 - \dfrac{3}{2} = +\dfrac{1}{2}$ mol

$\Delta H = \Delta U + \Delta n_g RT$
 $= -742.7$ kJmol$^{-1}$ + (+1/2 mol)
    $(8.314 \times 10^{-3}$ kJ mol$^{-1}$ K$^{-1}$ mol$^{-1})$ (298 K)
 $= -742.7 + 1.2$ kJ mol$^{-1}$ $= -741.5$ kJ mol$^{-1}$

**6.9** Calculate the number of kJ of heat necessary to raise the temperature of 60.0 g of aluminium from 35°C to 55°C. Molar heat capacity of Al is 24 J mol$^{-1}$ K$^{-1}$.

**Ans.** $q = n \times C \times \Delta T$

$$= \left(\frac{60 \text{ mol}}{27}\right) \times (24 \text{ J mol}^{-1} \text{ K}^{-1}) \times (328 - 308)\text{K}$$

$$= 1066.7\text{J} = 1.07 \text{ kJ}$$

**6.10** Calculate the enthalpy change on freezing of 1.0 mol of water at 10.0°C to ice at –10°C.
$\Delta_{\text{fus}} H = 6.03$ kJ mol$^{-1}$ at 0°C
$C_p [H_2O (\ell)] = 75.3$ J mol$^{-1}$ K$^{-1}$
$C_p [H_2O(s)] = 36.8$ J mol$^{-1}$ K$^{-1}$

**Ans.** Total $\Delta H = $ (1 mol water at 10°C $\longrightarrow$ 1 mol of water at 0°C) + (1 mole of water at 0°C $\longrightarrow$ 1mol ice at 0°C)+ (1 mole of ice at 0°C $\longrightarrow$ 1 mol of ice at –10°C)

$$= C_p[H_2O(l)] \times \Delta T + \frac{\Delta H_{\text{freezing}}}{T_f} + C_p[H_2O(s)] \times \Delta T$$

$$(\Delta T = T_2 - T_1)$$

$$= (75.3 \text{ JK}^{-1} \text{ mol}^{-1}) (0-10)\text{K} + (- 6.03 \text{ kJ mol}^{-1})$$
$$+ (36.8 \text{ JK}^{-1} \text{ mol}^{-1}) (-10 \text{ K})$$
$$= - 753 \text{ J mol}^{-1} - 6.03 \text{ kJ mol}^{-1} - 0.368 \text{ J mol}^{-1}$$
$$= - 0.753 \text{kJ mol}^{-1} - 6.03 \text{ kJmol}^{-1} - 0.368 \text{ kJ mol}^{-1}$$
$$= - 7.151 \text{ kJ mol}^{-1}$$

**6.11** Enthalpy of combustion of carbon to $CO_2$ is – 393.5 kJ mol$^{-1}$. Calculate the heat released upon formation of 35.2 g of $CO_2$ from carbon and dioxygen gas.

**Ans.** $C(s) + O_2(g) \longrightarrow CO_2(g), \Delta H = -393.5 \text{ kJ mol}^{-1}$
For $CO_2$, 1 mol = 44 g
Heat released when 44 g $CO_2$ is formed
= 393.5 kJ
$\therefore$ Heat released when 35.2 g $CO_2$ is formed

$$= \frac{393.5 \times 35.2 \text{ kJ}}{44} = 314.8 \text{ kJ}$$

**6.12** Enthalpies of formation of CO (g), $CO_2$ (g), $N_2O$ (g) and $N_2O_4$ (g) are –110, –393, 81 and 9.7 kJ mol$^{-1}$ respectively. Find the value of $\Delta_r H$ for the reaction :
$$N_2O_4(g) + 3CO(g) \longrightarrow N_2O(g) + 3 CO_2(g)$$

**Ans.** $\Delta_f H = \Sigma \Delta_f H \text{ (Products)} - \Sigma \Delta_f H \text{ (Reactants)}$
$$= (\Delta_f H (N_2O) + 3 \Delta_f H (CO_2)]$$
$$- [\Delta_f H (N_2O_4) + 3 \Delta_f H (CO)]$$
$$= [81 + 3 (-393)] - [9.7 + 3 (-110)]$$
$$= -777.7 \text{ kJ}$$

**6.13** Given : $N_2(g) + 3H_2(g) \rightarrow 2NH_3(g); \Delta_r H° = -92.4$ kJ mol$^{-1}$. What is the standard enthalpy of formation of $NH_3$ gas ?

**Ans.** Reaction for the enthalpy of formation of $NH_3$ (g) is

$$\frac{1}{2} N_2(g) + 3/2 H_2(g) \longrightarrow NH_3(g)$$

$$\Delta_f H° = -92.4 / 2 = - 46.2 \text{ kJ mol}^{-1}$$

**6.14** Calculate the standard enthalpy of formation of $CH_3OH$ (*l*) from the following data :

(i) $CH_3OH (l) + \frac{3}{2} O_2 (g) \longrightarrow CO_2 (g) + 2H_2O (l)$;
$\Delta_r H° = -726$ kJ mol$^{-1}$

(ii) C (graphite) + $O_2$ (g) $\longrightarrow CO_2$ (g) ;
$\Delta_c H° = -393$ kJ mol$^{-1}$

(iii) $H_2$ (g) $+ \frac{1}{2} O_2$ (g) $\longrightarrow H_2O (l)$ ;
$\Delta_f H° = - 286$ kJ mol$^{-1}$.

**Ans.** Aim : $C(s) + 2H_2(g) + \frac{1}{2} O_2(g) \longrightarrow CH_3OH(\ell), \Delta_f H° = ?$

Eqn. (ii) + 2 × Eqn. (iii) – Eqn. (i) gives the required eqn. with
$$\Delta H = - 393 + 2(- 286) - (- 726) \text{ kJ mol}^{-1}$$
$$= -239 \text{ kJ mol}^{-1}$$

**6.15** Calculate the enthalpy change for the process
$CCl_4 (g) \longrightarrow C (g) + 4Cl (g)$ and calculate bond enthalpy of C – Cl in $CCl_4$ (g)
$\Delta_{\text{vap}} H° (CCl_4) = 30.5$ kJ mol$^{-1}$
$\Delta_f H° (CCl_4) = -135.5$ kJ mol$^{-1}$
$\Delta_a H° (C) = 715.0$ kJ mol$^{-1}$ where $\Delta_a H°$ is enthalpy of atomisation
$\Delta_a H° (Cl_2) = 242$ kJ mol$^{-1}$

**Ans.** The given data imply as under :

(i) $CCl_4(\ell) \longrightarrow CCl_4(g), \Delta H = 30.5 \text{ kJ mol}^{-1}$

(ii) $C(s) + 2Cl_2(g) \longrightarrow CCl_4(\ell), \Delta H = - 135.5 \text{ kJ mol}^{-1}$

(iii) $C(s) \longrightarrow C(g), \Delta H = 715.0 \text{ kJ mol}^{-1}$

(iv) $Cl_2(g) \longrightarrow 2Cl(g), \Delta H = 242 \text{ kJ mol}^{-1}$

Aim : $CCl_4(g) \longrightarrow C(g) + 4Cl(g), \Delta H = ?$

Eqn. (iii) + 2 × Eqn. (iv) – Eqn. (i) – Eqn. (ii) gives the required equation with
$$\Delta H = 715.0 + 2(242) - 30.5 - (-135.5) \text{kJmol}^{-1}$$
$$= 1304 \text{ kJ mol}^{-1}$$

Bond enthalpy of C-Cl in $CCl_4$ (average value) $= \dfrac{1304}{4}$

$$= 326 \text{ kJ mol}^{-1}$$

**6.16** For an isolated system, $\Delta U = 0$, what will be $\Delta S$ ?

**Ans.** $\Delta U = 0$ means that energy factor has no role to play. Hence, for the process to be spontaneous, entropy factor should favour the process, i.e., $\Delta S$ must be positive i.e. $\Delta S > 0$. Consider the example of two gases contained separately in two bulbs connected by a stop-cock, and isolated from the surroundings as an example of an isolated system. On opening the stop-cock, the two gases mix up, i.e., the system becomes more disordered. This implies that $\Delta S > 0$, but $\Delta U = 0$ for the process.

**6.17** **For the reaction at 298 K, 2A + B $\longrightarrow$ C**
**$\Delta H = 400$ kJ mol$^{-1}$ and $\Delta S = 0.2$ kJ K$^{-1}$ mol$^{-1}$.**
**At what temperature will the reaction become spontaneous considering $\Delta H$ and $\Delta S$ to be constant over the temperature range.**

**Ans.** Let us first calculate the temperature at which the reaction will be in equilibrium, i.e., $\Delta G = 0$.

Now, $\Delta G = \Delta H - T\Delta S$ $\therefore$ $0 = \Delta H - T\Delta S$ or T $= \Delta H / \Delta S = 400$ kJ mol$^{-1}$ / 0.2kJ K$^{-1}$ mol$^{-1}$ $= 2000$ K

For reaction to be spontaneous, i.e., for $\Delta G$ to be –ve, T should be greater than 2000 K.

**6.18** **For the reaction, 2Cl (g) $\longrightarrow$ Cl$_2$ (g), what are the signs of $\Delta H$ and $\Delta S$?**

**Ans.** The given reaction represents the formation of bonds. Hence, energy is released, i.e., $\Delta H$ is –ve. Further, 2 moles of atoms have greater randomness than 1 mole of molecules. Hence, randomness decreases, i.e., $\Delta S$ is –ve.

**6.19** **For the reaction, 2A(g) + B(g) $\longrightarrow$ 2D(g),**
**$\Delta U° = -10.5$ kJ and $\Delta S° = -44.1$ JK$^{-1}$ Calculate $\Delta G°$ for the reaction, and predict whether the reaction may occur spontaneously.**

**Ans.** For the given reaction, $\Delta n_g = 2 - (3) = -1$

$\therefore \quad \Delta H° = \Delta U° + \Delta n_g RT$
$= -10.5$ kJ $+ (-1) (8.314 \times 10^{-3}$ k J) $\quad$ (298)
$= -10.5 - 2.48 = -12.98$ kJ

$\Delta G° = \Delta H° - T\Delta S°$
$= -12.98$ kJ $-298 (-44.1 \times 10^{-3}$ kJ)
$= -12.98$ kJ $+ 13.14$ kJ $= 0.16$ kJ

As $\Delta G°$ comes out to be +ve, the reaction will not occur spontaneously.

**6.20** **The equilibrium constant for a reaction is 10. What will be the value of $\Delta G°$ ? R = 8.314 JK$^{-1}$ mol$^{-1}$, T = 300 K.**

**Ans.** $\Delta G° = -2.303$ RT log K
$= -2.303 \times 8.314$ JK$^{-1}$ mol$^{-1} \times 300$K $\times \log 10$
$= -5744.1$ J

**6.21** **Comment on the thermodynamic stability of NO (g), given**

$$\frac{1}{2} N_2 (g) + \frac{1}{2} O_2(g) \longrightarrow NO(g) ;$$

$\Delta_r H° = 90$ kJ mol$^{-1}$

$$NO(g) + \frac{1}{2} O_2 (g) \longrightarrow NO_2 (g) ;$$

$\Delta_r H° = -74$ kJ mol$^{-1}$

**Ans.** As energy is absorbed in the first reaction, NO (g) is unstable. As energy is released in the second reaction, NO$_2$ (g) is stable. Thus, unstable NO (g) changes into the stable NO$_2$ (g).

**6.22** **Calculate the entropy change in surroundings when 1.00 mol of H$_2$O ($l$) is formed under standard conditions: $\Delta_f H° = -286$ kJ mol$^{-1}$.**

**Ans.** $H_2(g) + \frac{1}{2}O_2(g) \longrightarrow H_2O(\ell)$ $\Delta_f H° = -286$ kJ mol$^{-1}$

This means that when 1 mol of H$_2$O (l), is formed, 286 kJ of heat is released. This heat is absorbed by the surroundings, i.e., $q_{surr} = +286$ kJmol$^{-1}$.

$$\Delta S = q_{surr} / T = \frac{286 \,\text{kJ mol}^{-1}}{298 \,\text{K}}$$

$= 0.9597$ kJK$^{-1}$mol$^{-1}$ $= 959.7$ JK$^{-1}$mol$^{-1}$.

| SECTION B | PRACTICE QUESTIONS |
|---|---|

### MULTIPLE CHOICE QUESTIONS

**1.** Which of the following statements is not true regarding the laws of thermodynamics ?
   (a) It deal with energy changes of macroscopic systems.
   (b) It deal with energy changes of microscopic systems.
   (c) It does not depends on the rate at which these energy transformations are carried out.
   (d) It depends on initial and final states of a system undergoing the change.

**2.** Which of the following is closed system ?
   (a) Jet engine
   (b) Tea placed in a steel kettle
   (c) Pressure cooker
   (d) Rocket engine during propulsion

**3.** The state of a thermodynamic system is described by its measurable or macroscopic (bulk) properties. These are
   (a) Pressure and volume
   (b) Pressure, volume, temperature and amount
   (c) Volume, temperature and amount
   (d) Pressure and temperature

**4.** Among the following, the state function(s) is (are)
   (i) Internal energy
   (ii) Irreversible expansion work
   (iii) Reversible expansion work
   (iv) Molar enthalpy
   (a) (ii) and (iii)
   (b) (i), (ii) and (iii)
   (c) (i) and (iv)
   (d) (i) only

5. Read the following statements carefully and choose the correct option
   (i) Internal energy, $U$, of the system is a state function.
   (ii) $-w$ shows, that work is done on the system.
   (iii) $+w$ shows, that work is done by the system
   (a) (i) and (ii) are correct
   (b) (ii) and (iii) are correct
   (c) (i) and (iii) are correct
   (d) Only (i) is correct

6. The difference between $\Delta H$ and $\Delta U$ is usually significant for systems consisting of
   (a) only solids
   (b) only liquids
   (c) both solids and liquids
   (d) only gases

7. Which of the following is not true regarding thermo-chemical equations?
   (a) The coefficients in a balanced thermo-chemical equation refer to the number of moles of reactants and products involved in the reaction
   (b) The coefficients in a balanced thermo-chemical equation refer to the number of molecules of reactants and products involved in the reaction
   (c) The numerical value of $\Delta_r H$ refers to the number of moles of substances specified by an equation.
   (d) Standard enthalpy change $\Delta_r H^{\ominus}$ will have units as kJ mol$^{-1}$.

8. If enthalpies of formation of $C_2H_4(g)$, $CO_2(g)$ and $H_2O(l)$ at 25°C and 1atm pressure are 52, $-394$ and $-286$ kJ/mol respectively, the change in enthalpy for combustion of $C_2H_4$ is equal to
   (a) $-141.2$ kJ/mol
   (b) $-1412$ kJ/mol
   (c) $+14.2$ kJ/mol
   (d) $+1412$ kJ/mol

9. The enthalpy change for a reaction does **not** depend upon
   (a) use of different reactants for the same product
   (b) the nature of intermediate reaction steps
   (c) the differences in initial or final temperatures of involved substances
   (d) the physical states of reactants and products

10. The following two reactions are known :
    $$Fe_2O_3(s) + 3CO(g) \longrightarrow 2Fe(s) + 3CO_2(g);$$
    $$\Delta H = -26.8 \text{ kJ}$$
    $$FeO(s) + CO(g) \longrightarrow Fe(s) + CO_2(g);$$
    $$\Delta H = -16.5 \text{ kJ}$$
    The value of $\Delta H$ for the following reaction
    $$Fe_2O_3(s) + CO(g) \longrightarrow 2FeO(s) + CO_2(g) \text{ is;}$$
    (a) $+6.2$ kJ
    (b) $+10.3$ kJ
    (c) $-43.3$ kJ
    (d) $-10.3$ kJ

11. Hess's law is used to calculate :
    (a) enthalpy of reaction.
    (b) entropy of reaction
    (c) work done in reaction
    (d) All of the above

12. Standard enthalpy of vapourisation $\Delta_{vap} H°$ for water at 100°C is 40.66 kJ mol$^{-1}$. The change in internal energy of vaporisation of water at 100°C (in kJ mol$^{-1}$) is :
    (a) $+37.56$
    (b) $-43.76$
    (c) $+43.76$
    (d) $+40.66$
    (Assume water vapour to behave like an ideal gas).

13. In which of the following, entropy decreases?
    (a) Crystallization of sucrose solution
    (b) Rusting of iron
    (c) Melting of ice
    (d) Vaporization of camphor

## ASSERTION & REASON QUESTIONS

**DIRECTIONS (Qs. 1-6) :** *Each of these questions contains an assertion followed by reason. Read them carefully and answer the question on the basis of following options. You have to select the one that best describes the two statements.*
(a) If both Assertion and Reason are correct and the Reason is a correct explanation of the Assertion.
(b) If both Assertion and Reason are correct but Reason is not a correct explanation of the Assertion.
(c) If the Assertion is correct but Reason is incorrect.
(d) If the Assertion is incorrect but the Reason is correct.

1. **Assertion :** $T, P$ and $V$ are state variables or state functions.
   **Reason :** Their values depend on the state of the system and how it is reached.

2. **Assertion :** Absolute value of internal energy of a substance cannot be determined.
   **Reason :** It is impossible to determine exact values of constituent energies of the substances.

3. **Assertion :** A process is called adiabatic if the system does not exchange heat with the surroundings.
   **Reason :** It does not involve increase or decrease in temperature of the system.

4. **Assertion :** Many endothermic reactions that are not spontaneous at room temperature become spontaneous at high temperature.
   **Reason :** Entropy of the system increases with increase in temperature.

5. **Assertion :** An exothermic process which is non-spontaneous at high temperature may become spontaneous at a low temperature.
   **Reason :** There occurs a decrease in entropy factor as the temperature is decreased.

6. **Assertion :** When a solid melts, decrease in enthalpy is observed.
   **Reason :** Melting of a solid is endothermic.

## CASE/PASSAGE BASED QUESTIONS

**DIRECTIONS (Qs. 1-5) :** *Read the following case/passage and answer the questions.*

Work is said to have been done whenever the point of application of a force is displaced in the direction of the force which is given by the equation w = F × dl, where F is the magnitude of the force and dl is the displacement of the point of application in the direction in which the force acts. Two main types of work used in the aerodynamics are electrical work and P – V work. Electrical work done is given by the product of E.M.F and the quantity of electricity flowing through the circuit. Another type of work i.e., work of expansion or compression or P – V work is involved in system consisting of gases. This is the most important from of work used in the study of thermodynamics. It is the work done when the gas expands or contracts against the external pressure. It is a kind of mechanical work. The expression for such a work for irreversible process $w = -P_{ext}\Delta V$ may be given by the following equation. Work done in isothermal reversible expansion of an ideal gas is given by the expression $w = -2.303\ nRT \log \dfrac{V_2}{V_1}$

1. For an isothermal reversible expansion process, the value of $q$ can be calculated by the expression

   (a) $q = 2.303 nRT \log \dfrac{V_2}{V_1}$

   (b) $q = -2.303 nRT \log \dfrac{V_2}{V_1}$

   (c) $q = -P_{exp} nRT \log \dfrac{V_1}{V_2}$

   (d) None of these

2. Under isothermal condition for one mole of ideal gas what is the ratio of work done under reversible to irreversible process, initially held at 20 atm undergoes expansion from 1L to 2L, at 298K, under external pressure of 10 atm?
   (a) 1.7          (b) 2.0
   (c) 1.4          (d) 1.0

3. During isothermal expansion of an ideal gas, its
   (a) internal energy increases
   (b) enthalpy decreases
   (c) enthalpy remains unaffected
   (d) enthalpy reduces to zero.

**DIRECTIONS (Qs. 4-5) :** *Each of these questions contains an assertion followed by reason. Read them carefully and answer the question on the basis of following options. You have to select the one that best describes the two statements.*
   (a) If both Assertion and Reason are correct and the Reason is a correct explanation of the Assertion.
   (b) If both Assertion and Reason are correct but Reason is not a correct explanation of the Assertion.
   (c) If the Assertion is correct but Reason is incorrect.
   (d) If the Assertion is incorrect but the Reason is correct.

4. **Assertion :** At constant temperature and pressure, whatever heat absorbed by the system, is used in doing work.
   **Reason :** Internal energy change is zero.

5. **Assertion :** For an isothermal reversible process $Q = -w$ *i.e.* work done by the system equals the heat absorbed by the system.
   **Reason :** Enthalpy change ($\Delta H$) is zero for isothermal process.

## VERY SHORT ANSWER QUESTIONS

1. State why heat changes in physical and chemical processes are indicated by enthalpy changes and not internal energy changes.

2. In the equation $N_2(g) + 3H_2(g) \rightleftharpoons 2NH_3(g)$, what whould be the sign of work done?

3. Give an example of following energy conversions:
   (i) Radiation energy into chemical energy.
   (ii) Radiation energy into electrical energy.

4. Hydrogen iodide is put in a glass bulb which is sealed and is then heated to decompose hydrogen iodide into $H_2$ and $I_2$. What type of system does the reaction mixture represent.

5. A system is changed from an initial state to a final state by a manner such that $\Delta H = q$. If the change from the initial state to a final state were made by a different path, would $\Delta H$ be the same as that for the first path? Would q too be the same?

6. Can the absolute value of internal energy be determined ?

7. One mole of $CO_2$ at 300 K and 1 atm pressure is heated in a closed vessel so that temperature is 500 K and pressure is 5 atm. Then, it is cooled back to temperature of 300 K and pressure 1 atm. What is the change in internal energy of the gas ?

8. Water decomposes by absorbing 286·2 kJ of electrical energy per mole. When $H_2$ and $O_2$ combine to form one mole of $H_2O$, 286.2 kJ of heat is produced. Which law is proved ? What statement of the law follows from it ?

9. Neither q nor w is a state function, yet q + w is a state function. Explain why.

10. For the same increase in volume, why work done is more if the gas is allowed to expand reversibly at higher temperature ?

11. Give an example of reaction where $\Delta H = \Delta U$

12. What are the limitations of first law of thermodynamics?

13. One kg of graphite is burnt in a closed vessel. The same amount of the same sample is burnt in an open vessel. Will the heat evolved in the two cases be same? If not, in which case it would be greater?

**14.** What is the importance of 'free energy' concept for chemical reaction?

**15.** An endothermic process, $A \rightarrow B$, proceeds to completion. What is sign of $\Delta S$?

**16.** Does an aqueous solution of $Mg^{2+}$ ions have a larger entropy before or after hydration of the ions?

**17.** Why is entropy of a solution higher than that of pure liquid?

**18.** The enthalpy change for the conversion of liquid water to steam is 40.8 kJ at 100°C. Calculate $\Delta S$ for the process.

**19.** If an equation for a reaction is multiplied by 2 and then reversed, how is the value of $\Delta H$ changes?

**20.** What property of enthalpy provides the basis of Hess's law?

**21.** For the reaction $2A + B \rightleftharpoons A_2B$, the $K_p = 2.3 \times 10^2$ at 25°C. Predict the sign of $\Delta G_r°$.

**22.** Why standard heat of formation of diamond is not zero though it is an element ?

**23.** Water can be lifted into the water tank at the top of the house with the help of a motor pump. Then why this change is not considered to be spontaneous ?

**24.** Rank the following in the order of increasing entropy :
   (a) 1 mole of $H_2O$ ($l$) at 25 °C and 1 atm. pressure.
   (b) 2 mole of $H_2O$ (s) at 0 °C and 1 atm. pressure.
   (c) 1 mole of $H_2O$ (g) at 100 °C and 1 atm. pressure.
   (d) 1 mole of $H_2O$ ($l$) at 0 °C and 1 atm. pressure.

**25.** Under what condition, the heat evolved or absorbed in a reaction is equal to its free energy change ?

**26.** The standard free energy of a reaction is found to be zero. What is its equilibrium constant ?

**27.** Place the following systems in order of increasing randomness :
   (a) 1 mol of a gas X
   (b) 1 mol of a solid X
   (c) 1 mol of a liquid X.

**28.** Which out of the following can be determined? Absolute internal energy, absolute enthalpy, absolute entropy.

**29.** Is the bond energy of all the four C — H bonds in $CH_4$ molecule equal? If not then why ? How is the C—H bond energy then reported ?

## SHORT ANSWER QUESTIONS

**1.** What are the sign conventions for heat and work?

**2.** Prove that the change in internal energy is equal to the heat exchanged between the system and the surrounding.

**3.** Prove that the change in enthalpy is equal to the heat exchanged between the system and the surrounding at constant T and P.

**4.** 0.562 g of graphite kept in a bomb calorimeter in excess of oxygen at 298 K and 1 atmospheric pressure was burnt according to the equation
$$C(\text{graphite}) + O_2(g) \rightarrow CO_2(g)$$

During the reaction, temperature rises from 298 K to 298.89 K. If the heat capacity of the calorimeter and its contents is 20.7 kJ/K. What is the enthalpy change for the above reaction at 298 K and 1 atm?

**5.** What would be the heat released when:
   (i) 0.25 mol of hydrochloric acid solution is neutralised by 0.25 mol of sodium hydroxide solution?
   (ii) 0.02 mol of sulphuric acid solution is mixed with 0.2 mol of potassium hydroxide solution?

**6.** Why is it important to give the states of the reactants and products when giving an equation for $\Delta H$?

**7.** Separate out the following into extensive and intensive: Volume, Temperature, Pressure, Boiling point, Free energy

**8.** State whether each of the following processes will increase or decrease the total energy content of the system
   (a) Heat transferred to the surroundings
   (b) Work done by the system
   (c) Work done on the system
   (d) Heat transferred to the system

**9.** A chemist while studying the properties of gaseous $C_2Cl_2F_2$, a chlorofluorocarbon refrigerant, cooled 1.25 g sample at constant atmospheric pressure of 1.0 atm from 320 K to 293 K. During cooling, the sample volume decreased from 274 to 248 mL. Calculate $\Delta H$ and $\Delta U$ for the chlorofluorocarbon for this process. The value of molar heat capacity is 80.7 J mol$^{-1}$ K$^{-1}$.

**10.** What is meant by the reference form of an element? What is the standard enthalpy of formation of an element in its reference form?

**11.** Propane has the structure

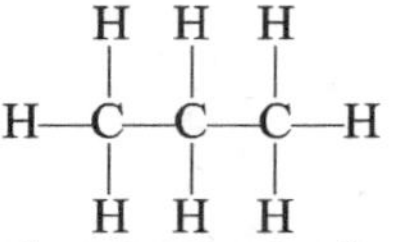

If standard enthalpy change for the reaction ($\Delta_r H°$) $C_3H_8(g) + 5O_2(g) \rightarrow 3CO_2(g) + 4H_2O(g)$ is $-2.05 \times 10^3$ kJ/mol and bond energies of C—C, C—H, C$=$O and O—H are 347, 414, 741 and 464 respectively. Calculate the energy of oxygen-oxygen bond in $O_2$ molecule.

**12.** The reaction $2Mg(s) + O_2(g) \rightarrow 2MgO(s)$ has $\Delta_r S°$ $= -217$ J K$^{-1}$ mol$^{-1}$ and
$\Delta_r H° = -1202$ kJ mol
Predict whether the reaction will be spontaneous or not.

**13.** Silane, $SiH_4$ burns in air. The products are solid $SiO_2$ and gaseous water.

$$SiH_4(g) + 2O_2(g) \longrightarrow SiO_2(s) + 2H_2O(g)$$

**Given :**

| $\Delta_f G°$(kJ/mol: | $-805$ | $-228.6$ | $52.3$ | $0$ |
|---|---|---|---|---|
| Substance : | $SiO_2$ | $H_2O$ | $SiH_4$ | $O_2$ |

Predict the spontaneity of the reaction.

**14.** For the reaction

$$2Fe_2O_3(s) + 3C(s) \rightarrow 4Fe(s) + 3CO_2(g)$$

$$\Delta_r H° = + 467.9 \text{ kJ/mol and}$$

$$\Delta_r S° = + 0.56 \text{ kJ/mol K}$$

Calculate the temperature at which the $\Delta_r G°$ becomes zero. What will be the direction of reaction above this temperature?

**15.** What is the equilibrium constant K for the following reaction at 400 K?

$$2NOCl(g) \rightleftharpoons 2NO(g) + Cl_2(g)$$

Given : $\Delta_r H° = 77.2$ kJ/mol

and $\Delta_r S° = 122$ JK$^{-1}$ mol$^{-1}$ at 400 K.

**16.** Which of the following conditions predict spontaneity:
(a) $\Delta H = +$ ve, $\Delta S = -$ ve, high temperature
(b) $\Delta H = -$ ve, $\Delta S = +$ ve, low temperature
(c) $\Delta H = +$ ve, $\Delta S = +$ ve, high temperature
(d) $\Delta H = -$ve, $\Delta S = -$ ve, low temperature?

**17.** Calculate $\Delta H_f°$ for chloride ion from the following data:

$$\frac{1}{2} H_2 (g) + \frac{1}{2} Cl_2 (g) \longrightarrow HCl (g) ;$$

$$\Delta_f H° = -92.8 \text{ kJ mol}^{-1}$$

$$HCl (g) + H_2O (l) \longrightarrow H_3O^+ (aq) + Cl^- (aq),$$

$$\Delta_{diss} H° = -75.2 \text{ kJ mol}^{-1}$$

**18.** Predict whether following reaction will be exothermic or endothermic. Give reason for your answer

$$H–H (g) + Cl–Cl (g) \longrightarrow 2H–Cl (g)$$

**19.** What do you mean by a spontaneous process ? Explain your answer with a suitable examples.

**20.** Which of the following processes are accompanied by increase of entropy ?
(a) Dissolution of iodine in a solvent,
(b) HCl is added to $AgNO_3$ solution to form a ppt. of AgCl.
(c) A partition is removed to allow gases to mix.
(d) Formation of $NH_3$ from $N_2$ and $H_2$

**21.** Predict the sign of entropy change for each of the following changes of state :
(a) $Hg(l) \longrightarrow Hg(g)$
(b) $AgNO_3(s) \longrightarrow AgNO_3(aq)$
(c) $I_2(g) \longrightarrow I_2(s)$
(d) $C(graphite) \longrightarrow C(diamond)$

**22.** An exothermic reaction $A \longrightarrow B$ is spontaneous in the backward direction. What will be the sign of $\Delta S$ for the forward reaction ?

**23.** Which of the following processes are accompanied by increase of entropy ?

(a) Stretching of rubber band,
(b) Boiling of an egg
(c) A deodrant is sprayed.

**24.** At a certain temperature 'T', the endothermic reaction A $\longrightarrow$ B proceeds virtually to the end. Determine
(i) sign of $\Delta S$ for this reaction (ii) sign of $\Delta G$ for the reaction B $\longrightarrow$ A at the temperature T, and (iii) the possibility of reaction B $\longrightarrow$ A proceeding at a low temperature.

## Long Answer Questions

**1.** A system containing an ideal gas was subjected to a number of changes as shown in the P-V diagram below. Temperatures at different points are indicated in the diagram.
(i) Name the type of process at each step.
(ii) What will be the value of $\Delta E$ for the complete process?
(iii) At which point, the number of moles of the gas will be maximum ?

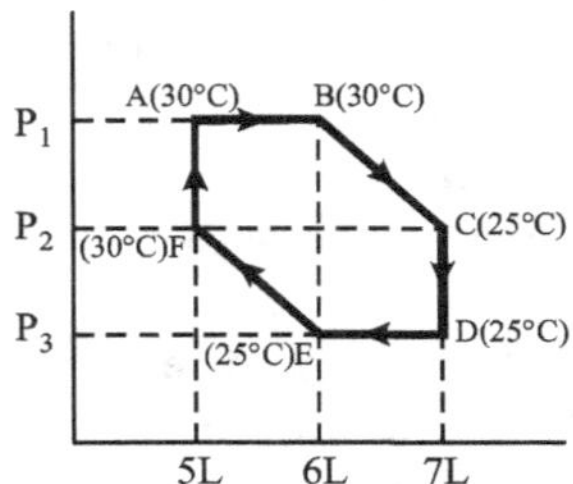


**2.** Define the following terms :
(a) System
(b) Isothermal processes
(c) Adiabatic processes
(d) State variables/state functions
(e) Work

**3.** (i) Calculate the standard molar entropy change for the following reactions at 298 K.
(a) $4 Fe (s) + 3 O_2 (g) \longrightarrow 2 Fe_2O_3(s).$
(b) $Ca (s) + 2 H_2O (l) \longrightarrow Ca(OH)_2 (aq) + H_2 (g)$
**Given:**

$$S°_{Fe(s)} = 27.28, \quad S°_{O_2(g)} = 205.14,$$

$$S°_{Fe_2O_3 (s)} = 87.4$$

$$S°_{Ca(s)} = 41.42, \quad S°_{H_2O(l)} = 69.9,$$

$$S°_{Ca(OH)_2(aq)} = 74.5, \quad S°_{H_2(g)} = 130.68$$

(ii) Calculate the standard molar Gibbs energy of formation of $CS_2$, given that its standard enthalpy of formation is 89.7 kJ mol$^{-1}$ and the standard molar entropies of graphite, S and $CS_2$ are 5.7, 31.8 and 151.3 JK$^{-1}$mol$^{-1}$ respectively.

**4. (i)** Why standard entropy of an elementary substance is not zero whereas standard enthalpy of formation is taken as zero?

**(ii)** Under what conditions will the reaction occur, if

(a) both $\Delta H$ and $\Delta S$ are positive

(a) both $\Delta H$ and $\Delta S$ are negative

**5.** Derive Gibbs – Helmholtz equation.

**6.** Calculate the enthalpy of formation of anhydrous aluminium chloride, $Al_2Cl_6$ from the following data:

(i) $2Al\ (s) + 6HCl\ (aq) \rightarrow Al_2Cl_6\ (aq.) + 3H_2(g);$

$$\Delta H = -1004.0\ kJ$$

(ii) $H_2(g) + Cl_2(g) \rightarrow 2HCl(g);\ \Delta H = -183.9\ kJ$

(iii) $HCl\ (g) \rightarrow HCl\ (aq);$

$\Delta H = -73.2\ kJ$

(iv) $Al_2Cl_6(s) + (aq) \rightarrow Al_2Cl_6\ (aq);\ \Delta H = -643\ kJ$

**7.** For the reaction

$$2H_2O_{(l)} \rightleftharpoons 2H_{2(g)} + O_{2(g)}$$

at 25°C, the equilibrium constant is $7.0 \times 10^{-84}$.

(i) Calculate the standard Gibbs energy formations of water at 25°C.

(ii) $\Delta_r\ H°_{H_2O} = -280\ kJ\ mol^{-1}$. Calculate the entropy change for the reaction.

## SOLUTIONS

### *Multiple Choice Questions*

**1. (b)** The laws of thermodynamics deal with energy changes of macroscopic systems involving a large number of molecules rather than microscopic systems containing a few molecules.

**2. (c)** Closed system can exchange energy but not matter with surroundings. Pressure cooker provides closed system.

**3. (b)** We can describe the state of a gas by quoting its pressure ($P$), volume ($V$), temperature ($T$), amount ($n$) etc.

**4. (c)** Internal energy and molar enthalpy are state functions. Work (reversible or irreversible) is a path function.

**5. (d)** The positive sign expresses when work is done on the system. Similarly, negative sign expresses when work is done by the system.

**6. (d)** The difference between $\Delta H$ and $\Delta U$ is not usually significant for systems consisting of only solids or liquids. Solids and liquids do not suffer any significant volume changes upon heating. The difference, however, becomes significant when gases are involved.

**7. (b)** The coefficients in a balanced thermo-chemical equation refer to the number of moles (not to molecules) of reactants and products involved in the reaction.

**8. (b)** (Given): Enthalpy of formation of $C_2H_4, CO_2$ and $H_2O$ are 52, – 394 and – 286 kJ/ mol respectively.

The reaction is

$C_2H_4 + 3O_2 \rightarrow 2CO_2 + 2H_2O.$

$(\Delta H)_{reaction} = \Delta H_{products} - \Delta H_{reactants}$

$= 2 \times (-394) + 2 \times (-286) - (52 + 0)$

$= -1412\ kJ/\ mol$

**9. (b)** Enthalpy change is a state function.

**10. (a)** $Fe_2O_3(s) + CO(g) \longrightarrow 2FeO(s) + CO_2(g)$

$[(i) - 2 \times (ii)]$

$\Delta H = -26.8 + 33.0 = +6.2\ kJ$

**11. (a)** Hess's law is used for calculating enthalpy of reaction.

**12. (a)** $H_2O\ (l) \rightleftharpoons H_2O\ (g) + Q\ ;\ \Delta n_g = 1$

$\Delta H = \Delta E + \Delta n_g\ RT$

$40660 = \Delta E + 1 \times 8.314 \times 373$

$\Delta E = 37558\ J\ /\ mol$

$\Delta E = 37.56\ kJ\ mol^{-1}$

**13. (a)** Crystallization of sucrose solution. Entropy is a measure of randomness during the crystallisation of sucrose solution liquid state is changing into solid state hence entropy decreases.

### *Assertion & Reason Questions*

**1. (c)** Values of state functions depend only on the state of the system and not on how it is reached.

**2. (a)** It is fact that absolute values of internal energy of substances cannot be determined. It is also true that it is not possible to determine exact values of constitutent energies of a substance.

**3. (c)** It may involve increase or decrease in temperature of the system. Systems in which such processes occur, are thermally insulated from the surroundings.

**4. (b)** The factor $T\Delta S$ increases with increase in temperature.

**5. (b)** Both assertion and reason are true but reason is not the correct explanation of assertion.

For a process to be spontaneous $\Delta G$ must be negative.

$\Delta G = \Delta H - T\Delta S$

Exothermic process ($\Delta H$ is negative) is non-spontaneous if $\Delta S$ is negative and temperature is high because in such condition $T\Delta S > \Delta H$. ($\Delta G = \Delta H - T\Delta S$ = +ve). When temperature is decreased, $T\Delta S < \Delta H$ ($\Delta G = \Delta H - T\Delta S = $ —ive) and so the reaction becomes spontaneous.

6. **(d)** When a solid melts, increase in enthalpy is observed.

### *Case/Passage Based Questions*

1. **(a)** $q = -w = 2.303nRT \log \dfrac{V_2}{V_1}$

2. **(a)** $-w_{\text{irreversible}} = P_{ext}(V_2 - V_1)$
$= 10 \, \text{atm} \, (2L - 1L) = 10 \, \text{atm} - L$

$-w_{\text{reversible}} = 2.303 \, nRT \log \dfrac{V_2}{V_1}$

$= 1 \times 2.303 \times 0.0821 \times 298 \, \text{atm–L/K/mol} \times \log \dfrac{2}{1}$

$= 16.96 \, \text{atm–L}$

$\dfrac{w_{\text{reversible}}}{w_{\text{irreversible}}} = \dfrac{16.96}{10.00} = 1.69 \approx 1.7$

3. **(c)** During isothermal expansion of an ideal gas,
$\Delta T = 0$. Now $H = E + PV$
$\because \Delta H = \Delta E + \Delta(PV)$
$\therefore \Delta H = \Delta E + \Delta(nRT)$;
Thus if $\Delta T = 0$., $\Delta H = \Delta E$
*i.e.*, remain unaffected

4. **(a)** if $\Delta E = 0$, $\Delta E = \Delta Q - w \Rightarrow \Delta Q = w$

5. **(b)** In an isothermal process change in internal energy ($\Delta E$) is zero (as it is a function of temperature).
$\therefore$ According to first law of thermodynamics
$\because \quad Q + w = \Delta E$. Hence $Q = -w$ (if $\Delta E = 0$)
If a system undergoes a change in which internal energy of the system remains constant (i.e. $\Delta E = 0$) then $-w = Q$. This means that work done by the system equals the heat absorbed by the system.

### *Very Short Answer Questions*

1. Most of the processes are carried out in open container, i.e., at constant pressure. Therefore, enthalpy changes are indicated and not internal energy changes.

2. The sign of work done will be +ve i.e. work will be done on the system due to decrease in volume.

3. (i) Photosynthesis
(ii) Photoelectric effect.

4. The reaction mixture represents a closed system as there is an exchange of energy between the system and the surrounding.

5. $\Delta H$ is the same, since it is a state function, but q will be different for the different paths.

6. No, because it is the sum of different types of energies some of which cannot be determined.

7. No change because internal energy is a state function and in this case system has returned to its original state.

8. Law of conservation of energy (or 1st law of thermodynamics). According to this law energy can neither be created or destroyed, although it may be converted from one form to another.

9. For a given change in state, q and w can vary depending on how the change is carried out. However, q + w = $\Delta E$ will depend only on initial and final state. It will be independent of the way the change is carried out.

10. For isothermal reversible expansion,
w = $-P_{int} \times \Delta V$. At higher temperature, internal pressure of the gas is more.

11. $H_2 (g) + Cl_2 (g) \rightarrow 2HCl(g)$, as $\Delta n_g = 0$

12. It could not give information about the spontaneity of chemical reactions.

13. Same in both cases because $\Delta n_g = 0$.

14. Free energy helps in determining spontaneity of the process.

15. $\Delta S$ is positive.

16. $Mg^{2+}$ has more entropy before hydration of ions.

17. In solution, there is more disorderness than in pure liquid.

18. $\Delta S = \dfrac{\Delta H_{vap}}{T} = \dfrac{40.8}{373} = 0.1094 \, \text{kJ mol}^{-1} \, \text{K}^{-1}$.

19. When a thermochemical equation is multiplied by 2, the value of $\Delta H$ becomes double, i.e. $2\Delta H$. When a chemical equation is reversed, the value of $\Delta H$ is reversed in sign i.e. $- 2\Delta H$.

20. (a) Enthalpy is a state function and (b) law of conservation of energy are the two basis of Hess's law. Hess's law enables us to predict the enthalpies of reactions that we cannot measure directly in the laboratory.

21. We know that $\Delta G_r^\circ = - 2.303 \, RT \log K_p$
If $K_p > 1$, then $\Delta G_r^\circ < 0$
In this reaction, $K_p = 2.3 \times 10^2$ is greater than 1, therefore, $\Delta G_r^\circ$ will have a negative sign.

22. It is because standard state chosen for carbon is graphite and not diamond.

23. A spontaneous process is one which should continue by itself after initiation. But this is not so in the given case because water will go up so long as the pump is working.

24. (b) < (d) < (a) < (c).

25. As $\Delta G = \Delta H - T\Delta S$. Thus, $\Delta G = \Delta H$ only when either the reaction is carried out at 0 K or the reaction is not accompanied by any entropy change, i.e., $\Delta S = 0$.

26. $\Delta G^\circ = - 2.303 \, RT \log K$. Hence, $\log K = 0$ or $K = 1$.

**27.** 1 mol of solid X < 1 mol of liquid X < 1 mol of gas X.

**28.** Absolute entropy.

**29.** No because after breaking of C—H bonds one by one, the electronic environments change. The reported value is the average value of the bond dissociation energies of the four C—H bonds.

### Short Answer Questions

**1.** The sign conventions for heat (q) are:
Heat absorbed by the system is positive, $q > 0$
Heat released by the system is negative, $q < 0$
The sign conventions for work (w) are:
work done on the system is positive, $w_{on} > 0$
work done by the system is negative, $w_{by} < 0$

**2.** $\Delta E = q + w$
(First law of thermodynamics)
$q$ = energy supplied to the system as heat
$w$ = work done on the system
If the work is a $P - V$ work, then $w = P\Delta V$
Therefore, $\Delta E = q + P\Delta V$
If the system is closed (like bomb calorimeter), then $\Delta V = 0$
$\therefore \quad \Delta E = q_v$
Hence, the heat exchange between the system and the surrounding is equal to change in internal energy.

**3.** $\Delta H = \Delta E + P\Delta V$ (at constant P)
But $\Delta E = q + w$ (Ist law of thermodynamics)
or $\Delta E = q - P\Delta V$ ($\because w = -P\Delta V$)
$\therefore \quad \Delta H = q - P\Delta V + P\Delta V$
$\Delta H = q_p$

**4.** $\Delta H = \Delta E + \Delta n_g RT$
For the reaction C(graphite) $+ O_2(g) \rightarrow CO_2(g)$, $\Delta n_g = 0$
$\therefore \quad \Delta H = \Delta U = q_v$
$\Delta H = q_v = C_v (\Delta T)$
$= 20.7$ kJ K$^{-1}$ $\times 0.89$ K $= 18.4$ kJ
As the reaction is a combustion reaction (exothermic) $\Delta H = -18.4$ kJ for the combustion of 0.562 g of C (graphite)
For 1 mol C (graphite),

$$\Delta H = -18.4 \times \frac{12.0}{0.562}$$

$\Delta H = -392.88$ kJ/mol
The enthalpy of combustion of graphite is $-392.88$ kJ mol$^{-1}$

**5.** (i) 0.25 mole HCl(aq) + 0.25 mole NaOH(aq)
The net reaction is
$H^+$ (0.25 mole) $+ OH^-$ (0.25 mole) $\rightarrow H_2O$ (0.25 mole)
Therefore heat released = $57.1 \times 0.25$ kJ
$= 14.3$ kJ

(ii) 1 mole of $H_2SO_4$ contains 2 mole of $H^+$
$\therefore$ 0.02 mole of $H_2SO_4$ contains 0.04 mole of $H^+$

The net reaction is
$H^+$ (0.04 mole) $+ OH^-$ (0.2 mole) $\rightarrow H_2O$ (0.04 mole)
Therefore heat released would be
$0.04 \times 57.1 = 2.284$ kJ

**6.** It is important to specify the states (whether a gas, liquid, solid or aqueous) of the reactants and products while writing the thermochemical equation because the enthalpy change, $\Delta H$ depends on the state of the substances. Consider the reaction of hydrogen and oxygen to produce water. If the product is water vapour, 2 moles of $H_2$ burn to release 483.7 kJ of heat.

$2H_2(g) + O_2(g) \rightarrow 2H_2O(g)$; $\Delta H = -483.7$ kJ
On the other hand, if the product is liquid water, the heat released is 571.7 kJ

$2H_2(g) + O_2(g) \rightarrow 2H_2O(l)$; $\Delta H = -571.7$ kJ
In this case, additional heat is released when water vapour condenses to liquid.

**7.** The properties which depend upon the quantity of the substance or substances present in the system. The properties which are independent of the quantity of the substance present in the system volume and free energy are extensive, others are intensive.

**8.** (a) decrease       (b) decrease
(c) increase       (d) increase

**9.** $q = \Delta E = -C\Delta T$
$q = -80.7$ J mol$^{-1}$ K$^{-1}$ $\times 27$ K
$= -2178.9$ J mol$^{-1}$
$\Delta E = -2178.9$ J mol$^{-1}$ $\times \dfrac{1.25g}{133g\,mol^{-1}}$
$\Delta E = -20.48$ J
$\Delta H = \Delta E + P\Delta V$
$P\Delta V = 1$ atm $\times (274 - 248) \times 10^{-3}$ L
$= 0.026$ L atm
$= 0.026 \times 101$ J $= 2.626$ J
$\therefore \quad \Delta H = -20.48$ J $- 2.626$ J
$\Delta H = -23.11$ J

**10.** The reference form of an element is the stablest form (physical state and allotrope) of the elements under standard thermodynamics conditions. The reference form of oxygen at 298 K is $O_2(g)$, the reference form of carbon at 298K is graphite.
The standard enthalpy of formation ($\Delta_f H°$) of an element in its reference form is zero.

**11.** $\Delta_r H° = \Sigma$ BE(reactants) $- \Sigma$ BE (products)
$\Delta_r H° = [8\,BE(C—H) + 2\,BE(C—C) + 5\,BE(O=O)] - [6\,BE(C=O) + 8\,BE(O—H)]$
$-2.05 \times 10^3 = [8 \times 414 + 2 \times 347 + 5\,BE\,(O=O)] - [6 \times 741 + 8 \times 464]$
$-2050 = 4006 + 5\,BE\,(O=O) - 8158$
$5BE\,(O=O) = 2102$
$BE(O=O) = 420.4$ kJ mol$^{-1}$

**12.** The criterion for spontaneity is that $\Delta S_{total} > 0$ and
$\Delta S_{total} = \Delta S_{system} + \Delta S_{surr}$.
Given : $\Delta S_{system} = -217\ J\ K^{-1}\ mol^{-1}$
As the reaction is exothermic, the heat evolved will increase the entropy of the surrounding.

$$\Delta S_{surr.} = -\Delta S_{sys} = \frac{-\Delta H_{sys}}{T}$$

$$= \frac{-(-1202 \times 10^3)}{298}$$

$\Delta S_{surr} = 4.03 \times 10^3\ J\ K^{-1}\ mol^{-1}$

$\therefore\quad \Delta S_{total} = \Delta S_{sys} + \Delta S_{surr}$
$= -217 + 4030$
$= 3813\ J\ K^{-1}\ mol^{-1}$

As $\Delta S_{total} > 0$, the reaction will be spontaneous.

**13.** To predict whether the reaction is spontaneous or not, we should first calculate $\Delta_r G^\circ$. For the reaction

$$SiH_4(g) + 2O_2(g) \longrightarrow SiO_2(s) + 2H_2O(g)$$

$$\Delta_r G^\circ = [\Delta_f G^\circ_{(SiO_2)} + 2\Delta_f G^\circ_{(H_2O)}]$$

$$-[\Delta_f G^\circ_{(SiH_4)} + 2\Delta_f G^\circ_{(O_2)}]$$

$\Delta_r G^\circ = [-805 + 2(-228.6)] - [+52.3 + 2 \times 0]$
$\Delta_r G^\circ = [-805 - 457.2] - 52.3$
$\Delta_r G^\circ = -1314.5\ kJ/mol$

The reaction would be spontaneous as $\Delta_r G^\circ$ is negative.

**14.** We know the Gibbs energy equation is
$\Delta_r G^\circ = \Delta_r H^\circ - T\Delta_r S^\circ$
Temperature at which the $\Delta_r G^\circ$ become zero is given by

$$0 = \Delta_r H^\circ - T\Delta_r S^\circ \text{ and } T = \frac{\Delta_r H^\circ}{\Delta_r S^\circ}$$

$$T = \frac{467.9\ kJ\ mol^{-1}}{0.56\ kJ\ mol^{-1}\ K^{-1}}$$

$T = 835.5\ K$

Above this temperature, sign of $\Delta_r G^\circ$ will be negative, $\Delta_r G^\circ < 0$. Therefore, the forward direction will be favourable.

**15.** Step (1) is to calculate $\Delta_r G^\circ$
$\quad\quad \Delta_r G^\circ = \Delta_r H^\circ - T\Delta_r S^\circ$
$= (77.2\ kJ\ mol^{-1}) - 400\ K \times (122 \times 10^{-3}\ kJ\ K^{-1}\ mol^{-1})$
$\Delta_r G^\circ = (77.2 - 48.8)\ kJ\ mol^{-1}$
$\Delta_r G^\circ = 28.4\ kJ\ mol^{-1}$
Step (2) is to calculate K

$$\log K = \frac{-\Delta_r G^\circ}{2.303\ RT}$$

$$= \frac{-28.4\ kJ\ mol^{-1}}{2.303 \times 8.314 \times 10^{-3}\ kJ\ mol^{-1}\ K^{-1} \times 400\ K}$$

$\log K = -3.708$
$K = \text{antilog } (\overline{4}.292)$
$K = 1.96 \times 10^{-4}$

**16.** (a) $\Delta H = +\ ve$, $\Delta S = -\ ve$, high temperature
$\quad\quad \Delta G = (+) - T(-) = +\ ve$
$\quad\quad$ Non-spontaneous at all temperatures.

(b) $\Delta H = -\ ve$, $\Delta S = +\ ve$, low temperature
$\quad\quad \Delta G = (-) - T(+) = -\ ve$
$\quad\quad$ Spontaneous at all temperature.

(c) $\Delta H = +\ ve$, $\Delta S = +\ ve$, high temperature
$\quad\quad \Delta G = (+) - T(+)$ At high temperature
$\quad\quad (T\Delta S > \Delta H)$, $\Delta G = -\ ve$ and therefore reaction will be spontaneous.

(d) $\Delta H = -\ ve$, $\Delta S = -\ ve$, low temperature
$\quad\quad \Delta G = (-) - T(-)$ ; at low temperature
$\quad\quad (T\Delta S < \Delta H)$
$\quad\quad \Delta G = -\ ve$ and therefore reaction will be spontaneous.

**17.** From the second reaction,
$\Delta_r H^\circ = \{\Delta_f H^\circ\ [H_3O^+\ (aq)] + \Delta_f\ H^\circ\ [Cl^-\ (aq)]\} - \Delta_f H^\circ$ (HCl)
But enthalpy of formation of $H^+$ ion in dilute aqueous solution is taken as zero, i.e.,
$\Delta_f H^\circ [H_3O^+(aq)] = 0$
Also from the first reaction,
$\Delta_f H^\circ$ (HCl) $= -92 \cdot 8\ kJ\ mol^{-1}$
$-75.2 = 0 + \Delta_f H^\circ[Cl^-(aq)] - (-92.8)$
$\Delta_f H^\circ[Cl^-\ (aq)] = -75.2 - 92.8 = -168.0\ kJ\ mol^{-1}$.

**18.** This reaction is accompanied by decrease of randomness, i.e., decrease of entropy. For the reaction to be spontaneous total entropy change should be negative. A reaction would be exothermic with respect to the system if it adds entropy to the surroundings and endothermic if it reduces entropy of surrounding.
$\Delta S_{surr} > 0 \Rightarrow$ exothermic $\Delta S_{surr} < 0 \Rightarrow$ endothermic.

**19.** Process which takes place by itself or by some initiation. Example- water flowing down hill is a spontaneous process but the reverse is a non-spontaneous process. Burning of coal has to be initiated by igniting some coals to fire but once ignited it will continue burning even if the igniting flame is removed.

**20.** (a) When solid iodine is dissolved in a suitable solvent it forms iodine solution. Thus entropy increases.

(b) HCl (aq) + $AgNO_3$(aq) $\rightarrow$ AgCl(s) + $HNO_3$(aq)
$\quad\quad$ Formation of solid ppt. (AgCl) entropy decreases.

(c) When a partition is removed to allow intermixing of gases. The volume increases and hence entropy also.
$\quad\quad N_2(g) + 3H_2(g) \rightarrow 2NH_3(g)$

(d) As per above equation total number of moles of gaseous species decreases. Thus entropy decreases.

**21.** (a) $\Delta S = +ve$     (b) $\Delta S = +ve$
    (c) $\Delta S = -ve$     (d) $\Delta S = -ve$.

**22.** Backward reaction will be endothermic. Thus, energy factor opposes the backward reaction. As backward reaction is spontaneous, randomness factor must favour, i.e., $\Delta S$ will be $+$ ve for backward reaction or it will be $-ve$ for forward reaction.

**23.** (b) and (c).

**24.** (i) As we know that $\Delta G = \Delta H - T\Delta S$. For endothermic reactions $\Delta H = +ve$. Thus for $\Delta G = -ve$, $\Delta S$ must be positive.

(ii) For $A \longrightarrow B$, $\Delta G$ is $-ve$, therefore, for $B \longrightarrow A$, $\Delta G$ will be $+ve$.

(iii) For $B \longrightarrow A$, $\Delta H = -ve$ and $\Delta S$ is also $-ve$, i.e., $\Delta S$ opposes the process but at low temp., $T\Delta S$ may be so low that $\Delta H$ is greater in magnitude than $T\Delta S$ and the process will be spontaneous.

### Long Answer Questions

**1.** (i) AB = isothermal and isobaric expansion
BC = adiabatic expansion (temperature falls)
CD = isochoric and isothermal
DE = isothermal and isobaric compression
EF = adiabatic compression (temperature rises)
FA = isothermal and isochoric.

(ii) As complete process is cyclic, therefore, $\Delta U = 0$.

(iii) Process AB is accompanied by increase of volume due to increase in the number of moles. Process BC is accompanied by increase in volume due to fall of temperature. Process CD is accompanied by fall of pressure due to decrease in the number of moles. Process DE is due to decrease in the number of moles. In process EF, there will be no change in the number of moles. Process FA is accompanied by increase of pressure due to higher number of moles at A. But as already explained, at B number of moles is greater than that at A. Hence, the number of moles is maximum at point B.

**2.** (a) It is that part of the universe which is under observation.

(b) Process in which temperature remains constant throughout the process is known as isothermal process. When such a process occurs, heat can flow from the system to the surrounding and vice-versa.

(c) Adiabatic process is a process which is carried out in such a manner that no heat can flow from the system to the surrounding or vice-versa.

(d) Functions or variable which depend on the initial and the final state of the system.

(e) Work is said to have been done whenever the point of application of a force is displaced in the direction of force.

**3.** (i) (a) $\Delta S^\circ = S^\circ_{(Products)} - S^\circ_{(Reactants)}$
$= [2 \times S^\circ_{(Fe_2O_3)\,(s)}] - [4 \times S^\circ_{Fe\,(s)} + 3 \times S^\circ_{O_2\,(g)}]$
$= (2 \times 87.4) - (4 \times 27.28 + 3 \times 205.14) JK^{-1}\,mol^{-1}$
$= 174.8 - (109.12 + 615.42)\,JK^{-1}\,mol^{-1}$
$= -549.74\,JK^{-1}\,mol^{-1}$

(b) $\Delta S^\circ = \left[ S^\circ_{Ca(OH)_2\,(aq)} + S^\circ_{H_2\,(g)} \right]$
$\quad\quad - \left[ S^\circ_{Ca(s)} + 2 \times S^\circ_{H_2O(l)} \right]$
$= [74.5 + 130.68] - [41.42 + 2 \times 69.9]$
$= 205.18 - 181.22 = 23.96\,JK^{-1}\,mol^{-1}$

(ii) $C + 2S \longrightarrow CS_2$
$\Delta S^\circ = [S^\circ_{CS_2} - (S^\circ_C + 2\,S^\circ_S]$
$= 151.3 - (5.7 + 2 \times 31.8) = 82\,JK^{-1}\,mol^{-1}$
$= 0.082\,kJ\,K^{-1}\,mol^{-1}$
$\Delta G^\circ = \Delta H^\circ - T\Delta S^\circ = 89.7\,kJ\,mol^{-1}$
$-298 \times (0.082\,kJ\,K^{-1}mol^{-1}) = 65.27\,kJ\,mol^{-1}$.

**4.** (i) Substance has perfectly ordered arrangement of its constituent particles only at absolute zero. When the element formed from itself. This means no heat change. Thus, $\Delta_f H = 0$

(ii) (a) If both $\Delta H$ and $\Delta S$ are positive $\Delta G$ can be $-ve$ only $T\Delta S > \Delta H$ in magnitude.
Thus the temperature should be high.
(b) If both $\Delta H$ and $\Delta S$ are negative $\Delta G$ can be negative only $T\Delta S < \Delta H$ is magnitude. Thus the value of T should be low.

**5.** Gibbs – Helmholtz equation is
$$\Delta G = \Delta H - T\Delta S$$
where $\Delta G$ = Change in free energy
$\Delta H$ = Change in enthalpy
$T$ = Kelvin temperature
$\Delta S$ = Change in entropy

**Derivation :** Let us consider a reactions being carried out at constant temperature, T and constant pressure, P.
Let $G_R$ = Free energy of reactants
$H_R$ = Enthalpy of reactants
$S_R$ = Entropy of reactants
$G_P$ = Free energy of products
$H_P$ = Enthalpy of products
$S_P$ = Entropy of products.
We know that, $G = H - T_S$
For reactants, $G_R = H_R - TS_R$
For products, $G_P = H_P - TS_P$
$\Delta G = G_P - G_R$
$\quad\quad = (H_P - TS_P) - (H_R - TS_R)$
$\quad\quad = H_P - TS_P - H_R + TS_R$
$\quad\quad = (H_P - H_R) - T(S_P - S_R)$
$\Delta G = \Delta H - T\Delta S$
which is Gibbs –Helmholtz equation.

**6.** The formation of $Al_2Cl_6$ from its elements may be represented as:

$$2Al\,(s) + 3Cl_2\,(g) \rightarrow Al_2Cl_6\,(s)$$

Multiply Eq. (ii) by 3 and Eq. (iii) by 6 and adding,

$$3H_2(g) + 3Cl_2(g) \rightarrow 6HCl(g);\ \Delta H = -551.7\ kJ \quad ...(ii)$$

$$6HCl(g) + (aq) \rightarrow 6HCl(aq);\ \Delta H = -439.2 kJ \quad ...(iii)$$

$$3H_2(g) + 3Cl_2(g) + (aq) \rightarrow 6HCl\,(aq);\ \Delta H = -990.9\ kJ \quad ...(v)$$

Add eq. (i) and eq. (v)

$$2Al(s) + 6HCl(aq) \rightarrow Al_2Cl_6(aq) + 3H_2(g);$$
$$\Delta H = -1004.0\ kJ \quad ...(i)$$

$$3H_2(g) + 3Cl_2(g) + (aq) \rightarrow 6HCl\,(aq);$$
$$\Delta H = -990.9\ kJ \quad ...(v)$$

$$2Al(s) + 3Cl_2(g) + (aq) \rightarrow Al_2Cl_6(aq);$$
$$\Delta H = -1994.9\ kJ \quad ...(vi)$$

Subtract eq. (iv) from eq. (vi)

$$2Al(s) + 3Cl_2(g) + (aq) \rightarrow Al_2Cl_6\,(aq);$$
$$\Delta H = -1994.9\ kJ \quad ...(vi)$$

$$Al_2Cl_6(s) + (aq) \rightarrow Al_2Cl_6(aq);$$
$$\Delta H = -643\ kJ \quad ...(iv)$$

$$2Al(s) + 3Cl_2(g) \rightarrow Al_2Cl_6(s);\ \Delta H = -1351.9\ kJ.$$

Thus, enthalpy of formation or anhydrous $Al_2Cl_6$
$$= -1351.9\ kJ$$

**7.** Using equation $\Delta_r\,G° = -2.303\ RT \log K_p$

(i) $\Delta_r\,G° = -2.303 \times 8.314\ J\ mol^{-1}\ K^{-1} \times 298\ K \times \log 7.0 \times 10^{-84}$

$\Delta_r\,G° = -2.303 \times 8.314 \times 298 \times (-83.15)\ J\ mol^{-1}$

$\Delta_r\,G° = 474441\ J\ mol^{-1} = 474.44\ kJ\ mol^{-1}$

For the reaction $2H_2O_{(l)} \rightleftharpoons 2H_{2(g)} + O_{2(g)}$

$\Delta_r G° = [2\Delta_r\,G°_{H_2} + \Delta_f\,G°_{O_2}] - 2\,\Delta_f\,G°_{H_2O}$

$474.44 = (0 + 0) - 2\Delta_f\,G°_{H_2O}$

$\therefore \quad \Delta_f G°_{H_2O} = -\dfrac{474.44}{2}$

$\qquad = -237.22\ kJ\ mol^{-1}$

(ii) $\Delta_r H° = [2\,\Delta_f\,H°_{H_2} + \Delta_f\,H°_{O_2}] - 2\Delta_f H°_{H_2O}$

$\Delta_r\,H° = (0 + 0) - 2\,(-286)$

$\Delta_r\,H° = 572\ kJ\ mol^{-1}$

Using equation $\Delta_r G° = \Delta_r\,H° - T\,\Delta_r\,S°$
we calculate $\Delta_r\,S°$

$$\Delta_r\,S° = \frac{\Delta_r H° - \Delta_r G°}{T}$$

$$\Delta_r\,S° = \frac{(572\,kJ\,mol^{-1}) - (474.44\,kJ\,mol^{-1})}{298\,K}$$

$\Delta_r S° = 0.327\ kJ\ mol^{-1}\ K^{-1}$

$\Delta_r S° = 327\ J\ mol^{-1}\ K^{-1}$

---

## SECTION C — NCERT EXEMPLAR QUESTIONS 

### MULTIPLE CHOICE QUESTIONS

**1.** Thermodynamics is not concerned about
   (a) energy changes involved in a chemical reaction
   (b) the extent to which a chemical reaction proceeds
   (c) the rate at which a reaction proceeds
   (d) the feasibility of a chemical reaction

**2.** Which of the following statement is correct?
   (a) The presence of reacting species in a covered beaker is an example of open system.
   (b) There is an exchange of energy as well as matter between the system and the surroundings in a closed system.
   (c) The presence of reactants in a closed vessel made up of copper is an example of a closed system.
   (d) The presence of reactants in a thermos flask or any other closed insulated vessel is an example of a closed system.

**3.** The state of a gas can be described by quoting the relationship between
   (a) pressure, volume, temperature
   (b) temperature, amount, pressure
   (c) amount, volume, temperature
   (d) pressure, volume, temperature, amount

**4.** The volume of gas is reduced to half from its original volume. The specific heat will be
   (a) reduce to half
   (b) be doubled
   (c) remain constant
   (d) increase four times

**5.** $\Delta_f U°$ of formation of $CH_4(g)$ at certain temperature is $-393\ kJ\ mol^{-1}$. The value of $\Delta_f H°$ is
   (a) zero
   (b) $< \Delta_f U°$
   (c) $> \Delta_f U°$
   (d) equal to $\Delta_f U°$

**6.** In an adiabatic process, no transfer of heat takes place between system and surroundings. Choose the correct option for free expansion of an ideal gas under adiabatic condition from the following.
   (a) $q = 0,\ \Delta T \neq 0,\ W = 0$
   (b) $q \neq 0,\ \Delta T = 0,\ W = 0$
   (c) $q = 0,\ \Delta T = 0,\ W = 0$
   (d) $q = 0,\ \Delta T < 0,\ W \neq 0$

## ASSERTION & REASON QUESTIONS

**DIRECTIONS (Qs. 1-2) :** *Each of these questions contains an assertion followed by reason. Read them carefully and answer the question on the basis of following options. You have to select the one that best describes the two statements.*

(a) If both Assertion and Reason are correct and the Reason is a correct explanation of the Assertion.

(b) If both Assertion and Reason are correct but Reason is not a correct explanation of the Assertion.

(c) If the Assertion is correct but Reason is incorrect.

(d) If the Assertion is incorrect but the Reason is correct.

1. **Assertion :** Combustion of all organic compounds is an exothermic reaction.
   **Reason :** The enthalpies of all elements in their standard state are zero.

2. **Assertion :** Spontaneous process is an irreversible process and may be reversed by some external agency.
   **Reason :** Decrease in enthalpy is a contributory factor for spontaneity.

## SHORT ANSWER QUESTIONS

1. Given that $\Delta H = 0$ for mixing of two gases. Explain whether the diffusion of these gases into each other in a closed container is a spontaneous process or not?

2. Expansion of a gas in vacuum is called free expansion. Calculate the work done and the change in internal energy when 1 litre of ideal gas expands isothermally into vacuum until its total volume is 5 litre?

3. Enthalpy diagram for a particular reaction is given in Fig. (A). Is it possible to decide spontaneity of a reaction from given diagram. Explain.

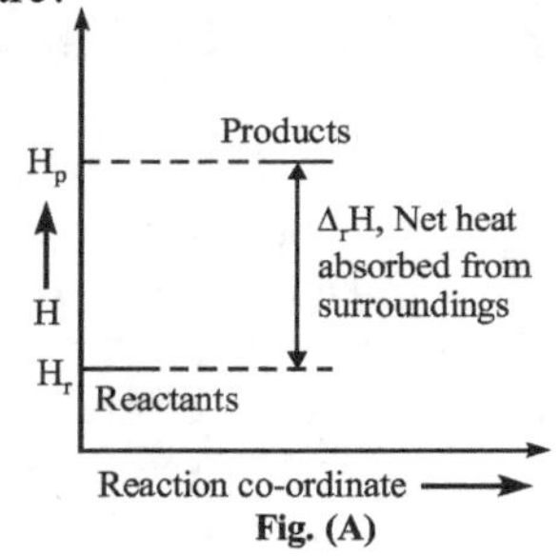


**Fig. (A)**

4. 18.0 g of water completely vapourises at 100°C and 1 bar pressure and the enthalpy change in the process is 40.79 kJ mol$^{-1}$. What will be the enthalpy change for vapourising two moles of water under the same conditions? What is the standard enthalpy of vapourisation for water?

5. A sample of 1.0 mol of a monoatomic ideal gas is taken through a cyclic process of expansion and compression as shown in fig. What will be the value of $\Delta H$ for the cycle as a whole?

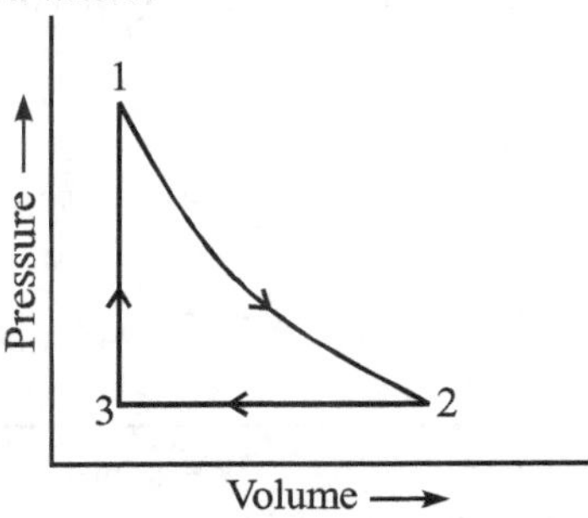


## LONG ANSWER QUESTIONS

1. The lattice enthalpy of an ionic compound is the enthalpy when one mole of an ionic compound present in its gaseous state, dissociates into its ions. It is impossible to determine it directly by experiment. Suggest and explain an indirect method to measure lattice enthalpy of NaCl(s).

2. Graphically show the total work done in an expansion when the state of an ideal gas is changed reversibly and isothermally from $(p_i, V_i)$ to $(p_f, V_f)$. With the help of a pV plot compare the work done in the above case with that carried at against a constant external pressure $p_f$.

3. $\Delta G$ is net energy available to do useful work and is thus a measure of "free energy", Show mathematically that $\Delta G$ is a measure of free energy. Find the unit of $\Delta G$. If a reaction has positive enthalpy change and positive entropy change, under what condition will the reaction be spontaneous?

## SOLUTIONS

### Multiple Choice Questions

1. **(c)** Thermodynamics deals with the energy change, feasibility and extent of a reaction, but not with the rate and mechanism of a process.
2. **(c)** For a closed vessel made of copper, there will be no exchange of matter between the system and the surroundings but energy exchange can occur through its walls.
3. **(d)** The state of a gas can be described by quoting the relationship between pressure, volume, temperature and amount. The ideal gas equation is
$PV = nRT$
4. **(c)** Specific heat is an intensive property which depends only on the nature of the gas. Hence, if the volume of gas is reduced to half from its original volume the specific heat will remain constant.
5. **(b)** $\Delta_f H^\circ = \Delta_f U^\circ + \Delta n_g RT$
For the reaction,
$C(s) + 2H_2(g) \rightarrow CH_4(g)$
$\Delta ng = 1 - 2 = -1$
$\therefore \quad \Delta_f H^\circ = \Delta U - 1 \times RT$
$\therefore \quad \Delta_f H^\circ < \Delta_f U^\circ$
6. **(c)** For free expansion, $W = 0$ ; and
For Adiabatic process, $q = 0$
According to first law of thermodynamics,
$\Delta U = q + W = 0$
Since, there is no change in $\Delta U$ hence, temperature change will be zero *i.e.*, $\Delta T = 0$

### Assertion & Reason Questions

1. **(b)** In combustion reaction, enthalpy of the reactants is always greater than the enthalpy of the product.
2. **(b)** For spontaneous process, energy factor should be favourable means $\Delta H$ is + ve and randomness should be positive.

### Short Answer Questions

1. It is spontaneous process. Although enthalpy change is zero but randomness or disorder (i.e., $\Delta S$) increase. Therefore, in equation $\Delta G = \Delta H - T\Delta S$, the term $T\Delta S$ will be negative. Hence, $\Delta G$ will be negative.
2. $(-w) = p_{ext} (V_2 - V_1) = 0 \times (5 - 1) = 0$
For isothermal expansion q = 0
By first law of thermodynamics
$q = \Delta E + (-w)$
$\Rightarrow \quad 0 = \Delta E + 0$ so $\Delta E = 0$
3. No.
Enthalpy is one of the contributory factors in deciding spontaneity but it is not the only factor. One must look for contribution of another factor i.e., entropy also, for getting the correct result.
4. + 81.58 kJ, $\Delta_{vap} H^\circ = + 40.79$ kJ mol$^{-1}$
5. $\Delta H$ (cycle) = 0.

### Long Answer Questions

1. • $Na(s) + \dfrac{1}{2}Cl_2(g) \rightarrow Na^+(g) + Cl^-(g)$;

$\Delta_{lattice} H^\circ$
• Born - Haber Cycle
• Steps to measure lattice enthalpy from Born - Haber cycle
• Sublimation of sodium metal

(1) Na (s) $\rightarrow$ Na (g) ; $\Delta_{sub}H$

(2) Ionisation of sodium atoms

Na (g) $\rightarrow$ Na$^+$ (g) + e$^-$(g) ; $\Delta_r H$

i.e., Ionisation enthalpy

(3) Dissociation of chlorine molecule

$\dfrac{1}{2}Cl_2(g) \rightarrow Cl(g); \dfrac{1}{2}\Delta_{bond}H$

i.e., One-half of bond dissociation enthalpy

(4) Cl(g) + e$^-$ (g) $\rightarrow$ Cl$^-$ (g) ; $\Delta_{eg}H$

i.e., electron gain enthalpy

Na$^+$ (g) + Cl (g)

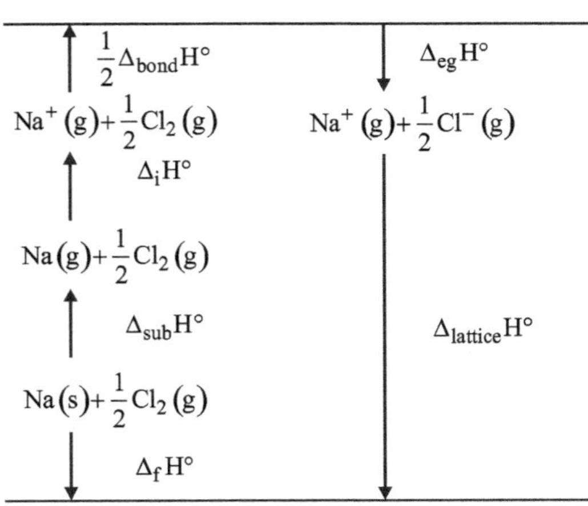

**2.**

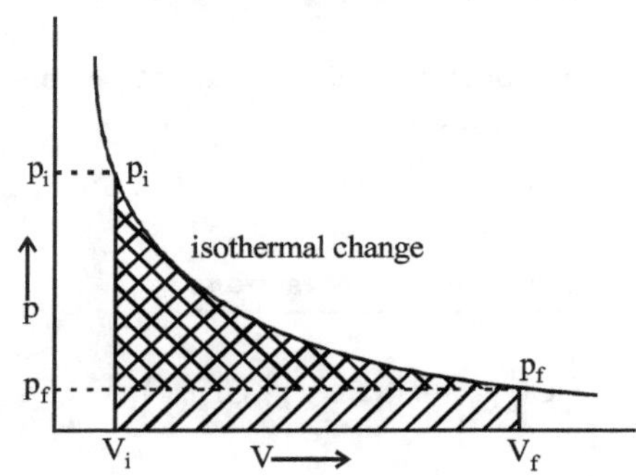



(i)   Reversible work is represented by the combined ▨ area and ▨.

(ii)  Work against constant pressure., $p_f$ is represented by the area ▨

Hence, work (i) > work (ii)

**3.**

$$\Delta S_{Total} = \Delta S_{sys} + \Delta S_{surr}$$

$$\Delta S_{Total} = \Delta S_{sys} + \frac{-\Delta H_{sys}}{T}$$

$$T\Delta S_{Total} = T\Delta S_{sys} - \Delta H_{sys}$$

For spontaneous change, $\Delta S_{sys} > 0$

$\therefore \quad T\Delta S_{sys} - \Delta S_{sys} > 0$

$\Rightarrow \quad (\Delta H_{sys} - T\Delta S_{sys}) > 0$

But, $\Delta H_{sys} - T\Delta S_{sys} = \Delta G$

$\therefore \quad -\Delta G_{sys} > 0$

$\Rightarrow \quad \Delta G_{sys} - \Delta H_{sys} - T\Delta S_{sys} < 0$

$\Delta H_{sys}$ = Enthalpy change of a reaction.

$T\Delta S_{sys}$ = Energy which is not available to do useful work.

$\Delta G_{sys}$ = Energy available for doing useful work.

- Unit of $\Delta G$ is Joule
- The reaction will be spontaneous at high temperature.

# 7

# Chemical Equilibrium



# NCERT EXERCISES

**7.1** A liquid is in equilibrium with its vapour in a sealed container at a fixed temperature. The volume of the container is suddenly increased.
(a) What is the initial effect of the change on vapour pressure?
(b) How do rates of evaporation and condensation change initially?
(c) What happens when equilibrium is restored finally and what will be the final vapour pressure?

**Ans.** (a) Initially, the vapour pressure will decrease.
(b) The rate of evaporation remains constant at constant temperature in a closed vessel. However, the rate of condensation will be low initially because there are fewer molecules per unit volume in the vapour phase and hence the number of collisions per unit time with the liquid surface decreases.
(c) When equilibrium is restored, rate of evaporation = rate of condensation. The final vapour pressure will be same as it was initially.

**7.2** What is $K_c$ for the following equilibrium when the equilibrium concentration of each substance is : $[SO_2] = 0.60M$, $[O_2] = 0.82M$ and $[SO_3] = 1.90M$?
$$2SO_2(g) + O_2(g) \rightleftharpoons 2SO_3(g)$$

**Ans.**
$$K_c = \frac{[SO_3]^2}{[SO_2]^2[O_2]} = \frac{(1.90M)^2}{(0.60M)^2(0.82M)}$$
$$= 12.229\,M^{-1} \text{ or } 12.229\,L\,mol^{-1}$$

**7.3** At a certain temperature and total pressure of $10^5$ Pa, iodine vapour contains 40% by volume of Iodine atoms
$$I_2(g) \rightleftharpoons 2\,I(g). \text{ Calculate } K_p \text{ for the equilibrium.}$$

**Ans.** Partial pressure of I atoms
$$(P_I) = 40/100 \times 10^5\,Pa = 0.4 \times 10^5\,Pa$$
Partial pressure of $I_2\,(P_{I_2}) = \frac{60}{100} \times 10^5\,Pa = 0.6 \times 10^5\,Pa$
$$\therefore K_p = \frac{P_I^2}{P_{I_2}} = \frac{(0.4 \times 10^5)^2}{0.60 \times 10^5} = 2.67 \times 10^4\,Pa$$

**7.4** Write the expression for the equilibrium constant, $K_c$ for each of the following reactions :
(i) $2NOCl(g) \rightleftharpoons 2NO(g) + Cl_2(g)$
(ii) $2Cu(NO_3)_2\,(s) \rightleftharpoons 2CuO(s) + 4NO_2(g) + O_2(g)$
(iii) $CH_3COOC_2H_5\,(aq) + H_2O\,(\ell) \rightleftharpoons$
$\qquad\qquad\qquad CH_3COOH\,(aq) + C_2H_5OH\,(aq)$
(iv) $Fe^{3+}(aq) + 3\,OH^-\,(aq) \rightleftharpoons Fe\,(OH)_3\,(s)$
(v) $I_2(s) + 5F_2 \rightleftharpoons 2IF_5$

**Ans.** (i) $K_c = \dfrac{[NO(g)]^2[Cl_2\,(g)]}{[NOC1(g)]^2}$

(ii) $K_c = \dfrac{[CuO(s)]^2[NO_2(g)]^4[O_2(g)]}{[Cu(NO_3)_2(s)]^2}$
$\qquad = [NO_2(g)]^4[O_2(g)]$

(iii) $K_c = \dfrac{[CH_3COOH(aq)][C_2H_5OH(aq)]}{[CH_3COOC_2H_5(aq)[H_2O(\ell)]}$
$\quad K_c = \dfrac{[CH_3COOH(aq)][C_2H_5OH(aq)]}{[CH_3COOC_2H_5(aq)]}$

(iv) $K_c = \dfrac{[Fe(OH)_3(s)]}{[Fe^{3+}(aq)][OH^-(aq)]^3}$
$\qquad = \dfrac{1}{[Fe^{3+}(aq)][OH^-(aq)]^3}$

(v) $K_c = \dfrac{[IF_5]^2}{[I_2(s)][F_2]^5} = \dfrac{[IF_5]^2}{[F_2]^5}$

**7.5** Find out the value of $K_c$ for each of the following equilibria from the value of $K_p$
(a) $2NOCl\,(g) \rightleftharpoons 2NO(g) + Cl_2(g);$
$\qquad\qquad\qquad K_p = 1.8 \times 10^{-2}$ at 500 K
(b) $CaCO_3(s) \rightleftharpoons CaO(s) + CO_2(g);$
$\qquad\qquad\qquad K_p = 167$ at 1073K

**Ans.** (a) $\Delta n_g = 3 - 2 = 1$, $K_p = K_c\,(RT)^{\Delta n_g}$
or $K_c = K_p / RT = (1.8 \times 10^{-2})/(0.0831 \times 500)$
$(R = 0.0831$ bar litre $mol^{-1}\,K^{-1}) = 4.33 \times 10^{-4}$
(b) $\Delta n_g = 1$, $K_c = K_p/RT = \dfrac{167}{0.0831 \times 1073} = 1.87$

**7.6** For the following equilibrium, $K_c = 6.3 \times 10^{14}$ at 1000 K

$$NO(g) + O_3(g) \rightleftharpoons NO_2(g) + O_2(g)$$

**Both the forward and reverse reactions in the equilibrium are elementary bimolecular reactions. What is $K_c$ for the reverse reaction ?**

**Ans.** For the reverse reaction $K'_c = 1/K_c = \dfrac{1}{6.3 \times 10^{14}}$

$$= 1.587 \times 10^{-15}$$

**7.7** **Explain why pure liquids and solids can be ignored while writing the equilibrium constant expression?**

**Ans.** [Pure liquid] or [Pure solid]

$$= \frac{No.\, of\, moles}{Volume\, in\, L} = \frac{Mass/Mol.mass}{Volume}$$

$$= \frac{Mass}{Volume} \times \frac{1}{Mol.\, mass} = \frac{Density}{Mol.\, mass}$$

As density of a pure liquid or pure solid is constant at constant temperature and molecular mass is also constant, therefore, their molar concentrations are constant and thus not included into the equilibrium constant.

**7.8** **Reaction between $N_2$ and $O_2$ takes place as follows :**

$$2N_2(g) + O_2(g) \rightleftharpoons 2N_2O(g)$$

**If a mixture of 0.482 mol $N_2$ and 0.933 mol of $O_2$ is placed in a 10 L reaction vessel and allowed to form $N_2O$ at a temperature for which $K_c = 2.0 \times 10^{-37}$. Determine the composition of equilibrium mixture.**

**Ans.**

|  | $2N_2(g)$ | $+\ O_2(g)$ | $\rightleftharpoons\ 2N_2O(g)$ |
|---|---|---|---|
| Initial | 0.482 mol | 0.933 mol | |
| At eqm. | $0.482 - x$ | $0.933 - x/2$ | $x$ |
| Molar | $\dfrac{0.482 - x}{10}$ | $\dfrac{0.933 - x/2}{10}$ | $\dfrac{x}{10}$ |

As $K_c = 2.0 \times 10^{-37}$ is very small, this means that the amount of $N_2$ and $O_2$ reacted $(x)$ is very very small and can be neglected. Hence, at equilibrium, we have
$[N_2] = 0.0482$ mol $L^{-1}$,
$[O_2] = 0.0933$ mol $L^{-1}$, $[N_2O] = 0.1\, x$

$$K_c = \frac{(0.1x)^2}{(0.0482)^2 (0.0933)} = 2.0 \times 10^{-37}$$

On solving, this gives $x = 6.57 \times 10^{-20}$
$[N_2O] = 0.1\, x = 6.57 \times 10^{-21}$ mol $L^{-1}$

**7.9** **Nitric oxide reacts with $Br_2$ and gives nitrosyl bromide as per reaction given below:**

$$2NO(g) + Br_2(g) \rightleftharpoons 2\ NOBr(g)$$

**When 0.087 mol of NO and 0.0437 mol of $Br_2$ are mixed in a closed container at constant temperature, 0.0518 mol of NOBr is obtained at equilibrium. Calculate equilibrium amount of NO and $Br_2$.**

**Ans.** 0.0518 mol of NOBr is formed from 0.087 mol of NO and 0.0437 mol of $Br_2$.

At equilibrium, amount of NO $= 0.087 - 0.0518$
$$= 0.0352 \text{ mol}$$
Amount of $Br_2 = 0.0437 - 0.0259 = 0.0178$ mol.

**7.10** **At 450 K, $K_p = 2.0 \times 10^{10}$ bar for the given reaction at equilibrium.**

$$2SO_2(g) + O_2(g) \rightleftharpoons 2SO_3(g)$$

**What is $K_c$ at this temperature ?**

**Ans.** For the given reaction, $\Delta n_g = 2 - 3 = -1$

$K_p = K_c (RT)^{\Delta n}$ or $K_c = K_p (RT)^{-\Delta n} = K_p(RT)$
$= (2.0 \times 10^{10}$ bar$^{-1})(0.0831\, L\, bar\, K^{-1}mol^{-1})(450K)$
$= 74.8 \times 10^{10}$ L mol$^{-1} = 7.48 \times 10^{11}$ L mol$^{-1}$

**7.11** **A sample of HI (g) is placed in flask at a pressure of 0.2 atm. At equilibrium, the partial pressure of HI (g) is 0.04 atm. What is $K_p$ for the given equilibrium ?**

**Ans.**

|  | $2HI(g)$ | $\rightleftharpoons\ H_2(g)\ +$ | $I_2(g)$ |
|---|---|---|---|
| Initial pressure | 0.2 atm | 0 | 0 |
| At eqm. | 0.04 atm | 0.16/2 atm $= 0.08$ atm | 0.16/2 atm $= 0.08$ atm |

(Decrease in the pressure of HI $= 0.2 - 0.04 = 0.16$ atm.)

$$\therefore\ K_p = \frac{p_{H_2} \times p_{I_2}}{p^2_{HI}} = \frac{0.08\,atm \times 0.08\,atm}{(0.04\,atm)^2} = 4.0$$

**7.12** **A mixture of 1.57 mol of $N_2$, 1.92 mol of $H_2$ and 8.13 mol of $NH_3$ is introduced into a 20 L reaction vessel at 500 K. At this temperature, the equilibrium constant, $K_c$ for the reaction**
**$N_2(g) + 3H_2(g) \rightleftharpoons 2NH_3(g)$ is $1.7 \times 10^2$. Is the reaction mixture at equilibrium ? If not, what is the direction of the net reaction ?**

**Ans.** Given reaction is:

$$N_2(g) + 3H_2(g) \rightleftharpoons 2\ NH_3(g)$$

$$Q_c = \frac{[NH_3]^2}{[N_2][H_2]^3}$$

$$= \frac{(8.13/20\, mol\, L^{-1})^2}{(1.57/20\, mol\, L^{-1})(1.92/20\, mol\, L^{-1})^3}$$

$$= 2394.20$$

As $Q_c \neq K_c$, the reaction mixture is not in equilibrium. As $Q_c > K_c$, the net reaction will be in the backward direction.

**7.13** **The equilibrium constant expression for a gas reaction is.**

$$K_c = \frac{[NH_3]^4 [O_2]^5}{[NO]^4 [H_2O]^6}$$

**Write the balanced chemical equation corresponding to this expression.**

**Ans.** $4\, NO(g) + 6\, H_2O(g) \longrightarrow 4\, NH_3(g) + 5\, O_2(g)$

**7.14** **One mole of $H_2O$ and one mole of CO are taken in 10 litre vessel and heated to 725 K. At equilibrium 40% of water (by mass) reacts with CO according to the equation,**

$H_2O(g) + CO(g) \rightleftharpoons H_2(g) + CO_2(g)$
**Calculate the equilibrium constant for the reaction.**
**Ans.** At equilibrium,
$[H_2O] = (1 - 0.40) / 10 \ mol \ L^{-1} = 0.06 \ mol \ L^{-1}$
$[CO] = 0.06 \ mol \ L^{-1}$
$[H_2] = 0.04 \ mol \ L^{-1}$
$[CO_2] = 0.04 \ mol \ L^{-1}$

$$K = \frac{[H_2][CO_2]}{[H_2O][CO]} = \frac{0.04 \times 0.04}{0.06 \times 0.06} = 0.444$$

**7.15 At 700 K, equilibrium constant for the reaction**
$H_2(g) + I_2 \ (g) \rightleftharpoons 2HI \ (g)$ **is 54.8. If 0.5 mol $L^{-1}$ of HI (g) is present at equilibrium at 700 K, what are the concentration of $H_2$ (g) and $I_2$ (g) assuming that we initially started with HI (g) and allowed it to reach equilibrium at 700 K?**

**Ans.** $2HI(g) \rightleftharpoons H_2(g) + I_2(g)$, K = 1/54.8
At equilibrium, $[HI] = 0.5 \ mol \ L^{-1}$,
$[H_2] = [I_2] = x \ mol \ L^{-1}$

$$\therefore \quad K = \frac{x \times x}{(0.5)^2} = 1 / 54.8 \text{ (Given)}$$

This gives $x = 0.068$, i. e., $[H_2] = [I_2] = 0.068 \ mol \ L^{-1}$.

**7.16 What is the equilibrium concentration of each of the substances in the equilibrium when the initial concentration of ICl was 0.78 M ?**

$2 \ ICl(g) \rightleftharpoons I_2(g) + Cl_2(g)$, $K_c = 0.14$

**Ans.** Suppose at equilibrium, $[I_2] = [Cl_2] = x \ mol \ L^{-1}$. Then

|  | 2ICl | $\rightleftharpoons$ | $I_2(g)$ | + | $Cl_2(g)$ |
|---|---|---|---|---|---|
| Initial conc. | 0.78M |  | 0 |  | 0 |
| At eqm. | 0.78 – 2x |  | x |  | x |

$$K_c = \frac{[I_2][Cl_2]}{[ICl_2]^2} \quad \therefore \quad 0.14 = \frac{(x)(x)}{(0.78 - 2x)^2}$$

or $\quad x^2 = 0.14 \ (0.78 - 2x)^2$

or $\quad x / (0.78 - 2x) = \sqrt{0.14} = 0.374$

or $\quad x = 0.292 - 0.748 \ x$

or $\quad 1.748x = 0.292 \quad$ or $\quad x = 0.166$

Hence, at equilibrium, $[I_2] = [Cl_2] = 0.166$ M,
$[ICl] = 0.78 - (2 \times 0.166$ M = 0.448 M

**7.17 $K_p$ = 0.04 atm at 899 K for the equilibrium shown below. What is the equilibrium concentration of $C_2H_6$, when it is placed in a flask at 4.0 atm pressure and allowed to come to equilibrium ?**

$C_2H_6(g) \rightleftharpoons C_2H_4(g) + H_2(g)$

**Ans.**

|  | $C_2H_6(g)$ | $\rightleftharpoons$ | $C_2H_4(g)$ | + | $H_2(g)$ |
|---|---|---|---|---|---|
| Initial pressure | 4.0 atm |  | 0 |  | 0 |
| At. eqm. | 4 – p |  | p |  | p |

$$K_p = \frac{p_{C_2H_4} \times p_{H_2}}{p_{C_2H_6}}$$

$\therefore \quad 0.04 = p^2 / (4 - p) \quad$ or $\quad p^2 = 0.16 - 0.04 \ p$
or $\quad p^2 + 0.04p - 0.16 = 0$

$$\therefore \ p = \frac{-0.04 \pm \sqrt{0.0016 - 4(-0.16)}}{2} = \frac{-0.04 \pm 0.80}{2}$$

Taking positive value, $p = 0.76 / 2 = 0.38$

$\therefore \ [C_2H_6]_{eq} = [4 - 0.38] \ atm = + 3.62 \ atm$

**7.18 Ethyl acetate is formed by the reaction between ethanol and acetic acid and the equilibrium is represented as**
$CH_3COOH \ (\ell) + C_2H_5OH(\ell) \rightleftharpoons CH_3COOC_2H_5 \ (\ell) + H_2O \ (\ell)$
**(i) Write the concentration ratio (reaction quotient), $Q_c$, for this reaction (Note: water is not in excess and is not a solvent in this reaction)**
**(ii) At 293 K, if one starts with 1.00 mol of acetic acid and 0.18 mol of ethanol, there is 0.171 mol of ethyl acetate in the final equilibrium mixture. Calculate the equilibrium constant.**
**(iii) Starting with 0.5 mol of ethanol and 1.0 mol of acetic acid and maintaining it at 293 K, 0.214 mol of ethyl acetate is found after sometime. Has equilibrium been reached ?**

**Ans.** (i) $$Q_c = \frac{[CH_3COOC_2H_5][H_2O]}{[CH_3COOH][C_2H_5OH]}$$

(ii)

|  | $CH_3COOH$ | + | $C_2H_5OH$ | $\rightleftharpoons$ | $CH_3COOC_2H_5$ | + | $H_2O$ |
|---|---|---|---|---|---|---|---|
| Initial | 1.00 mol |  | 0.180 mol |  |  |  |  |
| At eqm. | 1 – 0.171 |  | 0.180 – 0.171 |  | 0.171 mol |  | 0.171 mol |
|  | = 0.829 mol |  | = 0.009 mol |  |  |  |  |

Let V be the volume of reaction vessel.

| Molar conc. | 0.829/V | | 0.009/V | | 0.171/V | | 0.171/V |
|---|---|---|---|---|---|---|---|

$$K_c = \frac{[CH_3COOC_2H_5][H_2O]}{[CH_3COOH][C_2H_5OH]} = \frac{(0.171/V)(0.171/V)}{(0.829/V)(0.009/V)} = 3.94$$

(iii)

|  | $CH_3COOH$ | + | $C_2H_5OH$ | $\rightleftharpoons$ | $CH_3COOC_2H_5$ | + | $H_2O$ |
|---|---|---|---|---|---|---|---|
| Initial | 1.000 mol |  | 0.500 mol |  |  |  |  |
| After time 't' | 1 – 0.214 |  | 0.500 – 0.214 |  | 0.214 mol |  | 0.214 mol |
|  | = 0.786 mol |  | = 0.286 mol |  |  |  |  |

Let V be the volume of reaction vessel.

$$\text{Reaction quotient } (Q_c) = \frac{(0.214/V)(0.214/V)}{(0.786/V)(0.286/V)} = 0.203$$

As $Q_c \neq K_c$, equilibrium has not been attained.

**7.19** **A sample of pure $PCl_5$ was introduced into an evacuated vessel at 473 K. After equilibrium was attained, concentration of $PCl_5$ was found to be $0.5 \times 10^{-1}$ mol $L^{-1}$. If value of $K_c$ is $8.3 \times 10^{-3}$, what are the concentrations of $PCl_3$ and $Cl_2$ at equilibrium?**

$$PCl_5(g) \rightleftharpoons PCl_3(g) + Cl_2(g)$$

**Ans.** At eqn.

$$\underset{0.5 \times 10^{-1}\,mol\,L^{-1}}{PCl_5(g)} \rightleftharpoons \underset{x\,mol\,L^{-1}}{PCl_3(g)} + \underset{x\,mol\,L^{-1}}{Cl_2(g)}$$

$$K_c = \frac{x^2}{(0.5 \times 10^{-1})} = 8.3 \times 10^{-3} \text{ (Given)}$$

or $\quad x^2 = (8.3 \times 10^{-3})(0.5 \times 10^{-1}) = 4.15 \times 10^{-4}$

or $\quad x = \sqrt{4.15 \times 10^{-4}}$

$\qquad = 2.03 \times 10^{-2}\,M = 0.02\,M$

**7.20** **One of the reaction that takes place in producing steel from iron ore is the reduction of iron (II) oxide by carbon monoxide to give iron metal and $CO_2$.**
**$FeO(s) + CO(g) \rightleftharpoons Fe(s) + CO_2(g)$;**
**$K_p = 0.265$ atm at 1050 K**
**What are the equilibrium partial pressures of CO and $CO_2$ at 1050 K if the initial partial pressures are : $p_{CO} = 1.4$ atm and $p_{CO_2} = 0.80$ atm?**

**Ans.**

$$\underset{}{FeO(s)} + \underset{1.4\,atm}{CO(g)} \rightleftharpoons \underset{}{Fe(s)} + \underset{0.80\,atm}{CO_2(g)}$$

Initial pressures

$$Q_p = \frac{P_{CO_2}}{P_{CO}} = \frac{0.80}{1.4} = 0.571$$

As $Q_p > K_p$, reaction will move in the backward direction, i.e. pressure of $CO_2$ will decrease and that of CO will increase to attain equilibrium. Hence, if P is decrease in pressure of $CO_2$, increase in pressure of CO = P

At equilibrium, $P_{CO_2} = (0.80 - P)$ atm,

$P_{CO} = (1.4 + P)$ atm

$$K_p = \frac{P_{CO_2}}{P_{CO}} \therefore 0.265 = \frac{0.80 - P}{1.4 + P}$$

or $\quad 0.265\,(1.4 + P) = 0.80 - P$

or $\quad 0.371 + 0.265\,P = 0.80 - P$

or $\quad 1.265\,P = 0.429 \quad$ or $\quad P = 0.339$ at equilibrium

$\therefore \quad P_{CO} = 1.4 + 0.339 = 1.739$ atm

and $P_{CO_2} = 0.80 - 0.339 = 0.461$ atm

**7.21** **Equilibrium constant, $K_c$ for the reaction $N_2(g) + 3H_2(g) \rightleftharpoons 2NH_3(g)$ at 500 K is 0.061. At a particular time, the analysis shows that composition of the reaction mixture is 3.0 mol $L^{-1}$ $N_2$, 2.0 mol $L^{-1}$ $H_2$ and 0.5 mol $L^{-1}$ $NH_3$. Is the reaction at equilibrium? If**

**not in which direction does the reaction tend to proceed to reach equilibrium?**

**Ans.**
$$Q_c = \frac{[NH_3]^2}{[N_2][H_2]^3} = \frac{(0.5)^2}{(3.0)(2.0)^3} = 0.0104$$

As $Q_c \neq K_c$ reaction is not in equilibrium.
As $Q_c < K_c$ reaction will proceed in the forward direction.

**7.22** **Bromine monochloride, BrCl decomposes into bromine and chlorine and reaches the equilibrium $2BrCl(g) \rightleftharpoons Br_2(g) + Cl_2(g)$ for which $K_c = 32$ at 500K. If initially pure BrCl is present at a concentration of $3.3 \times 10^{-3}$ mol $L^{-1}$, what is its molar concentration in the mixture at equilibrium ?**

**Ans.**
$$\underset{}{2BrCl} \rightleftharpoons \underset{}{Br_2} + \underset{}{Cl_2}$$
Initial $\quad 3.30 \times 10^{-3}$ mol $L^{-1}$
At eqbm. $(3.30 \times 10^{-3} - x) \qquad\qquad x/2 \qquad x/2$

$$K_c = \frac{(x/2)(x/2)}{(3.30 \times 10^{-3} - x)^2} = 32 \text{ (Given)}$$

$$\therefore \frac{x/2}{(3.30 \times 10^{-3} - x)} = \sqrt{32}$$

or $x/2 = 5.66 \times (3.30 \times 10^{-3} - x)$
$\qquad x = 11.32(3.30 \times 10^{-3} - x)$
or $\quad 12.32x = 11.32(3.30 \times 10^{-3})$ or $x = 3.03 \times 10^{-3}$
at eqn. $[BrCl] = (3.30 \times 10^{-3} - 3.0 \times 10^{-3})$
$= 0.30 \times 10^{-3} = 3.03 \times 10^{-4}$ mol $L^{-1}$

**7.23** **At 1127 K and 1 atm pressure, a gaseous mixture of CO and $CO_2$ in equilibrium with solid carbon has 90.55% CO by mass,**
**$C(s) + CO_2(g) \rightleftharpoons 2CO(g)$.**
**Calculate $K_c$ for this reaction at the above temperature.**

**Ans.** If total mass of mixture of CO and $CO_2$ is 100 g, then CO $= 90.55$g and $CO_2 = 100 - 90.55 = 9.45$ g.
Number of moles of CO $= 90 \times 55/28 = 3.234$
Number of moles of $CO_2 = 9 \times 45/44 = 0.215$
$p_{CO} = 3.234 / (3.234 + 0.215) \times 1$ atm
$\qquad = 0.938$ atm
$p_{CO_2} = 0.215 / (3.234 + 0.215) \times 1$ atm $= 0.062$ atm

$$K_p = \frac{p^2_{CO}}{p_{CO_2}} = \frac{(0.938)^2}{0.062} = 14.19$$

$\Delta n_g = 2 - 1 = 1$
$\therefore \quad K_p = K_c (RT)^{\Delta n_g}$
or $\quad K_c = K_p / RT = 14.19 / (0.0821 \times 1127)$
$\qquad = 0.153$

**7.24** **Calculate (a) $\Delta G^\ominus$ and (b) the equilibrium constant for the formation of $NO_2$ from NO and $O_2$ at 298K**

$$NO(g) + \frac{1}{2}\,O_2(g) \rightleftharpoons NO_2(g)$$

**where $\Delta G^\ominus (NO_2) = 52.0$ kJ/mol,**
**$\Delta G^\ominus (NO) = 87.0$ kJ/mol,**
**$\Delta_f G^\ominus (O_2) = 0$ kJ/mol.**

**Ans.** (a) $\Delta_r G° = \Sigma_f G°$ (Products) $— \Sigma_f G°$ (Reactants)

$= \Delta_f G° (NO_2) - [\{\Delta_f G°(NO) + \dfrac{1}{2} \Delta_f G°(O_2)\}]$

$= 52.0 - (87.0 + \dfrac{1}{2} \times 0) = -35.0 \text{ kJ mol}^{-1}$

(b) $-\Delta G° = 2.303 \text{ RT log K}$

Hence,$- (- 35000) = 2.303 \times 8.314 \times 298 \times \log K$

or $\log K = 6.1341$ or $K = 1.361 \times 10^6$

**7.25** **Does the number of moles of reaction products increase, decrease or remain same when each of the following equilibria is subjected to a decrease in pressure by increasing the volume ?**

(a) $PCl_5(g) \rightleftharpoons PCl_3(g) + Cl_2(g)$

(b) $CaO(s) + CO_2(g) \rightleftharpoons CaCO_3(s)$

(c) $3Fe(s) + 4H_2O(g) \rightleftharpoons Fe_3O_4(s) + 4H_2(g)$

**Ans.** Applying Le Chatelier's principle, on decreasing the pressure, moles of reaction products will

(a) increase

(b) decrease

(c) remain same ($\because n_p = n_r$ gaseous)

**7.26** **Which of the following reactions will get affected by increasing the pressure? Also, mention whether change will cause the reaction to go into forward or backward direction?**

(i) $COCl_2(g) \rightleftharpoons CO(g) + Cl_2(g)$

(ii) $CH_4(g) + 2S_2(g) \rightleftharpoons CS_2(g) + 2H_2S(g)$

(iii) $CO_2(g) + C(s) \rightleftharpoons 2CO(g)$

(iv) $2H_2(g) + CO(g) \rightleftharpoons CH_3OH(g)$

(v) $CaCO_3(s) \rightleftharpoons CaO(s) + CO_2(g)$

(vi) $4NH_3(g) + 5O_2(g) \rightleftharpoons 4NO(g) + 6H_2O(g)$

**Ans.** Reactions affected will be those in which $(n_p \neq n_r)$ (gaseous). Hence, reactions (i), (iii), (iv), (v) and (vi) will be affected. By applying Le Chatelier's principle, we can predict the direction.

(i) $n_p = 2, n_r = 1$ i.e., $n_p > n_r$ reaction will proceed in the backward direction

(ii) $n_p = 3, n_r = 3$ i.e., $n_p = n_r$ reaction will not be affected by pressure.

(iii) $n_p = 2, n_r = 1$, i.e., $n_p > n_r$ reaction will proceed in the backward direction.

(iv) $n_p = 1, n_r = 3$ i.e., $n_p < n_r$ reaction will proceed in the forward direction.

(v) $n_p = 1, n_r = 0$ i.e., $n_p > n_r$ reaction will proceed in the backward direction.

(vi) $n_p = 10, n_r = 9$, i.e., $n_p > n_r$ reaction will proceed in the backward direction.

**7.27** **The equilibrium constant for the following reaction is $1.6 \times 10^5$ at 1024 K**

$H_2(g) + Br_2(g) \rightleftharpoons 2HBr(g)$

**Find the equilibrium pressure of all gases if 10.0 bar of HBr is introduced into a sealed container at 1024K.**

**Ans.** $\qquad 2HBr(g) \rightleftharpoons H_2(g) + Br_2(g), K = 1/(1.6 \times 10^5)$

Initial $\quad$ 10 bar

At eqm. $\quad 10 - p \qquad\quad p/2 \qquad p/2$

$K_p = \dfrac{(p/2)(p/2)}{(10-p)^2} = \dfrac{1}{1.6 \times 10^5}$

or $\dfrac{p^2}{4(10-p)^2} = \dfrac{1}{1.6 \times 10^5}$

Taking square root of both sides, we get

$\dfrac{p}{2(10-p)} = \dfrac{1}{(4.0 \times 10^2)}$

or $4 \times 10^2 p = 2(10-p)$ or $402p = 20$ or $p = 20/402 = 4.97 \times 10^{-2}$ bar

Hence, at equilibrium $P_{H_2} = P_{Br_2} = P/2$

$= 2.48 \times 10^{-2}$ bar,

$P_{HBr} = 10 - p \approx 10$ bar

**7.28** **Dihydrogen gas is obtained from natural gas by partial oxidation with steam as per following endothermic reaction:**

$CH_4(g) + H_2O(g) \rightleftharpoons CO(g) + 3H_2(g)$

(a) **Write an expression for $K_p$ for the above reaction.**

(b) **How will the values of $K_p$ and composition of equilibrium mixture be affected by**

(i) **increasing the pressure ?**

(ii) **increasing the temperature ?**

(iii) **using a catalyst ?**

**Ans.** (a) $K_p = \dfrac{p_{CO} \times (p_{H_2})^3}{p_{CH_4} \times p_{H_2O}}$

(b) (i) By Le Chatelier's principle, equilibrium will shift in the backward direction, and value of $K_p$ decreases.

(ii) By Le Chatelier's principle, equilibrium will shift in the forward direction, and value of $K_p$ increases.

(iii) Equilibrium composition will not be disturbed but equilibrium will be attained quickly and value of $K_p$ remains unaffected.

**7.29** **Describe the effect of :**

(a) **addition of $H_2$**

(b) **addition of $CH_3OH$**

(c) **removal of CO**

(d) **removal of $CH_3OH$, on the equilibrium of the reaction:**

$2H_2(g) + CO(g) \rightleftharpoons CH_3OH(g)$

**Ans.** (a) Equilibrium will shift in the forward direction.

(b) Equilibrium will shift in the backward direction.

(c) Equilibrium will shift in the backward direction.

(d) Equilibrium will shift in the forward direction.

**7.30** **At 473 K, equilibrium constant, $K_c$, for decomposition of phosphorus pentachloride, $PCl_5$ is $8.3 \times 10^{-3}$. If decomposition is depicted as :**

$PCl_5(g) \rightleftharpoons PCl_3(g) + Cl_2(g), \Delta rH° = 124.0 \text{ kJ mol}^{-1}$

(a) **write an expression for $K_c$ for the reaction ?**

(b) **what is the value of $K_c$ for the reverse reaction at the same temperature ?**

(c) **what would be the effect on $K_c$ if (i) more $PCl_5$ is added (ii) pressure is increased (iii) the temperature is increased ?**

**Ans.** (a)   $K_c = \dfrac{[PCl_3(g)][Cl_2(g)]}{[PCl_5(g)]}$

(b)   $K' = 1/K_c = \dfrac{1}{8.3 \times 10^{-3}} = 120.48$

(c) (i) No effect as $K_c$ is constant at constant temperature.
(ii) No effect
(iii) As given reaction is endothermic, on increasing the temperature $K_f$ will increase as $K_c = K_f / K_b$
Hence $K_c$ will increase with increase of temperature.

**7.31 Dihydrogen gas used in Haber's process is produced by reacting methane from natural gas with high temperature steam. The first stage of two stage reaction involves the formation of CO and $H_2$. In second stage, CO formed in first stage is reacted with more steam in water gas shift reaction.**

**CO (g) + $H_2O$ (g) $\rightleftharpoons$ $CO_2$ (g) + $H_2$ (g).**

**If a reaction vessel at 400°C is charged with an equimolar mixture of CO and steam such that $P_{CO} = P_{H_2O} = 4.0$ bar, what will be the partial pressure of $H_2$ at equilibrium ?**

**$K_p = 10.1$ at 400°C.**

**Ans.** Suppose the partial pressure of $H_2$ at equilibrium = p bar

$$CO(g) + H_2O(g) \rightleftharpoons CO_2(g) + H_2(g)$$

Initial
pressure      4.0 bar    4.0 bar
At eqm.       $(4-p)$    $(4-p)$         $p$      $p$
$K_p = p^2 /(4-p)^2 = 10.1$ (Given)

$\therefore \; p/(4-p) = \sqrt{10.1} = 3.178$

or   $p = 3.042$ bar

**7.32 Predict which of the following reaction will have appreciable concentration of reactants and products:**
(a)   $Cl_2$ (g) $\rightleftharpoons$ 2Cl (g), $K_c = 5 \times 10^{-39}$
(b)   $Cl_2$ (g) + 2NO(g) $\rightleftharpoons$ 2NOCl (g), $K_c = 3.7 \times 10^8$
(c)   $Cl_2$ (g) + $2NO_2$(g) $\rightleftharpoons$ $2NO_2Cl$ (g), $K_c = 1.8$

**Ans.** For reaction (c), as $K_c$ is neither high nor very low, reactants and products will be present in comparable amounts. In reaction (a) $K_c$ is very small and in reaction (b) $K_c$ is very large.

**7.33 The value of $K_c$ for the reaction**
**$3O_2(g) \rightleftharpoons 2O_3(g)$ is $2.0 \times 10^{-50}$ at 25°C. If the equilibrium concentration of $O_2$ in air at 25°C is $1.6 \times 10^{-2}$, what is the concentration of $O_3$ ?**

**Ans.** $K_c = \dfrac{[O_3]^2}{[O_2]^3}$

$\therefore \; 2.0 \times 10^{-50} = \dfrac{[O_3]^2}{(1.6 \times 10^{-2})^3}$

or   $[O_3]^2 = (2.0 \times 10^{-50})(1.6 \times 10^{-2})^3$
      $= 8.192 \times 10^{-56}$
or   $[O_3] = 2.86 \times 10^{-28}$ M

**7.34 The reaction,**
**CO (g) + $3H_2(g) \rightleftharpoons$ $CH_4$ (g) + $H_2O$ (g), is at equilibrium at 1300 K in a 1L flask. It also contain 0.30 mol of CO, 0.10 mol of $H_2$ and 0.02 mol of $H_2O$ and an unknown amount of $CH_4$ in the flask. Determine the concentration of $CH_4$ in the mixture. The equilibrium constant, $K_c$, for the reaction at the given temperature is 3.90.**

**Ans.** $K_c = \dfrac{[CH_4][H_2O]}{[CO][H_2]^3}$

$\therefore \; 3.90 = \dfrac{[CH_4][0.02]}{(0.30)(0.10)^3}$

(Molar conc. = No. of moles because vol. of flask = 1L)
or   $[CH_4] = 0.0585$ M = $5.85 \times 10^{-2}$ M

**7.35 What is meant by the conjugate acid–base pair ? Find the conjugate acid/base for the following species: $HNO_2$, $CN^-$, $HClO_4$, $F^-$, $OH^-$, $CO_3^{2-}$ and $S^{2-}$**

**Ans.** An acid-base pair which differ by a proton is called conjugate acid base pair. $NO_2^-$, HCN, $ClO_4^-$, HF, $H_2O$ (acid) or $O^{2-}$ (base), $HCO_3^-$ and $HS^-$.

**7.36 Which of the following are Lewis acids ?**
**$H_2O$, $BF_3$, $H^+$, $NH_4^+$.**

**Ans.** $BF_3$, $H^+$ and $NH_4^+$ are Lewis acids as they can accept a lone pair of electrons (Remember that all cations are Lewis acids).

**7.37 What will be the conjugate bases for the Bronsted acids: HF, $H_2SO_4$ and $HCO_3^-$ ?**

**Ans.** Bronsted acid = Conjugate base + $H^+$
or Conjugate base = Bronsted acid – $H^+$
$\therefore$ Conjugate bases of the given acids will be
$F^-$, $HSO_4^-$, $CO_3^{2-}$.

**7.38 Write the conjugate acids for the following Bronsted bases:**
**$NH_2^-$, $NH_3$ and $HCOO^-$**

**Ans.** $NH_3$, $NH_4^+$ and HCOOH

**7.39 The species: $H_2O$, $HCO_3^-$, $HSO_4^-$ and $NH_3$ can act both as Bronsted acids and bases. For each case give the corresponding conjugate acid and base.**

**Ans.** Conjugate acids: $H_3O^+$, $H_2CO_3$, $H_2SO_4$ and $NH_4^+$

Conjugate bases: $OH^-$, $CO_3^{2-}$, $SO_4^{2-}$ and $NH_2^-$.

**7.40 Classify the following species into Lewis acids and Lewis bases and show how these act as Lewis acid/ base:**
(a)   $OH^-$                (b)   $F^-$
(c)   $H^+$                  (d)   $BCl_3$

**Ans.** (a)   $OH^-$ can donate electron pair. Hence, it is a Lewis base.
(b)   $F^-$ can donate electron pair. Hence, it is a Lewis base.
(c)   $H^+$ can accept electron pair. Hence, it is a Lewis acid.
(d)   $BCl_3$ is deficient in electrons as its octet is incomplete. Hence, it can accept electron pair and is, therefore, a Lewis acid.

**7.41 The concentration of hydrogen ion in a sample of soft drink is $3.8 \times 10^{-3}$ M. What is its pH ?**

**Ans.** $pH = -\log[H^+] = -\log(3.8 \times 10^{-3})$

$\qquad = -\log 3.8 + 3 = 3 - 0.5797 = 2.4203 = 2.42$

**7.42 The pH of a sample of vinegar is 3.76. Calculate the concentration of hydrogen ion in it**

**Ans.** $pH = -\log[H^+]$ or $\log[H^+] = -pH$

$\qquad [H^+] = $ antilog $[-pH] = $ antilog $(-3.76)$

$\therefore \qquad = 1.737 \times 10^{-4}$ M

$\qquad = 1.74 \times 10^{-4}$ M

**7.43 The ionization constants of HF, HCOOH and HCN at 298 K are $6.8 \times 10^{-4}$, $1.8 \times 10^{-4}$ and $4.8 \times 10^{-9}$ respectively. Calculate the ionization constant of the corresponding conjugate base.**

**Ans.** For $F^-$, $K_b = K_w / K_a = 10^{-14}/(6.8 \times 10^{-4})$

$\qquad = 1.47 \times 10^{-11} \approx 1.5 \times 10^{-11}$.

$\qquad$ For $HCOO^-$, $K_b = 10^{-14}/(1.8 \times 10^{-4}) = 5.6 \times 10^{-11}$

$\qquad$ For $CN^-$, $K_b = 10^{-14}/(4.8 \times 10^{-9}) = 2.08 \times 10^{-6}$

**7.44 The ionization constant of phenol is $1.0 \times 10^{-10}$. What is the concentration of phenolate ion in 0.05 M solution of phenol? What will be its degree of ionization if the solution is also 0.01 M in sodium phenolate?**

**Ans.**

$$C_6H_5OH \rightleftharpoons C_6H_5O^- + H^+$$

Initial conc. $\quad 0.05$ M $\qquad 0 \qquad\qquad 0$

After dissociation $\quad 0.05 - x \qquad x \qquad\qquad x$

$\therefore \; K_a = (x)(x) / 0.05 - x = 1.0 \times 10^{-10}$ (Given)

or $\quad x^2 / 0.05 = 1.0 \times 10^{-10}$

or $\quad x^2 = 5 \times 10^{-12}$

or $\quad x = 2.23 \times 10^{-6}$ M

In presence of $0.01$ M $C_6H_5ONa$, suppose y is the amount of phenol dissociated, then at equilibrium

$[C_6H_5OH] = 0.05 - y \approx 0.05$

$[C_6H_5O^-] = 0.01 + y \approx 0.01$ M, $[H^+] = y$ M

$K_a = (0.01)(y) / 0.05 = 1.0 \times 10^{-10}$ (Given)

or $\quad y = 5 \times 10^{-10}$

$$\alpha = \frac{y}{c} = \frac{5 \times 10^{-10}}{5 \times 10^{-2}} = 10^{-8}$$

**7.45 The first ionization constant of $H_2S$ is $9.1 \times 10^{-8}$. Calculate the concentration of $HS^-$ ions in its 0.1 M solution. How will this concentration be affected if the solution is 0.1 M in HCl also ? If the second dissociation constant of $H_2S$ is $1.2 \times 10^{-13}$, calculate the concentration of $S^{2-}$ under both conditions.**

**Ans.** To calculate $[HS^{-1}]$

$$H_2S \rightleftharpoons H^+ + HS^-$$

Initial conc $\quad 0.1$ M $\qquad 0 \qquad\quad 0$

After dissociation $= 0.1$ $\qquad 0.1 - x \qquad x \qquad x$

$K_a = (x)(x)/0.1 = 9.1 \times 10^{-8}$ or $x^2 = 9.1 \times 10^{-9}$

or $\quad x = 9.54 \times 10^{-5}$.

In presence of 0.1 M HCl, suppose $H_2S$ dissociated is y. Then at equilibrium $[H_2S] = 0.1 - y \approx 0.1$,

$[H^+] = 0.1 + y \approx 0.1$, $[HS^-] = y$ M

$K_a = (0.1 \times y) / 0.1 = 9.1 \times 10^{-8}$ (Given)

or $\quad y = 9.1 \times 10^{-8}$ M

To calculate $[S^{2-}]$

$$H_2S \xrightleftharpoons{K_{a_1}} H^+ + HS^{-1}; HS^{-1} \xrightleftharpoons{K_{a_2}} H^+ + S^{2-}$$

For the overall reaction,

$$H_2S \rightleftharpoons 2H^+ + S^{2-}$$

$K_a = K_{a_1} \times K_{a_2} = 9.1 \times 10^{-8} \times 1.2 \times 10^{-13}$

$\qquad\qquad = 1.092 \times 10^{-20}$

$$K_a = \frac{[H^+]^2[S^{2-}]}{[H_2S]}$$

In the absence of 0.1 M HCl, $[H^+] = 2[S^{2-}]$

Hence, if $[S^{2-}] = x$, $[H^+] = 2x$

$(2x)^2 x / 0.1 = 1.092 \times 10^{-20}$

or $\quad 4x^3 = 1.092 \times 10^{-21}$

or $\quad x^3 = 273 \times 10^{-24}$

$\qquad x = 6.487 \times 10^{-8}$ M

In presence of $0.1$ M HCl,

suppose $[S^{2-}] = y$,

then $[H_2S] = 0.1 - y \approx 0.1$ M,

$[H^+] = 0.1 + y \approx 0.1$ M

$K_a = (0.1)^2 \times y / 0.1 = 1.09 \times 10^{-20}$

or $\quad y = 1.09 \times 10^{-19}$ M.

**7.46 The ionization constant of acetic acid is $1.74 \times 10^{-5}$. Calculate the degree of dissociation of acetic acid in its 0.05 M solution. Calculate the concentration of acetate ion in the solution and its pH.**

**Ans.**

$$CH_3COOH \rightleftharpoons CH_3COO^- + H^+$$

As $[CH_3COO^-] = [H^+]$

$$K_a = \frac{[CH_3COO^-][H^+]}{[CH_3COOH]} = \frac{[H^+]^2}{[CH_3COOH]}$$

or $\quad [H^+] = \sqrt{K_a[CH_3COOH]}$

$\qquad = \sqrt{(1.74 \times 10^{-5})(5 \times 10^{-2})}$

$\qquad = 9.33 \times 10^{-4}$ M

$[CH_3COO^-] = [H^+] = 9.33 \times 10^{-4}$ M

$pH = -\log(9.33 \times 10^{-4}) = 4 - 0.9699 = 4 - 0.97 = 3.03$

**7.47 It has been found that the pH of a 0.01 M solution of an organic acid is 4.15. Calculate the concentration of the anion, the ionization constant of the acid and its $pK_a$**

**Ans.** $HA \rightleftharpoons H^+ + A^-$

Here $[H^+] = [A^-]$

$pH = -\log[H^+]$ or $\log[H^+] = -pH = -4.15$

Taking antilog

$[H^+] = 7.08 \times 10^{-5}$ M

$[A^-] = [H^+] = 7.08 \times 10^{-5}$ M

$$K_a = \frac{[H^+][A^-]}{[HA]} = \frac{(7.08 \times 10^{-5})(7.08 \times 10^{-5})}{10^{-2}}$$

$\qquad = 5.012 \times 10^{-7}$

$pK_a = -\log K_a = -\log(5.012 \times 10^{-7}) = 7 - 0.7000 = 6.30$

**7.48 Assuming complete dissociation, calculate the pH of the following solutions:**

    **(a)  0.003 M HCl      (b)  0.005 M NaOH**

    **(c)  0.002 M HBr      (d)  0.002 M KOH**

**Ans.** (a)  $HCl(aq) \longrightarrow H^+ + Cl^-$,

      $\therefore\;\; [H^+] = [HCl] = 3 \times 10^{-3}$ M,

      $pH = -\log (3\times10^{-3}) = 2.52$

    (b)  $NaOH(aq) \longrightarrow Na^+ + OH^-$

      $[OH^-] = [NaOH]$

      $\therefore\;\; [OH^-] = 5 \times 10^{-3}$ M,

      $[H^+] = 10^{-14} / (5 \times 10^{-3})$

      $= 2 \times 10^{-12}$ M

      $pH = -\log(2\times 10^{-12}) = 11.699$

    (c)  $HBr(aq) \longrightarrow H^+ + Br^-, [H^+] = [HBr]$

      $\therefore\;\; [H^+] = 2 \times 10^{-3}$ M,

      $pH = -\log (2\times10^{-3}) = 2.699$

    (d)  $KOH(aq) \longrightarrow K^+ + OH^-, [OH^-] = [KOH]$

      $\therefore\;\; [OH^-] = 2 \times 10^{-3}$ M, $[H^+]$

      $= 10^{-14}/(2\times 10^{-3}) = 5 \times 10^{-12}$

      $pH = -\log (5\times10^{-12}) = 11.30$

**7.49 Calculate the pH of the following solutions:**

    **(a)  2g of TlOH dissolved in water to give 2 litre of solution**

    **(b)  0.3 g of $Ca(OH)_2$ dissolved in water to give 500 mL of solution**

    **(c)  0.3 g of NaOH dissolved in water to give 200 mL of solution**

    **(d)  1 mL of 13.6 M HCl is diluted with water to give 1 litre of solution.**

**Ans.** (a)  Molar conc. of TlOH

      $= 2g /(204 + 16 + 1)$ g mol$^{-1} \times 1 / 2L$

      $= 4.52 \times 10^{-3}$ M

      $[OH^-] = [TlOH] = 4.52\times10^{-3}$ M

      $[H^+] = 10^{-14}/(4.52 \times 10^{-3}) = 2.21\times10^{-12}$ M

      $pH = -\log(2.21\times10^{-12}) = 12 - (0.3424) = 11.655$

    (b)  Molar conc. of $Ca(OH)_2$

      $= 0.3 / [(40 + 34)$g mol$^{-1}] \times 1 / 0.5$ L

      $= 8.10 \times 10^{-3}$ M

      $Ca(OH)_2 \longrightarrow Ca^{2+} + 2 OH$

      $[OH^-] = 2[Ca(OH)_2] = 2 \times (8.10 \times 10^{-3})$M

      $= 16.2 \times10^{-3}$M

      $pOH = -\log(16.2\times10^{-3}) = 3 - 1.2101 = 1.79$

      $pH = 14 - 1.79 = 12.21$

    (c)  Molar conc. of NaOH

      $= 0.3g / 40g$ mol$^{-1} \times 1/ 0.2$L

      $= 3.75 \times10^{-2}$ M

      $pOH = -\log(3.75\times10^{-2})$

      $= 2 - 0.0574 = 1.426$

      $pH = 14 - 1.426 = 12.57$

    (d)  $M_1V_1 = M_2V_2$

      $\therefore\; 13.6M \times 1$ mL $= M_2 \times 1000$ mL

      $\therefore\; M_2 = 1.36 \times10^{-2}$ M

      $[H^+] = [HCl] = 1.36 \times10^{-2}$M,

      $pH = -\log(1.36 \times 10^{-2})$

      $= 2 - 0.1335 = 1.8665$

**7.50 The degree of ionization of a 0.1 M bromoacetic acid solution is 0.132. Calculate the pH of the solution and the $pK_a$ bromoacetic acid.**

**Ans.**       $CH_2(Br)COOH \rightleftharpoons CH_2(Br)COO^{-1} + H^+$

Initial conc.     c              0            0

Conc. at eqm.    $c - c\alpha$         $c\alpha$       $c\alpha$

Here $\alpha$ is the degree of ionisation of bromo acetic acid

$$K_a = \frac{c\alpha \times c\alpha}{c(1-\alpha)} = \frac{c\alpha^2}{1-\alpha}$$

        $= 0.1\times (0.132)^2 = 1.74 \times 10^{-3}$

$pK_a = -\log (1.74 \times10^{-3}) = 3 - 0.2405 = 2.76$

$[H^+] = c\alpha = 0.1\times 0.132 = 1.32 \times10^{-2}$M

    $pH = -\log(1.32\times10^{-2}) = 2 - 0.1206 = 1.88$

**7.51 The pH of 0.005 M codeine ($C_{18}H_{21}NO_3$) solution is 9.95. Calculate its ionization constant and $pK_b$**

**Ans.** $Cod + H_2O \rightleftharpoons CodH^+ + OH^-$

$pH = 9.95 \therefore pOH = 14 - 9.95 = 4.05$,

$[pH + pOH = 14]$

i.e.,$- \log [OH^-] = 4.05$

or    $\log[OH^-] = -4.05 = -5.95$

or    $[OH^-] = 8.913 \times10^{-5}$

$$K_b = \frac{[CodH^+][OH]}{[Cod]} = \frac{[OH^-]^2}{[Cod]} = \frac{(8.91\times10^{-5})^2}{5\times10^{-3}}$$

[at equilibrium $[Cod\,H^+] = [OH^-]$

$pK_b = -\log (1.588 \times10^{-6})$

$= -\log 1.59 + 6 \log 10$

$= 6 - \log 1.59 = 5.80$

**7.52 What is the pH of 0.001 M aniline solution ? The ionization constant of aniline is $4.27\times10^{-10}$. Calculate the degree of ionization of aniline in the solution. Also calculate the ionization constant of the conjugate acid of aniline.**

**Ans.** (i)  $C_6H_5NH_2 + H_2O \rightleftharpoons C_6H_5NH_3^+ + OH^-$

$$K_a = \frac{[C_6H_5NH_3^+][OH^-]}{[C_6H_5NH_2]} = \frac{[OH^-]^2}{[C_6H_5NH_2]}$$

    $\therefore$ at equilibrium $[C_6H_5NH_3^+] = [OH^-]$

    $[OH^-] = \sqrt{K_a[C_6H_5NH_2]}$

        $= \sqrt{(4.27\times10^{-10})(10^{-3})} = 6.534 \times 10^{-7}$ M

    $pOH = -\log (6.534 \times 10^{-7}) = 7 - 0.8152 = 6.18$

    $pH = 14 - 6.18 = 7.82$

(ii)  Also $C_6H_5NH_2 + H_2O \rightleftharpoons C_6H_5NH_3^+ + OH^-$

Initial      c

At. eqm.    $c - c\alpha$           $c\alpha$       $c\alpha$

    $K_b = (c\alpha)(c\alpha) / c(1-\alpha) = (c\alpha^2) / (1-\alpha)$

    $\therefore \alpha^2 = K_b /c = 4.27 \times 10^{-10} / 10^{-3}$

                  $(\because \alpha < < < 1, $ i.e., $ 1 - \alpha \approx 1)$

    $\alpha = 6.53 \times 10^{-4}$

(iii)  $pK_b + pK_a = 14$ (for a pair of conjugate acid and base)

$pK_b = -\log (4.27 \times 10^{-10}) = 10 - 0.62 = 9.37$

$pK_a = 14 - 9.37 = 4.63$

$-\log K_a = 4.62$ or $\log K_a = -4.62$

or $K_a = $ Antilog $-4.62 = 2.399 \times 10^{-5} \approx 2.4 \times 10^{-5}$

**7.53 Calculate the degree of ionization of 0.05 M acetic acid if its $pK_a$ value is 4.74. How is the degree of dissociation affected when its solution also contains (a) 0.01 M (b) 0.1M in HCl?**

**Ans.** $pK_a = 4.74$, i. e., $-\log K_a = 4.74$

or $\log K_a = -4.74$

Taking Antilog $K_a = $ Antilog $(-4.74)$

$\therefore$ $K_a = 1.82 \times 10^{-5}$

$\alpha^2 = K_a/c = (1.82 \times 10^{-5}) / (5 \times 10^{-2}) = 1.908 \times 10^{-2}$

In presence of HCl, due to high concentration of $H^+$ ion, dissociation equilibrium will shift backward, i.e. dissociation of acetic acid will decrease,

(a) In presence of 0.01 M HCl, if x is the amount dissociated, then

$$CH_3COOH \rightleftharpoons CH_3COO^- + H^+$$

Initial    0.05 M

After

disso.    $0.05 - x$          $x$        $0.01 + x$

       $= 0.05$                          $= 0.01$ M

(0. 01 M $H^+$ ions are obtained from 0. 01 M HCl)

$(\because x << 0.01$    $\therefore 0.01 + x \approx 0.01)$

$$\therefore K_a = \frac{[CH_3COO^-][H^+]}{[CH_3COOH]}$$

$\therefore \alpha = (1.82 \times 10^{-5}) / 10^{-2} = 1.82 \times 10^{-3}$

$$\left( since\ \alpha = \frac{Amount\ dissociated}{amount\ taken} \right)$$

(b) In the presence of 0.1 M HCl, if y is the amount of acetic acid dissociated, then at equilibrium

$[CH_3COOH] = 0.05 - y \approx 0.05$ M

$[CH_3COO^-] = y$, $[H^+] = 0.1M + y = 0.1M$

$K_a = (0.1) / 0.05$ or $y / 0.05 = K_a / 0.1$

$\therefore \alpha = (1.82 \times 10^{-5}) / 10^{-1} = 1.82 \times 10^{-4}$,

i. e. $\alpha = 1.82 \times 10^{-4}$

**7.54 The ionisation constant of dimethylamine is $5.4 \times 10^{-4}$. Calculate its degree of ionization in its 0.02 M solution. What percentage of dimethylamine is ionized if the solution is also 0.1 M NaOH ?**

**Ans.** $\alpha^2 = K_b / c = (5.4 \times 10^{-4}) / (2 \times 10^{-2}) = 0.027$; $\alpha = 0.164$

In presence of 0. 1 M NaOH, if x is the amount of dimethyl amine dissociated,

$$(CH_3)_2NH + H_2O \rightleftharpoons (CH_3)_2NH_2^+ + OH^-$$

Initial     c                      0         0

After     $c(1-\alpha)$          $c\alpha$      $c\alpha$

disso.

                       $\approx 0.1$ $([OH^-] = 0.1)$

$K_b = \dfrac{c\alpha}{c} 0.1$

$K_b = \alpha \times 0.1$

$[\alpha = \dfrac{5.4 \times 10^{-4}}{0.1}$ (% ionization = 0.54)$]$

$= 5.4 \times 10^{-3} = 0.0054$

**7.55 Calculate the hydrogen ion concentration in the following biological fluids whose pH are given below:**

(a) **Human muscle–fluid, 6.83**

(b) **Human stomach fluid, 1.2**

(c) **Human blood, 7.38**

(d) **Human saliva, 6.4**

**Ans.** (a) $\log [H^+] = pH = -6.83$

$\therefore [H^+] = $ Antilog $-6.83 = 1.479 \times 10^{-7}$M

(b) $\log [H^+] = -pH = -1.2$

$\therefore [H^+] = $ Antilog $-1.2 = 6.31 \times 10^{-2}$M

(c) $\log [H^+] = -pH = -7.38$

$\therefore [H^+] = $ Antilog $-7.38 = 4.169 \times 10^{-8}$ M

(d) $\log [H^+] = -pH = -6.4$

$\therefore [H^+] = $ Antilog $-6.4 = 3.981 \times 10^{-7}$M

**7.56 The pH of milk, black coffee, tomato juice, lemon juice and egg white are 6.8, 5.0, 4.2, 2.2 and 7.8 respectively. Calculate corresponding hydrogen ion concentration in each.**

**Ans.** Milk $\rightarrow$ $-\log[H^+] = pH = -6.8$

$\therefore$ $[H^+] = $ Antilog $(-6.8) = 1.58 \times 10^{-7}$ M

Black coffee $\rightarrow$ $-\log[H^+] = pH = -5.0$

$\therefore$ $[H^+] = 10^{-5}$ M

Tomato juice $\rightarrow$ $-\log[H^+] = pH = -4.2$

$\therefore$ $[H^+] = $ Antilog $(-4.2) = 6.31 \times 10^{-5}$M

Lemon juice $\rightarrow$ $-\log[H^+] = pH = -2.2$

$\therefore$ $[H^+] = $ Antilog $(-2.2) = 6.31 \times 10^{-3}$ M

Egg white $\rightarrow$ $-\log [H^+] = pH = -7.8$

$\therefore$ $[H^+] = $ Antilog $(-7.8) = 1.5 \times 10^{-8}$ M

**7.57 If 0.561 g of KOH is dissolved in water to give 200 mL of solution at 298 K. Calculate the concentration of potassium, hydrogen and hydroxyl ions. What is its pH ?**

**Ans.** $[KOH] = 0.561 / 56 \times 1000 / 200 = 0.05$M

As KOH $\longrightarrow$ $K^+ + OH^-$,

$[K^+] = [OH^-] = 0.05$ M

$[H^+] = K_w / [OH^-] = 10^{-14} / 0.05 = 10^{-14}/(5 \times 10^{-2})$

$= 2.0 \times 10^{-13}$ M.

$pH = -\log 2 \times 10^{-13}$

$= 13 - \log 2 = 12.69$

**7.58 The solubility of $Sr(OH)_2$ at 298K is 19.23 g/L of solution. Calculate the concentrations of strontium and hydroxyl ions and the pH of the solution.**

**Ans.** Molar mass of $Sr(OH)_2 = 87.6 + 34 = 121.6$ g $mol^{-1}$

Solubility of $Sr(OH)_2$ in moles $L^{-1}$

$= 19.23$ g$L^{-1} / 121.6$ g $mol^{-1} = 0.1581$ M

Assuming complete dissociation,

$Sr(OH)_2 \longrightarrow Sr^{2+} + 2 OH^-$

$\therefore$ $[Sr^{2+}] = 0.1581$M, $[OH^-] = 2 \times 0.1581 = 0.3162$M,

$pOH = -\log 0.3162 = 0.5$,

$\therefore$ pH $= 14 - 0. 5 = 13.5$

**7.59 The ionization constant of propanoic acid is $1.32 \times 10^{-5}$. Calculate the degree of ionization of the acid in its 0.05M solution and also its pH. What will be its degree of ionization if the solution is 0.01M in HCl also?**

**Ans.** Assuming $\alpha$ to be very small, applying formula directly, we have

$$\alpha = \sqrt{K_a/c} = \sqrt{(1.32\times10^{-5})/0.05} = 1.62 \times 10^{-2}$$

$$CH_3CH_2COOH \rightleftharpoons CH_3CH_2COO^- + H^+$$

In presence of HCl, equilibrium will shift in the backward direction, i.e. concentration of $CH_3CH_2COOH$ will increase hence amount of dissociation will be less. If 'c' is the initial concentration and 'x' is the amount now dissociated, then at equilibrium

$[CH_3CH_2COOH] = c(1-x)$

$[CH_3CH_2COO^-] = cx,$ $[H^+]$

$= c\alpha \approx 0.01 + x \approx 0.01$

$$\frac{cx \times 0.01}{c(1-x)} = x \times 0.01 = 1.32 \times 10^{-5}$$

$x = 1.32 \times 10^{-3}$.

**7.60 The pH of 0.1 M solution of cyanic acid (HCNO) is 2.34. Calculate the ionization constant of the acid and its degree of ionization in the solution.**

**Ans.** $HCNO \rightleftharpoons H^+ + CNO^-$

pH = 2.34 means

$-\log[H^+] = 2.34$

or   $\log[H^+] = -2.34 = -3.66$

or   $[H^+] = $ Antilog $-3.66 = 4.57 \times 10^{-3}$M

$[CNO^-] = [H^+] = 4.57 \times 10^{-3}$ M

$$K_a = \frac{(4.57\times10^{-2})^2}{0.1} = 2.09 \times 10^{-4}$$

$$\alpha = \sqrt{K_a/c} = \sqrt{(2.09\times10^{-4}/0.1)} = 0.0457$$

**7.61 The ionization constant of nitrous acid is $4.5 \times 10^{-4}$. Calculate the pH of 0.04 M sodium nitrite solution and also its degree of hydrolysis.**

**Ans.** Sodium nitrite is a salt of weak acid, strong base. Hence,

$K_h = K_w/K_a = 10^{-14}/(4.5 \times 10^{-4}) = 2.22 \times 10^{-11}$

$h = \sqrt{K_h/c} = \sqrt{(2.22\times10^{-11}/0.04)}$

$= \sqrt{5.5\times10^{-10}} = 2.36 \times 10^{-5}$

$$NO_2^- + H_2O \rightleftharpoons HNO_2 + OH^-$$

Initial   c

After   c(1–h)             ch         ch
hydrolysis

$[OH^-] = ch = 0.04 \times 2.36 \times 10^{-5} = 9.38 \times 10^{-7}$

$pOH = -\log(9.38 \times 10^{-7}) = 7 - 0.9722 = 6.03$

$pH = 14 - pOH = 14 - 6.03 = 7.97$.

**7.62 0.02 M solution of pyridinium hydrochloride has pH = 3.44. Calculate the ionization constant of pyridine.**

**Ans.** pH = 3.44, i. e., $\log [H^+] = -3.44 = -4.56$

Taking Antilog

$\therefore [H^+] = 3.63 \times 10^{-4}$

$$C_5H_5N^+HCl^- + aq \rightleftharpoons C_5H_5\overset{+}{N}Cl + \overset{-}{H}^+$$

$$K_a = \frac{[C_5N_5N^+Cl^-][H^+]}{[C_5H_5N^+HCl^-]}$$

$$= \frac{(3.63\times10^{-4})(3.63\times10^{-4})}{2\times10^{-2}} = 6.59 \times 10^{-6}$$

$pK_a = -\log(6.59 \times 10^{-6}) = 6 - 0.8187 = 5.18$

$pK_b + pK_b = 14$   $\therefore$ $pK_b = 14 - 5.18 = 8.82$

$-\log K_b = 8.82$ or $\log K_b = -8.82$ $\therefore K_b, = 1.514 \times 10^{-9}$

**7.63 Predict if the solutions of the following salts are neutral, acidic or basic:**
**$NaCl$, $KBr$, $NaCN$, $NH_4NO_3$, $NaNO_2$ and $KF$.**

**Ans.** $NaCN$, $NaNO_2$, $KF$ solutions are basic, as they are salts of strong base and weak acid. $NaCl$ and $KBr$ solutions are neutral, as they are salts of strong acid, strong base. $NH_4NO_3$ solution is acidic, as it is a salt of strong acid, weak base.

**7.64 The ionization constant of chloroacetic acid is $1.35 \times 10^{-3}$. What will be the pH of 0.1 M acid and its 0.1M sodium salt solution ?**

**Ans.** $ClCH_2COOH \rightleftharpoons ClCH_2COO^- + H^+$

$$K_a = \frac{[ClCH_2COO^-][H^+]}{[ClCH_2COOH]} = \frac{[H^+]^2}{c}$$

at equilibrium, $[ClCH_2COO^-] = [H^+]$

$[H^+] = \sqrt{K_a \times c} = \sqrt{1.35\times10^{-3}\times0.1} = 1.16 \times 10^{-2}$

$pH = -\log(1.16 \times 10^{-2}) = 2 - 0.06 = 1.94$

Sodium salt of chloroacetic acid is a salt of strong base and weak acid. Hence,

$pH = -1/2 [\log K_w + \log K_a - \log c]$

$\therefore$   $pH = -\dfrac{1}{2} [\log 10^{-14} + \log 1.35\times10^{-3} - \log 0.1]$

$= -\dfrac{1}{2} [-14 + (-3 + 0.1303) - (-1)]$

$= 7 + 1.44 - 0.5 = 7.94$

**7.65 The ionic product of water at 310 K is $2.7 \times 10^{-14}$. What is the pH of neutral water at this temperature?**

**Ans.** As $[H^+][OH^-] = K_w$

For neutral water $[H^+] = [OH^-]$

$\therefore$ $[H^+]^2 = 2.7 \times 10^{-14}$

or  $\sqrt{[H^+]^2} = \sqrt{2.7\times10^{-14}}$

$\therefore$ $[H^+] = 1.643 \times 10^{-7}$

$pH = -\log [H^+] = -\log (1.643 \times 10^{-7}) = 7 - 0.2156 = 6.78$

**7.66 Calculate the pH of the resultant mixtures**
**(a) 10 mL of 0.2 M $Ca(OH)_2$ + 25 mL of 0.1 M HCl**
**(b) 10 mL of 0. 01 M $H_2SO_4$ + 10 mL of 0. 01 M $Ca(OH)_2$**
**(c) 10 mL of 0.1 M $H_2SO_4$ + 10 mL of 0.1 M KOH**

**Ans. (a)** 10 mL of 0.2 M $Ca(OH)_2 = 10 \times 0.2$ millimoles = 2 millimoles of $Ca(OH)_2$

25 mL of 0.1 M HCl = $25 \times 0.1$ millimoles = 2.5 millimoles of HCl

$Ca(OH)_2 + 2 HCl \longrightarrow CaCl_2 + 2 H_2O$

∵  1 millimole of $Ca(OH)_2$ reacts with 2 millimoles of HCl

∴  2.5 millimoles of HCl will react with 1.25 millimoles of $Ca(OH)_2$

∴  $Ca(OH)_2$ left = 2 – 1.25 = 0.75 millimoles (HCl is the limiting reactant)
Total volume of the solution = 10 + 25 mL= 35 mL

∴  Molarity of $Ca(OH)_2$ in the mixture solution = 0.75/35 M = 0.0214 M
$[OH^-] = 2 \times 0.0214M = 0.0428$ M
$= 4.28 \times 10^{-2}$
$pOH = -\log(4.28 \times 10^{-2}) = 2 - 0.6314 = 1.3686 \approx 1.37$
$pH = 14 - 1.37 = 12.63$

(b)  10 mL of 0.01 M $H_2SO_4$ = 10 × 0.01 M mol
$= 0.1$ M mol
10 mL of 0.01 M $Ca(OH)_2$ = 10 × 0.01 M mol
$= 0.1$ M mol

$Ca(OH)_2 + H_2SO_4 \rightleftharpoons CaSO_4 + 2 H_2O$
1 mole of $Ca(OH)_2$ reacts with 1 mole of $H_2SO_4$
∴ 0.1 millimole of $Ca(OH)_2$ will react completely with 0.1 millimole of $H_2SO_4$. Hence, solution will be neutral with pH = 7.0

(c)  10 mL of 0.1 M $H_2SO_4$ = 1 millimole
10 mL of 0.1 M KOH = 1 millimole
$2 KOH + H_2SO_4 \longrightarrow K_2SO_4 + 2 H_2O$
1 millimole of KOH will react with 0.5 millimole of $H_2SO_4$

∴  $H_2SO_4$ left = 1 – 0.5 = 0.5 millimole
Volume of reaction mixture = 10 + 10 = 20 mL

∴  Molarity of $H_2SO_4$ in the mixture solution

$= \dfrac{0.5}{20} = 2.5 \times 10^{-2}$

$[H^+] = 2 \times 2.5 \times 10^{-2} = 5 \times 10^{-2}$
$pH = -\log(5 \times 10^{-2}) = 2 - 0.6989 = 1.3011$

**7.67 Determine the solubilities of silver chromate, barium chromate, ferric hydroxide, lead chloride and mercurous iodide at 298 K from their solubility product constants given in table 7.9. Determine also molarities of individual ions.**

**Ans.** 1.  $Ag_2CrO_4 \rightleftharpoons 2Ag^+ + CrO_4^{2-},$
        2s        s

$K_{sp} = (2s)^2(s) = 4s^3$

∴  $s^3 = K_{sp}/4$
$= (1.1 \times 10^{-12})/4 = 0.275 \times 10^{-12}$
$s = 6.5 \times 10^{-5} mol\ L^{-1}$
$[Ag^+] = 2 \times 6.5 \times 10^{-5} = 13.0 \times 10^{-5}M$
$= 1.30 \times 10^{-4}M$
$[CrO_4^{2-}] = 6.5 \times 10^{-5}M$

2.  For $BaCrO_4$; $BaCrO_4$ (s) $\rightleftharpoons Ba^{2+} + CrO_4^{-2}$
                s        s

$K_{sp} = s^2 = 1.2 \times 10^{-10}$,  ∴ $s = \sqrt{1.2 \times 10^{-10}}$
$= 1.1 \times 10^{-5}M = [Ba^{2+}] = [CrO_4^{-2}]$

3.  For $Fe(OH)_3$; $Fe(OH)_3 \rightleftharpoons Fe^{3+} + 3OH^-$
                  s              3s

$K_{sp} = s \times (3s)^3 = 27\ s^4$

∴  $s = \sqrt[4]{(K_{sp}/27)} = \sqrt[4]{(1 \times 10^{-38}/27)}$
Taking log

$\log s = \log\left(\dfrac{1 \times 10^{-38}}{27}\right)^{1/4}$

$= \dfrac{1}{4}[\log 10^{-38} - \log 27] = \dfrac{1}{4}[-38 - \log 27]$

$= \dfrac{1}{4}[-38 - 1.43136]$

$= \dfrac{1}{4}[-39.43] = -9.8578$

∴ $\log s = -9.8578$
Taking Antilog    $s = 1.35 \times 10^{-10}$
Hence $[Fe^{3+}] = 1.35 \times 10^{-10}M$ ;
$[OH^-] = 3 \times 1.35 \times 10^{-10} = 4.04 \times 10^{-10}M$

4.  For $PbCl_2$; $PbCl_2 \rightleftharpoons Pb^{2+} + 2Cl^-$
                s        2s

$K_{sp} = 4s^3$

∴  $s = \sqrt[3]{(K_{sp}/4)} = \sqrt[3]{(1.6 \times 10^{-5}/4)}$
$S = 1.59 \times 10^{-2}$
Hence $[Pb^{2+}] = 1.59 \times 10^{-2}M$ ;
$[Cl^-] = 2 \times 1.59 \times 10^{-2} = 3.18 \times 10^{-2}$ M

5.  For $Hg_2I_2$; $Hg_2I_2 \rightleftharpoons Hg_2^{2+} + 2I^-$
                s          2s

$K_{sp} = 4s^3$ solve as above, we get
$s = 2.24 \times 10^{-8}M = [Hg_2^{2+}]$
and $2 \times 2.24 \times 10^{-8} = 4.48 \times 10^{-8}M = [I^-]$

**7.68 The solubility product constants of $Ag_2CrO_4$ and AgBr are $1.1 \times 10^{-12}$ and $5.0 \times 10^{-13}$ respectively. Calculate the ratio of the molarities of their saturated solutions.**

**Ans.**  $Ag_2CrO_4 \rightleftharpoons 2Ag^+ + CrO_4^{2-},$
          2s      s

$K_{sp} = (2s)^2(s) = 4\ s^3,$  ∴ $s^3 = K_{sp}/4$
∴  $s = 6.5 \times 10^{-5}$
$AgBr \rightleftharpoons Ag^+ + Br^-$
        s      s
$K_{sp} = s^2 = 5 \times 10^{-13}$

∴  $s = \sqrt{5 \times 10^{-13}} = 7.07 \times 10^{-7}$

∴  ratio of $[Ag_2CrO_4] : [AgBr]$
$= 6.5 \times 10^{-5} : 7.07 \times 10^{-7}$
$= 91.9$
Silver chromate is more soluble than silver bromide.

**7.69 Equal volumes of 0.002 M solutions of sodium iodate and cupric chlorate are mixed together. Will it lead to precipitation of copper iodate? For cupric iodate, $K_{sp}$ = $7.4 \times 10^{-8}$.**

**Ans.** $2\,NaIO_3 + CuClO_4 \rightleftharpoons Na_2ClO_4 + Cu(IO_3)_2$

After mixing, $[NaIO_3] = [IO_3^-] = (2 \times 10^{-3})/2$
$= 10^{-3}\,M$

$[CuClO_4] = [Cu^{2+}] = (2\times10^{-3})/2 = 10^{-3}\,M$

Ionic product of $Cu(IO_3)_2 = [Cu^{2+}]\,[IO_3^-]^2$
$= (10^{-3})\,(10^{-3})^2 = 10^{-9}$

As ionic product is less than $K_{sp}$, no precipitation will occur.

**7.70** **The ionization constant of benzoic acid is $6.46 \times 10^{-5}$ and $K_{sp}$ for silver benzoate is $2.5 \times 10^{-13}$. How many times is silver benzoate more soluble in a buffer of pH 3·19 compared to its solubility in pure water ?**

**Ans.** $C_6H_5COOAg \rightleftharpoons C_6H_5COO^- + Ag^+$

**Solubility in water.** Suppose solubility in water
$= x\ mol\ L^{-1}$.

Then $[C_6H_5COO^-] = [Ag^+] = x\ mol\ L^{-1}$.

$\therefore\ x^2 = K_{sp}$ or $x = \sqrt{K_{sp}} = \sqrt{2.5\times10^{-13}}$

$= 5 \times 10^{-7}\ mol\ L^{-1}$

**Solubility in buffer of pH = 3.19**

pH = 3.19 means $-\log[H^+] = 3.19$

or $\log[H^+] = -3.19 = -4.81$

or $\log\ [H^+] = 6.457\times10^{-4}$

$C_6H_5COO^-$ ions now combine with the $H^+$ ions to form benzoic acid but $[H^+]$ remains almost constant because we have buffer solution. Now

$C_6H_5COOH \rightleftharpoons C_6H_5COO^- + H^+$

$$K_a = \frac{[C_6H_5COO^-][H^+]}{[C_6H_5COOH]}$$

or $$\frac{[C_6H_5COOH]}{[C_6H_5COO^-]}$$

$$= \frac{[H^+]}{K_a} = \frac{6.457\times10^{-4}}{6.46\times10^{-5}} = 10 \qquad \ldots(i)$$

Suppose solubility in the buffer solution is $y\ mol\ L^{-1}$. Then as most of the benzoate ions are converted into benzoic acid molecules (which remain almost ionized), we have

$y = [Ag^+] = [C_6H_5COO^-] + [C_6H_5COOH]$

$\quad = [C_6H_5COO^-] + 10\,[C_6H_5COO^-]$

$\quad = 11\,[C_6H_5COO^-]$ \hfill (using eqn. (i))

$[C_6H_5COO^-] = y/11$

$\therefore\ \ K_{sp} = [C_6H_5COO^-]\,[Ag^+]$

i. e., $2.5 \times 10^{-3} = y/11 \times y$

or $y^2 = 2.75 \times 10^{-12}$

or $y = 1.66 \times 10^{-6}$

$$\therefore\ y/x = \frac{1.66\times10^{-6}}{5\times10^{-7}} = 3.32$$

Silver benzoate is 3.32 times more soluble in buffer of pH 3.19 then in pure water.

**7.71** **What is the maximum concentration of equimolar solutions of ferrous sulphate and sodium sulphide so that when mixed in equal volumes, there is no precipitation of iron sulphide? For iron sulphide, $K_{sp} = 6.3 \times 10^{-18}$.**

**Ans.** Suppose the concentration of each of $FeSO_4$ and $Na_2S$ is $x\ mol\ L^{-1}$.

Then after mixing equal volumes,

$[FeSO_4] = [Na_2S]$
$= x/2\ M,$ i. e., $[Fe^{2+}] = [S^{2-}] = x/2\ M$

$K_{sp}$ for $FeS = [Fe^{2+}]\,[S^{2-}],$ i. e., $6.3 \times 10^{-18}$
$= (x/2) \times (x/2)$

or $x^2 = 25.2 \times 10^{-18},$ or $x = 5.01 \times 10^{-9}\,M.$

**7.72** **What is the minimum volume of water required to dissolve 1 g of calcium sulphate at 298K? (For calcium sulphate, $K_{sp}$ is $9.1\times10^{-6}$.)**

**Ans.** $CaSO_4\,(s) \rightleftharpoons Ca^{2+}\,(aq) + SO_4^{2-}\,(aq)$

If s is the solubility of $CaSO_4$ in moles $L^{-1}$, then
$K_{sp} = [Ca^{2+}] \times [SO_4^{2-}] = s^2$

or. $s = (K_{sp})^{1/2} = 3.02\times10^{-3}\ mol\ L^{-1}$
$= 3.02\times10^{-3} \times 136g\ L^{-1} = 0.4107\ gL^{-1}$

\hfill (Molar mass of $CaSO_4 = 136g\ mol^{-1}$)

Thus, for dissolving 0.4107 g, water required = 1 L

$\therefore$ For dissolving 1 g, water required
$= 1/(0.411)\ L = 2.43\ L.$

**7.73** **The concentration of sulphide ion in 0.1 M HCl solution saturated with hydrogen sulphide is $1.0 \times 10^{-19}$m. If 10 mL of this solution is added to 5 mL of 0.04 M solution of the following $FeSO_4$, $MnCl_2$, $ZnCl_2$ and $CdCl_2$. In which solutions precipitation will take place ?**

**Ans.** Precipitation will take place in the solution for which ionic product is greater than solubility product. As 10 mL of solution containing $S^{2-}$ ion is mixed with 5 mL of metal salt solution, after mixing

$[S^{2-}] = 1.0\times10^{-19}\times(10/15) = 6.67\times10^{-20}$

$[Fe^{2+}] = [Mn^{2+}] = [Zn^{2+}] = [Cd^{2+}]$
$= (5/15)\times 0.04 = 1.33\times10^{-2}\ M$

$\therefore$ Ionic product for each of these will be $= [M^{2+}]\,[S^{2-}]$
$= (1.33 \times 10^{-2})\,(6.67 \times 10^{-20}) = 8.87\times 10^{-22}$

As this is greater than the solubility product of ZnS and CdS, therefore, $ZnCl_2$ and $CdCl_2$ solutions be precipitated.

| SECTION B | PRACTICE QUESTIONS |

## MULTIPLE CHOICE QUESTIONS

**1.** A reaction is said to be in equilibrium when
(a) the rate of transformation of reactant to products is equal to the rate of transformation of products to the reactants.
(b) 50% of the reactants are converted to products.
(c) the reaction is near completion and all the reactants are converted to products.
(d) the volume of reactants is just equal to the volume of the products.

**2.** Which of the following is not a general characteristic of equilibria involving physical processes?
(a) Equilibrium is possible only in a closed system at a given temperature.
(b) All measurable properties of the system remain constant.
(c) All the physical processes stop at equilibrium.
(d) The opposing processes occur at the same rate and there is dynamic but stable condition.

**3.** A reaction is $A + B \rightleftharpoons C + D$. Initially we start with equal concentrations of $A$ and $B$. At equilibrium we find that the moles of $C$ is two times of $A$. What is the equilibrium constant of the reaction?
(a) $\dfrac{1}{4}$    (b) $\dfrac{1}{2}$    (c) 4    (d) 2

**4.** In the following equilibrium reaction
$$2A \rightleftharpoons B + C,$$
the equilibrium concentrations of $A$, $B$ and $C$ are $1 \times 10^{-3}$ M, $2 \times 10^{-3}$ M and $3 \times 10^{-3}$ M respectively at 300 K. The value of $K_c$ for this equilibrium at the same temperature is
(a) $\dfrac{1}{6}$    (b) 6    (c) $\dfrac{1}{36}$    (d) 36

**5.** If for the reaction
$$N_2 + 3H_2 \rightleftharpoons 2NH_3, \Delta H = -92.38 \text{ kJ/mol},$$
then what happens if the temperature is increased?
(a) Reaction proceed forward
(b) Reaction proceed backward
(c) No effect on the formation of product
(d) None of these

**6.** Conjugate acid of $NH_2^-$ is :
(a) $NH_4^+$   (b) $NH_3$   (c) $NH_2$   (d) $NH$

**7.** Which of the following molecules acts as a Lewis acid ?
(a) $(CH_3)_2 O$    (b) $(CH_3)_3 P$
(c) $(CH_3)_3 N$    (d) $(CH_3)_3 B$

**8.** Which of the following statements about pH and $H^+$ ion concentration is incorrect?
(a) Addition of one drop of concentrated HCl in $NH_4OH$ solution decreases pH of the solution.
(b) A solution of the mixture of one equivalent of each of $CH_3COOH$ and NaOH has a pH of 7
(c) pH of pure neutral water is not zero
(d) A cold and concentrated $H_2SO_4$ has lower $H^+$ ion concentration than a dilute solution of $H_2SO_4$

**9.** At 25°C, the solubility product of $Mg(OH)_2$ is $1.0 \times 10^{-11}$. At which pH, will $Mg^{2+}$ ions start precipitating in the form of $Mg(OH)_2$ from a solution of 0.001 M $Mg^{2+}$ ions?
(a) 9    (b) 10    (c) 11    (d) 8

**10.** pH of a saturated solution of $Ba(OH)_2$ is 12. The value of solubility product ($K_{sp}$) of $Ba(OH)_2$ is :
(a) $3.3 \times 10^{-7}$    (b) $5.0 \times 10^{-7}$
(c) $4.0 \times 10^{-6}$    (d) $5.0 \times 10^{-6}$

**11.** Why only $As^{3+}$ gets precipitated as $As_2S_3$ and not $Zn^{2+}$ as ZnS when $H_2S$ is passed through an acidic solution containing $As^{3+}$ and $Zn^{2+}$?
(a) Solubility product of $As_2S_3$ is less than that of ZnS
(b) Enough $As^{3+}$ are present in acidic medium
(c) Zinc salt does not ionise in acidic medium
(d) Solubility product changes in presence of an acid

## ASSERTION & REASON QUESTIONS

**DIRECTIONS (Qs. (1-8)) :** *Each of these questions contains an assertion followed by reason. Read them carefully and answer the question on the basis of following options. You have to select the one that best describes the two statements.*
(a) If both Assertion and Reason are correct and the Reason is a correct explanation of the Assertion.
(b) If both Assertion and Reason are correct but Reason is not a correct explanation of the Assertion.
(c) If the Assertion is correct but Reason is incorrect.
(d) If the Assertion is incorrect but the Reason is correct.

**1.** **Assertion :** $K_p$ can be less than, greater than or equal to $K_c$.
**Reason :** Relation between $K_p$ and $K_c$ depends on the change in number of moles of gaseous reactants and products ($\Delta n$).

**2.** **Assertion :** If a volume is kept constant and an inert gas such as argon is added which does not take part in the reaction, the equilibrium remains undisturbed.
**Reason :** It is because the addition of an inert gas at constant volume does not change the partial pressure or the molar concentrations of the substance involved in the reaction.

**3.** **Assertion :** For reaction
$$N_2(g) + 3H_2(g) \rightleftharpoons 2NH_3(g)$$
Unit of $K_c = L^2 mol^{-2}$
**Reason :** For the reaction
$$N_2(g) + 3H_2(g) \rightleftharpoons 2NH_3(g)$$
Equilibrium constant, $K_c = \dfrac{[NH_3]^2}{[N_2][H_2]^3}$

**4.** **Assertion :** The equilibrium constant is fixed and a characteristic for any given chemical reaction at a specified temperature.
**Reason :** The composition of the final equilibrium mixture at a particular temperature depends upon the starting amount of reactants.

**5.** **Assertion :** Addition of silver ions to a mixture of aqueous sodium chloride and sodium bromide solution will first precipitate AgBr rather than AgCl.
**Reason :** $K_{sp}$ of AgCl > $K_{sp}$ of AgBr.

**6.** **Assertion:** In a titration of weak acid and NaOH, the pH at half equivalence point is $pK_a$.
**Reason:** At half equivalence point, it forms an acidic buffer and the buffer capacity is maximum where [acid] = [salt]

**7.** **Assertion :** $[Al(H_2O)_6]^{3+}$ is a stronger acid than $[Mg(H_2O)_6]^{2+}$.
**Reason :** Size of $[Al(H_2O)_6]^{3+}$ is smaller than $[Mg(H_2O)_6]^{2+}$ and possesses more effective nuclear charge.

**8.** **Assertion :** KOH is more soluble in water than NaOH.
**Reason :** NaOH is a stronger base than KOH.

## CASE/PASSAGE BASED QUESTIONS

**DIRECTIONS (Qs. 1-5) :** *Read the following case/passage and answer the questions.*

The concentration of reactants and products, at equilibrium, are constant at a given temperature. Consider the following simple reversible reaction where A & B are the reactants whereas C & D are the products.

$$A + B \rightleftharpoons C + D$$

A mixture of products and reactants in a state of chemical equilibrium is known as an equilibrium mixture. There exists a relation between the concentration of products and the concentration of reactants for an equilibrium mixture. This relation can be equated as follows.

Kc = [C] [D] / [A] [B]

Here, $K_c$ is called the equilibrium constant. In this equation, the concentration of A at equilibrium is represented as [A] (similarly for B, C, and D), and the stoichiometric coefficients of the reactants and products are 1. $K_c$ is the equilibrium constant expressed in terms of the concentration of the reactants/products. Similarly, $K_p$ is the constant in terms of the partial pressures of the substances Relation between $K_c$, $K_p$ and $K_x$
$K_p = K_c(RT)^{\Delta ng}$

**1.** In $A + B \rightleftharpoons C$. The unit of equilibrium constant is :
(a) Litre $mol^{-1}$
(b) Mol litre
(c) Mol $litre^{-1}$
(d) No unit

**2.** In which of the following equilibrium $K_c$ and $K_p$ are not equal?
(a) $2NO(g) \rightleftharpoons N_2(g) + O_2(g)$
(b) $SO_2(g) + NO_2(g) \rightleftharpoons SO_3(g) + NO(g)$
(c) $H_2(g) + I_2(g) \rightleftharpoons 2HI(g)$
(d) $2C(s) + O_2(g) \rightleftharpoons 2CO_2(g)$

**3.** For the reaction $C(s) + CO_2(g) \rightleftharpoons 2CO(g)$, the partial pressures of $CO_2$ and CO are 2.0 and 4.0 atm respectively at equilibrium. The $K_p$ for the reaction is.
(a) 0.5 (b) 4.0 (c) 8.0 (d) 32.0

**4.** The $K_p/K_c$ ratio will be highest in case of
(a) $CO(g) + \dfrac{1}{2}O_2(g) \rightleftharpoons CO_2(g)$
(b) $H_2(g) + I_2(g) \rightleftharpoons 2HI(g)$
(c) $PCl_5(g) \rightleftharpoons PCl_3(g) + Cl_2(g)$
(d) $7H_2(g) + 2NO_2(g) \rightleftharpoons 2NH_3(g) + 4H_2O(g)$

**5.** Unit of equilibrium constant for the given reaction is
$Ni(s) + 4CO(g) \rightleftharpoons Ni(CO)_4(g)$
(a) $(mol/L)^{-3}$ (b) $(mol/L)^3$
(c) $(mol/L)^{-4}$ (d) $(mol/L)^4$

## VERY SHORT ANSWER QUESTIONS

**1.** In a reaction $a + b \rightleftharpoons c + d$ will addition of c to the system change the value of K?

**2.** In a reaction $a + b \rightleftharpoons c + d$ the change in enthalpy is $-10$ kcal. If heat is added to the system in which direction the reaction would proceed?

**3.** What is meant by the statement 'Equilibrium is dynamic in nature'?

**4.** At what temperature the solid and liquid are in equilibrium under 1 atm pressure ?

**5.** $A + B \rightleftharpoons AB; K = 1 \times 10^2$
$E + F \rightleftharpoons EF; K = 1 \times 10^{-3}$
Out of AB and EF, which one is more stable AB or EF ?

**6.** Which will have $CO_2$ to more extent, hot cold drink bottle or chilled cold drink bottle, why ?

**7.** Mention the conditions of temperature and pressure when gas will dissolve in liquid to maximum extent with decrease in volume and absorption of heat.

**8.** What is difference between strong electrolyte and weak electrolyte ?

**9.** Write the expression for equilibrium constant $K_p$, for the reaction.
$3Fe(s) + 4H_2O(g) \rightleftharpoons Fe_3O_4(s) + 4H_2(g)$

**10.** The equilibrium constant for a gas phase reaction is
$$K_c = \dfrac{[CS_2][H_2]^4}{[CH_4][H_2S]^2}$$
Write the balanced chemical equation corres- ponding to this expression.

**11.** In a gaseous reaction $a + b \rightleftharpoons c + 2d$, 3 mol of inert gas is introduced into the vessel at constant pressure. What will be its effect on equilibrium?

**12.** The equilibrium constants for HCN and HAc are $4.0 \times 10^{-10}$ and $1.9 \times 10^{-5}$ mole/L respectively. Which acid is stronger?

**13.** A certain metal sulphide MS, has a solubility product $1.3 \times 10^{-18}$ mole$^2$/L$^2$. What must be $[S^{-2}]$ be in a 0.10M solution of $M^{2+}$ when MS just starts to precipitate.

**14.** What is the effect of temperature on solubility of gases in liquids?

**15.** Is it possible to get precipitate of $Fe(OH)_3$ at pH = 2? Give reason.

**16.** What is the expression for $K_{sp}$ of $Ag_2CrO_4$?

**17.** $pK_a$ values of acids A, B, C, D are 1.5, 3.5, 2.0 and 5.0. Which of them is strongest acid ?

**18.** Give two applications of buffer solution.

**19.** Write an equation to show that $NH_3$ is an Arrhenius base.

**20.** Write two equations to show the amphiprotic (acid as well as base) property of water.

**21.** Which of the following is strongest Lewis acid ? $CCl_4$, $AlCl_3$, $NCl_3$, $OCl_2$.

**22.** All Bronsted acids are not Lewis acids. Explain.

**23.** Which of the following is strongest conjugate base? $CH_3^-$, $NH_2^-$, $OH^-$, $F^-$.

**24.** Which of the following salt will not be hydrolysed? $NaNO_3$, $CH_3COONa$

**25.** On what factor the choice of an indicator in acid-base titration depends?

**26.** Name the buffer present in blood.

## SHORT ANSWER QUESTIONS

**1.** For the reaction $2a \rightleftharpoons c + d$, the equilibrium constant is $1.0 \times 10^{-3}$. At equilibrium, the concentrations observed were $[c] = 1.2 \times 10^{-3}$ M, $[d] = 3.8 \times 10^{-6}$ M. What was $[a]$ at equilibrium?

**2.** For the reaction $d + 2e \rightarrow f$, the initial concentrations of 'd' and 'e' were 0.2 and 1.2 mole / litre. At equilibrium, the concentration of 'f' was found to be 0.1 mole / litre. What is 'K' for the reaction?

**3.** On the reaction $2NH_3 (g) \rightleftharpoons N_2 (g) + 3H_2(g)$; $\Delta H = + 93.6$ kJ. Tell us what would be effect of
(a) temperature
(b) pressure

**4.** Following data is given for the reaction :
$CaCO_3(s) \rightarrow CaO (s) + CO_2 (g)$

$\Delta_f U^{\ominus} [CaO(s)] = - 635.1$ kJ mol$^{-1}$

$\Delta_f U^{\ominus} [CO_2(g)] = - 393.5$ kJ mol$^{-1}$

$\Delta_f U^{\ominus} [CaCO_3(s)] = - 1206.9$ kJ mol$^{-1}$

Predict the effect of temperature on the equilibrium constant of the above reaction.

**5.** Which of the following reactions involve homogeneous equilibria and which involve heterogeneous equilibria?
(i) $2N_2O(g) \rightleftharpoons 2N_2(g) + O_2(g)$
(ii) $2NH_3(g) \rightleftharpoons N_2(g) + 3H_2(g)$
(iii) $2Cu (NO_3)_2(s) \rightleftharpoons 2CuO(s) + 4NO_2(g) + O_2(g)$
(iv) $CH_3COO\,C_2H_5(aq) + H_2O(l) \rightleftharpoons$
$\qquad\qquad CH_3\,COOH(aq) + C_2H_5OH(aq)$

**6.** Given :
(i) $Cu(g) + 2Ag^+ (aq) \rightleftharpoons Cu^{2+} (aq) + 2Ag(s)$

$$K = \frac{[Cu^{2+}(aq)]}{[Ag^+(aq)]^2} = 2.0 \times 10^{15}$$

(ii) $Cu(s) + Zn^{2+}_{(aq)} \rightleftharpoons Cu^{2+}(aq) + Zn(s)$

$$K = \frac{[Cu^{2+}(aq)]}{[Zn^{2+}(aq)]} = 2.0 \times 10^{-19}$$

Arrange the three metals in order of increasing reactivity.

**7.** One mole of $H_2O$ and one mole of CO are taken in a 10 L vessel and heated to 725 K. At equilibrium 40 percent of water (by mass) reacts with carbon monoxide according to the equation
$H_2O(g) + CO(g) \rightleftharpoons H_2(g) + CO_2(g)$
Calculate the equilibrium constant for the reaction.

**8.** The equilibrium constant for the following reaction is $1.6 \times 10^5$ at 1024 K
$$H_2(g) + Br_2(g) \rightleftharpoons 2HBr(g)$$
Find the equilibrium pressure of all gases if 10.0 bar of HBr is introduced into a sealed container at 1024 K.

**9.** For the reaction,
$CH_4(g) + 2H_2S(g) \rightleftharpoons CS_2(g) + 4H_2(g)$, at 1173 K, the magnitude of the equilibrium constant, $K_c$ is 3.6. For each of the following composition, decide whether the reaction mixture is at equilibrium. If it is not, decide to which direction the reaction should go
(i) $[CH_4] = 1.07$ M $[H_2S] = 1.20$ M, $[CS_2] = 0.90$ M, $[H_2] = 1.78$ M
(ii) $[CH_4] = 1.45$ M, $[H_2S] = 1.29$ M, $[CS_2] = 1.25$ M, $[H_2] = 1.75$ M

**10.** Vapour pressure of water, acetone and ethanol at 293 K are 2.34, 12.3 and 5.85 kPa respectively. Which of these has the lowest and the highest boiling point? At 293 K which of these evaporates least in a sealed container before equilibrium is reached?

**11.** $A \rightleftharpoons B$ $K_1 = 1$

$B \rightleftharpoons C$ $K_2 = 2$

$C \rightleftharpoons D$ $K_3 = 3$

$D \rightleftharpoons E$ $K_4 = 4$

What is value of K for $A \rightleftharpoons E$ ?

**12.** Calculate the molar concentration of an acetic acid solution which is 2% ionized? ($K_a = 1.8 \times 10^{-5}$)

**13.** (i) Why in detection of cations, group IV metals are not precipitated in group II radicals?
(ii) Why do we pass $H_2S$ gas in acidic medium in group 2?

**14.** Which has the greater molarity in water, AgCl or $Mg(OH)_2$ ($K_{sp}$ (AgCl) $= 1.8 \times 10^{-10}$, $K_{sp}Mg(OH)_2 = 1.2 \times 10^{-11}$)

**15.** Calculate the pH of the solution produced when an aqueous solution of pH = 5 is mixed with equal volume of an aqueous solution of pH = 3.

**16.** How much $CH_3COONa$ should be added to 1 litre of 0.1M $CH_3COOH$ to make a buffer of pH = 4.0? $K_a = 1.8 \times 10^{-5}$.

**17.** The species $H_2O$, $HCO_3^-$, $HSO_4^-$ and $NH_3$ can act as both Bronsted acids and bases. For each case give the corresponding conjugate acid and base.

**18.** At 298 K, a 0.1 M solutions of a weak acid, HA is 1.34 percent ionised. What is the ionization constant, $K_a$ for an acid?

**19.** Calculate the concentrations of hydrogen ion and hydroxide ion at 25° C in
(i) 0.15 M $HNO_3$ and
(ii) 0.01 M $Ca(OH)_2$

**20.** All Bronsted bases are also Lewis bases but all Lewis acids are not Bronsted acids. Justify.

**21.** What is the pH of 0.001 M aniline solution. The ionization constant of the base is $4.27 \times 10^{-10}$. Calculate the degree of ionization of aniline in the solution. Also, calculate the ionization constant of the conjugate acid of aniline.

**22.** 25.0 $cm^3$ of 0.001 M $AgNO_3$ solution is mixed with 75.0 $cm^3$ of 0.001 M $Na_2CO_3$ solution. Will it lead to the precipitation of $Ag_2CO_3$?
$K_{sp}$ of $Ag_2CO_3$ is $6.2 \times 10^{-12}$ at 298 K

## Long Answer Questions

**1.** Reaction between nitrogen and oxygen takes place as following:
$$2N_2(g) + O_2(g) \rightleftharpoons 2N_2O(g)$$
If a mixture of 0.482 mol $N_2$ and 0.933 mol of $O_2$ is placed in a reaction vessel of volume 10L and allowed to form $N_2O$ at a temperature for which $K_c = 2.0 \times 10^{-37}$. Determine the composition of the reaction mixture.

**2.** (i) How much volume of 0.1 M acetic acid should be added to 50 ml of 0.2M sodium acetate solution if we want to prepare a buffer solution of pH = 4.91. Given $pK_a$ for acetic acid is 4.76.
(ii) Prove that the pressure necessary to obtain 50% dissociation of $PCl_5$ at 500K is numerically equal to three times the value of $K_p$.

**3.** (i) What is the pH of a solution that contains 0.10 M HCl and 0.10 M $CH_3COOH$? For acetic acid, $K_a = 1.8 \times 10^{-5}$.
(ii) What are the concentrations of all the species present in a 0. 50 M solution of acetic acid. For $CH_3COOH$ $K_a = 1.8 \times 10^{-5}$.

**4.** Carbonic acid, $H_2CO_3$, is a weak diprotic acid formed by the reaction of carbon dioxide with water, For this acid, $K_{a_1} = 4.3 \times 10^{-7}$ and $K_{a_2} = 5.6 \times 10^{-11}$. What are the equilibrium concentrations of each species in a 0.10 M solution of carbonic acid?

**5.** How much of 0.3 M ammonium hydroxide should be mixed with 30 mL of 0.2 M solution of ammonium chloride to give buffer solution of pH 8.65 and 10?
$$[pK_b = 4.75]$$

---

## SOLUTIONS

### *Multiple Choice Questions*

**1.** (a) A reaction is said to be in equilibrium when rate of forward reaction is equal to the rate of backward reaction.

**2.** (c)

**3.** (c)
$$A + B \rightleftharpoons C + D$$
At eqm. $\quad x \quad\quad x \quad\quad\quad 2x \quad 2x$

$$K_c = \frac{2x \cdot 2x}{x \cdot x} = 4$$

**4.** (b) Given reaction, $2A \rightleftharpoons B + C$

$$K_c = \frac{[B][C]}{[A]^2}$$

$$K_c = \frac{2 \times 10^{-3} \times 3 \times 10^{-3}}{(10^{-3})^2} = 6$$

**5.** (b) Reaction proceed backward according to Le-chatelier's principle.

**6.** (b) Because $NH_3$ after losing a proton ($H^+$) gives $NH_2^-$
$$NH_3 + H_2O \rightleftharpoons NH_2^- + H_3O^+$$
(Conjugate acid-base pair differ only by a proton)

**7.** (d) $(CH_3)_3$ B - is an electron deficient, thus behave as a lewis acid.

**8.** (b) $CH_3COOH$ is weak acid while NaOH is strong base, so one equivalent of NaOH can not be neutralized with one equivalent of $CH_3COOH$. Hence the solution of one equivalent of each does not have pH value as 7. Its pH will be towards basic side as NaOH is a strong base. Hence, conc. of $OH^-$ will be more than the conc. of $H^+$.

**9.** (b) $Mg(OH)_2 \rightleftharpoons Mg^{2+} + 2OH^-$
$$K_{sp} = [Mg^{++}][OH^-]^2$$
$$1.0 \times 10^{-11} = 10^{-3} \times [OH^-]^2$$

$$[OH^-] = \sqrt{\frac{10^{-11}}{10^{-3}}} = 10^{-4}$$

$\therefore$    pOH $= 4$        $\therefore$   pH $+$ pOH $= 14$

$\therefore$    pH $= 10$

**10.**   **(b)**   Given   pH $= 12$

or     $[H^+] = 10^{-12}$

Since,    $[H^+][OH^-] = 10^{-14}$

$$\therefore \quad [OH^-] = \frac{10^{-14}}{10^{-12}} = 10^{-2}$$

$$Ba(OH)_2 \rightleftharpoons \underset{s}{Ba^{2+}} + \underset{2s}{2OH^-}$$

$[OH^-] = 10^{-2}$

$2s = 10^{-2}$

$$s = \frac{10^{-2}}{2}$$

$$K_{sp} = 4s^3 = 4 \times \left(\frac{10^{-2}}{2}\right)^3 = 5 \times 10^{-7}$$

**11.**   **(a)**   $K_{sp}$ of $As_2S_3$ is less than ZnS. In acid medium, ionisation of $H_2S$ is suppresed (common ion effect), thus, it an precipitate $As_2S_3$ only.

### Assertion & Reason Questions

**1.**   **(a)**   $K_p = K_c(RT)^{\Delta n}$

**2.**   **(a)**   If the volume is kept constant and an inert gas such as argon is added which does not take part in the reaction, the equilibrium remains undisturbed. It is because the addition of an inert gas at constant volume does not change the partial pressure or the molar concentration of the substance involved in the reaction. The reaction quotient changes only if the added gas is reactant or product involved in the reaction.

**3.**   **(a)**   For the given reaction,

$$K_c = \frac{[NH_3]^2}{[N_2][H_2]^3}$$

$$K_c = \frac{mol^2 \times L \times L^3}{L^2 \times mol \times mol^3} = L^2\,mol^{-2}$$

So, the unit for $K_c = L^2\,mol^{-2}$.

**4.**   **(c)**   The equilibrium constant is a fixed value for every reaction at a particular temperature. However, composition of final equilibrium mixture at a particular temperature does not depend upon the starting amount of the reactant.

**5.**   **(a)**   Ionic product of AgBr is greater than that of AgCl in comparison with their solubility product; hence AgBr will precipitate first rather than that of AgCl.

**6.**   **(a)**   Both assertion and reason are correct and reason is the correct explanation of assertion.

**7.**   **(a)**   Size of $[Al(H_2O)_6]^{3+}$ is smaller than $[Mg(H_2O)_6]^{2+}$. The former possesses more effective nuclear charge and thus, attracts electron pair from donor more effectively. This gives rise to relatively strong acidic nature of $[Al(H_2O)_6]^{3+}$.

**8.**   **(c)**   NaOH is a weaker base than KOH.

### Case/Passage Based Questions

**1.**   **(a)**   For $A + B \rightleftharpoons C$, $\Delta n = 1 - 2 = -1$ (assuming $A$, $B$ and $C$ are gases)

$$\text{Unit of } K_c = \left[\frac{mol}{litre}\right]^{\Delta n} = \left[\frac{mol}{litre}\right]^{-1}$$

$$= \text{Litre mol}^{-1}$$

**2.**   **(d)**   $2C(s) + O_2(g) \rightleftharpoons 2CO_2(g)$

$\Delta n = 2 - 1 = +1 \neq 0$

$\therefore$   $K_c$ and $K_p$ are not equal.

**3.**   **(c)**   $K_p = \dfrac{(P_{CO})^2}{(P_{CO_2})}$;   $K_p = \dfrac{4 \times 4}{2} = 8$ ; $C(s) = 1$

The concentration of solids and liquids are taken as unity.

**4.**   **(c)**   Using the relation $K_p = K_c(RT)^{\Delta n}$, we get

$$\frac{K_p}{K_c} = (RT)^{\Delta n}$$

Thus $\dfrac{K_p}{K_c}$ will be highest for the reaction having highest value of $\Delta n$.

The $\Delta n$ values for various reactions are

(a)   $\Delta n = 1 - \left(1 + \dfrac{1}{2}\right) = -\dfrac{1}{2}$

(b)   $\Delta n = 2 - (1 + 1) = 0$

(c)   $\Delta n = (1 + 1) - 1 = 1$

(d)   $\Delta n = (2 + 4) - (7 + 2) = -3$

Thus maximum value of $\Delta n = 1$

**5.**   **(a)**   $K = \dfrac{[Ni(CO)_4]}{[CO]^4} = \dfrac{mol\,L^{-1}}{(mol\,L^{-1})^4} = (mol\,L^{-1})^{-3}$

### Very Short Answer Questions

**1.**   No, K remains constant.

**2.**   As the reaction is exothermic hence on adding heat the reaction would move in the backward direction i.e. more '$a$' and '$b$' will be formed.

**3.**   At equilibrium, reaction does not stop rather it still continues, therefore, the equilibrium is dynamic in nature. It appears to stop because rate of forward reaction is equal to that of backward reaction.

**4.** Melting point or freezing point.

**5.** AB is more stable. Higher the value of K more will be the stability of product formed.

**6.** Chilled cold drink will dissolve more $CO_2$ because solubility of gases in liquid increases with decrease in temperature.

**7.** Since decrease in volume takes place, high pressure is favourable for gas to dissolve. Since absorption of heat takes place, high temperature will be suitable to dissolve maximum amount of gas.

**8.** Strong electrolytes can dissociate into ions completely in aqueous solution whereas weak electrolytes do not dissociate into ions completely and there exist an equilibrium between ions and unionised molecules, called Ionic Equilibrium.

**9.** $K_p = \dfrac{\left(p_{H_2}\right)^4}{\left(p_{H_2O}\right)^4}$ [Fe and $Fe_3O_4$ are solids]

**10.** $CH_4(g) + 2H_2S(g) \rightarrow 4H_2(g) + CS_2(g)$

**11.** Addition of inert gas at constant pressure will shift the equilibrium towards larger number of gases moles (right hand side) forward direction.

**12.** HAc is stronger since it has higher dissociation constant i.e. it would release more $H^+$ ion in solution than HCN.

**13.** $K_{sp} = [M^{2+}][S^{-2}] = 1.3 \times 10^{-18}$ mole$^2$/L$^2$

$[0.10][S^{-2}] = 1.3 \times 10^{-18}$

$[S^{-2}] = 1.3 \times 10^{-17}$ M

**14.** Solubility of gases in liquids decreases with increase in temperature.

**15.** No, because $Fe(OH)_3$ will dissolve in strongly acidic medium.

**16.** $Ag_2CrO_4(s) \rightleftharpoons 2Ag^+(aq) + CrO_4^{2-}(aq)$

$K_{sp} = [Ag^+]^2 [CrO_4^{2-}]$

**17.** Acid 'A' with $pK_a = 1.5$ is strongest acid, lower the value of $pK_a$ stronger will be the acid.

**18.** (i) Buffer solution is used in medicines.
(ii) Blood buffers maintain the pH of blood.

**19.** $\underset{\text{Base}}{NH_3} + H_2O \longrightarrow NH_4^+ + OH^-$

$NH_3$ is Arrhenius base because it gives $OH^-$ in aqueous solution.

**20.** $\underset{\text{Acid}_1}{HCl} + \underset{\text{Base}_2}{H_2O} \rightleftharpoons \underset{\text{Acid}_2}{H_3O^+} + \underset{\text{Base}_1}{Cl^-}$

$\underset{\text{Base}_1}{NH_3} + \underset{\text{Acid}_2}{H_2O} \rightleftharpoons \underset{\text{Acid}_1}{NH_4^+} + \underset{\text{Base}_2}{OH^-}$

**21.** $AlCl_3$ is strongest Lewis acid because its octet is not complete.

**22.** Bronsted acids can donate $H^+$ easily but they may not be able to donate electrons e.g., HCl, $H_2SO_4$, $HNO_3$. Therefore, all Bronsted acids are not Lewis acids.

**23.** $CH_3^-$ is strongest conjugate base.

**24.** $NaNO_3$ will not be hydrolysed as it is a salt derived from strong acid and strong base. It undergoes hydration, no change in pH is observed.

$NaNO_3(s) + H_2O(l) \rightarrow Na^+(aq) + NO_3^-(aq)$

**25.** The choice of an indicator depends on the abrupt change in the pH during neutralisation process near the equivalence point.

**26.** Carbonic acid/bicarbonate present as a buffer in blood which maintains the pH of blood in the range of 7.38 to 7.42

### *Short Answer Questions*

**1.** $K = \dfrac{[c][d]}{[a]^2} = 1.0 \times 10^{-3}$

$1.0 \times 10^{-3} = \dfrac{(1.2 \times 10^{-3})(3.8 \times 10^{-6})}{[a]^2}$

$[a]^2 = \dfrac{(1.2 \times 10^{-3})(3.8 \times 10^{-6})}{1.0 \times 10^{-3}}$

$= 4.56 \times 10^{-6}$ mol$^2$/L$^2$

$\therefore \ [a] = 2.13 \times 10^{-3}$ M

**2.** At equilibrium, $[d] = 0.2 - 0.1 = 0.1$M
$[e] = 1.2 - 2(0.1) = 1.0$M
$[f] = 0.1$ M

$K = \dfrac{[f]}{[d][e]^2} = \dfrac{(0.1)}{(0.1)(1.0)^2} = 1 L^2/$mole$^2$

**3.** (a) Since the forward reaction is endothermic, while the backward reaction is exothermic, increase in temperature would favour the forward reaction while decrease in temperature would favour the backward reaction.

(b) Increase in pressure favours the reaction towards less number of moles of gaseous species hence it would go in the backward direction while decrease in pressure will favour reaction to proceed in the forward direction.

**4.** $\Delta_r H^\ominus = \Delta_r H^\ominus [CaO(s)] + \Delta_r H^\ominus [CO_2(g)] + \Delta_r H^\ominus [CaCO_3(s)]$

$\therefore \ \Delta_r H^\ominus = 178.3$ kJ mol$^{-1}$

The reaction is endothermic. Hence, according to Le-Chatelier's principle, reaction will proceed in forward direction on increasing temperature.

**5.** (i) Homogeneous equilibrium
(ii) Homogeneous equilibrium
(iii) Heterogeneous equilibrium
(iv) Homogeneous equilibrium

**6.** $Cu(s) + 2Ag^+(aq) \rightleftharpoons Cu^{+2}(aq) + 2Ag(s)$
As $K = 2.0 \times 10^{15}$ (given), the reaction is favourable in

the forward direction in which Cu has displaced $Ag^+$ from its solution.

Therefore, Cu is more reactive than Ag.

In $Cu(s) + Zn^{+2}(aq) \rightleftharpoons Cu^{+2}(aq) + Zn(s)$, as $K = 2.0 \times 10^{-19}$ is very low, Cu cannot reduce $Zn^{+2}$ to Zn but Zn will displace $Cu^{+2}$ from its solution. Therefore Zn is more reactive than Cu. Hence, the increasing reactivity order of three metals is

$$Ag < Cu < Zn$$

**7.**
$$H_2O(g) + CO(g) \rightleftharpoons H_2(g) + CO_2(g); \Delta n = 0$$

| | | | | |
|---|---|---|---|---|
| Initial moles | 1.0 | 1.0 | 0 | 0 |
| Moles at | $1 - 0.4$ | $1 - 0.4$ | 0.4 | 0.4 |
| equilibrium | $= 0.6$ | $= 0.6$ | | |

As $\Delta n = 0$

$$K_c = K_p = K_n = \frac{n_{H_2} n_{CO_2}}{n_{H_2O} n_{CO}}$$

where $K_n$ = equilibrium constant in terms of number of moles.

$$K = \frac{0.4 \times 0.4}{0.6 \times 0.6} = \frac{4}{9} = 0.444$$

**8.**
$$H_2(g) + Br_2(g) \rightleftharpoons 2HBr(g)$$
$$K_p = 1.6 \times 10^5$$

For the reaction

$$2HBr(g) \rightleftharpoons H_2(g) + Br_2(g)$$

$$K_p = \frac{1}{1.6 \times 10^5} = 6.25 \times 10^{-6}$$

$$2HBr(g) \rightleftharpoons H_2(g) + Br_2(g)$$

| | | | |
|---|---|---|---|
| Initial pressure | 10.0 | 0 | 0 |
| at equilibrium | $10.0 - 2x$ | x | x |

$$\therefore \quad K_p' = \frac{p_{H_2} \, p_{Br_2}}{p_{HBr}^2}$$

$$6.25 \times 10^{-6} = \frac{x^2}{(10.0 - 2x)^2}$$

or $\dfrac{x}{10.0 - 2x} = 2.5 \times 10^{-3}$

and $x \approx 2.5 \times 10^{-2}$

$$p_{H_2} = p_{Br_2} = 2.5 \times 10^{-2} \text{ bar}$$
$$p_{HBr} = 10.0 - 5.0 \times 10^{-2} \approx 10.0 \text{ bar}$$

**9.**
$$Q_c = \frac{[CS_2][H_2]^4}{[CH_4][H_2S]^2}$$

(i) $Q_c = \dfrac{(0.90)(1.78)^4}{(1.07)(1.20)^2} = 5.86$

As $Q_c > K_c$ the reaction will proceed in the reverse direction (Reactant side)

(ii) $Q_c = \dfrac{(1.25)(1.75)^4}{(1.45)(1.29)^2}$, $Q_c = 4.86$

As $Q_c > K_c$, the reaction will proceed in the direction of reactants.

**10.** We know that with the rise in temperature, vapour pressure of a liquid increases and at the boiling point, vapour pressure of a liquid becomes equal to the atmospheric pressure.

A liquid with lower vapour pressure will boil at a higher temperature and vice-versa.

$\therefore$ Acetone has the lowest boiling point and water has the highest boiling point.

At 293 K, water evaporates least in the sealed container before equilibrium is reached.

**11.** $A \rightleftharpoons E \quad K = \dfrac{[E]}{[A]}$

$$K_1 = \frac{[B]}{[A]}; \quad K_2 = \frac{[C]}{[B]}; \quad K_3 = \frac{[D]}{[C]}; \quad K_4 = \frac{[E]}{[D]}$$

$$K = K_1 \times K_2 \times K_3 \times K_4 = \frac{[E]}{[A]}$$

$$= 1 \times 2 \times 3 \times 4 = 24$$

**12.** $CH_3COOH \rightleftharpoons CH_3COO^- + H^+$

Let x = molar concentration of acetic acid solution. Then $[H^+] = [CH_3COO^-] = 0.020x$ and $[CH_3COOH] = x - 0.020x \approx x$, since assumption is taken as dissociation constant of the acid is very small.

$$K_a = \frac{[CH_3COOH^-][H^+]}{[CH_3COOH]}$$

$$= \frac{(0.020x)(0.020x)}{x} = 1.8 \times 10^{-5}$$

On solving $x = 0.045$ M

**13.** (i) Group IV precipitate as sulphides like group II, but they do not precipitate in group II since the solubility products of group IV is higher than solubility products of group II sulphides.

(ii) It is done so as to reduce concentration of $[S^{2-}]$ by common ion effect so that only group 2 radicals get precipitated whereas higher group radicals do not.

**14.** $AgCl \rightleftharpoons Ag^+ + Cl^-$

If x is the solubility of the salt, then from the stoichiometry of the compound

$$K_{sp} = 1.8 \times 10^{-10} = [Ag^+][Cl^-] = x^2$$

Then $x = 1.34 \times 10^{-5}$ M

$$Mg(OH)_2 \rightleftharpoons Mg^{2+} + 2OH^-$$

$$K_{sp} = 1.2 \times 10^{-11} = [Mg^{2+}][OH^-]^2$$

$$= (x)(2x)^2 = 4x^3$$

On solving, $x = 1.4 \times 10^{-4}$ M hence $Mg(OH)_2$ has greater molarity.

**15.** Before mixing pH $= 5$ $\quad \therefore [H_3O^+] = 10^{-5}$ M

$$pH = 3 \quad \therefore [H_3O^+] = 10^{-3} M$$

After mixing the total volume becomes double, hence the new concentration of $[H_3O^+]$ becomes

$$= (10^{-5} + 10^{-3})/2 = 5 \times 10^{-4}$$

$$pH = -\log[H_3O^+] = -\log(5 \times 10^{-4})$$

$$= -(\log 5 - 4) = 4 - \log 5 = 4 - 0.699 = 3.301$$

**16.** According to Henderson's equation

$$pH = pK_a + \log\frac{[salt]}{[acid]}$$

$$pK_a = -\log K_a = -\log(1.8 \times 10^{-5}) = 4.745$$

Putting the values in above equation, we get

$$4 = 4.745 + \log\frac{[salt]}{[acid]}$$

$\log[salt]/0.1 = 4 - 4.745 = -0.745$

$[salt]/0.1 = $ antilog $-0.745 = 0.1798$

$[salt] = 0.1798 \times 0.1$

$\qquad = 0.01798 = 1.798 \times 10^{-2}$ mol/L

**17.**

| Species | Conjugate acid | Conjugate base |
|---------|----------------|----------------|
| $H_2O$ | $H_3O^+$ | $OH^-$ |
| $HCO_3^-$ | $H_2CO_3$ | $CO_3^{2-}$ |
| $HSO_4^-$ | $H_2SO_4$ | $SO_4^{2-}$ |
| $NH_3$ | $NH_4^+$ | $NH_2^-$ |

**18.**

$$HA(aq) + H_2O(l) \rightleftharpoons H_3O^+(aq) + A^-(aq)$$

Initial Conc. $\qquad$ c $\qquad\qquad$ 0 $\qquad$ 0

Conc. at equilibrium $\quad$ c(1–α) $\qquad$ cα $\quad$ cα

We know that

$$K_a = \frac{c\alpha^2}{1-\alpha} = \frac{0.1(0.0134)^2}{1-0.0134}$$

$$K_a = 1.82 \times 10^{-5}$$

**19.** (i) $HNO_3$ is a strong acid and is present in solution completely as ions.

Every mole of $HNO_3$ contributes one mole of $H^+$ ion.

$$\therefore [HNO_3] = [H^+]$$

The $H^+$ concentration is 0.15 M.

The $OH^-$ concentration is obtained from $K_w$ equation.

$$K_w = [H^+][OH^-] = 1.0 \times 10^{-14}$$

$$\therefore [OH^-] = \frac{1.0}{0.15} \times 10^{-14}$$

$$= 6.7 \times 10^{-14} \text{ M}$$

(ii) $Ca(OH)_2(aq) \xrightarrow{H_2O} Ca^{+2}(aq) + 2OH^-(aq)$

1 mol $Ca(OH)_2$ (aq) furnishes 2 mol $OH^-$

$\therefore$ 0.010 M $Ca(OH)_2$ will furnish $2 \times 0.010$ M $OH^-$

$[OH^-] = 0.020$ M

$$[H^+] = \frac{1.0 \times 10^{-14}}{0.020} = 5.0 \times 10^{-13} \text{ M}$$

**20.** Bronsted and Lewis bases are the same as the former accepts a proton, while the latter possesses a lone pair of electrons which readily accepts a proton.

However, Lewis acids are different from Bronsted acids, as former is an electron deficient species while the later furnishes a proton.

**21.** The ionization of aniline in water is represented by the equation

$$C_6H_5NH_2(aq) + H_2O(l) \rightleftharpoons C_6H_5NH_3^+(aq) + OH^-(aq)$$

$$[C_6H_5NH_3^+] = [OH^-] = c\alpha$$

$$\text{when } \alpha = \sqrt{\frac{K_b}{c}} = \sqrt{\frac{4.27 \times 10^{-10}}{0.001}}$$

$$\alpha = 6.53 \times 10^{-4}$$

Now, $[OH^-] = c\alpha$

$$= 0.001 \times 6.53 \times 10^{-4}$$

$$[OH^-] = 6.53 \times 10^{-7} \text{ M}$$

$$\text{and } [H^+] = \frac{10^{-14}}{6.53 \times 10^{-7}} = 1.53 \times 10^{-8} \text{ M}$$

and $pH = -\log(1.53 \times 10^{-8})$

$\qquad pH = 7.81$

For the ionization constant of the conjugate acid of aniline

$$C_6H_5NH_3^+ + H_2O \rightleftharpoons C_6H_5NH_2 + H_3O^+$$

$$K_a = \frac{[C_6H_5NH_2][H_3O^+]}{[C_6H_5NH_3^+]} = \frac{K_w}{K_b}$$

$K_a$ of the conjugate acid

$$= \frac{1.0 \times 10^{-14}}{4.27 \times 10^{-10}}$$

$$K_a = 2.34 \times 10^{-5}$$

**22.** At the instant of mixing, the total volume $= 100$ cm$^3$ $= 0.1$ L and concentration of silver ion is

$$[Ag^+] = \frac{0.001 \, mol/L \times 0.025L}{0.1L}$$

$$= 2.5 \times 10^{-4} \text{ M}$$

and $[CO_3^{2-}] = \dfrac{0.01\,mol/L \times 0.075L}{0.1L}$

$\qquad = 7.5 \times 10^{-4}\,M$

We are considering the reaction

$Ag_2CO_3(s) \rightleftharpoons 2Ag^+(aq) + CO_3^{2-}(aq)$

and $Q_{sp} = [Ag^+]^2\,[CO_3^{2-}]$

$\qquad = (2.5 \times 10^{-4})^2\,(7.5 \times 10^{-4})$

$Q_{sp} = 4.69 \times 10^{-11}$

As $Q_{sp} > K_{sp}$ the solution is saturated and $Ag_2CO_2$ will precipitate.

### Long Answer Questions

**1.**
$$2N_2(g) \;+\; O_2(g) \rightleftharpoons 2N_2O(g)$$

Initial moles :
$\qquad 0.482 \qquad\quad 0.933 \qquad\quad 0$

moles at equilibrium:
$\qquad (0.482 - 2x) \quad (0.933 - x) \qquad 2x$

Conc. at equilibrium:
$\qquad \left(\dfrac{0.482 - 2x}{10}\right) \left(\dfrac{0.933 - x}{10}\right) \quad \dfrac{2x}{10}$

$$K_c = \dfrac{[N_2O]^2}{[N_2]^2[O_2]} = \dfrac{\left(\dfrac{2x}{10}\right)^2}{\left(\dfrac{0.482 - 2x}{10}\right)^2\left(\dfrac{0.933 - x}{10}\right)}$$

$\qquad = 2.0 \times 10^{-37}$

$10x^2 + 1.016 \times 10^{-37}\,x - 0.1082 \times 10^{-37} = 0$

This is a quadratic equation, therefore

$$x = \dfrac{-1.016 \times 10^{-37} + \sqrt{1.03 \times 10^{-74} + 4.328 \times 10^{-37}}}{20}$$

$x = 3.3 \times 10^{-20}$

$[N_2O]_{eq} = \dfrac{2x}{10} = \dfrac{2}{10} \times 3.3 \times 10^{-20} = 6.6 \times 10^{-21}\,M$

$[N_2]_{eq} = \dfrac{0.482 - 2 \times 3.3 \times 10^{-20}}{10} \approx \dfrac{0.482}{10} = 0.0482\,M$

and $[O_2]_{eq} = \dfrac{0.933 - x}{10} \approx \dfrac{0.933}{10} = 0.0933\,M$

**2.** **(i)** $\quad pH = pK_a + \log\dfrac{[salt]}{[acid]}$

$\qquad 4.91 = 4.76 + \log\dfrac{[salt]}{[acid]}$

or $\quad \log\dfrac{[salt]}{[acid]} = 0.15$

or $\quad \dfrac{[salt]}{[acid]} = $ antilog $0.15 = 1.41$

$\qquad \dfrac{\text{moles of salt / litre}}{\text{moles of acid / litre}} = 1.41$

$\qquad = \dfrac{(0.2/1000) \times 50}{(0.1/1000) \times V} = 1.41$

or $\quad V = 10 / 1.41 = 70.92$ ml

**(ii)**
$\qquad\qquad\qquad PCl_5 \rightleftharpoons PCl_3 + Cl_2$

Initial moles $\qquad\qquad 1 \qquad\quad 0 \qquad\quad 0$

At equilibrium $\qquad\; 1 - 0.5 \quad 0.5 \qquad 0.5$

$\qquad$ (as it is 50% dissociated, $x = 0.5$)

$\qquad\qquad\qquad\qquad\quad = 0.5 \qquad 0.5 \qquad 0.5$

Total number of moles $= 1.5$

If $'P'$ is the total pressure, then $p(PCl_5) = \dfrac{0.5 \times P}{1.5}$,

$p(PCl_3) = \dfrac{0.5 \times P}{1.5}$, and $p(Cl_2) = \dfrac{0.5 \times P}{1.5}$

Now,

$\therefore K_p = \dfrac{p(PCl_3) \times p(Cl_2)}{p(PCl_5)} = \dfrac{(P/3)(P/3)}{(P/3)} = \dfrac{P}{3}$

or $\quad 3\,K_p = P$

**3.** **(i)** The 0.10 M solution of HCl contains 0.10 mol/L of $H^+$, because HCl is a strong acid. This is the concentration of $H^+$ before the $CH_3COOH$ is added. Then we add 0.10 M $CH_3COOH$ into it. The initial concentrations of $H^+$ and $CH_3COOH$

$[H^+]_{initial} = 0.10\,M$

$[CH_3COOH]_{initial} = 0.10\,M$

Now we have to consider the ionization of the acetic acid.

$CH_3COOH \rightleftharpoons H^+ + CH_3COO^-$

$K_a = \dfrac{[H^+][CH_3COO^-]}{[CH_3COOH]} = 1.8 \times 10^{-5}$

Since there is no $CH_3COO^-$ ion present initially, some of it must form by the dissociation of the $CH_3COOH$. Let the concentration of $CH_3COOH$ decreases by x and the concentration of $H^+$ and $CH_3COO^-$ increases by x, and then add the initial concentrations and the changes to get the equilibrium quantities.

| | Initial Molar Concentrations | Change | Equilibrium Molar Concentrations |
|---|---|---|---|
| $H^+$ | 0.10 | + x | $0.10 + x \approx 0.10$ |
| $CH_3COO^-$ | 0 | + x | x |
| $CH_3COOH$ | 0.10 | − x | $0.10 - x \approx 0.10$ |

When a solution contains both a strong acid and a weak acid, it is the concentration of the strong acid that determines the pH of the solution.

We expect x to be small, so we've assumed $0.10 \pm x \approx 0.10$. Substituting into the $K_a$ expression

$$1.8 \times 10^{-5} = K_a = \frac{[H^+][CH_3COO^-]}{[CH_3COOH]}$$

$$1.8 \times 10^{-5} = \frac{(0.10)(x)}{(0.10)}$$

$$x = 1.8 \times 10^{-5}$$

We see that x is very small as compared to 0.10, so in the solution $[H^+] = 0.10$ M. This gives pH of 1.00

**(ii)** We begin with the chemical equation and the equilibrium law,

$$CH_3COOH \rightleftharpoons H^+ + CH_3COO^-$$

$$K_a = \frac{[H^+][CH_3COO^-]}{[CH_3COOH]} = 1.8 \times 10^{-5}$$

$$H_2O + CH_3COOH \rightleftharpoons H_3O^+ + CH_3COO^-$$

Initial molarity  0.50    0  0

At equilibrium $(0.50 - x)$  x  x

Substituting these values into the equilibrium expression gives us $(x)(x) / (0.50 - x) = 1.8 \times 10^{-5}$

As x is very small thus x will be negligible compared to 0.50; thus

$$0.50 - x \approx 0.50$$

Our equation then becomes

$$x^2 /0.50 = 1.8 \times 10^{-5} \quad \text{or} \quad x = 3.0 \times 10^{-3}$$

Equilibrium Concentrations (M)

| | |
|---|---|
| $H^+$ | $3.0 \times 10^{-3}$ |
| $CH_3COO^-$ | $3.0 \times 10^{-3}$ |
| $CH_3COOH$ | 0.50 |

**4.** $H_2CO_3 \rightleftharpoons H^+ + HCO_3^{-1}$

$$K_{a_1} = [H^+][HCO_3^{-1}] / [H_2CO_3] = 4.3 \times 10^{-7}$$

And $HCO_3^- \rightleftharpoons H^+ + CO_3^{2-}$

$$K_{a_2} = [H^+][CO_3^{2-}] / [HCO_3^-] = 5.6 \times 10^{-11}$$

As $K_{a_1}$ is much larger than $K_{a_2}$, we can safely assume that nearly all the hydrogen ion in the solution is derived from the first step of the dissociation. In addition, only very little amount of the $HCO_3^-$ ion formed in the first step will undergo further dissociation. On the basis of this we can calculate the equilibrium concentrations of $H^+$ and $HCO_3^-$ by using the expression for $K_{a_1}$ alone.

$$K_{a_1} = [H^+][HCO_3^-] / [H_2CO_3]$$

If we consider x be the number of moles per litre of $H_2CO_3$ that dissociate, we obtain, from the stoichiometry of the first step, x mol/L of $H^+$ and x mol/L of $HCO_3^-$. At equilibrium, there will be $(0.10 - x)$ mol/L of $H_2CO_3$ remaining.

| | Initial Molar Concentrations | Change | Equilibrium Molar Concentrations |
|---|---|---|---|
| $H^+$ | 0.0 | + x | x |
| $HCO_3^-$ | 0.0 | + x | x |
| $H_2CO_3$ | 0.10 | −x | $0.10 - x \approx 0.10$ |

As x is very small, we may assume that x will be negligible in comparison to 0.10 and thus equilibrium concentration of

$$[H_2CO_3] = 0.10 - x = 0.10 \text{ M}$$

substituting these equilibrium concentration values into the expression for $K_{a_1}$ we have

$$(x)(x)/0.10 = 4.3 \times 10^{-7}$$
$$x^2 = 4.3 \times 10^{-8} \quad \text{or} \quad x = 2.07 \times 10^{-4}$$

therefore, the equilibrium concentrations from first dissociation are

$[H^+] = 2.07 \times 10^{-4}$M ; $[HCO_3^-] = 2.07 \times 10^{-4}$M ; $[H_2CO_3] = 0.10$ M

By employing $K_{a_2}$, we can now calculate the equilibrium concentration of $CO_3^{2-}$

$$HCO_3^- \rightleftharpoons H^+ + CO_3^{2-}$$

$$K_{a_2} = \frac{[H^+][CO_3^{2-}]}{[HCO_3^-]}$$

Consider y be the number of moles per litre of $HCO_3^-$ that dissociates. Thus, the total hydrogen ion concentration from both the first and second dissociations will be $(2.07 \times 10^{-4} + y)$, and y mol /L of $CO_3^{2-}$. At equilibrium, there will be $(2.07 \times 10^{-4} - y)$ mol / L of $HCO_3^-$

| | Initial Concentrations | Change | Equilibrium Concentrations |
|---|---|---|---|
| $H^+$ | $2.07 \times 10^{-4}$ | + y | $2.07 \times 10^{-4} + y$ |
| $CO_3^{2-}$ | 0.0 | + y | y |
| $HCO_3^-$ | $2.07 \times 10^{-4}$ | −y | $2.07 \times 10^{-4} - y$ |

Make the assumption that y will be negligible as compared to $2.07 \times 10^{-4}$. Our equilibrium concentrations then become

$$[H^+] = 2.07 \times 10^{-4} + y \approx 2.07 \times 10^{-4} \text{ M}$$

$$[CO_3^{2-}] = y$$

$$[HCO_3^-] = 2.07 \times 10^{-4} - y \approx 2.07 \times 10^{-4} \text{ M}$$

Note that the value of y is very much smaller than the value of x obtained for the first step in the dissociation.

By substituting these equilibrium concentration values in $Ka_2$, we obtain

$$Ka_2 = \frac{(2.1 \times 10^{-4})(y)}{(2.1 \times 10^{-4})} = 5.6 \times 10^{-11}$$

$$y = 5.6 \times 10^{-11}$$

Therefore equilibrium concentrations of all species,

$[H^+] = 2.07 \times 10^{-4}$ M ; $[HCO_3^-] = 2.07 \times 10^{-4}$ M;

$[CO_3^{2-}] = 5.6 \times 10^{-11}$ M ; $[H_2CO_3] = 0.10$ M

5.  $$pH = (14 - pK_b) + \log \frac{[base]}{[salt]}$$

$$pH = (14 - 4.75) + \log \frac{[base]}{[salt]}$$

For a buffer solution of pH 8.65, suppose V ml = volume of $NH_4OH$ added, then

$$8.65 = 9.25 + \log \left( \frac{\dfrac{0.3\,V}{30+V}}{\dfrac{0.2 \times 30}{30+V}} \right)$$

$$-0.6 = \log \left( \frac{0.3\,V}{6} \right)$$

$$\frac{0.1V}{2} = \text{antilog}\,(-0.6) = 0.25$$

$$\therefore \quad V = 5 \text{ mL}$$

For a buffer solution of pH 10, we have

$$10 = 9.25 + \log \left( \frac{\dfrac{0.3\,V}{30+V}}{\dfrac{0.2 \times 30}{30+V}} \right)$$

$$0.75 = \log \left( \frac{0.1V}{2} \right) \quad \text{and } V = 12.94 \text{ mL}$$

---

## SECTION C — NCERT EXEMPLAR QUESTIONS

### MULTIPLE CHOICE QUESTIONS

1.  $K_{a_1}, K_{a_2}$ and $K_{a_3}$ are the respective ionisation constants for the following reactions.

$$H_2S \rightleftharpoons H^+ + HS^-$$

$$HS^- \rightleftharpoons H^+ + S^{2-}$$

$$H_2S \rightleftharpoons 2H^+ + S^{2-}$$

The correct relationship between $K_{a_1}, K_{a_2}$ and $K_{a_3}$ is

(a)  $K_{a_3} = K_{a_1} \times K_{a_2}$     (b)  $K_{a_3} = K_{a_1} + K_{a_2}$

(c)  $K_{a_3} = K_{a_1} - K_{a_2}$     (d)  $K_{a_3} = K_{a_1} / K_{a_2}$

2.  Acidity of $BF_3$ can be explained on the basis of which of the following concepts?

(a)  Arrhenius concept

(b)  Bronsted Lowry concept

(c)  Lewis concept

(d)  Bronsted Lowry as well as Lewis concept

3.  Which of the following options will be correct for the stage of half completion of the reaction $A \rightleftharpoons B$?

(a)  $\Delta G^\ominus = 0$       (b)  $\Delta G^\ominus > 0$

(c)  $\Delta G^\ominus < 0$       (d)  $\Delta G^\ominus = -RT \ln K$

4.  What will be the correct order of vapour pressure of water, acetone and ether at 30°C? Given that among these compounds, water has maximum boiling point and ether has minimum boiling point?

(a)  Water < ether < acetone

(b)  Water < acetone < ether

(c)  Ether < acetone < water

(d)  Acetone < ether < water

5.  At 500 K, equilibrium constant, $K_c$, for the following reaction is 5.

$$\frac{1}{2} H_2(g) + \frac{1}{2} I_2(g) \rightleftharpoons HI(g)$$

What would be the equilibrium constant $K_C$ for the reaction ?

$$2HI(g) \rightleftharpoons H_2(g) + I_2(g)$$

(a)  0.04    (b)  0.4    (c)  25    (d)  2.5

### ASSERTION & REASON QUESTIONS

**DIRECTIONS (Qs. 1-3) :** *Each of these questions contains an assertion followed by reason. Read them carefully and answer the question on the basis of following options. You have to select the one that best describes the two statements.*

(a)  If both Assertion and Reason are correct and the Reason is a correct explanation of the Assertion.

(b)  If both Assertion and Reason are correct but Reason is not a correct explanation of the Assertion.

(c)  If the Assertion is correct but Reason is incorrect.

(d)  If the Assertion is incorrect but the Reason is correct.

1.  **Assertion :** A solution containing a mixture of acetic acid and sodium acetate maintains a constant value of pH on addition of small amounts of acid or alkali.
    **Reason :** A solution containing a mixture of acetic acid and sodium acetate acts as a buffer solution around pH of 4.75.

2.  **Assertion :** Aqueous solution of ammonium carbonate is basic.
    **Reason :** Acetic/basic nature of a salt solution of salt of weak acid and weak base depends on $K_a$ and $K_b$ value of the acid and the base forming it.

3.  **Assertion :** For any chemical reaction at a particular temperature, the equilibrium constant is fixed and is a characteristic property.
    **Reason :** Equilibrium constant is independent of temperature.

SHORT ANSWER QUESTIONS

1.  A sparingly soluble salt gets precipitated only when the product of concentration of its ions in the solution $(Q_{sp})$ becomes greater than its solubility product. If the solubility of $BaSO_4$ in water is $8 \times 10^{-4}$ mol dm$^{-3}$. Calculate its solubility in 0.01 mol dm$^{-3}$ of $H_2SO_4$.

2.  Calculate the pH of a solution formed by mixing equal volumes of two solutions A and B of a strong acid having pH = 6 and pH = 4 respectively.

3.  Calculate the volume of water required to dissolve 0.1 g lead (II) chloride to get a saturated solution. ($K_{sp}$ of $PbCl_2 = 3.2 \times 10^{-8}$, atomic mass of Pb = 207 u).

4.  On the basis of the equation pH = $-\log$ [H$^+$], the pH of $10^{-8}$ mol dm$^{-3}$ solution of HCl should be 8. However, it is observed to be less than 7.0. Explain the reason.

LONG ANSWER QUESTIONS

1.  Calculate the pH of a solution formed by mixing equal volumes of two solutions A and B of a strong acid having pH = 6 and pH = respectively.

2.  The solubility product of Al(OH) 3 is $2.7 \times 10^{-11}$. Calculate its solubility in gL$^{-1}$ and also find out the pH of this solution. (Atomic mass of Al = 27 u).

SOLUTIONS

### Multiple Choice Questions

1.  **(a)** For the reaction,
    $$H_2S \rightleftharpoons H^+ + HS^-$$
    $$K_{a_1} = \frac{[H^+][HS^-]}{[H_2S]} \qquad \dots (i)$$

    For the reaction,
    $$HS^- \rightleftharpoons H^+ + S^{2-}$$
    $$K_{a_2} = \frac{[H^+][S^{2-}]}{[HS^-]} \qquad \dots (ii)$$

    $$K_{a_3} = \frac{[H^+]^2[S^{2-}]}{[H_2S]} \qquad \dots (iii)$$

    Hence, $K_{a_3} = K_{a_1} \times K_{a_2}$

2.  **(c)** According to GN Lewis, an acid is a species which accepts an electron pair and base which donates an electron pair. Since $BF_3$ is an electron deficient species, hence, it is a Lewis acid.

3.  **(a)** $\Delta G° = -RT \ln K$
    At the stage of half completion of the reaction,
    $$[A] = [B] \text{ and } K = [B]/[A]$$

Therefore, $\quad K = 1$
As we know that
$$\Delta G^{\ominus} = -RT \ln K$$
$$\therefore \quad \Delta G^{\ominus} = 0$$

4.  **(b)** The order of boiling point of compounds given is
    $$\text{Water} > \text{acetone} > \text{ether}$$
    Lower the boiling point, higher is the vapour pressure of the solvent. Hence, the correct order of vapour pressure will be
    $$\text{Water} < \text{acetone} < \text{ether}$$

5.  **(a)** For the reaction, $\frac{1}{2}H_2(g) + \frac{1}{2}I_2(g) \rightleftharpoons HI(g)$

    $$K_c = \frac{[HI]}{[H_2]^{1/2}[I_2]^{1/2}} = 5$$

    Thus, for the reaction,
    $$2HI(g) \rightleftharpoons H_2(g) + I_2(g)$$
    $$K'_c = \frac{[H_2][I_2]}{[HI]^2}$$
    $$K'_c = \left(\frac{1}{K_c}\right)^2 = \left(\frac{1}{5}\right)^2 = \frac{1}{25} = 0.04$$

### Assertion & Reason Questions

1. **(a)** Both Assertion and Reason are correct and Reason is the correct explanation of Assertion.
2. **(a)** $K_a$ and $K_b$ are responsible for acidic and basic characters of substances.
3. **(c)** Assertion is correct but Reason is incorrect.

### Short Answer Questions

1.
$$BaSO_4(s) \rightleftharpoons Ba^{2+}(aq) + SO_4^{2-}(aq)$$

At t = 0      1      0      0

At equilibrium
in water      1–s      s      s

At equilibrium
in the      1–s      s      (s + 0.01)
presence of sulphuric acid

$K_{sp}$ for $BaSO_4$ in water $= [Ba^{2+}][SO_4^{-2}] = [s][s] = s^2$

But $s = 8 \times 10^{-4}$ mol dm$^{-3}$

$\therefore \quad K_{sp} = (8 \times 10^{-4})^2 = 64 \times 10^{-8}$      ...(i)

The expression for $K_{sp}$ in the presence of sulphuric acid will be as follows :

$K_{sp} = (s)(s + 0.01)$      ... (ii)

Since value of $K_{sp}$ will not change in the presence of sulphuric acid, therefore from (i) and (ii)

$(s)(s + 0.01) = 64 \times 10^{-8}$

$\Rightarrow \quad s^2 + 0.01\, s = 64 \times 10^{-8}$

$\Rightarrow \quad s^2 + 0.01\, s - 64 \times 10^{-8} = 0$

$$\Rightarrow \quad s = \frac{-0.01 \pm \sqrt{(0.01)^2 + (4 \times 64 \times 10^{-8})}}{2}$$

$$= \frac{-0.01 \pm \sqrt{10^{-4} + (256 \times 10^{-8})}}{2}$$

$$= \frac{-0.01 \pm \sqrt{10^{-4} + (1 + 256 \times 10^{-2})}}{2}$$

$$= \frac{-0.01 \pm 10^{-2}\sqrt{1 + 0.256}}{2}$$

$$= \frac{-0.01 \pm 10^{-2}\sqrt{1.256}}{2}$$

$$= \frac{-10^{-2} + (1.12 \times 10^{-2})}{2}$$

$$= \frac{-(-1 + 1.12) \times 10^{-2}}{2} = \frac{0.12}{2} \times 10^{-2}$$

$= 6 \times 10^{-4}$ mol dm$^{-3}$

2. pH of Solution A = 6

Therefore, concentration of $[H^+]$ ion in solution $A = 10^{-6}$ mol L$^{-1}$

pH of Solution B = 4

Therefore, Concentration of $[H^+]$ ion concentration of solution $B = 10^{-4}$ mol L$^{-1}$

On mixing one litre of each solution, total volume

$= 1\,L + 1\,L = 2L$

Amount of $H^+$ ions in 1L of solution A

$=$ Concentration $\times$ volume V

$= 10^{-6}$ mol $\times 1$ L

Amount of $H^+$ ions in 1L of solution B $= 10^{-4}$ mol $\times$ 1L

$\therefore$ Total amount of $H^+$ ions in the solution formed by mixing solution A and B is $(10^{-6}$ mol $+ 10^{-4}$ mol$)$

This amount is present in 2L solution.

$$\therefore \text{Total } [H^+] = \frac{10^{-4}(1 + 0.01)}{2}$$

$$= \frac{1.01 \times 10^{-4}}{2} \text{ mol L}^{-1}$$

$$= 0.5 \times 10^{-4} \text{ mol L}^{-1}$$

$$= 5 \times 10^{-5} \text{ mol L}^{-1}$$

$$pH = -\log[H^+] = -\log(5 \times 10^{-5})$$

$$= -[\log 5 + (-5 \log 10)]$$

$$= -\log 5 + 5$$

$$= 5 - \log 5$$

$$= 5 - 0.6990$$

$$= 4.3010 = 4.3$$

3. $K_{sp}$ of $PbCl_2 = 3.2 \times 10^{-8}$

Let S be the solubility of $PbCl_2$.

$$PbCl_2(s) \rightleftharpoons Pb^{2+}(aq) + 2Cl^-(aq)$$

Concentration
of species at t = 0      1      0      0

Concentration
of various      1–s      s      2s
species at equilibrium

$$K_{sp} = \left[Pb^{2+}\right]\left[Cl^{-1}\right]^2 = (s)(2s)^2 = 4s^3$$

$$K_{sp} = 4s^3$$

$$s^3 = \frac{K_{sp}}{4} = \frac{3.2 \times 10^{-8}}{4} \, mol \, L^{-1}$$

$$= 8 \times 10^{-9} \, mol \, L^{-1}$$

$$s = \sqrt[3]{8 \times 10^{-9}} = 2 \times 10^{-3} \, mol \, L^{-1}$$

$$\therefore \, s = 2 \times 10^{-3} \, mol \, L^{-1}$$

Molar mass of $PbCl_2 = 278$

$\therefore$ Solubility of $PbCl_2$ in g $L^{-1}$

$$= 2 \times 10^{-3} \times 278 \, g \, L^{-1}$$
$$= 556 \times 10^{-3} \, g \, L^{-1}$$
$$= 0.556 \, g \, L^{-1}$$

To get saturated solution, 0.556 g of $PbCl_2$ is dissolved in 1 L water.

0.1 g $PbCl_2$ is dissolved in $\dfrac{0.1}{0.556}$ L = 0.1798 L water.

To make a saturated solution, dissolution of 0.1 g $PbCl_2$ in 0.1798 L $\approx$ 0.2 L of water will be required.

4. Concentration of $10^{-8}$ mol dm$^{-3}$ indicates that the solution is very dilute. Hence, the contribution of $H_3O^+$ concentration from water is significant and should also be included for the calculation of pH.

### *Long Answer Questions*

1. Given, pH of solution A = 6

[H$^+$] of solution A = $10^{-6}$ mol/lit.

pH of solution B = 4

[H$^+$] of solution B = $10^{-4}$ mol/lit.

On mixing 1L of each solution we will get total 2L of solution.

Amount of [H$^+$] in 2L: solution A $= \dfrac{10^{-6}}{2}$

solution B $= \dfrac{10^{-4}}{2}$

Total [H$^+$] in solution $= \dfrac{10^{-6}}{2} + \dfrac{10^{-4}}{2}$

$$= 10^{-4} \, \frac{(1 + 0.01)}{2} = 10^{-4} \times 1.01/2$$

$= 5 \times 10^{-5}$ mol/L

pH $= -\log$ [H$^+$] $= -\log$ [5 $\times$ 10$^{-5}$]

$= -\log (5) + (-5 \log 10)$

$= -\log 5 + 5 = 4.3$

The pH of the solution formed by mixing will be 4.

2. The equation of dissociation of $Al(OH)_3$ will be:

$$Al(OH)_3 \rightleftharpoons Al^{3+} + 3OH^-$$

We know that,

$K_{sp} = [Al^{3+}][OH^-]^3$

$= (s) \times (3s)^3 = 27s^4$

$s^4 = K_{sp}/27$

$= 2.7 \times 10^{-11}/27$

$s^4 = 10^{-12}$

$s = (10^{-12})^{1/4} = 10^{-3}$ mol/L

Now, molar mass of $Al(OH)_3 = 78$

Solubility = molar mass $\times$ s

$= 78 \times 10^{-3}$

$= 7.8 \times 10^{-2}$ g/L

Now, we know that

pH = 14 – pOH

[OH] = 3s = 3 $\times$ 10$^{-3}$

POH = 3 – log(3)

pH = 14 – 3 + log(3)

= 11.4771

Hence the pH of the solution will be 11.4771 and solubility in g/L will be $7.8 \times 10^{-2}$ g/L.

# 8 Redox Reactions



**8.1 Assign oxidation number to the underlined elements in each of the following species :**

(a) $NaH_2\underline{P}O_4$     (b) $NaH\underline{S}O_4$

(c) $H_4\underline{P}_2O_7$     (d) $K_2\underline{Mn}O_4$

(e) $Ca\,\underline{O}_2$     (f) $Na\underline{B}H_4$

(g) $H_2\underline{S}_2O_7$

(h) $K\underline{Al}\,(\underline{S}O_4)_2.12H_2O$

**Ans.** (a) Let the oxidation number of P be x. Writing the oxidation number of each atom above its symbol, we have,

$$\overset{+1\;\;+1\;\;x\;\;-2}{Na\,H_2\,PO_4}$$

Sum of oxidation numbers of various atom in $NaH_2PO_4 = 1\,(+1) + 2\,(+1) + 1\,(x) + 4\,(-2) = x - 5$

But the sum of oxidation number of various atoms in $NaH_2PO_4$ (neutral) is zero

∴   $x - 5 = 0$   or $x = + 5$ Thus, the oxidation number of P in $NaH_2PO_4 = + 5$.

(b) $\overset{+1\;+1\,x\;\;-2}{Na\,H\,SO_4}$

$1(+1) + 1(+1) + x + 4\,(-2) = 0$

or $x = + 6$

Thus, the oxidation number of S in $NaHSO_4 = + 6$.

(c) $\overset{+1\;\;\;x\;\;-2}{H_4\,P_2\,O_7}$

$4(+1) + 2(x) + 7(-2) = 0$

or $x = + 5$

Thus, the oxidation number of P in $H_4P_2O_7 = + 5$.

(d) $\overset{+1\;\;x\;\;-1}{K_2\,MnO_4}$

$2(+1) + 1(x) + 4(-2) = 0$

or $x = + 6$

Thus, the oxidation number of Mn in $K_2MnO_4 = + 6$.

(e) Let the oxidation number of oxygen be x.

Thus, $\overset{+2\;\;\;x}{Ca\,O_2}$

∴   $2 + 2x = 0$,   $x = -1$

Thus, oxidation number of oxygen in $CaO_2 = -1$.

(f) In $NaBH_4$, H is present as hydride ion. Therefore, its oxidation number is $-1$. Thus,

$$\overset{+1\;\;x\;\;-1}{Na\,B\,H_4}$$

$1 + 1(x) + 4(-1) = 0$   or   $x = +3$

Thus, the oxidation number of B in $NaBH_4 = + 3$.

(g) $\overset{+1\;\;\;x\;\;-2}{H_2\,S_2\,O_7}$

$2(+1) + 2(x) + 7(-2) = 0$

or $x = +6$

Thus, the oxidation number of S in $H_2S_2O_7 = + 6$.

(h) $\overset{+1\;+3\;\;\;x-2\;\;\;\;\;+1}{K\,Al(SO_4)_2\,12(H_2O)}^{-2}$

or $+1 + 3 + 2x - 16 = 2x - 12$

or $x = + 6$

Alternatively, since $H_2O$ is a neutral molecule, therefore, sum of oxidation numbers of all the atoms in $H_2O$ may be taken as zero. As such water molecules may be ignored while computing the oxidation number of S.

∴   $+1 + 3 + 2x - 16 = 0$ or $x = + 6$

Thus, the oxidation number of S in $KAl\,(SO_4)_2.\,12H_2O = + 6$.

**8.2 What are the oxidation number of the underlined elements in each of the following and how do you rationalise your results ?**

(a) $K\underline{I}_3$     (b) $H_2\underline{S}_4O_6$

(c) $\underline{Fe}_3O_4$     (d) $\underline{C}H_3\underline{C}H_2OH$

(e) $\underline{C}H_3\underline{C}OOH$

**Ans.** (a) In $KI_3$, since the oxidation number of K is $+ 1$, therefore, the average oxidation number of iodine $= -1/3$. But the oxidation number cannot be fractional. Therefore, we must consider its structure, $K^+ [I - I \longleftarrow I]^-$. Here, a coordinate bond is formed between $I_2$ molecule and $I^-$ ion. The oxidation number of two iodine atoms forming the $I_2$ molecule is zero while that of iodine forming the coordinate bond is $-1$.

(b) By conventional method, $H_2S_4O_6$

$2\,(+1) + 4x + 6\,(-2) = 0$   or $x = + 2.5$ (wrong)

But it is wrong because all the four S atoms cannot be in the same oxidation state.

By chemical bonding method. the structure of $H_2S_4O_6$ is shown below :

$$H\text{—}O\overset{+5}{S}\text{—}\overset{0}{S}\text{—}\overset{0}{S}\overset{+5}{S}\text{—}OH$$

The O.N. of each of the S–atoms linked with each other in the middle is zero while that of each of remaining two S–atoms is + 5.

(c) By conventional method, $Fe_3O_4$

$3x + 4 (-2) = 0$ or $x = 8/3$

By stoichiometry $Fe_3O_4 = \overset{+2\ -2}{FeO}.\overset{+3\ -2}{Fe_2O_3}$

Fe has O. N. of + 2 and + 3

(d) By conventional method. $CH_3CH_2OH$

$= C_2H_6O$ or $2x + 6 (+1) + 1(-2) = 0$   or $x = -2$

By chemical bonding $C_2$ is attached to three H–atoms (less electronegative than carbon and one $CH_2OH$ group (more electronegative than carbon), therefore, O. N. of

$$H\text{—}\overset{H\ \ H}{\underset{H\ \ H}{\overset{|\ \ \ |}{\underset{|\ \ \ |}{C_2\text{—}C_1}}}}\text{—}OH$$

$C_2 = 3(+1) + x + 2 (+1) - 2 + 1(-1) = 0$ or $x = -2$ $C_1$ is, however, attached to one OH (O. N. –1) and one $CH_3$ (O. N. = +1) group, therefore,

O. N. of $C_1 = + 1 + 2(+1) + x + 1 (-1) = 0$ or $x = -2$

(e) By conventional method

$$CH_3COOH = \overset{x\ \ +1\ \ -2}{C_2H_4O_2}$$

$2x + 4(+1) + 2(-2) = 0$

or $2x + 4 - 4$ or $x = 0$

$$H\text{—}\overset{H\ \ \ O}{\underset{H}{\overset{|\ \ \ ||}{C_2\text{—}C_1}}}\text{—}OH$$

By chemical bonding method

$C_2$ is attached to three H–atoms (less electronegative than carbon)

And one–COOH group (more electro-negative than carbon), therefore,

O.N. of $C_2 = 3(+1) + x + 1(+1)$

$= 0$ or $x = + 4$

$C_1$ is however, attached to one oxygen atom by a double bond, one OH (O.N. = – 1) and one $CH_3$ (O.N. = +1) group, therefore O.N. of $C_1 = +1 + x + 1(-2) + 1(-1) = 0$ or $x = +2$

**8.3** **Justify that the following reactions are redox reactions.**

(a) $CuO(s) + H_2(g) \longrightarrow Cu(s) + H_2O(g)$

(b) $Fe_2O_3(s) + 3\,CO(g) \longrightarrow 2\,Fe(s) + 3\,CO_2(g)$

(c) $4\,BCl_3(g) + 3\,LiAlH_4(s) \longrightarrow$
$\qquad\qquad 2\,B_2H_6(g) + 3\,LiCl(s) + 3\,AlCl_3(s)$

(d) $2\,K(s) + F_2(g) \longrightarrow 2\,K^+F^-(s)$

(e) $4\,NH_3(g) + 5\,O_2(g) \longrightarrow 4\,NO(g) + 6\,H_2O(g)$

**Ans.** (a) $\overset{+2\ -2}{CuO(s)} + H_2(g) \longrightarrow Cu(s) + \overset{+1\ -2}{H_2O(g)}$

Here, O is removed from CuO, therefore, it is reduced to Cu while O is added to $H_2$ to form $H_2O$, therefore, it is oxidized. Further, O. N. of Cu decreases from + 2 in CuO to 0 in Cu but that of H increases from 0 in $H_2$ to + 1 in $H_2O$. Therefore, CuO is reduced to Cu but $H_2$ is oxidized to $H_2O$. Thus, this is a redox reaction.

(b) $\overset{+3\ -2}{Fe_2O_3(s)} + 3\,\overset{+2\,-2}{CO(g)} \longrightarrow 2Fe(s) + 3\,\overset{+4-2}{CO_2(g)}$

Here O.N. of Fe decreases from +3 is $Fe_2O_3$ to 0 in Fe while that of C increases from + 2 in CO to + 4 in $CO_2$. Further, oxygen is removed from $Fe_2O_3$ and added to CO, therefore. $Fe_2O_3$ is reduced while CO is oxidized. Thus, this is a redox reaction.

(c) $4\,\overset{+3-1}{BCl_3(g)} + 2\,\overset{+1\ +3\ -1}{LiAlH_4(s)} \longrightarrow$

$\qquad 2\,\overset{-3\ +1}{B_2H_6(g)} + 3\,\overset{+1\ -1}{LiCl(s)} + 3\,\overset{+3-1}{AlCl_3(s)}$

Here, O. N. of B decreases from + 3 in $BCl_3$ to –3 in $B_2H_6$ while that of H increases from –1 in $LiAlH_4$ to + 1 in $B_2H_6$. Therefore, $BCl_3$ is reduced while $LiAlH_4$ is oxidized. Further, H is added to $BCl_3$ but is removed from $LiAlH_4$, therefore, $BCl_3$ is reduced while $LiAlH_4$ is oxidized. Thus, it is a redox reaction.

(d) $2\,K(s) + F_2(g) \longrightarrow 2\,K^+F^-(s)$

Here, each K atom has lost one electron to form $K^+$ while $F_2$ has gained two electrons to form two $F^{-1}$ ions. Therefore, K is oxidized while $F_2$ is reduced. Thus, it is a redox reaction.

(e) $4\,\overset{-3+1}{NH_3(g)} + 5\,\overset{0}{O_2(g)} \longrightarrow 4\overset{+2\ -2}{NO(g)} + 6\overset{+1\ -2}{H_2O(g)}$

Here, O. N. of N increases from –3 in $NH_3$ to +2 in NO while that O decreases from 0 in $O_2$ to –2 in NO or $H_2O$. Therefore, $NH_3$ is oxidized while $O_2$ is reduced. Further H has been removed from $NH_3$ but added to $O_2$. Therefore, $NH_3$ has been oxidized while $O_2$ is reduced. Thus, this is a redox reaction.

**8.4** **Fluorine reacts with ice and results in the change:**

$H_2O(s) + F_2(g) \longrightarrow HF(g) + HOF(g)$

**Justify that this reaction is a redox reaction.**

**Ans.** Here, $F_2$ is reduced to HF and oxidized to HOF, therefore, it is a redox reaction. HOF is an highly unstable molecule and hence decomposes to form $O_2$ and HF

$$\overset{+1\ -2+1}{2H\ O\ F} \longrightarrow \overset{+1\ -1\ \ \ 0}{2H\ F} + O_2$$

In this reaction, F of HOF is reduced while O of HOF is oxidized. Therefore, it is a redox reaction but not a disproportionation reaction.

**8.5 Calculate the oxidation number of sulphur, chromium and nitrogen in $H_2SO_5$, $Cr_2O_7^{2-}$ and $NO_3^-$. Suggest structure of these three compounds. Count for the fallacy.**

**Ans.** (i) By conventional method, the O. N. of S in $H_2SO_5$ is
$2(+1) + x + 5(-2) = 0$ or $x = +8$

This is impossible because the maximum O.N. of S cannot be more than six since it has only six electrons in the valence shell. This fallacy is overcome if we calculate the O.N. of S by chemical bonding method.

$$\begin{array}{c} O \\ \parallel \\ H\!-\!O\!-\!S\!-\!O\!-\!O\!-\!H \\ \parallel \\ O \end{array}$$

$$\underset{\text{(for H)}}{2x\,(+1)} + \underset{\text{(for S)}}{x} + \underset{\text{for (O-O)}}{2(-1)} + \underset{\text{(for other O atoms)}}{3x(-2)} = 0 \text{ or } x = +6$$

(ii) Oxidation number of chromium in $Cr_2O_7^{2-}$ :

$$\begin{array}{c} O \qquad\qquad O \\ \diagup\!\diagup \quad\ \ \ \diagup\!\diagup \\ O^-\!-\!Cr\!-\!O\!-\!Cr\!-\!O^- \\ \diagup\!\diagup \qquad\ \diagup\!\diagup \\ O \qquad\qquad O \end{array}$$

Structure of dichromate.

Let the Oxidation number of chromium $= x$
$\therefore \quad 2x + 7(-2) = -2 \Rightarrow 2x - 14 = -2$
$\Rightarrow 2x = -2 + 14 \Rightarrow 2x = +12$
$\Rightarrow x = +6$

Thus the oxidation number of chromium $= +6$

(iii) O. N. of N in $NO_3^-$
According to conventional method, O. N. of N in
$NO_3^- = x + 3(-2) = -1$
or $x = +5$

$$^-O\!-\!N\overset{\displaystyle O}{\underset{\displaystyle O}{\diagdown}}$$

According to chemical bonding method,
$\underset{\text{(for O}^-)}{x + 1(-1)} + \underset{\text{(for = O)}}{1(-2)} + \underset{\text{(for O)}}{1(-2)} = 0$  or $x + 5$

Thus, there is no fallacy about the O. N. of N in $NO_3^-$ whether one calculates by conventional method or by chemical bonding method.

**8.6 Write formulas for the following compounds :**

**(a) Mercury (II) chloride**

**(b) Nickel (II) sulphate**

**(c) Tin (IV) oxide**

**(d) Thallium (I) sulphate**

**(e) Iron (III) sulphate**

**(f) Chromium (III) oxide**

**Ans.** (a) $Hg(II)Cl_2$      (b) $Ni(II)SO_4$
(c) $Sn(IV)O_2$      (d) $Tl(I)SO_4$
(e) $Fe_2(III)(SO_4)_3$    (f) $Cr_2(III)O_3$

**8.7 Suggest a list of the substances where carbon can exhibit oxidation states from $-4$ to $+4$ and nitrogen from $-3$ to $+5$.**

**Ans.**

| Compounds of Carbon | O. N. of Carbon |
| --- | --- |
| $CH_4$ | $-4$ |
| $CH_3CH_3$ | $-3$ |
| $CH_3Cl$ | $-2$ |
| $CH \equiv CH$ | $-1$ |
| $CH_2Cl_2$ | $0$ |
| $CHCl_3$ | $+2$ |
| $CCl_4$ | $+4$ |

| Compounds of Nitrogen | O. N. of Carbon |
| --- | --- |
| $NH_3$ | $-3$ |
| $NH_2NH_2$ | $-2$ |
| $NH = NH$ | $-1$ |
| $N \equiv N$ | $0$ |
| $N_2O$ | $+1$ |
| $NO$ | $+2$ |
| $N_2O_3$ | $+3$ |
| $N_2O_4$ | $+4$ |
| $N_2O_5$ | $+5$ |

**8.8 While sulphur dioxide and hydrogen peroxide can act as oxidising as well as reducing agents in their reactions, ozone and nitric acid act only as oxidants. Why ?**

**Ans.** (i) In $SO_2$, O.N. of S is $+4$. In principle, S can have a minimum O.N. of $-2$ and maximum of $+6$. Therefore, S in $SO_2$ can either decrease or increase its O.N. and hence can act both as an oxidizing as well as a reducing agent.

(ii) In $H_2O_2$, the O.N. of O is $-1$. In principle, O can have a minimum O.N. of $-2$ and maximum of zero ($+2$ is possible only with $OF_2$). Therefore, O in $H_2O_2$ can either decrease its O. N. from $-1$ to $-2$ or can increase its O.N. from $-1$ to zero. Therefore, $H_2O_2$ acts both as an oxidizing as well as a reducing agent.

(iii) In $O_3$, the O.N. of O is zero. It can only decrease its O. N. from zero to $-1$ or $-2$, but cannot increase to $+2$. Therefore, $O_3$ acts only as an oxidant.

(iv) In $HNO_3$, O, N. of N is $+5$ which is maximum. Therefore, it can only decrease its O. N. and hence it acts as an oxidant only.

**8.9** **Consider the reactions :**

(a) $6 CO_2 (g) + 6 H_2O (\ell) \longrightarrow$
$$C_6H_{12}O_6(aq) + 6 O_2 (g)$$

(b) $O_3 (g) + H_2O_2 (\ell) \longrightarrow H_2O (\ell) + 2 O_2 (g)$

**Why it is more appropriate to write these reactions as :**

(a) $6 CO_2 (g) + 12 H_2O (\ell) \longrightarrow$
$$C_6H_{12}O_6 (aq) + 6 H_2O (\ell) + 6 O_2 (g)$$

(b) $O_3 (g) + H_2O_2 (\ell) \longrightarrow H_2O(\ell) + O_2 (g) + O_2 (g)$

**Also suggest a technique to investigate the path of the above (a) and (b) redox reactions.**

**Ans.** (a) Although the mechanism of photosynthesis is very complex but broadly speaking it may be visualized to occur in two steps. In the first step, $H_2O$ decomposes to give $H_2$ and $O_2$ in presence of chlorophyll and the $H_2$ thus produced reduces $CO_2$ to $C_6H_{12}O_6$ in the second step. During the second step, some $H_2O$ molecules are also produced as shown below:

$$12 H_2O (\ell) \longrightarrow 12 H_2 (g) + 6 O_2 (g) \quad \ldots(i)$$
$$6 CO_2 (g) + 12 H_2 (g) \longrightarrow$$
$$C_6H_{12}O_6 (s) + 6 H_2O (\ell) \quad \ldots(ii)$$
$$6CO_2 (g) + 12 H_2O (\ell) \longrightarrow$$
$$C_6H_{12}O_6 (s) + 6 H_2O (\ell) + 6 O_2 (g) \quad \ldots(iii)$$

Therefore, it is more appropriate to write the equation for photosynthesis as (iii) because it emphasizes that $12 H_2O$ are used per molecule of carbohydrate formed and $6 H_2O$ are produced during the process.

(b) The purpose of writing $O_2$ two times suggests that $O_2$ is being obtained from each of the two reactants.

$$O_3 (g) \longrightarrow O_2 (g) + O (g)$$
$$H_2O_2 (\ell) + O (g) \longrightarrow H_2O (\ell) + O_2 (g)$$
$$O_3 (g) + H_2O_2 (\ell) \longrightarrow H_2O (\ell) + O_2 (g) + O_2(g)$$

The path of reactions (a) and (b) can be determined by using $H_2O^{18}$ in reaction (a) or by using $H_2O_2^{18}$ or $O_3^{18}$ in reaction (b).

**8.10** **The compound $AgF_2$ is unstable compound. However, if formed, the compound acts as a very strong oxidising agent. Why ?**

**Ans.** In $AgF_2$, oxidation state of Ag is +2 which is very very unstable. Therefore, it quickly accepts an electron to form the more stable +1 oxidation state.

$$Ag^{2+} + e^- \longrightarrow Ag^+.$$

Therefore, $AgF_2$, if formed, will act as a strong oxidising agent.

**8.11** **Whenever a reaction between an oxidising agent and a reducing agent is carried out, a compound of lower oxidation state is formed if the reducing agent is in excess and a compound of higher oxidation state is formed if the oxidising agent is in excess. Justify this statement giving three illustrations.**

**Ans.** (i) C is a reducing agent while $O_2$ is an oxidizing agent. If excess of carbon is burnt in a limited supply of $O_2$, CO is formed in which the oxidation state of C is

+ 2. If, however, excess of $O_2$ is used, the initially formed CO gets oxidized to $CO_2$ in which oxidation state of C is + 4.

$$2C(s) + O_2(g) \xrightarrow{\phantom{x}} 2\overset{+2-2}{C}O(g);$$
(Excess)

$$C(s) + O_2(g) \xrightarrow{\phantom{x}} \overset{+4-4}{C}O_2(g)$$
(Excess)

(ii) $P_4$ is a reducing agent while $Cl_2$ is an oxidizing agent. When excess of $P_4$ is used, $PCl_3$ is formed in which the oxidation state of P is + 3. If, however, excess of $Cl_2$ is used, the initially formed $PCl_3$ reacts further to form $PCl_5$ in which the oxidation state of P is + 5

$$P_4 + 6Cl_2(g) \xrightarrow{\phantom{x}} 4\overset{+3}{P}Cl_3\,;$$
(Excess)

$$P_4(s) + 10Cl_2 \xrightarrow{\phantom{x}} 4\overset{+5}{P}Cl_5$$
(Excess)

(iii) Na is a reducing agent while $O_2$ is an oxidizing agent. When excess of Na is used, sodium oxide is formed in which the oxidation state of O is –2. If, however, excess of $O_2$ is used, $Na_2O_2$ is formed in which the oxidation state of O is –1 which is higher than –2.

$$Na(s) + O_2(g) \xrightarrow{\phantom{x}} Na_2\overset{-2}{O}(s);$$
(Excess)

$$2Na(s) + 2O_2 (g) \xrightarrow{\phantom{x}} Na_2\overset{-1}{O_2}(s)$$
(Excess)

**8.12** **How do you count for the following observations?**

**(a)** **Though alkaline potassium permanganate and acidic potassium permanganate both are used as oxidants, yet in the manufacture of benzoic acid from toluene we use alcoholic potassium permanganate as an oxidant. Why ? Write a balanced redox equation for the reaction.**

**(b)** **When concentrated sulphuric acid is added to an inorganic mixture containing chloride, we get colourless pungent smelling gas HCl, but if the mixture contains bromide then we get red vapour of bromine. Why ?**

**Ans.** (a) In the manufacture of benzoic acid from toluene, alcoholic medium is preferred over acidic or alkaline medium due to following reasons:

(1) In alcoholic medium, neither acid nor base is added externally which reduces the cost of manufacturing process.

(2) Alcohol has non-polar alkyl groups as well as polar –OH group. Thus, if alcohol is used as a solvent, it will help in the formation of a homogeneous mixture between toluene (non-polar) and $KMnO_4$ (ionic).

The balanced reaction is :

$$CH_3\text{—}C_6H_5 (l) + 2MnO_4^-(aq) \longrightarrow$$

$$COO^-\text{—}C_6H_5 (aq) + 2\,MnO_2(s) + H_2O\,(l) + OH^-\,(aq)$$

(b) When conc. $H_2SO_4$ is added to an inorganic mixture containing chloride, a pungent smelling gas HCl is produced because a stronger acid displaces a weaker acid from its salt.

$$2\,NaCl + 2\,H_2SO_4 \longrightarrow 2\,NaHSO_4 + 2\,HCl$$
$$2\,HCl + H_2SO_4 \longrightarrow Cl_2 + SO_2 + 2\,H_2O$$

Since HCl is a very weak reducing agent, it can not reduce $H_2SO_4$ to $SO_2$ and hence HCl is not oxidized to $Cl_2$

However, when the mixture contains bromide ion, the initially produced HBr being a stronger reducing agent reduces $H_2SO_4$ to $SO_2$ and is itself oxidized to produce red vapour of $Br_2$.

$$2\,NaBr + 2\,H_2SO_4 \longrightarrow 2\,NaHSO_4 + 2\,HBr$$
$$2\,HBr + H_2SO_4 \longrightarrow Br_2 + SO_2 + 2\,H_2O$$

**8.13** **Identify the substance oxidised, reduced, oxidising agent and reducing agent for each of the following reactions :**

(a) $2\,AgBr\,(s) + C_6H_6O_2\,(aq) \longrightarrow$
$$2\,Ag\,(s) + 2\,HBr\,(aq) + C_6H_4O_2\,(aq)$$

(b) $HCHO(l) + 2\,[Ag(NH_3)_2]^+\,(aq) + 3OH^-\,(aq) \longrightarrow$
$$2Ag(s) + HCOO^-\,(aq) + 4NH_3(aq) + 2\,H_2O\,(l)$$

(c) $HCHO(l) + 2\,Cu^{2+}(aq) + 5OH^-\,(aq) \longrightarrow$
$$Cu_2O(s) + HCOO^-\,(aq) + 3H_2O(l)$$

(d) $N_2H_4(l) + 2H_2O_2\,(l) \longrightarrow N_2\,(g) + 4\,H_2O\,(l)$

(e) $Pb\,(s) + PbO_2\,(s) + 2\,H_2SO_4(aq) \longrightarrow$
$$2\,PbSO_4(s) + 2\,H_2O(l)$$

**Ans.**

| | Substance oxidised (Reducing agent) | Substance reduced (Oxidising agent) |
|---|---|---|
| (a) | $C_6H_6O_2$ (aq) <br> AgBr(s) | AgBr (s) <br> $C_6H_6O_2$ (aq) |
| (b) | HCHO (aq) <br> $[Ag(NH_3)_2]^+$ | $[Ag(NH_3)_2]^+$ <br> HCHO (aq) |
| (c) | HCHO (aq) <br> $Cu^{2+}$ (aq) | $Cu^{2+}$ (aq) <br> HCHO (aq) |
| (d) | $N_2H_4(l)$ <br> $H_2O_2$ $(l)$ | $H_2O_2$ $(l)$ <br> $N_2H_4(l)$ |
| (e) | Pb (s) <br> $PbO_2$(s) | $PbO_2$(s) <br> Pb (s) |

**8.14** **Consider the reactions:**
$$2S_2O_3^{2-}\,(aq) + I_2(s) \longrightarrow S_4O_6^{2-}(aq) + 2I^-\,(aq)$$
$$S_2O_3^{-2}\,(aq) + 2Br_2\,(l) + 5H_2O\,(l) \longrightarrow$$
$$2SO_4^{2-}\,(aq) + 4Br^-\,(aq) + 10\,H^+(aq)$$
**Why does the same reductant, thiosulphate react differently with iodine and bromine?**

**Ans.** The average O. N. of S in $S_2O_3^{2-}$ is $+2$ while in $S_4O_6^{2-}$ it is $+2.5$. The O.N. of S in $SO_4^{2-}$ is $+6$. Since $Br_2$ is a stronger oxidising agent that $I_2$, it oxidises S of $S_2O_3^{2-}$ to a higher oxidation state of $+6$ and hence forms $SO_4^{2-}$ ion. $I_2$, however, being a weaker oxidising agent oxidises S of $S_2O_3^{2-}$ ion to a lower oxidation state of $+2.5$ in $S_4O_6^{2-}$ ion. It is because of this reason that thiosulphate reacts differently with $Br_2$ and $I_2$.

**8.15** **Justify giving reactions that among halogens, fluorine is the best oxidant and among hydrohalic compounds, hydroiodic acid is the best reductant.**

**Ans.** The oxidizing power of halogens decreases in the order: $F_2 > Cl_2 > Br_2 > I_2$. This is evident from the observation that $F_2$ oxidizes $Cl^-$ to $Cl_2$, $Br^-$ to $Br_2$, $I^-$ to $I_2$ $Cl_2$ oxidizes $Br^-$ to $Br_2$ and $I^-$ to $I_2$ but not $F^-$ to $F_2$. $Br_2$, however, oxidizes $I^-$ to $I_2$ but not $F^-$ to $F_2$, and $Cl^-$ to $Cl_2$.
$$F_2(g) + 2Cl^-(aq) \longrightarrow 2\,F^-\,(aq) + Cl_2\,(g);$$
$$F_2(g) + 2\,Br^-(aq) \longrightarrow 2\,F^-(aq) + Br_2(l)$$
$$F_2\,(g) + 2\,I^-\,(aq) \longrightarrow 2\,F^-\,(aq) + I_2\,(s);$$
$$Cl_2(g) + 2\,Br^-(aq) \longrightarrow 2Cl^-(aq) + Br_2(l)$$
$$Cl_2\,(g) + 2I^-\,(aq) \longrightarrow 2\,Cl^-\,(aq) + I_2\,(s)$$
$$\text{and } Br_2\,(l) + 2\,I^-(aq) \longrightarrow 2\,Br^-\,(aq) + I_2\,(s)$$
Thus $F_2$ is the best oxidant

Among hydrohalic acids, the reducing power decreases in the order: $HI > HBr > HCl > HF$. Thus, HI and HBr reduce $H_2SO_4$ to $SO_2$ while HCl and HF do not.
$$2\,HBr + H_2SO_4 \longrightarrow Br_2 + SO_2 + 2\,H_2O$$
$$2\,HI + H_2SO_4 \longrightarrow I_2 + SO_2 + 2\,H_2O$$
Further $I^-$ reduces $Cu^{2+}$ to $Cu^+$ but $Br^-$ does not.
$$2\,Cu^{2+}\,(aq) + 4\,I^-\,(aq) \longrightarrow Cu_2I_2\,(s) + I_2\,(aq)$$
$$Cu^{2+}\,(aq) + 2Br^- \longrightarrow \text{No reaction.}$$
Further among HCl and HF, HCl is a stronger reducing agent than HF because HCl reduces $MnO_2$ to $Mn^{2+}$ but HF does not.
$$MnO_2\,(s) + 4\,HCl\,(aq) \longrightarrow$$
$$MnCl_2(aq) + Cl_2\,(g) + 2H_2O$$
$$MnO_2\,(s) + 4\,HF\,(l) \longrightarrow \text{No reaction.}$$

**8.16** **Why does the following reaction occur ?**
$$XeO_6^{4-}\,(aq) + 2\,F^-\,(aq) + 6\,H^+\,(aq) \longrightarrow$$
$$XeO_3\,(g) + F_2\,(g) + 3\,H_2O\,(l)$$
**What conclusion about the compound $Na_4XeO_6$ (of which $XeO_6^{4-}$ is a part) can be drawn from the reaction.**

**Ans.** $\overset{+8}{Xe}O_6^{-4}(aq) + 2\,\overset{-1}{F^-}\,(aq) + 6\,\overset{+}{H}\,(aq) \longrightarrow$

$$\overset{+6}{Xe}O_3(s) + F_2(g) + 3H_2O(l)$$

Here, O. N. of Xe decreases from $+8$ in $XeO_6^{4-}$ to $+6$ in $XeO_3$ while that of F increases from $-1$ in $F^-$ to $0$ in $F_2$. Therefore, $XeO_6^{4-}$ is reduced while $F^-$ is oxidized. This reaction occurs because $Na_4XeO_6^{4-}$ (or $XeO_6^{4-}$) is a stronger oxidizing agent than $F_2$.

**8.17 Consider the reactions:**

(a) $H_3PO_2$ (aq) $+ 4\ AgNO_3$ (aq) $+ 2\ H_2O(\ell)$
$\longrightarrow H_3PO_4$ (aq) $+ 4\ Ag$ (s) $+ 4\ HNO_3$ (aq)

(b) $H_3PO_2$ (aq) $+ 2\ CuSO_4$ (aq) $+ 2H_2O$ ($\ell$) $\longrightarrow$
$H_3PO_4$ (aq) $+ 2\ Cu$ (s) $+ H_2SO_4$ (aq)

(c) $C_6H_5CHO$ ($\ell$) $+ 2\ [Ag(NH_3)_2]^+$(aq) $+ 3\ OH^-$(aq)
$\longrightarrow C_6H_5COO^-$ (aq) $+ 2\ Ag$ (s) $+ 4\ NH_3$ (aq) $+ 2H_2O$ ($\ell$)

(d) $C_6H_5CHO$ ($\ell$) $+ 2\ Cu^{2+}$ (aq) $+ 5OH^-$ (aq)
$\longrightarrow$ **No change observed.**

**What inference do you draw about the behaviour of $Ag^+$ and $Cu^{2+}$ from these reactions?**

**Ans.** Reactions (a) and (b) indicate that $H_3PO_2$ (hypophosphorus acid) is a reducing agent and thus reduces both $AgNO_3$ and $CuSO_4$ to Ag and Cu respectively. Conversely, both $AgNO_3$ and $CuSO_4$ act as oxidizing agent and thus oxidize $H_3PO_2$ to $H_3PO_4$ (phosphorus acid) Reaction (c) suggests that $[Ag(NH_3)_2]^+$ oxidizes $C_6H_5CHO$ (benzaldehyde) to $C_6H_5COO^-$ (benzoate ion) but reaction (d) indicates that $Cu^{2+}$ ions cannot oxidize $C_6H_5CHO$ to $C_6H_5COO^-$. Therefore, from the above reactions, we conclude that $Ag^+$ ion is a stronger oxidizing agent than $Cu^{2+}$ ion.

**8.18 Balance the following redox reactions by ion –electron method:**

(a) $MnO_4^-$ (aq) $+ I^-$ (aq) $\longrightarrow MnO_2$ (s) $+ I_2$ (s)
(in basic medium)

(b) $MnO_4^-$ (aq) $+ SO_2$ (g) $\longrightarrow$
$Mn^{2+}$ (aq) $+ HSO_4^-$ (aq)
(in acidic solution)

(c) $H_2O_2$ (aq) $+ Fe^{2+}$ (aq) $\longrightarrow$
$Fe^{3+}$ (aq) $+ H_2O$ ($\ell$)
(in acidic solution)

(d) $Cr_2O_7^{2-}$ (aq) $+ SO_2$ (g) $\longrightarrow$
$Cr^{3+}$ (aq) $+ SO_4^{2-}$ (aq)
(in acidic solution)

**Ans.** (a) Oxidation half equation:
$$2I^- \longrightarrow I_2 + 2e^-$$
Reduction half equation:
$$MnO_4^- + 2H_2O + 3e^- \longrightarrow MnO_2 + 4OH^-$$
Now to cancel out the electrons multiply oxidation half by 3 and reduction half equation by 2 and add it. We get
$$6I^- \longrightarrow 3I_2 + 6e^-$$
$$2MnO_4^- + 4H_2O + 6e^- \longrightarrow 2MnO_2 + 8OH^-$$
$$2MnO_4^- + 6I^- + 4H_2O \longrightarrow 2MnO_2 + 3I_2 + 8OH^-$$

(b) Oxidation half equation:
$$SO_2\ (g) + 2H_2O\ (l) \longrightarrow$$
$$HSO_4^-\ (aq) + 3H^+\ (aq) + 2e^- \quad ...\ (i)$$
Reduction half equation:
$$MnO_4^-\ (aq) + 8H^+(aq) + 5e^- \longrightarrow$$
$$Mn^{2+}\ (aq) + 4\ H_2O\ (\ell) \quad ..\ (ii)$$
Multiply Eq. (i) by 5 and Eq. (ii) by 2 and add, we have,
$$2\ MnO_4^-(aq) + 5\ SO_2(g) + 2H_2O(\ell) + H^+(aq)$$
$$\longrightarrow 2\ Mn^{2+}\ (aq) + 5\ HSO_4^-(aq)$$

(c) Oxidation half equation:
$$Fe^{2+}\ (aq) \longrightarrow Fe^{3+}\ (aq) + e^- \qquad ...\ (i)$$
Reduction half equation:
$$H_2O_2\ (aq) + 2\ H^+\ (aq) + 2\ e^- \longrightarrow$$
$$2\ H_2O\ (\ell) \qquad ...\ (ii)$$
Multiply Eq. (i) by 2 and add it to Eq. (ii), we have,
$$H_2O_2\ (aq) + 2\ Fe^{2+}\ (aq) + 2\ H^+\ (aq) \longrightarrow$$
$$2\ Fe^{3+}\ (aq) + 2\ H_2O\ (\ell)$$

(d) Oxidation half equation:
$$SO_2\ (g) + 2\ H_2O\ (\ell) \longrightarrow$$
$$SO_4^{2-}\ (aq) + 4\ H^+\ (aq) + 2\ e^- ...\ (i)$$
Reduction half equation:
$$Cr_2O_7^{2-}\ (aq) + 14\ H^+\ (aq) + 6\ e^- \longrightarrow$$
$$2\ Cr^{3+}\ (aq) + 7\ H_2O\ (\ell) \quad ...\ (ii)$$
Multiply Eq. (i) by 3 and add it to Eq. (ii), we have,
$$Cr_2O_7^{2-}\ (aq) + 3\ SO_2\ (g) + 2\ H^+\ (aq) \longrightarrow$$
$$2\ Cr^{3+}\ (aq) + 3\ SO_4^-\ (aq) + H_2O\ (\ell)$$

**8.19 Balance the following equations in basic medium by ion electron method and oxidation number methods and identify the oxidising agent and the reducing agent.**

(a) $P_4(s) + OH^-$ (aq) $\longrightarrow PH_3(g) + HPO_2^-$ (aq)
(b) $N_2H_4(\ell) + ClO_3^-$ (aq) $\longrightarrow NO(g) + Cl^-$ (g)
(c) $Cl_2O_7(g) + H_2O_2(aq) \longrightarrow$
$ClO_2^-$ (aq) $+ O_2$ (g) $+ H^+$

**Ans.** (a) O. N. decreases by 3 per P atom

$$\overset{0}{P_4(s)} + OH^-(aq) \longrightarrow \overset{-3}{PH_3}(g) + \overset{+1}{H_2PO_2^-}$$

O. N. increases by 1 per P atom.

$P_4$ acts like both as an oxidizing as well as reducing agent.

**Oxidation number method :**

Total decrease in O. N. of $P_4$ in $PH_3 = 3 \times 4 = 12$

Total increase in O. N. of $P_4$ in $H_2PO_2^- = 1 \times 4 = 4$

Therefore, to balance increase/decreases in O. N. multiply $PH_3$ by 1 and $H_2PO_2^-$ by 3, we have,

$$P_4\ (s) + OH^-\ (aq) \longrightarrow PH_3\ (g) + 3H_2PO_2^-\ (aq)$$

To balance O atoms, multiply $OH^-$ by 6, we have,

$P_4 (s) + 6\ OH^-(aq) \longrightarrow PH_3 (g) + 3H_2PO_2^-(aq)$

To balance H atoms, add $3H_2O$ to deficient side and $3OH^-$ to the other side, now we have

$P_4(s) + 6OH^- (aq) + 3H_2O\ (\ell) \longrightarrow$
$$PH_3(g) + 3H_2PO_2^-\ (aq) + 3OH^-(aq)$$

To cancel out species present in both sides, we have

$P_4(s) + 3OH^- (aq) + 3H_2O(\ell) \longrightarrow$
$$PH_3(g) + 3H_2PO_2^-\ (aq)$$

This represents the correct balanced equation.

**Ion electron method :**

Oxidation half equation :

$$\overset{0}{P_4} \longrightarrow \overset{+1}{H_2PO_2^-}$$

Balance P atoms, $P_4 \longrightarrow 4\ H_2PO_2^-$

Balance H atom O atoms by adding $OH^-$

$P_4 + 8OH^- \longrightarrow 4H_2PO_2^-$

Now balance charge

$P_4 + 8OH^- \longrightarrow 4H_2PO_2^- + 4e^-$ ...... (i)

Thus, Eq. (i) represents the correct balanced oxidation half equation.

Reduction half equation :

$$\overset{0}{P_4} \longrightarrow \overset{-3}{PH_3}$$

Balance P atoms, $P_4 \longrightarrow 4PH_3$

Balance H atoms by adding $OH^-$ and $H_2O$,

$P_4 + 12H_2O + 12\ e^- \longrightarrow 4PH_3 + 12\ OH^-$ ... (ii)

Thus, Eq. (ii) represents the correct balanced reduction half equation.

To cancel out electrons gained and lost, multiply Eq. (i) by 3 and add with Eq. (ii) by cancelling common terms, we have,

$P_4(s) + 3OH^- (aq) + 3H_2O(\ell) \longrightarrow$
$$PH_3(g) + 3H_2PO_2^-\ (aq)$$

O.N. increases by 4 per N atom

(b) $\overset{-2}{N_2}H_4(l) + \overset{+5}{Cl}O_3^-(aq) \longrightarrow \overset{+2}{N}O(g) + \overset{-1}{Cl}^-(g)$

O.N. decreases by 6 per Cl atom

Thus, $N_2H_4$ is acting as a reducing agent while $ClO_3^-$ is acting as an oxidising agent.

**Oxidation number method :**

Total increase in O. N. of N in $NO = 4 \times 2 = 8$

Total increase in O. N. of Cl in

$ClO_3^- = 6 \times 1 = 6$

Therefore, to balance increase/decrease in O.N. multiply NO by 6 and $ClO_3^-$ by 4 we have

$N_2H_4 + 4\ ClO_3^- \longrightarrow 6NO + Cl^-$

Balance N and Cl atoms,

$3N_2H_4 + 4ClO_3^- \longrightarrow 6\ NO + 4Cl^-$

To balance H atoms, add $6H_2O$ to deficient side

$3N_2H_4(s) + 4ClO_3^- (aq) \longrightarrow$
$$6\ NO(g) + 4Cl^-(aq) + 6H_2O(\ell)$$

This represents the correct balanced equation.

**Ion electron method :** Oxidation half equation:

$$\overset{-2}{N_2}H_4(\ell) \longrightarrow \overset{+2}{N}O(g)$$

Balance N atoms, $N_2H_4\ (\ell) \longrightarrow 2\ NO\ (g)$

Balance H atom by adding $OH^-$ and $H_2O$

$N_2H_4 + 4OH^- \longrightarrow 2NO + 4H_2O$

Balance O atoms again by adding $H_2O$ and $OH^-$

$N_2H_4\ (\ell) + 4\ OH^-(aq) + 4OH^- \longrightarrow$
$$2\ NO\ (g) + 4\ H_2O\ (\ell) + 2H_2O$$

Now balance charge

$N_2H_4\ (l) + 8OH^-(aq) \longrightarrow 2NO + 6H_2O + 8e^-$ (i)

Thus, Eq. (i) represents the correct balanced oxidation half equation.

Reduction half equation $\overset{+5}{Cl}O_3^-\ (aq) \longrightarrow Cl^-\ (aq)$

Balance O. N. by adding electrons,

$ClO_3^-\ (aq) + 6\ e^- \longrightarrow Cl^-\ (aq)$

Balance charge by adding $OH^-$ ions,

$ClO_3^-\ (aq) + 6\ e^- \longrightarrow Cl^-\ (aq) + 6\ OH^-\ (aq)$

Balance O atoms by adding $3\ H_2O$,

$ClO_3^-\ (aq) + 3\ H_2O\ (\ell) + 6\ e^- \longrightarrow$
$$Cl^-\ (aq) + 6\ OH^-\ (aq)$$ ... (ii)

Thus, Eq. (ii) represents the correct balanced reduction half equation.

To cancel out electrons gained and lost, multiply Eq. (i) by 3 and Eq. (ii) by 4 and add, we have,

$3\ N_2H_4\ (\ell) + 4\ ClO_3^-\ (aq) \longrightarrow$
$$6\ NO\ (g) + 4\ Cl^-\ (aq) + 6\ H_2O\ (\ell)$$

This represents the correct balanced equation

(c)   O. N. decreases by 4 per Cl atom

$\overset{+7}{Cl_2}O_7(g) + \overset{-1}{H_2O_2}(aq) \longrightarrow \overset{+3}{Cl}O_2^-\ (g) + \overset{0}{O_2}(g) + H^+$

O. N. increases by 1 per O atom. Thus, $Cl_2O_7\ (g)$ acts an oxidizing agent while $H_2O_2\ (aq)$ as the reducing agent.

**Oxidation number method :** Total decrease in O. N. of $Cl_2O_7 = 4 \times 2 = 8$

Total increase in O. N. of $H_2O_2 = 2 \times 1 = 2$

$\therefore$ To balance increase/decrease in O. N. multiply $H_2O_2$ and $O_2$ by 4, we have,

$Cl_2O_7\ (g) + 4\ H_2O_2(aq) \longrightarrow ClO_2^-(aq) + 4\ O_2\ (g)$

To balance Cl atoms, multiply $ClO_2^-$ by 2, we have,

$Cl_2O_7 (g) + 4 H_2O_2(aq) \longrightarrow 2 ClO_2^- (aq) + 4 O_2 (g)$

To balance O atoms, add 3 $H_2O$ to R. H. S., we have,

$Cl_2O_7 (g) + 4 H_2O_2 (aq) \longrightarrow$
$$2 ClO_2^- (aq) + 4 O_2(g) + 3 H_2O (\ell)$$

To balance H atoms, add 2 $H_2O$ to R. H. S. and 2 $OH^-$ to L. H. S., we have,

$Cl_2O_7 (g) + 4 H_2O_2(g) + 2 OH^- (aq) \longrightarrow$
$$2 ClO_2^- (aq) + 4O_2 (g) + 5 H_2O$$

This represents the balanced redox equation.

**Ion electron method :** Oxidation half equation:

$H_2O_2 (aq) \longrightarrow O_2 (g)$

Balance O. N. by adding electrons,

$H_2O_2 (aq) \longrightarrow O_2 (g) + 2e^-$

Balance charge by adding $OH^-$ ions,

$H_2O_2 (aq) + 2 OH^- (aq) \longrightarrow O_2 (g) + 2 e^-$

Balance O atoms by adding $H_2O$,

$H_2O_2(aq) + 2 OH^- (aq) \longrightarrow O_2 (g) + 2 H_2O (\ell) + 2 e^-$
$$... (i)$$

Reduction half equation: $Cl_2O_7 (g) \longrightarrow ClO_2^- (aq)$

Balance Cl atoms; $Cl_2O_7 (g) \longrightarrow 2 ClO_2^- (aq)$

Balance O. N. by adding electrons,

$Cl_2O_7 (g) + 8 e^- \longrightarrow 2 ClO_2^- (aq)$

Add $OH^-$ ions to balance charge:

$Cl_2O_7 (g) + 8 e^- \longrightarrow 2 ClO_2^- (aq) + 6 OH^-$

Balance O atoms by adding 3 $H_2O$ to L. H. S., we have,

$Cl_2O_7 (g) + 3 H_2O (\ell) + 8 e^- \longrightarrow$
$$2 ClO_2^- (aq) + 6 OH^- (aq) \quad ... (ii)$$

To cancel out electrons, multiply Eq. (i) by 4 and add it to Eq. (ii), we have,

$4 H_2O_2(aq) + 8 OH^-(aq) + Cl_2O_7(g) + 3H_2O (\ell) \longrightarrow 2 ClO_2^- + (aq) + 6 OH^- (aq) + 4 O_2(g) + 8 H_2O (\ell)$

or $Cl_2O_7 (g) + 4 H_2O_2 (aq) + 2 OH^- (aq) \longrightarrow 2ClO_2^- (aq) + 4 O_2 (g) + 5 H_2O (\ell)$

**8.20 What sorts of information can you draw from the following reactions :**

$(CN)_2 (g) + 2 OH^- (aq) \longrightarrow$
$$CN^-(aq) + CNO^- (aq) + H_2O (\ell)$$

**Ans.** (i) It is a disproportionation reaction.

(ii) Cyanogen $(CN)_2$ gets simultaneously reduced to $CN^-$ ion as well as oxidized to cyanate ion.

(iii) O. N. of N in $(CN)_2$ is $-3$ while that in $CN^-$ is $-2$ and in $CNO^-$ is $-5$

(iv) The reaction occurs in basic medium.

**8.21 The $Mn^{3+}$ ion is unstable in solution and undergoes disproportionation to give $Mn^{2+}$, $MnO_2$ and $H^+$ ion. Write a balanced ionic equation for the reaction.**

**Ans.** The skeletal equation is: $Mn^{3+} (aq) \longrightarrow$
$$Mn^{2+} (aq) + MnO_2 (s) + H^+ (aq)$$

Oxidation half equation:

$\overset{+3}{Mn^{3+}} (aq) \longrightarrow \overset{+4}{Mn} O_2 (s)$

Balance O. N. by adding electrons,

$Mn^{3+} (aq) \longrightarrow MnO_2 (s) + e^-$

Balance charge by adding $H^+$ ions,

$Mn^{3+} (aq) \longrightarrow MnO_2 (s) + 4 H^+ (aq) + e^-$

Balance O atoms by adding $H_2O$:

$Mn^{3+} (aq) + 2 H_2O (\ell) \longrightarrow MnO_2 (s) + 4 H^+ (aq) + e^-$
$$... (i)$$

Reduction half equation : $\overset{+3}{Mn^{3+}} \longrightarrow \overset{+2}{Mn^{2+}}$

Balance O. N. by adding electron :

$Mn^{3+} (aq) + e^- \longrightarrow Mn^{2+} (aq)$ $\quad ... (ii)$

Adding Eq. (i) and Eq. (ii), the balanced equation for the disproportionation reaction is

$2 Mn^{3+} (aq) + 2 H_2O (\ell) \longrightarrow$
$$MnO_2 (s) + Mn^{2+} (aq) + 4H^+ (aq)$$

**8.22 Consider the elements : Cs, Ne, I and F only**

(a) **Identify the element that exhibits only – ve oxidation state.**

(b) **Identify the element that exhibits only + ve oxidation state**

(c) **Identify the element that exhibits both + ve and – ve oxidation states**

(d) **Identify the element which neither exhibits – ve nor + ve oxidation state.**

**Ans.** (a) Fluorine being most electronegative element shows only a –ve oxidation state of $-1$.

(b) Cs, Alkali metals because of the presence of a single electron in the valence shell, exhibit an oxidation state of $+ 1$.

(c) I, Because of the presence of seven electrons in the valence shell, I shows an oxidation state of $-1$ and because of the presence of $d$–orbitals it also exhibits +ve oxidation states of $+1$, $+3$, $+5$ and $+7$.

(d) Ne, It is an inert gas and hence it neither exhibits –ve nor +ve oxidation states.

**8.23 Chlorine is used to purify drinking water. Excess of chlorine is harmful. The excess chlorine is removed by treating with sulphur dioxide. Present a balanced equation for the reaction for this redox change taking place in water.**

**Ans.** The skeletal equation is:

$Cl_2 (aq) + SO_2 (aq) + H_2O (\ell) \longrightarrow$
$$2 Cl^- (aq) + SO_4^{2-} (aq)$$

Reduction half equation:

$Cl_2 (aq) \longrightarrow Cl^- (aq)$

Balance Cl atoms, $\overset{0}{Cl_2} (aq) \longrightarrow 2 Cl^- (aq)$

Balance O. N. by adding electrons:

$Cl_2$ (aq) + 2 e$^-$ ⟶ 2 Cl$^-$ (aq)      ...(i)

Oxidation half equation:

$\overset{+4}{S} O_2$(aq) ⟶ $\overset{+6}{S} O_4^{2-}$ (aq) + 2e$^-$

Balance O. N. by adding electrons:

$SO_2$ (aq) ⟶ $SO_4^{2-}$ (aq) + 2 e$^-$

Balance charge by adding H$^+$ ions:

$SO_2$ (aq) ⟶ $SO_4^{2-}$ (aq) + 4 H$^+$ (aq) + 2 e$^-$

Balance O atoms by adding 2 $H_2O$,

$SO_2$ (aq) + 2 $H_2O$ ($\ell$) ⟶
$$SO_4{}^{2-} \text{ (aq)} + 4 H^+ \text{ (aq)} + 2 e^- \quad ...(ii)$$

Adding Eq. (i) and Eq. (ii), we have,

$Cl_2$ (aq) + $SO_2$ (aq) + 2 $H_2O$ ($\ell$) ⟶
$$2 Cl^- \text{ (aq)} + SO_4{}^{2-} \text{ (aq)} + 4 H^+ \text{ (aq)}$$

This represents the balanced redox reaction.

**8.24 Refer to the periodic table given in your book and now answer the following questions.**

**(a) Select the possible non-metals that can show disproportionation reaction.**

**(b) Select three metals that can show disproportionation reaction.**

**Ans.** (a) The non–metals are: $P_4$, $Cl_2$ and $S_8$.

(i)   $P_4$ (s) + 3 OH$^-$ (aq) + 3 $H_2O$ ($\ell$) ⟶
$$PH_3 \text{ (g)} + 3 H_2PO_2^- \text{ (aq)}$$

(ii)   $Cl_2$ (aq) + 2 OH$^-$ (aq) ⟶
$$Cl^- \text{ (aq)} + ClO^- \text{ (aq)} + H_2O \text{ ($\ell$)}$$

(iii)   $S_8$ (s) + 12 OH$^-$ ⟶
$$4 S^{2-} \text{ (aq)} + 2 S_2O_3{}^{2-} \text{ (aq)} + 6 H_2O \text{ ($\ell$)}$$

(b) The metals are: Cu$^+$, Ga$^+$, In$^+$ etc.

$2 Cu^+$ (aq) ⟶ $Cu^{2+}$ (aq) + Cu (s)

$3 Ga^+$ (aq) ⟶ $Ga^{3+}$ (aq) + 2 Ga (s)

$3 In^+$ (aq) ⟶ $In^{3+}$ (aq) + 2 In (s)

**8.25 In Ostwald's process for the manufacture of nitric acid, the first step involves the oxidation of ammonia gas by oxygen gas to give nitric oxide gas and steam. What is the maximum weight of nitric oxide that can be obtained starting only with 10.0 g of ammonia and 20.0 g of oxygen?**

**Ans.** The balanced equation for the reaction is:

$$4NH_3(g) \ + \ 5O_2(g) \longrightarrow 4NO(g) \ + \ 6H_2O(g)$$

$4 \times 17$     $5 \times 32$     $4 \times 30$

= 68g      = 160g     = 120g

Here, 160 g of $O_2$ will react with $NH_3$ = 68 g

20g of $O_2$ will react with $NH_3$ = (68/160) × 20 = 8·5 g

Thus, $O_2$ is the limiting reagent, therefore, the calculations must be based upon the amount of $O_2$ taken and not on the amount of $NH_3$ taken.

From the equation,

160 g of $O_2$ produce NO = 120 g

20 g of $O_2$ will produce NO = (120/160) × 20 = 15 g

**8.26 Using the standard electrode potentials given in table 8.1 (NCERT), predict if the reaction between the following is feasible:**

**(a) Fe$^{3+}$(aq) and I$^-$ (aq)**

**(b) Ag$^+$(aq) and Cu(s)**

**(c) Fe$^{3+}$(aq) and Cu(s)**

**(d) Ag(s) and Fe$^{3+}$(aq)**

**(e) Br$_2$(aq) and Fe$^{2+}$(aq)**

**Ans.** A reaction is feasible if E.M.F. of the cell is + ve.

(a)   $E^o_{Fe^{3+}/Fe^{2+}} = + 0.77V$

$E^o_{I_2/2I^-} = + 0.54V$. Since we have to determine a reaction between Fe$^{3+}$ and I$^-$, the reaction should be

Fe$^{3+}$ + e$^-$ ⟶ Fe$^{2+}$ at cathode

2I$^-$ ⟶ I$_2$ + 2e$^-$ at anode .

We know that EMF = E$^o$$_{cathode}$ − E$^o$$_{anode}$ = 0.77 − 0.54 = 0.23 V as it is positive the reaction is feasible and the following reaction would occur.

2Fe$^{3+}$ + 2I$^-$ ⟶ 2Fe$^{2+}$ + I$_2$

(b)   $E^o_{Ag^+/Ag} = + 0.80V$ ;

$E^o_{Cu^{2+}/Cu} = + 0.34V$. Since we have to determine a reaction between Ag$^+$ and Cu, the reaction should be Ag$^+$ + e$^-$ ⟶ Ag at cathode

Cu ⟶ Cu$^{2+}$ + 2e$^-$ at anode.

We know that EMF = E$^o$$_{cathode}$ −E$^o$$_{anode}$ = 0.80 − 0.34 = 0.46 V as it is positive the reaction is feasible and the following reaction would occur.

2Ag$^+$ + Cu ⟶ 2Ag + Cu$^{2+}$

(c)   $E^o_{Fe^{3+}/Fe^{2+}} = + 0.77V$

$E^o_{Cu^{2+}/Cu} = + 0.34V$. Since, we have to determine a reaction between Fe$^{3+}$ and Cu, the reaction should be Fe$^{3+}$ + e$^-$ ⟶ Fe$^{2+}$ at cathode

Cu ⟶ Cu$^{2+}$ + 2e$^-$ at anode .

We know that EMF = E$^o$$_{cathode}$ − E$^o$$_{anode}$ = 0.77 − 0.34 = 0.43 V as it is positive the reaction is feasible and the following reaction would occur.

2Fe$^{3+}$ + Cu ⟶ 2Fe$^{2+}$ + Cu$^{2+}$

(d)   $E^o_{Fe^{3+}/Fe^{2+}} = + 0.77V$

$E^o_{Ag^+/Ag} = + 0.80V$. Since we have to determine a reaction between Fe$^{3+}$ and Ag, the reaction should be Fe$^{3+}$ + e$^-$ ⟶ Fe$^{2+}$ at cathode

Ag ⟶ Ag$^+$ + e$^-$ at anode

We know that EMF = E$^o$$_{cathode}$ − E$^o$$_{anode}$ = 0.77 − 0.80 = − 0.03 V as it is negative the reaction is not feasible.

(e) $E^o_{Fe^{3+}/Fe^{2+}} = + 0.77V$

$E^o_{Br_2/2Br^-} = + 1.09V$. Since, we have to determine a reaction between $Fe^{2+}$ and $Br_2$, the reaction should be $Fe^{2+} \longrightarrow Fe^{3+} + e^-$ at anode

$Br_2 + 2e^- \longrightarrow 2Br^-$ at cathode .

We know that $EMF = E^o_{cathode} - E^o_{anode}$ $= 1.09 - 0.77 = 0.32$ V as it is positive the reaction is feasible and the following reaction would occur.

$2Fe^{2+} + Br_2 \longrightarrow 2Fe^{3+} + 2Br^-$

**8.27 Predict the products of electrolysis in each of the following:**

**(i) An aqueous solution of $AgNO_3$ with silver electrodes**

**(ii) An aqueous solution of $AgNO_3$ with platinum electrodes**

**(iii) A dilute solution of $H_2SO_4$ with platinum electrodes**

**(iv) An aqueous solution of $CuCl_2$ with platinum electrodes**

**Ans.** (i) Electrolysis of aqueous solution of $AgNO_3$ with silver electrodes.

At cathode : $\quad Ag^+ + e^- \longrightarrow Ag$

At anode : $\quad Ag \longrightarrow Ag^+ + e^-$

(ii) Electrolysis of aqueous solution of $AgNO_3$ using platinum electrodes.

At cathode : $Ag^+ + e^- \longrightarrow Ag$ since reduction potential of Ag is higher than water.

At anode : $OH^- \longrightarrow OH + e^-$,

$4OH \longrightarrow 2H_2O + O_2$ since reduction potential of water is less than nitrate ion. Thus oxygen gas will be liberated.

(iii) Electrolysis of dil.$H_2SO_4$ with platinum electrode.

$H_2SO_4 \longrightarrow 2H^+(aq) + SO_4^{-2}(aq)$

$H_2O \longrightarrow H^+ + OH^-$

At cathode : $2H^+ + 2e^- \longrightarrow H_2$ hydogen gas will be liberated.

At anode: $OH^- \longrightarrow OH + e^-$,

$4OH \longrightarrow 2H_2O + O_2$

since reduction potential of water is less than sulphate ion. Thus oxygen gas will be liberated.

(iv) Electrolysis of $CuCl_2$ (aq) with platinum electrode.

$CuCl_2 \longrightarrow Cu^{2+} + 2Cl^-$

$H_2O \longrightarrow H^+ + OH^-$

At cathode : $Cu^{2+} + 2e^- \longrightarrow Cu$, copper will be liberated as copper has higher reduction potential than water.

At anode : $2Cl^- \longrightarrow Cl_2 + 2e^-$, chlorine will be discharged due to over–voltage.

**8.28 Arrange the following metals in the order in which they displace each other from the solution of their salts. Al, Cu, Fe, Mg, and Zn.**

**Ans.** This is based upon the relative positions of these metals in the activity series. The metal placed lower in the series can displace the metals occupying a higher position present as its salt. Based upon this, the correct order is: Mg, Al, Zn, Fe, Cu, Ag.

**8.29 Given the standard electrode potentials, $K^+/K = -2.93V$, $Ag^+/Ag = 0.80V$, $Hg^{2+}/Hg = 0.79V$, $Mg^{2+}/Mg = -2.37V$. $Cr^{3+}/Cr = -0.74V$ Arrange these metals in their increasing order of their reducing power.**

**Ans.** Lower the reduction potential, more easily the metal is oxidized and hence greater is the reducing power. Thus increasing order of reducing power will be

$$Ag < Hg < Cr < Mg < K.$$

**8.30 Depict the galvanic cell in which the reaction $Zn(s) + 2Ag^+(aq) \longrightarrow Zn^{2+}(aq) + 2Ag(s)$ takes place. Further show:**

**(i) which of the electrode is negatively charged,**

**(ii) the carriers of current in the cell, and**

**(iii) individual reaction at each electrode.**

**Ans.** $Zn\,|Zn^{2+}||Ag^+|Ag$; i.e. Zinc acts as anode and Ag acts as cathode.

(i) Zinc is negatively charged.

(ii) Electrons flow from Zn electrode to silver electrodes while current flows from silver electrodes toward zinc through wires fitted externally..

(iii) At cathode : $\quad Ag^+ + e^- \longrightarrow Ag$

At anode : $\quad Zn \longrightarrow Zn^{2+} + 2e^-$.

## SECTION B — PRACTICE QUESTIONS

### MULTIPLE CHOICE QUESTIONS

**1.** When a strip of metallic zinc is placed in an aqueous solution of copper nitrate the blue colour of the solution disappear due to formation of
(a) $Cu^{2+}$      (b) $Zn^{2+}$
(c) ZnS      (d) CuS

**2.** Oxidation numbers of chlorine atoms in $CaOCl_2$ are
(a) 0, 0      (b) $-1, -1$
(c) $-1, +1$      (d) None of these

**3.** The average oxidation state of sulphur in $Na_2S_4O_6$ is
(a) $+2.5$      (b) $+2$
(c) $+3.0$      (d) $+3.5$

**4.** In which of the following compounds oxygen has highest oxidation state and in which it has lowest oxidation state?
$OF_2$, $H_2O_2$, $KO_2$, $O_2F_2$
(a) Highest $= KO_2$, lowest $= H_2O_2$
(b) Highest $= OF_2$, lowest $= K_2O_2$
(c) Highest $= OF_2$, lowest $= KO_2$
(d) Highest $= KO_2$, lowest $= H_2O_2$

**5.** The average oxidation state of Fe in $Fe_3O_4$ is
(a) $+3$    (b) $8/3$    (c) $+6$    (d) $+2$

**6.** $2MnO_4^- + 5H_2O_2 + 6H^+ \rightarrow 2Z + 5O_2 + 8H_2O.$
In this reaction $Z$ is
(a) $Mn^{2+}$      (b) $Mn^{4+}$
(c) $MnO_2$      (d) Mn

**7.** Given :
$X\,Na_2HAsO_3 + Y\,NaBrO_3 + Z\,HCl \rightarrow$
$$NaBr + H_3AsO_4 + NaCl$$
The values of $X$, $Y$ and $Z$ in the above redox reaction are respectively
(a) 2, 1, 2      (b) 2, 1, 3
(c) 3, 1, 6      (d) 3, 1, 4

**8.** The values of $x$ and $y$ in the following redox reaction
$x\,Cl_2 + 6OH^- \longrightarrow ClO_3^- + y\,Cl^- + 3H_2O$ are
(a) $x = 5, y = 3$
(b) $x = 2, y = 4$
(c) $x = 3, y = 5$
(d) $x = 4, y = 2$

**9.** Consider the following reaction :
$$x\,MnO_4^- + y\,C_2O_4^{2-} + z\,H^+ \longrightarrow$$
$$x\,Mn^{2+} + 2y\,CO_2 + \frac{z}{2}H_2O$$
The value's of $x$, $y$ and $z$ in the reaction are, respectively:
(a) 5, 2 and 16      (b) 2, 5 and 8
(c) 2, 5 and 16      (d) 5, 2 and 8

**10.** For the reaction : $NH_3 + OCl^- \longrightarrow N_2H_4 + Cl^-$ in basic medium, the coefficients of $NH_3$, $OCl^-$ and $N_2H_4$ for the balanced equation are respectively
(a) 2, 2, 2      (b) 2, 2, 1
(c) 2, 1, 1      (d) 4, 4, 2

### ASSERTION & REASON QUESTIONS

**DIRECTIONS (Qs. 1-6) :** *Each of these questions contains an assertion followed by reason. Read them carefully and answer the question on the basis of following options. You have to select the one that best describes the two statements.*
(a) If both Assertion and Reason are correct and the Reason is a correct explanation of the Assertion.
(b) If both Assertion and Reason are correct but Reason is not a correct explanation of the Assertion.
(c) If the Assertion is correct but Reason is incorrect.
(d) If the Assertion is incorrect but the Reason is correct.

**1.** **Assertion :** Oxidation number of hydrogen in hydrogen containing compounds is always +1.
**Reason :** Hydrogen forms only covalent compounds.

**2.** **Assertion :** There is no way to convert $F^-$ to $F_2$ by chemical reaction.
**Reason :** This is because fluorine is the strongest oxidising agent.

**3.** **Assertion :** Redox reaction is also known as electron transfer reaction.
**Reason :** Because electrons are transferred from the reductant to the oxidant.

**4.** **Assertion :** $MnO_4^-$ act as self-indicator in titration.
**Reason :** The visible end point in this case is achieved.

**5.** **Assertion :** Iron liberates hydrogen form a solution of dilute hydrochloric acid.
**Reason :** Standard reduction potential of iron $\left( E^{\circ}_{Fe^{2+}/Fe} \right)$ is higher than hydrogen.

**6.** **Assertion :** If a iron wire is immersed in a blue colour solution of $CuSO_4$, the colour of the solution fades.
**Reason :** $E^{\circ}_{Fe^{2+}/Fe}$ is higher than $E^{\circ}_{Cu^{2+}/Cu}$.

### CASE/PASSAGE BASED QUESTIONS

**DIRECTIONS (Qs. 1-5) :** *Read the following case/passage and answer the questions.*

The electrochemical series helps to pick out substances that are good oxidizing agents and those which are good reducing agents. In an electrochemical series the species which are placed above hydrogen are more difficult to be reduced and their standard reduction potential values are negative. The Li : Li+ (aq) electrode has the least $E^0$ value and therefore, it is reduced with more difficulty. Therefore, Li+ cannot accept electrons easily and so loses electrons to behave as a reducing agent. Li is the strongest reducing agent.

The species which are easily reduced than hydrogen are placed below it in electrochemical series and their $E^0$ value is positive. The $F_2$ : 2F⁻(aq) electrode has the highest $E^0$ value and therefore, $F_2$ has the greatest tendency to get reduced, it is consequently the strongest oxidizing agent. In general, oxidizing agents have $+ E^0$ values.

Higher the positive value, stronger will be the oxidizing agent and reducing agents have $- E^0$ values, higher the negative value, stronger will be the reducing agent.

1. Given $E°$
   (i)   $Mg^{2+}/Mg(s)$, $E° = -2.36$
   (ii)  $Ag^+/Ag(s)$, $E° = 0.80$
   (iii) $Al^{3+}/Al(s)$, $E° = -1.66$
   (iv)  $Cu^{2+}/Cu(s)$, $E° = 0.52$
   Out of the above given elements which is the strongest oxidising agent and which is the weakest oxidising agent?
   (a) (iv) is the strong whereas (ii) is the weakest oxidising agent
   (b) (ii) is the strongest whereas (i) is the weakest oxidising agent
   (c) (i) is the strongest whereas (ii) is the weakest oxidising agent
   (d) (ii) is the strongest whereas (iii) is the weakest oxidising agent

2. Electrode potential data are given below :
   $$Fe^{+3}(aq) + e^- \longrightarrow Fe^{+2}(aq); \quad E° = +0.77 \text{ V}$$
   $$Al^{3+}(aq) + 3e^- \longrightarrow Al_{(s)}; \quad E° = -1.66 \text{ V}$$
   $$Br_2(aq) + 2e^- \longrightarrow 2Br^-(aq); \quad E° = +1.08V$$
   Based on the data, the reducing power of $Fe^{2+}$, Al and Br⁻ will increase in the order
   (a) $Br^- < Fe^{2+} < Al$
   (b) $Fe^{2+} < Al < Br^-$
   (c) $Al < Br^- < Fe^{2+}$
   (d) $Al < Fe^{2+} < Br^-$

3. Standard reduction potentials of the half reactions are given below :
   $$F_2(g) + 2e^- \longrightarrow 2F^-(aq); \quad E° = +2.85 \text{ V}$$
   $$Cl_2(g) + 2e^- \longrightarrow 2Cl^-(aq); \quad E° = +1.36 \text{ V}$$
   $$Br_2(l) + 2e^- \longrightarrow 2Br^-(aq); \quad E° = +1.06 \text{ V}$$
   $$I_2(s) + 2e^- \longrightarrow 2I^-(aq); \quad E° = +0.53 \text{ V}$$
   The strongest oxidising and reducing agents respectively are :
   (a) $F_2$ and I⁻          (b) $Br_2$ and Cl⁻
   (c) $Cl_2$ and Br⁻       (d) $Cl_2$ and $I_2$

4. Given :
   $$E°_{\frac{1}{2}Cl_2/Cl^-} = 1.36 \text{ V}, \quad E°_{Cr^{3+}/Cr} = -0.74 \text{ V},$$
   $$E°_{Cr_2O_7^{2-}/Cr^{3+}} = 1.33 \text{ V}, \quad E°_{MnO_4^-/Mn^{2+}} = 1.51 \text{ V}$$
   The correct order of reducing power of the species (Cr, $Cr^{3+}$, $Mn^{2+}$ and Cl⁻) will be
   (a) $Mn^{2+} < Cl^- < Cr^{3+} < Cr$
   (b) $Mn^{2+} < Cl^{3+} < Cl^- < Cr$
   (c) $Cr^{3+} < Cl^- < Mn^{2+} < Cr$
   (d) $Cr^{3+} < Cl^- < Cr < Mn^{2+}$

5. Which of the following statement(s) is/are correct ?
   (i)  A negative value of $E°$ means that the redox couple is a weaker reducing agent than the $H^+/H_2$ couple.
   (ii) A positive $E°$ means that the redox couple is weaker reducing agent than the $H^+/H_2$.
   Which of the following code is incorrect regarding above statements?
   (a) Only (i)                 (b) only (ii)
   (c) Both (i) and (ii)        (d) Neither (i) nor (ii)



1. Identify the oxidizing agent and the reducing agent in the following reaction
   $$H_2S + HNO_3 \longrightarrow NO + S + H_2O$$
2. In a binary compound of two non–metals, the positive oxidation state is assigned to which metal?
3. What is the oxidation number of C in $C_6H_6$ ?
4. What does negative electrode potential signify ?
5. Why is anode called oxidation electrode whereas cathode is called reduction electrode?
6. Fe decomposes steam while Cu does not, why?
7. What is meant by inert electrolyte used in salt bridge?
8. What is oxidation state of Cr in $CrO_5$ and why?
9. Find the oxidation number of Cl in HCl, HClO, $ClO^-_4$, and Ca(OCl)Cl.
10. Find the oxidation number of sulphur in $S_2O_7^2$.
11. Arrange the following in order of increasing oxidation number of iodine. $I_2$, HI, ICl.
12. Does the redox reaction in a cell go to completion?
13. What happens when a silver plate is dipped in copper sulphate solution?
14. What is electronation?
15. Is the valency of an element, same as its oxidation number?
16. At what concentration of $Cu^{2+}(aq)$, will its electrode potential become equal to its standard electrode potential?
17. Why can $CuSO_4$ solution not be stored in an iron vessel?
18. What is meant by oxidation potential of an electrode?
19. What is relationship between standard oxidation potential and standard reduction potential?
20. In the reaction given below which species is called a spectator ion and why?
    $$Zn(s) + Cu^{2+}(aq) + SO_4^{2-}(aq) \longrightarrow$$
    $$Zn^{2+}(aq) + Cu(s) + SO_4^{2-}(aq)$$

21. Out of zinc and copper vessel, which one will be more suitable to store 1M HCl solution?
22. A solution of silver nitrate solution was stirred with iron rod. Will it cause any change in concentration of silver and nitrate ions?

## SHORT ANSWER QUESTIONS

1. Show that oxidation and reduction go side by side by taking a suitable example.

2. $MnO_4^{2-}$ undergoes disproportionation reaction in acidic medium but $MnO_4^-$ does not. Give reason.

3. Nitric acid is an oxidising agent and reacts with $PbO$ but it does not react with $PbO_2$. Explain why?

4. Identify the oxidant and reductant in the following reactions:
   (i) $10H^+ (aq) + 4Zn(s) + NO^-_3(aq) \rightarrow$
   $$4Zn^{2+}(aq) + NH_4^+(aq) + 3H_2O(l)$$
   (ii) $I_2(g) + H_2S(g) \rightarrow 2HI(g) + S(s)$

5. Explain with example, the oxidation and reduction in terms of change in oxidation number.

6. Determine the oxidation number of elements marked with asterisk.

   (a) $[Cu(\overset{*}{N}H_3)_4](OH)_2$

   (b) $\overset{*}{O}_2 PtF_6$

   (c) $Rb_4Na[H\overset{*}{V}_{10}O_{28}]$

7. Which of the following are oxidizing agents and which are reducing agents? Justify your answer with half equations. $Br_2$, $Fe^{3+}$, $NO_3^-$, $I^-$, $Na$

8. Explain the difference between the electromotive force and the potential difference.

9. Zinc liberates hydrogen from dil.HCl while copper fails to do so. Why?

10. Balance the following equation using oxidation number method
    $HNO_3(aq) + Cu_2O(s) \rightarrow Cu(NO_3)_2 (aq) +$
    $$NO(g) + H_2O(l) + 2OH^-$$

11. Balance the following equation in acidic medium by both oxidation number and ion electron method and identify the oxidants and the reductants:
    $$H_2S (aq) + Cl_2(g) \rightarrow S(s) + Cl^- (aq)$$

12. Is it possible to store:
    (i) copper sulphate solution in a zinc vessel?
    (ii) copper sulphate solution in a nickel vessel?
    (iii) copper sulphate solution in a silver vessel?
    (iv) copper sulphate solution in a gold vessel?
    (Take help from electrochemical series)

13. Arrange A, B, C, D, E and H is order of increasing electrode potential in the electrochemical series:

$A + H_2SO_4 \rightarrow ASO_4 + H_2$
$ACl_2 + C \rightarrow CCl_2 + A$
$ECl_2 + C \rightarrow$ No reaction
$2BCl + D \rightarrow DCl_2 + 2B$
$H_2SO_4 + D \rightarrow$ No reaction

14. Can we find the reduction potential of a single electrode in an electrochemical cell?

15. With the help of the electro-chemical series, check the feasibility of the redox reaction:

$$Ni(s) + 2Ag^+ (aq) \longrightarrow Ni^{2+}(aq) + 2Ag(s)$$

## LONG ANSWER QUESTIONS

1. (i) Balance the following reaction by ion-electron method
   $K^+ MnO_4^- + H^+ Cl^- \longrightarrow$
   $$K^+Cl^- + Mn^{2+}(Cl^{-1})_2 + H_2O + Cl_2$$
   (ii) Balance the following reaction by oxidation number method
   $As_2S_5 + H^+ NO_3^-(conc.) \longrightarrow$
   $$H_3AsO_4 + 5H_2SO_4 + H_2O + NO_2$$

2. (i) Balance the following equations using half-reaction method in the acidic medium.

   (a) $Zn + NO_3^- \longrightarrow Zn^{2+} + NH_4^+$

   (b) $MnO_4^- + H_2C_2O_4 \longrightarrow Mn^{2+} + CO_2$

   (c) $Cr_2O_7^{2-} + Cl^- \longrightarrow Cr^{3+} + Cl_2$

   (ii) Balance the following redox reaction in basic medium using the half-reaction method:

   (a) $Mn^{2+} + ClO_3^- \rightarrow MnO_2 + ClO_2$

   (b) $Cl_2 \rightarrow Cl^- + ClO_3^-$

3. Calculate the oxidation number of the underlined atom in the following species:

   (i) $\underline{Zn} (OH)_4^{2-}$    (ii) $\underline{C}_6H_{12}O_6$

   (iii) $[\underline{Fe} (CN)_6]^{3-}$    (iv) $\underline{N}H_4^{+1}$

   (v) $K\underline{Br}O_4$

4. (i) What are the highest oxidation numbers of N, S and Cl?
   (ii) Is $Cr_2O_7^{2-} + H_2O \rightleftharpoons 2CrO_4^{2-} + 2H^+$ a redox reaction?
   (iii) Calculate oxidation number of:
   (a) Cr in $CrO_5$    (b) S in $H_2SO_5$
   (c) Fe in $Fe_3O_4$.

## SOLUTIONS

### *Multiple Choice Questions*

**1.** **(b)** Blue colour of the solution disappear due to formation of $Zn^{2+}$.

**2.** **(c)** $CaOCl_2$ or $Ca(OCl)Cl$ is the mixed salt of $Ca(OH)_2$ with HCl and HOCl.

**3.** **(a)** Let the oxidation state of S be $x$.

$$S_4O_6^{2-} \Rightarrow 4x - 12 = -2 \Rightarrow 4x = 10$$
$$\Rightarrow x = 10/4 = 2.5$$

**4.** **(c)** Oxidation number of oxygen in $OF_2 = +2$.

In $KO_2 = \dfrac{-1}{2}$

**5.** **(b)** Let the oxidation no. of Fe in $Fe_3O_4 = x$

$\therefore \quad 3x + (-2 \times 4) = 0$ or $3x = 8$

$\therefore \quad x = \dfrac{8}{3}$

**6.** **(a)**

$$2MnO_4^- + 5H_2O_2 + 6H^+ \to 2Mn^{2+} + 5O_2 + 8H_2O.$$

**7.** **(c)** On balancing the given reaction, we find
$$3Na_2HAsO_3 + NaBrO_3 + 6HCl \longrightarrow$$
$$6NaCl + 3H_3AsO_4 + NaBr$$

**8.** **(c)**

$$\overset{0}{x}Cl_2 + 6OH^- \longrightarrow \overset{+5}{Cl}O_3^- + y\overset{-1}{Cl}^- + 3H_2O$$

change in oxidation number $= -1$

on balancing the eq we get

$$3Cl_2 + 6OH^- \longrightarrow ClO_3^- + 5Cl^- + 3H_2O$$

**9.** **(c)** On balancing the given equations, we get

$$2MnO_4^- + 5C_2O_4^{2-} + 16H^+ \longrightarrow 2Mn^{2+} + 10CO_2 + 8H_2O$$

So, $x = 2, y = 5$ & $z = 16$

**10.** **(c)** The balanced equation :
$$2NH_3 + OCl^- \longrightarrow N_2H_4 + Cl^- + H_2O$$

### *Assertion & Reason Questions*

**1.** **(d)** Hydrogen when reacts with non-metals form covalent compounds where oxidation state of hydrogen is +1. Hydrogen when reacts with reactive metals form ionic compounds where oxidation state of hydrogen is –1. For example,

$$2Na + H_2 \longrightarrow \overset{+1\ -1}{Na\,H}$$

**2.** **(a)** The only way to achieve $F_2$ from $F^-$ is to oxidise electrolytically.

**3.** **(a)** Reduction is gain of electrons, oxidation is loss of electrons and electron transfer reactions are also called redox reactions.

**4.** **(a)** Potassium permanganate has a deep violet colour which is highly visible to the naked eye and when one titrates it and there is visible loss of colour. Thus, an indicator to observe the end point is not required.

**5.** **(c)** Fe is more reactive than hydrogen, therefore, liberate hydrogen from dilute hydrogen chloride.
$$Fe + 2HCl(dil) \longrightarrow FeCl_2 + H_2(g)$$

Standard reduction potential of iron $\left(E^{\circ}_{Fe^{2+}/Fe} = -ve\right)$ is

less than hydrogen $\left(E^{\circ}_{H^+/H_2} = 0\right)$.

**6.** **(c)** Iron is more reactive metal than copper metal, therefore, iron reacts with $CuSO_4$ (blue and form $FeSO_4$ light green), hence, blue colour of the solution fades away.
$$Fe(s) + CuSO_4(aq) \longrightarrow FeSO_4(aq) + Cu(s)$$

$E^{\circ}_{Fe^{2+}/Fe}$ is lower than $E^{\circ}_{Cu^{2+}/Cu}$.

### *Case/Passage Based Questions*

**1.** **(b)** Strongest oxidising agent = $Ag^+/Ag(s)$ ($E^{\circ}$ is max.)
Weakest oxidising agent = $Mg^{2+}/Mg(s)$ ($E^{\circ}$ is min.)

**2.** **(a)**

| Fe | Al | Br | |
|---|---|---|---|
| 0.77 | –1.66 | 1.08 | $E^{\circ}_{Red}$ |
| –0.77 | 1.66 | –1.08 | $E^{\circ}_{Oxi}$ |

Hence, reducing power $Al > Fe^{2+} > Br^-$

**3.** **(a)** Higher the value of reduction potential higher will be the oxidising power whereas the lower the value of reduction potential higher will be the reducing power.

**4.** **(a)** Lower the value of reduction potential higher will be reducing power hence the correct order will be
$Mn^{2+} < Cl^- < Cr^{3+} < Cr$

**5.** **(a)** By convention $E^{\circ}_{H^+/H_2} = 0$

### *Very Short Answer Questions*

**1.** $\overset{(-2)}{H_2S} + \overset{(+5)}{HNO_3} \longrightarrow \overset{(+2)}{NO} + \overset{0}{S} + H_2O$

In the reaction $HNO_3$ is an oxidizing agent since it itself gets reduced from +5 to +2. While $H_2S$ is an reducing agent since it itself gets oxidized from –2 to 0.

**2.** Less electronegative metal amongst the two.

**3.** It is –1.

**4.** It signifies that electrode has larger tendency to loose electrons than hydrogen electrode.

**5.** At anode, loss of electrons takes place, i.e., oxidation takes place whereas at cathode, gain of electrons takes place, i.e., reduction takes place therefore cathode is called reduction electrode and anode is called oxidation electrode.

**6.** Fe is more reactive than hydrogen, it has lower reduction potential than hydrogen whereas Cu has higher reduction potential than $H_2$.

**7.** Inert electrolyte is an electrolyte which does not react with any of the solution present in two half cells.

**8.** Cr has $+6$ oxidation state because it has 6 valence electrons, therefore, can form 6 covalent bonds

$$\underset{O}{\overset{O}{\underset{|}{\overset{\|}{Cr}}}}\begin{matrix}O\\ |\\ O\end{matrix}$$

**9.** Cl in HCl is $+1+x=0 \Rightarrow x=-1$
Cl in HClO is $+1+x-2=0 \Rightarrow x=+1$
Cl in $ClO_4^-$ is $x-8=-1 \Rightarrow x=+7$

In $Ca\!\!<^{OCl}_{Cl}$ there are two chlorine atoms, one of chlorine is in form of $Cl^-$ whose oxidation state is $-1$, other one is in form $ClO^-$ (hypochlorite ion) in which oxidation state is $+1$ ($x-2=-1 \Rightarrow x=+1$).
The average oxidation state of two Chlorine atoms in $CaOCl_2$ is 0 ($-1+1=0$) or $+2-2+2x=0$
$\Rightarrow x=0$

**10.** $+6, 2x-14=-2 \Rightarrow 2x=12$
$\Rightarrow x=+6$.

**11.** $I_2$ has oxidation number zero, in HI. iodine has oxidation number $-1$.
In ICl, iodine has oxidation number $+1$.
HI, $I_2$, ICl is order of increasing oxidation number.

**12.** No, it is not completed.

**13.** No change will be noticed.

**14.** The process in which gain of electrons takes place is called electronation.

**15.** No. they are not always same.

**16.** At 1 M concentration.

**17.** It is because $E°_{Fe^{2+}/Fe}=-0.44$ V which is lower than that of Cu
$E°_{cell}=E°_{Cu^{2+}/Cu}-E°_{Fe^{2+}/Fe}$
$=+0.34$ V $-(-0.44$ V$)=0.78$ V.
Since, $E°_{cell}=+$ ve, $\Delta G=-$ ve, i.e., reaction will take place. We cannot store $CuSO_4$ in an iron container.

**18.** Oxidation potential measures the tendency of an element or anion to lose electrons.

**19.** Both are equal in magnitude but opposite in sign.

**20.** $SO_4^{2-}$ ion is the spectator ion as it does not participate in the reaction.

**21.** Copper vessel.
[In electrochemical series copper lies above hydrogen].

**22.** Concentration of silver ions will change.

Short Answer Questions

**1.**
$$\overset{\text{loss of 2e}^-}{\overbrace{Zn(s)+Cu^{2+}(aq)\longrightarrow Zn^{2+}(aq)+Cu(s)}_{\text{gain of 2e}^-}}$$

In the above example, Zn has lost electrons to form $Zn^{2+}$ and therefore Zn is oxidised, releasing electrons, copper ion is reduced by gaining electrons from Zn.

**2.** In $MnO_4^-$, Mn is in the highest oxidation state i.e. $+7$. Therefore, it does not undergo disproportionation. $MnO_4^{2-}$ undergoes disproportionation as follows:
$$3MnO_4^{2-}+4H^+ \longrightarrow 2MnO_4^-+MnO_2+2H_2O$$

**3.** PbO is a basic oxide and simple acid base reaction takes place between PbO and $HNO_3$. On the other hand in $PbO_2$, lead is in $+4$ oxidation state and cannot be oxidised further. Therefore no reaction takes place. Thus, $PbO_2$ is passive, only PbO reacts with $HNO_3$.
$2PbO+4HNO_3 \rightarrow 2Pb(NO_3)_2+2H_2O$ (Acid base reaction)

**4.** (i) O.N. of Zn is changing from zero to $+2$ (increase in O.N.), therefore Zn is a reductant. O.N. of N is changing from $+5$ in $NO_3^-$ to $-3$ in $NH_4^+$. Therefore, $NO_3^-$ is oxidant.
(ii) $I_2$ is an oxidant as it is changing its O.N. from zero in $I_2$ to $-1$ in HI.
$H_2S$ is a reductant as S is changing its O.N. from $-2$ in $H_2S$ to zero in sulphur.

**5.** Oxidation is the part of an oxidation reduction reaction in which there is an increase in the oxidation number of an atom. Reduction is a reaction in which there is a decrease in the oxidation number of an atom.
Example:

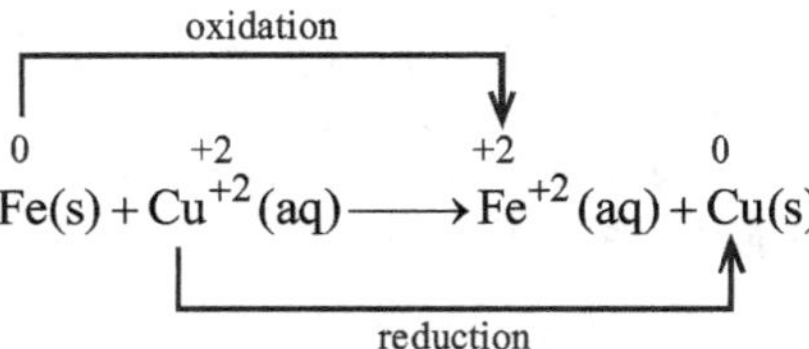
$$\overset{\text{oxidation}}{\overbrace{\underset{Fe(s)}{\overset{0}{}}+\underset{Cu^{+2}(aq)}{\overset{+2}{}}\longrightarrow \underset{Fe^{+2}(aq)}{\overset{+2}{}}+\underset{Cu(s)}{\overset{0}{}}}_{\text{reduction}}}$$

**6.** (a) $NH_3$ is a neutral ligand. Therefore oxidation state of nitrogen is same as in ammonia, i.e.,
$$x+3=0 \quad \text{or} \quad x=-3$$

(b) In this compound, platinum has maximum oxidation state of +4. Therefore oxidation state of $O_2$ is determined by taking $x$.

$2x + 4 - 6 = 0$    or    $x = +1$

(c) Let oxidation state of vanadium is $x$, then

$+ 4 + 1 + 1 + 10x - (28 \times 2) = 0$

or    $10x = 50$    or    $x = +5$

**7.** Oxidants : $Br_2$, $Fe^{3+}$, $NO_3^-$

$$Fe^{3+} + e \longrightarrow Fe^{2+}$$
$$N^{5+} + 2e \longrightarrow N^{3+}$$
$$Br_2 + 2e \longrightarrow 2Br^-$$

reductants : $I^-$, Na

$$Na \longrightarrow Na^+ + e$$
$$2I^- \longrightarrow I_2 + 2e$$

**8.**

| S.No. | E.M.F. | Potential Difference |
|---|---|---|
| 1 | It is the potential difference between the two electrodes when no current is flowing through the circuit i.e., in the open circuit. | It is difference between the electrode potentials of two electrodes when current is flowing through the circuit. |
| 2 | It is the maximum voltage obtainable from the cell. | It is always less than the emf of cell. |
| 3 | The work calculated from e.m.f. is the maximum work obtainable from the cell. | The work calculated from the potential difference is less than maximum work obtainable from the cell. |
| 4 | It is responsible for the flow of steady current through the circuit. | It is not responsible for the flow of steady current through the circuit. |

**9.** We know zinc has a negative reduction potential $Zn^{2+}/Zn = -0.76V$ and it lies below hydrogen in the electrochemical series. Therefore, the electron accepting tendency of zinc is less than that of hydrogen thus zinc can loose electrons to $H^+$ ions of the acid, as a result hydrogen gas is liberated.

Since copper has positive reduction potential value $(+0.34V)$ and it lies above hydrogen in the electrochemical series, therefore, it cannot lose electrons to $H^+$ and thus hydrogen is not liberated.

**10.** $HNO_3(aq) + Cu_2O(s) \rightarrow$

$$Cu(NO_3)(aq) + NO(g) + H_2O(l)$$

(i) The oxidation number of N changes from $+ 5$ in $HNO_3$ to $+ 2$ in NO.

(ii) The oxidation number of Cu changes from $+1$ in $Cu_2O$ to $+ 2$ in $Cu(NO_3)$

(iii) Electron balance diagrams can be written as follows

$$N^{+5} + 3e^- \rightarrow N^{+2} \qquad ...(1)$$
$$Cu^{+1} \rightarrow Cu^{+2} + e^- \qquad ...(2)$$

(iv) In order that the number of electrons lost shall be equal the number gained, multiply equation (1) by 2 and (2) by 6

$$2N^{+5} + 6e^- \rightarrow 2N^{+2}$$
$$6Cu^{+1} \rightarrow 6Cu^{+2} + 6e^-$$

Hence, the coefficients of $HNO_3$ and of NO are 2 and those of $Cu_2O$ is 3 and $Cu(NO_3)_2$ is 6. Part of the skeleton equation can now be written as

$$2HNO_3 + 3Cu_2O \rightarrow 2NO + 6Cu(NO_3)_2$$

The two atoms of H form one $H_2O$ on the right.

$$2HNO_3 + 3Cu_2O \rightarrow 2NO + 6Cu(NO_3) + H_2O$$

Although the N atoms that change oxidation number have been balanced, other N atoms are present as $NO_3^-$ ions in $6Cu(NO_3)_2$, For this reason, we add $12HNO_3$ to the $2HNO_3$ already on the left side and then balance $H_2O$ molecule. The complete balanced equation is

$$14HNO_3(aq) + 3Cu_2O(s) \rightarrow$$
$$6Cu(NO_3)_2(aq) + 2NO(s) + 7H_2O(l)$$

**11.** $H_2S(aq) + Cl_2(g) \rightarrow S(s) + Cl^-(aq)$

Oxidation number method

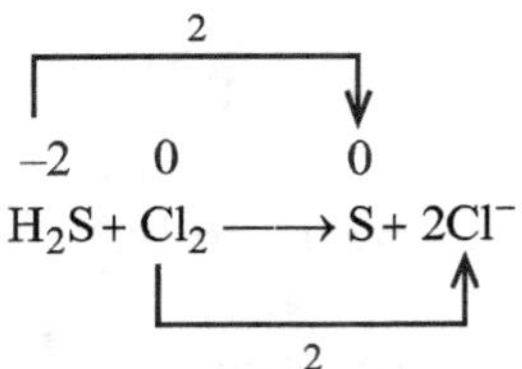


Net reaction is $H_2S + Cl_2 \rightarrow S + 2Cl^- + 2H^+$

Ion-electron method

Oxidation half-reaction:

$$H_2S \rightarrow S + 2H^+ + 2e^-$$

Reduction half-reaction:

$$Cl_2 + 2e^- \rightarrow 2Cl^-$$

Net reaction : $H_2S + Cl_2 \rightarrow S + 2Cl^- + 2H^+$

Oxidant : $Cl_2$ ; Reductant : $H_2S$

**12.** (i) No, zinc will displace copper from $CuSO_4$ solution because

$$E^o_{Zn^{2+}/Zn} < E^o_{Cu^{2+}/Cu}$$

(ii) No, copper sulphate solution can not be stored in nickel vessel.

(iii) Yes, copper sulphate solution can be stored in silver vessel as

$E^o_{Cu^{2+}/Cu} < E^o_{Ag^+/Ag}$. Silver will not displace copper from $CuSO_4$ solution.

(iv) Yes, gold vessel can easily store $CuSO_4$ solution.

**13.** $E < C < A < H < D < B$.

**14.** It is not possible to calculate the reduction potential of a single electrode in an electrochemical cell. Because, a single electrode constitutes a half cell, which can't work independently.

**15.** It is not possible to calculate the reduction potential of a single electrode in an electrochemical cell. Because, a single electrode constitutes a half cell, which can't work independently.

### *Long Answer Questions*

**1.**   (i)   $MnO_4^- + Cl^- \longrightarrow Mn^{2+} + Cl_2$

The half–reactions are : $\overset{+7}{MnO_4^-} \longrightarrow \overset{+2}{Mn^{2+}}$,

$MnO_4^- \longrightarrow Mn^{2+} + 4H_2O$

$8H^+ + MnO_4^- \longrightarrow Mn^{2+} + 4H_2O$

Balance total charge with adding electron on higher charge side . As the higher charge is +7 and it decreases to +2 thus add $5e^-$ to +7 side of reaction so that the total charge for this half reaction is balanced.

$5e^- + 8H^+ + MnO_4^{-1} \longrightarrow Mn^{2+} + 4H_2O$     ... (i)

$2Cl^- \longrightarrow Cl_2$

$2Cl^- \longrightarrow Cl_2 + 2e^-$     ... (ii)

Now combine equation (i) and (ii). The electrons should get cancelled out thus multiply eqn (i) by 2 and eqn (ii) by 5

$10e^- + 16H^+ + 2MnO_4^- \longrightarrow 2Mn^{2+} + 8H_2O$

$10Cl^- \longrightarrow 5Cl_2 + 10e^-$

Combining the half–reactions:

$10Cl^- + 16H^+ + 2MnO_4^- \longrightarrow 2Mn^{2+} + 8H_2O + 5Cl_2$

or    $16HCl + 2KMnO_4 \longrightarrow 2MnCl_2 + 8H_2O + 5Cl_2 + 2KCl$

(ii)

Net Loss in O. N of 'N' $(5 \rightarrow 4) = 4 - 5 = -1$

$$\overset{-2}{As_2S_5} + \underset{+5}{HNO_3} \longrightarrow H_3AsO_4 + 5H_2SO_4 + H_2O + \overset{+6}{\underset{+4}{NO_2}} \quad ...(i)$$

Net gain in O.N. of 'S' $(-2 \rightarrow +6) = 6 - (-2) = +8$

Here O.N. of 'N' decreases from + 5 to +4 while that of 'S' increases in from – 2 to +6. Since there are five 'S' atoms in reactants as well as in products and one 'N' atom in reactants as well as products in eqn(i), now balance increase / decrease in O.N. The total increase in O.N. of S is + 8 i.e. by a factor 40 since there are 5 'S' atoms and decrease in O.N. of N is –1. Multiply $As_2S_5$ by 1 and $HNO_3^-$ by 40 we get

Balance the elements which change oxidation state:

$As_2S_5 + 40HNO_3 \longrightarrow$
$$H_3AsO_4 + 5H_2SO_4 + H_2O + 40NO_2$$

Balance atoms other than "O" and "H".

$As_2S_5 + 40\, HNO_3 \longrightarrow$
$$2H_3AsO_4 + 5H_2SO_4 + H_2O + 40NO_2$$

Balance the 'O' and 'H' atoms. Since there are 120 'O' atoms on the reactant side and 109 'O' atoms on the product side add $11H_2O$ on the product side to balance the equation. There are 40 'H' atoms on reactant side and 18 'H' atoms on the product side initially but after adding 11 $H_2O$ the 'H' atoms get balanced.

$As_2S_5 + 40HNO_3 \longrightarrow$
$$2H_3AsO_4 + 5H_2SO_4 + 12H_2O + 40NO_2$$

**2.**   (i)

(a)
$$\overset{0}{Zn} + \overset{+5}{NO_3^-} \longrightarrow \overset{+2}{Zn^{+2}} + \overset{-3}{NH_4^+}$$

oxidation (top) / reduction (bottom)

Oxidation half-reaction:

$[Zn \rightarrow Zn^{+2} + 2e^-] \times 4$

Reduction half-reaction:

$NO_3^- + 10H^+ + 8e^- \rightarrow NH_4^+ + 3H_2O$

Net balanced redox reaction:

$4Zn + NO_3^- + 10H^+ \rightarrow 4Zn^{+2} + NH_4^+ + 3H_2O$

(b)
$$\overset{+7}{MnO_4^-} + \overset{+2}{H_2C_2O_4} \rightarrow \overset{+2}{Mn^{+2}} + \overset{+4}{CO_2}$$

reduction (top) / oxidation (bottom)

Oxidation half-reaction:

$[H_2C_2O_4 \rightarrow 2CO_2 + 2H^+ + 2e^-] \times 5$

Reduction half-reaction:

$[MnO_4^- + 8H^+ + 5e^- \rightarrow Mn^{+2} + 4H_2O] \times 2$

Net balanced redox reaction:

$5H_2C_2O_4 + 2MnO_4^- + 6H^+ \rightarrow$
$$10CO_2 + 2Mn^{+2} + 8H_2O$$

(c)
$$\overset{+6}{Cr_2O_7^{-2}} + \overset{-1}{Cl^-} \longrightarrow \overset{+3}{Cr^{+3}} + \overset{0}{Cl_2}$$

reduction (top) / oxidation (bottom)

Oxidation half-reaction:

$\{2Cl^- \rightarrow Cl_2 + 2e^-\} \times 3$

Reduction half-reaction:

$Cr_2O_7^{-2} + 14H^+ + 6e^- \rightarrow 2Cr^{+3} + 7H_2O$

Net balanced redox reaction :

$Cr_2O_7^{-2} + 6Cl^- + 14H^+ \rightarrow 2Cr^{+3} + Cl_2 + 7H_2O$

(ii)

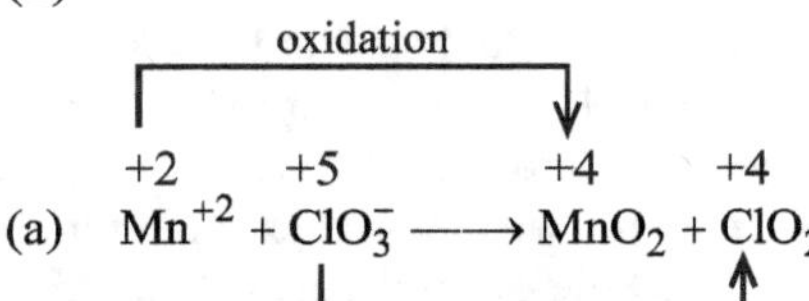

(a) $Mn^{+2} + ClO_3^- \longrightarrow MnO_2 + ClO_2$

Oxidation half-reaction:

$Mn^{+2} + 4OH^- \rightarrow MnO_2 + 2e^- + 2H_2O$

Reduction half-reaction:

$\{ClO_3^- + H_2O + e^- \rightarrow ClO_2 + 2OH^-\} \times 2$

Net balanced redox reaction:

$2ClO_3^- + Mn^{+2} \rightarrow 2ClO_2 + MnO_2$

(b) $Cl_2 \longrightarrow Cl^- + ClO_3^-$

Oxidation half-reaction:

$Cl_2 + 12OH^- \rightarrow 2ClO_3^- + 10e^- + 6H_2O$

Reduction half-reaction:

$\{Cl_2 + 2e^- \rightarrow 2Cl^-\} \times 5$

Net balanced redox reaction:

$6Cl_2 + 12OH^- \rightarrow 2ClO_3^- + 10Cl^- + 6H_2O$

**OR**

$3Cl_2 + 6OH^- \rightarrow ClO_3^- + 5Cl^- 3H_2O$

3. (i) $Zn(OH)_4^{-2} = x_{Zn} + 4x_{OH} = -2$

$= x_{Zn} + 4(-1) = -2$

$\therefore \quad x_{Zn} = +2$

(ii) $C_6H_{12}O_6 = 6x_C + 12(1) + 6(-2) = 0$

$\therefore \quad x_C = 0$

(iii) $[Fe(CN)_6]^{-3} = x_{Fe} + 6(-1) = -3$

$x_{Fe} = +3$

(iv) $NH_4^+ = x_N + 4(1) = +1$

$\therefore \quad x_N = -3$

(v) $K_{BrO4} = +1 + x_{Br} + 4(-2) = 0$

$\therefore \quad x_{Br} = +7$

4. (i) The highest oxidation numbers for N, S and Cl are +5, +6 and +7 respectively.

(ii) The reaction

$Cr_2O_7^{2-} + H_2O \rightleftharpoons 2CrO_4^{2-}$

$+2H^+$ cannot be regarded as a redox reaction because the O. No. of 'Cr' in $Cr_2O_7^{2-}$ and $CrO_4^{2-}$ is same $(+6)$.

(iii) (a)

Let the oxidation number of Cr in the compound be x.

$\therefore \quad x + 1 \times (-2) + 4(-1) = 0$

(For = 0)     (For peroxide linked oxygen atom)

$\Rightarrow x - 2 - 4 = 0$

$\Rightarrow x = +6$

(b) $H_2SO_5$

Let the oxidation number of S in the compound be x

$\therefore \quad 2(+1) + x + 3(-2) + 2(-1) = 0$

$\Rightarrow x = +6$

(c) Let the oxidation no. of Fe in $Fe_3O_4 = x$

$\therefore \quad 3x + (-2 \times 4) = 0 \text{ or } 3x = 8$

$\therefore \quad x = \dfrac{8}{3}$

<br>

## SECTION C — NCERT EXEMPLAR QUESTIONS

### MULTIPLE CHOICE QUESTIONS

1. Which of the following is not an example of redox reaction?
   (a) $CuO + H_2 \longrightarrow Cu + H_2O$
   (b) $Fe_2O_3 + 3CO \longrightarrow 2Fe + 3CO_2$
   (c) $2K + F_2 \longrightarrow 2KF$
   (d) $BaCl_2 + H_2SO_4 \longrightarrow BaSO_4 + 2HCl$

   Redox reactions are those reactions which involve change in oxidation number of the reactants.

2. The more positive the value of $E^\ominus$, the greater is the tendency of the species to get reduced. Using the standard electrode potential of redox couples given below find out which of the following is the strongest oxidising agent. $E^\ominus$ values : $Fe^{3+}/Fe^{2+} = +0.77V$ ; $I_2(s)/I^- = +0.54$; $Cu^{2+}/Cu = +0.34$; $Ag^+/Ag = 0.80 V$
   (a) $Fe^{3+}$            (b) $I_2(s)$
   (c) $Cu^{2+}$           (d) $Ag^+$

3. The largest oxidation number exhibited by an element depends on its outer electronic configuration. With which of the following outer electronic configurations the element will exhibit largest oxidation number ?
   (a) $3d^1 4s^2$        (b) $3d^2 4s^2$
   (c) $3d^5 4s^1$        (d) $3d^5 4s^2$

**4.** Which of the following arrangements represent increasing oxidation number of the central atom?

(a) $CrO_2^-, ClO_3^-, CrO_4^{2-}, MnO_4^-$

(b) $ClO_3^-, CrO_4^{2-}, MnO_4^-, CrO_2^-$

(c) $CrO_2^-, ClO_3^-, MnO_4^-, CrO_4^{2-}$

(d) $CrO_4^{2-}, MnO_4^-, CrO_2^-, ClO_3^-$

**5.** Identify disproportionation reaction

(a) $CH_4 + 2O_2 \longrightarrow CO_2 + 2H_2O$

(b) $CH_4 + 4Cl_2 \longrightarrow CCl_4 + 4HCl$

(c) $2F_2 + 2OH^- \longrightarrow 2F^- + OF_2 + H_2O$

(d) $2NO_2 + 2OH^- \longrightarrow NO_2^- + NO_3^- + H_2O$

## ASSERTION & REASON QUESTIONS

**DIRECTIONS (Qs. 1-3) :** *Each of these questions contains an assertion followed by reason. Read them carefully and answer the question on the basis of following options. You have to select the one that best describes the two statements.*

(a) If both Assertion and Reason are correct and the Reason is a correct explanation of the Assertion.

(b) If both Assertion and Reason are correct but Reason is not a correct explanation of the Assertion.

(c) If the Assertion is correct but Reason is incorrect.

(d) If the Assertion is incorrect but the Reason is correct.

**1. Assertion:** In the reaction between potassium permanganate and potassium iodide, permanganate ions act as oxidising agent.

**Reason :** Oxidation state of manganese changes from +2 to +7 during the reaction.

**2. Assertion :** The decomposition of hydrogen peroxide to form water and oxygen is an example of disproportionation reaction.

**Reason :** The oxygen of peroxide is in $-1$ oxidation state and it is converted to zero oxidation state in $O_2$ and $-2$ oxidation state in $H_2O$.

**3. Assertion :** Redox couple is the combination of oxidised and reduced form of a substance involved in an oxidation or reduction half cell.

**Reason :** In the representation $E^-_{Fe^{3+}/Fe^{2+}}$ and $E^-_{Cu^{2+}/Cu}$. $Fe^{3+}/Fe^{2+}$ and $Cu^{2+}/Cu$ are redox couples.

## SHORT ANSWER QUESTIONS

**1.** Nitric acid is an oxidising agent and reacts with PbO but it does not react with $PbO_2$. Explain why?

**2.** Calculate the oxidation number of each sulphur atom in the following compounds:

(a) $Na_2S_2O_3$      (b) $Na_2S_4O_6$

(c) $Na_2SO_3$      (d) $Na_2SO_4$

**3.** Balance the following equations by the oxidation number method.

(i) $Fe^{2+} + H^+ + Cr_2O_7^{2-} \rightarrow Cr^{3+} + Fe^{3+} + H_2O$

(ii) $I_2 + NO_3^- \rightarrow NO_2 + IO_3^-$

(iii) $I_2 + S_2O_3^{2-} \rightarrow I^- + S_4O_5^{2-}$

(iv) $MnO_2 + C_2O_4^{2-} \rightarrow Mn^{2-} + CO_2$

**4.** Calculate the oxidation number of phosphorus in the following species.

(a) $HPO_3^{2-}$ and $PO_4^{2-}$

**5.** Calculate the oxidation number of phosphorus in the following species.

(a) $Na_2S_2O_3$      (b) $Na_2S_4O_6$

(c) $Na_2SO_3$      (d) $Na_2SO_4$

## LONG ANSWER QUESTIONS

**1.** Based on standard electrode potential values, suggest which of the following reactions would take place? (Consult the book for E\degree value).

(i) $Cu + Zn^{2+} \rightarrow Cu^{2+} + Zn$

(ii) $Mg + Fe^{2+} \rightarrow Mg^{2+} + Fe$

(iii) $Br^{2+} 2Cl^- \rightarrow Cl^2 + 2B^{r-}$

(iv) $Fe + Cd^{2+} \rightarrow Cd + Fe^{2+}$

**2.** Which method can be used to find out the strength of reducant\oxidant in a solution? Explain with an example.

## SOLUTIONS

### *Multiple Choice Questions*

**1. (d)** Following are the examples of redox reaction

(a) $CuO + H_2 \longrightarrow Cu + H_2O$ (Red / Oxi)

(b) $Fe_2O_3 + 3CO \longrightarrow 2Fe + 3CO_2$ (Oxi / Red)

(c) $2K + F_2 \longrightarrow 2KF$ (Red / Oxi)

Option (d) is not an example of redox reaction as there is no change in oxidation number of any of the reactants.

**2. (d)** Since the redox couple $Ag^+/Ag$ has the highest positive value of $E^o$ *i.e.*, 0.80 V, therefore, $Ag^+$ is the strongest oxidising agent.

**3. (d)** Highest oxidation number of any transition element is the sum of $(n-1)$ $d$-electrons and $ns$ electrons. Hence, large the number of electrons in the $3d$-orbitals, higher is the maximum oxidation number.

**4. (a)** Calculating the oxidation number of central atom in the given species.
$$\overset{+3}{Cr}O_2^-, \overset{+5}{Cl}O_3^-, \overset{+6}{Cr}O_4^{2-}, \overset{+7}{Mn}O_4^-$$

**5. (d)** Reactions in which the same substance undergo oxidation as well as reduction are called disproportionation reactions. Writing the O.N. of each element above its symbol in the given reactions.

In reaction (d), N is both oxidised as well as reduced since the O. N. of N increases from +4 in $NO_2$ to +5 in $NO_3^-$ and decreases from +4 in $NO_2$ to +3 in $NO_2^-$.

$$\overset{+4}{N}O_2 + 2OH^- \longrightarrow \overset{+3}{N}O_2^- + \overset{+5}{N}O_3^- + H_2O$$

(oxidation / reduction)

### Assertion & Reason Questions

1. **(c)** $2KMnO_4 + 2KI \longrightarrow 2MnO_2 + I_2 + 4KO$

   (reduction / oxidation)

   Permagnate ion acts as an oxidising agent hence undergo reduction and O.S changes from +7 to +4. While iodine undergo oxidation from −1 to 0.

2. **(a)** $2H_2O_2(aq) \longrightarrow 2H_2O(l) + O_2(g)$

   (reduction / oxidation)

3. **(b)** A redox couple is defined as pair of compounds or elements having together the oxidised and reduced forms of its and taking part in an oxidation or reduction half reactions.

### Short Answer Questions

1. PbO is a basic oxide and simple acid base reaction takes place between PbO and $HNO_3$. On the other hand in $PbO_2$ lead is in +4 oxidation state and cannot be oxidised further. Therefore no reaction takes place. Thus, $PbO_2$ is passive, only PbO reacts with $HNO_3$.

   $2PbO + 4HNO_3 \longrightarrow 2Pb(NO_3)_2 + 2H_2O$
   (Acid base reaction)

2. (a) +2      (b) +5, 0, 0, +5
   (c) +4      (d) +6

3. (i) $Fe^{2+} + H^+ + \overset{+6}{Cr_2}O_7^{2-} \rightarrow 2Cr^{3+} + Fe^{3+} + H_2O$

   (decrease by 6 / increase by + 1)

   To make increase and decrease equal

   $6Fe^{2+} + 14H^- + Cr_2O_7^{2-} \rightarrow 2Cr^{3+} + 6Fe^{3+} + 7H_2O$

   (ii) $\overset{0}{I_2} + \overset{+5}{N}O_3^- \rightarrow \overset{+4}{N}O_2 + 2\overset{+5}{I}O_3^-$

   (decrease by 1 / increase by 10)

   $I_2 + 10NO_3^- + 4H_2 \rightarrow 10NO_2 + 2IO_3^- + 8OH^-$

   (iii) $I_2 + S_2O_3^{-2} \rightarrow I^- + S_4O_6^{2-}$

   $I_2 + 2S_2O_3^{-2} \rightarrow 2I^- + S_4O_6^{2-}$

   (iv) $MnO_2 + C_2O_3^{2-} \rightarrow Mn^{2-} + CO_2$

   $MnO_2 + C_2O_4^{2-} + \Delta H^- \rightarrow Mn^{2-} + 2CO_2 + 2H_2O$

4. $HPO_3^{2-}$ x = +3 ; $PO_4^{2-}$ x = +5
5. $Na_2S_2O_3$ x = +2; $Na_2S_4O_6$ x = +5
   $Na_2SO_3$ x = +4; $Na_2SO_4$ x = +6

### Long Answer Questions

1. (i) $Cu + Zn^{2+} \rightarrow Cu^{2+} + Zn$
   Here Cu undergoes oxidation so it acts as anode and Zn acts as the cathode. So from the table. For example E° anode = −0.76 V
   For anode E° anode = 0.52 V
   E° cell = −0.24 V
   As the EMF of the cell is negative the given reaction will not occur spontaneously if they were to form a cell placed as electrodes.
   (ii) $Mg + Fe^{2+} \rightarrow Mg^{2+} + Fe$
   Similarly, we can say that Mg undergoes oxidation and Fe undergoes reduction,
   E°cathode = −0.44 V
   E°anode = −2.36 V
   E°cell = +1.92 V
   Positive EMF implies that the reaction will give out energy and attain stability, thus it will occur spontaneously. So the given redox reaction will occur.
   (iii) $Br_2 + 2Cl^- \rightarrow Cl_2 + 2Br^-$
   Here Br undergoes reduction thus acting as cathode and Cl acting as the anode.
   For cathode E° cathode = 1.09 V
   For anode E° cathode = 1.36 V
   E°cell = −0.25
   The negative potential prevents easy reaction, so the redox reaction will not occur.
   (iv) $Fe + Cd^{2+} \rightarrow Cd + Fe^{2+}$
   Fe is the cathode and Cd is the anode
   For cathode E° cathode = −0.44V
   For anode E°anode = −0.40 V
   E°cell = −0.04V
   The negative potential prevents easy reaction, so the redox reaction will not occur.

2. Strength of a reductant (reducing agent) or oxidant (oxidising agent) can be found out by measuring the relative electrode potential when it's connected in a solution using a cell.
   For example, $Fe^{3+}/Fe$ is the element we want to test with the Standard Hydrogen electrode (SHE). The half-cell reaction for Fe and H are given below:
   $H^+ + e^- \rightarrow H_2$ ; $E° = 0.0V$
   $Fe^{3+} + e^- \rightarrow Fe^{2+}$ ; $E° = 0.77V$
   When any element needs to be evaluated it is placed as an electrode with SHE. The amount of emf it generates in the cell can be considered as the potential of the element.
   E°cell = 0 − 0.77
   E°cell = 0.77
   The above assumed configuration of Fe being anode can be reversed and hence strength Fe as a reductant can be established. Hence the strength of an oxidant can be determined.

# 9 Hydrogen



# NCERT EXERCISES

**9.1 Justify the position of hydrogen in the periodic table on the basis of its electronic configuration.**

**Ans.** Hydrogen is the first element in the periodic table but its position is ambiguous because of following reason:

(i) Since it has 1 valence electron in its s-subshell, it is placed in group-1 along with alkali metals.

(ii) It also shows properties of halogens of group-17 by picking up electron showing electronegative character like them.

(iii) In some yet another properties, hydrogen differs both from alkali metals and halogens.

**9.2 Write the names of isotopes of hydrogen. What is the mass ratio of these isotopes?**

**Ans.** Protium $_1H^1$, Deuterium $_1H^2$ or D, Tritium $_1H^3$ or T. The mass ratios of protium: deuterium: tritium = 1: 2: 3

**9.3 Why does hydrogen occur in a diatomic form rather than in a monoatomic form under normal conditions ?**

**Ans.** Hydrogen atom has only one electron and thus has one electron less than the stable inert gas configuration of helium. Therefore, to achieve stable inert gas configuration of helium, it shares its single electron with electron of other hydrogen atom to form a stable diatomic molecule.

**9.4 How can the production of dihydrogen, obtained from 'coal gasification', be increased?**

**Ans.** The process of producing syngas or synthesis gas from coal is called 'coal gasification'.

$$\underset{\text{Coal}}{C(s)} + \underset{\text{Steam}}{H_2O(g)} \xrightarrow[\text{Ni}]{1270\text{ K}} \underbrace{CO(g) + H_2(g)}_{\text{Syngas}}$$

The production of hydrogen can be increased by reacting carbon monoxide of syngas with steam in presence of iron chromate as catalyst at 673 K.

$$CO(g) + H_2O(g) \xrightarrow[\text{FeCrO}_4]{673\text{K}} CO_2(g) + H_2(g)$$

The $CO_2$ thus produced is removed by scrubbing with a solution of sodium arsenite.

**9.5 Describe the bulk preparation of dihydrogen by electrolytic method. What is the role of an electrolyte in this process ?**

**Ans.** Dihydrogen of high purity is usually obtained by electrolysis of water in presence of small amount of acid or base. During electrolysis, dihydrogen is collected at cathode while dioxygen is collected at anode.

At cathode: $H^+ + e^- \longrightarrow H$

$$H + H \longrightarrow H_2$$

At anode: $OH^- \longrightarrow OH + e^-$

$$4OH \longrightarrow 2H_2O + O_2$$

The role of the electrolyte is to make water conducting since pure water is bad conductor of electricity and is weakly ionized.

**9.6 Complete the following reactions:**

(i) $H_2(g) + M_mO_o\ (s) \xrightarrow{\Delta}$

(ii) $CO\ (g) + H_2\ (g) \xrightarrow[\text{Catalyst}]{\Delta}$

(iii) $C_3H_8(g) + 3H_2O(g) \xrightarrow[\text{Catalyst}]{\Delta}$

(iv) $Zn(s) + NaOH(aq) \xrightarrow{\text{heat}}$

**Ans.** (i) $H_2(g) + M_mO_o(s) \xrightarrow{\Delta} mM(s) + o\ H_2O\ (\ell)$

(ii) $CO(g) + 2H_2(g) \xrightarrow[\text{Catalyst}]{\Delta} \underset{\text{methanol}}{CH_3OH(\ell)}$

(iii) $C_3H_8(g) + 3H_2O(g) \xrightarrow[\text{1270K}]{\text{Ni}} 3CO(g) + 7H_2(g)$

(iv) $Zn(s) + 2NaOH(aq) \xrightarrow{\text{heat}} \underset{\text{Sodium zincate}}{Na_2ZnO_2(aq)} + H_2(g)$

**9.7** **Discuss the consequences of high enthalpy of H—H bond in terms of chemical reactivity of dihydrogen.**

**Ans.** Due to high enthalpy of H-H bond, hydrogen is quite unreactive at room temperature. However, at high temperatures or in presence of catalysts, it combines with many metals and non-metals to form hydrides.

**9.8** **What do you understand by**
(i) **electron-deficient,**
(ii) **electron-precise, and**
(iii) **electron-rich compounds of hydrogen ?**
**Provide justification with suitable examples.**

**Ans.** Molecular hydride is classified on the basis of the presence of the bonds and total number of electrons in their Lewis structures as:
1. Electron-deficient hydrides
2. Electron-precise hydrides
3. Electron-rich hydrides
1. An electron-deficient hydride has very less electrons, less than that required for representing its conventional Lewis structure.

E.g. $BH_3$, $AIH_3$ etc.

They exist in diameric forms such as $B_2H_6$, $AI_2H_6$ to they make up their deficiency.

In $B_2H_6$, there are 6 bonds in all, out of which only 4 bonds are regular 2 centered 2 electron bonds. The remaining 2 bonds are 3 centered 2 electron bonds i.e., 2 electrons are shared by 3 atoms.

2. An electron-precise hydride has a sufficient number of electrons to be represented to form covalent bond.

E.g. $CH_4$, $SiH_4$ etc.

In this compound 4 regular bonds are formed where 2 electrons are shared by 2 atoms.

3. An electron-rich hydride compounds contains excess valence electrons to form covalent bonds.

E.g. $NH_3$, $PH_3$

There are 3 regular bonds in all with a lone pair of electrons on the nitrogen atom.

**9.9** **What characteristics do you expect from an electron-deficient hydride with respect to its structure and chemical reactions.**

**Ans.** Electron deficient hydrides do not have sufficient electrons to form normal covalent bonds. Therefore, to make up this deficiency they generally exist in polymeric forms such as $B_2H_6$, $B_4H_{10}$, $(AlH_3)n$, etc. Further to make up this deficiency of electrons, they react with many metals, non-metals and their compounds. Hence, electron-deficient hydrides are very reactive as shown below:

$$B_2H_6 \text{ (g)} + 3O_2 \text{ (g)} \longrightarrow B_2O_3 \text{ (s)} + 3 H_2O \text{ (g)}$$

$$2NaH(s) + B_2H_6(g) \xrightarrow{\text{Diethyl ether}} 2Na^+[BH_4]^-\text{(s)}$$
Sod. borohydride

Being electron deficient compounds, they act as **Lewis acids** and thus form complex with Lewis bases.

For example.

$$B_2H_6 + 2NMe_3 \longrightarrow [2H_3B \longleftarrow NMe_3]$$
Diborane    Trimethylamine    Complex

$$B_2H_6 + 2CO \longrightarrow [2H_3B \longleftarrow CO]$$
Carbon       Complex<br>monoxide

**9.10** **Do you expect the carbon hydrides of the type $(C_nH_{2n+2})$ to act as Lewis acid or base ? Justify your answer.**

**Ans.** Carbon hydride of the type $(C_nH_{2n+2})$ are electron-precise hydrides. In other words, they have exact numbers of electrons required to form covalent bonds. Therefore, they do not have any tendency to either gain or lose electrons and hence they neither act as Lewis acids or Lewis bases.

**9.11** **What do you understand by the term" non-stoichiometric hydrides" ? Do you expect this type of the hydrides to be formed by alkali metals ? Justify your answer.**

**Ans.** Hydrides which are deficient in hydrogen and in which the ratio of the metal to hydrogen is fractional are called non-stoichiometric hydrides. Furthermore, this fractional ratio is not fixed but varies with the temperature and the pressure. These type of hydrides are formed by *d*-and *f*-block elements. In these hydrides, the hydrogen atoms occupy holes in the metal lattice. Usually some holes always remain unoccupied and hence these metals form non-stoichiometric hydrides. Since alkali metals are highly reducing, they transfer their lone electron to the H atom, thereby forming $H^-$ ions. In other words, alkali metal hydrides are ionic in which $H^-$ ions occupy holes in the lattice. Since a hydride ion is formed by complete transfer of an electron, therefore, the ratio of metal to hydrogen is always fixed and hence alkali metals form only stoichiometric hydrides. In other words, alkali metals do not form non-stoichiometric hydrides.

**9.12** **How do you expect the metallic hydrides to be useful for hydrogen storage ? Explain**

**Ans.** In metallic hydrides, hydrogen is absorbed as H-atoms. Due to the inclusion of H atoms, the metal lattice expands and thus becomes less stable. Therefore, when the metallic hydride is heated, it decomposes to form hydrogen and very finely divided metal.

The hydrogen thus evolved can be used as a fuel. Thus, transition metals or their alloys can be used to store and transport hydrogen to be used as a fuel. This is called hydrogen economy.

**9.13 How does the atomic hydrogen or oxy-hydrogen torch function for cutting and welding purposes? Explain.**

**Ans.** Atomic hydrogen is produced when molecular hydrogen is passed through an electric arc struck between tungsten electrodes (3773 – 4273 K).

$$H_2 \xrightarrow[\text{3773 – 4273K}]{\text{Electric arc,}} 2H; \Delta H = 435.9 \text{ kJ mol}^{-1}$$

The lifetime of atomic hydrogen is 0. 3 sec. and hence it immediately gets converted into the molecular form liberating a large amount of energy which is used for cutting and welding purposes in form of atomic hydrogen torch.

**9.14 Among $NH_3$, $H_2O$ and HF, which would you expect to have highest magnitude of hydrogen bonding and why?**

**Ans.** Due to greater electronegativity of N, O and F over H. all these molecules undergo intermolecular H-bonding.

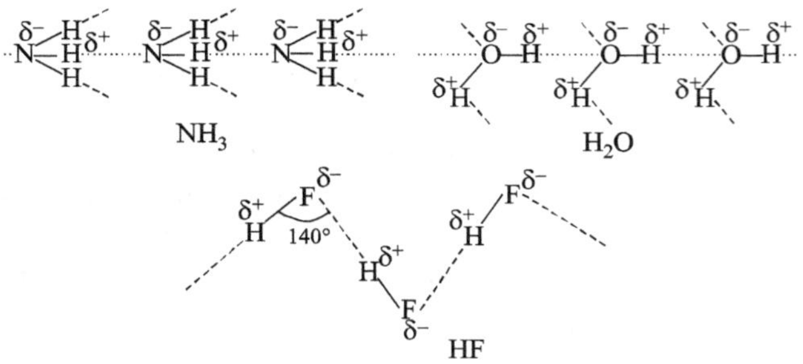

However, since electronegativity of F is highest, therefore, magnitude of the +ve charge on hydrogen and –ve charge on F is the highest and hence electrostatic attraction or the H-bonding is strongest in H-F.

**9.15 Saline hydrides are known to react with water violently producing fire: Can $CO_2$, a well known fire extinguisher, be used in this case ? Explain.**

**Ans.** Saline hydrides (such as NaH, $CaH_2$, etc. ), react with water violently to form the corresponding metal hydroxides with the evolution of dihydrogen.

$$NaH (s) + H_2O (\ell) \longrightarrow NaOH (aq) + H_2 (g)$$
$$CaH_2(s) + 2 H_2O (\ell) \longrightarrow Ca(OH)_2(aq) + 2 H_2(g)$$

The reactions are so much exothermic that the evolved $H_2$ catches fire. The fire so produced cannot be extinguished by $CO_2$ because it gets reduced by the hot metal hydride to form sodium formate.

$$NaH + CO_2 \longrightarrow HCOONa.$$

However, sand is useful since it is a highly stable solid.

**9.16 Arrange the following:**

**(i) $CaH_2$, $BeH_2$ and $TiH_2$ in order of increasing electrical conductance.**

**(ii) LiH, NaH and CsH in order of increasing ionic character.**

**(iii) H–H, D–D and F–F in order of increasing bond dissociation enthalpy.**

**(iv) NaH, $MgH_2$ and $H_2O$ in order of increasing reducing property.**

**Ans. (i)** $BeH_2$ is a covalent hydride, therefore, it does not conduct electricity at all. $CaH_2$ conduct electricity in the fused state while $TiH_2$ conduct electricity at room temperature. Thus, the order of increasing electrical conductance is: $BeH_2 < CaH_2 < TiH_2$.

**(ii)** Electronegativity decreases down the group from Li to Cs, therefore, the ionic character of their hydrides also increases in the same order, i. e., LiH < NaH < CsH.

**(iii)** Due to smaller size of D as compared to H, D-D bond has the highest bond dissociation enthalpy followed by H-H. However, due to repulsions between lone pairs of F and the bond pair, F-F bond dissociation enthalpy is the minimum. Thus the bond dissociation enthalpy increases in the order:

$$F-F < H-H < D-D.$$

**(iv)** Ionic hydrides are powerful reducing agents. Both $MgH_2$ and $H_2O$ are covalent hydrides but the bond dissociation energy of $H_2O$ is much higher than that of $MgH_2$. Therefore, the reducing character increases in the order: $H_2O < MgH_2 < NaH$

**9.17 Compare the structures of $H_2O$ and $H_2O_2$.**

**Ans.** In water, O is, $sp^3$-hybridized. Due to stronger lone pair-lone pair repulsions than bond pair-bond pair repulsions, the HOH bond angle decreases from 109. 5° to 104. 5°. Thus, water is a bent molecule. $H_2O_2$ has a non-planar structure. The two oxygen atoms are linked to each other by a single covalent bond (i.e., peroxide bond) and each oxygen is further linked to a hydrogen atom by a single covalent bond. The two O-H bonds are, however, in different planes. The dihedral angle between the two planes being 111. 5° in the gas phase. Thus, the structure of $H_2O_2$ is like that of an open book.

**9.18 What do you understand by the term 'auto-protolysis' of water? What is its significance?**

**Ans.** Auto-protolysis (self-ionization) of water is a chemical reaction in which 2 water molecules react to produce a hydroxide ion (OH) and a hydronium ion ($H_2O$). The reaction involved can be represented as :

$$H_2O(1) + H_2O(1) \leftrightarrow H_3O^+(aq) + OH^-(aq)$$

Auto-protolysis of water indicates its amphoteric nature i.e., its ability to act as an acid as well as a base. The acid-base reaction can be written as :

$$H_2O(1) + H_2O(1) \leftrightarrow H_3O^+(aq) + OH^-(aq)$$

**9.19 Consider the reaction of water with $F_2$ and suggest, in terms of oxidation and reduction which species are oxidised/reduced ?**

**Ans.** $2 F_2 (g) + 2H_2O (\ell) \longrightarrow O_2 (g) + 4 H^+ (aq)^+ 4 F^- (aq)$
  (Oxidant)        (Reductant)

  or   $3F_2(g) + 3H_2O(\ell) \longrightarrow O_3(g) + 6H^+(aq) + 6 F^-(aq)$
  (Oxidant)  (Reductant)

In these reactions, water acts as a reducing agent and hence itself gets oxidised to either $O_2$ or $O_3$. On the other hand, $F_2$ acts as an oxidising agent and hence itself gets to reduced $F^-$ion.

**9.20 Complete the following chemical reactions:**

  **(i)   PbS (s) + $H_2O_2$ (aq) $\longrightarrow$**

  **(ii)   $MnO_4^-$ (aq) + $H_2O_2$ (aq) $\longrightarrow$**

  **(iii)   CaO (s) + $H_2O$ (g) $\longrightarrow$**

  **(iv)   $AlCl_3$ (g) + $H_2O$ ($\ell$) $\longrightarrow$**

  **(v)   $Ca_3N_2$(s) + $H_2O$ ($\ell$) $\longrightarrow$**

  **Classify the above into (a) hydrolysis, (b) redox and (c) hydration reactions.**

**Ans.** (i)   $PbS (s) + 4 H_2O_2(aq) \longrightarrow PbSO_4(s) + 4H_2O (\ell)$

  (ii)   $2MnO_4^- (aq) + 5H_2O_2(\ell) + 6H^+(aq) \longrightarrow$
         $2Mn^{2+} (aq) + 8 H_2O (\ell) + 5 O_2 (g)$

  (iii)   $CaO(s) + H_2O(g) \longrightarrow Ca(OH)_2(aq)$

  (iv)   $AlCl_3 (s) + 3 H_2O (\ell) \longrightarrow$
         $Al(OH)_3 (s) + 3 HCl (aq)$

  (v)   $Ca_3N_2 (s) + 6 H_2O (\ell) \longrightarrow$
        $3 Ca(OH)_2 (aq) + 2 NH_3 (g)$

  (a)   Hydrolysis reactions : (iii), (iv), and (v).

  (b)   Redox reactions : (i) and (ii).

**9.21 Describe the structure of the common form of ice.**

**Ans.** Generally, ice is the crystalline form of water. It visibles in a hexagonal form if it is crystallized at atmosphereic pressure. When the temperature is very low, it condenses to cubic form.

**3-D structure of ice :**

It has hydrogen bonding and highly ordered structure. Each of the oxygen atoms is surrounded tetrahedrally by 4 other oxygen atoms at a distance of 276 pm. the structure of ice also contains wide holes that can hold molecules of particular sizes.

**9.22 What causes the temporary and permanent hardness of water?**

**Ans.** Due to the presence of soluble salts of magnesium and calcium in the form of chlorides in water, hardness remains permanent in water.

Due to the presence of soluble salts of calcium and magnesium in the form of hydrogen carbonates in water hardness remains temporary in water.

**9.23 Discuss the principle and method of softening of hard water by synthetic ion-exchange resins.**

**Ans.** Synthetic ion exchange resins are of two types : Cation exchange resins and anion exchange resins. **Cation exchange resins** are either carboxylic acids or sulphonic acids having the general formula, $R$-COOH or $R-SO_2OH$ where $R$ represents the giant hydrocarbon framework. These resins exchange their $H^+$ ions with $Ca^{2+}$ and $Mg^{2+}$ ions present in hard water.

$2R-COO^-H^+ + CaCl_2 \longrightarrow$
(Cation exchange        (From hard
resin)                  water)

$(RCOO)_2 Ca + 2H^+ + 2Cl^-$
(Exhausted resin)

$2R-SO_2O^-H^+ + MgSO_4 \longrightarrow$
(Cation exchange      (From hard
resin)                water)

$(RSO_2O)_2 Mg + 2H^+ + SO_4^{2-}$
(Exhausted resin)

**Anion exchange resins,** on the other hand, are substituted ammonium hydroxides having the general formula, $R - NH_3^+ OH$ where $R$ denotes the giant hydrocarbon framework. These resins exchange their $OH^-$ions with $Cl^-$ and $SO_4^{2-}$ ions present in hard water.

$R-NH_3^+OH^- + Cl^{-1} \longrightarrow R-\overset{+}{N}H_3Cl^- + OH^-$
Anion exchange    (From hard              (Exhausted resin)
resin)            water)

$2R-NH_3^+OH^- + SO_4^{2-} \longrightarrow$
(Anion exchange      (From hard
resin)               water)

$(R-\overset{+}{N}H_3)_2 SO_4 + 2OH^-$
(Exhausted resin)

Similarly, the $H^+$ ions produced from cation exchange resins and $OH^-$ ions produced from anion exchange resins combine to form $H_2O$.

The hard water is first passed through cation exchange resin and then through anion exchange resin. The resulting water is freed from both cations and anions and hence is called demineralised water or deionised water and is as good as distilled water.

**9.24 Write chemical reactions to show the amphoteric nature of water?**

**Ans.** The amphoteric nature of water can be described on the basis of the following reactions.

**1. Reaction with $H_2S$**

The reaction takes place as :

$$H_2O(l) + H_2S(aq) \rightleftharpoons H_3O^+(aq) + HS^-(aq)$$

In the forward reaction, $H_2O(l)$ accepts a proton from $H_2S(aq)$. Therefore, it acts as a Bronsted base.

**2. Reaction with $NH_3$**

The reaction takes place as :

$$H_2O(l) + NH_3(aq) \rightleftharpoons OH^-(aq) + NH_4^+(aq)$$

In the forward reaction, $H_2O(l)$ denotes its proton to $NH_3(aq)$. Therefore, it acts as Bronsted acid.

**3. Self-ionization of water**

2 water molecules reacts in this reaction as :

$$H_2O(l) + H_2O(l) \rightleftharpoons H_3O^+(aq) + OH^-(aq)$$

**9.25 Write chemical reactions to justify that hydrogen peroxide can function as an oxidising as well as reducing agent.**

**Ans.** Hydrogen peroxide acts as an oxidizing agent as well as reducing agent in both alkaline medium and acidic medium.

The reactino which are involved in oxidizing actions are:

(i) $Mn^{2+} + H_2O_2 \longrightarrow Mn^{4+} + 2OH^-$

(ii) $2Fe^{2+} + H_2O_2 \longrightarrow 2Fe^{3+} + 2OH^-$

(iii) $2Fe^{2+} + 2H^+ + H_2O_2 \longrightarrow 2Fe^{3+} + 2H_2O$

(iv) $PbS + 4H_2O_2 \longrightarrow PbSO_4 + 4H_2O$

The reaction which are involved in reduction actions are:

(i) $I_2 + H_2O_2 + 2OH^- \longrightarrow 2I^- + 2H_2O + O_2$

(ii) $2MnO_4^- + 3H_2O_2 \longrightarrow$
$$2MnO_2 + 3O_2 + 2H_2O + 2OH^-$$

(iii) $2MnO_4^- + 6H^+ + 5H_2O_2 \longrightarrow 2Mn^{2+} + 8H_2O + 5O_2$

(iv) $HOCl + H_2O_2 \longrightarrow H_3O^+ + Cl^- + O_2$

**9.26 What is meant by 'demineralised water' and how can it be obtained?**

**Ans.** Water which is free from all cations and anions is called demineralised water. It is obtained by passing hard water first through cation exchange resin and then through anion exchange resin.

**9.27 Is demineralised or distilled water useful for drinking purposes? If not, how can it be made useful?**

**Ans.** Demineralised or distilled water is not useful for drinking purposes since it does not contain even useful minerals. Therefore, to make it useful for drinking purposes, useful minerals in proper amounts should be added.

**9.28 Describe the usefulness of water in biosphere and biological systems.**

**Ans.** Water is essential for all forms of life. It constitutes about 65-70% of the body weight of animals and plants. In comparison to other liquids, water has a high specific heat, thermal conductivity, surface tension, dipole moment and dielectric constant, etc. These properties allow water to play a key role in biosphere. The high heat of vaporization and heat capacity are responsible for moderation of the climate and body temperature of living beings. It is an excellent solvent for transportation of minerals and other nutrients for plant and animal metabolism. Water is also required for photosynthesis in plants which releases $O_2$ into the atmosphere.

**9.29 What properties of water make it useful as a solvent? What types of compound can it (i) dissolve (ii) hydrolyse?**

**Ans.** Water has a high dielectric constant (79.39) and high dipole moment (1.84 D). Because of these properties, water dissolves most of the inorganic (ionic) compounds and many covalent compounds. That is why water is called an universal solvent whereas ionic compounds dissolve in water due to ion-dipole interaction or solvation of ions, covalent compounds such as alcohols, amines, urea, glucose, sugar, etc. dissolve in water due to H-bonding.

Water can hydrolyze many oxides (metallic or non-metallic), hydrides, carbides, nitrides, phosphides and other salts. In these reaction, $H^+$ and $OH^-$ ions of water interact with anions and cations respectively leading to the formation of an acid or a base or both as shown below:

$$CaO\,(s) + H_2O\,(\ell) \longrightarrow Ca(OH)_2\,(aq)$$
$$SO_2\,(g) + H_2O\,(\ell) \longrightarrow H_2SO_3(aq)$$
$$CaH_2\,(s) + 2\,H_2O\,(\ell) \longrightarrow Ca\,(OH)_2\,(aq) + 2\,H_2\,(g)$$
$$CaC_2\,(s) + 2\,H_2O(s) \longrightarrow Ca(OH)_2(aq) + \underset{\text{Acetylene}}{HC \equiv CH\,(g)}$$

**9.30 Knowing the properties of $H_2O$ and $D_2O$, do you think that $D_2O$ can be used for drinking purposes?**

**Ans.** Heavy water is injurious to human beings, plants and animals since it slows down the rates of reactions occurring in them. Thus, heavy water does not support life so well as does ordinary water.

**9.31 What is the difference between the terms 'hydrolysis' and 'hydration'?**

**Ans.** Interaction of $H^+$ and $OH^-$ ions of $H_2O$ with the anion and the cation of a salt respectively to give the original acid and the original base is called hydrolysis. For example,

$$\underset{\text{Salt}}{Na_2CO_3} + 2H_2O \longrightarrow \underset{\text{Base}}{2NaOH} + \underset{\text{Acid}}{H_2CO_3}$$

Hydration, on the other hand, means addition of $H_2O$ to ions or molecules to form hydrated ions or hydrated salts. For example,

$$\underset{\text{Colourless}}{CuSO_4} + 5H_2O \longrightarrow \underset{\text{Blue}}{CuSO_4 . 5H_2O}$$

**9.32 How can saline hydrides remove traces of water from organic compounds?**

**Ans.** Saline hydrides (i.e., $NaH$, $CaH_2$, etc.) react with water forming their corresponding metal hydroxides with the liberation of $H_2$ gas. Thus, traces of water present in organic solvents can be easily removed by distilling them over saline hydrides when $H_2$ escapes into the atmosphere, metal hydroxide is left in the flask while dry organic solvent distils over.

Alternatively, organic compounds containing traces of water can be dried by placing them in a desiccator containing saline hydrides at the bottom for a few hours or preferably overnight.

**9.33 What do you expect the nature of hydrides is, if formed by elements of atomic numbers 15, 19, 23 and 44 with dihydrogen ? Compare their behaviour towards water.**

**Ans.** (i)  Element with $Z = 15$ is a non-metal (i.e. P) and hence forms covalent hydride (i.e. $PH_3$).

(ii)  Element with $Z = 19$ is an alkali metal (i.e. K) and hence forms saline or ionic hydride ($K^+ H^-$).

(iii)  Element with atomic number $Z = 23$ is a transition metal (i.e. V) of group 3 and hence forms a metallic or interstitial hydride (i.e. $VH_{1.6}$)

(iv)  Element with $Z = 44$ is a transition metal (i.e. Ru) of group 8 and hence does not form any hydride.

**Behaviour towards water :** only ionic hydrides react with water evolving $H_2$ gas. Thus,

$$2 \text{ KH (s)} + 2 H_2O \text{ (s)} \longrightarrow 2 \text{ KOH (aq)} + 2 H_2 \text{ (g)}$$

**9.34 Do you expect different products in solution when aluminium (III) chloride and potassium chloride treated separately with (i) normal water (ii) acidified water, and (iii) alkaline water ? Write equations wherever necessary.**

**Ans.** KCl is the salt of a strong acid and a strong base. It does not undergo hydrolysis in normal water. It just dissociates to give $K^+$ (aq) and $Cl^-$(aq) ion.

$$KCl(s) \xrightarrow{\text{Water}} K^+ (aq) + Cl^- (aq)$$

Since the aqueous solution of KCl is neutral, therefore, in acidified water or in alkaline water, the ions do not react further and stay as such.

$AlCl_3$, on the other hand, is a salt of a weak base $Al(OH)_3$ and a strong acid (HCl). Therefore, in normal water, it undergoes hydrolysis to form, weak base $Al(OH)_3$ and a strong acid $H^+$ and $Cl^-$ ions.

$$AlCl_3 \text{ (s)} + 3 H_2O \text{ ($\ell$)} \longrightarrow$$
$$Al(OH)_3(s) + 3H^+ (aq) + 3 \, Cl^- (aq)$$

In acidic water, the $H^+$ ions react with $Al(OH)_3$ to form $Al^{3+}$ (aq) ions and $H_2O$. Thus, in acidic water, $AlCl_3$ exists as $Al^{3+}$(aq) and $Cl^-$(aq) ions.

$$AlCl_3 \text{ (s)} \xrightarrow{\text{Acidified water}} Al^{3+} (aq) + 3Cl^- (aq)$$

In alkaline water, $Al(OH)_3$ reacts to form soluble tetrahydroxoaluminate complex or meta-aluminate ion, i.e.,

$$Al(OH)_3 \text{ (s)} + OH^- (aq) \longrightarrow [Al(OH)_4]^- (aq)$$
Tetrahydroxoaluminate

or  $AlO_2^- \text{ (aq)}^+ \; + \; 2 H_2O \text{ ($\ell$)}$
meta-aluminate ion

The complete equation may be written as:

$$AlCl_3 \text{ (s)} \xrightarrow[\text{water}]{\text{Alkaline}} Al[(OH)_4]^- + 3 Cl^- \text{ (aq)}$$
$$\downarrow$$
$$AlO_2^- \text{ (aq)} + 2 H_2O(\ell) + 3 Cl^- \text{ (aq)}$$

**9.35 How does $H_2O_2$ behave as a bleaching agent ?**

**Ans.** The bleaching action of $H_2O_2$ is due to the nascent oxygen which it liberates on decomposition.

$$H_2O_2 \longrightarrow H_2O + O$$

The nascent oxygen combines with colouring matter which, in turn, gets oxidized. Thus, the bleaching action of $H_2O_2$ is due to the oxidation of colouring matter by nascent oxygen. It is used for the bleaching of delicate materials like ivory, feather, silk, wool, etc.

**9.36 What do you understand by the terms ?**

**(i)  hydrogen economy**

**(ii)  hydrogenation**

**(iii)  'syngas'**

**(iv)  water-gas shift reaction**

**(v)  fuel-cell**

**Ans.** (i)  **Hydrogen economy:** The proposal to use hydrogen as a fuel in industry, power plants and also in homes and motor vehicles is called hydrogen economy. The basic principle of hydrogen economy is the production, transportation and storage of energy in the form of liquid or gaseous dihydrogen.

(ii)  **Hydrogenation** means addition of hydrogen across double and triple bonds to form saturated compounds. The vegetables oils such as soyabean oil, cotton seed oil, groundnut oil, etc. are called polyunsaturated oils since they contain many $C = C$ bonds. When these oils are exposed to air for prolonged periods, the double bonds present in them undergo oxidation, i.e., develop unpleasant taste. To avoid this, double bonds are hydrogenated. For this purpose, dihydrogen is bubbled through edible oils in presence of finely divided nickel at 473 K when the oils are converted with solid fats.

$$\text{Vegatable oil} + H_2 \xrightarrow{\text{Ni, 473K}} \text{Vegetable Ghee}$$

This process is called hydrogenation or hardening of oils and is used in the manufacture of vegetable ghee like Dalda, Gagan, Rath, etc. from vegetable oils. It may, however, be noted that hydrogenation reduces the number of double bonds but does not completely eliminate them.

(iii)  **Syngas:** Syngas is a mixture of carbon monoxide and dihydrogen. Since the mixture of the two gases is used for the synthesis of methanol, it is called syngas snthesis gas, or water gas.

Syngas is produced on the action of steam with hydrocarbons or coke at a high temperature in the presence of a catalyst.

$$CnH_{2n+2} + nH_2O \longrightarrow nCO + (3n + 1)H_2$$

E.g.

$$CH_4(g) + H_2O(g) \longrightarrow CO(g) + 3H_2(g)$$

(iv) **Water-gas shift reaction :** It is a reaction of carbon monoxide of syngas mixture with steam in the presence of a catalyst as :

$$CO(g) + H_2O(g) \longrightarrow CO_2(g) + H_2(g)$$

This reaction is used to increase the yield of dihydrogen obtained from the coal gasification reaction as :

$$C(s) + H_2O(g) \longrightarrow CO(g) + H_2(g)$$

(v) **Fuel cell.** Fuel cell is a device which converts the energy produced during the combustion of a fuel directly into electrical energy. Dihydrogen is used in hydrogen–oxygen fuel cells for generating electrical energy. It has many advantages over the conventional fossil fuels. It does not produce any pollution, releases more amount of energy per unit mass of fuel as compared to gasoline and other fuels.

---

## SECTION B — PRACTICE QUESTIONS 

### MULTIPLE CHOICE QUESTIONS

1. Which of the following statements is correct ?
   (a) Hydrogen has same IP as alkali metals.
   (b) Hydrogen has same electronegativity as halogens.
   (c) It has oxidation number of $-1$ and $+1$.
   (d) It will not be liberated at anode.

2. Number of neutrons in three isotopes of hydrogen, protium, deuterium and tritium respectively is
   (a) 0, 1, 2     (b) 1, 1,1
   (c) 2, 1, 0     (d) 2, 0, 1

3. In Bosch's process which gas is utilised for the production of hydrogen gas ?
   (a) Producer gas     (b) Water gas
   (c) Coal gas     (d) None of these

4. Which of the following statements is correct?
   (a) Production of syn gas from coal is called coal gasification.
   (b) $CO(g) + H_2O(g) \xrightarrow[\text{catalyst}]{673K} CO_2(g) + H_2(g)$ represents water gas shift reaction.
   (c) $CO_2$ formed in water gas shift reaction is removed by scrubbing with sodium zincate solution.
   (d) Both (a) and (b)

5. Which one of the following pairs of substances will not produce hydrogen when reacted together?
   (a) Copper and conc. nitric acid
   (b) Ethanol and metallic sodium
   (c) Magnesium and steam
   (d) Phenol and metallic sodium

6. Hydrogen will not reduce
   (a) heated cupric oxide
   (d) heated ferric oxide
   (c) heated stannic oxide
   (d) heated aluminium oxide

7. Which of the following groups of ions makes the water hard?
   (a) Sodium and bicarbonate
   (b) Magnesium and chloride
   (c) Potassium and sulphate
   (d) Ammonium and chloride

8. Water possesses a high dielectric constant, therefore :
   (a) it always contains ions
   (b) it is a universal solvent
   (c) can dissolve covalent compounds
   (d) can conduct electricity

9. Permanent hardness of water can be removed by adding Calgon $(NaPO_3)_n$. This is an example of
   (a) Adsorption     (b) Exchange of ion
   (c) Precipitation     (d) None

10. In lab $H_2O_2$ is prepared by
    (a) Cold $H_2SO_4 + BaO_2$
    (b) $HCl + BaO_2$
    (c) Conc. $H_2SO_4 + Na_2O_2$
    (d) $H_2 + O_2$

11. Which of the following is the true structure of $H_2O_2$ ?
    (a) $H - O - O - H$
    (b) $H{\diagdown}O{-}O{\diagdown}H$
    (c) $\overset{H}{\underset{H}{\diagup}}\overset{+}{O} - \bar{O}$
    (d) $\overset{H}{\underset{H}{\diagup}}O \leftarrow O$

12. When $H_2O_2$ is oxidised the product is
    (a) $OH^-$  (b) $O_2$  (c) $O^{2-}$  (d) $HO_2^-$

### ASSERTION & REASON QUESTIONS

**DIRECTIONS (Qs. 1-6) :** *Each of these questions contains an assertion followed by reason. Read them carefully and answer the question on the basis of following options. You have to select the one that best describes the two statements.*
(a) If both Assertion and Reason are correct and the Reason is a correct explanation of the Assertion.
(b) If both Assertion and Reason are correct but Reason is not a correct explanation of the Assertion.
(c) If the Assertion is correct but Reason is incorrect.
(d) If the Assertion is incorrect but the Reason is correct.

1. **Assertion:** Dihydrogen is inert at room temperature.
   **Reason:** The H–H bond dissociation enthalpy is the highest for a single bond between two atoms of any elements.

2.  **Assertion:** *Ortho-* and *para*-dihydrogen are nuclear spin isomers.
    **Reason:** They have the same nuclear spins.
3.  **Assertion:** Hydrogen is known as future fuel.
    **Reason:** It does not produce any pollution and releases greater energy per unit mass of fuel.
4.  **Assertion:** Water dissolves many ionic compound and some covalent compounds.
    **Reason:** $H_2O$ has high dielectric constant, it has a very strong hydrating tendency.
5.  **Assertion:** Calculated amount of lime is added to hard water to remove temporary hardness.
    **Reason:** Because lime reacts with hard water and precipitates out $CaCO_3$ which can be filtered off.
6.  **Assertion:** Hard water enhances the efficiency of the boiler.
    **Reason:** Soft water deposits the salt in the form of scales.

## CASE/PASSAGE BASED QUESTIONS

**DIRECTIONS (Qs. 1-5) :** *Read the following case/passage and answer the questions.*

The most important covalent peroxide is hydrogen peroxide, $H_2O_2$. When pure, this syrupy, viscous liquid has a pale blue colour, although it appears almost colourless. Many of its physical properties resemble those of water. It has a larger liquid range than water, melting at $-0.43°$ C and boiling at $150.2°$ C, and it has a higher density (1.44 grams per cubic centimetre at $25°$ C) than water. The dielectric constant of pure $H_2O_2$ is, like that of water, quite high $-70.7$ at $25°$ C compared with a value of $78.4$ for water at $25°$ C. However, adding water, which is miscible in all proportions, causes the dielectric constant to increase to a maximum value of 121 at about 35 percent $H_2O_2$ and 65 percent $H_2O$.

1.  Which of the following is false about $H_2O_2$
    (a) Act as both oxidising and reducing agent
    (b) Two OH bonds lies in the same plane
    (c) Pale blue liquid
    (d) Can be oxidised by ozone
2.  Which of the following is not true for hydrogen peroxide?
    (a) $H_2O_2$ decomposes slowly on exposure to light.
    (b) It is kept away from dust because dust can induce explosive decomposition of the compound.
    (c) $H_2O_2$ is used as bleaching agent for textiles, paper pulp etc.
    (d) It is used as a moderator in nuclear reactor.
3.  Which of the following statements are correct?
    (i) Hydrogen peroxide is industrially prepared by the auto-oxidation of 2-alkylanthraquinols.
    (ii) One millilitre of 30% $H_2O_2$ means that solution will give 100 V of oxygen at STP.
    (iii) Dihedral angle of $H_2O_2$ in gas phase is $90.2°$ and in solid phase dihedral angle is $111.5°$.
    (a) (i), (ii) and (iii)   (b) (i) and (iii)
    (c) (ii) and (iii)   (d) (i) and (ii)



4.  **Assertion:** $H_2O_2$ is stored in dark places in air tight glass containers.
    **Reason:** $H_2O_2$ can be decomposed in presence of air and sunlight.
5.  **Assertion:** Dihedral angle of $H_2O_2$ in gas and solid phase is different.
    **Reason:** In $H_2O_2$, all the four atoms do not lie in the same place.

## VERY SHORT ANSWER QUESTIONS

1.  Give an example to show that ionic hydrides forms complexes.
2.  Why $H_2$ gas is not found in earth's atmosphere?
3.  Give the order of reactivity of dihydrogen with the halogens.
4.  Which isotope of hydrogen does not have neutron?
5.  Which types of hydrides are generally non-stoichiometric in nature?
6.  Why is hydrogen molecule highly polar?
7.  Arrange $H_2$, $D_2$ and $T_2$ in the decreasing order of their boiling points.
8.  What is the molecular mass of the compound formed by burning tritium in air?
9.  Name the phenomenon of adsorption of hydrogen on metal surface.
10. Which gas is used for filling airships and balloons?
11. Ionic hydrides are generally used to remove traces of water from organic compounds, why?
12. What is the use of hydrogen in the manufacture of vanaspati ghee?
13. Which type of elements form interstitial (metallic) hydrides?
14. Why is 2-ethylanthraquinone preferred in the commercial production of $H_2O_2$?
15. Which would have higher electrical conductivity $H_2O$ or $D_2O$?
16. Anhydrous $BaO_2$ is not used for preparing $H_2O_2$. Why?
17. What is the reason for hardness of water ?
18. Which gas is evolved when $Mg_3N_2$ (magnesium nitride) is treated with $H_2O$? Give chemical reaction.
19. How is heavy water produced from ordinary water?
20. Which compounds cause temporary hardness of water?
21. How would you prepare a sample of $ND_3$?
22. How does heavy water react with $Al_4C_3$?

**23.** What is the action of water on hydrolith?

**24.** What is the trade name of $H_2O_2$ used as antiseptic?

**25.** Give one example of zeolite used in softening of hard water.

**26.** Explain why dihedral angle ($111.5°$) of $H_2O_2$ reduces to $90.2°$ in the solid state?

## SHORT ANSWER QUESTIONS

**1.** How would you prepare dihydrogen gas from (i) acid (ii) alkali.

**2.** Discuss three characteristics in which hydrogen resembles alkali metals.

**3.** What are the advantages of using hydrogen as a fuel?

**4.** Give different types of hydrides along with examples.

**5.** The process $\frac{1}{2}H_2(g) + e^- \rightarrow H^-(g)$ is endo-thermic with $\Delta H = +151$ kJ/mol, yet salt like hydrides are known. How do you account for this?

**6.** Give two points of differences between hydrogen and alkali metals.

**7.** How hydrogen differs from halogens?

**8.** Statues coated with white lead on long exposure to atmosphere turn black and original colour can be restored on treatment with $H_2O_2$. Why?

**9.** How will you show that $H_2O_2$ will act like oxidizing agent in acidic as well as basic medium?

**10.** Why hard water is not used in industrial boilers for producing steam?

**11.** Why do lakes freeze from top towards bottom?

**12.** What happens when–
(i) Water reacts with cyanamide of calcium
(ii) Peroxosulphuric acid is hydrolysed.
(iii) Moist silver oxide reacts with $H_2O_2$

**13.** A mixture of hydrazine and $H_2O_2$ with Cu (II) catalyst is used as a rocket propellant. Why?

**14.** Give two tests for hydrogen peroxide.

## LONG ANSWER QUESTIONS

**1.** (i) What are the ways in which water molecules are bound to an anhydrous salt to form hydrate?
(ii) Why water is an excellent solvent?

**2.** Give the half reactions and the complete redox reactions for the following:
(i) oxidation of ferrous to ferric ion by $H_2O_2$ in acidic medium
(ii) oxidation of iodide to iodine by $H_2O_2$ in acidic medium
(iii) $H_2O_2$ oxidises basic manganese (II) sulphate
(iv) $H_2O_2$ reduces ferricyanide ion in alkaline medium to ferrocyanide
(v) $H_2O_2$ reduces permaganate ion in acidic medium.

**3.** Complete the following reactions :
(i) $P_4O_{10} + H_2O \rightarrow$
(ii) $AlCl_3 + H_2O \rightarrow$
(iii) $SiCl_4 + H_2O \rightarrow$
(iv) $Ca_3P_2 + H_2O \rightarrow$
(v) $NaH + H_2O \rightarrow$

## SOLUTIONS

### *Multiple Choice Questions*

**1.** **(c)** In metal hydrides the O.S. of hydrogen –1 otherwise it is +1.

**2.** **(a)** Number of neutrons in protium, deuterium and tritium respectively is = 0, 1 and 2

**3.** **(b)** $\underbrace{CO + H_2 + H_2O}_{\text{water gas}} \xrightarrow{\text{catalyst}} CO_2 + 2H_2$

**4.** **(d)** Carbon dioxide formed in water gas shift reaction is removed by scrubbing with sodium arsenite solution.

**5.** **(a)** $Cu + 4HNO_3(\text{conc.}) \longrightarrow$
$$Cu(NO_3)_2 + 2NO_2 + 2H_2O$$
$$C_2H_5OH + Na \longrightarrow C_2H_5O^-Na^+ + 1/2H_2 \uparrow$$
$$Mg + 2H_2O(\text{steam}) \longrightarrow Mg(OH)_2 + H_2 \uparrow$$
$$C_6H_5OH + Na \longrightarrow C_6H_5O^-Na^+ + 1/2H_2 \uparrow$$

**6.** **(d)** $H_2$ will not reduce heated $Al_2O_3$. As Al is more electro-positive than hydrogen. therefore, its oxide will not be reduced by hydrogen.

**7.** **(b)** Temporary hardness is due to presence of bicarbonates of calcium and magnesium and permanent hardness is due to the sulphates and chlorides of both of calcium and magnesium.

**8.** **(b)** Due to high dielectric constant, water acts as a good solvent therefore it is also called a universal solvent.

**9.** **(b)** When calgon added to hard water, following reactions takes place:
$$Na_2[Na_4(PO_3)_6] \rightarrow 2Na^+ + [Na_4(PO_3)_6]^{2-}$$
$$Ca^{2+} + [Na_4(PO_3)_6]^{-2} \rightarrow [Na_2Ca(PO_3)_6]^{2-} + 2Na^+$$
This is an example of exchange of ions.

**10.** **(a)** $H_2SO_4 + BaO_2 \rightarrow BaSO_4 + H_2O_2$

**11.** **(b)** $\overset{H}{\diagdown}O-O\overset{}{\diagdown}_H$ is the true structure of $H_2O_2$.

**12.** **(b)** $H_2O_2 + [O] \xrightarrow{\text{Oxidation}} H_2O + O_2 \uparrow$

## Assertion & Reason Questions

1. **(c)** Hydrogen atom has small size, therefore, $H_2$ molecule has high bond dissociation enthalpy and is very less reactive.

2. **(c)** When spins of the two protons are parallel in the hydrogen molecule (the resultant nuclear spin is one), it is known as *ortho* hydrogen. When the spins of the two protons are anti-parallel in the hydrogen molecule (the resultant proton spin is zero) it is known as *para* hydrogen.

3. **(a)** Burning hydrogen in air or dioxygen forms water and liberates a great deal of energy, without forming any other gaseous of particulate pollutants, as in the case of use of coal or oil as fuel. Due to these properties, hydrogen as a fuel could replace use of oil, coal and propane as in power stations, motor engines, etc.

4. **(a)** Water is highly polar and has high dipole moment. It has high dielectric constant, therefore, it has high dissolving power for ionic compounds and other polar covalent compounds.

5. **(a)** Sodium carbonate process is used for the removal of both temporary and permanent hardness and can be carried out either in cold or hot conditions. In this process, lime first removes impurities causing temporary hardness and then reacts with magnesium sulphate and chloride to form insoluble precipitates of $Mg(OH)_2$. Lime treatment is followed by the addition of calculated amount of soda ash ($Na_2CO_3$) as a result of which calcium ions in the hard water are removed as $CaCO_3$ and magnesium ions as $Mg(OH)_2$.

6. **(d)** Hard water has chloride and suitable salts of calcuim and magnesium which are deposited on the inners side of boiler, therefore, hard water reduces the efficiency of the boiler.

## Case/Passage Based Questions

1. **(b)** The value of dipole moment of $H_2O_2$ is 2.1 D, which suggest the structure of $H_2O_2$ cannot be planar.
   An open-book structure is suggested for $H_2O_2$ in which O – H bonds lie in different plane.

2. **(d)** $H_2O_2$ is not used as a moderator in nuclear reactors.

3. **(d)** Dihedral angle of $H_2O_2$ in gas phase is 111.5° and in solid phase it is 90.2°

4. **(a)** $H_2O_2$ decomposes in presence of air and sunlight, therefore stored in a dark place.

$$2H_2O_2(l) \xrightarrow{\text{sunlight}} 2H_2O(l) + O_2(g)$$

Urea can be added as stabiliser.

5. **(b)** $H_2O_2$ in gaseous state has a skew structure with restricted rotation about the O–O bond. A similar structure is retained in solid $H_2O_2$, but the length and angles are slightly changed due to hydrogen bonding, which is absent in gaseous phase.

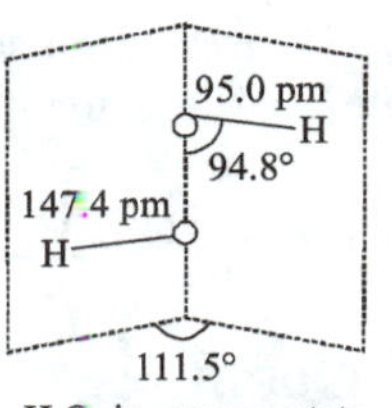

$H_2O_2$ in gaseous state

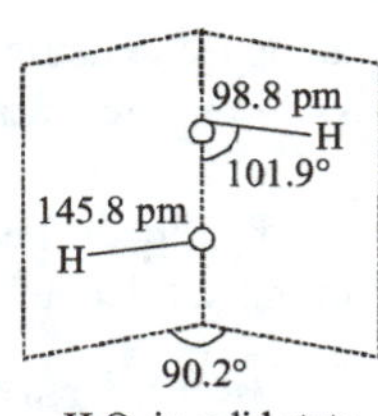

$H_2O_2$ in solid state

## Very Short Answer Questions

1. $8LiH + Al_2Cl_6 \longrightarrow 2LiAlH_4 + 6LiCl.$

2. Earth does not possess enough gravitational pull to retain light $H_2$ molecule, therefore it is not found in our atmosphere.

3. The decreasing order is $F_2 > Cl_2 > Br_2 > I_2$. The reaction with fluorine occurs even in the dark whereas with iodine it requires a catalyst.

4. $_1^1H$ does not have neutron. It is called protium or ordinary hydrogen.

5. Interstitial hydrides are generally non-stoichiometric in nature.

6. It is due to small size of hydrogen atom and high electronegativity.

7. $T_2 > D_2 > H_2.$

8. The compound $T_2O$ is formed having molecular mass 22 a.m.u.

9. Occulusion.

10. Since hydrogen is inflammable. A mixture of 85% He and 15% $H_2$ is used in filling of airships and balloons.

11. Ionic hydrides give $H^-$ ions which react with $H_2O$ to give $H_2$ gas.
$$Na^+ H^-\ H_2O \to NaOH + H_2$$
∴ Ionic hydrides are used to remove traces of water from organic compounds.

12. $H_2$ is used as reducing agent to convert vegetable oil into vegetable ghee.

13. *d*- and *f*-block elements.

14. It gets regenerated during the reaction by hydrogenation of 2–ethylanthrahydroquinone.

15. Water due its greater degree of dissociation
$$\left(pK_{H_2O} = 13.997\ pK_{D_2O} = 14.869\right).$$

16. Anhydrous $BaO_2$ is not used because the $BaSO_4$ formed during the reaction forms a protective layer around unreacted $BaO_2$ and the reaction stops after some time.

17. Hardness of water is due to the presence of bicarbonates, chlorides and sulphates of calcium and magnesium in water.

18. $NH_3$ gas is evolved.
$$Mg_3N_2 + 6H_2O \to 3Mg(OH)_2 + 2NH_3.$$

19. It is obtained by repeated electrolysis of ordinary water.

**20.** $Ca(HCO_3)_2$ and $Mg(HCO_3)_2$.

**21.** $Mg_3N_2 + 6D_2O \longrightarrow 3Mg(OD)_2 + 2ND_3$

$\qquad\qquad$ Heavy water $\qquad\qquad\qquad$ Deutero ammonia

**22.** $Al_4C_3 + 12D_2O \rightarrow 4Al(OD)_3 + 3CD_4$

**23.** $CaH_2 + 2H_2O \rightarrow Ca(OH)_2 + 2H_2 \uparrow$

**24.** $H_2O_2$ commercially is called perhydrol.

**25.** Hydrated sodium aluminium silicate,

$$Na_2Al_2Si_2O_8 \cdot xH_2O$$

**26.** The dihedral angle ($111.5°$) reduces to $90.2°$ in hydrogen peroxide crystal due to hydrogen bonding. The $H_2O_2$ has a non-planar structure.

### *Short Answer Questions*

**1.** (i) From acid :

$\qquad Zn + H_2SO_4 \longrightarrow ZnSO_4 + H_2$

(ii) From alkali :

$\qquad Zn + 2NaOH \longrightarrow Na_2ZnO_2 + H_2$

**2.** (i) Liberation at cathode:- When an aqueous solution of HCl is electrolysed, hydrogen is liberated at cathode in the same way as alkali metals are liberated during electrolysis of their salt in molten form

$\qquad 2HCl\,(aq) \longrightarrow H_2 + Cl_2$

$\qquad\qquad\qquad\qquad$ cathode

$\qquad 2NaCl \longrightarrow 2Na + Cl_2$

(ii) Reducing agent:- Like alkali metals, hydrogen also acts as a strong reducing agent.

$\qquad Fe_3O_4 + 4H_2 \longrightarrow 3Fe + 4H_2O$

$\qquad B_2O_3 + 6K \longrightarrow 2B + 3K_2O$

(iii) Electropositive nature:- Like alkali metals, hydrogen can also loose one electron to form unipositive ion.

$$[H \longrightarrow H^+ + e^-]$$

**3.** (i) High heat of combustion.

$$2H_2(g) + O_2(g) \xrightarrow{\text{Catalyst}} 2H_2O(l)$$

$$\Delta H = -285.9\ kJ\ mol^{-1}$$

(ii) No emission of polluting gases $CO_2$, $SO_2$, $NO_2$, etc

(iii) Fuel cells with hydrogen having efficiency 70-85% have been made and operated successfully.

**4.** **There are three types of hydrides :**

(i) Ionic hydrides —— NaH

(ii) Metallic or interstitial hydrides —— $LaH_2$

(iii) Molecular or covalent hydrides ——$H_2O$

**5.** Formation of $H^-$ is endothermic yet alkali and alkaline earth metals form salt like hydrides. This is due to the reason that high lattice energy released more than compensates the energy needed for the formation of $H^-$ ions from $H_2$ gas.

**6.** (i) The ionisation energy of hydrogen ($1312\ kJ\ mol^{-1}$) is very high as compared to those of alkali metals, e.g. Li ($520\ kJ\ mol^{-1}$), Na ($495\ kJ\ mol^{-1}$), etc.

(ii) At room temperature hydrogen is a gas while alkali metals are solids.

**7.** (i) Hydrogen has less tendency to take up electron to form hydride ion ($H^-$) as compared to the halogens which form halide ion ($X^-$) very easily.

(ii) Hydrogen molecule has no unshared pairs of electrons while halogen molecule has six unshared pairs of electrons i.e.

$$H{-}H, \qquad :\!\ddot{Cl}{-}\ddot{Cl}\!:$$

**8.** On long exposure to atmosphere, white lead is converted into black PbS due to action of $H_2S$ present in the atmosphere. As a result statues turn black

$$PbO + H_2S \longrightarrow PbS + H_2O$$

To restore the colour of lead paintings, it is dipped in aqueous solution of $H_2O_2$ then the lead sulphide is oxidised to lead sulphate which is white in colour.

$$PbS + 4H_2O_2 \longrightarrow PbSO_4 + 4H_2O$$

**9.** In $H_2O_2$, the oxidation state of O is $-1$. $H_2O_2$ can be reduced to $H_2O$ or $OH^-$ in which the oxidation number of O is $-2$. As this is a gain of electron, $H_2O$ is an oxidizing agent. $H_2O_2$ can act as oxidizing agent in acidic as well as in basic medium.

**Acidic :**

$$H_2O_2(aq) + 2H^+(aq) + 2e^- \rightarrow 2H_2O(l)$$

**Basic :**

$$H_2O_2(aq) + OH^-(aq) + 2e^- \rightarrow 3OH^-(aq)$$

**10.** Hard water cannot be used in industrial boilers as it contains the bicarbonates of calcium and magnesium. These bicarbonates decomposes on heating giving insoluble carbonates which settle at the bottom of the tanks as precipitate.

**11.** Ice is having less density than water and hence floats on it. But water's density is maximum at $4°C$. In cold upper layer of water freezes and protects the lower lying water from getting freezed as its density is heavier than solidified ice. This phenomenon helps in the existence of aquatic life in cold conditions.

**12.** (i) $Ca(CN)_2 + 4H_2O \rightarrow CaCO_3 + NH_4OH.$

$\qquad$ (Cal. cyanamide)

(ii) $H_2S_2O_8 + 2H_2O \rightarrow 2H_2SO_4 + H_2O_2$

$\qquad$ (Peroxosulphuric $\quad$ (Sulpuric $\quad$ (Hydrogen

$\qquad\quad$ acid) $\qquad\qquad$ acid) $\quad$ peroxide)

(iii) $H_2O_2 + Ag_2O \rightarrow 2Ag + H_2O + O_2$

**13.** The reaction between hydrazine and hydrogen peroxide in the presence of copper (II) is highly exothermic and is accompanied by a large increase in the volume of the product and hence this mixture is used as a rocket propellant.

$$NH_2{-}NH_2(l) + 2H_2O_2(l) \rightarrow N_2(g) + 4H_2(g) + 4H_2O(g) + \text{Heat}$$

**14.** (i) It decolourises the pink colour of acidified permanganate solution.

(ii) It liberates iodine from acidified KI solution which turns starch paper blue.

### Long Answer Questions

**1.** (i) Water molecules may be bounded to an anhydrous salts in the following three ways:

   (a) Water molecules are coordinated to the central metal ion in complex ions such as $[Ni(H_2O)_6]^+Cl$.

   (b) Water molecules may occupy, voids in the crystal lattice as interstitial water. e.g. $BaCl_2 . 2H_2O$.

   (c) Water molecules may be bonded by hydrogen bonds in certain oxygen containing anions.e.g. in $CuSO_4 . 5H_2O$, four water molecules are coordinated to a central $Cu^{2+}$ ion while the fifth water molecule is hydrogen bonded to sulphate $SO_4^{2-}$ group.

(ii) Water is highly polar solvent with high dielectric constant. It interacts with polar or ionic substances effectively with the liberation of considerable amount of energy that is responsible for breaking of crystal lattice and explain the solubility. The dissolution of covalent compounds like alcohols, urea glucose, etc. is due to tendency of these molecules to form hydrogen bond with water.

**2.** (i) $H_2O_2(aq) + 2H^+(aq) + 2e^- \rightarrow 2H_2O(l)$ [reduction]

$2Fe^{+2}(aq) \rightarrow 2Fe^{+3}(aq) + 2e^-$     [oxidation]

$$\overline{2Fe^{+2}(aq) + H_2O_2(aq) + 2H^+(aq) \rightarrow}$$
$$2Fe^{+3}(aq) + 2H_2O(l)$$

(ii) $H_2O_2(aq) + 2H^+(aq) + 2e^- \rightarrow 2H_2O(l)$ [reduction]

$2I^-(aq) \rightarrow I_2(s) + 2e^-$     [oxidation]

$$\overline{H_2O_2(aq) + 2I^-(aq) + 2H^+(aq) \rightarrow I_2(s) + 2H_2O(l)}$$

(iii) $H_2O_2(aq) + 2e^- \rightarrow 2OH^-(aq)$   [reduction]

$Mn^{+2}(aq) \rightarrow Mn^{+4}(aq) + 2e^-$   [oxidation]

$$\overline{Mn^{+2}(aq) + H_2O_2(aq) \rightarrow Mn^{+4}(aq) + 2OH^-(aq)}$$

(iv) $H_2O_2 + 2OH^-(aq) \rightarrow 2H_2O(l) + O_2(g) + 2e^-$
          [oxidation]

$2[Fe(CN)_6]^{-3}(aq) + 2e^- \rightarrow 2[Fe(CN)_6]^{-2}$

Ferricyanide ion        ferrocyanide ion   [reduction]

$$\overline{H_2O_2(aq) + 2[Fe(CN)_6]^{-3}(aq) + 2OH^- \rightarrow}$$
$$2H_2O(l) + O_2(g) + 2[Fe(CN)_6]^{-2}$$

(v) $H_2O_2(aq) \rightarrow O_2(g) + 2H^+(aq)^+ 2e^-] \times 5$ [oxidation]

$2MnO_4^-(aq) + 16H^+(aq) + 10e^- \rightarrow$
$$2Mn^{+2}(aq) + 8H_2O(l) \quad [reduction]$$

$$\overline{2MnO^-_4(aq) + 5H_2O_2(aq) + 6H^+(aq) \rightarrow}$$
$$2Mn^{+2}(aq) + 8H_2O(l) + 5O_2(g)$$

**3.** (i) $P_4O_{10} + 6H_2O \rightarrow 4H_3PO_4$

(ii) $AlCl_3 + 6H_2O \rightarrow [Al(H_2O)_6]Cl_3$

(iii) $SiCl_4 + 2H_2O \rightarrow SiO_2 + 4HCl$

(iv) $Ca_3P_2 + 6H_2O \rightarrow 3Ca(OH)_2 + PH_3$

(v) $NaH - H_2O \rightarrow NaOH + H_2$

---

## SECTION C — NCERT EXEMPLAR QUESTIONS 

### MULTIPLE CHOICE QUESTIONS

**1.** Hydrogen resembles halogens in many respects for which several factors are responsible. Of the following factors which one is most important in this respect?
  (a) Its tendency to lose an electron to form a cation.
  (b) Its tendency to gain a single electron in its valence shell to attain stable electronic configuration.
  (c) Its low negative electron gain enthalpy value.
  (d) Its small size.

**2.** Consider the reactions
  (i) $H_2O_2 + 2HI \longrightarrow I_2 + 2H_2O$
  (ii) $HOCl + H_2O_2 \longrightarrow H_3O^+ + Cl^- + O_2$

Which of the following statements is correct about $H_2O_2$ with reference to these reactions ? Hydrogen peroxide is .....
  (a) an oxidising agent in both (i) and (ii)
  (b) an oxidising agent in (i) and reducing agent in (ii)
  (c) a reducing agent in (i) and oxidising agent in (ii)
  (d) a reducing agent in both (i) and (ii)

**3.** Which of the following equations depict the oxidising nature of $H_2O_2$?
  (a) $2MnO_4^- + 6H^+ + 5H_2O_2 \longrightarrow 2Mn^{2+} + 8H_2O + 5O_2$
  (b) $2Fe^{3+} + 2H^+ + H_2O_2 \longrightarrow 2Fe^{2+} + 2H_2O + O_2$
  (c) $2I^- + 2H^+ + H_2O_2 \longrightarrow I_2 + 2H_2O$
  (d) $KIO_4 + H_2O_2 \longrightarrow KIO_3 + H_2O + O_2$

**4.** Which of the following equation depict reducing nature of $H_2O_2$?

(a) $2[Fe(CN)_6]^{4-} + 2H^+ + H_2O_2 \longrightarrow$
$$2[Fe(CN)_6]^{3-} + 2H_2O$$

(b) $I_2 + H_2O_2 + 2OH^- \longrightarrow 2I^- + 2H_2O + O_2$

(c) $Mn^{2+} + H_2O_2 \longrightarrow Mn^{4+} + 2OH^-$

(d) $PbS + 4H_2O_2 \longrightarrow PbSO_4 + 4H_2O$

**5.** When sodium peroxide is treated with dilute sulphuric acid, we get ......... .
(a) sodium sulphate and water
(b) sodium sulphate and oxygen
(c) sodium sulphate, hydrogen and oxygen
(d) sodium sulphate and hydrogen peroxide

**6.** Which of the following reactions is an example of use of water gas in the synthesis of other compounds?

(a) $CH_4(g) + H_2O(g) \xrightarrow[Ni]{1270\,K} CO(g) + H_2(g)$

(b) $CO(g) + H_2O(g) \xrightarrow[Catalyst]{673\,K} CO_2(g) + H_2(g)$

(c) $C_nH_{2n+2} + nH_2O(g) \xrightarrow[Ni]{1270\,K} nCO + (2n+1)H_2$

(d) $CO(g) + 2H_2(g) \xrightarrow[Catalyst]{Cobalt} CH_3OH(l)$

## ASSERTION & REASON QUESTIONS

**DIRECTIONS (Qs. 1-2) :** *Each of these questions contains an assertion followed by reason. Read them carefully and answer the question on the basis of following options. You have to select the one that best describes the two statements.*

(a) If both Assertion and Reason are correct and the Reason is a correct explanation of the Assertion.
(b) If both Assertion and Reason are correct but Reason is not a correct explanation of the Assertion.
(c) If the Assertion is correct but Reason is incorrect.
(d) If the Assertion is incorrect but the Reason is correct.

**1.** **Assertion :** Permanent hardness of water is removed by treatment with washing soda.
**Reason :** Washing soda reacts with soluble magnesium and calcium sulphate to form insoluble carbonates.

**2.** **Assertion :** Some metals like platinum and palladium, can be used as storage media for hydrogen.
**Reason :** Platinum and palladium can absorb large volumes of hydrogen.

## SHORT ANSWER QUESTIONS

**1.** Calculate the strength of 5 volume $H_2O_2$ solution.

**2.** Dihydrogen reacts with dioxygen ($O_2$) to form water. Write the name and formula of the product when the isotope of hydrogen which has one proton and one neutron in its nucleus is treated with oxygen. Will the reactivity of both the isotopes be the same towards oxygen? Justify your answer.

## LONG ANSWER QUESTION

**1.** What mass of hydrogen peroxide will be present in 2 litres of a 5 molar solution? Calculate the mass of oxygen which will be liberated by the decomposition of 200 mL of this solution.

## SOLUTIONS

### *Multiple Choice Questions*

**1.** **(b)** Hydrogen like halogens accept an electron readily to achieve nearest inert gas configuration.

**2.** **(b)** (i) $\overset{-1}{H_2}\overset{-1}{O_2} + 2\overset{-1}{HI} \longrightarrow \overset{0}{I_2} + 2\overset{-2}{H_2O}$
(Reduction / Oxidation)

Here, $H_2O_2$ oxidises HI into $I_2$ hence, behaves as an oxidising agent.

(ii) $H\overset{+1}{O}Cl + H_2\overset{-1}{O_2} \longrightarrow H_3O^+ + Cl^- + \overset{0}{O_2}$
(Reduction / Oxidation)

Here, $H_2O_2$ reduces HOCl to Cl, thus, behaves as reducing agent.

**3.** **(c)** $2I^- + 2H^+ + H_2\overset{-1}{O_2} \longrightarrow \overset{0}{I_2} + 2H_2\overset{-2}{O}$
(Reduction / Oxidation)

Here $H_2O_2$ oxidises $I^-$ to $I_2$, hence behaves as oxidising agent.

**4.** **(b)** The given below reaction show the reducing action in basic medium.

$\overset{0}{I_2} + H_2\overset{-1}{O_2} + 2OH^- \longrightarrow 2\overset{-1}{I^-} + 2H_2O + \overset{0}{O_2}$
(Reduction / Oxidation)

**5.** **(d)** $Na_2O_2 + dil.\,H_2SO_4 \longrightarrow Na_2SO_4 + H_2O_2$

**6.** **(d)** The water gas is a combination of carbon and hydrogen. It is used in manufacturing of methanol.

$$CO(g) + 2H_2(g) \xrightarrow[Catalyst]{Cobalt} CH_3OH(l)$$

### *Assertion & Reason Questions*

1.  **(a)**  Permanent hardness of water is due to the presence of soluble salts of magnesium and calcium in the form of chlorides and sulphates in water. Washing soda reacts with soluble calcium and magnesium chlorides and sulphonates in hard water to form insoluble carbonates.

$$MCl_2 + Na_2CO_3 \longrightarrow MCO_3\downarrow + 2NaCl$$
$$MSO_4 + Na_2CO_3 \longrightarrow MCO_3\downarrow + Na_2SO_4$$

(where M = Mg, Ca)

2.  **(a)**  Pd and Pt can accomodate a very large volume of hydrogen and therefore, can be used as its storage media.

### *Short Answer Questions*

1.  5 volume $H_2O_2$ solution means that hydrogen peroxide contained in 1 volume of this solution will decompose to give 5 volumes of oxygen at STP i.e. if 1L of this solution is taken, then 5 L of oxygen can be produced from this at STP. Chemical equation for the decomposition of $H_2O_2$ is

$$2H_2O_2(l) \longrightarrow O_2(g) + 2H_2O(l).$$

It shows that 68 g $H_2O_2$ gives 22.7 L of $O_2$ at STP, so 5 L oxygen will be obtained from :

$$\frac{68g \times 5L}{22.7L} = \frac{3400}{227}g\ H_2O_2$$

$$= 14.9\ g \approx 15g\ H_2O_2$$

i.e., 15 g $H_2O_2$ dissolved in 1 L solution will give 5 L oxygen or 1.5 g $H_2O_2$ / 100 mL solution will give 500 mL oxygen. Thus 15g/L or 1.5% solution is known as 5V solution of $H_2O_2$.

2.  [*Hint:* Heavy water; Bond dissociation energy of dihydrogen is less than dideuterium]

### *Long Answer Question*

1.  Total number of moles of $H_2O_2$ = M × V

$$= 5 \times 2 = 10\ mol$$

| 1 mol | 34 g |
| 10 mol | 340 g |

$$\text{Moles of } H_2O_2 \text{ in 200 mL} = 5 \times \frac{200}{1000}$$

$$= 1\ mol$$

$$= 34\ g$$

$$\underset{34\,g}{H_2O_2} \longrightarrow H_2O + \underset{16\,g}{\frac{1}{2}O_2}$$

Hence 34 g of $H_2O_2$ gives 16 g of $O_2$.

# The *s*-Block Elements



**10.1 What are the common physical and chemical features of alkali metals ?**

**Ans. Common physical properties**

(a) Large atomic radii. The atomic radii of alkali metals are largest in their respective periods. It increases as we travel down the group from Li to Cs.

(b) The ionization enthalpies of the alkali metals are lowest as compared to the elements in the other groups.

(c) They all show +1 oxidation state.

(d) The elements of this group are typical metals and are soft.

(e) All of them form ionic bond in their compound though the ionic character increases down the group.

(f) All alkali metals impart a characteristic colour to the flame.

**Common chemical properties.**

(a) All alkali metals are highly reactive and have the reducing property.

(b) Alkali metal react with water to release hydrogen.

(c) All the alkali metals on exposure to atmosphere (air and moisture) get converted into oxides, hydroxides and finally to carbonates.

(d) Alkali metals react vigorously with halogens to form metal halides of the type MX.

(e) The metals and their oxides on reaction with water give a strong alkali.

(f) All alkali metals dissolve in liquid ammonia giving highly conducting deep blue solutions.

**10.2 Discuss the general characteristics and gradation in properties of alkaline earth metals.**

**Ans. Trend in physical properties**

(a) The atomic radii of alkaline earth metals are fairly large though smaller than the corresponding alkali metals and they increase down the group.

(b) The alkaline earth metals have fairly low ionization enthalpies though greater than those of the corresponding elements of group–I and they decrease down the group.

(c) They all exhibit the oxidation state of +2 in their solid state as well as in solution.

(d) They are less electropositive than alkali metals but are fairly electropositive and metallic.

(e) Like alkali metals, alkaline earth metals predominantly form ionic bonds in their compounds but are less ionic than alkali metals.

(f) The alkaline earth metals are less reducing than alkali metals. Their reducing character increases down the group.

**Chemical properties :**

(a) They are less reactive than alkali metals. Be does not react with water while Mg can only react with steam. But as we go down the group, their reactivity with the water increases. They react with water to give hydroxides and hydrogen gas.

(b) Their reactivity towards air is less than alkali metals. Be and Mg are kinetically inert to oxygen but down the group their reactivity increases. They form oxides and nitrides when reacted in air.

(c) All alkaline earth metals combine with halogens at elevated temperature forming their halides of the type $MX_2$.

(d) The metals and their oxides are quite basic since they form alkali when treated with water. However they are less alkaline than group–I metals. The basicities of their oxides increase down the group.

(e) Like alkali metals , alkaline earth metals dissolve in liquid ammonia.

**10.3 Why are alkali metals not found in nature ?**

**Ans.** Alkali metals are highly reactive and hence they do not occur in the free state.

**10.4 Find out the oxidation state of sodium in $Na_2O_2$.**

**Ans.** Let x be the oxidation state of Na in $Na_2O_2$. Since $Na_2O_2$ contains a peroxide linkage in which O has an oxidation state of $-1$, therefore, $Na_2O_2$ or $2x + 2(-1) = 0$ or $x = +1$.

**10.5** **Explain why is sodium less reactive than potassium ?**

**Ans.** The ionization enthalpy ($\Delta_i H$) of potassium (496 kJ mol$^{-1}$) is less than that of sodium (496 kJ mol$^{-1}$) or more precisely the standard electrode potential (E°) of potassium (–2.925V) is more negative than that of sodium (–2.714V) and hence potassium is more reactive than sodium.

**10.6** **Compare the alkali metals and alkaline earth metals with respect to (i) ionisation enthalpy (ii) basicity of oxides and (iii) solubility of hydroxides.**

**Ans.** (i) **Ionization enthalpy ( $\Delta_i H$).** Because of higher nuclear charge, the $\Delta_i H$ of alkaline earth metals are higher than those of the corresponding alkali metals.

(ii) **Basicity of oxides.** The oxides of alkali and alkaline earth metals dissolve in water to form their respective hydroxides. These hydroxides are strong bases. However, since the ionization enthalpy of alkali metals is lower or the electropositive character of alkali metals is higher than that of the corresponding alkaline earth metal, therefore the M– OH bond in alkali metals can more easily ionize (MOH $\longrightarrow$ M$^+$ + OH$^-$), than in alkaline earth metals and hence alkali metal oxides are more basic than the corresponding alkaline earth metal oxides.

(iii) **Solubility of hydroxides.** Because of smaller size and higher ionic charge, the lattice enthalpies of alkaline earth metals are much higher than those of alkali metals and hence the solubility of alkali metal hydroxides is much higher than that of alkaline earth metal hydroxides. However, the solubility of the hydroxides of both alkali and alkaline earth metals increase down the group due to larger decrease in their lattices enthalpies as compared to their hydration enthalpies.

**10.7** **In what ways lithium shows similarities to magnesium in its chemical behaviour ?**

**Ans.** Lithium resembles magnesium mainly due to same charge/radius ratio or polarizing power. The main points of similarity are:

(a) Both LiOH and Mg(OH)$_2$ are weak bases.

(b) Both form ionic nitrides when heated in atmosphere of nitrogen, Li$_3$N and Mg$_3$N$_2$.

(c) The hydroxides and carbonates of both of them decompose on heating.

$$2LiOH \longrightarrow Li_2O + H_2O$$
$$Mg(OH)_2 \longrightarrow MgO + H_2O$$
$$Li_2CO_3 \longrightarrow Li_2O + CO_2$$
$$MgCO_3 \longrightarrow MgO + CO_2$$

(d) Both Li and Mg do not form solid bicarbonates.

(e) Li and Mg do not form peroxides and super oxides.

(f) Both Li and Mg nitrates decompose on heating producing NO$_2$.

$$4LiNO_3 \longrightarrow 2Li_2O + 4NO_2 + O_2$$
$$2Mg(NO_3)_2 \longrightarrow 2MgO + 4NO_2 + O_2$$

(g) The hydroxides, carbonates and fluorides of lithium and magnesium are sparingly soluble in water.

(h) LiCl and MgCl$_2$ are highly soluble in ethanol.

**10.8** **Explain why Alkali and Alkaline earth metals not be obtained by chemical reduction methods ?**

**Ans.** Alkali and alkaline earth metals are themselves strong reducing agents and reducing agents better than them are not available. Therefore, these metals cannot be obtained by reduction of their oxides or chlorides.

**10.9** **Why are potassium and caesium, rather than lithium used in photoelectric cells ?**

**Ans.** Potassium and caesium have much lower ionization enthalpy than that of lithium. As a result, these metals on exposure to light, easily emit electrons but lithium does not. Therefore, K and Cs rather than Li are used in photoelectric cells.

**10.10** **When an alkali metal dissolves in liquid ammonia, the solution can acquire different colours. Explain the reasons for this type of colour change.**

**Ans.** The dilute solutions of alkali metals in liquid ammonia exhibit dark blue colour because ammoniated electrons absorb energy corresponding the red region of the visible light.

$$M+ (x +y) NH_3 \longrightarrow [M(NH_3)_x]^{+} + e^-(NH_3)_y$$
$$\text{Ammoniated electrons}$$

However, if the concentration increases above 3M, the colour changes to copper–bronze and the solution acquires metallic lustre due to the formation of metal ion clusters.

**10.11** **Beryllium and magnesium do not give colour to flame whereas other alkaline earth metals do so. Why ?**

**Ans.** Because of the small size, the ionization enthalpies of Be and Mg are much higher than those of other alkaline earth metals. Therefore, they need large amount of energy for excitation of their valence electrons to higher energy levels. Since such a large amount of energy is not available in Bunsen flame, therefore, these metals do not impart any colour to the flame.

**10.12** **Discuss the various reactions that occur in the Solvay process.**

**Ans.** In Solvay ammonia process, CO$_2$ is passed through brine, (i.e., a concentrated solution of NaCl) saturated with ammonia where sodium bicarbonate being sparingly soluble gets precipitated.

$$NaCl + NH_3 + CO_2 + H_2O \longrightarrow$$
$$NaHCO_3 \downarrow + NH_4Cl \ \ ...(i)$$

Sodium bicarbonate on heating gives sodium carbonate.

$$2\,NaHCO_3 \longrightarrow Na_2CO_3 + CO_2 + H_2O \qquad ...(ii)$$

CO$_2$ needed for the reaction is prepared by heating calcium carbonate and the quick lime, CaO is dissolved in water to form slaked lime, Ca(OH)$_2$

$$CaCO_3 \longrightarrow CaO + CO_2$$
$$CaO + H_2O \longrightarrow Ca(OH)_2 \qquad ...(iii)$$

$NH_3$ needed for the purpose is prepared by heating $NH_4Cl$ obtained in Eq(i) with $Ca(OH)_2$ obtained in Eq(iii)

$$2NH_4Cl + Ca(OH)_2 \longrightarrow 2\,NH_3 + CaCl_2 + 2\,H_2O$$

Therefore, the only by product of the reaction is calcium chloride, $CaCl_2$.

**10.13 Potassium carbonate cannot be prepared by Solvay process. Why ?**

**Ans.** Potassium carbonate cannot be prepared by Solvay process because potassium bicarbonate being more soluble than sodium bicarbonate does not get precipitated when $CO_2$ is passed through a concentrated solution of KCl saturated with ammonia.

$$KCl + CO_2 + NH_3 + H_2O \longrightarrow KHCO_3 + NH_4Cl$$

**10.14 Why is $Li_2CO_3$ decomposed at a lower temperature whereas $Na_2CO_3$ at higher temperature?**

**Ans.** $Li_2CO_3$ is a salt of a weak acid ($H_2CO_3$) with a weak base (LiOH). Since the weak base cannot attract $CO_2$ strongly, therefore, $Li_2CO_3$ decomposes at lower temperature. On the other hand, NaOH is a much stronger base than LiOH and hence can attract $CO_2$ more strongly. Therefore, $Na_2CO_3$ is much more stable than $Li_2CO_3$ and hence decomposes at much higher temperature than $Li_2CO_3$

**10.15 Compare the solubility and thermal stability of the following compounds of the alkali metals with those of the alkaline earth metals (a) Nitrates (b) Carbonates (c) Sulphates.**

**Ans.** **Solubility :**

(a) **Alkali metals.** Nitrates, carbonates and sulphates of alkali metals are soluble in water. Their, solubility, however, increases as we move down the group since the lattice energies decrease more rapidly than the hydration energies.

(b) **Alkaline earth.** Nitrates of all alkaline earth metals are soluble in water. Their solubility, however, decreases as we move down the group because their hydration energies decrease more rapidly than the lattice energies. The size of $CO_3^{2-}$ and $SO_4^{2-}$ anions is much larger than the cations, therefore, within a particular group, lattice energies remain almost constant. Since the hydration energies decrease down the group, therefore, the solubility of alkaline earth carbonates' and sulphates decrease down the group. However, the hydration energy of $Be^{2+}$ and $Mg^{2+}$ ions overcome the lattice energy factor and therefore, $BeSO_4$ and $MgSO_4$ are readily soluble in water while the solubility of other sulphates decreases down the group from $CaSO_4$ to $BaSO_4$.

**Thermal stability :**

(a) **Nitrates.** Nitrates of both alkali and alkaline earth metals decompose on heating. All alkaline earth metal nitrates decompose to form metal oxide, $NO_2$ and $O_2$.

$$2M(NO_3)_2 \xrightarrow{\;\Delta\;} 2\,MO + 4\,NO_2 + O_2$$

(M = Be, Mg, Ca, Sr or Ba). The nitrates of Na, K, Rb and Cs decompose to form metal nitrites and $O_2$.

$$2MNO_3 \xrightarrow{\;\Delta\;} 2MNO_2 + O_2$$

(M = Na, K, Rb, Cs)

However, due to diagonal relationship between Li and Mg, lithium nitrate decomposes like $Mg(NO_3)_2$ to form metal oxide, $NO_2$ and $O_2$.

$$4LiNO_3 \xrightarrow{\;\Delta\;} 2Li_2O + 4NO_2 + O_2$$

(b) **Carbonates.** Carbonates of alkaline earth metals decompose on heating to form metal oxide and $CO_2$

$$MCO_3 \xrightarrow{\;\Delta\;} MO + CO_2$$

(M = Be, Mg, Ca, Sr, Ba)

Further as the electropositive character of the metal increases down the group, the stability of these metal carbonates increases and hence the temperature of their decomposition increases as shown below:

| $BeCO_3$ | $MgCO_3$ | $CaCO_3$ | $SrCO_3$ | $BaCO_3$ |
|---|---|---|---|---|
| <373 K | 813 K | 1173 K | 1563 K | 1633 K |

Due to diagonal relationship between Li and Mg, $Li_2CO_3$ decomposes in the same way as $MgCO_3$.

$$Li_2CO_3 \xrightarrow{\;\Delta\;} Li_2O + CO_2$$

All other alkali metal carbonates are stable and do not decompose even at high temperatures.

(c) **Sulphates.** Sulphates of alkaline earth metals decompose on heating giving the oxides and $SO_3$.

$$MSO_4 \longrightarrow MO + SO_3$$

The temperature of decomposition of these sulphates increases as the electropositive character of the metal or the basicity of the metal hydroxide increases down the group. For example,

| Compound: | Temp. of decomposition: |
|---|---|
| $BeSO_4$ | 773 K |
| $MgSO_4$ | 1168K |
| $CaSO_4$ | 1422K |
| $SrSO_4$ | 1644K |

Among alkali metals due to diagonal relationship, $Li_2SO_4$ decomposes like $MgSO_4$ to form the corresponding metal oxide and $SO_3$.

$$Li_2SO_4 \xrightarrow{\;\Delta\;} Li_2O + SO_3$$

$$MgSO_4 \xrightarrow{\;\Delta\;} MgO + SO_3$$

Other alkali metals are stable to heat and do not decompose easily.

**10.16 Starting with sodium chloride how would you proceed to prepare**

**(i) sodium metal**

**(ii) sodium hydroxide**

**(iii) sodium peroxide and**

**(iv) sodium carbonate?**

**Ans.** (i) Sodium metal is manufactured by electrolysis of a fused mixture of NaCl (40%) and $CaCl_2$ (60%) in Down's cell at 873 K using iron cathode and graphite anode. Na is liberated at the cathode while $Cl_2$ is evolved at the anode.

At cathode : $Na^+$ (melt) $+ e^- \longrightarrow Na$ $(l)$

At anode : $2\,Cl^-$ (melt) $\longrightarrow Cl_2$ (g) $+ 2e^-$

(ii) Sodium hydroxide: By electrolyzing a solution of sodium chloride, we can get sodium hydroxide. This process is commonly known as castner-Kellner process.

The process is carried out using a mercury cathode and a carbon anode. Sodium metal, deposited at cathode forms an Amalgam by combining with Mercury.

Cathode: $Na^+ + e^- \xrightarrow{Hg} Na$-Amalgam

$2Na$-$Hg + 2H_2O \rightarrow 2NaOH + H + Hg$

Anode: $Cl^- \longrightarrow 1/2\,Cl_2 + e^-$

(iii) Sodium peroxide is obtained by heating sodium in excess of air. The initially formed sodium oxide reacts with more $O_2$ to form $Na_2O_2$.

$4\,Na + O_2 \longrightarrow 2\,Na_2O$

$2\,Na_2O + O_2 \longrightarrow 2\,Na_2O_2$

(iv) Sodium hydrogen carbonate is obtained as a precipitate by reacting sodium chloride with ammonium hydrogen carbonate. The resultant crystals can be heated to obtain Sodium Carbonate.

$2NH_3 + H_2O + CO_2 \longrightarrow (NH_4)_2CO_3$

$(NH_4)_2CO_3 + H_2O + CO_2 \longrightarrow 2NH_4HCO_3$

$2NH_4HCO_3 + NaCl \longrightarrow NH_4Cl + NaHCO_3$

The resultant crystals can be heated to obtain Sodium Carbonate.

$2NaHCO_2 \longrightarrow Na_2CO_2 + C_2O + H_2O$

**10.17** **What happens when (i) magnesium is burnt in air (ii) quick lime is heated with silica (iii) chlorine reacts with slaked lime (iv) calcium nitrate is heated ?**

**Ans.** (i) $2\,Mg\,(s) + O_2\,(g) \xrightarrow{\Delta} 2\,MgO\,(s)$

(ii) $\underset{\text{Quick lime}}{CaO(s)} + \underset{\text{Silica}}{SiO_2(s)} \xrightarrow{\Delta} \underset{\text{Calcium silicate}}{CaSiO_3(s)}$

(iii) It reacts with $Cl_2$ to form calcium hypochlorite, $Ca(OCl)_2$–a constituent of bleaching powder

$\underset{\text{Slaked lime}}{2Ca(OH)_2} + 2\,Cl_2 \longrightarrow$

$$\underset{\text{Bleaching powder}}{\underbrace{CaCl_2 + Ca(OCl)_2}} + 2\,H_2O$$

(iv) $2Ca(NO_3)_2(s) \longrightarrow 2CaO(s) + 4\,NO_2(g) + O_2\,(g)$

**10.18** **Describe two important uses of each of the following: (i) caustic soda (ii) sodium carbonate (iii) quicklime.**

**Ans.** 1. Caustic soda :

(i) It is used in the manufacture of soap, paper, artificial silk, etc. and in petroleum refining and purification of bauxite.

(ii) It is used in the textile industries for mercerizing cotton fabrics.

2. Sodium carbonate :

(i) It is used in water softening laundering and cleaning.

(ii) It is used in the manufacture of glass, soap, borax, etc and in paper, paints and textile industries.

3. Quick lime :

(i) It is used in the manufacture of sodium carbonate from caustic soda,

(ii) It is employed in the purification of sugar and in the manufacture of dyestuffs.

**10.19** **Draw the structure of**
**(i) $BeCl_2$ (vapour)   (ii) $BeCl_2$ (solid).**

**Ans.** (i) In the vapour state, it exists as a chloro–bridged dimer.

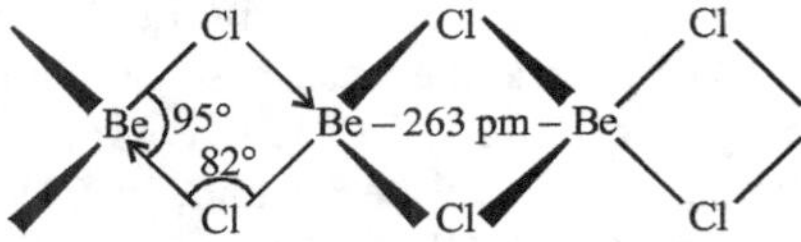


(ii) In the solid state, $BeCl_2$ has polymeric structure with chloro bridges.



**10.20** **The hydroxides and carbonates of sodium and potassium are easily soluble in water while the corresponding salts of magnesium and calcium are sparingly soluble in water. Explain.**

**Ans.** Due to larger size of Na and K as compared to that of Mg and Ca, the lattice energies of hydroxides and carbonates of sodium and potassium are much lower than those of the hydroxides and carbonates of magnesium and calcium. As a result, the hydroxides of Na and K are easily soluble in water while the corresponding salts of magnesium and calcium are sparingly soluble in water.

**10.21** **Describe the importance of the following:**
**(i) limestone**
**(ii) cement**
**(iii) Plaster of Paris.**

**Ans.** (i) **Limestone.** Specially precipitated $CaCO_3$ is extensively used in the manufacture of high quality paper. It is also used as an antacid, mild abrasive in toothpaste, a constituent of chewing gum and as a filler in cosmetics.

(ii) **Cement.** Uses of cement:
- Bridge construction
- Plastering
- Most important ingredient in concrete

(iii) **Plaster of Paris.** Uses of Plaster of Paris:
- Used to make casts and moulds
- Used to make surgical bandages

**10.22** **Why are lithium salts commonly hydrated and those of the other alkali metal ions usually anhydrous?**

**Ans.** Because of smallest size among alkali metals, $Li^+$ can polarize water molecules more easily than the other alkali metal ions and hence get attached to lithium salts as water of crystallization. For example, lithium chloride crystallizes as $LiCl.2\,H_2O$.

**10.23 Why is LiF almost insoluble in water whereas LiCl soluble not only in water but also in acetone?**

**Ans.** Difference in lattice energy and hydration energy of LiCl is higher i.e. $-31$ kJmol$^1$ [$-876 - (-845)$] than that of LiF i.e. $-14$ kJ mol$^{-1}$ [$-1019 - (-1005)$] and hence LiF is sparingly soluble in water while LiCl in soluble. In nut shell, we can say that LiF is almost insoluble in water because of much higher lattice energy ($-1005$ kJ mol$^{-1}$) than that of LiCl ($-845$ kJ mol$^{-1}$). Furthermore, Li$^+$ ion can polarize bigger Cl$^-$ ion more easily than the smaller F$^-$ion. As a result, according to Fajan rules, LiCl has more covalent character than LiF and hence is soluble in organic solvents like acetone

**10.24 Explain the significance of sodium, potassium, magnesium and calcium in biological fluids.**

**Ans.** **Sodium (Na):** They are found in our blood plasma and the interstitial fluids around the cells. They help in
(a) Transmission of nerve signals.
(b) They regulate the flow of water across the membranes of the neighbouring cells.
(c) Transport sugars and amino acids from and to cells.
**Potassium (K):** They are found mostly in the cell fluids in greater quantities. They help in
(a) Activating enzymes
(b) Oxidising glucose to form ATP
(c) Transmitting nerve signals.
**Magneslum (Mg) and calcium (Ca):** They are also called as macro-minerals named so because of their abundance in out body. Mg helps in
(a) Relaxing nerves and muscles
(b) Building and strengthening bones
(c) Maintaining blood circulation in our body
Ca helps in
(a) coagulation of blood
(b) Maintaining homeostasis.

**10.25 What happens when**
**(i) sodium metal is dropped in water ?**
**(ii) sodium metal is heated in free supply of air ?**
**(iii) sodium peroxide dissolves in water ?**

**Ans.** (i) H$_2$ gas is evolved which catches fire due to the exothermicity of the reaction.
$$2Na(s) + 2H_2O(\ell) \longrightarrow 2NaOH\,(aq) + H_2\,(g)$$
(ii) Na$_2$O$_2$ along with a small amount of Na$_2$O is formed.
$$2Na(s) + O_2 \longrightarrow \underset{\text{(minor)}}{Na_2O(s)}$$

$$Na_2O(s) + \tfrac{1}{2}O_2(s) \longrightarrow \underset{\text{(major)}}{Na_2O_2(s)}$$

(iii) H$_2$O$_2$ is formed.
$$Na_2O_2(s) + 2\,H_2O(\ell) \longrightarrow 2\,NaOH\,(aq) + H_2O_2\,(l)$$

**10.26 Comment on each of the following observations:**
**(a) The mobilities of the alkali metal ions in aqueous solution are**
$$Li^+ < Na^+ < K^+ < Rb^+ < Cs^+$$
**(b) Lithium is the only alkali metal to form a nitride directly.**
**(c) $E^{\ominus}$ for M$^{2+}$ (aq) $+ 2e^- \longrightarrow$ M (s)**
**(where M = Ca, Sr or Ba) is nearly constant.**

**Ans.** (a) Smaller the size of the ion, more highly it is hydrated and hence greater is the mass of the hydrated ion and hence smaller is its ionic mobility. Since the extent of hydration decreases in the order:
$$Li^+ > Na^+ > K^+ > Rb^+ > Cs^+$$
therefore, ionic mobility increases in the same order:
$$Li^+ < Na^+ < K^+ < Rb^+ < Cs^+$$
(b) Because of the diagonal relationship of Li and Mg, lithium like magnesium forms a nitride while other alkali metals do not.
$$6Li(s) + N_2(g) \xrightarrow{\Delta} 2Li_3N(s)$$
(c) $E^{\ominus}$ of any M$^{2+}$/M electrode depends upon three factors:
(i) enthalpy of vaporization,
(ii) ionization enthalpy
(iii) enthalpy of hydration.
Since the combined effect of these factors is approximately the same for Ca, Sr and Ba, therefore, their electrode potentials are nearly constant.

**10.27 State as to why**
**(a) A solution of Na$_2$CO$_3$ is alkaline?**
**(b) Alkali metals are prepared by electrolysis of their fused chlorides?**
**(c) Sodium is found to be more useful than potassium?**

**Ans.** (a) Na$_2$CO$_3$ is a salt of a weak acid, carbonic acid (H$_2$CO$_3$) and a strong base, sodium hydroxide (NaOH) therefore, it undergoes hydrolysis to produce strong base NaOH and hence its aqueous solution is alkaline in nature.
$$\underset{\text{Strong base}}{Na_2CO_3(s) + H_2O(\ell) \rightarrow 2NaOH(aq)} + \underset{\text{Weak acid}}{H_2CO_3(aq)}$$
(b) Since the discharge potential of alkali metals is much higher than that of hydrogen, therefore, when the aqueous solution of any alkali metal chloride is subjected to electrolysis. H$_2$ instead of the alkali metal is produced at the cathode. Therefore, to prepare alkali metals, electrolysis of their fused chlorides is carried out.

(c) Sodium ions are found primarily in the blood plasma and in the interstitial fluid which surrounds the cells while potassium ions are present within the cell fluids. Sodium ions help in the transmission of nerve signals, in regulating the flow of water across cell membranes and in the transport of sugars and amino acids into the cells. Thus, sodium is found to be more useful than potassium.

**10.28 Write balanced equations for the reactions between**

**(a) $Na_2O_2$ and water**

**(b) $KO_2$ and water**

**(c) $Na_2O$ and $CO_2$**

**Ans.** (a) $Na_2O_2(s) + 2\ H_2O\ (\ell) \longrightarrow$

$$2\ NaOH\ (aq) + H_2O_2\ (aq)$$

(b) $2\ KO_2(s) + 2\ H_2O\ (\ell) \longrightarrow$

$$2\ KOH\ (aq) + H_2O_2\ (aq) + O_2\ (g)$$

(c) $Na_2O + CO_2 \longrightarrow Na_2CO_3$

**10.29 How would you explain the following observations ?**

**(i) BeO is almost insoluble but $BeSO_4$ is soluble in water,**

**(ii) BaO is soluble but $BaSO_4$ is insoluble in water**

**(iii) LiI is more soluble than KI in ethanol.**

**Ans.** (i) Because of smaller size, higher ionization enthalpy and higher electro negativity, BeO is essentially covalent and hence is insoluble in water. In contrast, $BeSO_4$ is ionic. Further because of small size of $Be^{2+}$ ion, the hydration energy of $BeSO_4$ is much higher than its lattice energy and hence $BeSO_4$ is highly soluble in water.

(ii) Both BaO and $BaSO_4$ are ionic compounds. However, the size of $O^{2-}$ ion is much smaller than that of the $SO_4^{-2}$ ion. Since a bigger anion stabilizes a bigger cation more than a smaller anion stabilizes a bigger cation, therefore, the lattice energy of BaO is much smaller than that of $BaSO_4$ and hence BaO is soluble while $BaSO_4$ is insoluble in water.

(iii) $Li^+$ is much smaller than $K^+$ ion. Therefore, according to Fajan rule, $Li^+$ ion can polarize bigger $I^-$ ion to a greater extent than $K^+$ ion. As a result, LiI is more covalent than KI and hence is more soluble in organic solvents like ethanol.

**10.30 Which of the alkali metal is having least melting point?**

**(a) Na**        **(b) K**

**(c) Rb**        **(d) Cs**

**Ans.** As the size of the metal increases, the strength of metallic bonding decreases and hence its melting point decreases. Since the size of Cs is the biggest, therefore, its melting point is the lowest. Thus, option (d) is correct.

**10.31 Which one of the following alkali metals gives hydrated salts ?**

**(a) Li**        **(b) Na**

**(c) K**        **(d) Cs**

**Ans.** Among alkali metal ions, $Li^+$ is the smallest. Therefore, it has the highest charge density and hence attracts the water molecules more strongly than any other alkali metal cation. Thus, option (a) is correct.

**10.32 Which one of the alkaline earth metal carbonates is thermally the most stable ?**

**(a) $MgCO_3$**        **(b) $CaCO_3$**

**(c) $SrCO_3$**        **(d) $BaCO_3$**

**Ans.** As the electropositive character of the metal increases or the basicities of their hydroxides increases down the group, their thermal stability increases. Thus, $BaCO_3$ is the most stable and hence option (d) is Correct.

| SECTION B | PRACTICE QUESTIONS  |

## MULTIPLE CHOICE QUESTIONS

1. The elements of group 1 provide a colour to the flame of Bunsen burner due to
   (a) low ionization potential
   (b) low melting point
   (c) softness
   (d) presence of one electron in the outermost orbit

2. Select the correct statements
   (i) $Cs^+$ is more highly hydrated that the other alkali metal ions
   (ii) Among the alkali metals Li, Na, K and Rb, lithium has the highest melting point
   (iii) Among the alkali metals only lithium forms a stable nitride by direct combination with nitrogen
   (a) (i), (ii) and (iii)
   (b) (i) and (ii)
   (c) (i) and (iii)
   (d) (ii) and (iii)

3. Suppose an element is kept in air chamber, than air content was evaluated after sometime , oxygen and nitrogen content was found to be low comparitively. The given element will be
   (a) Li        (b) Rb
   (c) Na       (d) K

4. Which of the following statement(s) is/are correct regarding $Li_2CO_3$ and $Na_2CO_3$ ?
   (i) Sodium salt evolve $CO_2$ at higher temperature.
   (ii) Polarization of $Na^+$ is lesser than that of $Li^+$.
   (a) Both statements (i) and (ii) are correct
   (b) Both statements (i) and (ii) are incorrect
   (c) Statement (ii) is correct explanation for statement (i)
   (d) Statement (i) is correct explanation for statement (ii)

5. Suppose metal react with the oxygen to form oxide, than aqueous solution of this oxide when added to a solution of HI, solution turn yellowish brown in colour. This compound is
   (a) $Na_2O$      (b) $Li_2O$
   (c) NaOH     (d) $Na_2O_2$

6. Which of the following does not illustrate the anomalous properties of lithium?
   (a) The melting point and boiling point of Li are comparatively high
   (b) Li is much softer than the other group I metals
   (c) Li forms a nitride $Li_3N$ unlike group I metals
   (d) The ion of Li and its compounds are more heavily hydrated than those of the rest of the group

7. Li has the maximum value of ionisation potential among alkali metals i.e. lithium has the minimum tendency to ionise to give $LI^+$ ion. Thus, in aq. solution lithium is
   (a) strongest reducing agent
   (b) poorest reducing agent
   (c) strongest oxidising agent
   (d) poorest oxidising agent

8. The solubilities of carbonates decrease down the magnesium group due to a decrease in
   (a) hydration energies of cations
   (b) inter-ionic attraction
   (c) entropy of solution formation
   (d) lattice energies of solids

9. Which of the following statement(s) is/are correct?
   (i) The atomic and ionic radii of alkaline earth metals are smaller than those of the corresponding alkali metals in the same periods.
   (ii) Second ionisation enthalpies of the alkaline earth metals are smaller than those of the corresponding alkali metals.
   (iii) Compounds of alkaline earth metals are more extensively hydrated than those of alkali metals
   (a) (i) and (ii)
   (b) (ii) and (iii)
   (c) (i) and (iii)
   (d) (i), (ii) and (iii)

10. Which of the following is/are not characteristic property(ies) of alkaline earth metals ?
    (i) All alkaline earth metal oxides are basic in nature and forms sparingly soluble hydroxides with water.
    (ii) The hydrated chlorides, bromides and iodies of Ca, Sr and Ba on heating undergoes hydrolysis while corresponding hydrated halides of Be and Mg on heating undergo dehydration.
    (iii) Nitrates of alkaline earth metals decompose on heating as below
    $$2M(NO_3)_2 \rightarrow 2MO + 4NO_2 + O_2$$
    (a) (i) only      (b) (ii) only
    (c) (i) and (iii)    (d) (i) and (ii)

11. Magnesium burns in $CO_2$ to form
    (a) MgO + C      (b) MgO + CO
    (c) $MgCO_3$       (d) MgO.

12. Bleaching powder is obtained by the interaction of chlorine with
    (a) dil. solution of $Ca(OH)_2$
    (b) dry CaO
    (c) conc. solution of $Ca(OH)_2$
    (d) dry slaked lime

170 ——————————————————————————————————————————— *Chemistry*

**13.** Calcitonin and parathyroid hormone regulate concentration of which of the following element in plasma?

    (a)  Calcium           (b)  Magnesium

    (c)  Sodium            (d)  Potassium

## ASSERTION & REASON QUESTIONS

**DIRECTIONS (Qs. 1-5) :** *Each of these questions contains an assertion followed by reason. Read them carefully and answer the question on the basis of following options. You have to select the one that best describes the two statements.*

(a) If both Assertion and Reason are correct and the Reason is a correct explanation of the Assertion.

(b) If both Assertion and Reason are correct but Reason is not a correct explanation of the Assertion.

(c) If the Assertion is correct but Reason is incorrect.

(d) If the Assertion is incorrect but the Reason is correct.

**1.** **Assertion :** Group 1 elements of periodic table are known as alkali metals.

**Reason :** Because they form hydroxides on reaction with water which are strongly alkaline in nature.

**2.** **Assertion :** Order of hydration enthalpy is $Li^+ > Na^+ > K^+ > Rb^+ > Cs^+$.

**Reason :** This is because hydration enthalpy of alkali metal ions decreases with increases in ionic size.

**3.** **Assertion :** Alkali metal chlorides do not form hydrates except lithium.

**Reason :** LiCl is deliquescent in nature and crystallizes as a hydrate.

**4.** **Assertion :** The sulphate of Be and Mg are soluble in water.

**Reason :** The greater hydration enthalpy of $Be^{2+}$ and $Mg^2$ ions overcome the lattice enthalpy factor.

**5.** **Assertion :** Beryllium and aluminium exhibit diagonal relationship.

**Reason :** $Be^{2+}$ has almost same charge to size ratio as $Al^{3+}$.

## CASE/PASSAGE BASED QUESTIONS

**DIRECTIONS (Qs. 1-5) :** *Read the following case/passage and answer the questions.*

The alkali metals tend to form ionic solids in which the alkali metal has an oxidation number of +1. Therefore, neutral compounds with oxygen can be readily classified according to the nature of the oxygen species involved. Ionic oxygen species include the oxide, $O^{2-}$, peroxide, $O_2^{2-}$, superoxide, $O_2^-$, and ozonide $O_3^-$. Compounds that can be prepared that contain an alkali metal, M and oxygen are therefore the monoxide, $M_2O$, peroxide, $M_2O_2$, superoxide, $MO_2$ and ozonide $MO_3$. Rubidium and Ceasium and possibly, potassium also form the resquioxide $M_4O_6$, which contains two peroxide anions and one superoxide anion per formula unit. Lithium forms only the monoxide and the peroxide.

**DIRECTIONS (Qs. 1-5) :** *Each of these questions contains an assertion followed by reason. Read them carefully and answer the question on the basis of following options. You have to select the one that best describes the two statements.*

(a) If both Assertion and Reason are correct and the Reason is a correct explanation of the Assertion.

(b) If both Assertion and Reason are correct but Reason is not a correct explanation of the Assertion.

(c) If the Assertion is correct but Reason is incorrect.

(d) If the Assertion is incorrect but the Reason is correct.

**1.** **Assertion :** Only alkali metals form superoxide $(O_2^-)$ which are paramagnetic in nature.

**Reason :** Superoxides contain ion which has one unpaired electron.

**2.** **Assertion :** The carbonate of lithium decomposes easily on heating.

**Reason :** Lithium being very small in size polarizes large carbonate ion leading to the formation of more stable $Li_2O$ and $CO_2$.

**3.** **Assertion :** Alkali metals gives flame test.

**Reason :** This is due to their low ionisation energy.

**4.** **Assertion :** $Li_2O$ and MgO do not combine with excess $O_2$ to give any superoxide.

**Reason :** This is due to smaller size in comparison to large anion.

**5.** **Assertion :** The superoxide $(O_2^-)$ ion is stable only in the presence of large cation such as K, Rb, Cs.

**Reason :** This is due to the fact that a large anion is made stable by a large cation.

## VERY SHORT ANSWER QUESTIONS

**1.** Why are alkali metals used in photoelectric cells?

**2.** Why do alkali metals have low melting and boiling points?

**3.** Why do alkali metals have low density?

**4.** Why are alkali metals soft?

**5.** Complete the reaction : LiI + KF $\rightarrow$

**6.** Name the metal which floats on water without apparent reaction.

**7.** Can we store sodium metal in air or water?

**8.** Which method is commonly used to extract sodium metal from its ores?

**9.** Name the alkali metal which shows diagonal relationship with magnesium?

**10.** What happen when crystals of washing soda $(Na_2CO_3.10H_2O)$ are exposed to air?

**11.** Why is the solution of alkali metals in liquid ammonia conducting in nature?

**12.** What is the oxidation state of K in $KO_2$?

**13.** Sodium peroxide forms a white compound when it comes into contact with moist air. Explain.

14. Why caesium can be used in photoelectric cell while lithium can not be ?

15. Superoxides of alkali metals are coloured and paramagnetic in nature. Explain.

16. Why does a piece of burning magnesium ribbon continues to burn in sulphur dioxide ?

17. What is the function of adding gypsum to clinker cement?

18. Why is anhydrous $CaSO_4$ used as drying agent? Why not plaster of paris ?

19. How the caves are formed in limestone regions ?

20. Why group 2 elements (Mg and Ca) are harder and denser than group 1 elements?

21. The second ionization enthalpy of Ca is higher than first and yet calcium forms $CaCl_2$ and not $CaCl$, why?

22. Which is more basic, NaOH or $Mg(OH)_2$?

23. The crystalline salts of alkaline earth metals contain more water of crystallisation than the corresponding alkali metal salts, why?

24. Account for the following :
Be has less negative value of the reduction potential $(E°)$

## SHORT ANSWER QUESTIONS

1. Give reasons
   (i) Li & Mg show similar properties.
   (ii) Alkali metals show +1 oxidation state.
   (iii) Alkali metals have largest size in their period

2. Mention a few difficulties involved in the extraction of sodium from fused sodium chloride.

3. What is meant by 'diagonal relationship' in the periodic table? What is it due to?

4. Alkali metals are paramagnetic but their salts are diamagnetic. Explain.

5. How $LiNO_3$ and $NaNO_3$ differ from each other on the action of water?

6. Why it is not advisable to dry alcohols with sodium metal, though it is used for drying ether?

7. What is the use of $KO_2$ in oxygen masks?

8. KOH is preferred to NaOH to absorb $CO_2$, why?

9. Explain why a pellet of sodium is covered with sodium carbonate layer when exposed to atmosphere?

10. What happens when
    (i) calcium is treated with nitrogen.
    (ii) calcium is treated with dilute sulphuric acid.
    (iii) calcium is heated in the atmosphere of $SO_2$.
    (iv) calcium is treated with cold water .

11. How is quick lime prepared on a commercial scale ? How is it converted into slaked lime ?

12. What different changes occur when $CO_2$ is passed through lime water?

13. Why
    (i) is $Mg^+$ ion unstable ?
    (ii) does beryllium form $BeCl_2$ although it has no unpaired electrons ?

14. Magnesium metal burns in air to give a white ash. When this ash is treated with water, the odour of ammonia can be detected ? Explain.

15. Calcium burns in nitrogen to produce a white powder which dissolves in sufficient water to produce a gas (A) and an alkaline solution. The solution on exposure to air produces a thin solid layer of (B) on the surface. Identify the components A and B.

16. How will you distinguish between
    (i) Slaked lime
    (ii) Milk of lime
    (iii) Limewater

17. Arrange the following in the order of property indicated:
    (i) $CaCl_2$, $MgCl_2$, $BeCl_2$, $SrCl_2$ : Ionic character
    (ii) $Sr(OH)_2$, $Ba(OH)_2$, $Be(OH)_2$, $Mg(OH)_2$ : Basic character
    (iii) $BeSO_4$, $SrSO_4$, $CaSO_4$, $BaSO_4$ : Increasing solubility in water

18. Give reasons
    (i) $BeCl_2$ fumes in air.
    (ii) $BeCl_2$ differs from other halides of alkaline earth metals

19. Why is it that hydrated chlorides of Ca, Sr and Ba can be dehydrated by heating but those of Be and Mg suffer hydrolysis?

20. 'The chemistry of beryllium is not essentially ionic.' Justify the statement by making a reference to the nature of oxide, chloride and fluoride of beryllium.

21. Beryllium exhibits some similarities with aluminium. Point out three such properties.

22. Alkaline earth metal ions have a tendency to form complexes, whereas it is not so in case of alkali metals.

23. Why is MgO used as a refractory material ?

24. $BaSO_4$ is used during the X-ray of stomach, why?

25. Discuss thermal stability and the solubility of the oxosalts of alkaline earth metals.

26. Why is calcium preferred over sodium to remove last traces of moisture from alcohol?

## LONG ANSWER QUESTIONS

1. Give reasons
   (i) Alkali metals are good reducing agents.
   (ii) Alkali metals can be obtained only by electrolysis of their fused salts.
   (iii) Hydrogen is obtained on electrolysis of aqueous solution of salts of alkali metals.
   (iv) Alkali metals dissolve in liquid ammonia to give blue solutions.
   (v) The blue colour of metal–ammonia solution disappears on standing.

**2.** What happens when
   (i) Magnesium is heated with water.
   (ii) Magnesium is treated with nitrogen.
   (iii) Magnesium is heated in an atmosphere of carbon dioxide.
   (iv) Magnesium is treated with dilute sulphuric acid
   (v) Magnesium is burnt in air.

**3.** Contrast the action of heat on the following and explain your answer.
   (i) $Na_2CO_3$ and $CaCO_3$
   (ii) $MgCl_2.6H_2O$ and $CaCl_2.6H_2O$
   (iii) $Ca(NO_3)_2$ and $NaNO_3$.

**4.** Complete the following equations for the reaction between
   (i) $Ca + H_2O$     (ii) $Ca(OH)_2 + Cl_2$
   (iii) $BeO + NaOH$     (iv) $BeCl_2 + LiAlH_4$
   (v) $Ca_3N_2 + H_2O$

**5.** Give reasons
   (i) Unlike alkali metal compounds, compounds of Li are much less soluble in water.
   (ii) Although Li has highest I.E. in group −1 but it is the best reducing agent.
   (iii) Li differs from other members of its group.
   (iv) $LiOH$, $LiNO_3$, $Li_2CO_3$ decompose readily on heating, whereas the other alkali metal hydroxides & carbonates not decompose readily on heating.
   (v) Alkali & some alkaline earth metals impart colour to bunsen flame.

SOLUTIONS

### *Multiple Choice Questions*

**1.** **(a)** Electrons can easily excite due to low I.E.

**2.** **(d)** Amongst alkali metal, Li ions are highly hydrated.

**3.** **(a)** All the given elements react with oxygen to form oxides but only Li also react with nitrogen to form $Li_3N$.

**4.** **(c)** $Na_2CO_3$ is more stable than $Li_2CO_3$.

**5.** **(d)** (a) and (b) forms corresponding hydroxides (NaOH and LiOH) in aqueous solution

$$M_2O + H_2O \longrightarrow 2M^+ + 2OH^- \ (M = Na \text{ or } Li)$$

Therefore, reaction of HI with (a), (b) and (c) is simply a neutralization reaction, while aqueous solution of (d) form $H_2O_2$ which act as oxidizing agent, hence convert Iodide to Iodine($I_2$).

$$Na_2O_2 + 2H_2O \longrightarrow 2Na^+ + 2OH^- + H_2O_2$$

**6.** **(b)** Actually Li is harder than other alkali metals.

**7.** **(a)** The ionisation potential value of lithium is maximum among alkali metals *i.e.*, its tendency to ionise to give $Li^+$ ions should be the minimum *i.e.* Li should be the poorest reducing agent. But, lithium is the strongest reducing agent in aq. solution. This is due to the largest value of hydration energy of $Li^+$ ions.

**8.** **(a)** As we move down the group, the lattice energies of carbonates remain approximately the same. However, the hydration energies of the metal cation decreases from $Be^{2+}$ to $Ba^{2+}$, hence the solubilities of carbonates of the alkaline earth metal decrease down the group mainly due to decreasing hydration energies of the cations from $Be^{2+}$ to $Ba^{2+}$.

**9.** **(d)** All the given statements are correct.

**10.** **(d)** All alkaline earth metal oxides except BeO are basic in nature. BeO is amphoteric in nature.
Hydrated halides of Ca, Sr and Ba on heating undergo dehydration while corresponding hydrated halides of Be and Mg on heating suffer hydrolysis.

**11.** **(a)** Mg burns in $CO_2$ to give MgO and C.

**12.** **(d)** When cold calcium hydroxide reacts with chlorine, then bleaching powder is obtained.

$$\underset{\text{slaked lime}}{3Ca(OH)_2} + 2Cl_2 \longrightarrow$$

$$\underset{\text{Bleaching powder}}{Ca(OCl)_2.Ca(OH)_2.CaCl_2.2H_2O}$$

**13.** **(a)** The calcium concentration in plasma is regulated at about $100\ mgL^{-1}$. It is maintained by two hormones: calcitonin and parathyroid hormone.

### *Assertion & Reason Questions*

**1.** **(a)** Alkali metals react with cold water to form metal hydroxides (alkalis). Reactions are highly explosive in nature and evolve high amount of energy.

$$\underset{(M:Na,K)}{M} + H_2O \longrightarrow MOH + H_2(g)$$

**2.** **(a)** This is because hydration tendency depends on charge to radius ratio, therefore, hydration tendency decreases down the group form $Li^+$ to $Cs^+$.

**3.** **(a)** Alkali metals (except lithium) have lower tendency to hydrate due to bigger size, therefore, chlorides of alkali metals does not form hydrates. Li has small size and higher tendency for hydration. Hence, LiCl is deliquescent in nature and form hydrated salt.

**4.** **(b)** This is because of very large hydration enthalpies of the contains of the alkaline earth metals. These get very extensively hydrated in the presence of water, therefore, anhydrous halides of Mg and Ca are hygroscopic in nature.

**5.** **(a)** Be and Al has approximately same size. Their ions ($Be^{2+}$ and $Al^{3+}$) have approximately same charge to size ratio, therefore, they show diagonal relationship. They have similarity in chemical and physical properties.

### Case/Passage Based Questions

1. **(a)** $O_2^-$ has 17 electrons. Presence of unpaired electrons, $O_2^-$ is paramagnetic

2. **(a)** Lithium compounds are covalent in nature, therefore, has less thermal stability.

3. **(a)** Alkali metals have very low ionisation enthalpy, therefore, metals electrons get excited at flame temperature. Excited state is unstable and electrons return in ground state. When excited electrons return to the ground state, light of a particular colour is emitted out.

4. **(d)** $Li^+$ ion and $Mg^{2+}$ ions have small size and strong positive field around it which prevents the formation of peroxides and superoxides.

5. **(a)** The small cation can stabilise the small anion and the large cation can and stabilise the large anion. So, sodium metal forms peroxide and K, Rb and Cs give superoxide.

### Very Short Answer Questions

1. They have low ionisation energy and can lose electrons when light falls on them, that is why they are used in photoelectric cells.

2. It is due to weak metallic bonds which is due to bigger atomic size that is why they how low melting and boiling points.

3. Due to weak metallic bonds and large atomic size, their density is low.

4. They are soft metals due to less force of attraction between positively charged kernels and valence electrons cloud and due to large atomic size, i.e., weak metallic bond.

5. $LiI + KF \rightarrow LiF + KI$; larger cation stabilizes larger anion and smaller cation stabilizes smaller anion.

6. Beryllium

7. No, it reacts violently with water and catches fire.

8. Electrolytic reduction using *Down cell* is commonly used for the extraction of sodium metal.

9. Li.

10. Monohydrate ($Na_2CO_3. H_2O$) is formed as a result of efflorescence.

11. Due to ammoniated electrons and cations.

12. K is +1.

13. Sodium peroxide when exposed to moist air turns white due to formation of NaOH and $Na_2CO_3$.
$2Na_2O_2 + 2H_2O \rightarrow 4NaOH + O_2$
$2Na_2O_2 + 2CO_2 \rightarrow 2Na_2CO_3 + O_2$

14. Caesium has the lowest while lithium has the highest ionisation enthalpy. Hence caesium can lose electron very easily while lithium can not.

15. Superoxide contains a three electron bond which makes it paramagnetic and coloured.
$$[\ddot{O}\!\cdot\!\cdot\!\cdot\ddot{O}]$$

16. This is because magnesium has high affinity to combine with oxygen of $SO_2$ to form MgO and S.
$2Mg + SO_2 \longrightarrow 2MgO + S$

17. Gypsum is added to retard the rate of setting of cement. Gypsum reacts with tricalcium aluminate to form calcium sulphoaluminate.
$$3CaO.Al_2O_3 + 3CaSO_4 + nH_2O \longrightarrow$$
$$3CaO . Al_2O_3 .CaSO_4 . nH_2O$$

18. Anhydrous $CaSO_4$ can absorb water to form $CaSO_4 . 2H_2O$ and hence can be used as a drying agent. Plaster of paris is not used as a drying agent because it sets into a hard mass by absorbing water.

19. Caves in limestone regions get formed due to the dissolution of calcium carbonate in water containing carbon dioxide.
$$CaCO_3 + H_2O \longrightarrow Ca(OH)_2 + CO_2$$

20. They have strong metallic bonds due to smaller size and have more number of valence electrons.

21. The hydration energy of $Ca^{2+}$ overcomes the second ionisation energy of Ca, that is why Ca forms $CaCl_2$ and not CaCl. $Ca^+$ is not stable.

22. NaOH.

23. This is because alkaline earth metals have smaller size and higher nuclear charges as compared to alkali metals.

24. The less negative value for Be arises from the large hydration energy associated with the small size of $Be^{2+}$ and the relatively large value of the enthalpy of atomization of the metal.

### Short Answer Questions

1. (i) This is due to diagonal relationship as they have same electronegativity, ionisation enthalpy and charge/radius ratio.

   (ii) As alkali metal have $ns^1$ configuration , they loose one electron to achieve stable noble gas configuration.

   (iii) Since across the period the incoming electrons enters in the same energy shell and due to increase in nuclear charge the valence electrons feels more attraction from nucleus as we move from left to right in a period. As alkali metals are the first group along the period they have largest radius in their respective periods.

2. It is slightly difficult to obtain sodium from fused sodium chloride due to the following:

   (i) Sodium chloride melts at 1074 K and it is difficult to attain and maintain this temperature.

   (ii) Sodium boils at about 1165 K and hence at the temperature of electrolysis, the metal liberated will vapourize.

   (iii) Molten sodium forms a metallic fog (colloidal solution) with fused sodium chloride.

   (iv) The products of electrolysis, sodium and chlorine, corrode the material of the cell at this high temperature.

3. The similarity in properties of the first element of each group with the elements to the lower right of the next period i.e. diagonally opposite element, is known as 'diagonal relationship. This is due to
   (i) similarity in the size of the ions
      e.g. $r_{Li+}$ = 76 pm, $r_{Mg2+}$ = 72 pm
   (ii) similarity in polarizing power
$$\left[\frac{\text{ionic charge}}{(\text{ionic radius})^2}\right]$$
   (iii) similarity in electropositive character.

4. Alkali metals contain unpaired electrons and hence are paramagnetic. But in the salts of alkali metals there are alkali metal cations which don't have unpaired electrons. Hence these are diamagnetic.

5. $NaNO_3$ is very readily soluble in water because it is ionic in nature while $LiNO_3$ is not readily soluble in water because it is covalent in nature.

6. Alcohols react with sodium metal liberating hydrogen gas, hence it can not be dried with sodium metal. Ether, on the other hand, does not react with sodium metal.
$$2ROH + 2Na \rightarrow 2RONa + H_2\uparrow$$
   (Alcohol)

7. Potassium superoxide ($KO_2$) finds its application in oxygen masks used for emergency breathing purposes particularly in mines etc. It is also used as a source of oxygen in space crafts and submarines also. The moisture of breathing decomposes potassium superoxide to release oxygen.

8. Alkali metal hydroxides absorb carbon dioxide gas but KOH is preferred to NaOH because $K_2CO_3$ formed on absorption of $CO_2$ being more soluble in water does not separate.

9. A pellet of sodium hydroxide when exposed to moisture developes a liquid layer around it because of its hygroscopic nature. This liquid layer gradually turns into a white powdery mass as aqueous sol. Sodium hydroxide absorbs moisture and forms sodium Carbonate.

10. (i) Calcium nitride is formed.
$$3Ca(s) + N_2(g) \longrightarrow Ca_3N_2(s)$$
   (ii) Dihydrogen gas is liberated.
$$Ca(s) + H_2SO_4(aq) \longrightarrow CaSO_4(aq) + H_2(g)$$
   (iii) Calcium oxide is formed.
$$2Ca(s) + SO_2(g) \longrightarrow 2CaO(s) + S(s)$$
   (iv) Dihydrogen gas is liberated.
$$Ca(s) + 2H_2O(\ell) \longrightarrow Ca(OH)_2(aq) + H_2(g)$$

11. Quick lime is anhydrous calcium oxide (CaO) and is formed by heating lime stone ($CaCO_3$) in a specially designed kiln at 1070 – 1270 K
$$CaCO_3 \xrightleftharpoons{\text{Heat}} CaO + CO_2 ; \Delta H = +179.9 kJ$$

**Formation of slaked lime.** Slaked lime is formed when quick lime is added to water. The reaction is highly exothermic in nature and called slaking of lime.
$$CaO + H_2O \rightleftharpoons Ca(OH)_2 + \text{Heat}$$

12. On passing $CO_2$ through lime water, it turns milky due to the formation of insoluble calcium carbonate.
$$Ca(OH)_2(aq) + CO_2(g) \longrightarrow CaCO_3(s) + H_2O(\ell)$$
If carbon dioxide is passed in excess, a clear solution is again obtained. This is because the insoluble calcium carbonate changes into soluble calcium bicarbonate.
$$CaCO_3(s) + H_2O(\ell) + CO_2(g) \longrightarrow \underset{\text{Soluble}}{Ca(HCO_3)_2(aq)}$$
If the clear solution is heated, it again turns milky due to the decomposition of calcium bicarbonate into calcium carbonate.
$$\underset{\text{Soluble}}{Ca(HCO_3)_2} \xrightarrow{\text{Heat}} \underset{\text{Insoluble}}{CaCO_3(s)} + CO_2 + H_2O(\ell)$$

13. (i) Because $Mg^+$ ion has the tendency to lose another electron to form $Mg^{2+}$ ion which has stable noble gas configuration of the nearest inert gas (Neon).
   (ii) Beryllium (At.No.4) has electronic configuration $1s^2 2s^1 2p_x^1$ in the excited state. One $s$–orbital ($2s$) and one $p$–orbital ($2p$) can intermix to form two $sp$ hybrid orbitals which can be used to form $BeCl_2$.

14. Magnesium burns in air to form MgO and $Mg_3N_2$.
$$2Mg + O_2 \longrightarrow 2MgO$$
$$3Mg + N_2 \longrightarrow Mg_3N_2$$
Magnesium nitride on hydrolysis with $H_2O$ gives $NH_3$.
$$Mg_3N_2 + 6H_2O \longrightarrow 3Mg(OH)_2 + 2NH_3$$

15. Calcium burns in $N_2$ to produce $Ca_3N_2$.
$$3Ca + N_2 \rightarrow \underset{\text{White powder}}{Ca_3N_2}$$
Calcium nitride ($Ca_3N_2$) on hydrolysis with water gives ammonia gas (A)
$$Ca_3N_2 + 6H_2O \longrightarrow 3Ca(OH)_2 + \underset{(A)}{2NH_3}$$
The alkaline solution of $Ca(OH)_2$ thus formed reacts with $CO_2$ present in the air to form calcium carbonate, $CaCO_3$ (B)
$$Ca(OH)_2 + CO_2 \longrightarrow \underset{(B)}{CaCO_3} + H_2O$$
Thus A = $NH_3$ ; B = $CaCO_3$.

16. (i) **Slaked lime:** White amorphous solid, formed when quick lime is added to water
$$CaO + H_2O \longrightarrow \underset{\text{Slaked lime}}{Ca(OH)_2}$$
   (ii) **Milk of lime :** It is the suspension of slaked lime in water.
   (iii) **Lime water :** When milk of lime is kept for some time solid particles suspended in water settled down and clear solution is obtained which is decanted is known as lime water.

**17.** (i) Increasing order of ionic character $BeCl_2 < MgCl_2 < CaCl_2 < SrCl_2$

    (ii) Increasing order of basic character $Be(OH)_2 < Mg(OH)_2 < Sr(OH)_2 < Ba(OH)_2$

    (iii) Increasing order of solubility in water $BaSO_4 < SrSO_4 < CaSO_4 < BeSO_4$.

**18.** (i) $BeCl_2$ gives HCl gas in moist air due to which fumes are observed.

$$BeCl_2 + 2H_2O \longrightarrow Be(OH)_2 + 2HCl$$

    (ii) Be have small size and high ionization enthalpy, thus its halides are mostly covalent . But as we go down the group the size increases and ionization enthalpy decreases thus other members of the groups form ionic halides. The halides of beryllium do not form hydrates while other do form.

**19.** $$CaCl_2.6H_2O \xrightarrow{\text{heat}} CaCl_2 + 6H_2O$$

$$MgCl_2.6H_2O \xrightarrow{\text{heat}} MgO + 2HCl + 5H_2O$$

$MgCl_2. 6H_2O$ or $BeCl_2. 4H_2O$ on heating suffer hydrolysis due to the small size of $Mg^{2+}$ (or $Be^{2+}$).

**20.** Due to exceptionally small size and high ionization enthalpy, the compounds of beryllium are largely covalent. For example: BeO is amphoteric while oxide of other elements of group-2 are basic in nature. BeO dissolves in alkali to form beryllate

$$BeO + 2OH^- + H_2O \rightarrow [Be(OH)_4]^{2-}$$

$BeCl_2$ is largely covalent and is soluble in organic solvents. $BeF_2$ is also highly covalent and due to high lattice enthalpy, the solubility is very less.

**21.** (i) Both Be and Al react with conc. sodium hydroxide to form beryllate ion $[Be(OH)_4]^{2-}$ or aluminate ion $[Al(OH)_6]^{2-}$.

    (ii) Both BeO and $Al_2O_3$ are amphoteric in nature.

    (iii) $BeCl_2$ and $AlCl_3$ both are covalent.

**22.** For the complex formation the central metal ion must have a strong charge density to attract the ligands towards itself. The alkaline earth metal cation ($M^{2+}$) can do so whereas alkali metal ions ($M^+$) with smaller charge density cannot do so.

**23.** Magnesium oxide is used as a **refractory material** that is a material which can withstand high temperature without melting or decomposition. It is due to the reason that the lattice energy of MgO is very high and thus it does not decompose at high temperature.

**24.** During the X-ray of the stomach or the alimentary canal, a suspension of $BaSO_4$ in water known as **barium meal** is administered to the patient because it is insoluble in water, Coats the inner surface or walls of the alimentary canal making them opaque for X-ray. The poisonous $Ba^{2+}$ are not absorbed in blood due to the insoluble nature of $BaSO_4$.

**25.** Common oxosalts of alkaline earth metals are carbonates and sulphates. Thermal stability of carbonates, sulphates increases down the group because carbonates and sulphates are big anions which are more stabilized by bigger cations.

Solubility of the oxosalts also decreases down the group because hydration energy of the cations decrease down the group with increasing cationic size.

**26.** Both Na and K can react with water. But Na also reacts with alcohol whereas calcium does not or react slowly.

$$2C_2H_5OH + 2Na \rightarrow 2C_2H_5ONa + H_2 \uparrow$$

Sodium
ethoxide

Therefore, calcium is preferred over sodium to remove the last traces of moisture from alcohol.

### *Long Answer Questions*

**1.** (i) Due to their large size, their ionization enthalpies are very small and hence can loose electrons very easily. Thus alkali metals are strong reducing agents.

    (ii) Alkali metals are strong reducing agents and are also highly electropositive in nature, thus they cannot be displaced from aqueous solutions of their salts by other metals. Also they are more reducing than hydrogen thus they cannot be obtained from the electrolysis of their aqueous salts solution. Thus they are obtained only by electrolysis of their fused salts.

    (iii) As alkali metals are more reducing than hydrogen thus they cannot be obtained from the electrolysis of their aqueous salts solution. Thus during electrolysis of aqueous solution of alkali metals hydrogen is liberated at cathode as it has high reduction potential than alkali metals.

    (iv) These solutions contain ammoniated cations and ammoniated electrons as per the following reaction:

$$M + (x + y) NH_3 \rightarrow M^+(NH_3)_x + e^-(NH_3)_y$$

When ordinary light falls on these ammoniated electrons, they get excited to higher levels by absorbing energy corresponding to red region. As a result, transmitted light is blue which imparts blue colour to the solution.

    (v) The blue colour disappears after sometimes as the reaction goes for completion to form metal amides with liberation of hydrogen.

**2.** (i) Hydrogen gas is liberated.

$$Mg(s) + 2H_2O(\ell) \longrightarrow Mg(OH)_2(aq) + H_2(g)$$

    (ii) Magnesium nitride is formed.

$$3Mg(s) + N_2(g) \longrightarrow Mg_3N_2(s)$$

    (iii) Magnesium oxide is formed.

$$2Mg(s) + CO_2(g) \longrightarrow 2MgO(s) + C(s)$$

    (iv) Dihydrogen gas is liberated.

$$Mg(s) + H_2SO_4(aq) \longrightarrow MgSO_4(aq) + H_2(g)$$

    (v) A mixture of magnesium oxide and magnesium nitride is formed.

$$2Mg + O_2 \longrightarrow 2MgO$$

$$3Mg + N_2 \longrightarrow Mg_3N_2$$

**3.** (i) $Na_2CO_3$ and $CaCO_3$
No action of heat on $Na_2CO_3$ while $CaCO_3$ decomposes on heating.

$$CaCO_3 \xrightarrow{\text{Heat}} CaO + CO_2$$

(ii) $MgCl_2.6H_2O$ and $CaCl_2.6H_2O$.

$$MgCl_2 \cdot 6H_2O \xrightarrow{\text{Heat}} MgO + 2HCl + 5H_2O$$
$$CaCl_2 \cdot 6H_2O \xrightarrow{473K} CaCl_2 \cdot 2H_2O + 4H_2O$$

(iii) $Ca(NO_3)_2$ and $NaNO_3$
$$2Ca(NO_3)_2 \longrightarrow 2CaO + 4NO_2 + O_2$$
$$2NaNO_3 \longrightarrow 2NaNO_2 + O_2$$

**4.** (i) $Ca + 2H_2O \longrightarrow Ca(OH)_2 + H_2(g)$

(ii) $Ca(OH)_2 + Cl_2 \rightarrow \underset{\text{Bleaching Powder}}{CaOCl_2} + H_2O$

(iii) $BeO + 2NaOH \longrightarrow Na_2BeO_2 + H_2O$

(iv) $2BeCl_2 + LiAlH_4 \longrightarrow 2BeH_2 + LiCl + AlCl_3$

(v) $Ca_3N_2 + 6H_2O \longrightarrow 3Ca(OH)_2 + 2NH_3$

**5.** (i) Because of covalent character in the compounds of lithium they are less soluble in water.

(ii) Due to small size of lithium it readily gets hydrated and this high hydration enthalpy compensates high Ionization enthalpy which makes lithium the most reducing element.

(iii) The anomalous behaviour of lithium is due to following reasons:

(a) very small size of lithium and its ion.

(b) High polarizing power of $Li^+$ resulting in increased covalent character of its compounds which is responsible for their solubility in organic solvent.

(c) Comparatively high ionization enthalpy and low electropositive character as compared to other members.

(iv) Lithium being the first element in it's group, has very small size due to which it has high polarizing power resulting in the generation of covalent character in its compounds. Thus its salt easily decompose on heating.

(v) The alkali metals have very low ionisation enthalpies. The energy from the flame of bunsen burner is sufficient to excite the electrons of alkali metals to higher energy levels. The excited state is quite unstable and therefore when these excited electrons come back to their original energy levels, they emit extra energy, which fall in the visible region of the electromagnetic spectrum and thus appear coloured.

## SECTION C — NCERT EXEMPLAR QUESTIONS

### MULTIPLE CHOICE QUESTIONS

**1.** The alkali metals are low melting. Which of the following alkali metal is expected to melt if the room temperature rises to 30°C?

(a) Na    (b) K    (c) Rb    (d) Cs

**2.** Alkali metals react with water vigorously to form hydroxides and dihydrogen. Which of the following alkali metals reacts with water least vigorously?

(a) Li    (b) Na    (c) K    (d) Cs

**3.** Metals form basic hydroxides. Which of the following metal hydroxide is the least basic?

(a) $Mg(OH)_2$      (b) $Ca(OH)_2$

(c) $Sr(OH)_2$      (d) $Ba(OH)_2$

**4.** Some of the Group 2 metal halides are covalent and soluble in organic solvents. Among the following metal halides, the one which is soluble in ethanol is

(a) $BeCl_2$      (b) $MgCl_2$

(c) $CaCl_2$      (d) $SrCl_2$

**5.** The order of decreasing ionisation enthalpy in alkali metals is

(a) $Na > Li > K > Rb$     (b) $Rb < Na < K < Li$

(c) $Li > Na > K > Rb$     (d) $K < Li < Na < Rb$

**6.** Amphoteric hydroxides react with both alkalies and acids. Which of the following Group 2 metal hydroxides is soluble in sodium hydroxide?

(a) $Be(OH)_2$      (b) $Mg(OH)_2$

(c) $Ca(OH)_2$      (d) $Ba(OH)_2$

**7.** When sodium is dissolved in liquid ammonia, a solution of deep blue colour is obtained. The colour of the solution is due to

(a) ammoniated electron

(b) sodium ion

(c) sodium amide

(d) ammoniated sodium ion

**8.** Dead burnt plaster is

(a) $CaSO_4$      (b) $CaSO_4 \cdot \frac{1}{2} H_2O$

(c) $CaSO_4.H_2O$      (d) $CaSO_4.2H_2O$

9. Suspension of slaked lime in water is known as
   (a) lime water
   (b) quick lime
   (c) milk of lime
   (d) aqueous solution of slaked lime
10. The formula of soda ash is
   (a) $Na_2CO_3.10H_2O$     (b) $Na_2CO_3.2H_2O$
   (c) $Na_2CO_3.H_2O$     (d) $Na_2CO_3$

## ASSERTION & REASON QUESTIONS

**DIRECTIONS (Qs. 1-2) :** *Each of these questions contains an assertion followed by reason. Read them carefully and answer the question on the basis of following options. You have to select the one that best describes the two statements.*
(a) If both Assertion and Reason are correct and the Reason is a correct explanation of the Assertion.
(b) If both Assertion and Reason are correct but Reason is not a correct explanation of the Assertion.
(c) If the Assertion is correct but Reason is incorrect.
(d) If the Assertion is incorrect but the Reason is correct.

1. **Assertion :** The carbonate of lithium decomposes easily on heating to , form lithium oxide and $CO_2$.
   **Reason :** Lithium being very small in size polarizes large carbonate ion leading to the formation of more stable $Li_2O$ and $CO_2$.

2. **Assertion :** Beryllium carbonate is kept in the atmosphere of carbon dioxide.
   **Reason :** Beryllium carbonate is unstable and decomposes to give beryllium oxide and carbon dioxide:

## SHORT ANSWER QUESTIONS

1. Lithium resembles magnesium in some of its properties. Mention two such properties and give reasons for this resemblance.
2. Why are $BeSO_4$ and $MgSO_4$ readily soluble in water while $CaSO_4$, $SrSO_4$ and $BaSO_4$ are insoluble?

## LONG ANSWER QUESTIONS

1. When water is added to compound (A) of calcium, solution of compound (B) is formed. When carbon dioxide is passed into the solution, it turns milky due to the formation of compound (C). If excess of carbon dioxide is passed into the solution milkiness disappears due to the formation of compound (D). Identify the compounds A, B, C and D. Explain why the milkiness disappears in the last step.
2. Lithium hydride can be used to prepare other useful hydrides. Beryllium hydride is one of them. Suggest a route for the preparation of beryllium hydride starting from lithium hydride. Write chemical equations involved in the process.

## SOLUTIONS

### Multiple Choice Questions

1. **(d)** Alkali metals have low melting and boiling points. The melting point of alkali metals decreases from Li to Cs as cohesive force decreases with increase in atomic size.
2. **(a)** The reactivity of alkali metals with water increases on moving down the group from Li to Cs due to increase in electropositive character.
3. **(a)** The basic character of the given hydroxides increases down the group due to decrease in ionization enthalpies. On moving down the group, the ionic size increases, so M–O bond in metal hydroxides gets weaker and easily gives $OH^-$ in the solution and I.E. further decreases. Hence, $Mg(OH)_2$ will be least basic. The order of basicity will be:
   $Mg(OH)_2 < Ca(OH)_2 < Sr(OH)_2 < Ba(OH)_2$
4. **(a)** Ethanol is a covalent compound and only a compound which has more covalent character can be dissolved in it. Also the group ionic character increases and beryllium halide have covalent character due to its small size and high effective nuclear charge. Hence, among the given halides, $BeCl_2$ can be soluble in ethanol.

5. **(c)** On moving down the group from Li to Rb, increased atomic radii makes the removal of electron easier.
   Thus, the order of decreasing ionization enthalpy will be: Li > Na > K > Rb
   Also, LiF exhibit very high lattice energy.
6. **(a)** $Be(OH)_2$ is an amphoteric hydroxide thus gets dissolve both in acids and alkalies.
   Basic nature :
   $$Be(OH)_2 + 2HCl \longrightarrow BeCl_2 + 2H_2O$$
   Acidic nature:
   $$Be(OH)_2 + 2NaOH \longrightarrow \underset{\text{Sodium beryllate}}{Na_2BeO_2} + 2H_2O$$
7. **(a)** Alkali metals dissolve in liquid $NH_3$ giving deep blue coloured solution.
   $$Na + (x+y)NH_3 \longrightarrow$$
   $$\underset{\text{Ammoniated cation}}{\left[Na(NH_3)_x\right]^+} + \underset{\text{Ammoniated electron}}{e^-(NH_3)_y}$$
   When light fall on the solution, the ammoniated electrons get excite to higher energy level by absorbing certain wavelength and transmit blue colour.

8. **(a)** On heating plaster of Paris at certain temperature, it forms anhydrous calcium sulphate which is known to be dead burnt plaster and has no setting property as it absorbs water very slowly.

$$CaSO_4 . \frac{1}{2} H_2O \xrightarrow{200°C} \underset{(Anhydrous)}{CaSO_4} \xrightarrow{1100°C} CaO + SO_3$$

9. **(c)** Slaked lime $[Ca(OH)_2]$ is sparingly soluble in water and it forms a suspension of slaked lime in water which is called milk of lime. A clear solution obtained after the suspension settles is known as lime water.

10. **(d)** On heating washing soda, it loses its water of crystallisation. Above 373 K, it becomes completely anhydrous white powder called soda ash.

$$\underset{\text{Washing soda}}{Na_2CO_3 . 10H_2O} \xrightarrow{\text{Above 373K}} \underset{\substack{\text{Soda ash} \\ (\text{Anhydrous form})}}{Na_2CO_3}$$

### *Assertion & Reason Questions*

1. **(a)** Unlike other alkali metal carbonates, the carbonate of lithium decomposes on heating to form its oxide. Its oxide is stablised by polarization.

2. **(a)** $BeCO_3$ is kept in the atmosphere of $CO_2$, otherwise it will decompose to give its oxide and carbon dioxide.

### *Short Answer Questions*

1. (i) Lithium and magnesium are both lighter and harder than the other metals in their respective groups.
   (ii) Halides of both elements, LiCl and $MgCl_2$ are soluble in ethanol.

2. The greater hydration enthalpies of $Be^{2+}$ and $Mg^{2+}$ ions overcome the lattie enthalpy factor and therefore their sulphates are soluble in water.

### *Long Answer Questions*

1. Compound : A : CaO ; B : $Ca(OH)_2$ ; C : $CaCO_3$; D : $Ca(HCO_3)_2$

   $Ca(HCO_3)_2$ is soluble in water. Hence, milkiness of solution disappears on passing excess carbon dioxide into the solution of compound B.

2. $8\ LiH + Al_2Cl_6 \rightarrow 2Li\ AlH_4 + 6LiCl$

   $LiAl\ H_4 + 2BeCl_2 \rightarrow 2BeH_2 + LiCl + AlCl_3$

# 11 — The *p*-Block Elements



**11.1** **Discuss the pattern of variation in the oxidation states of (i) B to Tl (ii) C to Pb.**

**Ans.** (i) B and Al have no $d$–or $f$–electrons. Therefore, they do not exhibit inert pair effect. Consequently, they show an oxidation state of +3 only due to the presence of two electrons in the $s$–and one electron in the $p$–orbital of the valence shell. In contrast, all other elements from Ga to Tl contain only $d$–or $d$–and $f$–electrons and hence show two oxidation states of +1 and +3 due to inert pair effect. Further, as the number of $d$– and $f$–electrons increases down the group, the inert pair effect becomes more and more pronounced. In other words, as we move down the group from Ga to Tl, the stability of +1 oxidation state increases (i.e., Ga < In < Tl) while that of +3 oxidation state decreases (i.e. Ga > In > Tl).

Thus, +1 oxidation state of Tl is more stable than its +3 oxidation state.

(ii) Carbon and silicon have no $d$–or $f$–electrons. Therefore, they do not exhibit inert pair effect. Consequently, they show an oxidation state of + 4 due to the presence of two electrons in the $s$–and two electrons in the $p$–orbital of the valence shell. In contrast, all other elements from Ge to Pb contain only $d$– or $d$– and $f$–electrons and hence show two oxidation states of +2 and +4 due to inert pair effect. Further, as the number of $d$– and $f$–electrons increases, the inert pair effect becomes more and more pronounced. In other words, as we move down the group from Ge to Pb, the stability of +2 oxidation state increases (i.e., Ge < Sn < Pb) while that of +4 oxidation state decreases (i.e., Ge > Sn > Pb). Thus, +2 oxidation state of Pb is more stable than its +4 oxidation state.

**11.2** **How can you explain higher stability of $BCl_3$ as compared to $TlCl_3$?**

**Ans.** Due to the poor shielding of the $s$–electrons of the valence shell ($6s$) by the $3d$, $4d$, $5d$ and $4f$ electrons, inert pair effect is maximum in Tl. As a result, only $6p^1$ electron participates in bond formation and thus the most stable state of Tl is +1 and not +3. Therfore, $TlCl$ is stable but $TlCl_3$ is unstable. In contrast, due to the absence of $d$– and $f$– electrons in B, all the three valence electrons (i.e., two $2s$– and one $2p$–) take part in bond formation and hence B shows an oxidation state of +3 and thus forms $BCl_3$. Thus, $BCl_3$ is more stable than $TlCl_3$.

**11.3** **Why does boron triflouride behave as a Lewis acid ?**

**Ans.** The B atom in $BF_3$ has only 6 electrons in the valence shell and thus needs two more electrons to complete its octet. Therefore, it easily accepts a pair of electrons from nucleophiles such as $F^-$, $(C_2H_5)_2O$, $RCH_2OH$ etc. and thus behaves as a Lewis acid.

**11.4** **Consider the compounds, $BCl_3$ and $CCl_4$. How will they behave with water? Justify.**

**Ans.** The B atom in $BCl_3$ has only six electrons in the valence shell and hence is an electron–deficient molecule. It easily accepts a pair of electrons donated by water and hence $BCl_3$ undergoes hydrolysis to form boric acid $(H_3BO_3)$ and HCl.

$$BCl_3 + 3\ H_2O \longrightarrow H_3BO_3 + 3\ HCl$$

In contrast, C atom in $CCl_4$ has 8 electrons in the valence shell. Therefore, it is an electron–precise molecule and hence neither accepts nor donates a pair of electrons. In other words, it does not accept a pair of electrons from $H_2O$ molecule and hence $CCl_4$ does not undergo hydrolysis in water.

**11.5** **Is boric acid a protic acid ? Explain.**

**Ans.** It is a not a protic acid since it does not ionize in $H_2O$ to give a proton:

$$H_3BO_3 + H_2O \rightleftharpoons H_2BO_3^- + H_3O^+$$

because of the small size of boron atom and presence of only six electrons in its valence shell, $B(OH)_3$ accepts a lone pair of electrons from the oxygen atom of the $H_2O$ molecule to form a hydrated species.

The +ve charge on the O–atom, in turn, pulls the $\sigma$ electrons of the O–H bond towards itself thereby facilitating the release of a proton. As a result, $B(OH)_3$ acts as a weak monobasic Lewis acid and thus reacts with NaOH solution to form sodium metaborate.

$$B(OH)_3 + NaOH \longrightarrow Na^+[B(OH)_4]^-$$
Sod. metaborate

**11.6  Explain what happens when boric acid is heated?**

**Ans.** $H_3BO_3 \xrightarrow{\ \Delta\ } HBO_2 \xrightarrow{\ \Delta\ } B_2O_3$
Orthoboric acid    Metaboric acid    Boric oxide

**11.7  Describe the shapes of $BF_3$ and $[BH_4]^-$. Assign the hybridisation of boron in these species.**

**Ans.** In $BF_3$, boron is $sp^2$–hybridized and, therefore, $BF_3$ is a planar molecule. On the other hand, in $[BH_4]^-$ boron is $sp^3$–hybridized and hence $[BH_4]^-$ is a tetrahedral species.

**11.8  Write reactions to justify amphoteric nature of aluminium.**

**Ans.** It dissolves both in acids and alkalis evolving dihydrogen.

$$2\,Al\,(s) + 3\,H_2SO_4\,(aq) \longrightarrow Al_2(SO_4)_3(aq) + 3\,H_2\,(g)$$
$$2\,Al\,(s) + 2\,NaOH\,(aq) + 6\,H_2O\,(\ell) \longrightarrow$$
$$2\,Na^+\,[Al(OH)_4]^-\,(aq) + 3\,H_2\,(g)$$
Sod. tetrahydroxoaluminate (III)

**11.9  What are electron deficient compounds? Are $BCl_3$ and $SiCl_4$ electron deficient species? Explain.**

**Ans.** Species in which the central atom either does not have eight electrons in the valence shell or those which have 8 electrons in the valence shell but can expand their covalency beyond 4 due to the presence of $d$–orbital, are called electron deficient molecules. For example,

(i)  In $BCl_3$, the central boron atom has only six electrons. Therefore, it is an electron deficient compound. As such, it accepts a pair of electrons from $NH_3$ to form an adduct

$$Cl_3B + :NH_3 \longrightarrow Cl_3B \leftarrow NH_3$$

(ii) In $SiCl_4$, the central Si atom has 8 electrons but it can expand its covalency beyond 4 due to the presence of vacant $d$–orbitals.

**11.10  Write the resonance structures of $CO_3^{2-}$ and $HCO_3^-$.**

**Ans.** Resonance structures of $CO_3^{-2}$ and $HCO_3^-$ are:

$CO_3^{2-}$ :

**11.11  What is the state of hybridisation of carbon in (a) $CO_3^{2-}$ (b) diamond (c) graphite?**

**Ans.** (a) $sp^2$    (b) $sp^3$    (c) $sp^2$

**11.12  Explain the difference in properties of diamond and graphite on the basis of their structures.**

**Ans.** In diamond, carbon is $sp^3$ hybridized. Each carbon is tetrahedrally linked to four neighboring carbon atoms through four strong $C – C$, $sp^3$ $\sigma$ bonds, This network extends in three dimensions and is very rigid. Diamond is the purest form of carbon.

Since diamond exists as a 3D network solid, it is the hardest substance known with high density and melting point. It is a bad conductor of electricity as all the electrons are firmly held in $C$ –$C$ $\sigma$ bonds. Because of its high refractive index, diamond can reflect and refract light. It is therefore transparent substance.

Graphite has carbon having $sp^2$ hybridization. Each carbon is thus linked to three other carbon atoms forming hexagonal rings. Thus graphite has a two dimensional sheet like structure. The various sheets are held together by weak vander Waal's forces of attraction. The bond lengths in graphite are smaller than diamond. Since any two successive layers are held together by weak forces of attraction, one layer can slip over another. This makes graphite a good lubricating agent. As only three electrons of each carbon are used in making hexagonal rings in graphite, fourth valence electron is free to move. This makes graphite a good conductor of heat and electricity. Unlike diamond, graphite is black and possesses a metallic lustre.

**11.13  Rationalise the given statements and give chemical reactions :**

(i)  **Lead (II) chloride reacts with $Cl_2$ to give $PbCl_4$.**

(ii) **Lead (IV) chloride is highly unstable towards heat.**

(iii) **Lead is known not to form an iodide, $PbI_4$.**

**Ans.** (i)  Due to inert pair effect, Pb is more stable in $+2$ than in $+4$ oxidation state. Therefore, lead (II) chloride is more stable than lead (IV) chloride and hence lead (II) chloride does not react with $Cl_2$ to form lead (IV) chloride.

(ii) Due to greater stability of +2 over +4 oxidation state because of inert pair effect, lead (IV) chloride on heating decomposes to give lead(II)chloride and $Cl_2$.

$$PbCl_4(\ell) \xrightarrow{\Delta} PbCl_2(s) + Cl_2(g)$$

(iii) $I^-$ being a powerful reducing agent reduces $Pb^{4+}$ to $Pb^{2+}$ in solution. Thus, $PbI_2$ is formed.

$$Pb^{4+} + 2I^- \longrightarrow Pb^{2+} + I_2$$

**11.14 Suggest reasons why the B–F bond lengths in $BF_3$ (130 pm) and $BF_4^-$ (143 pm) differ ?**

**Ans.** $BF_3$ is a planar molecule in which B is $sp^2$-hybridized. It has an empty $2p$–orbital. F–atom has three lone pairs of electrons in the $2p$–orbitals. Because of similar sizes, $p\pi$ –$p\pi$ back bonding occurs in which a lone pair is transferred from F to B as shown below :

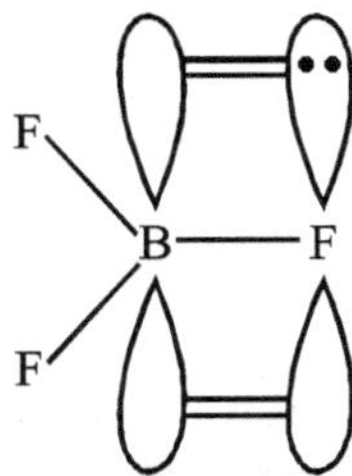

As a result of this back bonding, B–F bond acquires some double bond character. In contrast, in $[BF_4]^-$ ion, B is $sp^3$– hybridized and hence does not have an empty $p$–orbital available to accept the electrons donated by the F atom. Consequently, in $[BF_4]^-$, B–F is a purely single bond. Since double bonds are shorter than single bonds. Therefore, the B–F bond length in $BF_3$ is shorter (130 pm) than B–F bond length (143 pm) in $[BF_4]^-$.

**11.15 If B–Cl bond has a dipole moment, explain why $BCl_3$ molecule has zero dipole moment?**

**Ans.** Due to electro negativity difference between B (E.N. = 2.0) and Cl (E.N. = 3.0), the B–Cl bond is polar and hence has a finite dipole moment. The overall dipole moment of a molecule, however, depends upon its geometry. Now $BCl_3$ is a planar molecule in which the three B–Cl bonds are inclined at an angle of 120°. Therefore, the resultant of two B–Cl bonds is cancelled by equal and opposite dipole moment of the third B–Cl bond as shown below :

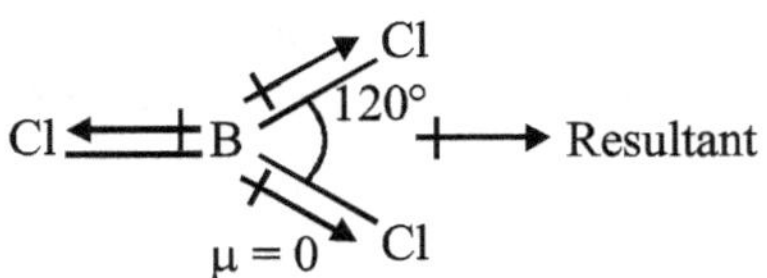

As a result, overall dipole moment of $BCl_3$ is zero.

**11.16 Aluminium trifluoride is insoluble in anhydrous HF but dissolves on addition of NaF. Aluminium trifluoride precipitates out of the resulting solution when gaseous $BF_3$ is bubbled through. Give reasons.**

**Ans.** (i) Anhydrous HF is a covalent compound and is strongly H– bonded. Therefore, it does give $F^-$ ions

hence $AlF_3$ does not dissolve in HF. In contrast, NaF being an ionic compound contains $F^-$ ions and hence combines with $AlF_3$ to form the soluble complex.

$$3NaF + AlF_3 \longrightarrow Na_3[AlF_6]$$
Sod.<br>hexafluoroaluminate (III)<br>(soluble complex)

(ii) Because of smaller size and higher electronegativity, B has much higher tendency to form complexes than Al, therefore, when $BF_3$ is added to the above solution, $AlF_3$ gets precipitated.

$$Na_3[AlF_6] + 3BF_3 \longrightarrow 3Na[BF_4] + AlF_3(S)$$
Sod. Tetra fluoro borate (III)<br>(soluble complex)

**11.17 Suggest a reason as to why CO is poisonous?**

**Ans.** In the lungs, haemoglobin present in red blood cells combines with molecular oxygen loosely and reversibly to form oxyhaemoglobin.

$$\text{Haemoglobin} + O_2 \rightleftharpoons \text{Oxyhaemoglobin}$$

Oxyhaemoglobin thus formed in the lungs then travels to different parts of the body through blood stream and delivers $O_2$ to the various tissues of the body. However, CO combines with haemoglobin irreversibly to form carboxyhaemoglobin which is about 300 times more stable than the oxyhaemoglobin.

$$\text{Haemoglobin} + CO \rightarrow \text{Carboxyhaemoglobin}$$

As a result, the oxygen carrying capacity of haemoglobin is destroyed and the man dies of suffocation. Thus, the highly poisonous nature of CO arises due to its ability to form a complex with haemoglobin which is about 300 times more stable than the oxygen– haemoglobin complex.

**11.18 How is excessive content of $CO_2$ responsible for global warming?**

**Ans.** $CO_2$ is produced during combustion. It is utilized by plants during photosynthesis and $O_2$ is released into the atmosphere. As a result of this $CO_2$ cycle, a constant percentage of 21% $O_2$ in the atmosphere is maintained. However, if the concentration of $CO_2$ increases beyond a certain level due to excessive combustion, some of the $CO_2$ will always remain unutilized. This excess $CO_2$ absorbs heat radiated by the earth. Some of it is dissipated into the atmosphere while the remaining part is radiated back to the earth and other bodies present on the earth. As a result, temperature of the earth and other bodies on the earth increases. This is called greenhouse effect and $CO_2$ is called a green house gas.

As a result of greenhouse effect, global warming occurs which has serious consequences.

**11.19 Explain structures of diborane and boric acid.**

**Ans.** (a) **Diborane :** $B_2H_6$ is a compound that lacks an electron. $B_2H_6$ only has 12 electrons – 6 $e^-$ of 6H atoms and 3 $e^-$ of 2B atoms each. so none of the boron atoms has any electrons left after being mixed with 3H atoms. X-ray diffraction studies showed the diborane structure as :

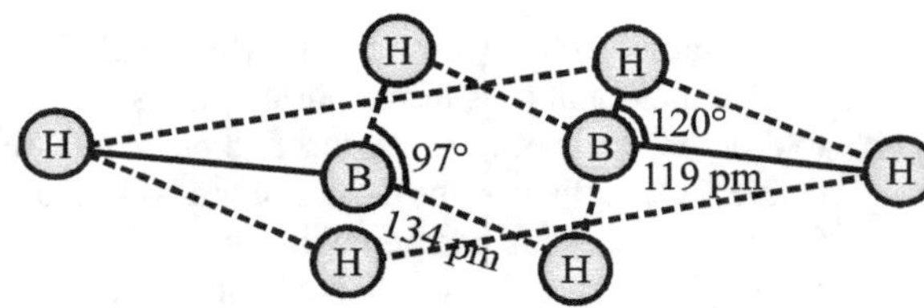



Two boron and four terminal atoms of hydrogen ($H_1$) lie in one direction, while the other two bridging atoms of hydrogen (H1) are on the surface perpendicular to the plane of boron atoms. Once, of the two atoms of hydrogen bridging one atom of H lies above the plane, and the other below the plane. The terminal bonds are regular two-centre two-electron ($2c - 2e^-$) bonds, while the two bridgings ($B - H - B$) bonds are three-centre two-electron ($3c - 2e^-$) bonds.



**(b) Boric acid :** Boric acid is structured in a layered form. Each planar unit $BO_3$ is connected by atoms H to each other. The H atoms form a covalent bond with a $BO_3$ unit whereas another $BO_3$ unit forms a hydrogen bond. The dotted lines, in the given figure represent hydrogen bonds.



**11.20 What happens when**
**(a) Borax is heated strongly,**
**(b) Boric acid is added to water**
**(c) Aluminium is treated with dilute NaOH**
**(d) BF₃ is reacted with ammonia?**

**Ans.** (a) $Na_2B_4O_7 \cdot 10H_2O \xrightarrow{\text{Heat}} Na_2B_4O_7 \xrightarrow{\text{Head}}$

$$2NaBO_2 + B_2O_3$$

Sodium    Boric
metaborate    anhydride

$\underbrace{\qquad\qquad}$
Transparent bead

(b) Boric acid acts as a weak Lewis acid by accepting a hydroxide ion of water and releasing a proton into the solution.

$$H—OH + B(OH)_3 \longrightarrow [B(OH)_4]^- + H^+$$

(c) Aluminum reacts to sodium tetrahydroxoaluminate (III) by forming dilute NaOH. In this process, hydrogen gas is liberated.

$$2Al(s) + 2NaOH(aq) + 6H_2O(l) \longrightarrow$$
$$2Na^+[Al(OH)_4]^-(aq) + 3H_2(g)$$

(d) $BF_3$ being a Lewis acid accepts a pair of electrons from $NH_3$ to form the corresponding complex.

$$F_3B + :NH_3 \longrightarrow F_3B \longleftarrow NH_3$$

Lewis acid   Lewis base     Complex

**11.21 Explain the following reactions**
**(a) Silicon is heated with methyl chloride at high temperature in the presence of copper**
**(b) Silicon dioxide is treated with hydrogen fluoride**
**(c) CO is heated with ZnO**
**(d) Hydrated alumina is treated with aqueous NaOH solution.**

**Ans.** (a) A mixture of mono–, di– and trimethylchlorosilanes along with a small amount of tetramethylsilane is formed.

$$CH_3Cl + Si \xrightarrow[373\ K]{\text{Cu power}} CH_3SiCl_3 + (CH_3)_2SiCl_2$$
$$+ (CH_3)_3\ SiCl + (CH_3)_4Si$$

(b) When the hydrogen fluoride (HF) heats silicon dioxide ($SiO_2$), it forms silicon tetrafluoride ($SiF_4$). The Si – O bonds is usually a strong bond, avoiding any attack by halogens and most acids even at high temperatures. It is being attacked by HF though.

$$SiO_2 + 4HF \longrightarrow SiF_4 + 2H_2O$$

The $SiF_4$ formed in this reaction can further react with HF to form hydro-flourosilicic acid.

$$SiF_4 + 2HF \longrightarrow H_2SiF_6$$

(c) When CO reacts with ZnO, it reduces ZnO to Zn. CO acts as a reducing agent.

$$ZnO(s) + CO(g) \longrightarrow Zn(s) + CO_2(g)$$

(d) Alumina dissolves to form sodium meta-aluminate

$$Al_2O_3.H_2O(s) + 2NaOH(aq) \xrightarrow{\text{Heat}}$$
Hydrated alumina

$$2NaAlO_2 + 3H_2O$$
Sod. meta aluminate
of Bauxite

**OR**

$$Al_2O_3.2\ H_2O\ (\ell) + 2\ NaOH\ (aq) + H_2O\ (\ell)$$
$$\longrightarrow 2\ Na[Al(OH)_4]\ (aq)$$
Sod. tetrahydroxoaluminate (III)

**11.22 Give reasons :**
   **(i) Conc. $HNO_3$ can be transported in Aluminium container.**
   **(ii) A mixture of dilute NaOH and Aluminium pieces is used to open drain.**
   **(iii) Graphite is used as lubricant**
   **(iv) Diamond is used as an abrasive.**
   **(v) Aluminium alloys are used to make aircraft body.**
   **(vi) Aluminium utensils should not be kept in water overnight.**
   **(vii) Aluminium wire is used to make transmission cables.**

**Ans.** (i) As it reacts with aluminium to form a thin protective oxide layer on the aluminium surface, concentrated $HNO_3$ can be stored and transported in aluminium containers.
   (ii) Sodium hydroxide and aluminium react to form sodium tetra hydro aluminate (III) and hydrogen gas.
   $$2Al + 2NaOH + 6H_2O \longrightarrow 2Na^+[al(OH)_4]^- + 3H_2$$
   (iii) Graphite has a layered structure, and the forces of weak van der Waals bind different layers of graphite together. These layers may slide one over another. Graphite is slippery and soft. Graphite can, therefore, be utilized as a lubricant.
   (iv) Carbon is $sp^3$ hybridized in Diamond with the help of strong convalent bonds, each carbon atom is bound to four other carbon atoms. These covalent bonds exist all over the surface, giving it a very rigid 3-D structure. This extended covalent bonding is very hard to break and for this reason, diamond is the hardest known substance. It is therefore used as an abrasive and for cutting instruments.
   (v) Aluminium alloys such as duralumin is light, tough and resistant to corrosion and hence is used to make aircraft body.
   (vi) Al reacts with $H_2O$ and dissolved $O_2$ to form a thin film of Aluminium oxide.
   $$2Al(s) + O_2(g) + H_2O(\ell) \longrightarrow Al_2O_3(s) + H_2(g)$$
   A very small amount of $Al_2O_3$ may dissolve to give a few ppm of $Al^{3+}$ ions in the solution. Since $Al^{3+}$ ions are injurious to health, therefore, drinking water should not be kept in Aluminium utensils overnight.
   (vii) On weight to weight basis, Aluminium conducts twice as Cu. Therefore, it is used in transmission cables.

**11.23 Explain why is there a phenomenal decrease in ionization enthalpy from carbon to silicon?**

**Ans.** Carbon ionizing enthalpy (the first element in group 14) is very high (1086 kJ/mol), that is expected because of its small size. However, there is a sharp decrease in enthalpy (786 kJ) when moving down the group to silicon. This is due to a considerable increase in the atomic sizes of elements when the group is moving down.

**11.24 How would you explain the lower atomic radius of Ga as compared to Al ?**

**Ans.** Due to poor shielding of the valence electrons of Ga by the inner $3d$–electrons, the effective nuclear charge of Ga is greater in magnitude than that of Al. As a result, the electrons in gallium experience greater force of attraction by the nucleus than in Al and hence atomic size of Ga (135 pm) is slightly less than that of Al (143 pm).

**11.25 What are allotropes? Sketch the structure of two allotropes of carbon namely diamond and graphite. What is the impact of structure on physical properties of two allotropes?**

**Ans.** The phenomenon of existence of an element in two or more forms having different physical properties but identical chemical properties are called allotropy and the different forms are called allotropes. (For rest answers see Ans. 12 above)

**11.26 (a) Classify following oxides as neutral, acidic, basic or amphoteric CO, $B_2O_3$, $SiO_2$, $CO_2$, $Al_2O_3$, $PbO_2$, $Tl_2O_3$**
   **(b) Write suitable chemical equations to show their nature.**

**Ans.** (a) Neutral oxides: CO; Acidic oxides: $B_2O_3$, $SiO_2$, $CO_2$ Amphoteric oxides : $Al_2O_3$, $PbO_2$ Basic oxide : $Tl_2O_3$
   (b) (i) Being acidic, $B_2O_3$, $SiO_2$ and $CO_2$ react with alkalis to form salts.
   $$B_2O_3 + 2NaOH \longrightarrow 2NaBO_2 + H_2O$$
   $$SiO_2 + 2NaOH \longrightarrow Na_2SiO_3 + H_2O$$
   $$CO_2 + 2NaOH \longrightarrow Na_2CO_3 + H_2O$$
   (ii) Being basic, $Tl_2O_3$ dissolves in acids
   $$Tl_2O_3 + 6HCl \longrightarrow 2TlCl_3 + 3H_2O$$
   (iii) Being amphoteric, $Al_2O_3$ and $PbO_2$ react with both acids and bases.
   $$Al_2O_3 + 2NaOH \longrightarrow 2NaAlO_2 + H_2O$$
   $$Al_2O_3 + 3H_2SO_4 \longrightarrow Al_2(SO_4)_3 + 3H_2O$$
   $$PbO_2 + 2NaOH \longrightarrow Na_2PbO_3 + H_2O$$
   $$2PbO_2 + 2H_2SO_4 \longrightarrow 2PbSO_4 + 2H_2O + O_2$$

**11.27 In some of the reactions, thallium resembles aluminium, whereas in others it resembles with group I metals. Support this statement by giving some evidences.**

**Ans.** Aluminium shows a uniform oxidation of +3. Like Aluminium, Tl also shows +3 oxidation state in some of its compounds like $TlCl_3$, $Tl_2O_3$, etc. Like Al, Tl also forms octahedral complexes: $[AlF_6]^{3-}$ and $[TlF_6]^{3-}$ Group 1 metals shows +1 oxidation state. Tl also shows +1 oxidation state due to inert pair effect. Thus it resembles with group 1 metals.

**11.28** When metal X is treated with sodium hydroxide, a white precipitate (A) is obtained, which is soluble in excess of NaOH to give soluble complex (B). Compound (A) is soluble in dilute HCl to form compound (C). The compound (A) when heated strongly gives (D), which is used to extract metal. Identify (X), (A), (B), (C) and (D). Write suitable equations to support their identities.

**Ans.** As the metal given in question on treatment with NaOH given a white ppt (A) which dissolves in excess of NaOH to given metal complex (B) therefore the given metal must be Al. the reactions may given as

$$2Al + 3NaOH \longrightarrow \underset{(A)}{Al(OH)_3 \downarrow} + 3Na^+$$

$$\underset{(excess)}{Al(OH)_3 + NaOH} \longrightarrow \underset{\substack{sodium\ tetra\ Hydorxy \\ aluminate\ (III)}}{Na^+[Al(OH)_4]^-}$$
$$\quad (A) \qquad\qquad\qquad (B)$$

As $Al(OH)_3$ is amphoteric in nature, it reacts with dil HCl to form $AlCl_3$(C).

$$\underset{(A)}{Al(OH)_3} + 3HCl \longrightarrow \underset{(C)}{AlCl_3} + 3H_2O$$

(A) when heated strongly give alumina which is used to extract meal.

$$\underset{(A)}{2Al(OH)_3} \xrightarrow{\Delta} \underset{(D)}{Al_2O_3} + 3H_2O$$

**11.29** What do you understand by (a) inert pair effect (b) allotropy and (c) catenation?

**Ans.** **(a)** As one moves down the group, *s*-block electrons decrease their tendency to participate in chemical bonding. This effect is called the intert pair effect. The electronic configuration for group 13 elements is $ns^2np^1$, and its group valence is +3. However, the oxidation state of + 1 becomes more stable when moving down the group. This is because the $ns^1$ electrons are poorly shielded by the d- and f-electrons. The $ns^2$ electrons are held tightly by the nucleus as a result of poor shielding, and thus they can not engage in chemical bonding.

**(b)** Allotropy is the presence of an element in more than one form, having different physical properties but the same chemical properties. This different forms of anelement are called allotropes. Carbon occurs in three allotropical forms, for example, diamond, graphite and fullerenes.

**(c)** The atoms of some elements (such as carbon) may connect with each other via strong covalent bonds to form long chains or branches. This characteristic is known as catenation. It is most common in carbon and important in Si and S.

**11.30** A certain salt X, gives the following results.
**(i)** Its aqueous solution is alkaline to litmus.
**(ii)** It swells up to a glassy material Y on strong heating.
**(iii)** When conc. $H_2SO_4$ is added to a hot solution of X, white crystal of an acid Z separates out.

Write equations for all the above reactions and identify X, Y and Z.

**Ans.** **(i)** Since the aqueous solution of X is alkaline to litmus, here it must be a salt of strong base and weak acid.

$$\underset{Borax\,(X)}{Na_2B_4O_7.10H_2O} \xrightarrow{\text{Water}}$$

$$\underset{\substack{Strong\ alkali \quad weak\ acid}}{2NaOH + H_2B_4O_7 + BH_2O}$$

**(ii)** Since (X) on strong heating swells up to a glassy material (Y). i.e. giving Borax Bead test thus it is now confirm that the compound X is Borax.

$$\underset{(X)}{Na_2B_4O_7.10H_2O} \xrightarrow{\Delta}$$

$$Na_2B_4O_7 + 10H_2O_2 \xrightarrow{\Delta} \underbrace{2NaBO_2 + B_2O_3}_{\text{(Y) Glassy material}}$$

**(iii)** When conc. $H_2SO_4$ is added to a hot solution of X, white crystal of an acid separate out, thus Z must be ortho boric acid.

$$Na_2B_4O_7.10H_2O + H_2SO_4 \longrightarrow$$

$$\underset{\substack{boric\ acid \\ (Z)}}{4H_3BO_3 + Na_2SO_4 + 5H_2O}$$

**11.31** Write balanced equations for :
**(i)** $BF_3 + LiH \longrightarrow$
**(ii)** $B_2H_6 + H_2O \longrightarrow$
**(iii)** $NaH + B_2H_6 \longrightarrow$
**(iv)** $H_3BO_3 \xrightarrow{\Delta}$
**(v)** $Al + NaOH \longrightarrow$
**(vi)** $B_2H_6 + NH_3 \longrightarrow$

**Ans.** **(i)** $\quad 2BF_3 + 6LiH \longrightarrow \underset{\text{Diborane}}{B_2H_6} + 6LiF$

**(ii)** $\quad \underset{\text{Diborane}}{B_2H_6} + 6H_2O \longrightarrow \underset{\substack{\text{Orthoboric} \\ \text{acid}}}{2H_3BO_3} + 6H_2$

**(iii)** $\quad 2NaH + B_2H_6 \longrightarrow \underset{\text{Sod. borohydride}}{2Na^+[BH_4]^-}$

**(iv)** $\quad \underset{\text{Boric acid}}{H_3BO_3} \longrightarrow \underset{\text{Metaboric acid}}{HBO_2} + H_2O$

$$\underset{\text{Meta boric acid}}{4HBO_2} \xrightarrow{\Delta} \underset{\text{Tetra boric acid}}{H_2B_4O_7} \xrightarrow{\Delta}$$

$$\underset{\text{Boron trioxide}}{2B_2O_3} + H_2O$$

**(v)** $2Al + 2NaOH + 6H_2O \longrightarrow$

$$\underset{\text{Sodium tetrahydroxyaluminate (III)}}{2\overset{+}{Na}[Al(OH)_4]^- + 3H_2}$$

**(vi)** $B_2H_6 + 2NH_3 \longrightarrow \underset{\text{Borane-ammonia complex}}{2BH_3.NH_3}$

**11.32 Give one method for industrial preparation and one for laboratory preparation of CO and $CO_2$ each.**

**Ans.** Industrial method:

$$2\,C\,(s) + O_2\,(g) \xrightarrow[\text{air}]{\text{Limited}} 2\,CO\,(g)$$

$$C\,(s) + O_2\,(g) \xrightarrow[\text{Air}]{\text{Excess}} CO_2(g)$$

**Laboratory method:** $HCOOH \xrightarrow{H_2SO_4} CO + H_2O$

$$CaCO_3\,(s) + 2HCl\,(aq) \longrightarrow$$
$$CaCl_2(aq) + CO_2\,(g) + H_2O\,(1)$$

**11.33 An aqueous solution of borax is**
(a) neutral
(b) amphoteric
(c) basic
(d) acidic

**Ans.** Borax is a salt of a strong base (NaOH) and a weak acid ($H_3BO_3$), therefore, it is basic in nature, i.e., option (c) is correct.

**11.34 Boric acid is polymeric due to**
(a) its acidic nature
(b) the presence of hydrogen bonds
(c) its monobasic nature
(d) its geometry

**Ans.** Boric acid is polymeric due to the presence of H–bonds. Therefore, option (b) is correct.

**11.35 The type of hybridisation of boron in diborane is**
(a) $sp$      (b) $sp^2$
(c) $sp^3$      (d) $dsp^2$

**Ans.** In $B_2H_6$, B is $sp^3$–hybridized. Therefore, option (c) is correct.

**11.36 Thermodynamically the most stable form of carbon is**
(a) diamond
(b) graphite
(c) fullerenes
(d) coal

**Ans.** Thermodynamically the most stable form of carbon is graphite, i.e., option (b) is correct.

**11.37 Elements of group 14.**
(a) exhibit oxidation state of + 4 only
(b) exhibit oxidation state of +2 and +4
(c) form $M^{2-}$ and $M^{4+}$ ions
(d) form $M^{2+}$ and $M^{4+}$ ions.

**Ans.** Due to inert pair effect, elements of group 14 exhibit oxidation states of +2 and +4. Thus, option (b) is correct.

**11.38 If the starting material for the manufacture of silicones is $RSiCl_3$, write the structure of the product formed.**

**Ans.** $RSiCl_3 + 3H_2O \longrightarrow RSi(OH)_3 + 3HCl$

| SECTION B | # PRACTICE QUESTIONS |

## MULTIPLE CHOICE QUESTIONS

**1.** Which of the following is/are true regarding gallium?
(i) It has unusually low melting point (303 K).
(ii) It exist in liquid state during summer.
(iii) It has a high boiling point (2676 K).
The correct option is
(a) (i) and (ii)
(b) (i) and (iii)
(c) (i), (ii) and (iii)
(d) (ii) and (iii)

**2.** Which of the following statement(s) is/are incorrect ?
(i) Trichlorides on hydrolysis in water form tetrahedral $[M(OH)_4]^-$ species.
(ii) Hybridisation state of metal in tetrahedral species is $sp^3$.
(iii) Aluminium chloride in acidified aqueous solution forms $[Al(OH)_4]^-$ ion.
(a) (i) and (ii)
(b) (ii) only
(c) (iii) only
(d) (i) and (iii)

**3.** Which among the following oxides react with alkali?
$B_2O_3$, $Al_2O_3$ and $Tl_2O$
(a) $B_2O_3$ and $Al_2O_3$
(b) $Al_2O_3$ and $Tl_2O$
(c) Only $B_2O_3$
(d) $B_2O_3$ and $Tl_2O$

**4.** The factor responsible for weak acidic nature of B–F bonds in $BF_3$ is
(a) large electronegativity of fluorine
(b) three centred two electron bonds in $BF_3$
(c) $p\pi$ - $d\pi$ back bonding
(d) $p\pi$ - $p\pi$ back bonding

**5.** The bonds present in borazole or inorganic benzene are
(a) $9\,\sigma, 6\pi$
(b) $12\,\sigma, 3\pi$
(c) $6\,\sigma, 9\pi$
(d) $15\,\sigma$ only

**6.** Which one of the following is the correct statement?
(a) Boric acid is a protonic acid
(b) Beryllium exhibits coordination number of six
(c) Chlorides of both beryllium and aluminium have bridged structures in solid phase
(d) $B_2H_6.2NH_3$ is known as 'inorganic benzene'

**7.** Orthoboric acid when heated to red hot gives
(a) metaboric acid
(b) pyroboric acid
(c) boron and water
(d) boric anhydride

**8.** Unlike the other elements of its group, carbon and silicon does not form $MX_2$ type molecules because
(a) energetically this is not possible
(b) carbon undergoes catenation
(c) it is non-metallic
(d) carbon does not contain $d$-orbital

**9.** The stability of dihalides of Si, Ge, Sn and Pb increases steadily in the sequence
(a) $PbX_2 << SnX_2 << GeX_2 << SiX_2$
(b) $GeX_2 << SiX_2 << SnX_2 << PbX_2$
(c) $SiX_2 << GeX_2 << PbX_2 << SnX_2$
(d) $SiX_2 << GeX_2 << SnX_2 << PbX_2$.

**10.** The main reason that $SiCl_4$ is easily hydrolysed as compared to $CCl_4$ is that
(a) Si-Si bond is weaker
(b) $SiCl_4$ can form hydrogen bonds
(c) $SiCl_4$ is covalent
(d) Si can extend its coordination number beyond four

**11.** Lead pipes are not suitable for drinking water because
(a) lead forms basic lead carbonate
(b) lead reacts with water containing air to form $Pb(OH)_2$
(c) a layer of lead dioxide is deposited over pipes
(d) lead reacts with air to form litharge

**12.** A group 14 element is oxidised to form corresponding oxide which is gaseous in nature. When dissolved in water, pH of the water decreases; further addition of group 2 hydroxides leads to precipitation. This oxide can be
(a) $GeO_2$
(b) $C\,O$
(c) $CO_2$
(d) $SnO_2$

**13.** Lead is not affected by dil. HCl in cold because
(a) Pb is less electronegative than H
(b) PbO film is formed which resists chemical attack by acid
(c) $PbCl_2$ protective coating gets formed on Pb surface
(d) $PbO_2$ film is always present on Pb surface, which resist chemical attack

**14.** Carbon and silicon belong to group 14. The maximum coordination number of carbon in commonly occurring compounds is 4, whereas that of silicon is 6. This is due to
(a) large size of silicon
(b) more electropositive nature of silicon
(c) availability of $d$-orbitals in silicon
(d) Both (a) and (b)

## ASSERTION & REASON QUESTIONS

**DIRECTIONS (Qs. 1-6) :** *Each of these questions contains an assertion followed by reason. Read them carefully and answer the question on the basis of following options. You have to select the one that best describes the two statements.*
(a) If both Assertion and Reason are correct and the Reason is a correct explanation of the Assertion.
(b) If both Assertion and Reason are correct but Reason is not a correct explanation of the Assertion.
(c) If the Assertion is correct but Reason is incorrect.
(d) If the Assertion is incorrect but the Reason is correct.

**1.** **Assertion:** $B(OH)_3$ and $In(OH)_3$ are basic in nature.
**Reason:** This is due to the presence of $OH^-$ ions.

2. **Assertion:** $B_2H_6$ has 3c–2e bonding.
   **Reason:** $B_2H_6$ on reaction with $NH_3$ forms inorganic benzene.
3. **Assertion:** Size of aluminium atom is smaller than gallium atom.
   **Reason:** Down the group, nuclear charge decreases and size of atom increases.
4. **Assertion:** Graphite is used as a lubricant, where oil cannot be used.
   **Reason:** Graphite cleaves easily between the layers, so it's very soft and slippery.
5. **Assertion:** In group 14, the tendency of heavier elements to show +2 oxidation state increases as Ge < Sn < Pb.
   **Reason:** It is due to the inability of $ns^2$ electrons of valence shell to particular in bonding.
6. **Assertion:** Pyrosilicate anion is $[Si_2O_7]^{6-}$.
   **Reason:** Pyrosilicate anion has Si–Si linkages.

## CASE/PASSAGE BASED QUESTIONS

**DIRECTIONS (Qs. 1-5) :** *Read the following case/passage and answer the questions.*

Diamond is the very best understand allotrope of carbon. It is the hardest recognized natural mineral that makes it very rough. In the structure of diamond, each carbon atom is covalently bounded to four other carbon atoms and has a tetrahedral shape, suggesting it is a non-planar molecule. Graphite is the second allotrope of carbon. Its atoms of carbon are arranged in layers. Within each layer of carbon atoms, the atoms join to form six-membered rings and such carbon atom is linked to three others. Two of the three bonds is a single covalent bond and the other bond is a double covalent bond. A 3rd allotrope of carbon is the fullerenec. Each atom is bounded to three other atoms of carbon much like in the graphite structure, however, the atoms sign up with to form both five membered ringes and six membered rings. The chemical properties of fullerenes are still being researched by scientists and they are likewise studied for potential medical usage in the belief that they can be part into specific antibiotics to target bacteria and cancer cells. Another allotropes of carbon is carbon nanotubes. They have a cylindrical as circular cylinder shape. The name nanotube comes from their size because they only have a diameter of a few nanometers. They are extremely strong and they have special electrical properties. Their unique electrical properties make them a very good conductor of heat.

1. The hybridisation state of carbon in fullerene is
   (a) *sp*
   (b) *sp$^2$*
   (c) *sp$^3$*
   (d) *sp$^3$d*
2. In graphite, electrons are
   (a) localised on every third C-atom
   (b) present in anti-bonding orbital
   (c) localised on each C-atom
   (d) spread out between the structure
3. Which one of the following allotropic forms of carbon is isomorphous with crystalline silicon?

   (a) Graphite
   (b) Coal
   (c) Coke
   (d) Diamond
4. Buckminster fullerene is
   (a) pure graphite
   (b) C-60
   (c) diamond
   (d) C-90
5. The element that does not show catenation among the following *p*-block elements is
   (a) carbon
   (b) silicon
   (c) germanium
   (d) lead

## VERY SHORT ANSWER QUESTIONS

1. Name the element of group 13 which forms only covalent compounds.
2. Why boron forms electron deficient compounds?
3. Why boron halides do not exist as dimer while $AlCl_3$ exists as $Al_2Cl_6$?
4. Why B–X bond distance in $BX_3$ is shorter than theoretically expected value?
5. The +1 oxidation state is more stable than the + 3 oxidation state for thallium.
6. Between $AlF_3$ and $AlCl_3$ which one will have a higher melting point.
7. $BCl_3$ exists but $BH_3$ does not. Explain.
8. Explain why boron halides don't conduct electricity in the liquid state?
9. What is the use of boron nitride?
10. Consider the reaction
$$BCl_3 + 6NH_3 \longrightarrow B(NH_2)_3 + 3NH_4Cl$$
What do you infer about acidic/basic character of $BCl_3$?
11. What type of bond would you expact when elements of the *p*-block combine with elements of *s*-block?
12. What are the basic units of layer structure of orthoboric acid? How are they bonded to one another?
13. The $p\pi$-$p\pi$ back bonding occurs in the halides of boron but not in the halides of aluminium. Explain.
14. Explain why silicon shows a higher covalency than carbon?
15. Why is diamond a bad conductor of electricity but a good conductor of heat?
16. Which oxide of carbon is an anhydride of carbonic acid ?
17. What name is given to the compounds formed by more electropositive elements with carbon?
18. Is carbon dioxide poisonous or not?
19. Graphite is used as solid lubricant but charcoal is not, why?
20. What are silicates?
21. Silanes gets hydrolysed by water whereas alkanes do not, why?
22. Explain the following statement with reason.
    The fullerene is considered as purest allotrope of carbon.
23. Give one example each of ionic and covalent carbides.
24. Why a silicon analogue of graphite does not exist?
25. Name an oxide of carbon that is poisonous. Why is it poisonous?

## SHORT ANSWER QUESTIONS

1. (a) Complete and balance the following chemical equations.

    (i) $BF_3 + N(CH_3)_3 \longrightarrow$

    (ii) $BCl_3 + H_2O \longrightarrow$

   (b) Give the structure of anhydrous Aluminium chloride and boron trifluoride.

2. (a) Molten aluminium bromide is a poor conductor of electricity. Explain.

   (b) Anhydrous aluminium chloride is used as a catalyst. Explain.

   (c) White fumes appear around the bottle of anhydrous aluminium chloride. Give reason.

3. Standard electrode potential values, E° of $Al^{3+}/Al$ is –1. 66 V and that of $Tl^{3+}/Tl$ is 1.26 V. Predict about the formation of $M^{3+}$ ion in solution and compare the electropositive character of the two metals.

4. Account for the following :

   (a) Aluminium sulphide gives a foul odour when it becomes damp.

   (b) Although aluminium is above hydrogen in the electrochemical series, still it is stable in moist air.

5. (a) $CO_2$ is a gas while $SiO_2$ is a solid. Explain.

   (b) Give one chemical reaction to show that:

    (i) Tin (II) is a reducing agent whereas Pb (II) is not.

    (ii) Tin (II) reduces mercuric salt to mercurous salt.

6. (a) Carbon monoxide is readily absorbed by ammonical cuprous chloride solution but carbon dioxide is not. Explain.

   (b) Silanes are few in number whereas alkanes are large in number. Explain.

7. Select the member(s) of group 14 that (i) forms the most acidic dioxide, (ii) is commonly found in +2 oxidation state, (iii) is used as semiconductor(s).

8. Give reason :

   (a) Silicon form compounds with coordination number of 5 and 6.

   (b) Si—F bond is stronger than C—F bond although Si is larger in size than C.

9. Arrange the following in increasing order of the property indicated:

   (a) $CCl_2$, $SiCl_2$, $GeCl_2$, $SnCl_2$ and $PbCl_2$
       (stability)

   (b) CO, SiO, SnO, GeO, PbO (basicity)

   (c) $SiF_4$, $SiCl_4$, $SiI_4$, $SiBr_4$ (stability)

10. Out of $CCl_4$ and $SiCl_4$ which one reacts with water?

11. $[SiF_6]^{2-}$ is known whereas $[SiCl_6]^{2-}$ is not. Give possible reasons.

## LONG ANSWER QUESTIONS

1. (i) Compound X on reduction with $LiAlH_4$ gives a hydride Y. The compound Y reacts with air explosively resulting in boron trioxide. Identify X and Y. Give balanced equations involved in the formation of Y and its reaction with air.

   (ii) Assign reasons for each of the

     (a) Gallium (+1) undergoes disproportionation reactions.

     (b) Unlike $In^+$, $Tl^+$ is more stable with respect to disproportionation.

     (c) InCl undergoes disproportionation but TlCl does not.

2. (i) (a) Why $N(CH_3)_3$ is pyramidal but $N(SiH_3)_3$ is planar ?

      (b) Why $(SiH_3)_3N$ is a weaker base than $(CH_3)_3N$?

   (ii) Account for the following:

      $PbO_2$ is a stronger oxidizing agent than $SnO_2$.

      **OR**

      $PbO_2$ can act as an oxidizing agent.

3. Write balanced equations for the following reactions :

   (i) SnO is treated with dilute $HNO_3$.

   (ii) Tin is heated with excess of chlorine gas.

   (iii) An aqueous solution of sodium hydroxide is added dropwise to a solution of gallium chloride in water. A precipitate is formed initially which dissolves on further addition of NaOH solution.

   (iv) Lead sulphide is heated in air.

   (v) Lead tetrachloride is heated.

## SOLUTIONS

### Multiple Choice Questions

**1.** **(c)**

**2.** **(c)** Aluminium chloride in acidified aqueous solution forms octahedral $[Al(H_2O)_6]^{3+}$ ion.

**3.** **(a)** $B_2O_3$ is acidic and $Al_2O_3$ is amphoteric.

**4.** **(d)** It is $p\pi - p\pi$ back bonding involving B and F. The smaller atoms show more back bonding.

**5.** **(b)**

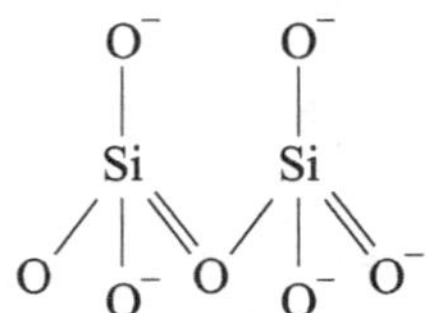

$$12\ \sigma \text{ bonds} \qquad\qquad 12\ \sigma \text{ and } 3\ \pi \text{ bonds}$$

**6.** **(c)** The correct formula of inorganic benzene is $B_3N_3H_6$ so (d) is incorrect statement

Boric acid ($H_3BO_3$ or $\overset{\displaystyle OH}{\underset{\displaystyle OH}{B-OH}}$ ) is a lewis acid so (a) is incorrect statement.

The coordination number exhibited by beryllium is 4 and not 6 so statement (b) is incorrect.

Both $BeCl_2$ and $AlCl_3$ exhibit bridged structures in solid state so (c) is correct statement.

**7.** **(d)** $H_3BO_3 \xrightarrow{100°C} HBO_2 \xrightarrow{160°C}$
$H_2B_4O_7 + H_2O \xrightarrow{330°C} 2B_2O_3 + H_2O$
(boric acid anhydride)

**8.** **(a)** The stability of dihalides ($MX_2$) increases down the group. Except C and Si, the other members form dihalides.

**9.** **(d)** Reluctance of valence shell electrons to participate in bonding is called inert pair effect. The stability of lower oxidation state (+2 for group 14 element) increases on going down the group. So the correct order is
$$SiX_2 < GeX_2 < SnX_2 < PbX_2$$

**10.** **(d)** Carbon halides are not hydrolysed due to absence of $d$-orbitals. On the other hand, $SiCl_4$ is easily hydrolysed due to the availability of $d$-orbitals in Si.
$$SiX_4 + 4H_2O \rightarrow Si(OH)_4 + 4HX$$

**11.** **(b)** $2Pb + 2H_2O + O_2 \rightarrow 2Pb(OH)_2$

**12.** **(c)** $CO_2$ forms carbonic acid $H_2CO_3$, when dissolved in water. When group 2 hydroxide like $Ca(OH)_2$ is added, a precipitation will form: $Ca(OH)_2 + CO_2 \rightarrow CaCO_3\downarrow +$ $H_2O$. CO is neutral, whereas other two $GeO_2$ and $SnO_2$ are solids.

**13.** **(c)** Pb with dil HCl forms protective coating of $PbCl_2$.

**14.** **(c)** Due to non-availability of vacant $d$-orbitals, it cannot exceed its coordination number more than four. Thus, carbon never forms complexes *e.g.*, $[CCl_6]^{2-}$ does not exist but $[SiCl_6]^{2-}$ exists.

### Assertion & Reason Questions

**1.** **(d)** B has small size and $B(OH)_3$ has incomplete octet, thus, accept $OH^-$ from $H_2O$, hence, acts as a Lewis acid
$$B(OH)_3 + H_2O \rightarrow [B(OH)_4]^+ + H^+$$
However, due to large size and low ionisation enthalpy of In, $-OH$ bond readily breaks and release $OH^-$ ion, thus, $In(OH)_3$ acts as a base.

**2.** **(b)** Four terminal hydrogens ($H_t$) have normal covalent bonding (2c–2e). $B_2H_6$ has $sp^3$ hybridization. $B_2H_6$ completes its electron deficiency by banana bonding (3c–2e).



$$3B_2H_6 + 6NH \longrightarrow 3[BH_2(NH_3)_2]^+ [BH_4]^- \xrightarrow{Heat}$$
$$12H_2 + \underset{\substack{\text{Borazine}\\ \text{(Inorganic Benzene)}}}{2B_3N_3H_6}$$

**3.** **(d)** The presence of additional 10 $d$-electrons offer only poor screening effect for the outer electrons from the increased nuclear charge in gallium. Consequently, the atomic radius of gallium (135 pm) is less than of aluminium (143 pm).

**4.** **(a)** Because it is a solid material, it is known as a dry lubricant.

**5.** **(a)** In 14th group, down the group, stability of +2 oxidation state increases due to inert pair effect.

**6.** **(c)** The two $[SiO_4]^{4-}$ tetrahedral share a common oxygen to form pyrosilicate $[Si_2O_7]^{6-}$.

### *Case/Passage Based Questions*

1. **(b)** In fullerene, each carbon atom is bonded to three other carbon atoms and is $sp^2$ hybridised.

2. **(d)** In graphite, each carbon is $sp^2$-hybridised and the single occupied unhybridised $p$-orbitals of C-atoms overlap side wise to give $\pi$-electron cloud which is delocalized and thus, the electrons are spread out between the structure.

3. **(d)** Diamond and crystalline silicon are isomorphous. The C atom in diamond and Si atom in crystalline silicon is coordinated to 4 other atoms, resulting in tetrahedral structure.

4. **(b)** Buckminster fullerene is $C_{60}$. The molecule has shape of soccer ball.

5. **(d)** The order of tendency of catenation for elements of C family is

   $C \gg Si > Ge \approx Sn > Pb$

### *Very Short Answer Questions*

1. B forms only covalent compounds.

2. Boron has three electrons in the outermost shell which it can share with other atoms. Hence, in its compounds, only 6 electrons are present around B–atom, i.e., octet is not complete. Thus boron forms electron deficient compounds.

3. Boron atom being small in size is unable to accommodate four large sized halogen atoms around it to form dimer. Thus $BCl_3$ exists as a monomer whereas $AlCl_3$ exists as a dimer $Al_2Cl_6$.

4. This is due to $p\pi - p\pi$ back bonding of the fully filled $p$–orbital of halogen (X) atom with the empty $p$–orbital of boron atom.

5. As we move down the group 13 elements, nuclear charge increases while shielding effect due to intervening $d$ and $f$ orbitals decreases, hence elements in $ns$-orbitals are held more tightly and do not participate in bonding. As a result only $p$-orbital electron may be involved in bonding. Thus stability of +1 oxidation state increases down the group.

6. $AlF_3$ is more ionic, therefore, has higher melting point.

7. In $BCl_3$, Cl donates lone pair of electrons to vacant $p$-orbital of boron (back-bonding) making it more stable whereas in $BH_3$ back-bonding is not possible, therefore, it exists as dimer. Secondly, in $BCl_3$, chlorine being bigger in size cannot form bridged bonds.

8. Boron halides don't conduct electricity in the liquid state because they are covalent compounds.

9. Boron nitride is harder than diamond and is used as an abrassive.

10. It shows the acidic character of $BCl_3$.

11. Such compounds will feature ionic bonds.

12. The basic unit of layer structure of orthoboric acid is $BO_3$. They are bonded through hydrogen bonds.

13. The tendency to show $p\pi$-$p\pi$ back bonding is maximum in boron halides and decreases very rapidly with increase in size of central atom and halogen atom. Since A1 is larger in size than B and thus do not show back bonding.

14. Si because of the presence of vacant $d$–orbitals can show a covalency upto six while C because of the absence of $d$– orbitals cannot have a covalency of more than four.

15. In diamond all the valence electrons are involved in forming carbon-carbon bonds and does not have free electrons and, therefore, it is a bad conductor of electricity. Conduction of heat does not necessarily require movement of electrons thus diamond is a conductor of heat.

16. $CO_2$ is an anhydride of carbonic acid:
$$H_2CO_3 \longrightarrow H_2O + CO_2.$$

17. Ionic compounds.

18. No, it is not poisonous.

19. Graphite is soft due to which it can be used as solid lubricant whereas charcoal is hard due to which it cannot be used as lubricant.

20. Silicates are minerals which consist of $SiO_4^{4-}$ units arranged in different ways.

21. Silane gets hydrolysed because silicon has vacant $d$-orbital whereas alkane cannot due to non-availability of vacant $d$-orbital in carbon.

22. It is because it does not have edges, therefore, impurities cannot be adsorbed on it.

23. $CaC_2$ is ionic carbide while SiC is the covalent carbide.

24. The graphite structure is considered to contain $\pi$-bonds with in planes. Since $\pi$-bonds are far weaker in lower member of a group as compared to top member so the silicon analogue of graphite does not exist.

25. CO (Carbon monoxide) is poisonous oxide of carbon. It attaches more strongly, in comparison to oxygen, to the iron in the haemoglobin and so prevents the transport of sufficient oxygen. Thus a person who breathes in carbon monoxide is liable to suffocate.

### *Short Answer Questions*

1. (a) (i) $BF_3 + :N(CH_3)_3 \longrightarrow [F_3B \longleftarrow N(CH_3)_3]$

   (ii) $BCl_3 + 3H_2O \longrightarrow H_3BO_3 + 3HCl$

   (b)
   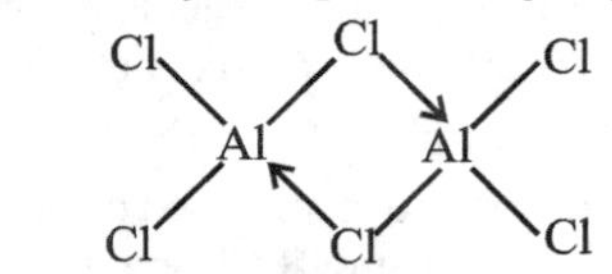

   Structure of anhydrous $Al_2Cl_6$

   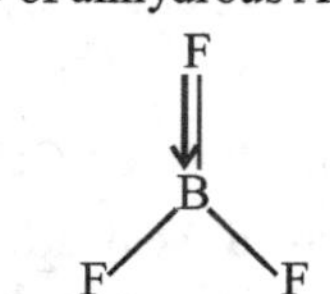

   Structure of anhydrous $BF_3$

**2.** (a) Aluminium bromide is a covalent molecule. Even in the molten state, it ionizes only to a very small extent and hence is a poor conductor of electricity.

(b) The Al atom in $AlCl_3$, has only 6 electrons in its valence shell. It needs two more electrons to complete its octet. It is, therefore, acts as a lewis acid catalyst in Friedel–Crafts alkylation and acylation reactions of benzene and other aromatic compounds. In these reactions, it helps to generate the electrophile ($R^+$ or $RCO^+$) which attacks the benzene/aromatic ring.

(c) Anhydrous aluminium chloride is partially hydrolyzed by atmospheric moisture to liberate HCl gas. Moist HCl appears white in colour.
$$AlCl_3 \, (s) + 3 \, H_2O \, (\ell) \longrightarrow Al(OH)_3 \, (s) + 3 \, HCl \, (g)$$

**3.** The negative value of $E°$ for $Al^{3+}/Al$ suggests that Al has a strong tendency to form $Al^{3+}$ (aq) ions. On the other hand, the positive value of $E°$ for $Tl^{3+}/Tl$ suggests that Tl does not have high tendency to form $Tl^{3+}$ ions. Since Al can form $Al^{3+}$ ions more easily than Tl does to form $Tl^{3+}$ ions, therefore, Al is more electropositive than Tl.

**4.** (a) The foul smell is due to the formation of $H_2S$.
$$Al_2S_3 + 6H_2O \rightarrow 3H_2S + 2Al \, (OH)_3$$

(b) In the presence of water and air, aluminium gets covered with a protective layer of aluminium oxide. Aluminium oxide does not allow further reaction. Therefore, aluminium is stable in moist air.

**5.** (a) Carbon atom has a small size and forms stable multiple covalent bonds because of close interaction between the $2p$ orbitals on carbon and $2p$ orbitals on oxygen. This is because the energy of $2p$ orbitals of carbon and $2p$ orbitals of oxygen are nearly the same and they can easily overlap. However, silicon has large size and so the $3p$-orbitals of Si do not overlap effectively with $2p$ orbitals of oxygen. Therefore, Si – O are not formed. The tetravalency of silicon is satisfied by the formation of Si – O bonds which result in a network structure.

(b) (i) Both tin and lead show two oxidation states of +2 and +4. But the inert pair effect is more prominent in case of Pb than in Sn. In other words +2 oxidation state of Sn is less stable than its +4 oxidation state. Therefore, Sn (II) acts as a reducing agent and gets converted into more stable Sn (IV) by losing two electrons. In contrast, + 2 oxidation state of Pb is more stable than its + 4 oxidation state. In other words, Pb (II) does not lose electrons easily and hence does not act as a reducing agent.

(ii) Being a reducing agent, tin (II) chloride reduces mercuric chloride ($HgCl_2$) to mercurous chloride ($Hg_2Cl_2$)
$$SnCl_2 + 2 \, HgCl_2 \longrightarrow SnCl_4 + Hg_2Cl_2$$

**6.** (a) Due to the presence of a lone pair of electrons on carbon in CO, it acts as a Lewis base (or ligand) and thus forms a soluble complex with ammonical cuprous chloride solution.
$$CuCl + NH_3 + : CO \longrightarrow [Cu(CO)NH_3]^+ Cl^-$$
$$\text{Soluble complex}$$
On the other hand, $CO_2$ does not act as a Lewis base since it does have a lone pair of electrons on the carbon atom and hence does not dissolve in ammonical cuprous chloride solution.

(b) Carbon has the maximum tendency for catenation due to stronger C–C ($355 \, kJmol^{-1}$) bonds. As a result, it forms a large number of alkanes. Silicon, on the other hand, due to weaker Si–Si ($200 \, kJ \, mol^{-1}$) bonds has much lesser tendency for catenation and hence forms only a few silanes.

**7.** (i) Carbon is the most non–metallic element of group 14 and hence its dioxide is most acidic.

(ii) Lead is most stable in +2 oxidation state due to inert pair effect.

(iii) Silicon and germanium are used as semiconductors.

**8.** (a) Silicon shows a coordination number higher than four by using empty $3d$ atomic orbitals. Si can expand its octet beyond eight electrons.

(b) Si—F bond is stronger than C—F bond due to dative pi bonding involving filled $p$-atomic orbital of fluorine and empty $d$-atomic orbital of silicon.

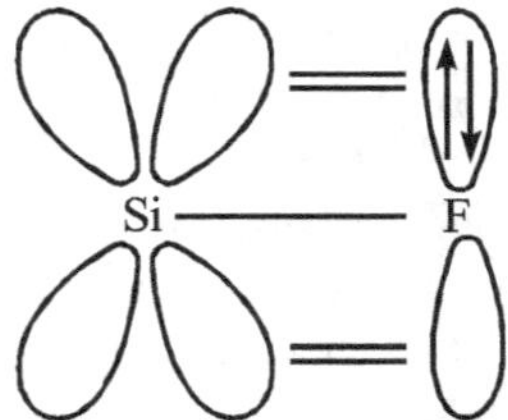


**9.** (a) The stability of dihalides increasing down the group because divalent state becomes more and more stable as we move down the group.
$$CCl_2 < SiCl_2 < GeCl_2 < SnCl_2 < PbCl_2$$

(b) Basicity of oxides increases down the group as metallic character increases.
$$CO < SiO < GeO < SnO < PbO$$

(c) Si — X bond strength decreases as the size of the halogen increases. The correct order is
$$SiI_4 < SiBr_4 < SiCl_4 < SiF_4$$

**10.** Carbon has only $s$ and $p$-orbitals. As a result carbon cannot increase its coordination number beyond four and therefore, it cannot accept electrons from water molecules. On the other hand, $SiCl_4$ is readily hydrolysed by water because silicon has vacant $3d$ orbitals in its outermost shell. As a result, silicon extends its coordination number beyond four. The vacant $3d$ orbitals of silicon accept electrons from water. and $SiCl_4$ can be hydrolysed as shown below :

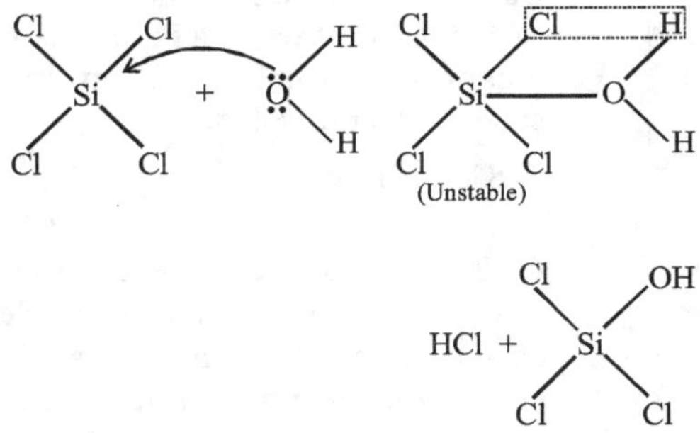

(Unstable)

$$HCl + \underset{\underset{\displaystyle Cl}{|}}{\overset{\underset{\displaystyle OH}{}}{Si}}$$

**11.** The main reasons are:

(i) Due to smaller size of F as compared to Cl, six F atoms can be easily accommodated around Si atom but six large sized Cl atoms cannot.

(ii) The lone pair of electrons in F are present in a smaller $2p$–orbital but is Cl they are present in a larger $3p$–orbital. Therefore, interaction of F lone pair electrons with $d$–orbitals of silicon are stronger than that of Cl lone pairs of electrons.

### *Long Answer Questions*

**1.** (i) $4BF_3 + 3\,LiAlH_4 \longrightarrow 2\,B_2H_6 + 3\,LiAlF_4$

The equation representing the reaction of Y with $O_2$ may be written as follows:

$B_2H_6 + 3O_2 \longrightarrow B_2O_3 + 3H_2O$

Thus $X = BF_3$ and $Y = B_2H_6$

(ii) (a) Due to inert pair effect, gallium shows both $+1$ and $+3$ oxidation states but its $+3$ oxidation state is more stable than $+1$ oxidation state. In other words, $+1$ gallium is less stable than $+3$ gallium and hence undergoes disproportionation to form gallium metal and the more stable $+3$ oxidation ions in aqueous solution as shown below:

$3GaX(s) \longrightarrow 2Ga(s) + Ga^{3+}(aq) + 3X^-(aq\}$

or $3\,Ga^+(aq) \longrightarrow 2\,Ga\,(s) + Ga^{3+}\,(aq)$

(b) Although both In and Tl can show oxidation states of $+1$ and $+3$, but inert pair effect is more prominent in Tl than in In. Therefore, $+1$ oxidation of Tl is more stable than its $+3$ oxidation state while $+3$ oxidation state of In is more stable than its $+1$ oxidation state. Consequently, in aqueous solution, less stable $In^+$ undergoes disproportionation to more stable

$In^{3+}$ but $+1$ thallium being more stable does not undergo dispro-portionation to $+3$ thallium.

$3\,In^+\,(aq) \longrightarrow 2\,In\,(s) + In^{3+}\,(aq)$

(c) As stated above, $+3$ oxidation state of In is more stable than its $+1$ oxidation state, therefore, InCI undergoes disproportionation in aqueous solution.

$3\,InCl\,(aq) \longrightarrow 2\,In\,(s) + In^{3+}\,(aq) + 3\,Cl^-$

Since the $+1$ oxidation state of Tl is more stable than its $+3$ state, therefore, TlCl does not undergo disproportionation in aqueous solution.

**2.** (i) (a) In $N(CH_3)_3$, N is $sp^3$–hybridized with one lone pair of electrons and hence $N(CH_3)_3$ is pyramidal. In $N(SiH_3)_3$, Si is $sp^3$–hybridized and forms three – bonds with H and fourth with the N–atom. Further due to the presence of $d$–orbitals, Si has a strong tendency to form $p\pi$–$d\pi$ double bond with O or N–atoms. For this to occur, N must be $sp^2$–hybridized so that the $p$–orbital on N containing the lone pair of electrons overlaps with the empty $d$–orbital of Si. As a result, $N(SiH_3)_3$ is planar.

(b) This is because the lone pair of electrons present on N (present in the $2p$ orbital) is transferred to the empty $d$–orbital of Si ($p\pi - d\pi$ overlapping) and hence is not available for protonation.

(ii) In $PbO_2$ and $SnO_2$ both lead and tin are present in $+$ 4–oxidation state. But due to stronger inert pair effect, $Pb^{2+}$ ion is more stable than $Sn^{2+}$ ion. In other words, $Pb^{4+}$ ions (i.e. $PbO_2$) is more easily reduce to $Pb^{2+}$ ions than $Sn^{4+}$ ions are reduced to $Sn^{2+}$ ions. Thus, $PbO_2$ acts as a stronger oxidizing agent than $SnO_2$.

**3.** (i) $3SnO + 2HNO_3\,(dil) \rightarrow 2SnO_2 + 2NO + H_2O$

(ii) $Sn + 2Cl_2 \xrightarrow{\Delta} SnCl_4$

(iii) $GaCl_3 + 3NaOH \rightarrow \underset{\text{white ppt.}}{Ga(OH)_3} + 3NaCl$

$Ga(OH)_3 + NaOH \rightarrow \underset{\text{Soluble}}{Na\,[Ga(OH)_4]}$

(iv) $2Pbs + 3O_2 \xrightarrow{\Delta} 2PbO + 2SO_2$

(v) $PbCl_4 \xrightarrow{\Delta} PbCl_2 + Cl_2$

## SECTION C | NCERT EXEMPLAR QUESTIONS

### MULTIPLE CHOICE QUESTIONS

1. The elements which exists in liquid state for a wide range of temperature and can be used for measuring high temperature is
   (a) B  (b) Al
   (c) Ga  (d) In

2. Which of the following is a Lewis acid?
   (a) $AlCl_3$  (b) $MgCl_2$
   (c) $CaCl_2$  (d) $BaCl_2$

3. Which of the following oxides is acidic in nature?
   (a) $B_2O_3$  (b) $Al_2O_3$
   (c) $Ga_2O_3$  (d) $In_2O_3$

4. The exhibition of highest coordination number depends on the availability of vacant orbitals in the central atom. Which of the following elements is not likely to act as central atom in $MF_6^{3-}$ ?
   (a) B  (b) Al
   (c) Ga  (d) In

5. Quartz is extensively used as a piezoelectric material, it contains .............. .
   (a) Pb  (b) Si
   (c) Ti  (d) Sn

6. Dry ice is
   (a) solid $NH_3$  (b) solid $SO_2$
   (c) solid $CO_2$  (d) solid $N_2$

7. The geometry of a complex species can be understood from the knowledge of type of hybridisation of orbitals of central atom. The hybridisation of orbitals of central atom in $[B(OH_4)]^-$ and the geometry of the complex are respectively.
   (a) $sp^3$, tetrahedral
   (b) $sp^3$, square planar
   (c) $sp^3d^2$, octahedral
   (d) $dsp^2$, square planar

8. Boric acid is an acid because its molecule
   (a) contains replaceable $H^+$ ion
   (b) gives up a proton
   (c) accepts $OH^-$ from water releasing proton
   (d) combines with proton from water molecule

9. Catenation *i.e.*, linking of similar atoms depends on size and electronic configuration of atoms. The tendency of catenation in group 14 elements follows the order
   (a) C > Si > Ge > Sn
   (b) C >> Si > Ge ≈ Sn
   (c) Si > C > Sn > Ge
   (d) Ge > Sn > Si > C

### ASSERTION & REASON QUESTIONS

**DIRECTIONS (Qs. 1-2)** : *Each of these questions contains an assertion followed by reason. Read them carefully and answer the question on the basis of following options. You have to select the one that best describes the two statements.*
(a) If both Assertion and Reason are correct and the Reason is a correct explanation of the Assertion.
(b) If both Assertion and Reason are correct but Reason is not a correct explanation of the Assertion.
(c) If the Assertion is correct but Reason is incorrect.
(d) If the Assertion is incorrect but the Reason is correct.

1. **Assertion** : If aluminium atoms replace a few silicon atoms in three dimensional network of silicon dioxide, the overall structure acquires a negative charge.
   **Reason** : Aluminium is trivalent while silicon is tetravalent.

2. **Assertion** : Silicones are water repelling in nature.
   **Reason** : Silicones are organosilicon polymers, which have ($-R_2SiO-$) as repeating unit.

### SHORT ANSWER QUESTIONS

1. Aluminium dissolves in mineral acids and aqueous alkalies and thus shows amphoteric character. A piece of aluminium foil is treated with dilute hydrochloric acid or dilute sodium hydroxide solution in a test tube and on bringing a burning matchstick near the mouth of the rest tube, a pop sound indicates the evolution of hydrogen gas. The same activity when performed with concentrated nitric acid, reaction doesn't proceed. Explain the reason.

2. Identify the compounds A, X and z in the following reactions:
   (i) $A + 2HCl + 5H_2O \rightarrow 2NaCl + X$
   $$X \xrightarrow[370K]{\Delta} HBO_2 \xrightarrow[>370K]{\Delta} Z$$

3. Complete the following chemical equations:
   $$Z + 3LiAlH_4 \longrightarrow X + 3LiF + 3AlF_3$$
   $$X + 6H_2O \longrightarrow Y + 6H_2$$
   $$3X + 3O_2 \xrightarrow{\Delta} B_2O_3 + 3H_2O$$

### LONG ANSWER QUESTIONS

1. A compound (A) of boron reacts with $NMe_3$ to give an adduct (B) which on hydrolysis gives a compound (C) and hydrogen gas. Compound (C) is an acid. Identify the compounds A, B and C. Give the reactions involved.

2. $BCl_3$ exists as monomer whereas $AlCl_3$ is dimerised through halogen bridging. Give reason. Explain the structure of the dimer of $AlCl_3$ also.

3. A compound (A) of boron reacts with $NMe^3$ to give an adduct (B) which on hydrolysis gives a compound (C) and hydrogen gas. Compound (C) is an acid. Identify the compounds A, B and C. Give the reactions involved.

## SOLUTIONS

### *Multiple Choice Questions*

1. **(c)** Among these elements, in gallium, the crystal structure is different which suggests that Ga consists of almost discrete $Ga_2$ molecule, so its melting point is lowest. Ga exists as liquid from $30°C$ upto $2000°C$ and hence, it is used in high temperature measurement.

2. **(a)** Alkaline earth metals (Mg, Ca, Ba) form ionic chloride whereas aluminium form covalent chloride. Despite of sharing electrons with chlorine, the octet of aluminium is incomplete. To complete the octet, it needs electrons and thus, acts as a Lewis acid.

3. **(a)** On moving down the group the acidic nature of oxides changes from acidic to basic through amphoteric

$$\underset{\substack{\text{More acidic} \\ \text{less basic}}}{B_2O_3} \quad , \quad \underset{\text{Amphoteric}}{Al_2O_3 \text{ and } Ga_2O_3}, \quad \underset{\text{Basic}}{In_2O_3 \text{ and } Tl_2O_3}$$

4. **(a)** Among these elements boron has the lowest atomic number. It has atomic number 5 and do not have vacant $d$-orbital. Boron can show maximum coordination number of 4. The element M in the complex ion $MF_6^{3-}$ has a coordination number of six. Hence, B can not form complex of the type $MF_6^{3-}$.

5. **(b)** Quartz is a crystalline form of silica. Quartz is extensively used as a piezoelectric material.

6. **(c)** Carbon dioxide can be obtained as a solid in the form of dry ice, allowing the liquified $CO_2$ to expand rapidly.

    It is used to maintain the low temperature in laboratory.

    Dry ice is solid $CO_2$

7. **(a)** Structure of $B(OH)_4^-$ is

$$HO - \underset{\underset{OH}{|}}{\overset{\overset{OH}{|}}{B}} \longleftarrow \overset{\ominus}{O}H$$

4 bond pair + 0 lone pair

Hybridisation — $sp^3$

Geometry — Tetrahedral

8. **(c)** Boric acid is a monobasic weak acid. It does not liberate $H^+$ ion but accepts electrons from $OH^-$ ion.

$$H_3BO_3 + H_2O \longrightarrow B(OH)_4^- + H^+$$

9. **(b)** The tendency of forming long open or closed chains by combination of some atoms in themselves is known as catenation. The tendency of catenation is maximum in carbon and decreases on moving down the group.

$$C >> Si > Ge \approx Sn > Pb$$

This is due to high bond energy of C — C bonds. On moving down the group, atomic size increases and electronegativity decreases, hence, tendency to show catenation decreases.

### *Assertion & Reason Questions*

1. **(a)** In aluminosilicates (anion), some of the silicon atoms are replaced by aluminium. Since, aluminium is trivalent while silicon is tetravalent, hence we get negatively charged ion.

2. **(b)** Silicones are organosilicon polymers and they are hydrophobic in nature. Silicones neither react nor absorb water molecules.

### *Short Answer Questions*

1. Al being amphoteric dissolves both in acids and alkalies evolving $H_2$ gas which burns with a pop sound.

$$2Al + 6HCl \rightarrow 2AlCl_3 + 3H_2$$
$$2Al + 2NaOH + 2H_2O \rightarrow \underset{\text{Sod. meta aluminate}}{2NaAlO_2} + 3H_2$$

Conc $HNO_3$ renders aluminium passive by forming a protective oxide layer on the surface.

$$2Al + 6HNO_3 \rightarrow Al_2O_3 + 6NO_2 + 3H_2O$$

2. A : $Na_2B_4O_7$ (Borax)
   X : $H_3BO_3$
   Z : $B_2O_3$

3. Z : $BF_3$
   X : $B_2H_6$
   Y : $H_3BO_3$

### *Long Answer Questions*

1. $A = B_2H_6$, $B = BH_3.NMe_3$, $C = B(OH)_3$ i.e., $H_3BO_3$.

2. **Hint:** Absence of $d$-orbitals in boron.

    $BCl_3$ is electron deficient species and has $6e^-$ in the valence shell of central atom B. But it does not form dimer to complete its octet due to small size of boron. Bridging Cl comes very closer in dimer and dimer becomes unstable. Therefore $BCl_3$ exists as monomer.

    $AlCl_3$ has the presence of 6 electrons, so, to complete its octet it exists as dimer. It has vacant $3d$ orbitals, so it can extend its coordination beyond 3. Hence, it completes its octet by forming coordinate bond with Cl atom of the other $AlCl_3$.

Structure of anhydrous $Al_2Cl_6$

3. $A = B_2H_6$, $B = BH_3.NMe_3$, $C = B(OH)_3$ i.e., $H_3BO_3$.

# 12 General Principles of Organic Chemistry



**12.1** What are hybridisation states of each carbon atom in the following compounds?
$CH_2 = C = O$, $CH_3CH = CH_2$, $(CH_3)_2CO$, $CH_2 = CHCN$, $C_6H_6$.

**Ans.** 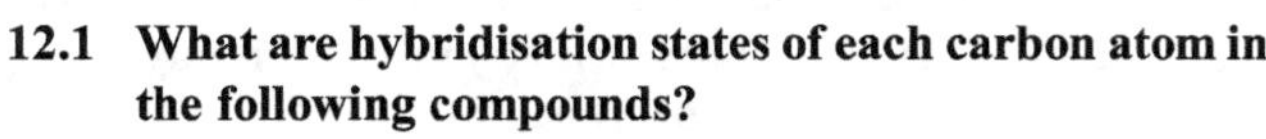

$$\overset{sp^2}{H_2C} = \overset{sp}{C} = O; \quad \overset{sp^3}{H_3C} - \overset{sp^3}{C}H = \overset{sp^2}{C}H_2$$

$$\overset{sp_3}{H_3C} - \overset{O}{\overset{\|}{C}} - \overset{sp_3}{C}H_3; \quad \overset{sp^2}{H_2C} = \overset{sp^2}{C}H - \overset{sp}{C} \equiv N;$$

Each C is $sp^2$ hybridized.

**12.2** Indicate the σ– and π–bonds in the molecules: $C_6H_6$, $C_6H_{12}$, $CH_2Cl_2$, $CH_2=C=CH_2$, $CH_3 NO_2$, $HCONHCH_3$

**Ans.** (i) $C_6H_6$      (ii) $C_6H_{12}$

12 σ-bonds 3π-bonds     18 σ-bonds 0π-bonds

(iii) $CH_2Cl_2$      (iv) $CH_2 = C = CH_2$

4 σ-bonds        6 σ-bonds
0 π-bonds        2π-bonds

(v) $CH_3NO_2$      (vi) $HCONHCH_3$

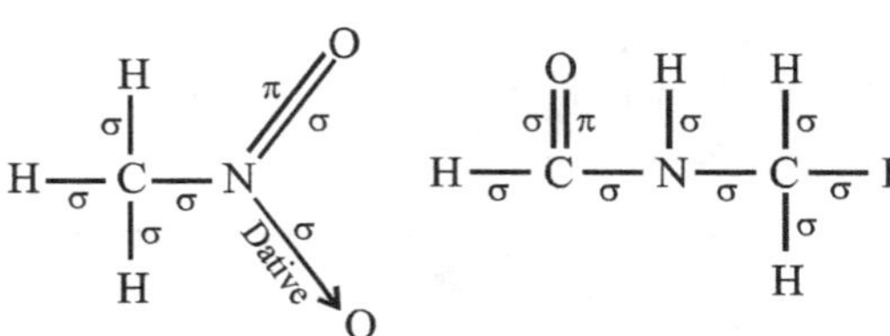

6 σ-bonds         8 σ-bonds
1π-bond          1π-bond

**12.3** Write bond line formulas for : Isopropyl alcohol, 2, 3-Dimethyl butanal, Heptan-4-one.

**Ans.** 

Isopropyl alcohol     2, 3-Dimethylbutanal

Heptan-4-one

**12.4** Give the IUPAC names of the following compounds:

(a)           (b) CN

(c)           (d) Cl Br

(e) Cl ... H      (f) $Cl_2CHCH_2OH$

**Ans.** (a) Propylbenzene
      (b) 3–Methylpentanenitrile

(c)  2,5–Dimethylheptane

(d)  3–Bromo–3–chloroheptane

(e)  3–Chloropropanal

(f)  2, 2–Dichloroethanol

**12.5  Which of the following represents the correct IUPAC name for the compounds concerned?**

(a)  **2, 2-Dimethylpentane or 2-Dimethylpentane**

(b)  **2,4,7-Trimethyloctane or 2, 5, 7-Trimethyloctane**

(c)  **2-Chloro-4-methylpentane or 4-Chloro-2-methylpentane**

(d)  **But-3-yn-1-ol or But-4-ol-1-yne.**

**Ans.**  (a)  2, 2 Dimethylpentane

(b)  2,4,7-Trimethyloctane.2,4, 7-locant set sum is lower than 2, 5, 7.

(c)  2-Chloro-4-methylpentane. Alphabetical order of substituents.

(d)  But-3-yn-1-ol. Lower locant for principal functional group, i.e., alcohol.

**12.6  Draw formulas for the first five members of each homologous series beginning with the following compounds.**

(a)  **H – COOH**          (b)  **$CH_3COCH_3$**

(c)  **$CH_2= CH_2$**

**Ans.**  (a)  $HCOOH, CH_3COOH, CH_3CH_2 COOH,$

$CH_3CH_2 CH_2COOH,$

$CH_3CH_2 CH_2 CH_2COOH$

(b)  $CH_3COCH_3, CH_3 CH_2COCH_3,$

$CH_3 CH_2 CH_2COCH_3,$

$CH_3 CH_2 CH_2CH_2COCH_3,$

$CH_3 CH_2 CH_2 CH_2 CH_2COCH_3$

(c)  $CH_2 = CH_2, CH_3 CH = CH_2,$

$CH_3 CH_2 CH = CH_2,$

$CH_3 CH_2 CH_2 CH = CH_2,$

$CH_3 CH_2 CH_2CH_2 CH = CH_2$

**12.7  Give condensed and bond line structural formulas and identify the functional group(s) present, if any, for:**

(a)  **2,2,4-Trimethylpentane**

(b)  **2-Hydroxy-1,2,3-propanetricarboxylic acid**

(c)  **Hexanedial**

| Condensed | Bond line | Functional Group |
|---|---|---|
| (a) $(CH_3)_3CCH_2CH(CH_3)_2$ | 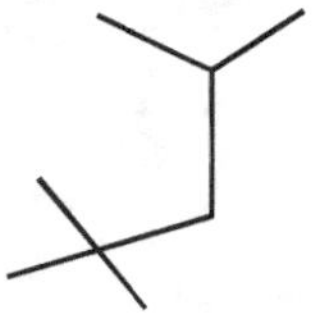 | – |
| (b) $HOOCCH_2CH(OH)COOH – CH_2COOH$ | 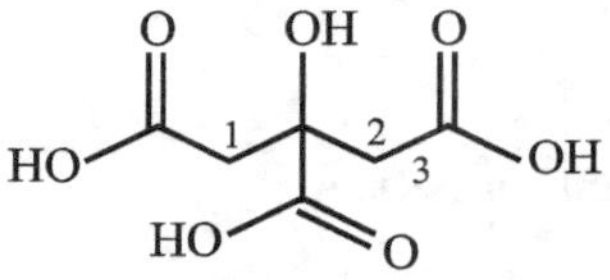 | 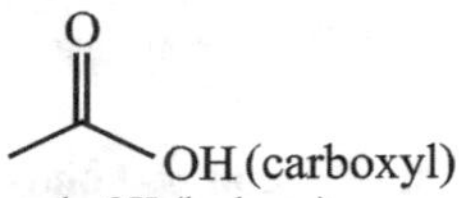 OH (carboxyl) and –OH (hydroxy) |
| (c) $OHC(CH_2)_4CHO$ | 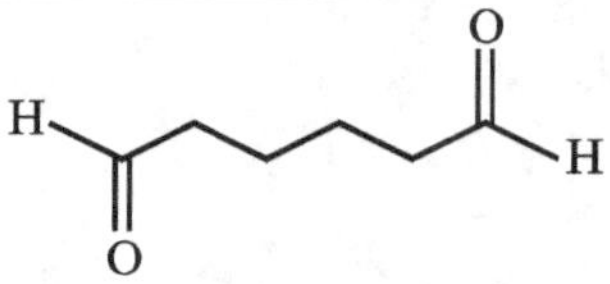 | 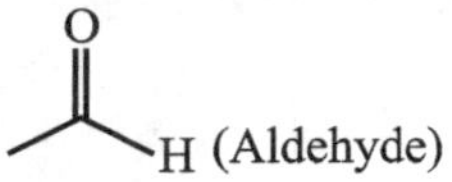 H (Aldehyde) |

**12.8  Identify the functional groups in the following compounds:**

(a)

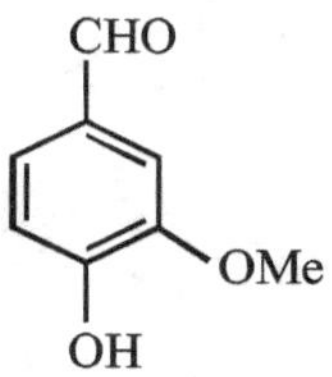

(b)

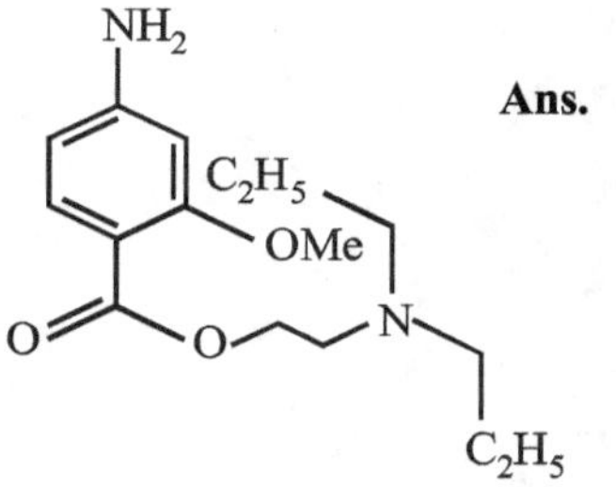

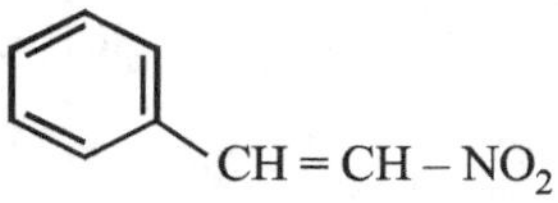

**Ans.**  (a) 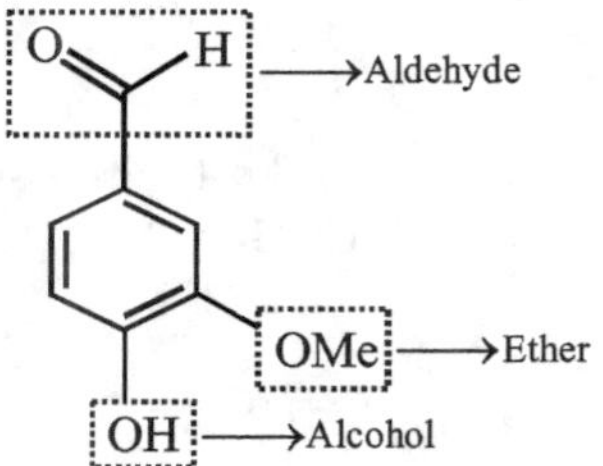  Aldehyde, OMe → Ether, OH → Alcohol

(c)  $CH = CH – NO_2$

(b) 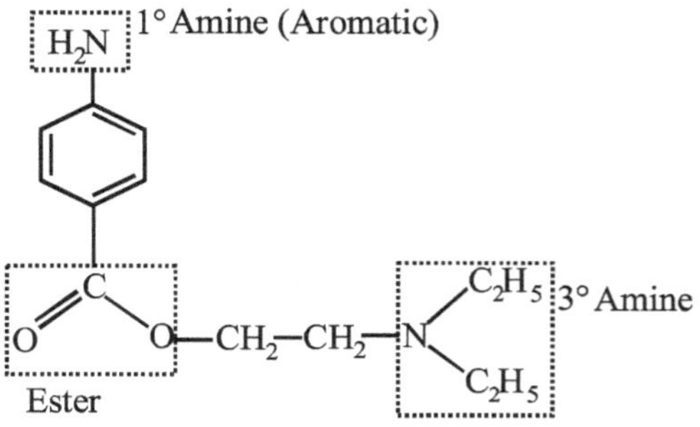  1° Amine (Aromatic)

Ester / C₂H₅ 3° Amine

(c) 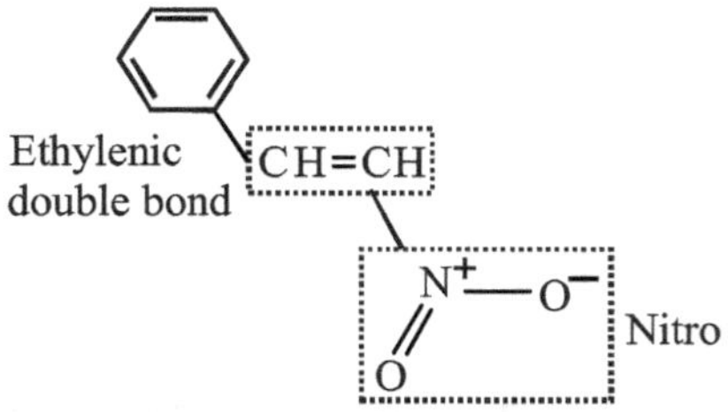 Ethylenic double bond / Nitro

## 12.9 Which is expected to be more stable, $O_2NCH_2\,CH_2O^-$ or $CH_3CH_2O^-$ and why?

**Ans.** $O_2N \leftarrow CH_2 \leftarrow CH_2 \leftarrow O^-$ is more stable than $CH_3 \rightarrow CH_2 \rightarrow O^-$ because $NO_2$ group has –I effect and hence it tends to disperse the –ve charge on the O-atom. In contrast, $CH_3CH_2$ has +I effect. It therefore, tends to intensify the –ve charge and hence destabilizes it.

## 12.10 Explain why alkyl groups act as electron donors when attached to a π-system.

**Ans.** Due to hyper conjugation, alkyl group acts as electron donors when attached to π -system as shown below:

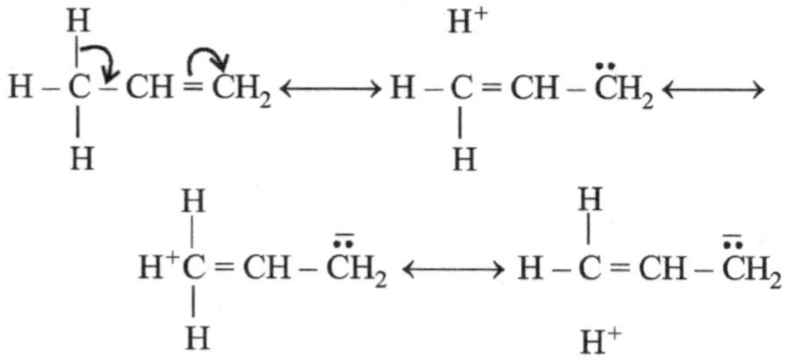

## 12.11 Draw the resonance structures for the following compounds. Show the electron shift using curved - arrow notation.

(a)  $C_6H_5OH$

(b)  $C_6H_5NO_2$

(c)  $CH_3\,CH = CHCHO$

(d)  $C_6H_5 - CHO$

(e)  $C_6H_5 - \overset{+}{C}H_2$

(f)  $CH_3CH = CH\overset{+}{C}H_2$

**Ans.** (a)

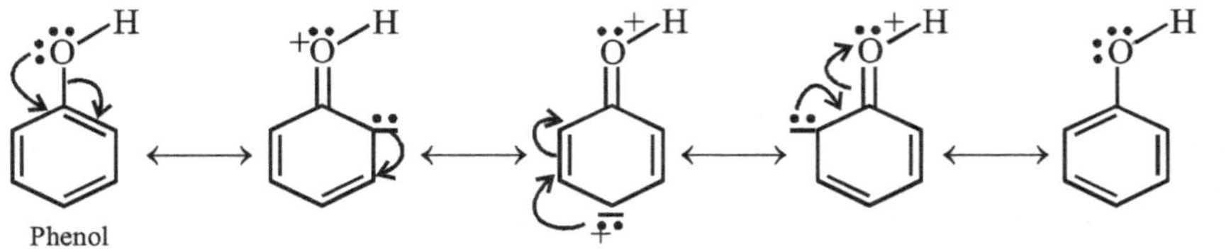

Phenol

(b)

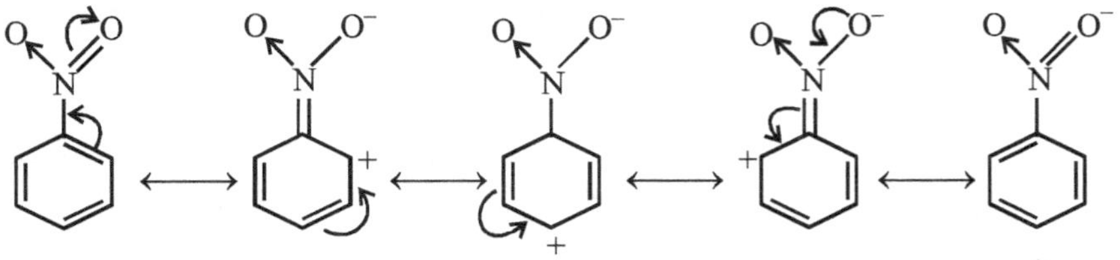

(c)

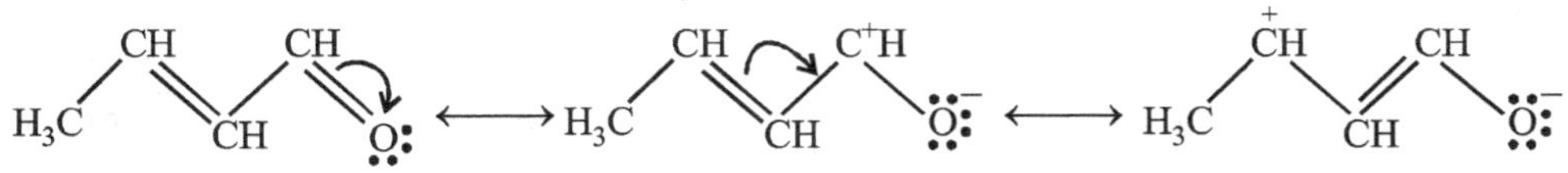

But-2-en-1-al

(d)

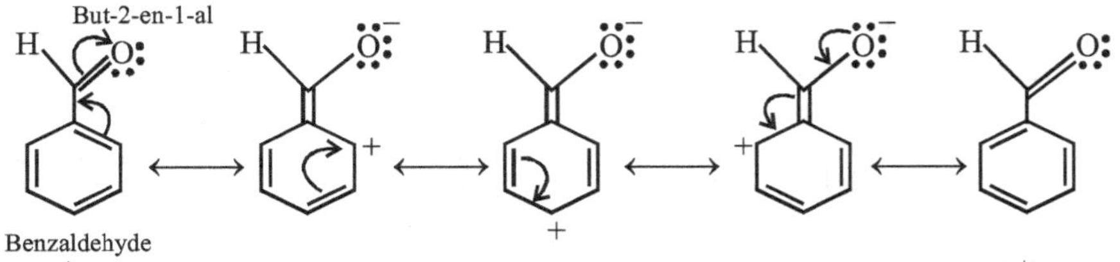

Benzaldehyde

(e)

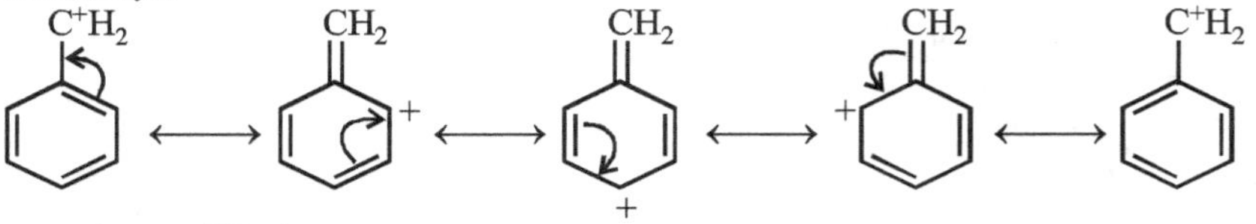

(f)  $CH_3 - CH = CH - \overset{\oplus}{C}H_2 \longleftrightarrow CH_3 - \overset{\oplus}{C}H - CH = CH_2$

**12.12 What are electrophiles and nucleophiles? Explain with examples.**

**Ans.** Electrophiles: Those species which are attracted towards electronic pairs are called electrophiles, e.g.,

$$NO_2^+ , \overset{+}{C}H_3Cl^+, CH_3\overset{+}{C}=O$$

Nucleophile: Those species which unshared pair of electron are attracted towards positive charge are called Nucleophile.

e.g., $OH^-, :NH_3, H_2\overset{..}{O}, H_2\overset{..}{N}:^-, HS^-$

**12.13 Identify the reagents shown in bold in the following equations as nucleophiles or electrophiles**

(a) $CH_3COOH + \mathbf{HO^-} \longrightarrow CH_3COO^- + H_2O$

(b) $CH_3 COCH_3 + \mathbf{^-CN} \longrightarrow (CH_3)_2 C\,(CN)\,(OH)$

(c) $C_6H_5 + \mathbf{CH_3\overset{+}{C}O} \longrightarrow C_6H_5COCH_3$

**Ans.** Nucleophiles: (a) and (b)

Electrophile: (c).

**12.14 Classify the following reactions in one of the reaction type studied in this unit.**

(a) $CH_3CH_2Br + HS^- \longrightarrow CH_3CH_2SH + Br^-$

(b) $(CH_3)_2C = CH_2 + HCl \longrightarrow (CH_3)_2\,CCl–CH_3$

(c) $CH_3CH_2 Br + HO^- \longrightarrow$
$$CH_2 = CH_2 + H_2O + Br^-$$

(d) $(CH_3)_3C–CH_2OH + HBr \longrightarrow$
$$(CH_3)_2CBr\,CH_2CH_3 + H_2O$$

**Ans.** (a) Nucleophilic substitution

(b) Electrophilic addition

(c) Elimination

(d) Nucleophilic substitution with rearrangement.

**12.15 What is the relationship between the members of following pairs of structures ? Are they structural or geometrical isomers or resonance contributors?**

(a)

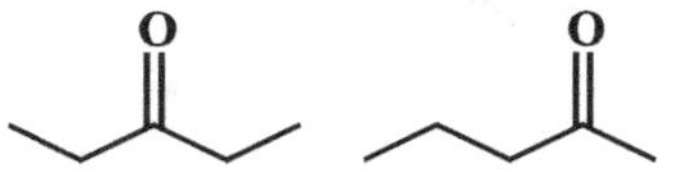

(b)

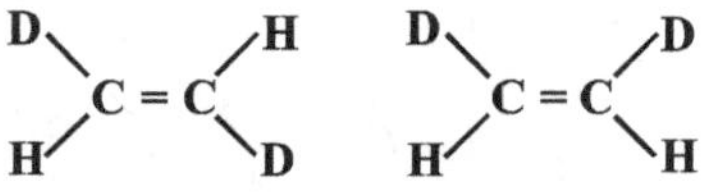

(c) $H – \overset{+OH}{\overset{\|}{C}} – OH \qquad H – \overset{OH}{\overset{\|\,+}{C}} – OH$

**Ans.** (a) Structural isomers (actually position isomers as well as metamers)

(b) geometrical isomers

(c) resonance contributors because they differ in the position of electrons but not atoms.

**12.16 For the following bond cleavages, use curved-arrows to show the electron flow and classify each as homolysis or heterolysis. Identify reactive intermediate produced as free radical, carbocation and carbanion.**

(a) $CH_3O – OCH_3 \longrightarrow CH_3\overset{.}{O} + \overset{.}{O}CH_3$

(b) $\overset{}{\rangle}{=}O + {}^-OH \longrightarrow \overset{}{\rangle}{=}O + H_2O$

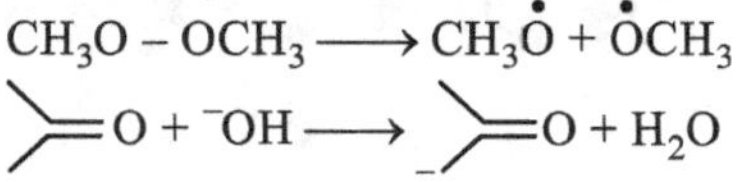

(c) 

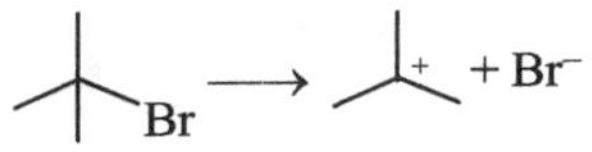

(d) 

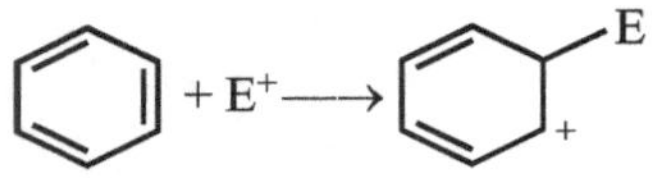

**Ans.** (a) $CH_3O \overset{\frown\frown}{} OCH_3 \xrightarrow{\text{Homolysis}} CH_3\overset{.}{O} + \overset{.}{O}CH_3$
Free radicals

(b) $HO^- + H \xrightarrow{\text{Heterolysis}} \rangle{=}O + H_2O$
Carbanion

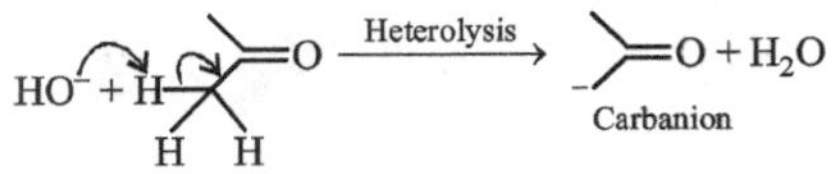

(c) $\xrightarrow{\text{Heterolysis}}$ + $Br^-$
Carbocation

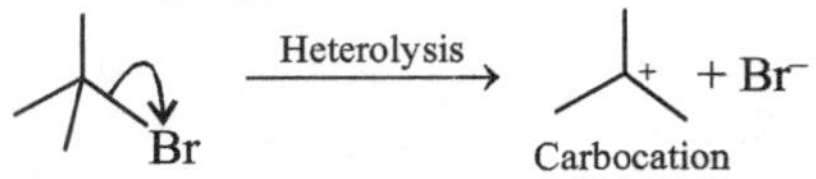

(d) $+ E^+ \xrightarrow{\text{Heterolysis}}$
Carbocation

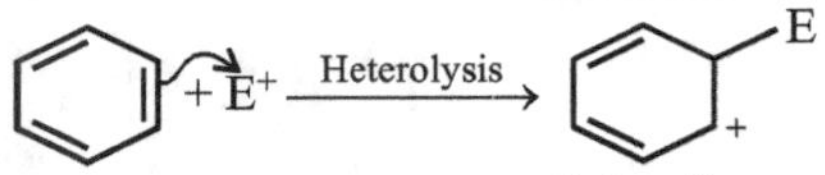

**12.17 Explain the terms Inductive and Electromeric effects. Which electron displacement effect explains the following correct orders of acidity of the carboxylic acids?**

(a) $Cl_3CCOOH > Cl_2CHCOOH > ClCH_2COOH$

(b) $CH_3CH_2COOH > (CH_3)_2CHCOOH$
$$> (CH_3)_3CCOOH$$

**Ans.** **Inductive effect:** Polarisation of sigma bond ($\sigma$) due to electron with drawing or electron donating group of adjacent atom is termed as inductive effect. It is a permanent effect.

**Electromeric effect:** Complete transfer of a shared pair of $\pi$ electrons to one of the atoms joined by a multiple bond on the demand of attacking reagent is called electromeric effect. It is a temporary effect. When inductive and electromeric effects operate in opposite directions, the electromeric effect predominates.

(a) –I effect as shown below :

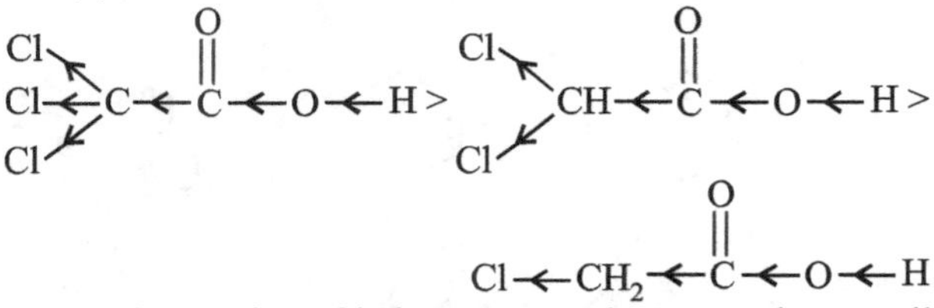

As the number of halogen atoms decreases, the overall –I effect decreases and the acid strength decreases accordingly,

(b) +I–effect as shown below :

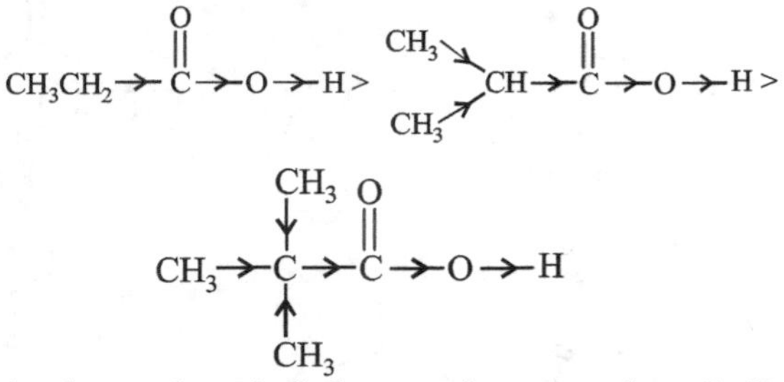

As the number of alkyl groups increases, the + I-effect increases and the acid strength decreases accordingly.

**12.18 Give a brief description of the principles of the following techniques taking an example in each case :**
**(a) Crystallisation  (b) Distillation**
**(c) Chromatography**

**Ans.** **(a) Crystallisation:** This technique is based on the difference in the solubilities of the compound and the impurities in a suitable solvent. In this method, impure compound is dissolved in suitable solvent at high temperature to form a saturated solution. On cooling the solution, pure compound crystallises out and is removed by filtration. This method is used for purification of solid organic compound.

**(b) Distillation:** Distillation is important separation method and used to separated (i) volatile liquid from non-volatile impurities. (ii) the liquids having sufficient different in their boiling point. Types of distillation.

| S. No. | Method | Principle | Example |
|---|---|---|---|
| (i) | Simple Distillation: | Liquids having sufficiently different boiling points vaporises at different temperature. These vapour at cooled and collected separately this method is called simple distillation. | Separation of chloroform (334K) and aniline (457 K). |
| (ii) | Fractional distillation: | This method is used if the difference in boiling points of two liquids is not much. In this technique vapours of a liquid mixture are passed through a fractionating column before condensation. Vapours of the liquid with higher boiling point condense before the other liquid with lower b.pt. | Separation of fraction of crude oil. |
| (iii) | Distillation under reduced pressure: | This method is used to purify liquids having very high b.pt. or those liquid which decomposes on heating. A liquid boils at its atmospheric or external pressure. If this pressure is reduced, liquid will boil before its boiling point. | Glycerol can be separated from spent lye in soap industry. |
| (iv) | Steam Distillation: | This method is used to purify those organic compound, which is steam volatile and immiscible in water. On passing steam the compound gets heated up and the steam gets condensed to water. After some time, the mixture of water and liquid starts to boil and passes through condenser. The condensed mixture of water and liquid is then separated by using separating funnel. | Mixture of water and aniline is separated by this method. |

**(c) Chromatography:** It is an entensively used to separate mixture into their componds, purify compounds and also to test, the purity of compounds: Types of chromotography.

| (i) | Adsorption Chromatography: | Different compounds are adsorbed on an adsorbent to different categories. There are two phase stationary phase : solid (Alumina, silica gel MgO etc.) Mobile phase: liquid (liquid solid) | Two main types of chromatographic technique based on the principle of different adsorption. (a) Column chromatography (b) Thin layer chromatography |
|---|---|---|---|
| (ii) | Partition Chromatography: | It is based on continuous differential partitioning of components of a mixture between stationary and mobile phases. Stationary phase : Liquid Mobile phase : Liquid | It mainly includes paper chromatography in which a strip of chromatographic paper is spotted with the solution mixture is suspended in a suitable solvent or a mixture solvent which acts as mobile phase. |

**12.19 Describe the method, which can be used to separate two compounds with different solubilities in a solvent S.**
**Ans.** Refer ans. 12.18(a).

**12.20 What is the difference between distillation, distillation under reduced pressure and steam distillation?**
**Ans.** Refer ans. 12.18(b).

**12.21 Discuss the Chemistry of Lassaigne's test.**
**Ans.** During fusion, carbon and nitrogen of the organic compound combine to form sodium cyanide.

$$Na + C + N \longrightarrow NaCN$$
(From organic compound)    Sodium cyanide

On heating the filtrate with ferrous sulphate solution, sodium ferrocyanide, i.e. sodium hexacyanoferrate (II) is formed and at the same time some $Fe^{2+}$ ions are oxidized to $Fe^{3+}$ ions. These $Fe^{3+}$ ions then react with sodium hexacyanoferrate (II) to produce iron (III) hexacyanoferrate (II) which is Prussian blue in colour.

$$2NaCN + FeSO_4 \longrightarrow Na_2SO_4 + Fe(CN)_2$$
$$Fe(CN)_2 + 4NaCN \longrightarrow Na_4[Fe(CN)_6]$$
$$3Na_4[Fe(CN)_6] + 4Fe^{3+} \longrightarrow Fe_4[Fe(CN)_6]_3 + 12Na^+$$
Prussian blue

If nitrogen and Sulphur both are present, they may combine during fusion to form sodium thiocyanate due to insufficient sodium. This when heated with ferrous sulphate produces a blood red coloration due to ferric thiocyanate.

$$Na + C + N + S \rightarrow NaSCN$$

$$Fe^{3+} + 3NaSCN \longrightarrow Fe(SCN)_3 + 3Na^+$$

Blood red coloration

**12.22 Differentiate between the principle of estimation of nitrogen in an organic compound by**

**(i) Duma's method**

**(ii) Kjeldahl's method.**

**Ans. (i) Duma's method:** The nitrogen containing organic compounds, when heated with copper oxide in an atmosphere of carbon dioxide, yields free nitrogen in addition to carbon dioxide and water. % nitrogen is measured as follows :

$$C_xH_yN_2 + \left(\frac{2x+y}{2}\right)CuO \rightarrow xCO_2 + \frac{y}{2}H_2O$$
$$+ \frac{z}{2}N_2 + \left(\frac{2x+y}{2}\right)Cu$$

$$\% \text{ of Nitrogen} = \frac{28 \times V \times 100}{22400 \times m}$$

**(ii) Kjeldahl method:** Nitrogen containing compound is treated with conc. $H_2SO_4$ to get ammonium sulphate which liberates ammonia on treating with NaOH: ammonia is absorbed in known volume of standard acid with the help of this % nitrogen is calculated.

$$- \text{ Organic compound} + H_2SO_4 \longrightarrow (NH_4)_2SO_4$$
$$\xrightarrow{2NaOH} Na_2SO_4 + 2NH_3 + 2H_2O$$
$$2NH_3 + H_2SO_4 \longrightarrow (NH_4)_2SO_4$$

$$\% \text{ of nitrogen} = \frac{1.4 \times M \times 2(V - V_1/2)}{m}$$

– V and $V_1$ are volume (mL) of $H_2SO_4$ and volume (mL) of NaOH respectively.

**12.23 Discuss the principle of estimation of halogens, sulphur and phosphorus present in an organic compound.**

**Ans. Qualitative Analysis:** Lassaigne's test is used for the detection of halogen and sulphur.

| S. No. | Element | Sodium Extract | Procedure | Reaction |
|---|---|---|---|---|
| (i) | Halogen | $Na + X \rightarrow NaX$ (S.E.)<br><br>$X - I, Br, I$ | • **White ppt.** soluble in aq. $NH_3$ confirms Cl.<br>• **Pale yellow ppt.** partially soluble in excess aq. $NH_3$ confirms Br.<br>• **Yellow ppt.** insoluble in aq. $NH_3$ confirms I. | $NaX + AgNO_3 \rightarrow AgX$<br>$AgCl + 2NH_3(aq.) \rightarrow [Ag(NH_3)_2]Cl$ Whiteppt.<br>$AgBr + 2NH_3(aq.) \rightarrow [Ag(NH_3)_2]Br$ Yellowppt.<br>$AgINH_3(aq.) \rightarrow$ Insoluble |
| (ii) | Sulphur | $2Na + S \rightarrow Na_2S$ (S.E.) | (a) S.E. + Sodium nitro prusside $\rightarrow$ A **deep violet colour.**<br>(b) S.E. + $CH_3COOH + (CH_3COO)_2Pb \rightarrow$ **Black ppt.** | $Na_2S + Na_2[Fe(CN)_5NO] \rightarrow Na_4[Fe(CN)_5(NO_5)]$<br>$Na_2S + (CH_3COO)_2 Pb \rightarrow PbS + 2CH_3COONa$ |
| (iii) | Phosphorus | — | Organic compound containing phosphorus $+ Na_2O_2 \xrightarrow{\Delta}$ phosphorus is oxidised to phosphate $\rightarrow$ Boiled with $HNO_3$ and then treated with ammonium molybdate. | $-Na_3PO_4 + 3HNO_3 \rightarrow H_3PO_4 + 3NaNO_3 - H_3PO_4 + 12(NH_4)_2 + MoO_4 + 21HNO_3 \rightarrow (NH_4)_3PO_4.12MoO_3 + 21NH_4NO_3 + 12H_2O$ ppt |

**Quantitative Analysis:** Let's look at the various methods involved in the estimation of halogens, sulphur and phosphorus.

Let mass of organic compound taken = m

And, mass of precipitate for analysis = $m_1$

**Estimation of halogens:** Halogens are estimated by the process known as Carius method. In this method a known quantity of the organic compound is reacted with fuming nitric acid in the presence of silver nitrate. Carbon and hydrogen get oxidized and the halogen is converted to silver halide. It is then collected, filtered, washed and dried.

$$\text{Percentage of halogen} = \frac{\text{At. mass of} \times m_1 \times 100}{\text{mol. mass of Ag X} \times m}$$

**Estimation of sulphur:** A small amount of organic compound is reacted with fuming nitric acid. The sulphur present is oxidized to sulphuric acid. An excess amount of barium chloride is added to precipitate out the sulphur present as barium sulphate. It is then filtered, washed and dried.

$$\text{Percentage of sulphur} = \frac{32 \times m_1 \times 100}{233 \times m}$$

Where 233g is the molar mass of barium sulphate.

**Estimation of phosphorus:** A small amount of organic acid is reacted with fuming nitric acid. The phosphorus present is oxidized to phosphoric acid. Ammonia and ammonium molybdate are then added to get the phosphorus as ammonium phosphomolybdate as a precipitate. It is then filtered, washed and dried.

$$\text{Percentage of phosphorous} = \frac{31 \times m_1 \times 100}{1877 \times m}\%$$

Where 1877 is the molar mass of ammonium phosphomolybdate.

**12.24 Explain the principle of paper chromatography.**

**Ans.** Paper chromatography is a type of partition chromatography and is based on continuous differential partitioning of components of a mixture between stationary and mobile phase.

–    In this method, a strip of chromatography paper spotted at the base with the solution of the mixture is suspended in a suitable solvent which acts as mobile phase.

–    The solvent rises up the paper and it selectively retains different compounds according to their differing partition in two different phases (mobile phase and stationary phase).

–    The paper strip so developed is known as a chromatogram.

–    The spots of the separated coloured compounds are visible at different heights. The spots of components of colourless mixture are observed under UV light.

**12.25 Why is nitric acid added to sodium extract before adding silver nitrate for testing halogens?**

**Ans.** Sodium extract is boiled with nitric acid to decompose NaCN and Na$_2$S, if present, otherwise these will react with AgNO$_3$ and hence will interfere with the test.

NaCN + AgNO$_3$ $\longrightarrow$ NaNO$_3$ + AgCN (white ppt)

Na$_2$S + AgNO$_3$ $\longrightarrow$ 2NaNO$_3$ + Ag$_2$S (black ppt)

Hence to remove them i.e. NaCN and Na$_2$S, HNO$_3$ is added.

NaCN + HNO$_3$ $\longrightarrow$ NaNO$_3$ + HCN

Na$_2$S + 2HNO$_3$ $\longrightarrow$ 2NaNO$_3$ + H$_2$S

**12.26 Explain the reason for the fusion of an organic compound with metallic sodium for testing nitrogen, Sulphur and halogens.**

**Ans.** The organic compound is fused with sodium metal to convert these elements which are present in the covalent form to ionic form.

**12.27 Name a suitable technique of separation of the components from a mixture of calcium sulphate and camphor.**

**Ans.** A mixture of camphor and CaSO$_4$ can be separated by the following methods:

(i)    Camphor is a sublimable solid while CaSO$_4$ is not, therefore, sublimation of mixture gives camphor on the sides of funnel while CaSO$_4$ is left in the china dish.

(ii)    Camphor is soluble in organic solvents like CHCl$_3$,CCl$_4$ etc while CaSO$_4$ is not. Therefore, when the mixture is shaken with the solvent, camphor goes into solution while CaSO$_4$ remains as residue. It is filtered and evaporation of solvent gives camphor.

**12.28 Explain, why an organic liquid vaporises at a temperature below its boiling point in its steam distillation?**

**Ans.** In steam distillation, the mixture consisting of the organic liquid and water boils at a temperature when the sum of the vapour pressure of organic liquid (p$_1$) and that of water (p$_2$) becomes equal to the atmospheric pressure (p), i. e, p = p$_1$ + p$_2$. Since the vapour pressure of water around the boiling point of the mixture is quite high and that of liquid is quite low (10–15 mm), therefore, the organic liquid distils at a pressure much lower than the pressure. In other words, the organic liquid vapourizes at a temperature much lower than its normal boiling point.

**12.29 Will CCl$_4$ give white precipitate of AgCl on heating it with silver nitrate ? Give reason for your answer.**

**Ans.** When CCl$_4$ is heated with AgNO$_3$ solution, white ppt. of AgCl will not be formed. The reason being that CCl$_4$ is a covalent compound, therefore, it does not ionize to give Cl$^-$ ions needed for the formation of ppt. of Ag Cl.

**12.30 Why is a solution of potassium hydroxide used to absorb carbon dioxide evolved during the estimation of carbon present in an organic compound ?**

**Ans.** CO$_2$ is acidic in nature, therefore, it reacts with the strong base KOH to form K$_2$CO$_3$.

2 KOH + CO$_2$ $\longrightarrow$ K$_2$CO$_3$ + H$_2$O

The increase in the mass of U-tube containing KOH then gives the mass of CO$_2$ produced and from its mass the percentage of carbon in the organic compound can be estimated by using the equation % of C = 12/44 × (Mass of CO$_2$ formed) /(Mass of substance taken) × 100

**12.31 Why is it necessary to use acetic acid and not sulphuric acid for acidification of sodium extract for testing sulphur by lead acetate test ?**

**Ans.** For testing sulphur, the sodium extract is acidified with acetic acid because lead acetate is soluble and does not interfere with the test. If H$_2$SO$_4$ were used, lead acetate itself will react with H$_2$SO$_4$ to form white ppt. of lead sulphate which will interfere with the test.

Pb(OCOCH$_3$)$_2$ + H$_2$SO$_4$ $\longrightarrow$ PbSO$_4$ $\downarrow$ + 2CH$_3$COOH

Lead acetate                                                     (White ppt.)

**12.32 An organic compound contains 69% carbon and 4. 8% hydrogen, the remainder being oxygen. Calculate the masses of carbon dioxide and water produced when 0.20 g of this substance is subjected to complete combustion.**

**Ans.** We know that %C = 12/44 × (Mass of CO$_2$ formed)/( Mass or substance taken) × 100

Substituting the values of % of C and mass of the substance taken, we have,

$$69 = \frac{12}{44} \times \frac{\text{mass of CO}_2 \text{ formed} \times 100}{\text{mass of substance taken}}$$

or Mass of CO$_2$ formed $= \dfrac{69 \times 44 \times 0.2}{12 \times 100} = 0.506 \text{ g}$

Similarly, % H = 2/18 × (Mass of H$_2$O formed)/ mass of substance taken ×100

Substituting the values of % H and the mass of substance taken, we have,

$$4.8 = \frac{2 \times \text{mass of water formed}}{18 \times 0.2} \times 100 \text{ or}$$

$$\text{mass of water formed} = \frac{4.8 \times 18 \times 0.2}{2 \times 100} = 0.0864 \text{ g}$$

**12.33 A sample of 0.50 g of an organic compound was treated according to Kjeldahl's method. The ammonia evolved was absorbed in 50 ml of 0.5 M $H_2SO_4$. The residual acid required 60 mL of 0.5 M solution of NaOH for neutralisation. Find the percentage composition of nitrogen in the compound.**

**Ans.** **Step 1.** To determine the volume of $H_2SO_4$ used.
Volume of acid taken = 50 ml of 0.5 M $H_2SO_4$ = 25 ml of 1 M $H_2SO_4$
Volume of alkali used for neutralization of excess acid
= 60 ml of 0.5 M NaOH = 30 ml of 1M NaOH.
Now 1 mole of $H_2SO_4$ neutralizes 2 moles of NaOH
(i. e. $H_2SO_4 + 2$ NaOH$\longrightarrow Na_2SO_4 + 2$ $H_2O$)
30 ml of 1 M NaOH = 15 ml of 1 M $H_2SO_4$
$\therefore$  Volume of acid used by ammonia
$$= 25 - 15 = 10 \text{ ml}$$
**Step 2.** To determine percentage of nitrogen.
Again 1 mole of $H_2SO_4$ neutralizes 2 moles of $NH_3$

$$\left( \text{i.e. } 2NH_3 + H_2SO_4 \longrightarrow \left(NH_4\right)_2 SO_4 \right)$$

10 ml of 1 M $H_2SO_4 \equiv$ 20 ml of 1 M $NH_3$
$\because$  1000 ml of 1 M $NH_3$ contain nitrogen = 14 g
20 ml of 1M $NH_3$ will contain nitrogen
= 14/1000 ×20 g
But this much amount of nitrogen is present in 0.5 g of the organic compound.
Percentage of nitrogen = 14/1000 × 20/0.5 × 100 = 56%.
**Alternatively,** % of N can be determined by applying the following equation,

$$\%N = \frac{1.4 \times \text{Molarity of the acid} \times \text{Basicity of the acid} \times \text{Vol. of the acid used}}{\text{Mass of substance taken}}$$

Substituting the values of all the items in the above equation, we have,

$$\%N = \frac{1.4 \times 1 \times 2 \times 10}{0.5} = 56.0$$

**12.34 0.3780 g of an organic chloro compound gave 0.5740 g of silver chloride in Carius estimation. Calculate the percentage of chlorine present in the compound.**

**Ans.** Here, the mass of the substance taken = 0.3780 g
Mass of AgCl formed = 0.5740 g
Now 1 mole of AgCl $\equiv$ 1 g atom of Cl  or
$(108 + 35.5) = 143.5$ g of AgCl $\equiv$ 35.5 g of Cl
Applying the relation,  Percentage of chlorine

$$= \frac{35.5}{143.5} \times \frac{\text{Mass of AgCl formed}}{\text{Mass of substance taken}} \times 100$$

$$= \frac{35.5}{143.5} \times \frac{0.5740}{0.3780} \times 100 = 37.56\%$$

**12.35 In the estimation of sulphur by Carius method, 0.468 g of an organic sulphur compound afforded 0.668 g of barium sulphate. Find out the percentage of sulphur in the given compound.**

**Ans.** Here, the mass of the substance taken = 0.468 g
Mass of $BaSO_4$ formed = 0.668 g
Now 1 mole of $BaSO_4 \equiv$ 1g atom of S
or $(137 + 32 + 4 \times 16) = 233$g of $BaSO_4 \equiv 32$ g of S
Applying the relation, Percentage of Sulphur

$$= \frac{32}{233} \times \frac{\text{Mass of } BaSO_4 \text{ formed}}{\text{Mass of substance taken}} \times 100$$

$$= \frac{32}{233} \times \frac{0.668}{0.468} \times 100 = 19.603\%$$

**12.36 In the organic compound $CH_2 = CH–CH_2–CH_2– C\equiv CH$, the $C_2$–$C_3$ bond is the pair of hybridised orbitals involved in the formation of**
(a) $sp–sp^2$      (b) $sp – sp^3$
(c) $sp^2 – sp^3$      (d) $sp^3– sp^3$

**Ans.** (c) When both double and triple bonds are present, double bond is given preference while numbering the carbon chain. Thus,

$$\underset{sp^2}{\overset{1}{CH_2}} = \underset{sp^2}{\overset{2}{CH}} - \underset{sp^3}{\overset{3}{CH_2}} - \underset{sp^3}{\overset{4}{CH_2}} - \underset{sp}{\overset{5}{C}} \equiv \underset{sp}{\overset{6}{CH}}$$

$\therefore$  $C_2$–$C_3$ bond is formed by overlap of $sp^2 - sp^3$ orbital. Thus, option (c) is correct.

**12.37 In the Lassaigne's test for nitrogen in an organic compound, the Prussian blue colour is obtained due to the formation of:**
(a) $Na_4[Fe(CN)_6]$    (b) $Fe_4[Fe(CN)_6]_3$
(c) $Fe_2[Fe(CN)_6]$    (d) $Fe_3[Fe(CN)_6]_4$

**Ans.** (b) The prussian blue colour is due to the formation $Fe_4[Fe(CN)_6]_3$. Thus, option (b) is correct.

**12.38 Which of the following carbocation is most stable ?**
(a) $(CH_3)_3CC^+H_2$      (b) $(CH_3)_3C^+$
(c) $CH_3CH_2C^+H_2$      (d) $CH_3C^+HCH_2CH_3$

**Ans.** (b) The order of stability of carbocation is:
$3° > 2° > 1°$

(a) $(CH_3)_3C - \overset{+}{C}H_2$      (b) $(CH_3)_3C^+$
      1°Carbocation           3°Carbocation

(c) $CH_3CH_2CH_2^+$      (d) $CH_3 \overset{+}{C}HCH_2CH_3$
      1°Carbocation           2°Carbocation

Thus, option (b) is correct.

**12.39 The best and latest technique for isolation, purification and separation of organic compounds is;**
(a) **Crystallisation**      (b) **Distillation**
(c) **Sublimation**      (d) **Chromatography**

**Ans.** (d) Chromatography. Thus, option (d) is correct.

**12.40 The following reaction is classified as :**
$$CH_3CH_2I + KOH \text{ (aq)} \longrightarrow CH_3CH_2OH + KI$$
(a) **electrophilic substitution**
(b) **nucleophilic substitution**
(c) **elimination**
(d) **addition.**

**Ans.** (b) This is an example of nucleophilic substitution reaction since the nucleophile $I^-$ is replaced by the nucleophile $OH^-$ ion. Thus, option (b) is correct.

## SECTION B | PRACTICE QUESTIONS

### MULTIPLE CHOICE QUESTIONS

**1.** The compound in which $\overset{x}{C}$ uses its $sp^3$ - hybrid orbitals for bond formation is

(a) $H\overset{X}{C}OOH$

(b) $(H_2N)_2\overset{X}{C}O$

(c) $(CH_3)_3\overset{X}{C}OH$

(d) $CH_3\overset{X}{C}HO$

**2.** 2- Pentene contains

(a) 15 σ- and one π- bond

(b) 14 σ-and one π- bond

(c) 15 σ- and two π- bonds

(d) 14 σ- and two π- bonds

**3.** The compound which has one isopropyl group is

(a) 2, 2, 3, 3 - Tetramethylpentane

(b) 2, 2 - Dimethylpentane

(c) 2, 2, 3- Trimethylpentane

(d) 2- Methypentane

**4.** IUPAC name of following compound is :

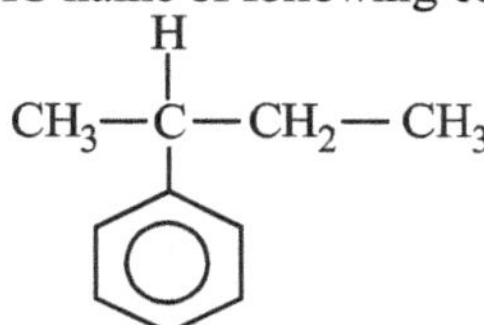

(a) 2 - cyclohexylbutane

(b) 2 - phenylbutane

(c) 3 - cyclohexylbutane

(d) 3 - phenylbutane

**5.** What is the IUPAC name of the following compound?

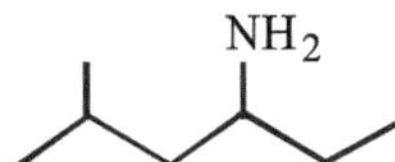

(a) 2-methyl-4-hexanamine

(b) 5-methyl-3-hexanamine

(c) 2-methyl-4-amino hexane

(d) 5-methyl-3-amino hexane

**6.** IUPAC name of $(CH_3)_3\,CCl$ is

(a) 1-butyl chloride

(b) 3-chloro butane

(c) 2-chloro-2-methylpropane

(d) 2-butyl chloride

**7.** IUPAC name of the following compound

(a) N, N-dimethylcyclopropane carboxamide

(b) N-methylcyclopropanamide'

(c) cyclopropionamide

(d) None of these

**8.** The organic reactions which proceed through heterolytic bond cleavage called _________

(a) ionic

(b) polar

(c) non-polar

(d) Both (a) and (b)

**9.** The shape of methyl carbanion is similar to that of –

(a) $BF_3$

(b) $NH_3$

(c) methyl free radical

(d) methyl carbocation

**10.** Homolytic fission of C–C bond in ethane gives an intermediate in which carbon is

(a) $sp^3$-hybridised

(b) $sp^2$-hybridised

(c) $sp$-hybridised

(d) $sp^2d$-hybridised

**11.** Which of the following is strongest nucleophile?

(a) Br

(b) : $OH^-$

(c) : $CN^-$

(d) $C_2H_5\bar{O}$ :

**12.** Which of the following represents a set of nucleophiles?

(a) $BF_3, H_2O, NH_2^-$

(b) $AlCl_3, BF_3, NH_3$

(c) $CN^-, RCH_2^-, ROH$

(d) All of these

**13.** Which of the following species does not act as a nucleophile?

(a) ROH

(b) ROR

(c) $PCl_3$

(d) $BF_3$

**14.** The best method for the separation of naphthalene and benzoic acid from their mixture is:

(a) distillation

(b) sublimation

(c) chromatography

(d) crystallisation

**15.** In steam distillation the vapour pressure of volatile organic compound is

(a) equal to atmospheric pressure

(b) double the atmospheric pressure

(c) less than atmospheric pressure

(d) more than atmospheric pressure

**16.** Distillation under reduced pressure is employed for

(a) $C_6H_6$

(b) petrol

(c) $CH_2OHCHOHCH_2OH$

(d) organic compounds used in medicine

**17.** Kjeldahl method is not applicable to which of the following?

(a) Nitro compounds

(b) Azo compounds

(c) Pyridine

(d) All of these

## ASSERTION & REASON QUESTIONS

**DIRECTIONS (Qs. 1-5) :** *Each of these questions contains an assertion followed by reason. Read them carefully and answer the question on the basis of following options. You have to select the one that best describes the two statements.*

(a) If both Assertion and Reason are correct and the Reason is a correct explanation of the Assertion.

(b) If both Assertion and Reason are correct but Reason is not a correct explanation of the Assertion.

(c) If the Assertion is correct but Reason is incorrect.

(d) If the Assertion is incorrect but the Reason is correct.

1. **Assertion :** IUPAC name of the following organic compound is 3, 4, 7 – trimethyloctane

$$CH_3-CH-CH_2-CH_2-CH-CH-CH_2-CH_3$$
$$\quad\quad | \quad\quad\quad\quad\quad\quad | \quad | $$
$$\quad\quad CH_3 \quad\quad\quad\quad CH_3 \ CH_3$$

   **Reason :** The numbering is done in such a way that the branched carbon atoms get the lowest possible numbers.

2. **Assertion :** The styrene molecule does not exhibit geometrical isomerism.
   **Reason :** All the carbon atoms of styrene molecule lie in a plane.

3. **Assertion :** Diastereomers have different solubilities in the same solvent.
   **Reason :** Diastereomers may or may not be optically active.

4. **Assertion :** Aniline is better nucleophile than anilium ion.
   **Reason :** Anilium ion has +ve charge.

5. **Assertion :** Different number of electron pairs are present in resonance structures.
   **Reason :** Resonance structures differ in the location of electrons around the constituent atoms.

## CASE/PASSAGE BASED QUESTIONS

**DIRECTIONS (Qs. 1-4) :** *Read the following case/passage and answer the questions.*

The word "isomer" is derived from the Greek words "isos" and "meros", which mean "equal parts". This term was coined by the Swedish chemist Jacob Berzelius in the year 1830. Isomerism is the phenomenon in which more than one compounds have the same chemical formula but different chemical structures. Chemical compounds that have identical chemical formulae but differ in properties and the arrangement of atoms in the molecule are called **isomers**. Therefore, the compounds that exhibit isomerism are known as isomers. There are two primary types of isomerism, which can be further categorized into different subtypes. These primary types are **Structural Isomerism** and **Stereoisomerism.** Structural isomerism is commonly referred to as constitutional isomerism. The functional groups and the atoms in the molecules of these isomers are linked in different ways. The different types of structural isomerism are Chain Isomerism, Position Isomerism,

Functional Isomerism, Metamerism etc. Stereoisomerism arises in compounds having the same chemical formula but different orientations of the atoms belonging to the molecule in three-dimensional space. This phenomenon can be further categorized into two subtypes, optical and geometric isomerism.

**DIRECTIONS (Qs. 1-4) :** *Each of these questions contains an assertion followed by reason. Read them carefully and answer the question on the basis of following options. You have to select the one that best describes the two statements.*

(a) If both Assertion and Reason are correct and the Reason is a correct explanation of the Assertion.

(b) If both Assertion and Reason are correct but Reason is not a correct explanation of the Assertion.

(c) If the Assertion is correct but Reason is incorrect.

(d) If the Assertion is incorrect but the Reason is correct.

1. **Assertion :** Ethyl alcohol and dimethyl ether are functional isomers.
   **Reason :** They possess same molecular formula but different functional groups.

2. **Assertion :** But-1-ene shows geometric isomerism and but-2-ene does not shows geometric isomerism.
   **Reason :** But-1-ene and but-2-ene are position isomers.

3. **Assertion :** 2- butyne shows geometric isomerism.
   **Reason :** geometrical isomerism is shown by alkenes and other compounds.

4. **Assertion :** $CHBr = CHCl$ exhibit geometrical isomerism, but $CH_2Br-CH_2Cl$ does not.
   **Reason :** $CH_2Br-CH_2Cl$ have free rotation around C-C bond.

**OR**

**Assertion :** Optically active molecules are chiral molecules.
**Reason :** Chiral carbon has four different groups attached to it.

## VERY SHORT ANSWER QUESTIONS

1. What type of isomerism is shown by butane and isobutane?
2. Write the metamer of diethyl ether. What is its IUPAC name?
3. What primary and secondary suffixes are as applied to IUPAC nomenclature?
4. Give the IUPAC name of the compound:
   $$CH_2 = CH - CH(CH_3)_2$$
5. Define homologous series.
6. Give the IUPAC names of the following compound:

$$CH_3-CH-C-CH-CH_3$$
$$\quad\quad | \quad\ || \ \ |$$
$$\quad\quad Br \ \ O \ \ CH_3$$

7. Write the IUPAC name of

$$CH_3-CH-CH_2-CH-COOH$$
$$\quad\quad | \quad\quad\quad\quad |$$
$$\quad\quad CHO \quad\quad\ CH_3$$

8.   Is neopentyl radical, 4°?
9.   Write the structural formula of the compound 4-formyl - 3-methylbutanoic acid.
10.  An organic liquid decomposes below its boiling point. How will you purify it ?
11.  Two volatile compounds A and B differ in their boiling points by 15K. Suggest a suitable method for their separation.
12.  How will you separate a mixture of *o–* and *p–* nitro phenols?
13.  Name two methods which can be safely used to purify aniline.
14.  Define the term 'elution' as applied to column chromatography.
15.  Name the process of separating benzoic acid and naphthalene.
16.  What is the suitable adsorbent in the process of column chromatography?
17.  Which gas is liberated in Kjeldahl's method?
18.  What is the value of 'x' in an organic compound with molecular formula $C_xH_{12}$ with vapour density 42?
19.  Which gas is liberated in Duma's method?
20.  Why are melting point and refractive index used as the criteria of purity of organic compounds?
21.  A student was given the compound $H_2N - C_6H_4 - SO_3H$ for elemental analysis. While performing Lassaigne's test for N, what colour will he get and why?
22.  In order to determine the molecular mass of benzene, which method would you use?
23.  Why does hydrazine not give test for Lassaigne's extract?
24.  It is advisable to prepare Lassaigne's extract in distilled water. Why?

## SHORT ANSWER QUESTIONS

1.   A compound is formed by the substitution of two chlorine atoms for two hydrogen atoms in propane. What is the number of structural isomers possible?
2.   Give IUPAC names for
     (i)   $CH_3 - CH = C(NO_2) CH_2CH_3$
     (ii)  $H_2C = CHCH - \overset{|}{C}HCH - CHCHMe_2$
           $\overset{|}{C}H(Me)CH_2CH_3$
     (iii) 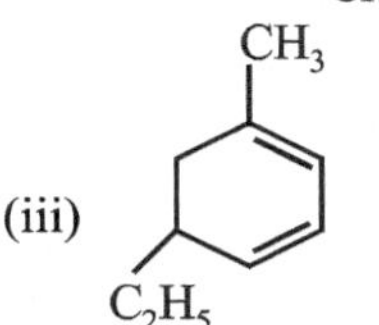
     (iv)  $(H_2C = CH)_2 CHCH_2CH = CHCH_3$
3.   Write the condensed structural formula of
     (i)   4-ethyl-3-methyl heptane
     (ii)  3, 3-dimethyl octane
4.   Write the structural formula of
     (i)   *o*-methoxyethylbenzene
     (ii)  2,3-dibromo-1-phenylpentane
     (iii) 4-ethyl-1-fluoro-2-nitrobenzene

5.   An alcohol with no carbon-carbon double bond has the formula $C_4H_8O$. What are the possible structures?
6.   Draw all possible isomers for a compound with molecular formula $C_8H_{10}$ containing benzene ring. Also, give IUPAC name to these isomers.
7.   An aliphatic amine has a molecular mass of 59. Draw all its possible isomers.
8.   Give IUPAC names for the following compounds.

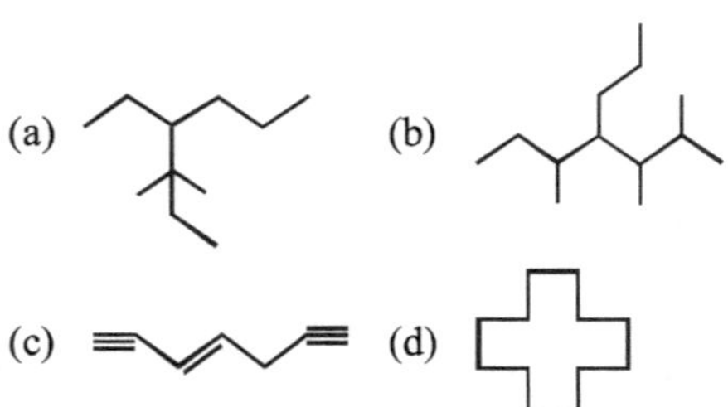

9.   What are carboanions? Discuss their types.
10.  Explain the relative stabilities of primary, secondary and tertiary free radicals.
11.  What are carbocations (carbonium ion)? Discuss their types.
12.  What are free radicals ? Discuss their types.
13.  In Carius method of estimation of halogen, 0.15 g of an organic compound gave 0.12 of AgBr. Find the percentage of bromine in the compound.
14.  Which of the following species behaves as (i) a nucleophile, (ii) an electrophile, (iii) both, or (iv) neither?

$$:\overset{..}{\underset{..}{I}}:^- H_3N:, BeCl_2, NO_2^+, CH_3C \equiv N:,$$
$$H_2, H_2C = \overset{..}{C}:, CH_4$$

15.  Explain why an organic liquid vapourizes at a temperature below its boiling point in its steam distillation?
16.  What type of compounds are purified by sublimation?
17.  How will you separate iodine from sodium chloride?
18.  What are the advantages of using the chromatography method over other methods of separation?
19.  Suggest a method to purify:
     (i)   Camphor containing traces of common salt.
     (ii)  Kerosene oil containing water.
     (iii) A liquid which decomposes at its boiling point.
20.  Pick up the species which can act as
     (a)  both *i.e.* electrophile as well as nucleophile and
     (b)  neither electrophile or nucleophile.
          $H^+, H_2, H_2O, Cl^+, Cl^-, Cr^{3+}, CH_4, NO_2^+, BeCl_2,$
          $CH_2O, CH_3CH = CH_2, SnCl_4, CH_3CN, SiF_4$

## LONG ANSWER QUESTIONS

1.   What are reaction intermediates ? How are they generated by bond fission ?
2.   (i)   Select electrophiles out of the following:
           $H^+, Na^+, Cl^-, C_2H_5OH, AlCl_3, SO_3, CN^-, CH_3CH_2^+,:$
           $CCl_2, R–X$
     (ii)  Select nucleophiles from the following: $BF_3, NH_3, ^-OH, R–X, C_2H_5OH.$

**3.** Name each of the following :

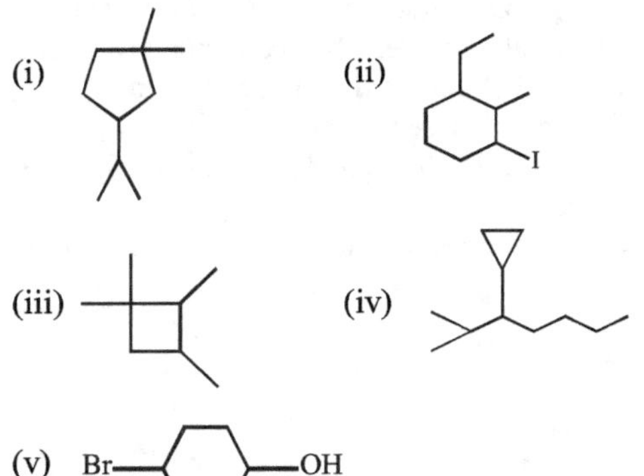

(i)        (ii)

(iii)        (iv)

(v)  Br⟶◯⟶OH

**4.** Draw all possible isomers of a compound with molecular formula, $C_4H_{10}O$. Classify them as chain and position isomers.

**5.** (i) On combustion, 0.3650 g of compound (A) gave 0.88 g $CO_2$ and 0.495 g $H_2O$. Further, 0.1186 g of the same compound gave, on combustion by Dumas' method, 20 ml of nitrogen measured at 27°C and 779 mm Hg pressure. (Aqueous tension at 27°C = 19 mm Hg). What is the percentage composition of the compound?

(ii) A 3.87 mg sample of organic compound give 5.80 mg $CO_2$ and 1.58 mg $H_2O$ on combustion. What is the percentage composition of this compound? The organic compound contains only C, H and O.

## SOLUTIONS

### Multiple Choice Questions

**1.** **(c)** See the number of σ bonds formed by $\overset{x}{C}$ in each case. In $H\overset{x}{C}OOH$, $(H_2N)_2\overset{x}{C}O$ and $CH_3\overset{x}{C}HO$, $\overset{x}{C}$ forms 3σ bonds and 1 π bond, hence hybridisation is $sp^2$. In $(CH_3)_3\overset{x}{C}OH$, $\overset{x}{C}$ forms 4σ bonds, so hybridisation will be $sp^3$.

**2.** **(b)**

$$H-\underset{H}{\overset{H}{C}}-C=C-\underset{H}{\overset{H}{C}}-\underset{H}{\overset{H}{C}}-H\ ;$$

2 – Pentene

No. of σ bonds = 14,  No. of π bond = 1

**3.** **(d)**

$$CH_3-\underset{CH_3}{\overset{CH_3}{C}}-\underset{CH_3}{\overset{CH_3}{C}}-CH_2CH_3$$

(a)

$$CH_3-\underset{CH_3}{\overset{CH_3}{C}}-CH_2CH_3 \qquad CH_3\underset{CH_3}{\overset{CH_3}{C}}-\overset{CH_3}{C}HCH_2CH_3$$

(b)              (c)

$$\boxed{CH_3} \rightarrow \text{isoprophl group}$$
$$CH_3\overset{|}{C}H\,CH_2CH_2CH_3$$

(d)

**4.** **(b)** The compound is a derivative of butane.

**5.** **(b)** The compound contains longest chain of 6C atoms and amino group. Hence it is an alkanamine.

**6.** **(c)**

$$\overset{1}{CH_3}-\overset{\overset{\displaystyle Cl}{|}}{\underset{\underset{\displaystyle CH_3}{|}}{\overset{2}{C}}}-\overset{3}{CH_3}$$

2-Chloro-2-methyl propane

**7.** **(a)** N, N-dimethylcy clopropane carborcamide

**8.** **(d)** The organic reaction which proceed through heterolytic bond cleavage are called ionic or heteropolar or just polar reactions.

**9.** **(b)** Methyl carbanion is $sp^3$ hybridised, with three bond pairs and one lone pair same is the case with $NH_3$.

**10.** **(b)** Homolytic fission of the C – C bond gives free radicals in which carbon is $sp^2$- hybridised.

**11.** **(c)** The strength of nucleophile depends upon the nature of alkyl group R on which nucleophile has to attack and also on the nature of solvent. The order of strength of nucleophiles follows the order :

$$CN^- > C_6H_5O^- > OH^- > Br^- > Cl^-$$

**12.** **(c)** $CN^-$, $RCH_2^-$ carry negative charge while $R\overset{..}{\underset{..}{O}}H$ has lone pair. Hence option (c) represents nucleophiles.

**13.** **(d)** $BF_3$ has incomplete octet. Hence it does not act as nucleophile.

**14.** **(b)** Among the given compounds naphthelene is volatile but benzoic acid is non-volatile (it forms a dimer). So, the best method for their separation is sublimation, which is applicable to compounds which can be converted directly into the vapour phase from its solid state on heating and back to the solid state on cooling. Hence it is the most appropriate method.

**15.** **(d)** In steam distillation a liquid boils when the sum of vapour pressures due to organic liquid $(p_1)$ and that due to water $p_2$ becomes equal to atmospheric pressure (p) i.e., $p = p_1 + p_2$. Since $p_1$ is lower than p, the organic liquid vaporises at lower temperature than its boiling point. Hence vapour pressure of volatile organic compound is less than atmospheric pressure.

**16.** (c) Glycerol decomposes at its boiling point, hence it should be purified by distillation under reduced pressure.

**17.** (d) Kjeldahl method is not applicable to any of the given compounds. As nitrogen of these compounds does not change to ammonium sulphate on heating with conc. $H_2SO_4$.

### Assertion & Reason Questions

**1.** (d) The correct name of the given compound is 2, 5, 6 -trimethyloctane.

**2.** (b) In styrene $(C_6H_5CH = CH_2)$ the terminal carbon atom has two identical groups i.e. H-atoms.

**3.** (b) Diastereomers are not mirror images of each other and hence have different solubilities in the same solvent.

**4.** (a) It is fact that aniline is better nucleophile than anilium ion. Anilium ion has +ve charge, which reduces the tendency to donate lone pair of electron $C_6H_5NH_3^+$ .

Anilium ion

**5.** (d) Resonance structures have the same number of electron pairs. However, they differ in the way of distribution of electrons.

### Case/Passage Based Questions

**1.** (a) $C_3H_6O$: $CH_3CH_2OH$, $CH_3$—$\overset{\overset{\displaystyle O}{\|}}{C}$—$CH_3$

     ethyl alcohol     dimethyl ether

**2.** (d) but-1-ene does not shows geometric isomerism and but-2-ene shows geometric ispmerism.

**3.** (d) alkynes have linear structure and do not show geometric isomerism.

**4.** (a)

### OR

(b) Because chiral molecules are able to rotate the plane of polarization differently by interacting with the electric field differently, they are said to be optically active.

### Very Short Answer Questions

**1.** Chain or nuclear isomerism.

**2.** 1-Methoxypropane, $CH_3OCH_2CH_2CH_3$ or 2-methoxypropane, $CH_3$-$OCH(CH_3)_2$.

**3.** The primary suffix indicates whether the carbon chain is saturated or unsaturated while the secondary suffix indicates the functional group present in the molecule.

**4.** 3-Methylbut-1-ene.

**5.** Refer theory

**6.** 2-Bromo-4-methylpentan-3-one.

**7.** 2, 4-dimethyl-5-oxopentanoic acid.

**8.** No. It is 1°.

**9.**
$$\overset{4}{CH_2}-\overset{3}{CH}-\overset{2}{CH_2}\overset{1}{COOH}$$
$$\quad\ \ |\qquad |$$
$$\ CHO\quad CH_3$$

**10.** Distillation under reduced pressure, i. e., vacuum distillation.

**11.** By fractional distillation.

**12.** *o*–nitro phenol is steam volatile while *p*–nitro phenol is not and hence these can be separated by steam distillation.

**13.** Vacuum distillation and steam distillation.

**14.** It is the process of extraction of different compounds adsorbed on the column by means of a suitable solvent called eluent.

**15.** Fractional crystallisation using benzene as a solvent.

**16.** $Al_2O_3$ (alumina).

**17.** Ammonia gas $(NH_3)$.

**18.** V.D. is 42, Mol. wt. $= 2 \times$ V.D. $= 2 \times 42 = 84$ therefore, molecular formula is $C_6H_{12}$.

**19.** $N_2$.

**20.** Every pure substance has fixed melting point and refractive index. Impurities reduce the melting point and change refractive index.

**21.** Blood red, because compound contains both N and S.

**22.** Victor-Meyer's method because it is volatile liquid.

**23.** It does not contain carbon, therefore, it is not an organic compound.

**24.** Tap water usually contains dissolved chlorine which gives test for halogens.

### Short Answer Questions

**1.** Four: 1, 1–dichloropropane $(CH_3CH_2CHCl_2)$, 1, 2–dichloropropane $(CH_3CHClCH_2Cl)$, 2, 2–dichloropropane $(CH_3CCl_2CH_3)$ and 1, 3–dichloropropane $(ClCH_2CH_2CH_2Cl)$.

**2.** (i) 3-Nitro-2-pentene

(ii)
$$\overset{1}{H_2}\overset{\ }{C}=\overset{2}{C}H\overset{3}{C}H\overset{4}{\underset{|}{C}}H-\overset{5}{C}H=\overset{6}{C}H\overset{7}{C}H\diagdown\overset{8}{CH_3}$$

with $Cl$ on C-4, and side chain $CH_3$—$CH$—$CH_2$—$CH_3$, other branch $CH_3$

4-Chloro-3-(1-methyl propyl or sec-butyl)-7-methyl-1, 5-octadiene

(iii) 1-Methyl-5-ethylcyclohexa-1, 3-diene

(iv)
$$\overset{1}{H_2}C=\overset{2}{C}H-\overset{3}{C}H-\overset{4}{C}H_2-\overset{5}{C}H=\overset{6}{C}H\overset{7}{C}H_3$$
with side chain $CH$ double bond $CH_2$

3-ethenyl (or vinyl) Hepta-1, 5-diene

**3.** (i)
$$CH_3CH_2CHCHCH_2CH_3$$
with substituents $CH_2CH_3$ and $CH_3$

(ii)
$$H_3CCH_2-\underset{|}{\overset{|}{C}}-CH_2CH_2CH_2CH_2CH_3$$
with $CH_3$ groups

**4.** (i)

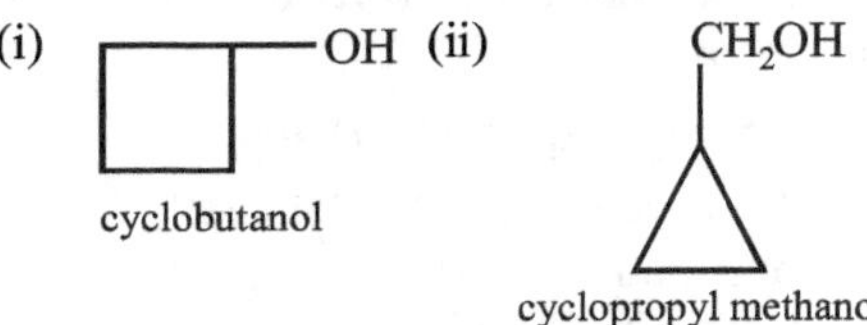

(ii)

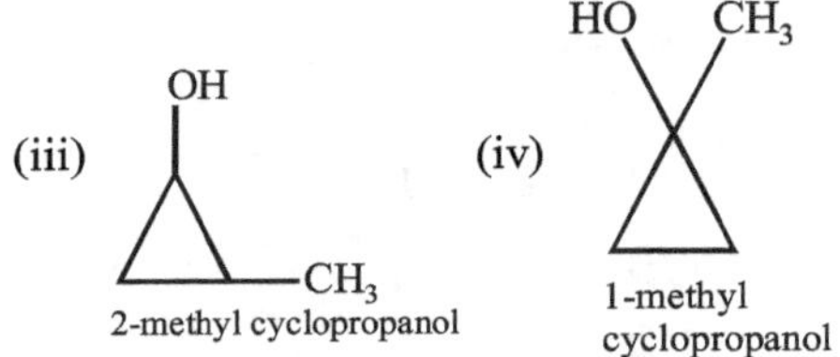

(iii) $H_5C_2$—⟨ ⟩—F , $NO_2$

**5.** The possible structures of an alcohol with molecular formula, $(C_4H_8O)$ and with no carbon-carbon double bond are

(i) ☐—OH
cyclobutanol

(ii) $CH_2OH$ △
cyclopropyl methanol

(iii) OH △—$CH_3$
2-methyl cyclopropanol

(iv) HO, $CH_3$
1-methyl cyclopropanol

**6.** The possible isomers are:

$CH_2CH_3$
Ethyl benzene

$CH_3$, $CH_3$
1,2-dimethyl benzene

$CH_3$, $CH_3$
1,3-dimethyl benzene

$CH_3$, $CH_3$
1,4-dimethyl benzene

**7.** $C_nH_{2n+1}NH_2$ or $C_nH_{2n+3}N$ is the molecular formula of aliphatic amine. Molecular mass is 59.

$\therefore \quad 12n + 2n + 3 + 14 = 59$

$$n = \frac{59-17}{14} = \frac{42}{14} = 3$$

Thus, the molecular formula is $C_3H_9N$.

The possible isomers are:

(i) $CH_3$—$CH_2$—$CH_2$—$NH_2$

(ii) $CH_3$—CH—$NH_2$ , $CH_3$

(iii) $CH_3$—$CH_2NHCH_3$

(iv) $CH_3$—N—$CH_3$ , $CH_3$

**8.** (a) 4-Ethyl-3,3-dimethylheptane.

(b) 2,3,5-Trimethyl-4-propylheptane

(c) Hept-3-ene-1,6-diyne (-ene is written first because it comes first in alphabetic order).

(d) Cyclododecane (it is having 12 C's)

**9.** Carbanion is defined as a group of atoms in which a carbon atom carries a negative charge. For example, when group Z attached to the carbon leaves without electron pair, the methyl anion (carbanion) is formed Carbanions are unstable and highly reactive species.

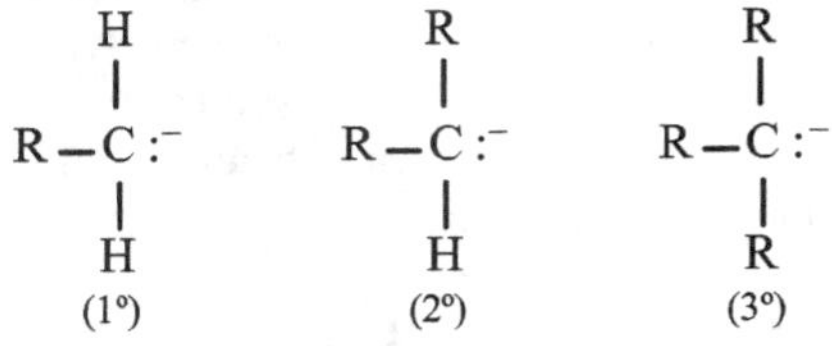

Types of carboanions. Carbanions are of three types namely primary (1°), secondary (2°) and tertiary (3°) carbanions.

$$R-\overset{H}{\underset{H}{C}}:^- \qquad R-\overset{R}{\underset{H}{C}}:^- \qquad R-\overset{R}{\underset{R}{C}}:^-$$
$$(1°) \qquad\qquad (2°) \qquad\qquad (3°)$$

**10.** The order of stability of free radicals is

$$R_3\overset{\bullet}{C} > R_2\overset{\bullet}{C}H > R\overset{\bullet}{C}H_2$$

This order is due to hyperconjugation. More the hyperconjugation, more will be the stability of free radical.

**11.** Carbocation is defined as the group of atoms in which a carbon atom carries a positive charge i. e., has only six electrons in its valence shell. For example, in the heterolytic fission of a carbon halogen bond in alkyl halides an alkyl carbocation is formed.

$$CH_3Cl \longrightarrow CH_3^+ + Cl^-$$

**Types of carbocations**

Carbocations are classified as primary (1°, secondary (2°) and tertiary (3°)

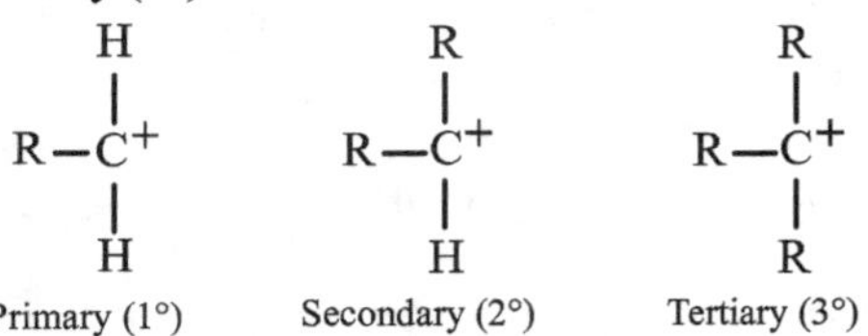

On the basis of number of alkyl groups present on central carbon atom. Carbocations are short lived and highly reactive species as they have a strong tendency to complete their octet.

**12.** Free radical is defined as an atom or group of atoms having an odd or unpaired electron. Due to the presence of unpaired electron, free radicals are paramagnetic in character. Free radicals are highly reactive and short lived due to their tendency to pair up the odd electron. Free radicals are formed due to the homolytic fission of covalent bond by the effect of heat or UV light.

$$R \overset{\curvearrowleft\curvearrowright}{\longrightarrow} X \xrightarrow{\text{Heat Light}} \dot{R} + \dot{X}$$

**Types of Free radicals.** Free radicals are classified as primary (1°), secondary (2°) and tertiary (3°) free radicals depending upon whether the carbon carrying the odd electron is primary, secondary or tertiary respectively.

$$\begin{array}{ccc}
H & R & R \\
| & | & | \\
R-\dot{C} & R-\dot{C} & R-\dot{C} \\
| & | & | \\
H & H & R \\
(1°) & (2°) & (3°)
\end{array}$$

The structure of free radical is planar due to $sp^2$-hybridization of carbon atom carrying odd electron.

**13.** Mass of the organic compound = 0.15 g
Mass of AgBr obtained = 0.12 g
Molecular mass of AgBr = 108 + 80
= 188 g mol$^{-1}$
Percentage of Br

$$= \frac{(\text{at. mass of Br})}{\text{MW(AgBr)}} \times \frac{\text{mass of AgBr}}{\text{mass of org. compound}} \times 100$$

$$= \frac{80}{188} \times \frac{0.12}{0.15} \times 100 = 34.04\%$$

**14.** (i) Nucleophiles : $\ddot{\underset{..}{I}}\,\overset{-}{}$, $H_3N\!:$

(ii) Electrophiles : $BeCl_2$ (Be has vacant $\pi$-atomic orbital available) and $NO_2^+$ (the electrophilic character completely masks the potential nucleophilic behaviour of the unshared electron-pairs on the O's).

(iii) Both : $CH_3C \equiv N\!:$, $H_2C = \ddot{O}\!:$, since C in each of these species is $\pi$-bonded to an electrophilic site.
The electronegative N and O also have unshared e$^-$-pairs and are the nucleophilic sites.

(iv) Neither : $CH_4$, $H_2$.

**15.** **(d)** In steam distillation a liquid boils when the sum of vapour pressures due to organic liquid ($p_1$) and that due to water $p_2$ becomes equal to atmospheric pressure (p) i.e., $p = p_1 + p_2$. Since $p_1$ is lower than p, the organic liquid vaporises at lower temperature than its boiling point. Hence vapour pressure of volatile organic compound is less than atmospheric pressure.

**16.** Substances whose vapour pressures become equal to the atmospheric pressure much below their melting points.

**17.** Either by sublimation or by extraction with $CCl_4$ followed by evaporation.

**18.** Advantages of using chromatography over other methods of separation are as follows:
(i) It is used to separate the complex mixture of substances.
(ii) It is also used in biology to separate the plant pigments.
(iii) It is more accurate and efficient.

**19.** (i) Sublimation. Camphor sublimes while common salt remains as residue in the china dish.
(ii) Solvent extraction using a separatory funnel. The lower water layer is run off when kerosene oil is obtained. It is dried over anhydrous $CaCl_2$ and then distilled to give pure kerosene oil.
(iii) Distillation under reduced pressure.

**20.** (a) **Both (Ambiphile).** $CH_2=\ddot{O}\!:$, $CH_3C \equiv N\!:$ (In these, C is electrophilic ; while O and N acts is as nucleophilic site).

(b) $H_2$, $CH_4$ (absence of charge, $\pi$ electrons, lone pair of electrons or $\delta+$ and $\delta-$ charges).

### *Long Answer Questions*

**1.** The highly reactive species formed from the reactants during the reaction are called reaction intermediates. The moment these are formed in the reaction, they get consumed. The high reactivity of reaction intermediates is due to the fact that these are charged species and moreover have incomplete octet. These are (i) free radicals (ii) carbocations (iii) carbanions.
**Generation of reaction intermediates**
**(i) Free radicals.** Refer short ans. 12
**(ii) Carbocations.** Refer short ans. 11
**(iii) Carbanions.** Refer short ans. 9

**2.** (i) $H^+$, $Na^+$, $AlCl_3$, $SO_3$, $CH_3CH_2^+$: $CCl_2$, R–X.

In $SO_3$, $O = \overset{\overset{\displaystyle O}{\|}}{S} - O^-$ , S atom carries a positive charge and hence acts as an electrophile. In $AlCl_3$, Al atom has six and in: $CCl_2$, C atom has six electrons in the valence shell and hence each one of these needs two more electrons to complete their respective octets. As a result, both $AlCl_3$ and: $CCl_2$ act as electrophiles. In R–X, due to greater electro negativity of X, R carries a partial positive charge and hence acts as an electrophile.

(ii) $NH_3$, $^-OH$, $C_2H_5OH$.

**3.** (i) 1, 1-Dimethyl-3-isopropylcyclopentane

(ii) 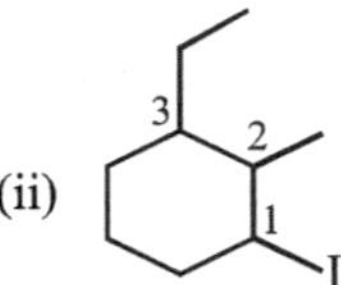

3-Ethyl-1-iodo-2-methyl cyclohexane

(iii) 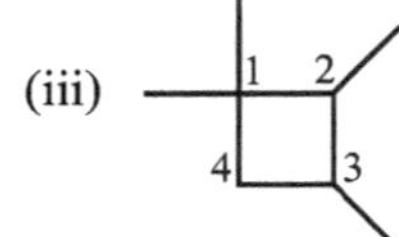

1, 1, 2, 3-tetramethyl cyclobutane

(iv)

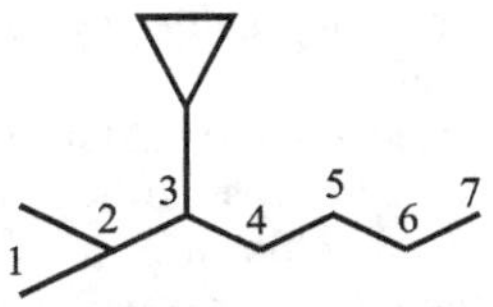

3-cyclopropyl-2-methly heptane

(v) 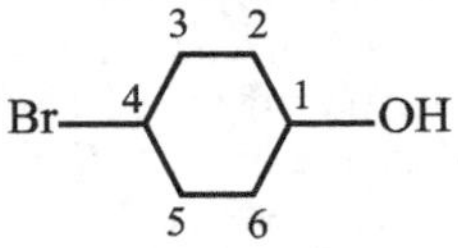  Br—4—⬡—1—OH

4-Bromo cyclohexanol

**4.** (i)  $CH_3 - CH_2 - CH_2 - CH_2 - OH$
Butanol-1

(ii)  $CH_3 - CH - CH_2 - OH$
$\quad\quad\quad | $
$\quad\quad\quad CH_3$
2-methyl propanol-1

(iii)  $CH_3 - CH_2 - CH - CH_3$
$\quad\quad\quad\quad\quad | $
$\quad\quad\quad\quad\quad OH$
Butanol-2

(iv)
$\quad\quad\quad\quad CH_3$
$\quad\quad\quad\quad | $
$CH_3 - C - OH$
$\quad\quad\quad\quad | $
$\quad\quad\quad\quad CH_3$
2-methyl propanol-2

(v)  $CH_3 - CH_2 - O - CH - CH_3$
Ethoxy ethane

(vi)  $CH_3 - CH_2 - CH_2 - O - CH_3$
Methoxy propane

(vii)  $CH_3 - CH - OCH_3$
$\quad\quad\quad\quad | $
$\quad\quad\quad\quad CH_3$
2-methoxy propane

Chain isomers:  [i and ii], [iii and iv]
Position isomers : [i and iii], [ii and iv]
$\quad\quad\quad\quad$ and  [vi and vii]

**5.** (i)  Calculation of percentage of C and H mass of organic
compound = 0.3650 g
mass of $CO_2$ = 0.88 g
mass of $H_2O$ = 0.495 g

$$\%C = \frac{12x}{44w} \times 100 = \frac{12 \times 0.88}{44 \times 0.3650} \times 100$$
$$= 65.75\%$$

$$\%H = \frac{2y}{18w} \times 100 = \frac{2 \times 0.495}{18 \times 0.3650} \times 100$$
$$= 15.07\%.$$

Calculation of percentage of nitrogen
T = 27 + 273 = 300 K, w = 0.1186 g
P of dry gas = 779 – 19 = 760 mm Hg
V at 300 K = 20 ml
V of $N_2$ of STP

$$= \frac{760\,mm\,Hg \times 20ml \times 273K}{760\,mmHg \times 300K} = 18.2\ ml$$

$$\%N = \frac{28 \times V_{STP}}{22,400 \times w} \times 100$$

$$\frac{28 \times 18.2 \times 100}{22,400 \times 0.1186} = 19.18\%.$$

(ii)  Mass of organic compound = 3.87 mg
mass of carbon dioxide = 5.80 mg
mass of water = 1.58 mg

$$\%C = \frac{12x}{44w}.100 = \frac{12 \times 5.80mg}{44 \times 3.87mg} \times 100$$
$$= 40.87\%$$

$$\%H = \frac{2y}{12w}.100 = \frac{2 \times 1.58mg}{18 \times 3.87mg} \times 100$$
$$= 4.54\%$$

∴  % of Oxygen = 100 – (40.87 + 4.54)
$$= 54.59\%$$

---

## SECTION C  NCERT EXEMPLAR QUESTIONS

### MULTIPLE CHOICE QUESTIONS

**1.** Which of the following is the correct IUPAC name?
(a)  3-Ethyl-4, 4-dimethylheptane
(b)  4, 4-Dimethyl-3-ethylheptane
(c)  5-Ethyl-4, 4-dimethylheptane
(d)  4, 4-Bis(methyl)-3-ethylheptane

**2.** The IUPAC name for

$$CH_3 - \overset{\overset{\displaystyle O}{\|}}{C} - CH_2 - CH_2 - \overset{\overset{\displaystyle O}{\|}}{C} - OH \text{ is}$$

(a)  1-hydroxypentane-1, 4-dione
(b)  1, 4-dioxopentanol
(c)  1-carboxybutan-3-one
(d)  4-oxopentanoic acid

**3.** Electronegativity of carbon atoms depends upon their state
of hybridisation. In which of the following compounds,
the carbon marked with asterisk is most electronegative?
(a)  $CH_3 - CH_2 - {}^*CH_2 - CH_3$
(b)  $CH_3 - {}^*CH = CH - CH_3$
(c)  $CH_3 - CH_2 - C \equiv {}^*CH$
(d)  $CH_3 - CH_2 - CH = {}^*CH_2$

4. In which of the following functional groups, isomerism is not possible?
   - (a) Alcohols
   - (b) Aldehydes
   - (c) Alkyl halides
   - (d) Cyanides

5. The principle involved in paper chromatography is
   - (a) adsorption
   - (b) partition
   - (c) solubility
   - (d) volatility

6. In which of the following compounds the carbon marked with asterisk is expected to have greatest positive charge?
   - (a) $*CH_3 — CH_2 — Cl$
   - (b) $*CH_3—CH_2—Mg^+Cl^-$
   - (c) $*CH_3 — CH_2 — Br$
   - (d) $*CH_3 — CH_2 — CH_3$

7. Electrophilic addition reactions proceed in two steps. The first step involves the addition of an electrophile. Name the type of intermediate formed in the first step of the following addition reaction. $H_3C – HC = CH_2 + H^+ \longrightarrow ?$
   - (a) $2°$ carbanion
   - (b) $1°$ carbocation
   - (c) $2°$ carbocation
   - (d) $1°$ carbanion

8. During hearing of a court case, the judge suspected that some changes in the documents had been carried out. He asked the forensic department to check the ink used at two different places. According to you which technique can give the best results?
   - (a) Column chromatography
   - (b) Solvent extraction
   - (c) Distillation
   - (d) Thin layer chromatography

## ASSERTION & REASON QUESTIONS

**DIRECTIONS (Qs. 1-2) :** *Each of these questions contains an assertion followed by reason. Read them carefully and answer the question on the basis of following options. You have to select the one that best describes the two statements.*
- (a) If both Assertion and Reason are correct and the Reason is a correct explanation of the Assertion.
- (b) If both Assertion and Reason are correct but Reason is not a correct explanation of the Assertion.
- (c) If the Assertion is correct but Reason is incorrect.
- (d) If the Assertion is incorrect but the Reason is correct.

1. **Assertion :** Energy of resonance hybrid is equal to the average of energies of all canonical forms.

   **Reason :** Resonance hybrid cannot be presented by a single structure.

2. **Assertion :** Simple distillation can help in separating a mixture of propan-1-ol (boiling pt.97°C) and propanone (boiling pt. 56°C).

   **Reason :** Liquids with a difference of more than 20°C in their boiling points can be separated by distillation.

## SHORT ANSWER QUESTIONS

1. The structure of triphenylmethyl cation is given below. This is very stable and some of its salts can be stored for months. Explain the cause of high stability of this cation.

2. Name the compounds whose line formulae are given below:

   (i)       (ii)

3. Identify the most stable species in the following set of ions giving reasons:

   (i) $\overset{+}{C}H_3 , \overset{+}{C}H_2Br, \overset{+}{C}HBr_2 , \overset{+}{C}Br_3$

   (ii) $\overset{\ominus}{C}H_3 , \overset{\ominus}{C}H_2Cl, \overset{\ominus}{C}HCl_2 ,\overset{\ominus}{C}Cl_3$

4. Why does $SO_3$ act as an electrophile?

5. Write structures of various carbocations that can be obtained from 2-methylbutane. Arrange these carbocations in order of increasing stability.

6. What is the hybridization of each carbon in $H_2C = C = CH_2$?

## LONG ANSWER QUESTION

1. What is meant by hybridisation? Compound $CH_2 = C = CH_2$ contains $sp$ or $sp^2$ hybridised carbon atoms. Will it be a planar molecule?

## SOLUTIONS

### *Multiple Choice Questions*

1. **(a)**
$$\overset{7}{C}H_3 – \overset{6}{C}H_2 – \overset{5}{C}H_2 – \overset{4}{\underset{\underset{CH_3C_2H_5}{|}}{C}} – \overset{3}{\underset{}{C}H} – \overset{2}{C}H_2 – \overset{1}{C}H_3$$
   with $CH_3$ on carbon 4

   3-Ethyl-4, 4-dimethyl heptane

2. **(d)** $\overset{5}{C}H_3 – \overset{4}{\overset{O}{\overset{\|}{C}}} – \overset{3}{C}H_2 – \overset{2}{C}H_2 – \overset{1}{\overset{O}{\overset{\|}{C}}}-OH$

   4-oxopentanoic acid

**Note :** Carboxylic acid (—COOH) has more priority than ketone ($>C= O$).

3. **(c)** Electronegativity of carbon atom depends on its state of hybridisation. More the $s$-character more will be the electronegativity.

$$sp^3 < sp^2 < sp$$

$s$-character :   25%   33%   50%

Thus, $sp$-carbon ($CH_3 – CH_2 – C \equiv *CH$) has the highest electronegativity.

**4.** **(c)** Two or more compounds having the same molecular formula but different functional groups are called functional isomers. Functional isomer of alcohol is ether, aldehyde is ketone and cyanide is isocyanide. But alkyl halides do not show functional isomerism.

**5.** **(b)** Partition chromatography is based on continuous differential partitioning of components of a mixture between stationary and mobile phases. Paper chromatography is a type of partition chromatography.

**6.** **(a)** Electronegativity of Cl, Br, C and Mg follows the order Cl > Br > C > Mg, thus chlorine has the greatest –I-effect and disperse the positive charge on 'C' atom most effectively. Hence, $^*CH_3 — CH_2 — Cl$ has the greatest positive charge.

**7.** **(c)** When an electrophile attacks $CH_3 – CH = CH_2$, there are two possibilities of an intermediate formed:

$$CH_3—CH=CH_2 + H^+ \longrightarrow CH_3—\overset{\oplus}{CH}—CH_3$$
(2° carbocation)

$$CH_3—CH=CH_2 + H^+ \longrightarrow CH_3—CH_2—\overset{\oplus}{CH}_2$$
(1° carbocation)

As 2° carbocation is more stable than 1° carbocation thus first addition is more feasible.

**Note:** Stability of carbocations is the basis of Markownikoff's rule.

**8.** **(d)** Thin layer chromatography (TLC) involves separation of substances of a mixture over a thin layer of an adsorbent coated on a glass plate.

A thin layer of an adsorbent is spread over a glass plate and glass plate is placed in an eluant. As eluant rises, components of the mixture move up along with the eluant to different distances depending on their degree of adsorption and separation takes place. Therefore, TLC technique will give the best results in identifying the different types of ink used at different places in the documents.

### Assertion & Reason Questions

**1.** **(d)** Canonical structures always have more energy than resonance hybrid. Resonance hybrids are always more stable than any of the canonical structures. The delocalisation of electron lowers the orbital energy and gives stability.

**2.** **(a)** Reason is the correct explanation of A.

### Short Answer Questions

**1.** Stabilised due to nine possible canonical structures.

Other canonical structures

**2.** (i) 3-Ethyl-4-methylheptan-5-en-2-one
(ii) 3-Nitrocyclohex-1-ene.

**3.** (i) $\overset{\oplus}{CH_3}$, The replacement of hydrogen by bromine increases positive charge on carbon atom and destabilises the species.

(ii) $\overset{\ominus}{C} - Cl_3$ is most stable because electro-negativity of chlorine is more than hydrogen. On replacing hydrogen by chlorine, negative charge on carbon is reduced and species is stabilised.

**4.**

$$\underset{O}{\overset{O}{\underset{\big\|}{S}}}\diagdown_O \longleftrightarrow \underset{\overset{\ominus}{O}}{\overset{O}{\underset{\big\|}{\overset{\oplus}{S}}}}\diagdown_O$$

Three highly electronegative oxygen atoms are attached to sulphur atom. It makes sulphur atom electron deficient. Due to resonance also, sulphur acquires positive charge. Both these factors make $SO_3$ an electrophile.

**5.** Four possible carbocations are

$$CH_3 – \underset{\underset{CH_3}{|}}{CH} – CH_2 – \overset{+}{CH}_2$$
(I)

$$CH_3 – \underset{\underset{CH_3}{|}}{CH} – \overset{+}{CH} – CH_3$$
(II)

$$CH_3 – \underset{\underset{CH_3}{|}}{\overset{+}{C}} – CH_2 – CH_3$$
(III)

$$\overset{+}{CH}_2 – \underset{\underset{CH_3}{|}}{CH} – CH_2 – CH_3$$
(IV)

Order of increasing stability I < IV < II < III

**6.** In $H_2C = \overset{(1)\ (2)\ (3)}{C} = CH_2$, carbon (1) and (3) are $sp^2$ hybridised and carbon (2) is $sp$ hybridized.

Show the polarization of carbon-magnesium bond in the following structure.

$$CH_3 – CH_2 – CH_2 – CH_2 – Mg – X$$

$$CH_3 – CH_2 – CH_2 – CH_2 \longleftarrow \overset{\delta+}{Mg} – X$$

Carbon is more electronegative than magnesium.

### Long Answer Question

**1.** No. It is not a planar molecule.

Central carbon atom is $sp$ hybridised and its two unhybridised $p$-orbitals are perpendicular to each other. The $p$-orbitals in one plane overlap with one of the $p$-orbital of left terminal carbon atom and the $p$-orbital in other plane overlaps with $p$-orbital of right side terminal carbon atom. This fixes the position of two terminal carbon atoms and the hydrogen atoms attached to them in planes perpendicular to each other. Due to this the pair of hydrogen atoms attached to terminal carbon atoms are present in different planes.

# 13 Hydrocarbons



**13.1** How do you account for the formation of ethane during chlorination of methane ?

**Ans.** Chlorination of methane is a free radical reaction which occurs by the following mechanism:

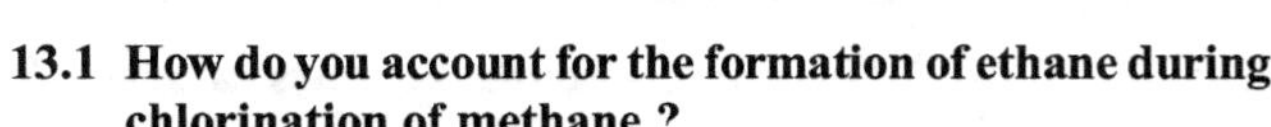

Initiation : $Cl—Cl \xrightarrow{\text{Homolytic fission}} 2Cl^\bullet$ (Chlorine free radical)

Propagation: $CH_3-H + \dot{C}l \longrightarrow \dot{C}H_3 + HCl$

$\dot{C}H_3 + Cl—Cl \longrightarrow CH_3-Cl + \dot{C}l$    ... (i)

Termination: $\dot{C}H_3 + \dot{C}H_3 \longrightarrow CH_3-CH_3$    ... (ii) (Ethane)

$\dot{C}H_3 + \dot{C}l \longrightarrow H_3C-Cl \; ; \dot{C}l + \dot{C}l \longrightarrow Cl-Cl$ ... (iii)

From the above mechanism, it is evident that during propagation step, $CH_3$ free radicals are produced which may undergo three reactions. In the chain termination step, the two $CH_3$ free radicals combine together to form ethane ($CH_3–CH_3$) molecule.

**13.2** Write IUPAC names of the following compounds:

(a) $CH_3CH = C(CH_3)_2$

(b) $CH_2 = CH - C \equiv C - CH_3$

(c) [structure]

(d) [phenyl]$-CH_2 - CH_2 - CH = CH_2$

(e) [2-methylphenol structure with $CH_3$ and OH]

(f) $CH_3(CH_2)_4CH(CH_2)_3CH_3$
   with branch $CH_2 - CH(CH_3)_2$

(g) $H_3C - CH = CH - CH_2 - CH = CH - CH - CH_2$
   with branches $C_2H_5$, $CH$ and $CH_2$ (double bond)

**Ans.** (a) $CH_3CH = \overset{\overset{\displaystyle CH_3}{|}}{C} - CH_3$

2–Methylbut–2–ene

(b) $CH_2 = CH - C \equiv C - CH_3$

Pent -1-en-3-yne

(c) [structure] Buta–1, 3–diene

(d) [phenyl]$-\overset{4}{C}H_2 - \overset{3}{C}H_2 - \overset{2}{C}H = \overset{1}{C}H_2$

4-Phenylbut-1~ene

(e) [benzene ring with $\overset{2}{C}H_3$ and $\overset{1}{O}H$]

2-Methylphenol

(f) $CH_3-(CH_2)_4-\underset{|}{CH}-(CH_2)_3-CH_3$
   $CH_2-\underset{|}{CH}-CH_3$
   $CH_3$

5-(2-Methylpropyl)-decane

(g) $H_3C - CH = CH - CH_2 - CH = CH - \underset{|}{CH} - CH_2$
   $C_2H_5 \quad \underset{||}{CH}$
   $CH_2$

4-Ethyldeca-1, 5, 8-triene

**13.3** For the following compounds, write structural formulas and IUPAC names for all possible isomers having the number of double or triple bond as indicated:

(a) $C_4H_8$ (one double bond)

(b) $C_5H_8$ (one triple bond)

**Ans.** (a) Isomers of $C_4H_8$ having one double bond are:

(a) $C_4H_8$

(i) $H_3C-CH_2-CH=CH_2$

But-1-ene

(ii)

$$H_3C, CH_3$$
$$C = C$$
$$H, H$$

*cis*-But-2-ene

(iii)

$$H_3C, H$$
$$C = C$$
$$H, CH_3$$

*trans*-But-2-ene

(iv)

$$CH_3$$
$$|$$
$$H_3C - C = CH_2$$

2-Methylprop-1-ene

**(b)** $C_5H_8$

(i) $\overset{5}{C}H_3 \overset{4}{C}H_2 - \overset{3}{C}H_2 \equiv \overset{2}{C} - \overset{1}{C}H$

Pent-1-yne

(ii) $\overset{5}{C}H_2 \overset{4}{C}H_2 - \overset{3}{C} \equiv \overset{2}{C} - \overset{1}{C}H_3$

Pent-2-yne

(iii) $CH_3 - CH - C \equiv CH$
$$|$$
$$CH_3$$

3–Methylbut–1–yne

**13.4 Write IUPAC names of the products obtained by the ozonolysis of the following compounds: (i) Pent–2–ene (ii) 3, 4–Dimethylhept–3–ene (iii) 2–Ethylbut–l–ene (iv) 1–Phenylbut–l–ene.**

**Ans.** (i) $\overset{5}{C}H_3 - \overset{4}{C}H_2 - \overset{3}{C}H = \overset{2}{C}H - \overset{1}{C}H_3$

Pent-2-ene

$$\xrightarrow[\text{(ii) Zn/H}_2\text{O}]{\text{(i) O}_3/\text{CH}_2\text{Cl}_2, 196\,\text{K}}$$

$$CH_3 - CH_2 - CH = O + O = CH - CH_3$$

Propanal    Ethanal

(ii)

$$H_3C - CH_2 \quad CH_3$$
$$CH_2 - C$$
$$C - CH_2$$
$$H_3C \quad CH_3$$

3,4-Dimethylhept-3-ene

$$\xrightarrow[\text{(ii) Zn/H}_2\text{O}]{\text{(i) O}_3, \text{CH}_2\text{Cl}_2, 196\,\text{K}}$$

$$\underset{\text{Pentan-2-one}}{\overset{O}{\underset{H_3C}{\overset{||}{\underset{CH_2}{\overset{CH_2}{\phantom{x}}}}C}CH_3}} + \underset{\text{Butan-2-one}}{O = \overset{CH_2}{\underset{CH_3}{C}}CH_3}$$

(iii) $\overset{4}{C}H_3 \overset{3}{C}H_2 - \overset{2}{C} = \overset{1}{C}H_2$
$$|$$
$$CH_2CH_3$$

2-Ethylbut-1-ene

$$\xrightarrow[\text{(ii) Zn/H}_2\text{O}]{\text{(i) O}_3.\text{CH}_2\text{Cl}_2, 196\,\text{K}}$$

$$O = CH_2 + CH_3 - CH_2 - \overset{O}{\overset{||}{C}} - CH_2 - CH_3$$

Methanal    Pentan-3-one

(iv) $\overset{4}{C}H_3 \overset{3}{C}H_2 - \overset{2}{C}H = \overset{1}{C}H - C_6H_5$

1–Phenylbut–1–ene

$$\xrightarrow[\text{(ii) Zn/H}_2\text{O}]{\text{(i) O}_3,\text{CH}_2\text{Cl}_2, 196\,\text{K}}$$

$$\underset{\text{Propanal}}{CH_3CH_2CH = O} + \underset{\text{Benzaldehyde}}{O = CH - C_6H_5}$$

**13.5 An alkene 'A' on ozonolysis gives a mixture of ethanal and pentan-3-one. Write structure and IUPAC name of 'A'.**

**Ans. Step 1:** Write the structure of the products side by side with their oxygen atoms pointing towards each other.

$$\underset{\text{Pentan-3-one}}{\overset{CH_3CH_2}{\underset{CH_3CH_2}{C}} = \boxed{O \quad O} = \underset{\text{Ethanal}}{CHCH_3}}$$

**Step 2 :** Remove the oxygen atoms and join the two ends by a double bond, the structure of the alkene 'A' is

$$\overset{CH_3CH_2}{\underset{CH_3CH_2}{C}} = CH - CH_3$$

3-Ethylpent-2-ene (A)

**13.6 An alkene 'A' contains three C–C, eight C–H σ–bonds, one C–C π–bond. 'A' on ozonolysis gives two moles of an aldehyde of molar mass 44 u. Write the IUPAC name of 'A'.**

**Ans.** (i) An aldehyde with molar mass of 44 u is ethanal, $CH_3CH = O$

(ii) Write two moles of ethanal side by side with their oxygen atoms pointing towards each other.

$$\underset{\text{Ethanal}}{CH_3CH} = \overset{..}{\underset{..}{O}} \cdots \overset{..}{\underset{..}{O}} = \underset{\text{Ethanal}}{CHCH_3}$$

(iii) Remove the oxygen atoms and join them by a double bond, the structure of alkene 'A' is

$$CH_3 - CH = CH - CH_3$$

But–2–ene

As required, but–2–ene has three C–C, eight C–H and one C–C π–bond.

**13.7 Propanal and pentan-3-one are the ozonolysis products of an alkene. What is the structural formula of the alkene?**

**Ans.** (i) Write the structures of propanal and pentan-3-one with their oxygen atoms facing each other, we have,

$$\underset{H_3C}{\overset{CH_2}{\diagup}}\overset{CH}{\diagup} = O \quad O = \overset{CH_2CH_3}{\underset{CH_2CH_3}{C}}$$

(ii) Remove oxygen atoms and join the two fragments by a double bond, the structure of the alkene is

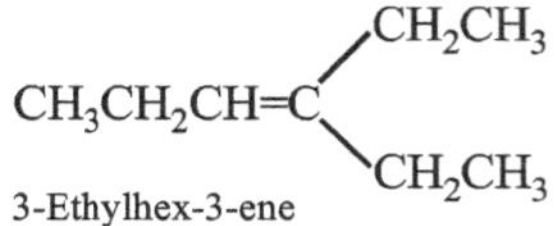

3-Ethylhex-3-ene

**13.8 Write chemical equations for the combustion reaction of the following hydrocarbons.**
**(i) Butane   (ii) Pentene   (iii) Hexyne   (iv) Toluene**

**Ans.** (i)  $C_4H_{10}$ (g) + 13/2 $O_2$ (g) $\xrightarrow{\Delta}$

Butane

$$4\ CO_2\ (g) + 5\ H_2O\ (g)$$

(ii)  $C_5H_{10}$ (g) + 15/2 $O_2$ (g) $\xrightarrow{\Delta}$

Pentene

$$5\ CO_2\ (g) + 5\ H_2O\ (g)$$

(iii)  $C_6H_{10}$ (g) + 17/2 $O_2$ (g) $\xrightarrow{\Delta}$

Hexyne

$$6\ CO_2\ (g) + 5\ H_2O\ (g)$$

(iv)

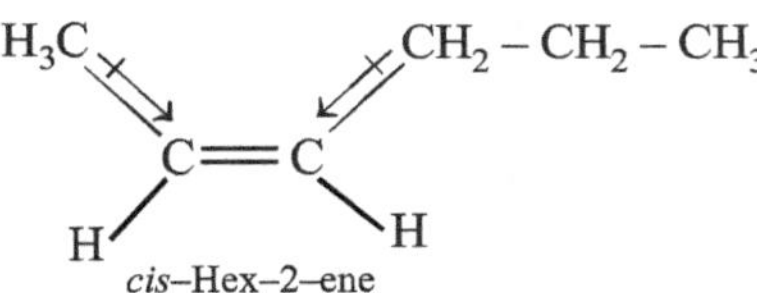

Toluene

or   $C_7H_8$ (g) + 9 $O_2$ (g) $\xrightarrow{\Delta}$

$$7\ CO_2\ (g) + 4\ H_2O\ (g)$$

**13.9 Draw the *cis*–and *trans*–structures for hex–2–ene. Which isomer will have higher b. p. and why ?**

**Ans.** The structure of *cis*–and *trans*–isomer of hex–2–ene are:

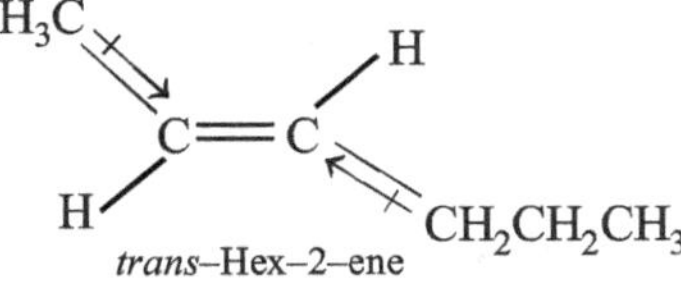

*cis*–Hex–2–ene

(Higher dipole moment, higher b.p.)

*trans*–Hex–2–ene

(Lower dipole moment, lower b. p.)

The dipole moment of a molecule depends upon dipole-dipole interactions. Since *cis*-isomer has higher dipole moment, therefore, it has higher boiling point.

**13.10 Why is benzene extra ordinarily stable though it contains three double bonds ?**

**Ans.** Resonance or delocalization of electrons usually leads to stability. Since in benzene all the six π–electrons of the three double bonds are completely delocalized to form one lowest energy molecular orbital which surrounds all the carbon atoms of the ring, therefore, it is extra–ordinarily stable.

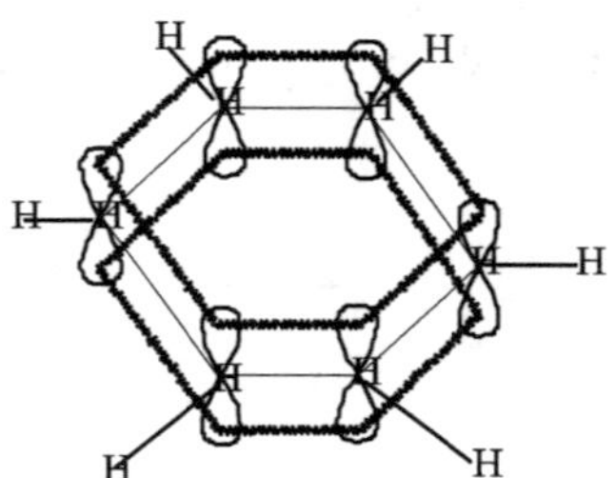

Delocalization of 6π-electrons in benzene

**13.11 What are the necessary conditions for any system to be aromatic ?**

**Ans.** Necessary conditions to be aromatic
   (i)   Molecule should be planar
   (ii)  It should have $(4n + 2\pi)e^-$ in the ring where $n = 0$, 1, 2...
   (iii) Complete delocalisation of the π electrons in the ring.

**13.12 Explain why the following systems are not aromatic?**

(i) 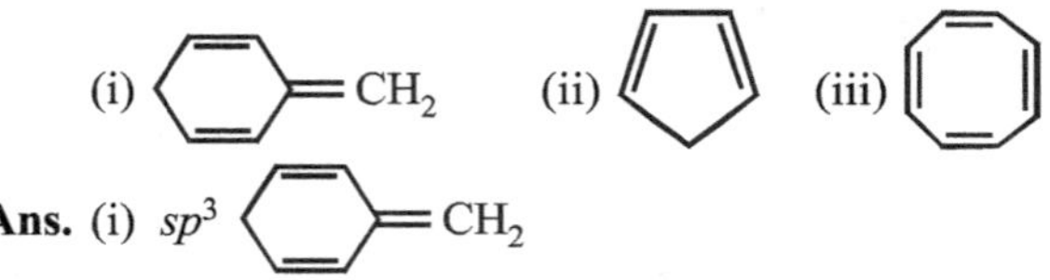   (ii)   (iii)

**Ans.** (i)  $sp^3$

Due to the presence of a $sp^3$–hybridized carbon, the system is not planar. It does contain six π-electrons but the system is not fully conjugated since all the six π-electrons do not form a single cyclic electron π cloud which surrounds all the atoms of the ring. Therefore, it is not an aromatic compound.

(ii)

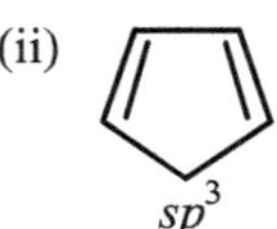

$sp^3$

Due to the presence of a $sp^3$-carbon, the system is not planar. Further, it contains only four π electrons, therefore, the system is not aromatic because it does not contain planar cyclic cloud having $(4n + 2)$ π-electrons.

(iii)

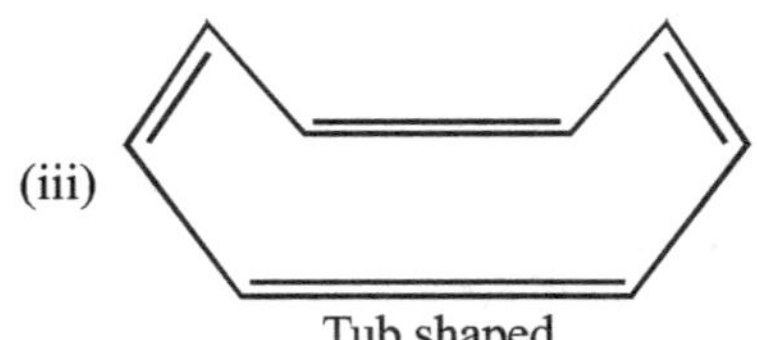

Tub shaped

Cyclooctatetraene is not planar but is tub shaped. It is, therefore, a non–planar system having 8 pi-electrons. Therefore, the molecule is not aromatic since it does not contain a planar cyclic cloud having $(4n + 2)$π-electrons.

**13.13 How will you convert benzene into**
   (i)   *p*-nitrobromobenzene
   (ii)  *m*-nitrochlorobenzene
   (iii) *p*-nitrotoluene
   (iv)  acetophenone ?

**Ans.** **(i)** The two substituents in the benzene ring are present at *p*-positions. Therefore, the sequence of reactions should be such that first an *o, p*-directing group, i.e., Br atom should be introduced in the benzene ring and this should be followed by nitration. Thus,

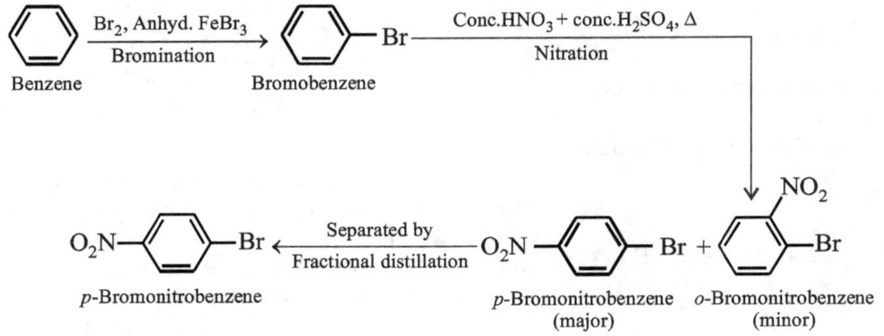

Benzene $\xrightarrow[\text{Bromination}]{\text{Br}_2,\text{ Anhyd. FeBr}_3}$ Bromobenzene (—Br) $\xrightarrow[\text{Nitration}]{\text{Conc.HNO}_3 + \text{conc.H}_2\text{SO}_4,\ \Delta}$

*p*-Bromonitrobenzene ($O_2N$—⬡—Br) $\xleftarrow[\text{Fractional distillation}]{\text{Separated by}}$ $O_2N$—⬡—Br (*p*-Bromonitrobenzene, major) + ⬡ with $NO_2$ and Br (*o*-Bromonitrobenzene, minor)

**(ii)** Here since the two substituents are at *m*– position w. r. t each other, therefore, the first substituent in the benzene ring should be a *m*–directing group (i. e., $NO_2$) and then the other group (i. e. Cl) should be introduced. Therefore, the sequence of reactions is:

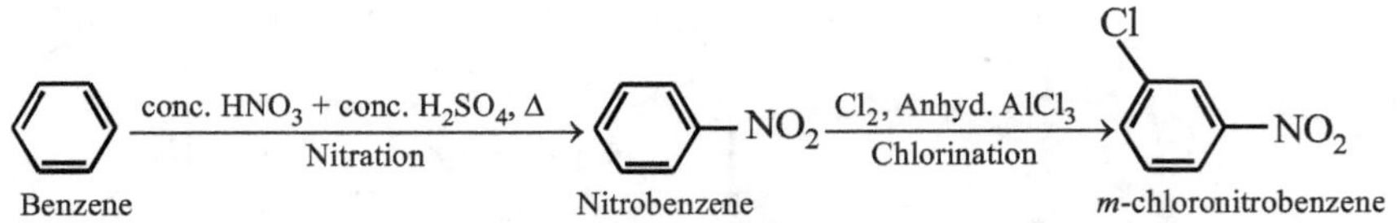

Benzene $\xrightarrow[\text{Nitration}]{\text{conc. HNO}_3 + \text{conc. H}_2\text{SO}_4,\ \Delta}$ Nitrobenzene (—$NO_2$) $\xrightarrow[\text{Chlorination}]{\text{Cl}_2,\text{ Anhyd. AlCl}_3}$ *m*-chloronitrobenzene (Cl—⬡—$NO_2$)

**(iii)** Here since the two substituents are at *p*–position w. r. t. each other, therefore, the first substituent in the benzene ring should be a *o, p*-directing group (i.e., $CH_3$) and then the other group (i.e., $NO_2$) should be introduced.

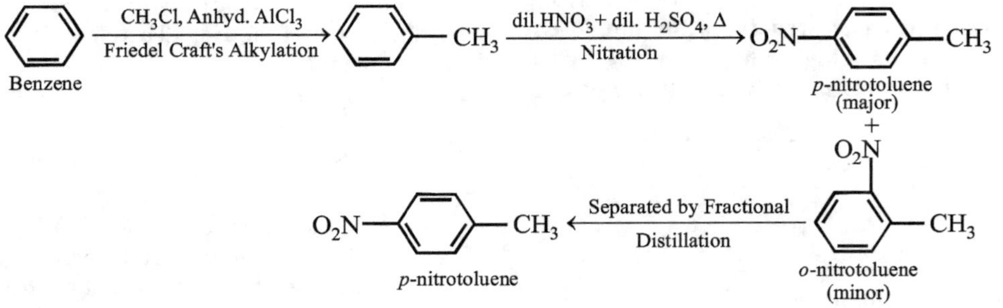

Benzene $\xrightarrow[\text{Friedel Craft's Alkylation}]{\text{CH}_3\text{Cl, Anhyd. AlCl}_3}$ (—$CH_3$) $\xrightarrow[\text{Nitration}]{\text{dil.HNO}_3 + \text{dil. H}_2\text{SO}_4,\ \Delta}$ $O_2N$—⬡—$CH_3$ (*p*-nitrotoluene, major)

+

*o*-nitrotoluene (minor) ($O_2N$, ⬡—$CH_3$) $\xrightarrow[\text{Distillation}]{\text{Separated by Fractional}}$ $O_2N$—⬡—$CH_3$ (*p*-nitrotoluene)

**(iv)** 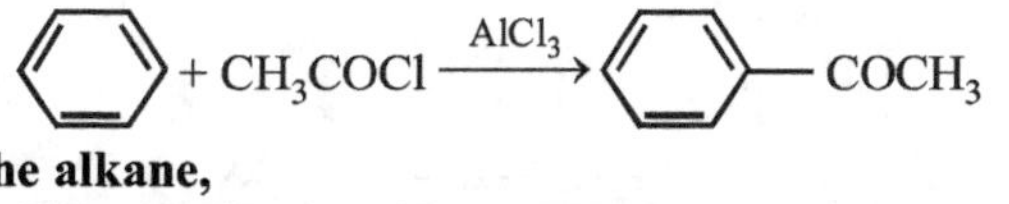 ⬡ + $CH_3COCl$ $\xrightarrow{\text{AlCl}_3}$ ⬡—$COCH_3$

**13.14 In the alkane,**

$CH_3CH_2 – C(CH_3)_2 – CH_2 – CH(CH_3)_2$ , **identify 1°, 2°, 3° carbon atoms and give the number of H – atoms bonded to each one of these.**

**Ans.** The expanded formula of the given compound is:

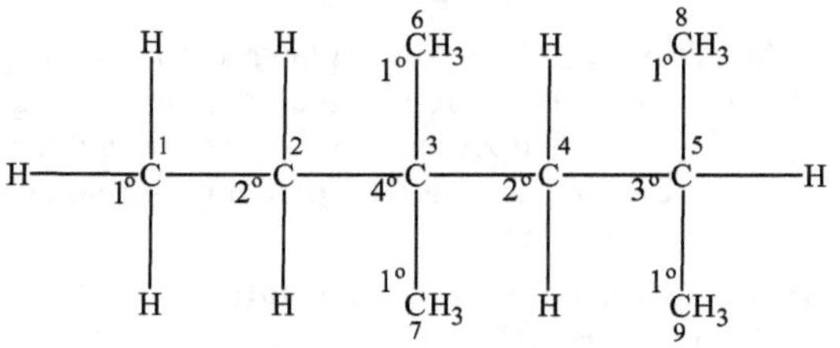

The number of H-atoms bonded to each carbon are:

$C_1$ : 3 H-atoms

$C_2$ : 2 H-atoms

$$C_3 \quad : \quad \text{0 H-atoms}$$
$$C_4 \quad : \quad \text{2 H-atoms } C_8 : \text{3 H-atoms}$$
$$C_5 \quad : \quad \text{1 H-atoms } C_9 : \text{3 H-atoms}$$
$$C_6 \quad : \quad \text{3 H-atoms}$$
$$C_7 \quad : \quad \text{3 H-atoms}$$

**13.15 What effect does branching of an alkane chain has on its boiling point?**

**Ans.** As branching increases, the surface area of the molecule decreases, hence vander waal's force of attraction also decreases. Therefore, boiling point of alkane decreases on increased branching.

**13.16 Addition of HBr to propene yields 2-bromopropane, while in the presence of benzoyl peroxide, the same reaction yields 1-bromopropane. Explain and give mechanism.**

**Ans. Addition of HBr to propene :**

$$CH_3CH = CH_2 + HBr \longrightarrow CH_3\underset{\underset{Br}{|}}{C}HCH_3$$

**Mechanism :**

$$H - Br \rightleftharpoons H^+ + Br^-$$

**Step I :**

$$H_3C - CH = CH_2 \quad + H^+ \xrightarrow{\text{Slow}} H_3C - \overset{+}{C}H - CH_3$$

Electrophile $\qquad$ 2° Carbocation (more stable)

**Step II :**

$$H_3C - \overset{+}{C}H - CH_3 + Br^- \xrightarrow{\text{Fast}} H_3C - \underset{\underset{Br}{|}}{C}H - CH_3$$

Nucleophile $\qquad$ 2-Bromopropane

Addition of HBr to propene in presence of benzoyl peroxide :

$$CH_3CH = CH_2 + HBr \xrightarrow[(C_6H_5CO)_2O]{} CH_3CH_2CH_2Br$$

**Mechanism :**

$$C_6H_5\overset{\underset{\parallel}{O}}{C} - O - O - \overset{\underset{\parallel}{O}}{C} \quad C_6H_5 \longrightarrow 2\overset{\bullet}{C}_6H_5 + 2CO_2$$

$$\overset{\bullet}{C}_6H_5 + H - Br \longrightarrow C_6H_6 + \overset{\bullet}{Br}$$

Benzene

**13.17 Write down the product of ozonolysis of 1,2 dimethylbenzene (*o*-xylene). How does the result support Kekulé structure for benzene.**

**Ans.**

$$\text{(I)} \xrightarrow{O_3} 2 CH_3 - \overset{\underset{\parallel}{O}}{C} - \overset{\underset{\parallel}{O}}{C} - H + H - \overset{\overset{O}{\parallel}}{C} - \overset{\overset{O}{\parallel}}{C} - H$$

Methyl glyoxal $\qquad$ Glyoxal

$$\text{(II)} \xrightarrow{O_3} CH_3 - \overset{\underset{\parallel}{O}}{C} - \overset{\underset{\parallel}{O}}{C} - CH_3 + 2H - \overset{\overset{O}{\parallel}}{C} - \overset{\overset{O}{\parallel}}{C} - H$$

1, 2-Dimethyl glyoxal

All the three products cannot be obtained from one of the two structures, this proves that *o*-xylene is a resonance hybrid of Kekulé structure I and II.

**13.18 Arrange benzene *n*-hexane and ethyne in decreasing order of acidic behaviour. Also give reason for this behaviour.**

**Ans.** Acidic behaviour of benzene, *n*-hexane and ethyne can be compared with the help of % *s* character of each. More the % *s* character more will be the acidic nature.

$$HC \equiv CH > \text{(benzene)} > n\,CH_3CH_2CH_2 - CH_2CH_2CH_3$$

|  |  |  |
|---|---|---|
| *sp* | *sp*$^2$ | *sp*$^3$ |
| 50% *s* | 33% *s* | 25% *s* |
| character | character | character |

**13.19 Why does benzene undergo electrophilic substitution reactions easily and nucleophilic substitutions with difficulty?**

**Ans.** Benzene has the presence of $\pi$ bonded electron which are delocalised. Hence, any electrophile can attack easily on the electrons of benzene ring. Thus Benzene favours electrophilic substitution reaction.

Nucleophile are electron rich species, electrons of benzene ring repels the nucleophile making nucleophilic substitution difficult to occur.

**13.20 How would you convert the following compounds into benzene?**

    **(i)   Ethyne**          **(ii)  Ethene**              **(iii)  Hexane**

**Ans. (i)**     $3\,HC \equiv CH \xrightarrow[\substack{873\ K}]{\substack{\text{Red hot}\\ \text{Iron tube}}}$ (benzene)

    **(ii)**   Ethene is first converted into ethyne and then to benzene as shown above.

$$CH_2 = CH_2 \xrightarrow{Br_2\,/CCl_4} Br - CH_2 - CH_2 - Br \xrightarrow[\substack{1,2-\text{Dibromoethane}\\ (\text{Dehydro bromination})}]{KOH(\text{alc}),\Delta}$$

$$HC \equiv CH \xrightarrow[\substack{873\ K}]{\text{Red hot Fe tube}} Benzene$$

    **(iii)** 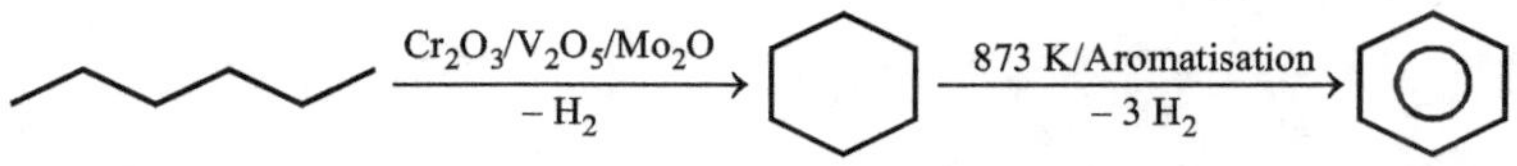    (skeletal structure) $\xrightarrow[- H_2]{Cr_2O_3/V_2O_5/Mo_2O}$ (cyclohexane) $\xrightarrow[- 3\ H_2]{873\ K/\text{Aromatisation}}$ (benzene)

         *n*-Hexane                      Cyclohexane            Benzene

**13.21 Write structures of all the alkenes which on hydrogenation give 2–methylbutane?**

**Ans.** The basic skeleton of 2–methylbutane is $^4C - ^3C - ^2\overset{\overset{\displaystyle C}{\displaystyle |}}{C} - ^1C$

Putting double bonds at various different positions and satisfying the tetracovalency of each carbon, the structures of various alkenes which give 2–methylbutane on hydrogenation are:

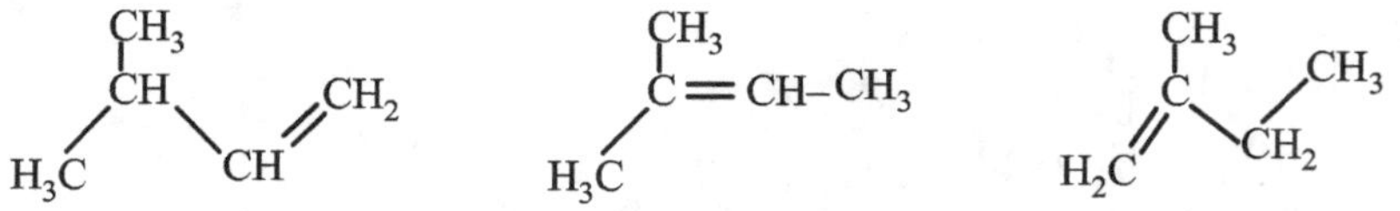

|  |  |  |
|---|---|---|
| 3-methyl but-1-ene | 2-methyl but-2-ene | 2-methyl but-1-ene |

**13.22 Arrange the following set of compounds in order of their decreasing relative reactivity with an electrophile, E⁺.**

    **(a)  Chlorobenzene, 2, 4–dinitrochlorobenzene , *p*–nitrochlorobenzene**

    **(b)  Toluene , $p - H_3C - C_6H_4 - NO_2$, $p - O_2N - C_6H_4 - NO_2$**

**Ans. (a)**   The typical reactions of benzene are electrophilic substitution reactions. Higher the electron density in the benzene ring, more reactive is the compound toward these reactions. Since $NO_2$ is more powerful electron–withdrawing group than Cl, therefore, more the number of nitro groups, less reactive is the compound. Thus, the overall reactivity decreases in order.

Chlorobenzene > *p*-nitrochlorobenzene > 2, 4-dinitrochlorobenzene.

(b) Here, $CH_3$ group is electron donating but $NO_2$ group is electron–withdrawing. Therefore, the maximum electron–density will be in toluene, followed by *p*–nitro toluene followed by *p*-dinitrobenzene.

Thus, the overall reactivity decreases in the order :

$$\text{Toluene} > p\text{–}H_3C\text{–}C_6H_4\text{–}NO_2 > p\text{–}O_2N\text{–}C_6H_4\text{–}NO_2$$

**13.23 Out of benzene, *m*–dinitrobenzene and toluene which will undergo nitration most easily and why ?**

**Ans.** $CH_3$ group is electron–donating while $-NO_2$ group is electron–withdrawing. Therefore, maximum electron density will be in toluene, followed by benzene and least in *m*–dinitrobenzene. Therefore, the ease of nitration decreases in the order: toluene > benzene > *m*–dinitrobenzene.

**13.24 Suggest the name of a Lewis acid other than anhydrous aluminium chloride which can be used during ethylation of benzene.**

**Ans.** Anhydrous $FeCl_3$, $SnCl_4$, $BF_3$, etc.

**13.25 Why is Wurtz reaction not preferred for the preparation of the alkanes containing odd number of carbon atoms? Illustrate your answer by taking one example.**

**Ans.** For preparation of alkanes containing odd number of carbon atoms, a mixture of two alkyl halides has to be used. Since two alkyl halides can react in three different ways, therefore, a mixture of three alkanes instead of the desired alkane would be formed. For example, Wurtz reaction between 1–bromopropane and 1– bromobutane gives a mixture of three alkanes, i. e., hexane, heptane and octane as shown below:

$$CH_3CH_2CH_2-Br \ + 2Na + Br \ CH_2CH_2CH_3 \xrightarrow{\text{Dry ether}} CH_3CH_2CH_2CH_2CH_2CH_3 \ + 2\,NaBr$$
1–Bromopropane         Hexane

$$CH_3CH_2CH_2-Br + 2Na + Br-CH_2CH_2CH_2CH_3 \xrightarrow{\text{Dry ether}} CH_3CH_2CH_2CH_2CH_2CH_2CH_3 + 2NaBr$$
1–Bromopropane    1–Bromopropane      Heptane

$$CH_3CH_2CH_2CH_2-Br + 2Na + Br-CH_2CH_2CH_2CH_3 \xrightarrow{\text{Dry ether}} CH_3CH_2CH_2CH_2CH_2CH_2CH_2CH_3 + 2NaBr$$
1-Bromobutane        Octane

| SECTION B | **PRACTICE QUESTIONS** ◆ |

## MULTIPLE CHOICE QUESTIONS

**1.** How many moles of $O_2$ are required for complete combustion of one mole of iso pentane?
 (a) 5    (b) 6    (c) 7    (d) 8

**2.** $n$–Butane $\xrightarrow[\text{HCl}]{\text{AlCl}_3}$ [X] $\xrightarrow{\text{KMnO}_4}$ [Y], [Y] is
 (a) Primary alcohol    (b) Secondary alcohol
 (c) Tertiary alcohol    (d) Diol

**3.** $CH_3CH_2COOH \longrightarrow CH_4$
 For this conversion sequence of reagents required are
 (a) NaOH / CaO / Δ
 (b) NaOH / CaO / Δ, $KMnO_4$, NaOH / CaO / Δ
 (c) NaOH / CaO / Δ, $(CH_3COO)_2$ Mn, NaOH / CaO / Δ
 (d) NaOH / CaO / Δ, $AlCl_3$ / HCl,
              $KMnO_4$, NaOH / CaO / Δ

**4.** Which of the following compound can be best prepared by Wurtz reaction?
 (a)     (b) 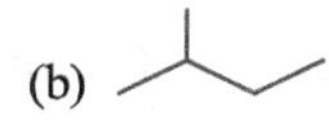
 (c) 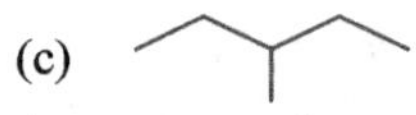    (d) 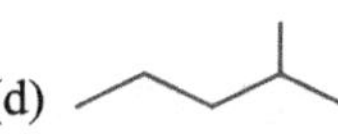

**5.** A reagent used to test unsaturation in alkene is -
 (a) ammonical $Cu_2Cl_2$
 (b) ammonical $AgNO_3$
 (c) solution of $Br_2$ in $CCl_4$
 (d) conc. $H_2SO_4$

**6.** One mole of a symmetrical alkene on ozonolysis gives two moles of an aldehyde having a molecular mass of 44 u. The alkene is
 (a) propene    (b) 1-butene
 (c) 2-butene    (d) ethene

**7.** Arrange in decreasing order of reactivity towards HCl
 (1) $F - CH = CH_2$    (2) $(CH_3)_2 C = CH_2$
 (3) $NO_2 - CH = CH_2$    (4) $(CN)_2 C = C(CN)_2$
 (a) 2 > 1 > 3 > 4    (b) 4 > 1 > 3 > 2
 (c) 1 > 4 > 2 > 3    (d) 3 > 2 > 4 > 1

**8.** Ammonical silver nitrate forms a white precipitate easily with
 (a) $CH_3C \equiv CH$    (b) $CH_3C \equiv CCH_3$
 (c) $CH_3CH = CH_2$    (d) $CH_2 = CH_2$

**9.** Which of these will not react with acetylene?
 (a) NaOH    (b) Ammo
 (c) Na    (d) HCl.

**10.** Which of the following polymer can be used as electrodes in batteries ?
 (a) Polypropene    (b) Polyacetylene
 (c) Polyethene    (d) Polyisoprene

**11.** The correct increasing order of acidity of the following alkynes
 (1) $CH_3 - C \equiv C - CH_3$    (2) $CH_3 - C \equiv CH$
 (3) $CH \equiv CH$
 (a) 1 < 2 < 3    (b) 2 < 3 < 1
 (c) 3 < 2 < 1    (d) 1 < 3 < 2

**12.** The conditions for aromaticity is :
 (a) molecule must have cyclic clouds of delocalised π electrons
 (b) molecule must contain $(4n + 2)\pi$ electrons
 (c) Both (a) and (b)
 (d) None of the above

**13.** Benzene can be directly obtained from
 (a) Acetylene    (b) Phenol
 (c) Chlorobenzene    (d) All the above

**14.** Catalytic hydrogenation of benzene gives
 (a) xylene    (b) cyclohexane
 (c) benzoic acid    (d) toluene

**15.** Benzene can be obtained in the reaction
 (a) Ethene + 1, 3-butadiene
 (b) Trimerisation of ethyne
 (c) Reduction of PhCHO
 (d) All of these

**16.** The carbon-carbon bond length in benzene is
 (a) Same as in $C_2H_4$
 (b) In between $C_2H_6$ and $C_2H_2$
 (c) In between $C_2H_4$ and $C_2H_2$
 (d) In between $C_2H_6$ and $C_2H_4$

## ASSERTION & REASON QUESTIONS

**DIRECTIONS (Qs. 1-8) :** *Each of these questions contains an assertion followed by reason. Read them carefully and answer the question on the basis of following options. You have to select the one that best describes the two statements.*
 (a) If both Assertion and Reason are correct and the Reason is a correct explanation of the Assertion.
 (b) If both Assertion and Reason are correct but Reason is not a correct explanation of the Assertion.
 (c) If the Assertion is correct but Reason is incorrect.
 (d) If the Assertion is incorrect but the Reason is correct.

**1.** **Assertion:** Decolourisation of $KMnO_4$ solution is used as a test for unsaturation.
 **Reason:** Alkenes on reaction with cold, dilute aqueous solution of potassium permanganate produce vicinal glycols.

**2.** **Assertion:** Melting point of neopentane is more than isopentane.
 **Reason:** More are van der Waals forces, more is the melting point.

**3.** **Assertion:** Chloromethane cannot show dehydrohalogenations reaction.
 **Reason:** H–Cl is stronger than H–Br bond and not cleaved by the free radical.

**4. Assertion:** Chlorination of cumene with $Cl_2$ in presence of UV mainly yields 2-chloro-2-phenyl propane.
**Reason:** The reaction occurs through intermediate formation of the radical, $C_6H_5\overset{\bullet}{C}HCH_2$.
$$\underset{CH_3}{|}$$

**5. Assertion:** Ethyne is acidic in nature in comparison to ethene and ethane.
**Reason:** *sp* hybridised orbitals of carbon atoms in ethyne have highest electronegativity, hence can attract shared $e^-$ pair of C–H bond to a greater extent.

**6. Assertion:** Benzene does not form ozonide with $O_3$.
**Reason:** Benzene has resonance effect due to closed ring.

**7. Assertion:** When benzene reacts with $CH_3Cl$ in the presence of anhydrous $AlCl_3$ forms toluene.
**Reason:** Anhydrous $AlCl_3$ is ionic compound and behaves as a catalyst.

**8. Assertion:** Acetylene on polymerisation gives benzene.
**Reason:** It involves carbocation formation.

## CASE/PASSAGE BASED QUESTIONS

**DIRECTIONS (Qs. 1-5) :** *Read the following case/passage and answer the questions.*

Modern bonding models (valence-bond and molecular orbital theories) explain the structure and stability of benzene in terms of delocalization of six of its electrons, where delocalization in this case refers to the attraction of an electron by all six carbons of the ring instead of just one or two of them. This delocalization causes the electrons to be more strongly held, making benzene more stable and less reactive than expected for an unsaturated hydrocarbon. As a result, the hydrogenation of benzene occurs somewhat more slowly than the hydrogenation of alkenes (other organic compounds that contain carbon-carbon double bonds), and benzene is much more difficult to oxidize than alkenes. Most of the reactions of benzene belong to a class called electrophilic aromatic substitution that leave the ring itself intact but replace one of the attached hydrogens. These reactions are versatile and widely used to prepare derivatives of benzene.

**1.** Benzene reacts with $CH_3COCl + AlCl_3$ to give
(a) chlorobenzene (b) toluene
(c) benzyl chloride (d) acetophenone

**2.** Benzene is highly unsaturated but it does not undergo addition reaction because
(a) $\pi$-electrons of benzene are delocalised.
(b) cyclic structures do not show addition reaction
(c) benzene is a non-reactive compound
(d) All of the above

**3.** (i) Chlorobenzene and (ii) benzene hexachloride are obtained from benzene by the reaction of chlorine, in the pesence of
(a) (i) Direct sunlight and (ii) anhydrous $AlCl_3$
(b) (i) Sodium hydroxide and (ii) sulphuric acid
(c) (i) Ultraviolet light and (ii) anhydrous $FeCl_3$
(d) (i) Anhydrous $AlCl_3$ and (ii) direct sunlight

**4.** A group which deactivates the benzene ring towards electrophilic substitution but which directs the incoming group principally to the *o*-and *p*-positions is
(a) $-NH_2$ (b) $-Cl$ (c) $-NO_2$ (d) $-C_2H_5$

**5.** Benzene can be obtained by heating either benzoic acid with X or phenol with Y. X and Y are respectively.
(a) Zinc dust and soda lime
(b) Soda lime and zinc dust
(c) Zinc dust and sodium hydroxide
(d) Soda lime and copper

## VERY SHORT ANSWER QUESTIONS

**1.** Name the products formed when an ethereal solution containing ethyl iodide and methyl iodide is heated with sodium metal.

**2.** How can ethylene be converted into ethane ?

**3.** Give the structure of the alkene ($C_4H_8$) which adds on HBr in the presence and in the absence of peroxide to give the same product, $C_4H_9Br$

**4.** Can eclipsed and staggered conformations of ethane be isolated? Give reason.

**5.** What is Lindlar's catalyst? What is it used for?

**6.** Arrange the three isomers of pentane in increasing order of their boiling points.

**7.** Can you separate the two conformations of ethane?

**8.** What is halogen carrier? Give one example.

**9.** Out of ethylene and acetylene which is more acidic and why?

**10.** Name two reagents which can be used to distinguish between ethene and ethyne.

**11.** What happens when benzene is treated with excess of $Cl_2$ in presence of sunlight? Give chemical reaction.

**12.** How will you distinguish between
$CH_3CH_2C \equiv CH$ and $CH_3 - C \equiv C - CH_3$

**13.** Although alkenes are more reactive than alkynes towards addition reaction, reverse is true regarding catalytic hydrogenation. Explain.

## SHORT ANSWER QUESTIONS

**1.** Arrange the following in increasing order of their release of energy on combustion.

(i)      (ii) 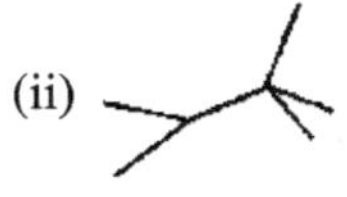

(iii)      (iv) 

**2.** Define the terms conformation and conformational isomerism.

**3.** Why is cyclopropane is more reactive as compared to cyclohexane?

**4.** How are alkenes obtained from alkyl halides ?

**5.** Which of the following shows geometrical isomerism ?
(i) $CHCl = CHCl$ (ii) $CH_2 = CCl_2$
(iii) $CCl_2 = CHCl$
Give the structures of its *cis* – and *trans* – forms.

6. What happens when (give chemical equation)
   (i) Sodium ethanoate is heated with sodalime,
   (ii) Sodium cyclohexane carboxylate is heated with sodalime?

7. What happens when
   (i) bromoethane is treated with zinc and hydrochloric acid
   (ii) hydrogen is passed into 2-bromopropane in the presence of palladium?

8. What is the role of red phosphorus in the reduction of alkyl halide using hydroiodic acid?

9. List the following alkenes in decreasing order of reactivity towards electrophilic addition:
   (i) $Cl\,CH_2CH = CH_2$
   (ii) $(CH_3)_2\,C = CH_2$
   (iii) $CH_3CH = CH_2$
   (iv) $CH_2 = CHCl$
   Explain your answer.

10. Write down the structural formulae of the product obtained in the following reaction:

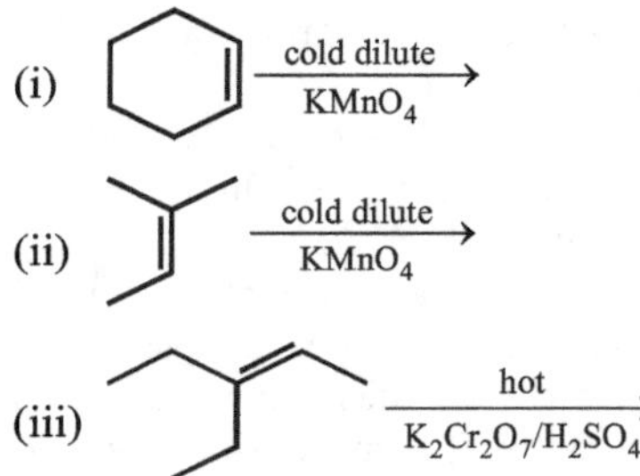

   (i) $\xrightarrow[\text{KMnO}_4]{\text{cold dilute}}$

   (ii) $\xrightarrow[\text{KMnO}_4]{\text{cold dilute}}$

   (iii) $\xrightarrow[\text{K}_2\text{Cr}_2\text{O}_7/\text{H}_2\text{SO}_4]{\text{hot}}$

11. What do you mean by cracking or pyrolysis?

12. Account for the fact that the chain-initiating step in thermal chlorination of $CH_4$ is

$$Cl_2 \xrightarrow{\text{heat}} 2Cl^{\bullet} \quad \text{and not} \quad CH_4 \xrightarrow{\text{heat}} CH_3^{\bullet} + H^{\bullet}$$

13. Give the major product formed when each of the following alcohol is heated in presence of conc. $H_2SO_4$.

(a) $CH_3CH_2CH_2\overset{\overset{\displaystyle OH}{|}}{C}HC(CH_3)_3$

(b) $CH_3CH_2CH_2CH_2CH_2OH$

14. Identify A, B and C in the following set :

$$B + C \xleftarrow[\text{MnO}_4^-]{\text{Hot}} \quad \xrightarrow{\text{Cold MnO}_4^-} A$$

15. Alkenes are more reactive than alkynes toward addition of electrophilic reagents (e.g. $Br_2$, HBr, etc.) yet it is easy to stop the reaction at the alkene stage when 1 molar equivalent of the reagent is used. Explain.

16. Explain the following :
   (a) Alkanes are inert
   (b) Pyrolysis of alkanes leads to cleavage of C–C bonds rather than C–H bonds
   (c) Although combustion of alkanes is a strongly exothermic process, it occurs only at high temperatures.

17. Which member of each pair is more reactive toward addition of HBr?
   (a) 1-Propene or 2-methylpropene
   (b) Cyclohexene of 1-methylcyclohexene
   (c) 1-Butene or 1,3-butadiene

18. Write all the possible isomers for a benzene derivative having the molecular formula $C_8H_{10}$.

19. How will you prepare 3-methylbut-1-yne by starting with ethyne?

20. Hydrocarbon A (MF is $C_5H_8$) gave a white precipitate with ammonical silver nitrate. Oxidation of A with hot alkaline $KMnO_4$ gave 2-methyl propanoic acid. What is the structural formula of A?

21. Explain why alkynes are less reactive than alkenes toward addition of $Br_2$.

22. How will you make the following conversions?
   (i) Propene into propyne
   (ii) 1, 1-dibromopentane into pentyne-1

23. Supply structures for the products of the reaction of Methyl benzene with
   (i) chlorine in the presence of light
   (ii) chlorine in the presence of $FeCl_3$
   (iii) $K_2Cr_2O_7 / H_2SO_4$

24. Classify the following substituent groups by their orientation and reactivity :

   (i) $-CH = CHNO_2$
   (ii) $-O\,CR$ with $\overset{||}{O}$

   (iii) $-\overset{\overset{\displaystyle}{||}}{\underset{O}{C}}-NH_2$
   (iv) $-O-$ (phenyl)

   (v) $-CH_2OH$
   (vi) $-\overset{||}{\underset{O}{C}}-NH_3$

25. How will you make the following conversions?
   (i) Benzene to benzoic acid
   (ii) Benzoic acid to ethylbenzene
   (iii) Benzoic acid to benzene sulphonic acid

26. Why do alkenes prefer to undergo electrophilic addition reaction while arenes prefer electrophilic substitution reactions? Explain.

## LONG ANSWER QUESTIONS

1. Discuss the different conformations of ethane.

2. (i) Why is the Wurtz synthesis not a good method for preparing propane?
   (ii) What alkanes would be expected from the reaction of sodium with 50 : 50 mixture of 1-chloropropane and 2-chloropropane ?

3. List alkanes, alkenes and terminal alkynes in order of decreasing acidity of their terminal C—H. Also, account for the order of acidities. Give two reactions to show acidic nature of terminal alkynes.

4. (i) Arrange the following compounds according to the increasing order of boiling point: Hexane, heptane, 3-methyl pentane, 2, 2-dimethyl butane.

   (ii) Account for the following :

      (a) The boiling points of hydrocarbon decreases with increase in branching.

      (b) Hydrocarbons with odd number of carbon atoms have a melting point lower than expected.

      (c) Boiling point of *n*-pentane is greater than that of neo-pentane but melting point of neo-pentane is greater than that of *n*-pentane.

5. The ring systems having following characteristics are aromatic.

   (i) Planar ring containing conjugated $\pi$ bonds.

   (ii) Complete delocalisation of the $\pi$-electrons in ring

system i.e, each atom in the ring has unhybridised *p*-orbital, and

(iii) Presence of $(4n + 2)$ $\pi$-electrons in the ring where *n* is an integer ($n = 0, 1, 2 \ldots\ldots\ldots$) [Huckel's rule]

Using this information classify the following compounds as aromatic/non-aromatic.

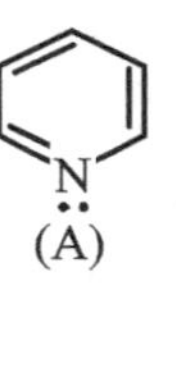  
(A)       (B)       (C)

   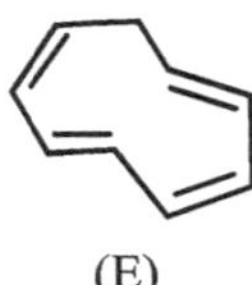
(D)         (E)

---

## SOLUTIONS

### *Multiple Choice Questions*

1. **(d)** Iso pentane ($C_5H_{12}$)

   $C_5H_{12} + 8\,O_2 \longrightarrow 5\,CO_2 + 6\,H_2O$

2. **(c)** $\xrightarrow[\text{HCl}]{\text{AlCl}_3}$ $\xrightarrow{\text{KMnO}_4}$ (—OH)

3. **(c)** $CH_3\!-\!CH_2COOH \xrightarrow[\text{CaO, }\Delta]{\text{NaOH}} CH_3CH_3$

   $\xrightarrow{(CH_3COO)_2\,Mn} CH_3COOH \xrightarrow[\text{CaO, }\Delta]{\text{NaOH}} CH_4$

4. **(a)** For (b), (c) and (d) we have to take mixture of alkyl halides and hence many side products will also form along with main products.

5. **(c)** Solution of $Br_2$ in $CCl_4$ is used to test unsaturation in alkene. It has red colour and when it is added to alkene red colour disappears due to formation of dibromo alkane.

6. **(c)** The given molecular formula suggests that the aldehyde formed will be acetaldehyde hence the alkene will be

   $$CH_3CH = CHCH_3 \xrightarrow[\text{(ii) Zn/H}_2\text{O}]{\text{(i) O}_3} 2CH_3CHO$$
   $$\text{2–Butene}$$

7. **(a)** Observe stability of $C^+$ ion.

8. **(a)** Terminal alkyenes give a white precipitate easily on reaction with ammonical silver nitrate solution.

9. **(a)** Acetylene reacts with the other three as:

   $$CH \equiv CNa \xleftarrow[\text{liq. NH}_3]{\text{Na}} CH \equiv CH \xrightarrow{+\,HCl}$$

   $$\begin{array}{ccc} CH_2 & & CH_3 \\ \| & \longrightarrow & | \\ CHCl & & CHCl_2 \end{array}$$

   $$CH \equiv CH \xrightarrow{[AgNO_3 + NH_4OH]}$$
   $$AgC \equiv CAg + NH_4NO_3$$
   $$\text{white ppt.}$$

10. **(b)** Thin film of polyacetylene can be used as electrodes in batteries. These films are good conductors, lighter and cheaper than the metal conductors.

11. **(a)** Only terminal alkynes show acidic nature. Ethyne is more acidic than propyne. But-2-yne is not acidic as it does not contain any hydrogen attached to *sp* hybridised carbon.

12. **(c)**

13. **(d)** Benzene can be obtained by all the compounds given.

   $$3CH \equiv CH \xrightarrow[\text{873 K}]{\text{Red hot tube}}$$

   (OH) $+ Zn \xrightarrow{\Delta}$

   (Cl) $+ 2\,[H] \xrightarrow[\text{NaOH}]{\text{Ni-Al alloy}}$

14. **(b)** (Benzene) $+ 3H_2 \xrightarrow{\text{Ni}}$ (Cyclohexane)

15. **(b)** Benzene can be obtained by polymerisation of acetylene.

   $$3HC \equiv CH \xrightarrow[\text{500°C}]{\text{Red hot tube}}$$

16. **(d)** In benzene due to delocalisation of $\pi$ - electrons, all the $C-C$ bond lengths are equal as each $C-C$ bond has some double bond character and thus the bond length is between single and double bond, i.e., between $C_2H_6$ and $C_2H_4$.

### *Assertion & Reason Questions*

**1. (a)**

$$\underset{\text{Alkene}}{\overset{}{>}C=C\overset{}{<}} \xrightarrow[\text{Cold violet}]{\text{Alkaline KMnO}_4} \underset{\underset{\text{Colourless}}{\overset{}{OH\ OH}}}{\overset{}{>}C-C\overset{}{<}}$$

**2. (b)** Melting point depends on intermolecular forces and symmetry of compound. Neo-pentane has radical symmetry, but isopentane does not, therefore, neo-pentane has higher melting point than isopentane.

**3. (b)** In dehydrohalogenation reaction, hydrogen eliminate from the β-carbon and gives alkene, but β-carbon is not present in chloromethane.

**4. (c)**

$$\underset{\text{Cumene}}{\overset{H_3C-CH-CH_3}{\bigcirc}} + Cl_2 \xrightarrow{UV} \underset{\underset{\text{propane}}{\text{2-Chloro, 2-phenyl}}}{\overset{\overset{Cl}{|}\ }{\overset{H_3C-C-CH_3}{\bigcirc}}}$$

The reaction occurs through intermediate stable bezylic radical.

$$(C_6H_5 - \overset{\overset{\bullet}{}}{\underset{\underset{CH_3}{|}}{C}} - CH_3)\ \text{ formation.}$$

**5. (a)** More is the *s*-character, more they are acidic in nature.

$$\underset{\underset{50\%}{sp}}{CH \equiv CH} > \underset{\underset{33\%}{sp^2}}{CH_2 = CH_2} > \underset{\underset{25\%}{sp^3}}{C_2H_6}$$

*s*-character   *s*-character   *s*-character

**6. (d)** Benzene reacts with ozone and forms triozonide, which on hydrolysis in presence of Zn gives glyoxal.

$$\bigcirc \xrightarrow[\text{(ii) Zn + H}_2\text{O}]{\text{(I) O}_3\ (3\ \text{mole})} 3\ \underset{\underset{CHO}{|}}{\overset{CHO}{}}\ \text{(glyoxal)}$$

Benzene has resonance effect, because it has conjugate system (double and single bond alternative).

**7. (c)** Electrophilic substitution reaction

$$\bigcirc + CH_3Cl \xrightarrow{AlCl_3\ (\text{anhydrous})} \overset{CH_3}{\bigcirc} + HCl$$

Anhydrous $AlCl_3$ is covalent and Lewis acid, therefore, acts as catalyst.

**8. (c)** Acetylene on polymerisation gives benzene and involve free radical formation

$$3CH \equiv CH \xrightarrow[874\ K]{\text{Red hot Fe tube}} \bigcirc$$

### *Case/Passage Based Questions*

**1. (d)**

**2. (a)** π-Electrons of benzene rings are delocalised throughout the molecule. This makes the molecule very stable. The stability resists breaking of double bonds for addition.

**3. (a)**

$$\underset{\text{Benzene}}{\bigcirc} \begin{cases} \xrightarrow{Cl_2,\ \text{anly AlCl}_3\ (\text{Substitution})} \underset{\text{Chlorobenzene}}{\overset{Cl}{\bigcirc}} + HCl \\[2em] \xrightarrow{3Cl_2,\ \text{sunlight (Addition)}} \underset{\underset{(BHC)}{\text{Benzene hexachloride}}}{\text{Benzene hexachloride}} \end{cases}$$

**4. (b)** –Cl group is *o*-, *p*-directing due to +R effect ; however it is deactivating due to strong –I effect of Cl (difference from other *o*-, *p*-directing groups which are activating). The net result is that chlorobenzene undergoes *o*, *p*-substitution, but with difficulty.

**5. (b)**

$$\underset{(X)}{C_6H_5COOH + NaOH} \xrightarrow[\Delta]{CaO} C_6H_6 + Na_2CO_3$$

$$\underset{(Y)}{C_6H_5OH + Zn} \xrightarrow{\text{distill}} C_6H_6 + ZnO$$

### *Very Short Answer Questions*

**1.** A mixture of ethane, propane and butane is formed.

**2.** By catalytic reduction with $H_2$ in presence of nickel at 523–573 K.

**3.** 2–Butene $H_3C$—$CH = CH$—$CH_3$ (being symmetrical gives the same product i. e., 2–bromobutane).

**4.** No, because the difference of energy between these two conformations is very small, so even at room temperature these two interconverts rapidly and hence cannot be isolated.

**5.** Pd deposited over $CaCO_3$ or $BaSO_4$ and partially poisoned by addition of lead acetate or sulphur or quinoline. This is used for partial reduction of alkynes to *cis*–alkenes.

**6.** Isomers are 2-methyl pentane, 2, 3-dimethyl butane and 2, 2-dimethyl butane.

All three are isomers with the same molecular formula but one with least branching will have the highest boiling point, this is due to large surface area and more dispersion, forces.

**7.** The two conformations of ethane cannot be separated but are readily convertible.

**8.** A halogen compound used during halogenation of benzene is called halogen carrier e.g. $FeCl_3$.

**9.** Acetylene, due to greater electronegativity of the *sp*–hybridized carbon.

**10.** Tollens' reagent and ammonical CuCl solution.

**11.**

Benzene $+ 3Cl_2 \xrightarrow{h\nu}$ Hexachlorocyclohexane

**12.** $CH_3 - C \equiv C - CH_3 + NaNH_2 \longrightarrow$ No reaction

$$CH_3CH_2 \equiv CH + NaNH_2 \longrightarrow CH_3CH_2C \equiv \overset{-\ +}{C}Na$$

**13.** Alkenes are adsorbed on the surface of the catalyst only when the plane of the $\pi$ bond approaches perpendicularly (head on). Because of cylindrical nature of the $\pi$ bonds. Any approach along the axis of the cylinder can be successful.

### *Short Answer Questions*

**1.** More the number of C–atoms having maximum hydrogens, i. e., $CH_3$ groups, greater is the heat of combustion.
Thus the increasing order of heat of combustion is (iii) < (iv) < (i) < (ii).

**2.** Conformation of a molecule refers to different three dimensional positions of atoms relative to each other, arising from rotation about single (s) bonds. The energy required for rotation about C–C bond is very low and such rotation usually occur readily. So, the various conformations of a molecule are freely interconvertible. This phenomenon of getting different conformations arising from rotation about a single or sigma bond is called conformational isomerism.

**3.** Cyclopropane is planar having bond angle of 60°. Cyclohexane does not have all the carbon atoms in one plane and bond angle is 109°.28'. Due to deviation from normal tetrahedron cyclopropane is very strained and hence very reactive. On the other hand, cyclohexane is free from angle strain hence known as strainless rings and hence is quite stable and unreactive.

**4.** By heating alkyl halides with alcoholic solution of potassium hydroxide. A molecule of halogen acid is eliminated. The reaction is known as dehydrohalogenation reaction.

$$RCH_2 - CH_2 - X \xrightarrow[\text{Heat}]{\text{Alc.KOH}} \underset{\text{Alkene}}{RCH = CH_2} + HX$$

(X = Cl, Br, I)

e.g.

$$H-\overset{\overset{\displaystyle H}{|}}{\underset{\underset{\displaystyle H}{|}}{C}}-\overset{\overset{\displaystyle Cl}{|}}{\underset{\underset{\displaystyle H}{|}}{C}}-H + \text{Alc.KOH} \longrightarrow$$

$$H - \overset{\overset{\displaystyle |}{C}}{\underset{\underset{\displaystyle H}{|}}{}} = \overset{\overset{\displaystyle |}{C}}{\underset{\underset{\displaystyle H}{|}}{}} - H + KCl + H_2O$$

This is an elimination reaction. The ease of dehydrohalogenation for different halogens is Iodine > Bromine > Chlorine, while for carbons it is tertiary > secondary > primary i. e., tertiary alkyl iodide is the most reactive.

**5.** Only (i) i. e. $ClCH = CHCl$ has two different substituents on each carbon atom of the double bond and hence shows geometrical isomerism. The other two compounds, i. e., (ii) and (iii) do not show geometrical isomerism because one of the carbon atoms of the double bond in each case has two identical atoms, i.e., Cl atoms as structure of cis and trans form of $CHCl = CHCl$, 1, 2-dichloroethene

*cis*         *trans*

**6.** (i) Methane is formed.

$$\boxed{CH_3 COONa + NaO} H \xrightarrow[\Delta]{CaO} CH_4 + Na_2CO_3$$

(ii) $\underset{COONa}{\bigcirc} + NaOH \xrightarrow[\text{Heat}]{CaO} \underset{\text{Cyclohexane}}{\bigcirc} + Na_2CO_3$

**7.** (i) Ethane is formed

$$CH_3CH_2 - Br + 2[H] \xrightarrow[\text{(reduction)}]{Zn/HCl} CH_3CH_3 + HBr$$

(ii) Propane is obtained.

$$CH_3 - \underset{\underset{\displaystyle CH_3}{|}}{CH} - Br + H_2 \xrightarrow[\text{(reduction)}]{Pd} \underset{\text{Propane}}{CH_3 - \underset{\underset{\displaystyle CH_3}{|}}{CH_2}} + HBr$$

**8.** Alkyl halides can be reduced to alkanes by using red phosphorus and hydroiodic acid.
For example,

$$\underset{\text{bromoethane}}{CH_3 CH_2 - Br} + 2HI \rightarrow \underset{\text{ethane}}{CH_3 CH_3} + HBr + I_2$$

The function of the red phosphorus is to remove the iodine liberated in this reaction as it can react further with the alkane.

$$3I_2 + 2P \longrightarrow 2PI_3$$

**9.** Electron-donating alkyl groups make the $\pi$-bond more electron-rich and more reactive. Conversely, electron withdrawing groups such as Cl make the $\pi$-bond more electron deficient and less reactive. The order is

$$\underset{\underset{\displaystyle CH_3}{|}}{CH_3 - C} = CH_2 \ > \ CH_3 - CH = CH_2$$

(two $CH_3$ groups)     (one $CH_3$ groups)

$$> Cl - CH_2CH = CH_2 \ > \ CH_2 = CH - Cl$$

(one alkyl group with Cl atom)     (Cl is directly bonded to double bonded carbon)

**10.** (i) 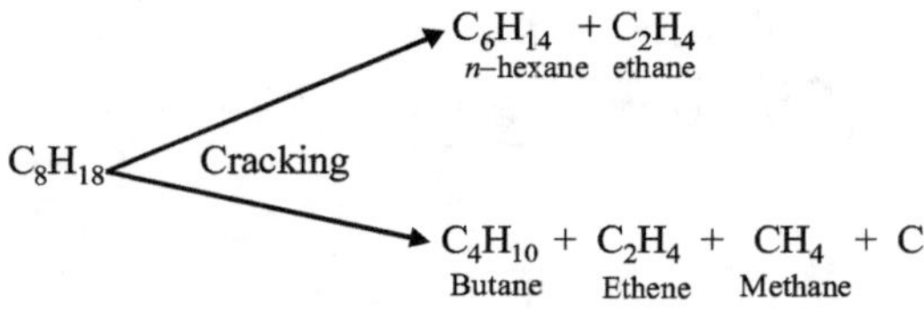 (Hydroxylation)

(ii)

OH          OH

(iii)         O

         +         O
              OH

Butanone        Ethanoic acid

**11.** Cracking is the process of breaking down the less volatile higher molecular mass hydrocarbon from petroleum into different types of more volatile lower molecular mass hydrocarbon. The cracking of alkanes involve the cleavage of C–C and C–H bonds. For example

$$C_8H_{18} \xrightarrow{\text{Cracking}} \begin{cases} C_6H_{14} + C_2H_4 \\ \text{n–hexane \quad ethane} \\ \\ C_4H_{10} + C_2H_4 + CH_4 + C \\ \text{Butane \quad Ethene \quad Methane} \end{cases}$$

**12.** We know that the value of $E_{act}$ of reactions involving only bond-breaking is equal to $\Delta H$, then

$$\underset{\text{(58 kCal)}}{Cl-Cl} \xrightarrow{\text{heat}} 2\overset{\bullet}{C}l\ ;\ \Delta H = 58;\ E_{act} = 58\ kCal$$

$$\underset{\text{(104 kCal)}}{CH_3-H} \xrightarrow{\text{heat}} \overset{\bullet}{C}H_3 + \overset{\bullet}{H}\ ;\ \Delta H = 104,$$

$$E_{act} = 104\ kCal$$

**13.** (a) $CH_3CH_2CH_2\overset{\overset{\displaystyle CH_3}{|}}{C} = C(CH_3)_2$

(b) $CH_3CH_2CH = CH\,CH_3$

**14.**

**15.** The high reactivity of alkenes than alkynes toward electrophiles can be explained on the basis of stability of their corresponding intermediate cyclic bromonium ion or carbocation.

$$\underset{\text{from alkyne}}{CH_2 = \overset{+}{C}H}\ \text{less stable than}\ \underset{\text{(from alkene)}}{CH_3 - \overset{+}{C}H_2}$$

**16.** (a) A reactive site in a molecule generally has at least one of the following features : (i) one or more unshared pair of electrons, (ii) a polar bond, (iii) an electron deficient atom, (iv) an atom with an expandable octet. Alkanes have none of these features, hence these are inert.

(b) The C—C bond has a lower average bond energy ($\Delta H = + 347\ kJ\ mol^{-1}$) than the C—H bond ($\Delta H = + 415\ kJ\ mol^{-1}$).

(c) The reaction is very slow at moderate temperatures because of a very high activation energy.

**17.** Species with more stable intermediate (carbocation) will be more reactive

(a) 2-Methylpropene (3° carbocation as intermediate)

(b) 1-Methylcycloehexene (3° carbocation as intermediate)

(c) 1, 3-Butadiene (Allylic carbocation as intermediate)

**18.** Four isomers; ethylbenzene (1), *o*–xylene (2), *m*–xylene (3) and *p*–xylene (4).

ethylbenzene        *o*-xylene        *m*-xylene        *p*-xylene

**19.** $$\underset{\text{Ethyne}}{HC \equiv CH} \xrightarrow[\text{196 K}]{Na, NH_3(l)} \underset{\text{Sod. acetylide}}{HC \equiv C^-Na^+}$$

$$HC \equiv C^-Na^+ + CH_3 \overset{\overset{\displaystyle CH_3}{|}}{\underset{\text{Isopropyl iodide}}{-CH}} \overset{\curvearrowright}{-I} \longrightarrow$$

$$\underset{1}{\overset{4}{CH_3}} - \underset{}{\overset{3}{CH}} \overset{\overset{\displaystyle CH_3}{|}}{} - \overset{2}{C} \equiv \overset{1}{CH} + NaI$$

3-Methylbut -1-yne

**20.** $$A(C_5H_8) \xrightarrow{AgNO_3/NH_4OH} \text{white ppt indicates the presence of triple bond at the terminal position.}$$

$A$ with hot alkaline $KMnO_4$ gives

$$\underset{\overset{\displaystyle |}{CH_3}}{CH_3 - CH\ COOH}$$

2-Methyl propanoic acid

Therefore, the structural formula of A is

$$CH_3 - \overset{\overset{\displaystyle CH_3}{|}}{CH} - C \equiv CH$$

3-Methy-1-butyne

**21.** The three-membered ring bromonium ion formed from the alkyne (A) has a full double bond causing it to be more strained and less stable than the other from the alkene (B).

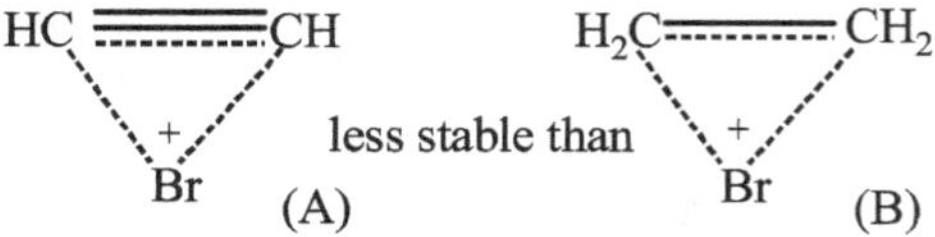



Also, the carbon's of (A) that are part of the bromonium ion have more *s*-character than (B), further making (A) less stable than (B).

**22.** (i) $CH_2 = CH - CH_2 + Br_2 \longrightarrow$

$$CH_3 - \underset{|}{\underset{Br}{C}}H - \underset{|}{\underset{Br}{C}}H_2 \xrightarrow[H^+]{NaNH_2} CH_3 - C \equiv CH$$

(ii) $CH_3 - CH_2 - CH_2 - CH_2 - \underset{|}{\underset{Br}{C}}H - Br$

$$\xrightarrow[H^+]{NaNH_2} CH_3 - CH_2 - CH_2 - C \equiv CH$$

**23.** (i) 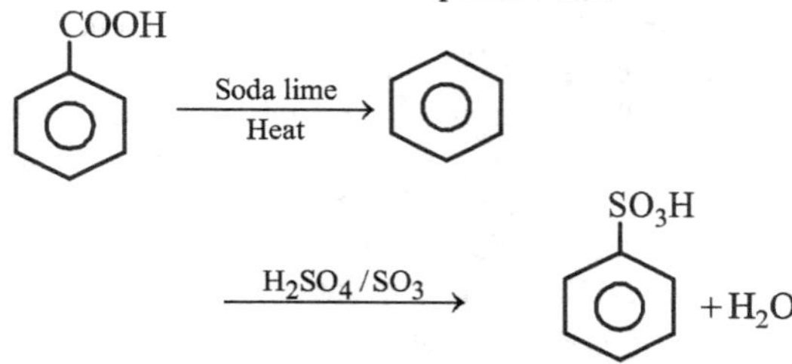

(ii) a mixture of

and

(iii)

**24.** ⇒ (ii), (iv), (v) ⟶ activating and *o, p*-directing.
⇒ (iii) and (vi) ⟶ deactivating and *m*-directing.
⇒ (i) is deactivating (by $NO_2$ group) but *o, p*-directing (due to $C = C$ group).

**25.** (i) 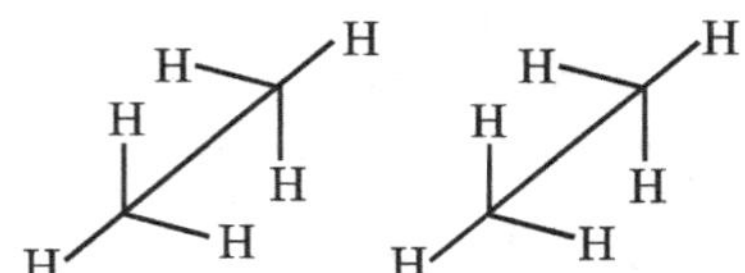

Toluene $\xrightarrow[KMnO_4]{alkaline}$ Benzoic acid

(ii) Benzoic acid to ethylbenzene

COOH $\xrightarrow[Heat]{Soda\ lime}$

$\xrightarrow[AlCl_3]{CH_3CH_2Cl}$ CH₂CH₃

Ethyl benzene

(iii) Benzoic acid to benzene sulphonic acid

COOH $\xrightarrow[Heat]{Soda\ lime}$

$\xrightarrow{H_2SO_4/SO_3}$ SO₃H $+ H_2O$

Benzene sulphonic acid

**26.** Both alkenes and arenes are electron-rich. Therefore undergo electrophilic reactions. Olefins undergo addition reactions because addition of a reagent to an olefin gives a more stable product as $sp^2$ hybridisation changes to $sp^3$ hybridisation. Addition to the double bond of arene would give a product with less or no resonance stability hence addition is difficult in arenes. On the other hand in substitution reaction, resonance stabilisation is retained therefore, arenes undergo substitution reaction.

Long Answer Questions

**1.** **Conformations of ethane:** Infinite no. of spatial arrangements of hydrogen atoms attached to one carbon atom with respect to the hydrogen atoms attached to another carbon atom are called conformational isomers. Ethane have following conformations :
**Sawhorse projections :**

In this, the molecule is viewed along the molecular axis. C – C bond is drawn in slightly tilted manner towards right or left side as shown in figure. Front carbon is shown at lower end while rear carbon is shown at upper end. Each carbon has three lines attached to it corresponding to three hydrogen atoms.

**Newman projections :** In this the molecule is viewed at C-C bond head on. Carbon atom towards the side of viewer is represented by dot or point and three 'H' atoms attached to this C are shown by lines at an angle of 120°. Carbon away from viewer or rear carbon is represented by circle and three 'H' atoms attached to this 'C' atom are represented by shorter line at an angle of 120°.

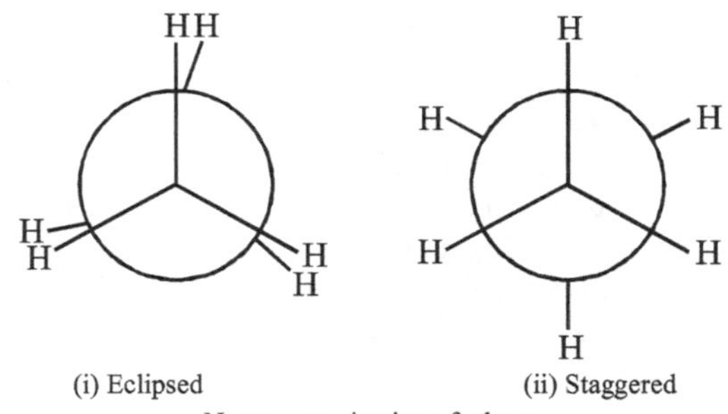

(i) Eclipsed   (ii) Staggered
Newman projection of ethane

The staggered form has the least torsional strain and the eclipsed form has the maximum torsional strain hence, staggered form is more stable.

**2.** **(i)** Wurtz reaction is suitable for synthesis of alkane containing even number of carbon. Propane contains odd number of carbon hence Wurtz reaction is not suitable for its preparation. Moreover, mixture of products may be obtained if reaction is done with chloroethane and chloromethane.

$$C_2H_5Cl + CH_3Cl \longrightarrow C_2H_5 - C_2H_5 +$$
$$\text{butane}$$
$$CH_3 - CH_3 + C_2H_5 - CH_3$$
$$\text{ethane} \qquad \text{propane}$$

**(ii)** Three alkanes are obtained from the reaction of sodium with equimolar mixture of 1-chloropropane and 2-chloropropane.

$$CH_3CH_2CH_2Cl + CH_3 - \underset{\underset{\text{2–chloropropane}}{\underset{\displaystyle Cl}{|}}}{CH} - CH_3 \xrightarrow[\text{ether}]{Na}$$
$$\underset{\text{1–chloropropane}}{\ }$$

$$\underset{\text{hexane}}{CH_3CH_2CH_2 - CH_2CH_2CH_3}$$

$$CH_3CH_2CH_2 - \underset{\underset{\text{2-methyl pentane}}{\underset{\displaystyle CH_3}{|}}}{CHCH_3} + CH_3\underset{\underset{\text{2, 3–dimethyl butane}}{\underset{\displaystyle CH_3}{|}}}{CH} - \underset{\underset{\ }{\underset{\displaystyle CH_3}{|}}}{C}HCH_3$$

**3.** The order of decreasing acidic strength

Alkyne > alkene > alkane

The acidic character of acetylene may be explained in terms of the $s$-character of the $sp$ hybridised orbital. An electron in an $s$-orbital is more tightly held than in a $p$-orbital because the $s$-electrons are closer to the nucleus. Since there is more $s$-character in $sp$ orbitals, the electrons in $sp$ orbitals are held more strongly by the nucleus than $sp^2$ and $sp^3$ electrons. In other words, the $sp$ hybridised carbon is more electronegative than $sp^2$ and $sp^3$ hybridised carbon atoms. Due to this, the hydrogen of acetylenic carbon develops a more positive charge and is acidic in character.

$$CH \equiv C - H + NaNH_2 \longrightarrow \underset{\text{sodium acetylide}}{CH \equiv C^- Na^+} + NH_3$$

$$CH \equiv CH + 2AgNO_3 \xrightarrow{2NH_4OH}$$

$$\underset{\text{silver acetylide}}{Ag^+C \equiv C^-Ag^+} + 2NH_4NO_3 + 2H_2O$$
$$\qquad\qquad\qquad\qquad \text{(white ppt)}$$

**4.** **(i)** The increasing order of boiling points is 2, 2- dimethyl butane < 3- methyl pentane < hexane < heptane.

Hexane, 3-methyl pentane and 2, 2-dimethyl butane are isomers. As we know that increase in branching reduces the extent of contact between the neighbouring molecules. The van der Waals forces decreases, boiling point also decreases. Heptane has the highest boiling point due to its high molecular mass.

**(ii)** **(a)** Branched chain alkanes have lower boiling points than their straight chain isomers, and as branching increases, the boiling point decreases still further. The explanation is that increased branching gives the molecule a more spherical shape and reduces the extent of contact between neighbouring molecules. Consequently, the attractive forces are reduced and the boiling point decreases.

**(b)** Hydrocarbon with odd number of carbon atoms have lesser melting point than expected. This is because, in the crystalline state the molecule adopt a highly ordered arrangement in which the carbon chains form a zig-zig pattern. For the even members, different chains peak closer together than for the odd numbered members, so that the attractive forces are larger for the even membered hydrocarbon than for odd membered hydrocarbons of similar size. Therefore, relatively more energy must be applied to separate the molecules with even numbers of carbon atoms and enable them to adopt the more random arrangement of the liquid state than to separate the molecules with odd numbers of carbon atoms.

**(c)** The $n$-pentane, due to large surface area, the extent of contact between neighbouring molecules is more. Therefore, the attractive forces are more and the boiling point increases. But the melting point of neo-pentane is greater than that of n-pentane because neo-pentane has a highly symmetrical structure and reduced surface area. Therefore, it is packed in the crystal systems more closely than $n$-pentane. So more energy is required to break the neo-pentane lattice than the $n$-pentane. Hence, neo-pentane has a higher melting point $n$-pentane.

**5.** A = Planar ring, all atoms of the ring $sp^2$ hybridised, has six delocalised $\pi$ electrons, follows Huckel rule. It is aromatic.

B = Six delocalised $\pi$-electrons ($4\pi$ electrons +2 unshared electrons on negatively charged carbon) in a planar ring, follows Huckel's rule. It is aromatic.

C = Has only four-delocalised $\pi$-electrons. It is non-aromatic.

D = Follows Huckel's rule, has $2\pi$ electrons i.e., $(4n + 2)$ $\pi$-electrons where $(n = 0)$, delocalised $\pi$-electrons. It is aromatic.

E = $8\pi$ electrons, does not follow Huckel's rule i.e, $(4n + 2)$ $\pi$-electrons rule. It is not aromatic.

## SECTION C | NCERT EXEMPLAR QUESTIONS 

### MULTIPLE CHOICE QUESTIONS

**1.** Arrange the following in decreasing order of their boiling points.

1. *n*–butane      2. 2-methylbutane

3. *n*–pentane     4. 2, 2-dimethylpropane

(a) $1 > 2 > 3 > 4$     (b) $2 > 3 > 4 > 1$

(c) $4 > 3 > 2 > 1$     (d) $3 > 2 > 4 > 1$

**2.** Arrange the halogens $F_2$, $Cl_2$, $Br_2$, $I_2$, in order of their increasing reactivity with alkanes.

(a) $I_2 < Br_2 < Cl_2 < F_2$     (b) $Br_2 < Cl_2 < F_2 < I_2$

(c) $F_2 < Cl_2 < Br_2 < I_2$     (d) $Br_2 < I_2 < Cl_2 < F_2$

**3.** The increasing order of reduction of alkyl halides with zinc and dilute HCl is

(a) $R - Cl < R - I < R - Br$

(b) $R - Cl < R - Br < R - I$

(c) $R - I < R - Br < R - Cl$

(d) $R - Br < R - I < R - Cl$

**4.** The correct IUPAC name of the following alkane is

$$H_3C - CH_2 - CH - CH_2 - CH_2 - CH - CH_2 - CH_3$$

with CH branch (CH₃ CH₃) on the first CH and CH₂–CH₃ branch on the second CH.

(a) 3, 6-diethyl-2-methyloctane

(b) 5-isopropyl-3-ethyloctane

(c) 3-ethyl-5-isopropyloctane

(d) 3-isopropyl-6-ethyloctane

**5.** The addition of HBr to 1-butene gives a mixture of products A, B and C.

(A) $H_5C_2 - C(Br)(H) - CH_3$

(B) $H - C(C_2H_5)(Br) - CH_3$

(C) $CH_3 - CH_2 - CH_2 - CH_2 - Br$

The mixture consists of

(a) A and B as major and C as minor products

(b) B as major, A and C as minor products

(c) B as minor, A and C as major products

(d) A and B as minor and C as major products

**6.** Which of the following will not show geometrical isomerism?

(a) $\begin{matrix} F \\ Cl \end{matrix} C = C \begin{matrix} H \\ D \end{matrix}$

(b) $\begin{matrix} F \\ Cl \end{matrix} C = C \begin{matrix} F \\ Cl \end{matrix}$

(c) $\begin{matrix} H_3C \\ H_5C_2 \end{matrix} C = C \begin{matrix} C_2H_5 \\ CH_3 \end{matrix}$

(d) $\begin{matrix} CH_3 \\ CH_3 \end{matrix} C = C \begin{matrix} CH_3 \\ C_2H_5 \end{matrix}$

**7.** Arrange the following hydrogen halides in order of their decreasing reactivity with propene.

(a) $HCl > HBr > HI$     (b) $HBr > HI > HCl$

(c) $HI > HBr > HCl$     (d) $HCl > HI > HBr$

**8.** Arrange the following carbanions in order of their decreasing stability.

A. $H_3C - C \equiv C^-$     B. $H - C \equiv C^-$

C. $H_3C - \bar{C}H_2$

(a) $A > B > C$     (b) $B > A > C$

(c) $C > B > A$     (d) $C > A > B$

**9.** Arrange the following alkyl halides in decreasing order of the rate of $\beta$ – elimination reaction with alcoholic KOH.

A. $CH_3 - C(H)(CH_3) - CH_2Br$

B. $CH_3 - CH_2 - Br$

C. $CH_3 - CH_2 - CH_2 - Br$

(a) $A > B > C$     (b) $C > B > A$

(c) $B > C > A$     (d) $A > C > B$

**10.** Which of the following reactions of methane is incomplete combustion?

(a) $2CH_4 + O_2 \xrightarrow{Cu/523\ K/100\ atm} 2CH_3OH$

(b) $CH_4 + O_2 \xrightarrow{Mo_2O_3} HCHO + H_2O$

(c) $CH_4 + O_2 \longrightarrow C(s) + 2H_2O(l)$

(d) $CH_4 + 2O_2 \longrightarrow CO_2(g) + 2H_2O(l)$

## ASSERTION & REASON QUESTIONS

**DIRECTIONS (Qs. (1-2)** : *Each of these questions contains an assertion followed by reason. Read them carefully and answer the question on the basis of following options. You have to select the one that best describes the two statements.*

(a) If both Assertion and Reason are correct and the Reason is a correct explanation of the Assertion.

(b) If both Assertion and Reason are correct but Reason is not a correct explanation of the Assertion.

(c) If the Assertion is correct but Reason is incorrect.

(d) If the Assertion is incorrect but the Reason is correct.

1. **Assertion:** Nitration of benzene with nitric acid requires the use of concentrated sulphuric acid.
   **Reason:** The mixture of concentrated sulphuric acid and concentrated nitric acid produces the electrophile, $NO_2^+$.

2. **Assertion:** Among isomeric pentanes, 2,2-dimethylpentane has highest boiling point.
   **Reason:** Branching affects the boiling point.

## SHORT ANSWER QUESTIONS

1. The relative reactivity of 1°, 2°, 3° hydrogen's towards chlorination is 1 : 3.8 : 5. Calculate the percentages of all monochlorinated products obtained from 2-methylbutane.

2. Rotation around carbon-carbon single bond of ethane is not completley free. Justify the statement.

3. An alkane $C_8H_{18}$ is obtained as the only product on subjecting a primary alkyl halide to Wurtz reaction. On monobromination this alkane yields a single isomer of a tertiary bromide. Write the structure of alkane and the tertiary bromide.

## LONG ANSWER QUESTIONS

1. An alkyl halide $C_5H_{11}Br$ (A) reacts with ethanolic KOH to give an alkene 'B', which reacts with $Br_2$ to give a compound 'C', which on dehydrobromination gives an alkyne 'D'. On treatment with sodium metal in liquid ammonia one mole of 'D' gives one mole of the sodium salt of 'D' and half a mole of hydrogen gas. Complete hydrogenation of 'D' yields a straight chain alkane. Identify A, B, C and D. Give the reactions involved.

2. An unsaturated hydrocarbon 'A' adds two molecules of $H_2$ and on reductive ozonolysis gives butane–1, 4-dial, ethanal and propanone. Give the structure of 'A', write its IUPAC name and explain the reactions involved.

## SOLUTIONS

### *Multiple Choice Questions*

1. **(d)** We know that, as the number of carbon atom increases, boiling point increases while for the same alkane, boiling point decreases with branching.

   2, 2-dimethyl propane,

   $$\begin{array}{c} CH_3 \\ | \\ H_3C - C - CH_3 \\ | \\ CH_3 \end{array}$$
   b.pt = 282.5 K

   $n$ – pentane, b.pt = 309.1 K

   2-methyl butane, $H_3C - H_2C - HC - CH_3$
   $$\begin{array}{c} | \\ CH_3 \end{array}$$
   b.pt = 301 K

   $n$-butane, b.pt = 273 K

2. **(a)** Reactivity of halogens decreases with decrease in electronegativity which decreases down the group.

   Hence the order of reactivity of alkanes with halogens is

   $$F_2 > Cl_2 > Br_2 > I_2.$$

   Also with $I_2$, the reaction is too slow that it requires a catalyst.

3. **(b)** The reactivity of halogens with alkanes follows the order : $F_2 > Cl_2 > Br_2 > I_2$. Further, the reactivity of reduction of alkyl halides with Zn & dilute HCl increases as the strength of $C - X$ (X = F, Cl , Br, I) bond decreases. Hence, reduction of alkyl halide with Zn and dilute HCl follows the order :

   $$R - I > R - Br > R - Cl.$$

4. **(a)** The correct IUPAC name of the alkane will be :

   $$H_3C - CH_2 - \underset{3}{CH} - \underset{4}{CH_2} - \underset{5}{CH_2} - \underset{6}{CH} - \underset{7}{CH_2} - \underset{8}{CH_3}$$
   $$\underset{2}{CH} \qquad\qquad CH_2$$
   $$\underset{1}{CH_3}\ CH_3 \qquad\qquad CH_3$$

   3, 6-Diethyl -2-methyloctane

5. **(a)** 1-butene is an unsymmetrical alkene and will follow Markovnikov's rule to give major product.

$$CH_3 - CH_2 - CH = CH_2 + H - Br \longrightarrow$$
I-Butene

$$CH_4(g) + O_2(g) \xrightarrow[\text{combustion}]{\text{Incomplete}} C(s) + 2H_2O(l)$$
Carbon black

### Assertion & Reason Questions

1. **(a)** In nitration, benzene is treating with nitrating mixture, i.e. conc. $HNO_3$ and $H_2SO_4$ and $H_2SO_4$ helps in furnishing $NO_2$ (Electrophile)

2. **(d)** Among isomeric pentanes 2, 2-dimethylpentane has lowest boiling point and on branching point decreases.

### Short Answer Questions

1. 2-Methyl butane is $CH_3 - \overset{\overset{\displaystyle CH_3}{|}}{CH} - CH_2 - CH_3$. Possible compounds are A, B and C given below:

$ClCH_2 - \overset{\overset{\displaystyle CH_3}{|}}{CH} - CH_2CH_3$
A(1°)

Nine possibilities for compound 'A' because nine methyl hydrogens are present in 2-methylbutane.

$\overset{H_3C}{\underset{H_3C}{>}} CH - \overset{\overset{\displaystyle}{\underset{\underset{\displaystyle Cl}{|}}{CH}}} - CH_3$
B(2°)

Two possibilities for 'B' compound because two CH hydrogens are present in 2-methylbutane.

$\overset{H_3C}{\underset{H_3C}{>}} \overset{\overset{\displaystyle}{\underset{\underset{\displaystyle Cl}{|}}{C}}} - CH_2 - CH_3$
C(3°)

Only one possibility for 'C' compound because one CH hydrogens is present in 2-methylbutane.

Relative amounts of A, B and C compounds =
Number of hydrogen × relative reactivity

| | A(1°) | B(2°) | C(3°) |
|---|---|---|---|
| Relative amount | $9 \times 1 = 9$ | $2 \times 3.8 = 7.6$ | $1 \times 5 = 5$ |

**Total amount of monohaloginated compounds**
**= 9 + 7.6 + 5 = 21.6**

Percentage of A = $\dfrac{9}{21.6} \times 100 = 41.7\%$

Percentage of B = $\dfrac{7.6}{21.6} \times 100 = 35.2\%$

Percentage of C = $\dfrac{5}{21.6} \times 100 = 23.1\%$

2. The rotation about C–C bond is restricted because of repulsion between electron cloud of C–H bonds on either carbon atoms.

6. **(d)** In option (d), a carbon with double bond has two same functional groups ($CH_3$) attached to it. The rotation around carbon will not produce a new compound. Hence, geometrical isomerism is not possible.

7. **(c)** Lesser the bond energy of hydrogen halide more will be its reactivity. Hence, the order of reactivity of given compounds with propene will be HI > HBr > HCl.

8. **(b)** + I-effect decreases the stability of carbanion. Since, $- CH_3$ group shows + I-effect, therefore, it intensifies the negative charge and hence destabilises the carbanion (A) relative to (B).

Also, $sp$ hybridised carbanion is more stabilised than $sp^3$.

$$\underset{\substack{(B) \quad sp}}{CH \equiv C} > \underset{\substack{(A) \quad sp}}{CH_3 - C \equiv C^-} > \underset{\substack{(C) \quad sp^3}}{CH_3 - \overset{..}{C}H_2}$$

Hence, the order of decreasing stability will be : B > A > C

9. **(d)** Alkyl halides on heating with alcoholic KOH eliminates halogen from α-carbon atom and hydrogen is eliminated from β-carbon atom to form an alkene.

(A) $\overset{3°\ \beta\text{–carbon}}{CH_3 - \underset{\underset{\displaystyle CH_3}{|}}{CH} - CH_2Br}$
(A)

(B) $\overset{1°\ \beta\text{–carbon}}{CH_3 - CH_2 - Br}$
2° β – carbon

(C) $CH_3 - CH_2 - CH_2 - Br$

More the number of β-substituents (alkyl groups) more stable alkene will be formed on β-elimination, more will be the reactivity. Thus the correct order is A > C > B

10. **(c)** During incomplete combustion of alkanes with insufficient amount of air carbon black is formed which is used in the manufacture of ink, printer ink, black pigments and as filters.

**3.**

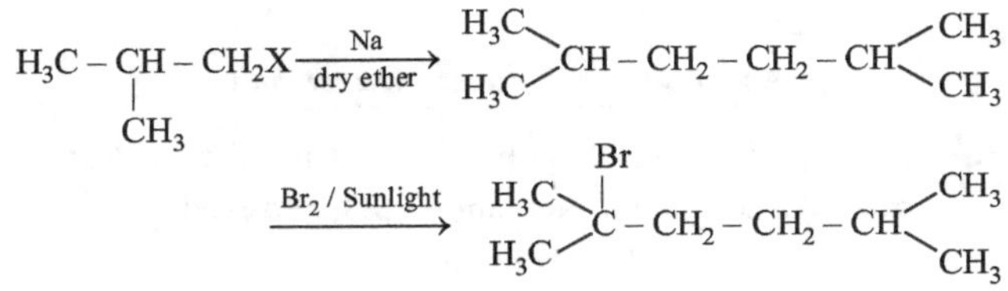

$$H_3C - \underset{\underset{CH_3}{|}}{CH} - CH_2X \xrightarrow[\text{dry ether}]{Na} \underset{H_3C}{\overset{H_3C}{\diagdown}} CH - CH_2 - CH_2 - CH \underset{CH_3}{\overset{CH_3}{\diagup}}$$

$$\xrightarrow{Br_2 / Sunlight} \underset{H_3C}{\overset{H_3C}{\diagdown}} \overset{\overset{Br}{|}}{C} - CH_2 - CH_2 - CH \underset{CH_3}{\overset{CH_3}{\diagup}}$$

### *Long Answer Questions*

**1.**

$$C_5H_{11}Br \xrightarrow{\text{alc.KOH}} \underset{\text{(B)}}{\text{Alkene}(C_5H_{10})} \xrightarrow{Br_2 \text{ in } CS_2} \underset{\text{(C)}}{C_5H_{10}Br_2}$$

$$\underset{\text{(A)}}{}$$

$$\xrightarrow[-2HBr]{\text{Alc.KOH}} C_5H_8 \xrightarrow{Na-liq.NH_3} C_5H_7 - Na + \frac{1}{2}H_2$$

$$\underset{\text{D (Alkyne)}}{} \qquad \underset{\text{Sodium alkylide}}{}$$

The reactions suggest that (D) is a terminal alkyne. This means triple bond is at the end of the chain. It could be either (I) or (II).

$$CH_3 - CH_2 - CH_2 - CH_2 \equiv CH$$
$$\text{I}$$

$$CH_3 - \underset{\underset{CH_3}{|}}{CH} - C \equiv CH$$
$$\text{II}$$

Since alkyne 'D' on hydrogenation yields straight chain alkane, therefore structure I is the structure of alkyne (D). Hence, the structures of A, B and C are as follows:

(A)  $CH_3 - CH_2 - CH_2 - CH_2 - CH_2Br$

(B)  $CH_3 - CH_2 - CH_2 - CH = CH_2$

(C)  $CH_3 - CH_2 - CH_2 - CH(Br) - CH_2Br$

**2.**  Two molecules of hydrogen add on 'A' this shows that 'A' is either an alkadiene or an alkyne.

On reductive ozonolysis 'A' gives three fragments, one of which is dialdehyde. Hence, the molecule has broken down at two sites. Therefore, 'A' has two double bonds. It gives the following three fragments:

$$OHC - CH_2 - CH_2 - CHO, \ CH_3CHO \ \text{and}$$

$$CH_3 - CO - CH_3$$

Hence, its structure as deduced from the three fragments must be

**Reactions:**

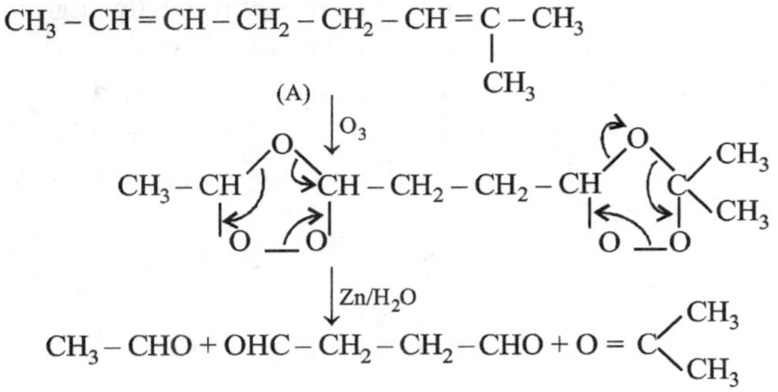

$$CH_3 - CH = CH - CH_2 - CH_2 - CH = \underset{\underset{CH_3}{|}}{C} - CH_3$$
$$\underset{\text{(A)}}{} \qquad \downarrow O_3$$

$$CH_3 - CH \overset{O}{\underset{O}{\diagup\diagdown}} CH - CH_2 - CH_2 - CH \overset{O}{\underset{O}{\diagup\diagdown}} \underset{CH_3}{\overset{CH_3}{C}}$$

$$\downarrow Zn/H_2O$$

$$CH_3 - CHO + OHC - CH_2 - CH_2 - CHO + O = C \underset{CH_3}{\overset{CH_3}{\diagup}}$$

# 14 Environmental Chemistry



**14.1 Define environmental chemistry.**

**Ans.** Environmental chemistry is defined as that branch of science which deals with the chemical phenomenon occurring in the environment, i.e., study of origin, transport, reactions, effects and the rates of chemical species in the environment.

**14.2 Explain tropospheric pollution in 100 words.**

**Ans.** Tropospheric pollution occurs due to the presence of undesirable gases and the solid particles in the air. The major gaseous and the particulate pollutants present in the troposphere are as follows:

(i) Gaseous air pollutants. These include mainly oxides of sulphur ($SO_2$, $SO_3$), oxides of nitrogen (NO, $NO_2$) and oxides of carbon (CO, $CO_2$) in addition to hydrogen sulphide ($H_2S$), hydrocarbons, ozone and other oxidants.

(ii) Particulate pollutants. These include dust, mist, fumes, smoke, smog, etc.

**14.3 Carbon monoxide gas is more dangerous than carbon dioxide gas. Why ?**

**Ans.** CO binds to haemoglobin for which it has 200 times more affinity than oxygen and forms carboxyhaemoglobin. In blood, when the concentration of carboxyhaemoglobin reaches 3.4%, the oxygen carrying capacity of the blood is greatly reduced. In other words, the body becomes oxygen–starved. This results into headache, nervousness, cardiovascular disorder, weak eye–sight etc. On the other hand, $CO_2$ does not combine with haemoglobin and hence is less harmful as pollutant. $CO_2$ is the main contributor towards green–house effect and global warming.

**14.4 Which gases are responsible for green–house effect? List some of them.**

**Ans.** $CO_2$ is the main gas responsible for green–house effect. Other green–house gases are methane, nitrous oxide, water vapors, chlorofluorocarbons (CFC's) and ozone.

**14.5 Statues and monuments in India are affected by acid rain. How?**

**Ans.** The air around the statues and monuments in India contains fairly high levels of the oxides of sulphur and nitrogen. This is mainly due to a large number of industries and power plants in the nearby areas. The problem has been further aggravated due to use of poor quality of coal, kerosene and firewood as fuel for domestic purposes. The resulting acid rain attacks the marble of these statues and monuments

$$CaCO_3 + H_2SO_4 \longrightarrow CaSO_4 + H_2O + CO_2$$

As a result, these monuments are being slowly eaten away and marble is getting discolored and lusterless.

**14.6 What is smog? How are classical and photochemical smog different?**

**Ans.** Smog is a combination of smoke and fog. Difference between Classical and photochemical smog

| Classical Smog | Photochemical Smog |
|---|---|
| 1. This was first time observed in London in 1952. | 1. This was observed in Los Angeles in 1950. |
| 2. It is formed due to presence of $SO_2$ and humidity in the air which combine to form $H_2SO_4$ fog which deposits on the particulates. | 2. It is formed due to photochemical reaction when air contains $NO_2$ and hydrocarbons. |
| 3. It involves smoke and fog. | 3. It does not involve any smoke or fog. |
| 4. It is formed in the months of winter particularly in the morning hours when the temperature is low. | 4. It is formed in the months of summer during afternoon when there is a bright sunlight so that photochemical reactions can take place. |
| 5. It causes bronchitis i.e. irritation in lungs. | 5. It causes irritation in the eyes. |
| 6. It is reducing in character. | 6. It is oxidizing in character. |

**14.7 Write down the reactions involved during the formation of photochemical smog.**

**Ans.** In the presence of sunlight, $NO_2$ undergoes photolysis to form NO and atomic oxygen. Atomic oxygen then combines with the molecular oxygen in the presence of some molecule which acts as a source of transfer of energy to form ozone, $O_3$. The ozone formed reacts with NO to form $NO_2$ and $O_2$. Thus $NO_2$ cycle is completed.

Reactions:– $NO_2 \xrightarrow{hv} NO + O$,

$$O + O_2 \longrightarrow O_3, \ O_3 + NO \longrightarrow NO_2 + O_2$$

When hydrocarbons are present, they combine with oxygen atom, produced in the first step during photolysis of $NO_2$, to form highly reactive free radicals as intermediates. These free radicals initiate a variety of reactions:

$$RCO + O_2 \longrightarrow RCO_3, \ RCO_3 + NO \longrightarrow$$
$$RCO_2 + NO_2,$$
$$RCO_3 + O_2 \longrightarrow O_3 + RCO_2, \ RCO_3 + NO_2$$
$$\longrightarrow RCO_3NO_2$$

(peroxyacetylnitrate – PAN)

As a result concentration of ozone, PAN and aldehydes and ketones is a build up in the atmosphere.

**14.8 What are the harmful effects of photochemical smog and how can they be controlled?**

**Ans.** The harmful effects of smog are:

(i) All these compounds like ozone, PAN etc. cause irritation in our eyes.

(ii) They damage many materials such as metals, stones, building materials.

(iii) Ozone destroys rubber.

(iv) It is also harmful to fabrics, crops and ornamental plants.

(v) $NO_2$ present in photochemical smog , reduces visibility. Hence pilots experience problems due to this smog.

**14.9 What are the reactions involved for ozone layer depletion in the stratosphere ?**

**Ans.** NO which may be produced at the ground level due to human activity react with ozone and form different oxides of nitrogen & oxygen

$$NO + O_3 \longrightarrow NO_2 + O_2, \ NO_2 + O \longrightarrow NO + O_2$$

Chlorofluorocarbons(CFC) are commonly known as freons which introduced in the atmosphere from aerosol sprays, refrigerating equipments and others. These compounds decompose to form Cl free radical

$$CF_2Cl_2 \longrightarrow CF_2Cl + \overset{\bullet}{C}l, \ CFCl_3 \longrightarrow CFCl_2 + \overset{\bullet}{C}l$$

The reactive chlorine atoms then destroys the ozone layer through the following sequence of reactions.

$$\overset{\bullet}{C}l + O_3 \longrightarrow Cl\overset{\bullet}{O} + O_2, \ Cl\overset{\bullet}{O} + O \longrightarrow \overset{\bullet}{C}l + O_2$$

**14.10 What do you mean by ozone hole? What are its consequences?**

**Ans.** Due to depletion of ozone in the atmosphere, large ozone holes are created in the ozone layer.

**Effects of Ozone depletion**

(i) The U.V. rays coming from the sun passes through the stratosphere and reach the surface of earth. This radiation is the cause of cancer in skin.

(ii) Exposure of eyes to the U.V. radiation can cause cataract or even blindness.

(iii) Exposure of plants to the U.V. radiations can adversely affect the plant proteins and results in destruction of chlorophyll and harmful mutation.

(iv) It has a very strong effect on our climate. It upsets the heat balance of the earth.

(v) If it is not controlled, it would cause ecological disturbances.

**14.11 What are the major causes of water pollution? Explain.**

**Ans.** The main causes for pollution in water are:

(i) Sewage and domestic wastes causes pathogens which are disease causing bacteria and also result in gastro–intestinal diseases.

(ii) The industrial effluents contain toxic and hazardous chemicals cause lead poisoning, kidney damage, etc.

(iii) The agricultural discharge includes fertilizers, pesticides, etc., causing harm to men and animals.

(iv) Siltation produces turbidity in water thereby hindering the free movement of aquatic organisms and their growth and productivity.

(v) The thermal pollutants increase the temperature of water adversely affecting the aquatic lives present in them.

(vi) The radioactive discharge from nuclear reactors are highly hazardous.

**14.12 Have you ever observed any water pollution in your area ? How can you control it ?**

**Ans.** We have water pollution due to sewage disposal in our area. It is controlled by spraying insecticides in the drains. Some places have been earmarked for water harvesting.

**14.13 What do you mean by Biochemical Oxygen Demand (BOD) ?**

**Ans.** The total amount of oxygen consumed by micro–organisms in decomposing the waste present in a certain volume of a sample of water is called Biochemical Oxygen Demand (BOD) of water.

**14.14 Do you observe any soil pollution in your neighbourhood? What efforts will you make for controlling the soil pollution ?**

**Ans.** Yes, we do observe soil pollution in our neighbourhood due to dumping of non–biodegradable waste like plastic bags and cans along with biodegradable wastes.

The best way to manage waste from house–hold is to keep two garbage bins, one for the biodegradable waste and the other for the non–biodegradable waste. Many combustible wastes can be burned and the ashes can be used for land–fill. However care must be taken for the toxic gases which can emit during combustion.

**14.15 What are pesticides and herbicides ? Explain giving examples.**

**Ans.** **Pesticides.** These are synthetic toxic chemicals which are used in agriculture to control the damages caused by insects, rodents, weeds and various crop diseases. Their repeated use gives rise to pests that are resistant to that group of pesticides. As a result, these pesticides become ineffective for those pests.

Earlier DDT was used. As insect resistance towards DDT increased, other organic toxins such as Aldrin and Dialdrin were introduced for use as pesticides. But these were non–biodegradable and slowly transferred to human being through food chain causing metabolic and physiological disorders, Consequently, a new series of pesticides, organophosphates and carbamates have been introduced. These are biodegradable but are severe nerve toxins and hence more harmful to humans and have caused even deaths. Thus, the insecticide industry is engaged in developing new insecticides.

**Herbicides.** These are the chemicals used to control weeds. Earlier, inorganic compounds such as sodium chlorate ($NaClO_3$) and sodium arsenite ($Na_3AsO_3$) were used but arsenic compounds, being toxic to mammals, are no longer preferred. Instead, organic compounds such as triazines, are now considered as better herbicides, especially for the corn–fields.

**14.16 What do you mean by green chemistry? How will it help decrease environmental pollution?**

**Ans..** Producing chemicals of our daily needs using such reactions and chemical processes which neither use toxic chemicals nor emit such chemicals into the atmosphere. It is evident that if concerted efforts are made to develop green chemical products, it will certainly help us to keep our environment pollution free.

**14.17 What would have happened if the greenhouse gases were totally missing in the earth's atmosphere ? Discuss.**

**Ans.** The solar energy radiated back from the earth surface is absorbed by the greenhouse gases (i.e., $CO_2$, $CH_4$, $O_3$, CFC's and water vapour) present near the earth's surface. Thus, they heat up the atmosphere near the earth's surface and keep it warm. As a result, they keep the temperature of the earth constant and help in the growth of plants and existence of life on the earth. If there were no greenhouse gases, there would have no vegetation and life on the earth.

**14.18 A large number of fish are suddenly found floating dead on a lake. There is no evidence of toxic dumping but you find an abundance of phytoplankton. Suggest a reason for the fish kill.**

**Ans.** Excessive phytoplankton (organic pollutants such as leaves, grass, trash etc. ) present in water is biodegradable. A large population of bacteria decomposes this organic matter in water. During this process, they consume the oxygen dissolved in water. Water has already limited dissolved oxygen (10 ppm). Thus, it is further depleted. When the level of dissolved oxygen falls below 6 ppm, the fish cannot survive. Hence, they die and float dead on the lake.

**14.19 How can domestic waste be used as manure?**

**Ans.** Domestic waste comprises of two types of materials, biodegradable such as leaves, rotten food etc. and non–biodegradable such as plastics, glass, metal scrap etc. The non–biodegradable waste is sent to industry for recycling. The biodegradable waste should be deposited in the land fills. With the passage of time, it is converted into manure (compost).

**14.20 For your agricultural field or garden, you have developed a compost producing pit. Discuss the process in the light of bad odour, flies and recycling of wastes for a good produce.**

**Ans.** The compost producing pit should be set up at a suitable place or in a tin to protect ourselves from bad odour and flies. It should be kept covered so that flies cannot make entry into it and the bad odour is minimized. The recyclable material like plastics, glass, newspapers etc. should be sold to the vendor who further sells it to the dealer. The dealer further supplies it to the industry involved in recycling process.

## SECTION B — PRACTICE QUESTIONS

### MULTIPLE CHOICE QUESTIONS

1. The gas emitted by supersonic jet planes that slowly depletes the concentration of ozone layer is
   (a) CO    (b) NO    (c) $SO_2$    (d) $O_2$

2. Non-biodegradable pollutant are created by
   (a) Forest Fires      (b) Natural Disasters
   (c) Humans      (d) Industrialization

3. Which of the following would be natural pollution
   (a) Forest fires
   (b) Eutrophication
   (c) Occurance of smog
   (d) Occurance of $NO_2$ in atmosphere

4. Environmental studies deal with the
   (a) Social and economical
   (b) Chemically and physically
   (c) Biological and physical
   (d) All of the above

5. Carbon monoxide (CO) is harmful to man because
   (a) it forms carbolic acid
   (b) it generates excess $CO_2$
   (c) it is carcinogenic
   (d) it competes with $O_2$ for haemoglobin

6. Classical smog occurs in places of
   (a) excess $SO_2$      (b) low temperature
   (c) high temperature      (d) excess $NH_3$

7. The biggest particulate matter is
   (a) $HNO_3$ droplets      (b) Soot
   (c) $H_2SO_4$ droplets      (d) Fly ash

8. The gas(es) not responsible for ozone depletion :
   (a) NO and freons      (b) $SO_2$
   (c) $CO_2$      (d) Both (b) and (c)

9. Which causes death of fish in water bodies polluted by sewage?
   (a) Foul smell      (b) Pathogens
   (c) Herbicides      (d) Decrease in D.O.

10. Brewery and sugar factory waste alters the quality of a water body by increasing
    (a) temperature      (b) turbidity
    (c) pH      (d) COD and BOD

11. Which is known as 'Third poison of environment' and also creates 'Blue baby syndrome'
    (a) Nitrate present in water
    (b) Phosphate and detergents found in water
    (c) Cyanide
    (d) Pesticides

12. Chief source of soil and water pollution is
    (a) mining
    (b) agro industry
    (c) thermal power plant
    (d) All of the above

13. Green chemistry means such reactions which :
    (a) produce colour during reactions
    (b) reduce the use and production of hazardous chemicals
    (c) are related to the depletion of ozone layer
    (d) study the reactions in plants

### ASSERTION & REASON QUESTIONS

**DIRECTIONS (Qs. 1-3) :** *Each of these questions contains an assertion followed by reason. Read them carefully and answer the question on the basis of following options. You have to select the one that best describes the two statements.*
(a) If both Assertion and Reason are correct and the Reason is a correct explanation of the Assertion.
(b) If both Assertion and Reason are correct but Reason is not a correct explanation of the Assertion.
(c) If the Assertion is correct but Reason is incorrect.
(d) If the Assertion is incorrect but the Reason is correct.

1. **Assertion :** Photochemical smog is oxidising in nature.
   **Reason :** Photochemical smog contains $NO_2$ and $O_3$, which are formed during the sequence of reactions.

2. **Assertion :** Ozone is destroyed by solar radiation in upper stratosphere.
   **Reason :** Thinning of the ozone layer allows excessive UV radiations to reach the surface of earth.

3. **Assertion :** Uncatalysed oxidation of sulphur dioxide is a slow process.
   **Reason :** Particulate matter in polluted air catalyses the oxidation of sulphur dioxide.

### CASE/PASSAGE BASED QUESTIONS

**DIRECTIONS (Qs. 1-5) :** *Read the following case/passage and answer the questions.*

Global warming is the long-term warming of the planet's overall temperature. Though this warming trend has been going on for a long time, its pace has significantly increased in the last hundred years due to the burning of fossil fuels. As the human population has increased, so has the volume of fossil fuels burned. Fossil fuels include coal, oil, and natural gas, and burning them causes what is known as the "greenhouse effect" in Earth's atmosphere. Global warming causes climate change, which poses a serious threat to life on earth in the forms of widespread flooding and extreme weather. Scientists continue to study global warming and its impact on Earth.

1. This is not a possible adverse effect of global warming
   (a) sea level rise
   (b) an increase of UVB radiation
   (c) retreat of glaciers
   (d) extraordinary weather patterns

2.  Correct descending order of relative contribution of various greenhouse gases to total global warming is
    (a)  carbon dioxide; methane; CFCs; nitrous oxide
    (b)  carbon dioxide; methane; nitrous oxide; CFCs
    (c)  carbon dioxide; CFCs; nitrous oxide; methane
    (d)  carbon dioxide; CFCs; methane; nitrous oxide
3.  Which of the following is not a major greenhouse gas?
    (a)  ozone
    (b)  water vapour
    (c)  methane
    (d)  carbon dioxide
4.  The greenhouse effect is because of the
    (a)  presence of gases, which in general are strong infrared absorbers, in the atmosphere
    (b)  presence of $CO_2$ only in the atmosphere
    (c)  pressure of $O_3$ and $CH_4$ in the atmosphere
    (d)  $N_2O$ and chlorofluorohydrocarbons in the atmosphere
5.  Which of the following is the major cause of global warming?
    (a)  re-radiation of U.V. rays by $CO_2$ and $H_2O$
    (b)  re-radiation of I.R. rays by $CO_2$ and $H_2O$
    (c)  re-radiation of I.R. rays by $O_2$ and $N_2$
    (d)  re-radiation of U.V. rays by $O_2$ and $N_2$

## VERY SHORT ANSWER QUESTIONS

1.  Name the different regions of the atmosphere alongwith their altitudes.
2.  In what regions of the atmosphere, the temperature increases with altitude and in which regions it decreases?
3.  What gas leaked to bring havoc in Bhopal tragedy?
4.  What is the %age of $CO_2$ in the pure dry air?
5.  Name three gases which are major air pollutants.
6.  What is the most important sink of CO pollutant?
7.  What is the compound formed when CO combines with blood?
8.  What is anoxia or asphyxiation?
9.  How are NO and $NO_2$ formed in the atmosphere?
10. How are fuel gases from industries freed from oxides of nitrogen and sulphur?
11. What is chlorosis?
12. What is the size range of particulates?
13. What type of aromatic compounds are present as particulates in the air?
14. Who are the people who usually suffer from 'black lung disease' and who are those who suffer from 'white lung disease'?
15. How particulates help in the cloud formation?
16. Which zone is called ozonosphere?
17. Which main compounds are causing damage to ozone layer?
18. Which gaseous species are present in the mesosphere and thermosphere?
19. Which disease is caused due to hole in the ozone layer and why?
20. What is the composition of 'London smog or reducing smog'?
21. In which season and of what time of the day, there is 'London smog or reducing smog' ?
22. What is the nature of 'London smog' ?
23. In which season and what time of the day, there is photochemical smog?
24. Which acids are present in the acid rain?
25. Name two important sinks of $CO_2$.
26. What is marine pollution?
27. What type of pollution affects the sea–birds?
28. What are the main sources of thermal pollution?
29. Why COD is preferred over BOD ?
30. What is humification?
31. What should be the tolerable limit of fluoride ions in drinking water? What happens if it is higher than 10 ppm?
32. Name any four methods for waste management.
33. What is the nature of 'photochemical smog'?
34. Name of source of energy which does not create pollution.
35. What are PCBs?
36. What are polar stratospheric clouds (PSCs)?
37. What is meant by polar vortex?
38. What is effect of excess of $SO_4^{2-}$ ion in drinking water?
39. Write the name of gas produced in Mathura refineries which can damage the great historical monument "Taj Mahal"?
40. What type of radiations are absorbed by $CO_2$ in the atmosphere?

## SHORT ANSWER QUESTIONS

1.  Name two natural sources of air pollution.
2.  What are 'asbestosis' and 'silicosis'?
3.  What is the composition of 'photochemical smog'?
4.  What is the role of $CO_2$ in the 'greenhouse effect'?
5.  What is COD ? Which chemical substance is generally used in its measurement?
6.  What are viable and non–viable particulates?
7.  (i)   Why there is ozone depletion mainly over Antarctica?
    (ii)  In which season the depletion of ozone on Antarctica takes place and when is it replenished?
8.  Give three examples in which green chemistry has been applied.
9.  Define environmental pollution. Give the causes of pollution.
10. What are primary and secondary pollutants? Explain with suitable examples.
11. What are biodegradable and non-biodegradable pollutants?

12. Depending upon the nature of pollutants, how can the pollution be classified into different types ?

13. What is the composition of pure dry air? What do you mean by the terms 'sink' and 'target' with respect to pollution?

14. How can $SO_x$ pollution be controlled?

15. How plant nutrients and pesticides acts as water pollutants?

16. Why is acid rains considered a threat to Taj Mahal?

17. Discuss the importance of dissolved oxygen in water. What processes are generally responsible for the deoxygenation of the water?

18. On the basis of chemical reactions involved, explain how do chlorofluorocarbons cause thinning of ozone layer in stratosphere.

19. What are the sources of dissolved oxygen in water?

20. How can lead poisoning be cured?

21. Oxygen plays a key role in the troposphere while ozone in the stratosphere. Elucidate.

22. What is BOD and COD?

## LONG ANSWER QUESTIONS

1. What is the strategy for control of Environmental pollution?

2. List industrial wastes which contaminate water.

## SOLUTIONS

### *Multiple Choice Questions*

1. **(b)** Nitric oxide (NO) which may be produced at the ground level due to human activity or natural sources or is produced in large amounts in the exhaust gases by the engine of supersonic transport planes and introduced directly into the stratosphere.
$$NO + O_3 \longrightarrow NO_2 + O_2$$

2. **(c)** Humans are the primary source of producing non-biodegradable pollutants.

3. **(a)** Forest fires

4. **(d)** All of the above.

5. **(d)** CO is highly toxic and impairs respiration. CO combine with haemoglobin of blood and reduces its $O_2$ carrying capacity.

6. **(b)** Classical smog occurs in places of low temperature.

7. **(d)** Fly ash is the biggest particulate matter.

8. **(d)** $SO_2$ and $CO_2$ are not responsible for ozone layer depletion.

9. **(d)** Decrease in dissolved oxygen causes death of fish.

10. **(d)** Biochemical and chemical oxygen demand increases.

11. **(a)** It affects oxygen carrying capacity of haemoglobin and parts of skin becomes blue in colour.

12. **(d)** All the given options are source of soil and water pollution.

13. **(b)** Green chemistry may be defined as the programme of developing new chemical products and chemical processes or making improvements in the already existing compounds and processes so as to make less harmful to human health and environment. This means the same as to reduce the use and production of hazardous chemicals.

### *Assertion & Reason Questions*

1. **(a)** Both $NO_2$ and $O_3$ are oxidising in nature.

2. **(d)** Ozone is destroyed by pollutant gases.

3. **(a)** The presence of particulate matter in polluted air catalyses the oxidation of $SO_2$ to $SO_3$.

### *Case/Passage Based Questions*

1. **(b)**      2. **(a)**      3. **(a)**

4. **(a)** Green house gases such as $CO_2$, ozone, methane, the chlorofluorocarbon compounds and water vapour form a thick cover around the earth which prevents the IR rays emitted by the earth to escape. It gradually leads to increase in temperature of atmosphere.

5. **(b)** $CO_2$ and water vapour can re-radiate I.R. rays.

### *Very Short Answer Questions*

1. Troposphere (0-10 km), stratosphere (10-50 km), mesosphere (50-85 km), thermosphere (85-500 km).

2. Temperature increases with altitude in stratosphere and thermosphere while it decreases in troposphere and mesosphere.

3. Methyl isocyanate (MIC).

4. About 0. 032%.

5. $CO_x$, $NO_x$, and $SO_x$

6. Soil micro–organism.

7. Carboxyhaemoglobin (HbCO).

8. Acute oxygen starvation in the body (due to CO poisoning) is called anoxia or asphyxiation.

9. NO is formed due to reaction between $N_2$ and $O_2$ during lightning or combustion of fossil fuels. It is further oxidized to $NO_2$.

10. By scrubbing them with conc. $H_2SO_4$ or with alkaline solutions like $Ca(OH)_2$ and $Mg(OH)_2$.

11. Slowing down the formation of chlorophyll in plants due to presence of $SO_2$ as pollutant is called chlorosis.

12. 5 nm to 500,000 nm.

13. Polycyclic aromatic hydrocarbons (PAH).

14. Coal miners suffer from black lung disease and textile workers suffer from white lung disease.

15. They act as nuclei for cloud formation.

16. Stratosphere.

17. NO and freons.
18. Gaseous ions like $NO^+$, $O_2^+$, $N_2^+$, $O^+$ and atoms of N and O.
19. Ultraviolet rays will reach the earth after passing through the hole and cause skin cancer.
20. Fog of $H_2SO_4$ droplets deposited on the particulates.
21. In winter during the morning hours.
22. Reducing.
23. In summer, in the afternoon.
24. $H_2SO_4$, $HNO_3$ and HCl.
25. Oceans (which dissolve it) and plants (which use it for photosynthesis).
26. Pollution of sea water due to discharge of wastes into it is called marine pollution.
27. Oil water pollution.
28. Thermal power plants and nuclear plants.
29. COD can be found in a few minutes whereas BOD requires at least 5 days.
30. The decomposition of organic material (leaves, roots etc.) in the soil by microorganism to produce humus is called humification.
31. 1 ppm or $1$ mg $dm^{-3}$. Higher concentration is harmful to bones and teeth.
32. Recycling, burning, incineration and sewage treatment.
33. It is oxidizing in nature.
34. Sun is source of energy which does not create pollution.
35. PCBs are **polychlorinated biphenyls**
36. **Polar stratospheric clouds.** PSC's are formed over Antarctica. They are of two types:
Type I clouds contain some solidified nitric acid trihydrate ($HNO_3$, $3H_2O$) formed at $-77°C$.
Type II clouds contain some ice, formed at $-85°C$
These clouds play an important role in ozone depletion.
37. **Polar vortex.** When polar stratospheric clouds are formed over Antarctica during winters, stable wind patterns in the stratosphere are called **polar vortex** which encircle the continent.
38. Excess of $SO_4^{2-}$ in drinking water (>500 ppm) may cause a laxative effect.
39. Sulphur dioxide.
40. Infrared radiations.

### *Short Answer Questions*

1. (i) Volcanic eruptions
   (ii) Forest fires
2. The lung disease caused by particulates of asbestos is called 'asbestosis' and that caused by those of silica is called 'silicosis'.
3. It is a mixture of a number of irritation causing compounds like $NO_2$, $O_3$, peroxyacylnitrates (PAN), aldehydes, ketones, hydrocarbons and CO.
4. Heat from the sun after being absorbed by the earth is remitted by the earth and absorbed by $CO_2$ and then radiated back to the earth, thereby resulting in the increase of temperature of earth.

5. COD stands for Chemical Oxygen Demand. It is a measure of all types of oxidisable impurities present in the sewage. COD values are higher than BOD values.

It is measured by treating the given sample of water with an oxidizing agent, generally $K_2Cr_2O_7$ in presence of dilute $H_2SO_4$.

6. Viable particulates are small size living organisms such as bacteria, fungi, moulds, algae etc.
Non–viable particulates are formed by disintegration of large size materials or condensation of small size particles or droplets, e. g., mist, smoke, fume and dust.

7. (i) This is because in other parts of the stratosphere, chlorine free radicals combine to form compounds which goes away but in Antarctica, the compounds formed are converted back into chlorine free radicals which deplete the ozone layer.
   (ii) During spring season (i. e., in the months of September and October), depletion of ozone takes place and after spring (i. e., in the month of November), it is replenished.

8. (i) In dry cleaning, use of liquefied $CO_2$ in place of tetrachloroethene ($Cl_2C = CCl_2$).
   (ii) In bleaching of paper by using $H_2O_2$ in place of chlorine.
   (iii) In the manufacture of chemicals like ethanal using environment–friendly chemicals and conditions.

$$CH_2 = CH_2 + O_2 \xrightarrow[\text{Pd(II)/Cu(II)(in water)}]{\text{Catalyst}}$$

$$CH_3CHO(90\%)$$

9. The addition of undesirable material to air, water and soil by a natural sources or due to human activity which adversely affects the quality of environment is called environmental pollution. The undesirable material thus added to the environment are called pollutants. Environmental pollution model includes:
   (i) Atmospheric pollution
   (ii) Water pollution
   (iii) Land pollution
   The main causes of pollution are
   (i) Fast population growth
   (ii) Use of excessive pesticides in agriculture
   (iii) Rapid urbanization
   (iv) Excessive industrialization

10. Primary pollutants are those which after their formation enter into environment and remain as such. For example, NO formed by bacterial decay or by lightning flashes becomes pollutant if present in excessive amount.

Secondary pollutants are those which are formed due to chemical reactions between the primary pollutants in the atmosphere or hydrosphere. For example, hydrocarbons and oxides of nitrogen which are primary pollutants react together in the presence of sunlight to form certain compounds like PAN which are also harmful. Thus the harmful compounds formed from primary pollutants are called secondary pollutants.

11. Bio-degradable pollutants are materials such as domestic sewage, cow dungs etc. which are easily decomposed by the micro-organisms either by nature or by suitable treatment and thus are not harmful but if these are present in excess in the environment, they do not undergo degradation completely and thus become pollutants.
    Non-biodegradable pollutants are materials such as mercury, DDT etc. which do not undergo degradation or degrade very slowly but may react with the compound present in the environment and produce even more toxic product.

12. It can be classified in two different ways:
    (a) Depending upon the part of the environment polluted. For example
        (i)   Air pollution
        (ii)  Water pollution
        (iii) Soil pollution
    (b) Depending upon the nature of the pollutant added into the environment. A few common examples are:
        (i)    Radioactive pollution
        (ii)   Plastic pollution
        (iii)  Soap and detergent pollution
        (iv)   Oil pollution
        (v)    Chemical pollution
        (vi)   Noise pollution
        (vii)  Acid rain pollution
        (viii) Smog pollution
        (ix)   Effluent pollution and many others

13. The composition of the pure dry air is as follows:
    $N_2$(78.1%), $O_2$(20.95%), Ar(0.93%), $CO_2$(0.032%), Ne (18 ppm), He (5.2ppm), $CH_4$(1.3 ppm) , Kr(1 ppm), $H_2$(0.5 ppm), $N_2O$ (0.25 ppm), CO (0.10 ppm), $O_3$ (0.02 ppm), $SO_2$ (0.001 ppm), $NO_2$(0.001 ppm).
    In nature, some amount of certain pollutants is taken up by medium present in the environment. Such medium is called 'sink' for that pollutant. Ocean acts as sink for $SO_2$ and $CO_2$. The living organisms like animals and plants or the materials like metals and buildings which are affected by pollutants are called targets.

14. (i)   By use of low sulphur or sulphur free fuels like natural gas.
    (ii)  By removing sulphur from fuel before burning.
    (iii) By making sulphur free liquefied gaseous fuels from coal.
    (iv)  By using alternate source of energy rather then sulphur containing fossil fuels.

15. The plant nutrients containing N and P, which flows into lakes where they support the growth of aquatic plants. These plants on decay produce unpleasant odour . Further, the micro-organisms in decomposing these plants consume oxygen. As a results, the amount of dissolved oxygen in the water decreases which proves that these are fatal for aquatic life. Pesticides are organic compounds which are used to protect plants from pests. These are used to stop the growth of weeds. These are mild poisons. When plants are watered or during rain, these chemicals flow down into lakes or rivers and cause problems to aquatic as well as human lives.

16. Oxides of N and S released by the Mathura refinery and by the automobile causes acid rain formation over Agra. This acidic rain water reacts with marble of Taj Mahal causing pitting, therefore acid rain is a threat to Taj Mahal.
$$CaCO_3 + H_2SO_4 \longrightarrow CaSO_4 + H_2O + CO_2$$

17. Dissolved oxygen is very important for the support of aquatic life. The phytoplanktons and zooplanktons will die and their growth will be inhibited if the dissolved $O_2$ concentration decreases.
    Processes of deoxygenation of water
    1. Micro-organisms consume oxygen and oxidises the organic matter
       Carbohydrate + $O_2$ (aq) $\longrightarrow$ $CO_2$ (aq) + $H_2O$ (l)
    2. By biochemical oxidation
       $$4Fe^{2+}(aq) + O_2(aq) + 10H_2O(l) \longrightarrow$$
       $$4Fe(OH)_3(aq) + 8H^+(aq)$$
    3. Mediated oxidation of organic matters, it also consumed by the bioxidation of nitrogenous materials.
       $$NH^+_4(aq) + 2O_2(aq) \longrightarrow$$
       $$2H^+(aq) + NO_3^-(aq) + H_2O(l)$$

18. CFC's are stable compounds. These undergo decompositions in presence of sunlight, as shown below :
    **Reactions**
    $$CF_2Cl_2(g) \xrightarrow{\text{UV}} \dot{C}l(g) + \dot{C}F_2Cl(g)$$
    $$\dot{C}l(g) + O_3(g) \longrightarrow Cl\dot{O}(g) + O_2(g)$$
    $$Cl\dot{O}(g) + O(g) \longrightarrow \dot{C}l(g) + O_2(g)$$
    Chain reactions continue in which ozone layer is depleted.

19. Sources of dissolved oxygen in water
    (i)   Photosynthesis
    (ii)  Natural aeration
    (iii) Mechanical aeration

20. Lead poisoning can be cured by feeding the patient with an aqueous solution of calcium complex of EDTA.
    $$Ca-EDTA + Pb^{2+} \longrightarrow Ca^{2+} + Pb-EDTA$$
    The soluble Pb–EDTA is excreted through urine.

**21.** The portion of the atmosphere closest to the earth up to the height of ~ 10 km from the sea level is called troposphere. Oxygen plays an important role in this sphere to support animal life and other chemical processes such as combustion etc. Beyond 11 km up to the altitude of 50 km is stratosphere. Ozone is the important chemical compound of this region which absorbs ultraviolet radiations and raised the temperature in this zone. This act of ozone protects us from the harmful effects of sun's ultraviolet radiations.

**22.** BOD gives the idea of extent of organic waste present in water. It is defined as the amount of oxygen in milligrams dissolved in water needed to break down the organic matter present in one litre of water for five days at 20°C. COD is a parameter for measuring the amount of oxygen in ppm that would be required to oxidize the organic and inorganic waste present in the water.

### Long Answer Questions

**1.** The management of waste for control of environmental pollution can be done by:
(a) **Recycling.** For example :
   (i) the collection and recycling of glass.
   (ii) the use of scrap metal in the manufacture of steel.
   (iii) The recovery of energy by burning combustible waste.
(b) **Sewage treatment.** It can be carried out in three steps.

   (i) Removal of solid matter.
   (ii) Degradation of the organic content by microbial oxidation.
   (iii) Application of various physical and chemical processes like coagulation, filtration and disinfection using chlorine.
(c) **Incineration.** It is the conversion of organic materials to $CO_2$ and $H_2O$ at 1000°C and in excess of oxygen.
(d) **Digestion.** It is the anaerobic digestion when micro-organisms degrade wastes in the absence of oxygen.

$$2(CH_2O) \longrightarrow CO_2(g) + CH_4(g)$$

(e) **Dumping.** The controlled dumping of wastes in ocean and soil is a useful practice.

**2.** Industrial wastes which contaminate water are following :
(a) **Detergents and fertilizers.** They may contain phosphates additives, which encourage the formation of algae and reduces the dissolved oxygen. This process is called Eutrophication.
(b) **Heavy metals.** The industrial or mining waste may contain Cd, Pb, Hg etc. These metals can damage the kidneys, liver, brain and central nervous system.
(c) **Acid polluted water.** The water having pH less than 3 is deadly to most forms of aquatic life.
(d) **Polychlorinated biphenyls** (PCBs) PCBs used in transformers, capacitors are resistant to oxidation and can cause skin disorders promote cancer.

# SECTION C | NCERT EXEMPLAR QUESTIONS

## MULTIPLE CHOICE QUESTIONS

**1.** Photochemical smog occurs in warm, dry and sunny climate. One of the following is not amongst the components of photochemical smog, identify it.
(a) $NO_2$
(b) $O_3$
(c) $SO_2$
(d) Unsaturated hydrocarbon

**2.** Which of the following statements is not true about classical smog?
(a) Its main components are produced by the action of sunlight on emissions of automobiles and factories
(b) Produced in cold and humid climate
(c) It contains compounds of reducing nature
(d) It contains smoke, fog and sulphur dioxide

**3.** Sewage containing organic waste should not be disposed in water bodies because it causes major water pollution. Fishes in such a polluted water die because of

(a) large number of mosquitoes
(b) increase in the amount of dissolved oxygen
(c) decrease in the amount of dissolved oxygen in water
(d) clogging of gills by mud

**4.** Which of the following statements about photochemical smog is wrong?
(a) It has high concentration of oxidising agents
(b) It has low concentration of oxidising agent
(c) It can be controlled by controlling the release of $NO_2$, hydrocarbons, ozone etc
(d) Plantation of some plants like pinus helps in controlling photochemical smog

**5.** The gaseous envelope around the earth is known as atmosphere. The lowest layer of this is extended upto 10 km from sea level, this layer is
(a) stratosphere      (b) troposphere
(c) mesosphere      (d) hydrosphere

**6.** Which of the following statements is correct?
   (a) Ozone hole is a hole formed in stratosphere from which ozone oozes out
   (b) Ozone hole is a hole formed in troposphere from which ozone oozes out
   (c) Ozone hole is thinning of ozone layer of stratosphere at some places
   (d) Ozone hole means vanishing of ozone layer around the earth completely

**7.** Which of the following practices will not come under green chemistry?
   (a) If possible, making use of soap made of vegetable oils instead of using synthetic detergents.
   (b) Using $H_2O_2$ for bleaching purpose instead of using chlorine based bleaching agents
   (c) Using bicycles for travelling small distances instead of using petrol/ diesel based vehicles
   (d) Using plastic cans for neatly storing substances

**8.** Which of the following gases in not a green house gas?
   (a) CO
   (b) $O_3$
   (c) $CH_4$
   (d) $H_2O$ vapour

**9.** Biochemical Oxygen Demand, (BOD) is a measure of organic material present in water. BOD value less than 5 ppm indicates a water sample to be
   (a) rich in dissolved oxygen
   (b) poor in dissolved oxygen
   (c) highly polluted
   (d) not suitable for aquatic life

**10.** Which of the following statement(s) is/are wrong?
   (a) Ozone is not responsible for green house effect
   (b) Ozone can oxidise sulphur dioxide present in the atmosphere to sulphur trioxide
   (c) Ozone hole is thinning of ozone layer present in stratosphere
   (d) Ozone is produced in upper stratosphere by the action of UV rays on oxygen

**11.** Dinitrogen and dioxygen are main constituents of air but these do not react with each other to form oxides of nitrogen because ............... .
   (a) the reaction is endothermic and requires very high temperature
   (b) the reaction can be initiated only in presence of a catalyst
   (c) oxides of nitrogen are unstable
   (d) $N_2$ and $O_2$ are unreactive

**12.** The pollutants which come directly in the air from sources are called primary pollutants. Primary pollutants are sometimes converted into secondary pollutants. Which of the following belongs to secondary air pollutants?
   (a) CO
   (b) Hydrocarbon
   (c) Peroxyacetyl nitrate
   (d) NO

## ASSERTION & REASON QUESTIONS

**DIRECTIONS (Qs. 1-2) :** *Each of these questions contains an assertion followed by reason. Read them carefully and answer the question on the basis of following options. You have to select the one that best describes the two statements.*
   (a) If both Assertion and Reason are correct and the Reason is a correct explanation of the Assertion.
   (b) If both Assertion and Reason are correct but Reason is not a correct explanation of the Assertion.
   (c) If the Assertion is correct but Reason is incorrect.
   (d) If the Assertion is incorrect but the Reason is correct.

**1.** **Assertion :** The pH of acid rain is less than 5.6.
   **Reason :** Carbon dioxide present in the atmosphere dissolves in rain water and forms carbonic acid.

**2.** **Assertion :** Carbon dioxide is one of the important greenhouse gases.
   **Reason :** It is largely produced by respiratory function of animals and plants.

## SHORT ANSWER QUESTIONS

**1.** Green house effect leads to global warming. Which substances are responsible for green house effect.

**2.** What is the importance of measuring BOD of a water body?

**3.** Acid rain is known to contain some acids. Name these acids and where from they come in the rain?

**4.** Ozone is a toxic gas and is a strong oxidizing agent even then its presence in the stratosphere is very important. Explain what would happen if ozone from this region is completely removed?

**5.** Dissolved oxygen in water is very important for aquatic life. What processes are responsible for the reduction of dissolved oxygen in water?

**6.** What could be the harmful effects of improper management of industrial and domestic solid waste in a city?

**7.** During an educational trip, a student of botany saw a beautiful lake in a village. She collected many plants from that area. She noticed that villagers were washing clothes around the lake and at some places waste material from houses was destroying its beauty.
   After a few years, she visited the same lake again. She was surprised to find that the lake was covered with algae, the stinking smell was coming out and its water had become unusable. Can you explain the reason for this condition of the lake?

**8.** Water are biodegradable and non-biodegradable pollutants?

**9.** What are the sources of dissolved oxygen in water?

## LONG ANSWER QUESTION

**1.** Explain how does green house effect cause global warning.

## SOLUTIONS

### *Multiple Choice Questions*

1. **(c)** The smog which is formed in presence of sunlight is called photochemical smog. The main components of the photochemical smog results from the action of sunlight on unsaturated hydrocarbons and nitrogen oxides produced by automobiles and factories.

2. **(a)** Classical smog occurs in cold humid climate. It is a mixture of smoke, fog and sulphur dioxide.

3. **(c)** The large population of bacteria decomposes organic matter present in water. They consume oxygen dissolved in water. Hence, oxygen from water decreases. It is harmful for aquatic life.

4. **(b)** Photochemical smog has high concentration of oxidants such as $O_3$, organic oxidant and is therefore called as oxidising smog.

5. **(b)** The lowest region of the atmosphere in which human beings along with other organisms live is called troposphere. It extends upto the height of $\sim 10$ km from sea level. Troposphere is a turbulent, dusty zone containing air, much water vapour and clouds.

6. **(c)** Ozone hole is thinning of ozone layer of stratosphere at some places. NO and chlorofluorocarbon have been found to be the most responsible for depleting the ozone layer.

7. **(d)** Using plastic cans for neatly storing substances will not come under green chemistry. The plastic materials are non-biodegradable.

8. **(a)** Those gases which absorb sunlight near the earth's surface and then radiates back to the earth are called green house gases.
Carbon dioxide, water vapour, methane, ozone, oxides of nitrogen, chlorofluoro carbons (CFCs) etc; are green house gases. CO is not a green house gas.

9. **(a)** Water considered to be clean if it has BOD less than 5 ppm whereas highly polluted water has BOD more than 17 ppm.
Therefore, water having BOD less than 5 ppm is rich in dissolved oxygen.

10. **(a)** $O_3$ is responsible for greenhouse effect. Its contribution is about 8%.

11. **(a)** Nitrogen and oxygen do not react with each other at normal temperature. At high altitude when lightning strikes, they combine to form oxides of nitrogen.

$$N_2\,(g) + O_2\,(g) \xrightarrow{\;3000^\circ C\;} 2NO\,(g)$$

12. **(c)** Hydrocarbons present in atmosphere combine with oxygen atom produced by the photolysis of $NO_2$ to form highly reactive intermediate called free radical. Free radical initiates a series of reaction.

Peroxyacetyl nitrates are formed, which can be said as secondary pollutants.

$$\text{Hydrocarbon} + O \rightarrow RCO^{\cdot}\ (\text{free radicals})$$

$$RCO^{\cdot} + O_2 \rightarrow RCO_3$$

$$RCO_3^{\cdot} + NO_2 \rightarrow \underset{\text{Peroxyacetyl nitrate}}{RCO_3NO_2}$$

### *Assertion & Reason Questions*

1. **(b)** When the pH of rain water is less than 5.6 is known as acid rain and this will occur due to presence of oxide of sulphur and nitrogen in the air.

2. **(b)** The increasing amount of $CO_2$ in the atmosphere is responsible for the global warming. It is produced by respiratory function, automobiles burning of fuel, wood etc. Excess of $CO_2$ from the atmosphere is utilized by green plants.

### *Short Answer Questions*

1. Trapping of heat occurs by green house gases, namely carbon dioxide, methane, nitrous oxide, ozone and chlorofluorocarbons, which leads to global warming.

2. BOD is the mesure of level of pollution caued by organic biodegradable material. Low value of BOD indicates that water contains less organic matter.

3. Acid rain is the result of human activities that emit the oxides of sulphur and nitrogen in the atmosphere.
$$2SO_2\,(g) + O_2\,(g) + 2H_2O\,(l) \rightarrow 2H_2SO_4\,(aq)$$
$$4NO_2\,(g) + O_2\,(g) + 2H_2O\,(l) \rightarrow 4HNO_3\,(aq)$$
Nitric acid and sulphuric acid are acids present in acid rain which causes harmful effects to both living and non-living things.

4. If ozone is removed the ultravoidet rediation comes directly in contact with living things and cause damages such as skin cancers and many other serious diseases. Ozone in the stratosphere absorbs this UV radiation from the sun and does not allow to pass it to the inner atmosphere.

5. Eutrophication is the process responsible for the reduction of dissolved oxygen in the water. It is a process in which nutrient-enriched water bodies support a dence plant population, which kill animal life by depriving of oxygen and result in subsequent loss of biodiversity.

6. The improper management of industrial and domestic waste in a city can cause serious damages to both living and non-living things.
   1. Domestic waste if not disposed of property it will lead to the blockage of sewage lines and thus

    mosquitoes will grow in the water and cause dengue-like diseases.

2. Improper management of such domestic wastes contributes to soil pollution to a large extent and also water pollution.

3. Soil pollution is caused by the dumping of harmful chemicals generated by industries which penetrate in soil and get mixed with groundwater.

7. Due to the disposal of domestic waste in the lake can provide nutrients for algae to grow rapidly and also aquatic plants. The decomposition of these with the help of bacteria can cause foul smell also. This development of plants in the nutrient rich lake is due to the process called cutrophication.

8. Biodegradable pollutants are those which can be decomposed by bacteria or any other environmental factors like fruits, sewages etc. Non-biodegradable pollutants are not easily decomposed by bacteria. It remains as such in the environment. Examples like DDT, mercury etc.

9. Oxygen reaches the water through the atmosphere where there is direct contact of water with atmospheric air. Photosynthesis by green aquatic plants at day time. In the night the photosynthesis does not take place but the plants respire but the amount of oxygen is reduced.

### *Long Answer Question*

1. The greenhouse effect is the process during which radiation from the sun is trapped within the earth's atmosphere, which warms the planet. This effect occurs naturally. Since the industrial revolution, the greenhouse effect has been magnified due to greenhouse gases emitted into the atmosphere by humans. Global warming refers to the increase in annual average temperatures across the globe. As the amount of greenhouse gases in the atmosphere increases, the planet becomes warmer and warmer on average. Thus, as humans emit more greenhouse gases and those gases are trapped in the atmosphere, more heat is retained. This causes an average annual warming across the globe.